Memoirs of a
Yorkshire Bastard

Memoirs of a Yorkshire Bastard

A Chronicle of the Life and Times of a Gay Medieval Historian

Keith Dockray

AMBERLEY

First published 2008

Amberley Publishing plc
Cirencester Road, Chalford,
Stroud, Gloucestershire, GL6 8PE
www.amberley-books.com

© Keith Dockray, 2008

The right of Keith Dockray to be identified as the Author
of this work has been asserted in accordance with the
Copyrights, Designs and Patents Act 1988.

All rights reserved. No part of this book may be reprinted
or reproduced or utilised in any form or by any electronic,
mechanical or other means, now known or hereafter invented,
including photocopying and recording, or in any information
storage or retrieval system, without the permission in writing
from the Publishers.

British Library Cataloguing in Publication Data.
A catalogue record for this book is available from the British Library.

ISBN 978-1-84868-016-6

Typesetting and origination by Amberley Publishing
Printed in Great Britain

Contents

	Prologue	11
1	Unpromising Beginnings in Post-war Huddersfield	15
2	Grammar School Boy at Huddersfield (New) College	31
3	Escapes From Reality in Huddersfield	57
4	Bristol University Student	79
5	Plymouth College Schoolmaster	99
6	Pleasures and Pastimes in Bristol and Plymouth	123
7	Coming to Terms with Homosexuality	141
8	Huddersfield Polytechnic Lecturer	161
9	Huddersfield Polytechnic/University Lecturer	193
10	Early Historical Research and Writing	221
11	Pleasures and Pastimes in Huddersfield	253
12	From Huddersfield to Bristol	283
13	Open University Tutor in Yorkshire and the South West	303
14	Part-time Lecturer in Bristol	329
15	Later Historical Research and Writing	347
16	Pleasures and Pastimes in Bristol	377
17	Out of the Closet	401
	Epilogue	427

Foreword

Having suffered a horrid twelve months when the avarice and dishonesty of others has astonished me, it is refreshing to be able to write about someone who represents the absolute opposite of these traits.

I have known Keith for almost thirty years. We first met in Swansea at the Fifteenth Century Conference in 1979 and his mischievous irreverence made a deep impression on me. Over the years I have got to know him extremely well and a close friendship developed where mutual respect and sincerity were the abiding hallmarks of the relationship as if it were a form of glue. On my part I cannot accept insincerity in anyone I have dealings with and Keith cannot accept pomposity. On many occasions he has made light of bringing me down to earth whenever he thinks I have gone beyond myself! And yet, even when such demonstrations of one's failings are briskly punctured, it is impossible but to declare that he was right, and then smile at the absurdities of life.

Keith cares not for material wealth and is happy if his basic needs are catered for. Although he makes light of things he is, deep down, a very caring person and one quickly realises that his dramatic statements are more often for effect than for real. Whenever a friend is in need, Keith is a person who genuinely cares. All those close to him know him and love him for what really matters in life — sincere and genuine friendship.

On more than one occasion Keith has quoted a favourite passage of his from C. S. Lewis, and I can think of no better place to narrate it than in this foreword:

Of all tyrannies, a tyranny sincerely exercised for the good of its victims may be the most oppressive. It would be better to live under robber barons than under omnipotent moral busybodies. The robber baron's cruelty may sometimes sleep, his cupidity may at some point be satiated; but those who torment us for our own good will torment us without end, for they do so with the approval of their own conscience.

There is little more to say. Political correctness is not part of Keith's ideal world, or mine. Perhaps we would have lived more happily in earlier times? Anyway, before wandering from my subject, may I close this short notice by commending Keith's book to his friends with the hope that it provides a better understanding of this sometimes contradictory character while at the same time entertaining and amusing.

Alan Sutton, May 2008

List of Illustrations

1. KRD's birth certificate.
2. Earliest surviving photograph of KRD.
3. John Saunders, outside Huddersfield council house, Huddersfield, mid-1950s.
4. Actors Fred Ferris (left) and Trevor Maskell (right), with KRD (centre).
5. Huddersfield College, October 1955.
6. Form IY, Huddersfield College, October 1955.
7. Staff, Huddersfield College, October 1955.
8. Yard containing Moldgreen house, Huddersfield, later 1950s.
9. KRD and Edith Wood, later 1950s.
10. KRD, later 1950s.
11. 1.30pm 'Double Header' Newcastle to Liverpool express, arriving at Huddersfield station; later 1950s.
12. A4 Pacific ('Streak') locomotive, arriving at York station, later 1950s.
13. Upper Sixth Arts, Huddersfield New College, September 1961.
14. Staff, Huddersfield New College, September 1961.
15. Roger Kitching and KRD, 1962/3.
16. KRD as Charles VI of France in William Shakespeare's *Henry V*, Huddersfield New College, 1963.
17. Huddersfield New College State Scholars, *Huddersfield Examiner*, 1963.
18. Churchill Hall, Bristol University, 1960/5.
19. KRD, student house, Bristol University, 1965/6.
20. KRD *en route* to student house, Bristol University, 1965/6.
21. Michael Stammers, student house, Bristol University, 1965/6.
22. Peter, Allender, student house, Bristol University, 1965/6.
23. Bernard Jarvis, student house, Bristol University, 1965/6.
24. Caricatures by Ian Faulkner, mid-1960s: KRD (left) and K. G. Davies (right).
25. KRD's Graduation Photograph, 1966.
26. Miriam Saunders (left), Edith Wood (centre) and KRD (right), later 1960s.
27. Patrick Scott (left) and KRD (right), *Hatchet* pub, Bristol, 1968.
28. Patrick Scott *Hatchet* pub, Bristol, 1968.
29. Alfred Josephson (left) and KRD (right), Cotham flat, Bristol, 1968.
30. Alfred Josephson (left), KRD (centre) and Miriam Saunders (right) Cotham flat, Bristol, 1968.
31. Alfred Josephson (left), Edith Wood (centre) and Miriam Saunders (right), Cotham flat, 1968.
32. Charles Ross (left) and KRD (right), France, 1969.
33. KRD (left) and Charles Ross (right), France, 1969.

34. Charles Ross, France, 1969.
35. Plymouth College, 1970.
36. KRD, Colson House, Plymouth College, 1970.
37. KRD, Colson House, Plymouth College, 1970
38. Curtain call, *The Happiest Days of Your Life*, Plymouth College, 1971.
39. Post-production party, *The Happiest Days of Your Life*, Plymouth College, 1971.
40. Miriam Saunders (left), Patrick Scott (centre) and Edith Wood (right).
41. Miriam Saunders (left), KRD (centre) and Edith Wood (right.
42. Elsie Dockray, Newsome house, Huddersfield, later 1970s.
43. Elsie Dockray and Puss Puss, Newsome house, Huddersfield, later 1970s.
44. Edith Wood (left), Tony Dockray (centre) and Miriam Saunders (right).
45. Tony Saul (left), John O'Connell (centre) and Peter Durrans (right), later 1970s.
46. Peter Wood (first from left), John O'Connell (second from right) and Peter Durrans (first from right), later 1970s.
47. Peter Durrans (second from left), Keith Laybourn (third from left) and Pauline Stafford (second from right), later 1970s.
48. Nancy Alexander (first from left) John O'Connell (second from right) and Pauline Stafford (first from right), later 1970s.
49. Darrolyn Lowe (first from left) and Alison Shaw (centre), later 1970s.
50. Special Subject group, Middleham Castle, 1979.
51. Special Subject group, Middleham Castle, 1979.
52. KRD wearing a Campaign for Homosexual Equality badge.
53. KRD (left), Vivienne Haley (centre) and Peter Durrans (right), *Coach House* club, Huddersfield, December 1979.
54. KRD and Hazel Durrans, Newsome house, Huddersfield, January 1980.
55. Puss Puss, January 1980.
56. Edith Wood (left), KRD (centre) and Miriam Saunders (right).
57. History and Political Studies Department, Huddersfield Polytechnic, 1980.
58. Peter Allender and KRD, Bristol, early 1980s.
59. Oxford Union Debate on Richard III, Oxford University, November 1983.
60. Stratford-upon-Avon, July 1984.
61. Last photograph of Edith Wood (left), KRD (centre) and Miriam Saunders (right).
62. Graduation Day, Huddersfield Polytechnic, 1985.
63. Richard Bell (with Laurel and Hardy!), 1990/1.
64. Snubby, Bristol house, August 1991.
65. Snitch, Bristol house, August 1991.
66. Graduation Day, Huddersfield Polytechnic, 1991.
67. University of Huddersfield.
68. Steve Garrett and KRD, Bristol house, 1992.
69. Peter Allender and KRD, Bristol house, 1992.
70. Brendan Evans and KRD, joint 50th birthday party.
71. 50th birthday party, March 1994.
72. 50th birthday party, March 1994.

73. 50th birthday party, March 1994.
74. 50th birthday party, March 1994.
75. 50th birthday party, March 1994.
76. 50th birthday party, March 1994.
77. Graduation Day, Huddersfield University, 1994.
78., 79. and 80. KRD's retirement card, Huddersfield University, 1994.
81. *Representation and Reality of War*, book launch, Huddersfield, May 1999.
82. *Representation and Reality of War*, book launch, Huddersfield, May 1999.
83. *Representation and Reality of War*, book launch, Huddersfield, May 1999.
84. Peter Allender (left), KRD (centre) and Alan Sutton (right), Chinon, France, July 2000.
85. Alan Sutton (left), KRD (centre) and Peter Allender (right), Tours, France, July 2000.
86. KRD (left) and Peter Fleming (right), contemplating the battlefield of Nibley Green, July 2001.
87. Peter Fleming (left), KRD (centre) and an archer, Nibley Green battlefield, July 2001.
88. Fifteenth-century conference, University of the West of England, September 2001.
89. Reunion of 1966 Bristol English and History graduates, Bristol, July 2002.
90. Richard III Debate, University of the West of England, October 2002.
91. 'Black Stanier' locomotive, Severn Valley Railway, 2003.
92. Smoky, 2004.
93. KRD's final public performance, University of the West of England, December 2004.
94. KRD, towards the end of an extended session in the *Sportsman* and *Annexe* pubs, Bristol, 2005.
95. KRD (left) and Roger Kitching (right), August 2007.
96. KRD (left) and Roger Kitching (right), August 2007.
97. KRD (left) and Peter Allender (right), August 2007.
98. Discussing *Memoirs of a Yorkshire Bastard*, Annexe garden, 9 August 2007.
99. Discussing *Memoirs of a Yorkshire Bastard*, Annexe garden, 9 August 2007.
100. *Annexe* garden, August 2007.

Prologue

On completing my biography of Henry V in the summer of 2003, I felt I had written myself out on fifteenth-century England; moreover, I had no desire whatever to embark on a new programme of medieval historical research. Indeed, I was rather surprised to find myself still alive at all! Way back in 1978 I had deliberately settled for a hedonistic lifestyle, regardless of any implications for future longevity: hence why, in the autumn of that year, I'd resumed smoking cigarettes after over a year's abstention and abandoned any attempt to curb my penchant for regular session drinking of real ale. Living to a decrepit and maybe senile old age, I concluded, was a profoundly unappealing prospect, so why increase the risk of doing so? Similar considerations underpinned my decision to take early retirement from the University of Huddersfield in 1994: the prospect of a few years free of full time employment while I was still young enough to enjoy them. By the summer of 2003 over a quarter of a century of seriously unhealthy living had certainly left its mark but, strangely, I wasn't yet quite ready to hang up my pen altogether. So, when a couple of regular drinking mates suggested in the pub one night that I have a go at writing a history of my own life and times, I put together a synopsis of what such a volume of memoirs might contain. Early responses to it were sufficiently encouraging to solidify a vague idea into a firm project, not least those of former student Graham Townend ('I think you have a very interesting and compelling story to tell'), historian Ralph Griffiths ('You are a brave man to contemplate autobiography and I admire the frank scope you plan to take') and publisher Alan Sutton ('An admirable thing to do and I believe you will get much pleasure out of it').

From the start I settled on *Memoirs of a Yorkshire Bastard* as a deliberately ambiguous title and, before long, came up with the subtitle 'A Chronicle of the Life and Times of a Gay Medieval Historian' as well. Early on, too, I rejected any notion of penning a conventional autobiography or striving to make my ramblings commercially viable. As I wrote to Alan Sutton in December 2003:

> I'm embarking on these *Memoirs* primarily for my own entertainment and, hopefully, that of friends, former colleagues and ex-students. Only when (if!) they're completed might I contemplate publication. My own life and experiences will provide the core and narrative thread holding the story together but with a great deal of less personal stuff thrown in as well: for instance, working class mentalité and life in post-war Huddersfield; the ethos of, and education on offer at, Huddersfield (New) College, a traditional northern grammar school in the later 1950s and early 1960s; Bristol University, its history department and teaching in the mid-1960s; Plymouth College and boarding school life in the early 1970s; Huddersfield Polytechnic, its history staff, students and teaching in the later 1970s, 1980s and early 1990s; the Open University and its Arts courses in the 1970s, 1980s and 1990s; fifteenth-century historiography, research and writing; theatre and theatre-going in the later twentieth-century; and the impact of changing political and social attitudes towards homosexuality during my lifetime. Whether all this will hang together as a coherent whole only time will tell.

The sheer pleasure of donning the mantle of a medieval chronicler was very appealing as well, not least since I had spent so much of my academic career teaching and writing about such luminaries. At their best medieval and early modern annalists, chroniclers and historians might be conscientious enough when researching earlier times but, for more recent events, they tended to rely mainly on personal memories and experiences, supplemented by the not always reliable oral testimony of other men and women within their own circle. I decided to do precisely the same. Since my unknown natural father never figured in my life at all, however, I haven't even attempted to find out who he was. As for my natural mother, whom I did know, she certainly provides a salutary warning of the possible dangers of oral testimony. For years I took at face value the countless stories she told about herself and her life experiences until, eventually, coming to the conclusion that many of them were pure fiction. Under the influence of alcohol, indeed, I've occasionally been known to let my own imagination run riot too. Fortunately, when sober, I can still distinguish between myth and reality well enough!

Once I embarked on the *Memoirs* I soon realised I had a considerable personal archive to draw upon, not least a daunting quantity of material covering over thirty years teaching and research. I also unearthed copies or originals of many revealing letters sent or received since the mid-1970s, an impressive run of theatre programmes (the earliest dated 1960) and loads of memory-triggering and thought-provoking photographs. What I didn't have were diaries but, at least, this reduced any temptation to become bogged down in the trivia of yesteryear. The nearest equivalent to diaries were a series of tape recordings. In 1990 Robert Perks, a former student at Huddersfield Polytechnic who had become curator of oral history for the British Library National Sound Archive, persuaded me to record a couple of hours of reminiscences of my life and times for him; in December 2003 he kindly sent me copies of the resulting tapes; and, it soon became clear, my memory in 1990 had been considerably sharper than it is now. No less valuably, in the early 1980s, I had myself recorded several cassettes of conversation about their lives and times with Miriam Saunders and Edith Wood, both of whom played vital roles in my upbringing. Several friends have also sent me relevant material: for instance, former schoolmate Roger Kitching rooted in his attic and unearthed several copies of Huddersfield New College magazines dating from the early 1960s; Ian Faulkner and Michael Stammers, fellow history undergraduates at Bristol University in the mid-1960s, came up with a series of evocative photographs (particularly useful since, not possessing a camera at the time, I had virtually none of my own); and helpfully informative, too, was a very personal account by Cliff Burhouse (a mature student I taught at the end of the 1980s) of his working class upbringing in Honley, a suburb of Huddersfield, during the 1930s and 1940s. Another former school friend John Mackay, moreover, put me in touch with John Pearson who generously allowed me access to his unpublished *Memories of a Huddersfield Childhood*, particularly valuable as a source for Huddersfield College about the time I became a pupil there in 1955. Ex-colleague and dean of faculty John O'Connell even penned an immensely helpful mini-history of Huddersfield Polytechnic 1970-1992 specifically for my use. For context, I have also consulted Hazel Wheeler, *Huddersfield in Old Photographs* (1989) and *Huddersfield in Old Photographs: A Second Selection* (1990); E.A.Hilary Haigh (ed), *Huddersfield: A Most Handsome Town* (1992); Bryan Little, *The City and County of Bristol* (1955); Brian Chalkley, David Dunkerley and Peter Gripaies (eds), *Plymouth: Maritime City in Transition* (1991); and Chris Robinson, *Plymouth College: The First Hundred Years* (2005).

Towards the end of 2003 I approached over fifty friends, ex-colleagues and former students requesting reminiscences of me and our shared experiences. In 2004 and 2005 I asked another thirty or so. Amazingly, over seventy people responded and I've drawn on the resulting archive (filling three box files) heavily. Much of what they've written has been gratifyingly positive—indeed, sometimes embarrassingly flattering—but their recollections have certainly enhanced and enriched my own memories of the last half century. Several couldn't resist commenting on the project itself and how I was proposing to tackle it; again, their remarks were almost always encouraging. Peter Hammond, whom I first got to know through the Richard III Society in the 1980s, was particularly positive:

What a splendid idea to write a chronicle of your life and times. I thought the synopsis read very well and wanted to know more. You have certainly had a varied life and one which is becoming ever more remote from the experiences of people growing up and being educated nowadays.

As for John O'Connell, his 'main reaction' to the synopsis was 'one of admiration for the sheer facts of your life, your courage and resilience in overcoming disadvantage, and the candid and honest self-analysis'. 'Is the world ready for *Memoirs of a Yorkshire Bastard?*', asked former student Richard Bell rhetorically, adding firmly that 'it probably is'; Andy Hook, another ex-student, judged my 'smashing title for the chronicle certainly different, and why not?'; and longtime Huddersfield colleague Bill Roberts simply concluded that I had 'undoubtedly got the title right'. Reactions to my decision not only to use but also incorporate relevant material from the reminiscences of others were far from uniform but, again, mainly encouraging. Bernard Jarvis, whom I have known since grammar school days, found the notion of consulting in advance people who were to figure in an autobiography interesting, wondered if many did it, and even speculated that my intention to quote extensively from them maybe reflected my sheer inability, as a historian, to resist primary sources. Graham Townend felt including 'bite-size chunks of comments' from my contemporaries 'an excellent idea that ought to enhance the story', as should seeking to locate myself 'in the cultural, social and political context of the times'. Most thought provokingly Peter Allender, whom I first met in 1963, even wondered if the whole project was 'an exercise in self-validation' and 'giving speeches to bit-part players' an irresistible opportunity to read my own obituaries while I still could. Maybe so, but drawing on such material has certainly proved invaluable in helping construct a fuller and rounder picture of my life and times. Hopefully too, the *Memoirs* have acquired a more distinctive edge as a result, almost amounting to a Socratic-type dialogue in places. Now and again, though, I've judiciously concealed people's identities in order to prevent any possible embarrassment and, in particular, rendered most former sexual partners anonymous. Where I wasn't sure what to do, I consulted the individuals concerned. The response of my oldest friend Roger Kitching was typical: 'I have no objection whatsoever to being named in *any* of your chapters'. Roger's wife Bernice, too, urged me to 'go for the truth every time'. Let's hope that, at the very least, I've managed to fulfil Alan Sutton's expectation that 'your *Memoirs* will be a revelation since I'm sure you will not be frightened to speak your mind and honestly recount your experiences'.

Bristol, September 2007

1

Unpromising Beginnings in Post-war Huddersfield

When I was born on Monday 13 February 1944 my natural mother Elsie Dockray, then aged thirty-nine, was no longer married; her husband had deserted her a few years earlier; and she was struggling, on very little money, to bring up her legitimate eight year old son Tony. My conception, not the product of a long-term relationship, came as a complete bolt from the blue (not least since, at her age in 1943, she'd thought herself virtually immune from such a catastrophe). I was certainly not wanted and had it been legally possible at the time, so she once admitted, she'd probably have had an abortion. Instead, such was the social stigma of carrying an illegitimate child, she did her best to conceal her condition. Once my arrival was imminent, so she told me years later, she took a taxi from Halifax (her home town in the West Riding of Yorkshire) to St. Luke's Hospital in nearby Huddersfield where I was duly born in the early hours of the morning. So desperate was her situation at the time, or so she always claimed, that she had to carry on working and couldn't look after a baby as well. As a result, for most of my first six months I was in care, during which time, on 3 July 1944, I was baptized at Crosland Moor Church, not far from the hospital where I was born. After that I was fostered by a poor working class couple in Huddersfield. Both my mother and foster mother told me quite early on that this was facilitated by a photograph of me as an infant published in the *Huddersfield Examiner*. John and Miriam Saunders were the only couple who showed any interest, apparently. Local social services were far from happy about them: a recently married couple, not young, and living in a virtual slum dwelling in Almondbury, a short trolley-bus ride from the centre of Huddersfield. Even so, as a marginally preferable alternative to a children's home presumably, they reluctantly went along with the arrangement. I remained with these foster parents until I went to university in the autumn of

1963. Yet, in effect, I was fostered by three not two people since Edith Wood, an unmarried woman who lived next door to Miriam and John, also played a very active role in my upbringing.

Of my three foster parents, John Saunders was the oldest. Born in Scotland in 1895, he had been seriously wounded during the First World War, came to Huddersfield in 1932 and married Miriam Armitage at Huddersfield Registry Office in 1942. By then both were already living in the Almondbury terrace house where I spent my early years. Throughout my childhood John worked intermittently as an unskilled labourer in local textile factories but my most vivid memories relate to his penchant for heavy drinking and its domestic impact. When sober, which he was for most of the time, he had little to say for himself, often sitting quietly smoking his pipe for hours on end or, after we acquired a rented television set towards the end of the 1950s, watching the box. My schoolmate Roger Kitching recalls that when he visited me at home:

> John always seemed to be sitting in a corner smoking his pipe or watching TV. One afternoon, unusually, neither Keith nor Miriam were in so he answered the door. He was desperate for tobacco (the black wadded stuff) and pressed money into my hand to go and get him some. I did. He couldn't thank me enough when I came back with the right brand and the change.

To some extent at least John was dominated by Miriam, a notably strong-willed woman, for (except when strongly under the influence of alcohol) he was an amiable enough man; he was quite kind hearted and, as far as I can remember, never hit me; and, although he rarely showed it very much, he probably had quite a lot of affection for me. Even so, I suspect he found me very puzzling, especially once I became a grammar school boy and began to acquire knowledge and develop interests entirely beyond his limited comprehension. On reflection, he seems rather a sad figure. Maybe, indeed, he never recovered from his experience of the First World War, about which he was rarely prepared to talk at all. Only when well oiled with beer, Roger Kitching remembers me once telling him, did John occasionally open up about the war, particularly and poignantly recalling 'not being allowed to stay around if his army mates got some women in because he was regarded as too young for such hanky panky'. As the years went by, moreover, he suffered from ever more frequent bouts of ill health; he had a kidney removed (no doubt wrecked by years of intermittent heavy drinking); and I never had the chance to get to know him as an adult. He died in June 1964 and, although I have no memory of doing so, perhaps I provided the information for an obituary in the *Huddersfield Examiner*:

A Huddersfield man Mr John Saunders, who walked about for forty-five years with an inch-long piece of shrapnel in his head, has died at the age of sixty-nine. He served with the Royal Scots Fusiliers during the First World War and received a head wound at the battle of Neuve Chapelle in 1915. It was patched up without an operation and the shrapnel remained undiscovered. After a long hospital stay he returned to his regiment, only to be wounded again, this time in the arm. For six months he had suffered from head pains and, only after an X-ray revealed the shrapnel, did he at last have an operation for its removal in 1960.

Born near Selby in 1905, the same year as my natural mother, Miriam Brown was the daughter of a farm labourer who came to Huddersfield as a child. John Saunders was her second husband: an earlier marriage in June 1930 to Joe Armitage, an engineer's labourer, had ended less than two years later when he died of consumption. Perhaps mainly remarrying for conventional working class reasons of respectability and security, I doubt very much that love ever entered the equation; indeed, talking to Miriam later in life, I came seriously to doubt whether the marriage had much of a sexual dimension either, if any at all. Until her second marriage Miriam had been a weaver in various local mills. After it she never worked again so, for all the problems of my childhood, I was at least never a 'latch-key' kid. An overweight working class woman, she had a broad Yorkshire accent and, particularly when angry, tended to express herself loudly and volubly (a characteristic of many northern weavers, no doubt partly because of years battling to make themselves heard above the noise of looms). Yet she was also extremely kind-hearted and, throughout my childhood, looked after me as well as she possibly could. Roger Kitching also remembers her as 'very pleasant and kind, always welcoming' when he came to visit me. She was an excellent plain cook and, however hard up we were (and, clearly, we must have been not infrequently, since John had considerable difficulty holding down a job for long), I never went short of food or, for that matter, a bit of pocket money. Most of the time, too, she and I hit it off reasonably well, although there were occasional flare-ups as I got older. Like her husband she found it unnerving when I showed few signs of behaving like a conventional working class lad; nevertheless, she almost always encouraged me, even if she didn't fully understand what I was up to and why.

Edith Wood lived next door to Miriam and John Saunders in Almondbury until I was about nine and played a key role in my upbringing. An unmarried Roman Catholic (who, I have no doubt whatsoever, lived and died a virgin) and a native of Huddersfield, again from a poor working class background, she had been born in 1900 and worked in the same woollen textile mill from about 1916 until 1963, when she finally retired. Shortly before the outbreak of the Second

World War, following the death of her father whom she looked after during his last years, she moved from a tenement dwelling in Moldgreen to the terrace house next to Miriam's in Almondbury and, before long, they became friends. Although she strongly disapproved of John's heavy drinking (her father had been semi-alcoholic) and even counselled Miriam against marrying him, the two nevertheless remained very close. Always loving, supportive and generous with what little she had, nothing ever fazed Edith and she got on well with everybody; she was both more intelligent and more dependable than my foster parents proper; and, in another time and another place, she might well have left more of a mark than she did. She was also the nicest of the three of them and I probably felt more affection for her than anyone else as a child. Roger Kitching's judgement is spot on:

> Edith always seemed to me to be much more worldly wise than Miriam and had a glint of mischief in her eyes. There certainly would have been in younger days. I always thought she was quite canny, in a complimentary way. She seemed to know when to be involved and when to give you space. A sort of non-interfering guardian angel.

Both Miriam and. Edith, he adds

> ... seemed like two loving women who accepted their lot and, in most ways, were perfectly content: a pair of quite remarkable ladies. I suspect you played an enormous role in their lives, even more perhaps than you realised at the time.

From very early on I knew John and Miriam Saunders were my foster parents but this never worried me overmuch: it just didnt seem very important. My natural father never figured in my life at all and I have no firm memory of ever meeting him. According to my mother he was considerably older than her (another reason, perhaps, why my conception took her so much by surprise) and I got the strong impression that I was the product of a one night stand not a sustained relationship. Apparently, too, he ran a clothing business in Huddersfield and was a married man with a family. Beyond that I know nothing about him at all, not even his name, and he never recognised me as his son: Dockray was my mother's married name and the 'name of father' column on my birth certificate is blank. Nor have I ever had any desire to investigate my paternal roots. As for my mother herself, she was temperamentally highly strung, a compulsive talker and very much preoccupied with her own personal problems and well being. Even as a child I felt little affection for her: indeed, if anything, I disliked her, maybe even resented her very existence. She seemed a remote and rather irrelevant figure most of the time, far more concerned with my half brother Tony (who lived with her in Halifax) than her bastard son in Huddersfield. Much more powerful was my fear of local welfare officers and resentment at their unwelcome role in my life. Since I was a foster child living in conditions hardly likely to inspire the confidence of social service professionals, for years they had a habit of regularly arriving unannounced to check on my progress. Yet the only specific memory I have of these women, and they changed with bewildering frequency, is of an unusually pleasant young lady who owned a car and once gave me a ride in it: virtually the only car journey I ever experienced as a young child. Otherwise, welfare officers were the enemy, to be duped if necessary (for instance, concerning John Saunders drinking and its domestic impact) and I soon became adept at pulling the wool over their eyes. In a nutshell, I was scared stiff of most of them, terrified they might put me in a childrents home. Perhaps not surprisingly, I retain a deep-seated dislike, even contempt, for social workers to this day, as men and women employed by the nanny state to interfere in people's lives and promote whatever happens to be the fashionable social model of the time. I hope I never become decrepit enough to fall into their clutches again: no wonder I'm such an enthusiastic advocate of voluntary euthanasia.

In later life Miriam Saunders recalled that, when I was a little boy, my mother used to travel from Halifax to see me about once a week (usually on Thursdays); however, she added vehemently, Elsie Dockray did not want me herself. Edith Wood, more sympathetically, thought her 'a nice woman who occasionally stayed for tea'. My own memory is of less frequent visits, perhaps every three weeks or so, when I was more bewildered by her mildly maternal overtures than anything else. Until I was about fifteen or so she did at least contribute to the cost of my upbringing but never more than sixteen shillings a week, When she told me years later that, had she swallowed her pride and claimed the child allowance to which she was probably entitled (five shillings a week under the Family Allowance Act of 1945), it could have been more, I wasn't impressed and told her so in no uncertain terms. During her visits to Huddersfield I dimly recollect conversations between my mother and Miriam. Edith was frequently present too but, as for John, he just kept out of the way. The relationship between Elsie Dockray and Miriam Saunders was always uncomfortable, though, perhaps a reflection of class difference: my mother was essentially lower middle class (in attitude if not in wealth), not unintelligent (if no intellectual) and well spoken; Miriam was solidly West Riding working class, not frantic with brains, and had the dialect to prove it. For most of the time a sort of armed neutrality prevailed but, even in my presence, this carefully maintained facade did slip occasionally and increasingly, as I got older, I found myself acting as go-between. Deep down my mother simply didn't approve of either Miriam or her husband; they, in turn, neither understood or liked her; and nor, in all honesty, did I very much.

From about the age of nine, when I began travelling regularly to Halifax to see my mother, her own visits to Huddersfield became less and less frequent. This involved two bus journeys, lasting almost an hour, followed by a twenty minute walk to my mother's house. Only very rarely did either Miriam or Edith come with me. Today, it's difficult to imagine even most working class parents allowing a young lad to undertake such expeditions on his own virtually every week but, in the early 1950s, neither Miriam, Edith nor my mother seem to have had any real fears for my safety. Nor had I. After two or three years, indeed., I sometimes caught a train from Huddersfield to Halifax just for a change, requiring an even longer trek to my mother's place. Only very infrequently did I stay overnight with her and, since these visits were almost always made in the evening after school, I often had to travel back in the dark, rarely getting home much before ten o'clock at night. Amazingly, I only once encountered a paedophile. More importantly, I sampled my first illicit cigarette (pinched from a packet in my mother's living room) on the upper deck of a Halifax-Huddersfield bus when I was about twelve or thirteen and, before long, this became a regular ritual. By the time I got to my mid-teens, however, such journeys had become a real chore (especially as I had to do my school homework very early next morning) and, perhaps, this helps explain why I've never enjoyed travelling as an adult. Nor, in all honesty, did I much relish my mother's company, still less sampling her appalling cooking on occasion. Perhaps my most vivid memory is of at last meeting my half-brother Tony, resplendent in RAF uniform since he was doing his National Service at the time. I don't recollect my mother ever bringing him to Huddersfield with her. I certainly never had any desire to live with my mother myself. When at the age of about thirteen or fourteen, it seemed a real possibility for a time, I firmly resisted the suggestion. The burgeoning cost of my upbringing, and my mother's contribution to it, was at the root of the problem but, somehow, I managed to persuade her to leave me where I was. The fact that I was progressing well at a local Huddersfield grammar school by then was probably the clinching factor.

At the time of my birth in February 1944 the Second World War in Europe still had over a year to run but, obviously, I have no personal recall of its last few months. As a little boy, however, I do remember Miriam and Edith talking about the war and, even in old age, both still retained vivid memories of what were clearly the most traumatic years of their lives. Since there was an anti-aircraft battery not far from where they lived in Almondbury, the sound of guns firing at German bombers was, according to them, not infrequent. Yet, despite the presence of a large chemical complex which, throughout the war, was given over to manufacturing explosives, hardly any bombs were dropped on Huddersfield (unlike nearby Bradford, where a long-time friend of Edith now lived): indeed., Roger Kitching remembers his father, who was in the Home Guard, telling him that only a couple of bombs ever fell on Huddersfield, both narrowly missing the ICI. Fear was the main emotion Miriam and Edith conjured up: the sirens, the noise of planes flying overhead and, most of all, the guns. Specifically, Miriam recalled getting up in the dark when the sirens sounded, rushing to a neighbour's house for comfort or, even, cowering in the coal cellar of her own. There was no air raid shelter nearby, apparently. Her most persistent memory, dating from before her wartime marriage to John, was of fire watching during the night at the local factory where she worked and being petrified much of the time. Edith, similarly, vividly remembered the noise of gunfire, feeling scared stiff and wishing she'd never moved from Moldgreen. A particular nightmare, so she once told me, was that the Germans would drop a bomb while she was sitting on the lavatory, knickers around her ankles, and the sheer humiliation of being killed under such circumstances. Once they became close friends, moreover, she and Miriam often took to sharing a bed together if the sirens sounded. Both were clearly almost as intimidated by the blackout (probably the cause of more injuries and fatalities in Huddersfield than enemy action), hated being out alone after dark, and felt profoundly relieved when the war in Europe ended in May 1945.

Post-war Britain was undoubtedly bleak since, for all the no doubt honourable intentions of Clement Attlee's Labour government to promote welfare and social justice, austerity was very much the name of the game. Many foodstuffs were still rationed; Miriam, John and Edith hadn't much money anyway; and, as a result, I hardly ever enjoyed the luxury of either fruit or chocolate as a young child. Jam and bread, on the other hand, were regularly on the menu, and even beef dripping was a treat when John was out of work. Wholesome stews usually appeared at weekends, though, and very occasionally funds ran to a tin of salmon for tea (shared between three of us). Unfortunately, there never seemed to be any shortage of cod liver oil! Nevertheless, I seem to have been healthy enough, apart from contracting childhood illnesses like measles and chicken pox, then almost unavoidable. Also, when I was about four or five, I had my tonsils out, a fashionable procedure at the time. This entailed spending a few thoroughly unpleasant days in Huddersfield Royal Infirmary, the only time I've ever been a hospital in-patient (although I was an out-patient at about the age of fifteen when I broke an ankle). Occasionally, too, I was dragged along to see a school dentist, almost invariably to have decayed teeth extracted under a general anaesthetic: working class kids like me were rarely, if ever, offered the option of fillings in the 1950s. I loathed these visits and didn't like doctors much either. No doubt this helps explain why, as an adult, I've kept contact with both dentists and general practitioners to an absolute bare minimum: indeed, for several years in both the 1970s and 1990s I wasn't even registered with a dentist or doctor at all.

My earliest personal memory is of the exceptionally severe winter and heavy snowfalls of 1947 and, again while I was still an infant, a very dry summer when we had to get water from standpipes in the street. Another firm memory is of a lady who delivered milk from door to door, ladling it from a portable churn into jugs and bowls provided by customers. She even let me accompany her on her round occasionally. I also remember a nearby fish and chip shop; its owner was very friendly; and, a great boon for a small boy with hardly any money, free samples came my way now and again. Then there were the regular visits to Miriam's older sister Annie Moxon, more often than not for tea on Sundays; she lived in a tiny house that had no electricity and was lit by gas; and I certainly found this extraordinary to say the least. A formidable woman who had spent many years in domestic service, she oozed traditional working class morality; Edith, who often accompanied us, didn't like her much at all; and, as for me, I found her alarmingly severe and censorious. She obviously didn't think her younger sister was fit to bring up a child, disapproved strongly of my foster father (who, wisely, never came with us) and invariably found my table manners below standard. She even spanked me once for some minor misdemeanour or other, much to Miriam's embarrassment. Later, she was to express her strongly held view that boys of my background ought not to go to grammar school. Perhaps Miriam was as scared of her sister as I was but, fortunately, rarely took any notice of either her forthright opinions or frequently tendered advice about my upbringing. Much the most vivid memories of my early years, however, are of lying in bed on Friday and Saturday nights listening to Miriam and John loudly arguing whenever he returned home drunk from the pub: a frequent occurrence, at any rate until his health began to deteriorate in the later 1950s, and a source of deep anxiety for an already insecure little boy. Now and again he would become violent; I dimly remember a crockery-smashing incident and once running to a local policeman's house to get help; and, as I grew older, I became more and more adept as a conciliator and diffuser of potential conflict and violence. In the mid-1950s I even took to meeting him at the factory gate on Friday teatimes in the hope of persuading him to come straight home with me rather than squandering his meagre wages in the pub. Presumably John was a virtual alcoholic. If he stuck to beer it didn't tend to be too bad but, if he had sufficient funds for whisky, the ensuing strife (almost invariably preluded by his loudly singing in the street as he wended his unsteady way home) could be very frightening indeed. No wonder I dreaded the onset of weekends for years.

John's alcoholic excesses tended to blight Christmas as well, despite the efforts of Miriam and Edith to make it as enjoyable as possible. The pair of them always scraped together enough cash for presents, however modest, most memorably a splendid glove puppet of Mr Punch one year; however, if John went to the pub the night before or at lunchtime, Christmas Day afternoon could all too easily be ruined. Perhaps, indeed, it was the anxieties of Christmas (combined with involuntary attendance at Sunday school for several years!) that first led me to have doubts about Christianity, doubts that had made me an agnostic by my mid-teens and an atheist by the time I departed for university in 1963. Until I went to primary school, moreover, I was a very solitary child and knew hardly anybody of my own age. I only recollect ever playing with one other little lad and, once his parents realised where I lived, they rapidly put an end to our meetings. I was obviously a most unsuitable companion for their son. This probably brought home to me, for the first time, just how desperately poor a hand I had been dealt by life.

For centuries far more important than Huddersfield itself, Almondbury, where I spent most of my first eight or nine years, had a well recorded history; the village's Norman lords had constructed a castle there in the early twelfth century (on a hill now occupied by the Victoria or Jubilee Tower, first opened to the public in 1899); and its much restored parish church dated back to later medieval times. In terms of living conditions, moreover, the Almondbury terrace house rented by John and Miriam Saunders was probably no great advance on its medieval equivalents (as my mother, for reasons best known to herself, was forever reminding me in later years). A one-up one-down slum dwelling, it had no kitchen, no bathroom, no hot water even; the door opened straight into an all-purpose living room, with very basic cooking facilities, and heated by a coal fire (sometimes unlit, even in winter, if money was short); and upstairs lay a single unheated bedroom, dominated by a huge double bed. Internal walls, I vividly remember, were distempered a depressing shade of green, there wasn't much furniture and, I dimly recall, the three of us even shared the double bed. The outside lavatory, shared with at least two other residences, was at the bottom of an unkempt communal garden; its door had no lock or bolt; torn up newspaper served for loo paper; and, when the temperature dropped below freezing in winter, its plumbing tended to seize up as well. For night use, all three of us had a chamber pot in the communal bedroom and slopping out was the first ritual every morning. Edith's house next door was precisely the same as ours. Nevertheless, Miriam in particular was extremely houseproud, no doubt partly in order to fill the long days while John was at work. Monday was washday and, since she had no washing machine, this was a laborious business requiring a tub (filled with water heated in a gas boiler), rubbing board, posser and mangle.

Drying took place on a washing line outside if the weather was fine but, if it wasn't, wet garments were placed in sequence on a clothes horse in front of the coal fire. This resulted, inevitably, in a steam-filled living room before long. Tuesday was devoted to ironing, again a long drawn-out routine since the flat iron had to be reheated frequently on an ancient gas stove. On Wednesdays and Thursdays the house was cleaned, another massively time-consuming operation since Miriam didn't have a vacuum cleaner either, always insisted on black-leading the cast iron fire surround, washing the windows and even donkey-stoning the doorstep. When I once questioned the point of all this, she became extremely annoyed, muttering darkly about what the neighbours would think if she didn't. Perhaps observing all this cleaning as a child helps explain why, as an adult householder, I've never given it any sort of priority. Friday was shopping day for the weekend, particularly at the local coop where there was the important bonus of dividend stamps, as well as bath night: an embarrassing semi-public ritual featuring a battered tin bath in front of the fire and hot water transported by bucket from the faithful gas boiler. Alternatively, and very much my preferred option as I grew older, there was the head-to-foot weekly wash at the stone sink in the corner of the living room. I don't remember washing much any other day and, if I did, it was almost invariably in cold water. As for my teeth, I hardly ever brushed them at all until I was about nine or ten: no wonder so many decayed. Like many northern working class women of the time, both Miriam and Edith had had false teeth since their early twenties and, as for John, he seemed to have virtually no teeth at all. Personal hygiene certainly took second place in our home to keeping the house spick-and-span:

When I was about nine, perhaps because social services determined I was now too old to share a bedroom (let alone a bed) with my foster parents, we were offered and moved into a small semi-detached council house on a newly built housing estate in Dalton, an ill-defined Huddersfield suburb about twenty minutes from the town centre. For the first time in my life I now experienced the luxury of a kitchen, a 'front room' (which we only tended to use at weekends), an internal lavatory, a bathroom, hot water on tap (when we could afford to switch on the immersion heater) and, best of all, a small bedroom of my own. Even so, the estate itself left a great deal to be desired, as did some of the residents, and it could be distinctly scary after dark. Not that we lived there very long. When my mother refused to increase her weekly payments to Miriam and John, at a time when his health and capacity to work were deteriorating, there were only two options: either I went to live with her (a prospect I dreaded) or we found cheaper accommodation. Hence why, at the age of about fourteen, I found myself back in a sub-standard house. This was in Moldgreen, a largely working class district only a few minutes from the centre of Huddersfield and awash with nondescript terrace housing mainly built towards the end of the nineteenth century. Cliff Burhouse, whom I taught as a mature student in the late 1980s, remembers his own home in Honley, just outside Huddersfield, in the 1930s and 1940s:

> We lived in a back-to-back end terrace house with one large and one small bedroom and an attic. We had just one downstairs room which served as a sitting room and dining room. There was also a large cellar and a cellar head kitchen, referred to as a scullery, which contained the only sink in the house. There was, of course, no bathroom: instead, diagonally opposite, was a row of outside toilets.

The Moldgreen house we rented from about 1957 or 1958 was very similar (although lacking an attic and not back-to-back): an end terrace property virtually unaltered since it was built over half a century earlier, privately owned (the landlord collected his modest rent in person every Saturday morning) and located at the bottom of a yard. Once more there was no running hot water, no bathroom and no inside lavatory (but at least the outside loo was exclusively ours and had a door that locked!). Most importantly, I still had a tiny bedroom of my own (a boxroom really) and, a real bonus, Edith Wood now lived in a one-room underdwelling in the same yard. Bernard Jarvis, a middle class lad I got to know as a sixth former, vividly remembers:

> ... coming to tea with you in Moldgreen on more than one occasion. It must have been a bit of an eye opener for me, coming from the other (posher) side of town. Where your foster parents lived was traditional working class terrace housing, with outside lavatories where you had to take the key when you wanted to go. It was the nearest I got to the D.H.Lawrence novel *Sons and Lovers* we were studying at the time—but with more warmth and more fun.

I continued to live in this house until I went to university in 1963 and stayed there during vacations until 1972. Miriam and Edith, after John's death in 1964, eventually moved in together (and shared an ancient double bed whenever I was at home). There they remained until, back in Huddersfield myself and lecturing at the recently established polytechnic, I bought a modernised Moldgreen terrace for them in 1978. Bernard Jarvis recalls this too:

> After Miriam was widowed, she and Edith lived together, eventually in the house in Moldgreen you bought for them. And they lived together, with you to keep an eye on them and help when needed, until they died.

'Not many people do that for foster parents', he adds gratifyingly, 'nor, for that matter, birth parents'.

In the autumn of 1949, at the age of five, I joined the infant class of a local Almondbury school. Despite the 1944 Education Act (providing free secondary education for all up to the age of fifteen in grammar, technical or secondary modern schools), Almondbury County School continued to cater for children of both sexes between the ages of five and fifteen. Only in 1955, the year I left, was it finally split at eleven and a brand new primary school opened. It was not an establishment for wimps. The headmaster, a large bald man, was hardly progressive even by the standards of the time. On the contrary, he seemed to operate on the general principle, if it transgresses, cane it. Indeed, he was only marginally less brutal than Cliff Burhouse's vividly remembered junior school head of the later 1930s:

> There is no doubt in my mind that he derived great pleasure from administering punishment. He looked for and loved any excuse to apply the cane; moreover, the procedure entailed a performance which could not be rushed. Each element was enacted in its own time-honoured way, designed to extend the punishment, a psychological tool of terror. First there was a sermon expressing disappointment in the wrong-doer, then the sentence, from six strokes of the cane on the hand, the minimum, to twelve strokes bent over, the maximum. Serious misdemeanours earned a caning bent over a chair in front of the whole school at assembly.

My own starkest memories, too, are of morning assembly when the whole school came together, tightly crammed into an area barely adequate to contain us all. This provided a perfect setting for the head to harangue his temporary prisoners and, all too frequently, such gatherings culminated in the despatch of a senior lad to his study to fetch the cane, a fearsome instrument of correction whose vigorous employment was clearly the highpoint of his day. More often than not several offenders now suffered an obviously painful caning across the palms of both hands (generally two or three strokes on each hand but sometimes more) in full view of the entire school. Some of his victims, almost invariably older boys, were tough and took their punishment with scarcely a whimper; others he rapidly reduced to floods of tears; and, throughout, there was a deathly hush. For we little boys the warning was only too clear: such a brutal and ritualistic infliction of pain and humiliation must surely come our way, too, when we got older, if we ever stepped out of line. Except for assembly, however, juniors hardly ever encountered the head and only once do I remember him chastising anyone in my own class. It was certainly a dramatic occasion, probably deliberately so. Suddenly materialising one day in the middle of a lesson, he seized a startled six or seven year old lad, pulled his pants down, put him across his knee and spanked him so hard that he cried and sobbed for at least ten minutes. Only once, too, do I recall him in a jovial mood: on 2 June 1953, Elizabeth II's coronation day, when every child received a dimpled glass (inscribed with the royal coat of arms) and a copy of the New Testament. Most junior misdemeanours were dealt with by class teachers or, very occasionally, the deputy head but, again, corporal punishment was a frequently employed sanction. Even during our first two or three years at the school naughty boys—and, occasionally, girls too—might find themselves at the receiving end of sharp slaps to legs and buttocks; by the age of eight or nine a well worn gym shoe or leather slipper was often put to effective use on the rumps of miscreants; and by the time we got to ten teachers were permitted, perhaps encouraged, to cane our hands and bottoms as well. No wonder the more timorous of us knuckled down and learnt for all we were worth. Now strictly taboo of course, and perhaps rightly so, corporal punishment nevertheless helped produce a disciplined learning environment for working class children in the 1950s.

Almondbury County School itself must have been built decades earlier and lacked virtually all modern facilities. The classrooms were dingy, the layout inconvenient for staff and children alike, and even infants and juniors had to use outside lavatories that were basic to say the least. Classes were large, teaching methods traditional and rote-learning very much the order of the day. As for physical education, what little there was occurred in the playground and mainly took the form of drill; the school had no playing fields; and there was no attempt, either, to teach us to swim. Yet, perversely, I responded well to a curriculum consisting almost entirely of reading, writing and arithmetic. Within a year I had learned to read fluently; writing came easily to me as well and I soon came to enjoy the eccentricities of English grammar and spelling; and, although I found arithmetic more challenging, I was probably smarter than most when it came to the mysteries of addition, subtraction, multiplication and division. As a result I managed to escape corporal punishment almost entirely; the odd slap and occasional slippering came my way but I was never caned; and I could witness the sufferings of my more unruly and less able classmates almost as an outside observer. Indeed, as the years went by, I felt more and more at ease with myself in the school and, even after we moved from Almondbury to Dalton, I remained a pupil, running the two miles there and back twice a day. I never stayed for school dinners either at junior or secondary school. Years later Edith Wood recalled that I was 'a good little boy who worked very hard at school'; moreover, she added, everyone took to me. Yet, in fact, I was always a bit of a loner, mixing well enough with most of my classmates when I had to and never becoming the target of bullies but rarely joining in boisterous playground games or ever becoming close friends with anybody.

Everyone knew, of course, that the only avenue of exit from Almondbury County School before the age of fifteen was the 11+ examination. Here I was very fortunate. Miss Clarke, the school's deputy headmistress, was also the 11+ teacher. A middle-aged woman and a first-rate traditional schoolmistress, she was certainly formidable, not least when wielding a cane. Yet, perhaps, she needed to be if she was to have any chance of getting even the brighter kids in a class of over forty children through a notoriously tricky series of three exam papers: English, Arithmetic and General Knowledge. Cliff Burhouse remembers the 'dauntingly formal exams' he took to gain entrance to Holme Valley Grammar School, near Huddersfield, in 1940 and they hadn't changed much fifteen years later. Many middle class kids, no doubt, received help, even coaching, at home but, obviously, I didn't. Indeed, even at school there was almost no teaching specifically directed at the General Knowledge paper. As for most of my fellow pupils at Almondbury (mainly of working class origins like me), they probably had little or no prospect of making it to grammar school, however well taught they were; moreover, although virtually all my classmates were both literate and numerate by the age of eleven, this was confirmed when the results were published. Only a handful, of us had reached the level required. What I most remember about Miss Clarke's lessons, however, is not the teaching most overtly aimed at the 11+ (beginning, each morning, with a list of words whose spelling we were expected to have mastered before the day was out) but the sheer amount of poetry we were required to learn by heart. William Wordsworth's pastoral poems were a particular passion of hers and, for me, this was to provide an unexpected bonus years later when sitting an A-Level English Literature examination: I found, to my surprise, that I could still quote passages from several of them, so firmly had they been committed to memory at Miss Clarke's direction.

Boys from Almondbury County School who got through the 11+ very often opted to go to nearby Almondbury Grammar School. Since I now lived in Dalton, and had had more than my fill of journeying four miles a day by foot (not least negotiating a long and steep hill), I opted, instead, for Huddersfield College, mainly because it was near the town centre and easily reached by trolley bus. The fact that it was also Huddersfield's most prestigious grammar school, even if I knew that at the time (probably not), didn't enter the equation at all. None of my classmates applied for that school or, if they did, they failed to make it. Hence why, at the beginning of my first term at grammar school in September 1955, I knew no one at all among the thirty-three boys in Form 1Y. Peter Allender, a friend for over forty years, muses:

> What is it that makes Keith so intensely question the point of everything, even life itself? Perhaps the answer lies in his early years and upbringing. I have come

to understand that one of the results of emotional abuse in childhood is to rob you of the self-confidence which is everyone's birthright and that it never returns in the same form. Instead, along with the unresolved anger, there is a sense of always performing a role that is not the real you. Some are driven inwards on themselves. Others, like Keith, push ever outward with a will not just to succeed but to exceed in everything.

Maybe passing the 11+ and becoming a pupil at Huddersfield College, on top of the traumas I'd already experienced, set me irrevocably on just such a path.

2

Grammar School Boy at Huddersfield (New) College

When it became clear during my last year or two at junior school that I wasn't going to turn out to be the conventional working class boy, my foster parents must have found it very puzzling. Yet, as the evidence mounted that I was reasonably intelligent and making real progress at school, both Miriam and Edith (and even John) were very supportive and, when I passed the 11+ and obtained a place at Huddersfield College, they were delighted. This needn't necessarily have been the case. Cliff Burhouse recalls that, when he obtained a place at Holme Valley Grammar School, near Huddersfield, in 1940, his father had to be persuaded to let him go there because of the school's 'lofty aspirations which those of our social position and financial status had no business to expect'. Even fifteen years later the notion that grammar schools were for the posh, the middle class, not the likes of them, remained commonplace in northern working class circles. There was also the perception that grammar schools took working class children away from their roots, the fear that they might become alienated from their backgrounds, even that they might become snooty and begin to despise their parents. Such apprehensions were not without justification and, certainly, Huddersfield College did nothing to prevent this happening (quite the contrary in fact). Equally daunting was the sheer expense of going to grammar school, particularly the cost of fitting out children with uniforms. Cliff Burhouse remembers the problem of getting the money together for his uniform and my foster parents were very worried about this too. Fortunately, for once, my mother came to the rescue: she was very keen indeed that the negative consequences of my upbringing by Miriam, John and Edith (as she saw it) be countered, not least my rather strong Yorkshire accent.

John Pearson, who left the school in 1956, recalls that:

The College, as Huddersfield College was usually known (nicely reflecting the self-confidence of the place), was a traditional boys-only grammar school with a remarkable record of getting lots of people into Oxbridge and other universities. It was selective and took those Huddersfield boys who had done best in the 11+ examination.

Dating back to Victorian times, the school certainly had a very distinctive uniform, most notably a black blazer sporting Huddersfield's coat of arms and the town's motto *Juvat Impigros Deus: God Helps the Industrious*. 'That', comments John Pearson wryly, 'says it all'. For me, wearing a uniform at all was an entirely novel experience and it made me feel distinctly vulnerable on the Dalton housing estate where I lived until I was about fourteen: in particular, I hated the college cap and kept it stuffed in my pocket most of the time. Yet, on reflection, I'm glad uniform was a requirement. At least it meant I looked like everyone else at school. After all, Huddersfield College was a huge culture shock for me and, for quite a while, I wondered what the hell I was doing in such a deeply alien environment. My classmate Roger Kitching, another working class lad, is spot on here:

> We must have arrived at Huddersfield College after similar experiences at junior school and we reacted similarly too: a new start surrounded by strange faces and, all around us, middle class boys whose parents lived in posh houses, possessed cars and had homes full of books.

It was obviously very different for Bernard Jarvis (whom I got to know in the sixth form):

> My memory of schooldays is of a remarkably uncritical acceptance of things as they were. It wasn't that I either approved or disapproved of the set-up at grammar school: it just didn't occur to me that it could be other than it was. I suppose this was because the ambience of the place suited a middle class boy like me better than a working class lad.

My own reaction to Huddersfield College in the autumn of 1955 was very much more akin to that of Cliff Burhouse who, when he'd arrived at Holme Valley Grammar School fifteen years earlier, had 'felt very much like a small fish in a large pond'. The place had about it an entirely unfamiliar muscular Christian ethos and, horror of horrors, an expectation that all boys would participate actively in sport. This was the worst feature of all for me. No less strangely, all the staff were men; they wore academic gowns both at morning assembly and in class; and they almost invariably called us by our surnames (as we did each other!). Early on, too, I experienced my first school Speech Day in Huddersfield Town Hall, a most serious event featuring not only an uplifting address by the headmaster to assembled pupils and parents but even speeches in Latin and French delivered by senior boys, and brought to an end by us all singing the remarkably stirring and tuneful school song to the accompaniment of the town hall's splendid organ:

> We're boys of the sturdy northland,
> Midst mills and mines we live,
> And for our well-loved homeland
> The best we can we'll give...
> We're sons of the school,
> We'll hold fast the rule,
> And all do our best
> For the School, School, School.

I now recognise that the school was, in fact, permeated by a Protestant work ethic, an acceptance of the strange notion that 'a healthy mind' and 'a healthy body' formed an inseparable unity, and a belief that encouraging a sense of loyalty to house, to school and, by extension, to country, was an entirely desirable objective: in a nutshell, Huddersfield College sought to import into the state sector of education many of the features of contemporary public schools. No wonder when, between 1969 and 1972, I myself taught at Plymouth College (a partially residential HMC Direct Grant School), I found the parallels with Huddersfield College striking to say the least.

Although there were plenty of working class lads at Huddersfield College, they were far outnumbered by middle class boys (or so it seemed to me); moreover, even among the ranks of working class kids, I soon became acutely conscious that my background and home circumstances were worse than most. Hence why, during the first year or two at least, I was so reluctant to invite anyone to the council estate where I lived. We were positively discouraged, moreover, from mixing with non-grammar school boys, as Roger Kitching recalls:

> At the meeting all parents of new boys were supposed to attend they were told by the headmaster that their children would now be expected to mix with other boys from the college and not their former friends if they were at secondary moderns. The reason given was that they would now be getting a lot of homework whereas other children wouldn't. My mother, in response, told me I wouldn't be able to play out with some of my old mates anymore.

I didn't even tell John, Miriam and Edith about this meeting! What really got to me early on was the lack of understanding by many staff of the problems faced by a boy like me in such a privileged, academic work-orientated environment. Most of them had no idea how it was for us working class lads plucked from everything that was familiar and plunged into this strange new world with its very different priorities and values. A particular memory stands out here when the headmaster A. Ronald Bielby (a mathematician and Methodist lay preacher), perhaps when I was in the second year, deliberately went round the class asking (without any concern for individual privacy or sensitivity) what our parents' jobs were. I was mortified at having to admit, within the hearing of others, that my foster father was a mere unskilled factory worker and I still squirm at the sense of humiliation I experienced that day. Always lurking at the back of my mind, too, was the fear of it becoming known that I was not only a poor working class boy living on a council house estate but a bastard as well. Such was the stigma of illegitimacy in the 1950s.

During his time at Huddersfield College, John Pearson recalls, there were 'no serious disciplinary problems' nor much rough or violent behaviour among the boys'. This was equally true of the later 1950s. Nevertheless, one school friend at least does 'vividly recall being bullied' in the lower school and believes 'a lot of the teachers turned a blind eye'; however, he adds, 'I also seem to remember that you were better than me at keeping out of the way of bullies'. This is probably true, not least because I deliberately befriended the most persistent bully in my form and even tried to discourage his excesses. Nor did I ever attract much in the way of punishment. This mainly took the form of detention after lessons for the day were over (even on Saturday mornings for persistent offenders): one lad I knew even managed to get himself detained on one occasion for 'taking the name of a prefect in vain'! Roger Kitching also recollects, as a punishment for being late for school, once having to report to a member of staff at 8.00am next morning. A couple of detentions came his way as well but he can't remember me ever receiving one. Nor can I, maybe because I became adept at covering my tracks (especially after I started smoking a bit). What was almost entirely lacking at Huddersfield College, in contrast to both my junior school and many public schools of the time, was corporal punishment. Only one boy in my class, as I recall, was ever caned: on the bottom by the headmaster and, so the lad reported, very painful. Judging by the weals on his backside, closely inspected by several of us in the showers later, the middle-aged headmaster was fitter than he looked! Otherwise, an art teacher very occasionally put a T-square to unorthodox use on a boy's rump; an exasperated English master once applied his own gym shoe to another's; and, most memorably, there was an isolated occasion when a lad's bare behind was vigorously spanked by a games teacher in the changing rooms. That was it.

Once I embarked on my grammar school career, there were all sorts of pressures liable to distance me from my foster parents and conventional working class home life, not least the sheer amount of homework I was expected to do both in the evenings and at weekends. They really couldn't see what the point of it was. Nor, probably, could I at first. Nevertheless, both they and Edith Wood strove to provide as good an atmosphere as they could for me to do my work. Years later Miriam Saunders recalled that I obviously wanted to learn and had lots of homework; moreover, even though she couldn't understand a great deal of what I was doing, she admitted to always feeling proud of my progress at grammar school. The nearest Miriam and Edith got to personal involvement was by subjecting themselves to school parents' evenings, as Roger Kitching speculates:

> Did Miriam and Edith go to parents' evenings? I'll bet they did, as a pair, and they'd fasten onto anything and everything that was said. I also wonder what the staff would have made of them: not the middle class mother and father they were used to.

I certainly admired Miriam and Edith for subjecting themselves to such alien experiences yet was probably more embarrassed for them than they were for themselves. Even so, they must have found entering such an aggressively middle class environment and talking to middle class masters about subjects that were often a completely closed book to them very strange. Fortunately, the feedback they received on me seems to have been largely positive, as indeed were my school reports (all of which have long since vanished, unfortunately), and the encouragement they (and even John Saunders) gave me deserves more credit than I ever acknowledged at the time. Both in the council house at Dalton and, later, the terrace in Moldgreen, I had my own bedroom and could retreat there from the ever blaring radio (later TV) downstairs. I have particularly vivid memories of my tiny bedroom in the Moldgreen house: much of it was occupied by a bed and, since there was no table (no space for one), I did most of my homework on a piece of hardboard laid across it. In winter I was provided with a one bar electric fire but soon realised that the cost of running even this was a worry to my foster parents. Hence why I took to wearing two, sometimes three, pullovers and a pair of fingerless gloves to keep my hands warm. Even in bed I often kept a pullover on, not to mention socks, and getting dressed in the morning in a freezing bedroom was never a pleasant experience. Soon I began acquiring books (mainly bought out of my pocket money but occasionally obtained by more dubious means) and Miriam even persuaded a local joiner she knew to knock together a bookcase for me. I still have it, in the utility room of my Bristol house. This bedroom, in fact, became my little domain and I even took to entertaining friends like Roger Kitching. God knows how we managed to squeeze in and, once we started smoking cigarettes there as well, the atmosphere must have been unhealthy to say the least. Even Miriam eventually baulked at cleaning the room too thoroughly, no doubt put off by the sheer amount of closely packed clutter.

As a sixth former in 1962 I wrote an article entitled 'Bi-Lingual' for the Huddersfield New College magazine, obviously reliving my early years at the school:

> For the new boy grammar school is a bewildering environment: teachers (only they are called masters now!) in black gowns; new subjects such as physics (whatever that is!); and, worst of all, homework. The initial strangeness of these features of school life is common to most first formers but, for a minority, there are other problems: working class boys also feel the contrast between primary school (with its substantial proportion of working class lads) and grammar school (with its much smaller percentage) sharply. These boys, speaking the 'Broad Yorkshire' of their working class homes, find that almost all the masters and a fair number of the boys at grammar school speak 'BBC English'. Inevitably, they feel inferior to both. Possibly, too, their shortcomings of speech will lead to them becoming shy; or, instead, they may adopt a 'couldn't-care-less' attitude towards both their speech and the school. In most cases, however, they will attempt to rid themselves of the embarrassing Yorkshire accent when at school. Often, owing to conscious or unconscious determination, they become able to speak more or less good English in class. Yet, at home, they continue to speak as they always have: it would embarrass them to do anything else. Both they and their families would feel uncomfortable otherwise and they would cease to feel part of their local community.

'It is hardly desirable that a significant minority of grammar school boys should be bi-lingual', I concluded boldly, 'but it does emphasise the gulf which still exists between the working-class home and the essentially middle-class school, a gulf neither side seems fully able to bridge'. This obviously came from the heart and, maybe, even the headmaster read and pondered it.

Not too long after leaving Huddersfield New College in 1963 I began to cultivate an extrovert, friendly, devil-may-care image and, eventually, image and reality became virtually inseparable. There was very little sign of this in the nervous, insecure schoolboy of the mid-1950s. I didn't find it easy to make friends at grammar school and wasn't even sure if I wanted to. There was one lad Bryn Moody (in the year above me at Huddersfield College), whom I'd known a bit at junior school and with whom I now often travelled to town on the trolley bus from Dalton, but we were never close. I also got to know Roger Kitching, another fellow traveller on the early morning bus, who nevertheless recalls that:

> Early on, apart from seeing you on the bus most days, I didn't know you very well because you sat with a second year boy called Bryn, a pleasant self-confident fellow who probably gave you lots of important information such as masters' nicknames.

Both of us remember that we most frequently found ourselves on the upper deck of two of the most ancient trolley buses in the fleet and, more specifically, 'Minnie, the tubby little bad-tempered clippie, all bust, bus tickets and bag o'money'. There was certainly no juvenile rowdiness on the bus when she was in charge! Roger lived not too far from me, but not on a council estate, and he enjoyed a much more secure (if still working class) home environment: indeed, his parents were terrific and, once they got to know me, always welcomed me with open arms. Before long I realised that Roger himself was a super lad and, fifty years on, see no reason to revise my judgement. I also soon came to envy him a great deal, not least for his prowess at sport, and, ironically enough, it was football that first helped forge our long-lasting friendship:

> I nervously approached you towards the end of our first term when I was picked to play for the school first year team against Almondbury Grammar School and had to get hold of a green football shirt. Since you were in Lancaster house you had such a shirt and, at 4.0pm one day when we were packing our bags for homework in Room 1 (we had to be quick because our form room was also the detention room!), I asked you for a loan. Your response was magnificent. Not only did you say I could borrow the shirt, you promptly brought it out of your desk and let me have it, commenting that there was no hurry to get it back and I didn't even have to wash it afterwards.

As I detested games anyway, I was probably only too glad to see the back of a pestilential football shirt: indeed, the only constructive use it ever had was when Roger wore it! Occasionally, he and I were joined on the morning trolley bus by John Mackay, another local lad who had been at the same junior school as Roger, and I was most impressed to discover his aunt was a primary school head teacher. As an 'A' stream boy, however, John was little more than an acquaintance at this stage and it wasn't until the sixth form that we became firm friends. Otherwise, I only really knew a lad called Michael Duke, another working class boy (albeit a notch up from me) whose small stature and gaucheness made him a natural target for bullies. Sad to say, I found his impressive model railway layout more interesting than he was and even persuaded my foster parents to buy me an electric train set. That must have created a nasty hole in their tight finances.

Only gradually did I become confident enough to invite the occasional boy to my own home but only if their backgrounds were not dissimilar to mine. I continued to remain very wary of middle class lads (especially once we'd moved back into a sub-standard terrace house). Not until I entered the sixth form did I get to know Bernard Jarvis. His father was something important in the ICI, his mother a notably cultivated woman (she read serious books for pleasure and went to classical music concerts, for God's sake!), and he lived in a splendid house with a younger brother and two or three sisters. Being invited to tea at his home was a revelation and, eventually, I took the bull by the horns and nervously brought him back to my place one day. My foster mother must have been rather taken-aback by this confident, well-spoken middle class teenager but, oddly enough, my very different background served to cement rather than inhibit our friendship; we both went to Bristol University; and, in 1966/7, even shared a flat together. Throughout my lower school years, however, Roger Kitching was my best mate, a friendship much solidified once we discovered a shared love of the theatre. 'Although I haven't seen our first year form photograph for years', he mused in January 2004:

> ... I can remember exactly what you looked like in it: on the end of a row, with a pre-Beatle mop of hair. After that it was combed back straight in good adolescent manner.

'We were little boys when we went to Huddersfield College', he adds, 'but we had to grow up quite quickly and fit into a mould that didn't necessarily suit'.

Fortunately for me, I found myself in the 'B' stream at Huddersfield College. Perhaps this reflected the level I'd achieved in the 11+ although, I suspect, the junior school I had attended and my council estate background might well have been factors as well. At the end of the first term I almost got promoted from 1Y to 1X (or 1B and 1A as they now became, as all pretence that there wasn't streaming was abandoned), and at the end of the first year (as a result of good examination results) I did qualify to transfer to the 'A' stream. I didn't want to. The 'A' stream seemed to be even more awash with confident middle class kids than the 'B' stream, the pressure on them was greater (the 'A' stream were expected to take several 'O' Levels after four years) and, anyway, I'd only just begun to feel fairly comfortable where I was. In the end I wasn't forced into it and probably just as well. I hadn't got much faith in my academic ability as it was. At least in the 'B' stream I generally managed to come near the top of the class in most subjects; this gradually led to a growth in my self-confidence; and, eventually, I passed the eight O-Levels I sat. I can't help wondering if, had I been fast-tracked in the 'A' stream, I might well have come badly unstuck and, maybe, even dropped out of grammar school altogether.

My memories of Huddersfield College itself coincide almost precisely with those of John Pearson:

> Huddersfield College, a group of soot-blackened buildings in Halifax Road about half a mile from the town centre, was the main focal point and formative influence of my adolescence. The physical environment of the school is imprinted on my mind: the square, castellated main building, then, down some steps and across a small yard, 'the House', with three or four classrooms. And, across a lane, 'Highfields', a large building with a lot of stairs.

Roger Kitching particularly remembers:

> ... the 'House', across the quad at the old school. It's amazing that the best grammar school in Huddersfield could have conditions like that. It was completely unsuitable for classrooms. No wonder they were so keen to move us to new buildings.

Conditions certainly were dire. The main building was clearly in a poor state of repair; the roof leaked and, on very wet days, buckets might be found littering its narrow corridors; and once, during the night fortunately, a corner turret came crashing down. The 'House' must surely have been a serious fire and safety hazard. As for Highfield Hall, a tall building containing both a large assembly room and classrooms, I seem to remember that it didn't even belong to the school but was rented from the Congregational Church. Nor was the furniture much better. Many of the boys' desks, in particular, looked as if they'd been there for years. Yet, paradoxically, when we moved to brand new premises at Oakes in the spring of 1958 (irritatingly located much further from the town centre), I suddenly realised just how much affection I'd developed for the castellated if ramshackle late Victorian building we'd left behind and the rather cosy introverted grammar school ethos now irrevocably lost.

What I most remember about the typical school day at Huddersfield College is how very tightly organized it was. Each day began with registration, the responsibility of whoever happened to be our form master that year, followed by morning assembly in Highfield Hall: a daily dose of nondenominational Christianity (hymn, Bible reading and prayer) enthusiastically led by the headmaster. Although never explicitly revealing his Methodist credentials, A. R. Bielby's Christianity was only too evident and, perhaps, most boys felt comfortable enough with it. I never did and, instead, my nascent agnosticism became more and more solid. The ritual ended with announcements of the day's sporting activities, school society meetings and, not infrequently, a morality-charged homily by the head himself. At his best, moreover, he could put in a remarkably charismatic and compelling performance. John Mackay could mimic him splendidly and, indeed, still can. As for the rest of the day, Roger Kitching recalls its structure precisely:

9.0am:	Period 1
9.45am:	Period 2
10.30am:	Break (Milk!)
10.50am:	Period 3
11.35am:	Period 4
12.20pm:	Lunch (Dinner!)
1.55pm:	Registration
2.0pm:	Period 5
2.40pm:	Period 6
3.20pm:	Period 7 (God! What a long pm!)
4.0pm:	Finish

'How's that for memory', he comments ruefully, 'it's all to do with anxiety!'.

Even more firmly etched in my mind is the sheer range of academic subjects we studied. From the start we were taught Latin and French, as well as chemistry and physics in specialist laboratories. They were all new to me: indeed, I didn't even know what physics was. In the first year we were taught French by our form master 'Garry' Gowans and, so Roger Kitching assures me, I began joining in lessons quite early on, 'even to the extent of taking part in little plays acted out in front of the class'; moreover, in his opinion at least, my accent was excellent! Sadly, my enthusiasm for French didn't last and, today, I can hardly string together a couple of sentences in the language. Early on, too, I enjoyed chemistry, particularly as taught by the deputy head 'Joss' Browning: 'a genuinely kind and caring man', recalls Bernard Jarvis, 'as well as someone who thought teaching and pupils were at least as important as the subject—a pretty dangerous and radical view at the time'. I soon acquired a chemistry set and, so Roger reminds me, 'even had a bunsen burner attached to a gas tap at home: very impressive'. Once chemistry became increasingly mathematical, however, I rapidly lost interest and, at the end of the third form, gave it up in favour of history. Clearly, by the age of fourteen, we were considered ready to choose between a predominantly 'arts' or 'science' pathway. Physics was always less appealing but here, too, Roger has a striking memory of:

> ... a physics homework when we had to find out how the valve in a bicycle pump worked. Since you didn't have a bike, I came round to your house and brought my own bicycle pump with me. We took it apart. You explained how you thought it worked but I wasn't too sure. We agreed to differ. You got full marks, I got very few, but you had shared the right answer with me.

Since we were offered no choice in the matter, I reluctantly carried on with physics to O-Level and, amazingly, clocked up a B grade (perhaps an examiner's mistake!). Mathematics I never liked and struggled to cope with it for several years, not least because I couldn't see the point of algebra and geometry (and no one ever tried to explain it). The headmaster himself taught us geometry in the first form, presumably in order to get to know new boys, even using a textbook he had written himself: I was suitably impressed! He wasn't a bad teacher and certainly preferable to 'Benny' Barker whose mathematics lessons we also endured in the first couple of years. In a nutshell, this seriously obese man, who would often manicure his nails while sitting at a tall old-fashioned schoolmaster's desk in an upper room of the 'House', simply frightened us to death as he relentlessly ridiculed our efforts. He only ever once cracked a joke at his own expense when, after almost tripping over a boy's feet one day, he pointed out the possible fatal outcome had he actually fallen on top of him! God help anyone he took a serious dislike to and, as a result, a couple of lads in our form suffered absolute hell. Fortunately, I managed to keep a low profile most of the time and only rarely attracted his sadistic attention. Yet, as far as I was concerned, even maths with 'Benny' Barker was preferable to P.E., swimming and, worst of all, games. Why so many boys seemed to enjoy them was a complete mystery to me.

No doubt John Mackay particularly has our early years at the school in mind when he comments:

> I didn't think much of most of the teaching we received and laugh when people talk about the high standards in old grammar schools. There's no comparison between the quality and commitment of teachers I worked with as head of a comprehensive school in North Wales and many of the time servers at Huddersfield College.

This is a bit harsh. There were highly qualified staff at the school (several could have taught at degree level) and a few first-rate teachers. Unfortunately, they were rarely saddled with first, second or third form 'B' stream pupils. Eventually, I opted to study English, history and geography to A-Level but, early on, my enjoyment of these subjects was seriously marred by frequently uninspired teaching. For the first couple of years I was taught English by music masters and they obviously felt far more at ease with grammar than literature. Fortunately, if perversely, I didn't mind this but even I never fully got the hang of clause analysis. The senior geography master 'Jake' Ormondroyd, who did teach us and knew his stuff, was both a firm disciplinarian and boring with it: it was certainly very unwise to turn up at his lessons without an atlas. History was a complete disaster. 'Bessie' Baldick, who attempted to teach us Latin as well, simply didn't have a clue. Since he was slightly deaf, too, he found it extremely difficult to maintain order in class and, all too often, completely failed to do so. His idea of history teaching was to get us to read a textbook chapter for homework and set a twenty question factual test next period. Our aim was to delay and disrupt proceedings as much as possible, if only to facilitate cheating when it came to marking each other's answers. Nevertheless, since his favourite punishment for mild unruliness was the deduction of marks, not a few boys must have ended up with virtually negative scores by the end of term. Detentions and lines, too, he scattered like confetti but since, more often than not, he forgot to register such punishments, they were no deterrent. As there were two periods of history per week but only one homework, there was also the problem of how to occupy us during the second lesson. More often than not, he simply set the class to copy a map, battle plan or any other illustration he could find in the textbook. How I retained my nascent interest in history during two years of his tuition I'll never know. Fortunately, we never suffered him again. His teaching of Latin (a subject in which, as he freely admitted on more than one occasion, he had little expertise) was no better and we endured three years of him for that: no wonder I only just scraped through O-Level. Over half a century I have encountered plenty of lousy teachers but none more appalling than 'Bessie' Baldick. Yet he was certainly loyal to a school he had known, as boy and man, for over fifty years. He was also a fundamentally decent man (as I discovered one summer vacation when I enjoyed a long conversation with him in a local park) and deserved a better fate than to be killed by a passing train when, in old age, he blundered onto a local railway line.

Despite so much indifferent teaching in the lower school at Huddersfield College, I tended to do well enough in most subjects, as Roger Kitching confirms:

> I remember you as one of the brighter boys who was very alert but always kept a low profile. In some ways you were a teacher's delight because when it came to the

really hard question, and no one else volunteered, you would often then answer and seemed almost invariably to be right. I could put always right because I don't think you would answer unless you were certain. You always did your homework, always seemed well organised and rarely did badly in a test. In the termly alpha race, you were invariably up with the leaders. Boys gained an alpha for a good piece of work and, if a lad obtained one for each week of term, he got a half day holiday at the end. You always made the number with several to spare yet never seemed desperate to get the last few in the final weeks as some were. A few even pleaded!

Since, as John Pearson recalls, 'any boy who was in the least unusual stood out sharply from the crowd', I was always very careful not to do that.

When I was in the third form Huddersfield College combined with Hillhouse Technical School, doubled in size and moved into brand new premises as Huddersfield New College. Roger Kitching, moreover, is right to 'suspect that Keith, like me, did not relish the move to the new school'; indeed, he adds, 'it was a real worry and hung over me for months beforehand'. I felt precisely the same. The huge four storey building we moved into at the start of the summer term in 1958 was designed by John Poulson, an architect who later achieved considerable criminal notoriety, and perhaps cost-cutting helps explain its lack of any real character, its early teething troubles and its many practical drawbacks. In particular, we boys seemed to be forever trudging up and down long and crowded flights of stairs; connecting corridors were notable by their absence; and there was but a single lift (strictly off limits for us, of course). This must have been a real challenge to older masters and virtually impossible for anyone who was disabled. As for the school stage, it seemed to have been designed to make mounting productions as difficult as possible. Since lower school boys were not present anyway, I have no memory of the *Official Opening* of *Huddersfield New College 1957—58: An Inheritance of Learning from the College and Hillhouse Technical School* in March 1958. The programme of what amounted to a service of dedication says it all, however, not least the 'ceremony of the open book' (whatever that was!) and an anthem 'I Saw a New Heaven and a New Earth' (composed by the music master and performed by the school choir). Inevitably, there was a heavy Christian content and this spurious ceremony of pompous self-congratulation culminated in an address by Sir Edward Boyle, Parliamentary Secretary to the Ministry of Education. Needless to say, too, A. R. Bielby (not his Hillhouse Technical School equivalent) became headmaster of the new hybrid and, clearly, he was determined to carry across as much of the ethos of Huddersfield College as he possibly could. Not only did masters continue to wear gowns, for instance, before long prefects started doing so as well. As Bernard Jarvis recalls, moreover, Huddersfield New College continued to have a 'Christian middle class aura' about it and the 'implicit values of its hidden curriculum' remained essentially unchanged; nevertheless, he also emphasises that, even if 'shot through with a desire to ape public schools' (in sport, for instance), the college at least lacked the 'raging anti-intellectualism' of its Victorian muscular Christian forbears and, in more enlightened moments, even aspired to stimulate 'an independent critical intelligence'. This is evident in a school magazine report of A.R.Bielby's homily at the 'Upper School Speech Day' in the autumn of 1962:

> The headmaster recalled some of the outstanding achievements of the school during the past year. On the academic side, he mentioned the large number of university places which pupils have won; he remarked that we run nearly twenty sports teams; and that, on Saturdays, a hundred and fifty boys represent the school.

Inevitably, however, since there were now four or five streams instead of two, a wider range of subjects on offer and far more working class boys, the traditional grammar school ethos became increasingly hard to sustain (whether the headmaster liked it or not).

Perhaps even a headmaster as remote as A. R. Bielby became aware, by the time we entered the third or fourth form, that we were not progressing as well as we should be. At least we now began to get a few of the better masters. In the autumn of 1957, for instance, we got a first-rate mathematics teacher and, for the first time, I began to make real progress in the subject I'd always found hardest. Unfortunately, at the end of 1958, he suddenly left, rumour had it for showing rather too much interest in a homophobic sixth former. No doubt this explained the hasty recruitment of a local clergyman to take his place and he proved almost as hopeless as 'Bessie' Baldick. He couldn't control even a class of grammar school boys and his foolish admission, after two or three weeks trying to teach us the mathematics of the cone, that the cone was no longer in the O-Level syllabus only served to make matters worse. No wonder many of us performed so badly in the end of year exams. As a result, no doubt, we got 'Ivor' Barron in the fifth form, a master who usually taught only 'A' stream boys and sixth formers. Thanks to his encouragement, patience and excellent teaching, I progressed from a near-fail at the end of the fourth year to a B grade at O-Level: remarkable: He was a splendid form master too, even seeing the funny side of our occasional pranks at his expense. We got decent Latin, French and physics masters as well and, most importantly for me, Alan Thorpe for English and James Crump for history. 'Burp' Thorpe had been head of English at Hillhouse Technical School and now saw himself as a bit of a rebel against the establishment; I enjoyed his down-to-earth approach to teaching; and, as a result, obtained high grades in both English Language and English Literature. As for Jim Crump, a young Oxford history graduate, he was a revelation. Not that he was a progressive teacher. Quite the contrary. More often than not, he talked and we took notes. Yet, and this is what mattered, he clearly knew a lot, and could put it across vigorously and inspiringly, even when constrained by a less than exhilarating syllabus: indeed he, more than anyone else, must bear the blame for my eventually becoming a professional historian. In the end, I passed all eight O-Levels I took: English Language, English Literature, History, Geography, Latin, French, Mathematics and Physics (both written and practical!).

Once I'd secured my O-Levels, both my natural mother and my foster parents expected that I would leave school and get a job. This was certainly my intention as well until, belatedly to say the least, Huddersfield New College suddenly realised that I might be an academic high flyer, perhaps even a potential Oxbridge entrant. No doubt this explains why, for the first time in my school career, I was summoned to the headmaster's study; he'd obviously been well briefed by the likes of Alan Thorpe and Jim Crump; and he now unleashed his not inconsiderable persuasive powers in order to convince me that I ought to enter the sixth form. For a while I resisted, convinced that I owed it to my foster parents to start earning, especially since John Saunders had just retired and money seemed tighter than ever at home. A. R. Bielby now pulled his master stroke. Not only did he pen a letter to John and Miriam, he wrote to my mother Elsie Dockray as well, powerfully putting the case for my embarking on A-Levels. As a result, for the one and only time, even my mother visited the school and met the headmaster; he convinced her that I ought to set my sights on going to university (an idea that rather appealed to her vanity); and, most importantly, he drew attention to the possibility of my getting a bit of funding. Miriam, John and Edith all made it clear, too, that they would back whatever decision I came to and help me as much as they could. This was the main reason, in fact, why Edith carried on working beyond retirement age. The upshot was that, armed with a small but vital bursary, I entered the sixth form in September 1960. In the intervening summer vacation, though, knowing full well the financial implications of my staying on at school, I did get a job in a local department store for several weeks. Once in the sixth form, of course, I joined lads who had arrived there via the 'A' stream. This seemed a very daunting prospect at first until, over the first couple of terms, it gradually dawned on me that I was academically up with the best of them: a real surprise but a most agreeable one as well.

That I chose to study history to A-Level was virtually inevitable. Nor was I disappointed by the periods we were now required to study. Jim Crump inspired an immediate interest in Tudor England, especially its kings, queens and politics, which has remained strong ever since. Perhaps, too, it was reading and discussing G. R. Elton's controversial *England under the Tudors* (1955) that first sparked a taste for historiography. Roger Kitching's enthusiasm for history was also fired by this first-rate teacher and, apparently, I did my bit as well:

> You were a lad I found it inspiring to talk to about history. If I couldn't get to grips with a Crump essay, half an hour talking it over with you made me want to rush back home and start it. I'd dropped history in the third form, Jim Crump got me interested again, but it was you who gave me so great an enthusiasm that I resolved to go to university to study history and eventually become a history teacher myself.

Harold Richardson, the middle-aged head of history and our form master in the second year sixth, was a highly intelligent man whose teaching I had already experienced in 1957/8. Rather to our consternation, however, he now announced that we were to study medieval Europe 800—1500. By 1960 he was no longer *au fait* with recent research: indeed, he even recommended that we frequently consult T. F. Tout's *The Empire and the Papacy* (first published way back in 1898), perhaps because he himself had been touched by Tout's powerful legacy at Manchester University thirty years earlier. Fortunately, our main textbook was R. H. C. Davis's much more recent and stimulating *History of Medieval Europe* (1957). Nor was Richardson's teaching all that inspired, not least because of his tendency to rely on William Edwards' notorious, and none too reliable, *Notes on European History*. Nevertheless, he certainly fired my interest in a fascinating and formative era of European history and, when diverted from virtually dictating notes to us (not too difficult), his own enthusiasm for history was still very evident. Again, I was particularly drawn to personality, politics and the exercise of power: the Emperors Charlemagne, Otto the Great and Frederick Barbarossa, for instance, and the Capetian kings who ruled France from 987 to 1328. Harold Richardson was also an extremely civilised man who took a real interest in my progress, encouraged me to read beyond the textbooks and even invited me to his Almondbury home once or twice. He was also a great hit with Miriam and Edith at parents' evenings. I remained in contact with him for years after leaving school and got to know him quite well following my return to Huddersfield in 1972. Long retired by then, he remained a stalwart supporter of the local branch of the Historical Association and looked set to reach a ripe old age (as a staunch Methodist, he'd never drank, or smoked for that matter). Sadly, he was tragically killed in a car accident in Spain.

There was never any doubt, either, that I would study English literature to A-Level. Ted Darke ('Sambo' as we'd known him in the lower school!), head of

English and our form master in the lower sixth, was an avuncular and gentle man (as befitted a Quaker), as well as an accomplished traditional teacher: he introduced us to Chaucer, for which I remain eternally grateful, and even managed to make sense of Shakespeare's *Anthony and Cleopatra* (no mean achievement). Alan Thorpe drew the short straw, I suspect, and had to engage our interest in John Milton's *Paradise Lost* Books 1 and 2: he certainly succeeded with me and, over twenty years later, I hope I managed to do the same with Open University students. He was on an altogether easier wicket with Shakespeare's *The Tempest*. Not until the second year sixth did I experience, for the first time, the English teaching of Michael Gillard, perhaps the most charismatic and dynamic young master on the staff. For Bernard Jarvis he was 'an inspirational English teacher whose enthusiasm for literature fired me to go on and study it at university'; indeed, Bernard adds, 'I can still remember some of his lessons quite clearly'. Even John Mackay, for all his criticisms of the school, is entirely positive about Mike Gillard:

> He was a real role model for me, as he was for many. More than that, he introduced me to a new world of culture in its widest sense.

Unfortunately, I found it impossible to share Gillard's enthusiasm for either D. H. Lawrence's *Sons and Lovers* or the poetry of Gerard Manly Hopkins. I'd had enough experience of working class life in Huddersfield without sampling Lawrence's Nottinghamshire equivalent and, as for poetry, Wordsworth (whom we studied with Ted Darke) was far more to my taste. Indeed, it wasn't until the third year sixth, when I got to know him much better, that I fully came to appreciate Michael Gillard's remarkable qualities both as a teacher and a friend outside the classroom. Even Edith and Miriam, when they met him at a parents' evening, were completely charmed.

Why I chose geography as my third A-Level remains a minor mystery to this day. Maybe it was because, in the early 1960s, it had the reputation of being a soft option. I enjoyed geomorphology with Frank Ormondroyd, head of geography, although his monotonous presentation could be a real challenge, particularly in the late afternoon; Tony Hague entirely failed to engage my interest in climatology (but I doubt if anyone else could have succeeded either); and as for regional geography, an antidote to intellect if ever there was one, the less said the better. Since 'Jake' Ormondroyd, although a considerate enough man beneath the surface, had scared me to death in the lower school, and 'Ernie' Hague hadn't exactly endeared himself to me as my housemaster for several years (I'm sure the feeling was mutual), perhaps I wasn't predisposed to appreciate their efforts anyway. There's no doubt they knew their stuff. Even so, how I managed to get a B grade in geography I'll never know. It was my lowest grade. I obtained an A* in English, an A in history, and managed to pass a couple of more demanding 'Special' papers in history and (amazingly) geography as well. As a result I obtained a State Scholarship (in the last year of the existence of such awards) and, alongside the other two lads who won them (Jeremy Anscombe and W. S. Sheldrick, both scientists), even got my picture in the *Huddersfield Examiner*.

Huddersfield College and its hybrid successor both offered a bewildering range of after school activities in which boys were expected to participate. For a start, there was sport: athletics, cricket, cross-country running, football, hockey, rugby, tennis—the list seems endless. Then there were societies: chess, debating, geographic, literary and dramatic, music, natural history, photographic, scientific, to name but a few. Regular school trips were organised too. During my sixth form years, for instance, school magazines report expeditions to Wharfedale, North Wales, Paris, Switzerland and Norway. Almost from the start, I resolved to avoid sport, especially team games, like the plague. I rarely attended society meetings either: too alarmingly full of self-confident middle class lads. As for the Student Christian Movement, its very existence seemed yet another reason to embrace agnosticism. School trips were beyond my foster parents' financial means so I missed out on them as well: indeed, I wasn't to venture abroad until 1969. The only exception to my all round non-participation was a geography field trip to the south coast in the spring of 1962, when Frank Ormondroyd persuaded the powers-that-be to cough up the necessary funds; as a result, I visited the New Forest and Isle of Wight for the only time in my life.

At Huddersfield College, recalls John Pearson, 'the big hall in the middle of the main building was used as a gym and equipped with wall bars and ropes'. From the very first moment I saw this torture chamber in September 1955, I knew it wasn't for me. The sight of school playing fields, and boys playing team games, had much the same impact. As for Cambridge Road Baths, the only positive feature of swimming lessons was the mug of cocoa we got afterwards; moreover, although I soon mastered the basics of swimming, I never let on since the next stage, learning to dive, was too profoundly unappealing even to contemplate. Early on, Roger Kitching remembers:

> ... you were only too happy to play for the 1Y (1B) third soccer team. As there were only thirty-three boys in our form, this was always low in numbers, due to the sick, the lame and the lazy. It didn't seem to bother you.

Another unpleasant feature of P.E., swimming and games in the first couple of years was having to shower naked, no doubt because of deep-seated working class prudery. As puberty set in, this became more embarrassing still, even for an accomplished games player like Roger who recalls a gym master, as late as the fourth form, once demanding that:

> ... everyone who had a towel go for a shower together. About ten of us (you and me included) obeyed. To take our shorts off in public was difficult: it felt a bit like Jews going to the gas chamber. It was alright once we were in the shower, and we certainly returned to the changing room as superior beings: the truly brave who had showered naked!

The only consolation, as my homosexual orientation began to emerge, was the opportunity to observe the finer points of nicely put together classmates. Otherwise, I felt much the same as John Mackay, who believes the ethos of games for non-sportsmen like us was:

> ... beautifully evoked in the late 1960s film *Kes*: cold days, huge boots, agonised warming of hands on radiators after the match (in the third team for football, of course). The boy in the film swinging miserably on the goal post could certainly have been me.

The contrast between us and Roger Kitching could hardly have been greater. Yet, Roger reckons, sport was 'the only thing' that gave him 'pleasure and some prestige: I felt the school valued me for that but nothing else'. He was particularly skilled at rugby (which, fortunately, I managed to avoid playing altogether), as indicated by a school magazine report on the rugby first fifteen in the autumn term of 1962:

> In the pack R. A. Kitching, G. H. Field and A. G. Oldfield have formed a formidable back row and have outplayed their counterparts in every match this season. Kitching, the scorer of ten tries, has been most adept at pouncing on a loose ball, and his strength has usually brought his tries.

No wonder, as I struggled to come to terms with my homosexuality, I fell so deeply in love with this athletic heterosexual lad who was everything I wasn't as a teenager. No wonder, either, that relations between 'Ernie' Hague, my housemaster at Huddersfield New College, and I were less than cordial. He had no sympathy at all for boys like me who cared not a jot for the 'honour of the house' and did everything I could to avoid sport, even forging my natural mother's signature on bogus sick notes from time to time. Only once did I ever make any sort of impact when, instructed to open a window to let in some fresh air during a house meeting, I responded so vigorously that it smashed to smithereens, scattering broken glass everywhere. 'Well', I commented dryly, 'you've certainly got plenty of fresh air now!'. Even the housemaster was unable to suppress a chortle at that.

The only sport I was any good at was cross-country running, as John Mackay rather ruefully reminds me:

> Like me, I recall you being both unathletic and uninterested in sport. Yet I also remember your talent for running, at which I always struggled. There was one annual cross-country race when we ran together. I was wheezing along in much pain and you were bouncing alongside to keep me company, as though out for a gentle stroll. When we got about two thirds of the way round I think you must have got bored, declared 'I'll just run on a bit', and vanished in about ten seconds. You couldn't have cared less about 'getting the standard' for the house, or competition of any kind, but running at my pace had understandably become tedious.

'You weren't into sport', echoes Roger Kitching:

> ... but nearly made a bad decision by demonstrating, in the first and second year cross-country races, an ability to do distance running. I think you must have come in the top ten. This form was not replicated in subsequent races, so it must either have been nandrolene or a desire not to get noticed.

Definitely the latter. Better to maintain a low profile in all sports, I decided, so as to get myself written off as universally useless. Only in the lower sixth did I suddenly rediscover an aptitude for running on games afternoons, but only as far as the nearby *Spotted Cow* pub, accompanied by two or three other like-minded lads. The landlord must have known we were Huddersfield New College boys, and probably under age, but that never stopped him serving us beer. As for cigarettes, we stashed those in pockets carefully sewn into the inside of our shorts. Indeed, in the sixth form, I even smoked on school premises now and again, either in a tiny windowless room next to the library (very risky) or a lavatory much frequented by a chain-smoking member of staff. A fitting end to a non-sporting career in a school where fortunately, as Bernard Jarvis points out, it was possible to flourish even without being good at games.

Of all the after school activities on offer at Huddersfield New College, only drama had any real appeal for me. Occasionally, I went on school visits to the theatre. In the autumn of 1962, for instance, I joined a coachload of sixth formers for a trip to Manchester Opera House to see the Old Vic Company in William Shakespeare's *The Tempest* (one of our A-Level set texts). Alastair Sim, as Prospero, certainly gave a compelling if highly unconventional performance. I remember, too, Michael Gillard taking a group of us to Leeds Grand Theatre (in a thick fog) for an electrifying staging of Leonard Bernstein's musical *West Side Story*. I went to the odd school production as well, most memorably a rendering of A. A. Milne's *Toad of Toad Hall*, splendidly performed by a cast of younger boys under Mike Gillard's direction. Only by accident, however, did I become involved in drama myself, playing Thomas Mowbray Earl of Nottingham in Gordon Daviot's *Richard of Bordeaux*. This was in the lower sixth and, rather to my surprise, I enjoyed myself enormously, camping it up quite outrageously in a small but vital part (played by Donald Wolfit in the original West End production of 1933). John Mackay has an evocative memory of one particular performance:

> In Mike Gillard's production of *Richard of Bordeaux*, when I was John of Gaunt Duke of Lancaster, there was a bit of gauntlet play. You hit Barry Kergan across the face with your felt gauntlet; he let rip with the heavyweight version he'd been given; three blobs of sweat flew from your forehead into the wings; and you staggered back half way across the stage in a daze. I even remember smothering a snigger!

A couple of years later, in the spring of 1963, I played Charles VI of France in a production of Shakespeare's *Henry V*. A report in the school magazine judged the production 'consistently and excitingly entertaining throughout', not least the performance of John Mackay who brought 'a truly regal glory' to the part of Henry V, 'leaving us in no doubt that here was a king in the grand style, born to control and succeed'. Even I penned a short article entitled 'A View from the Throne':

> No question of lack of enthusiasm on the stage: In those dreadful few seconds before the curtains drew back on my scenes, I found myself frantically and almost unconsciously rushing through lines, adjusting my costume and trying, usually with little success, to make myself comfortable on the hard wooden seat of the throne. Around me were others performing similar operations: one pacing up and down the stage trying to avoid the creak, another trying not to cough, and the rest finding their correct positions for the start of the scene. Then—dreaded moment—the preceding front-of-stage scene ended and, with a loud fanfare, the curtains parted to reveal—US. While trying to appear regal, how unlike a king I always felt at this point—the climax of nervousness for me. Yet once the action had begun all nervousness disappeared. Not only was I attempting to look like Charles VI, I was beginning to feel like him too. This, for me, is why acting can

be such a satisfying experience, the feeling of coming to understand a character well enough to interpret him on stage.

Looking back, I have no doubt that sixth form acting increased my self-confidence and, maybe, even helps explain why, in later years, I treated lectures very much as if they were stage performances.

Once I arrived at university in the autumn of 1963, I soon realised that most of my fellow students had obtained places conditional on their A-Level results that year. Huddersfield New College, perhaps here reflecting its large and well-heeled middle class intake into the sixth form, had a firm policy of requiring boys to get their results the year *before* applying. The main reason for this, I suspect, was the headmaster's determination to maximise the number of lads obtaining places, better still open scholarships and exhibitions, at Oxford and Cambridge. In the summer of 1961 the school magazine contained a letter from a sixth former, describing himself as 'a rebel', complaining of the work load and calling for greater freedom:

> ... to learn for oneself. The only way out is to pluck up courage, break down the hurdles and leave school. I do not know if this is possible, but I am tempted to try; for this much praised sixth form life has deprived me of the things I enjoy. The sixth form is no place for the highly emotional, highly strung or temperamental person; for he will soon realise he is trapped and may perhaps reach his breaking point.

Even in my final months at Huddersfield New College I never felt as disorientated as that but I did find the third year sixth a strange, even mildly surrealistic, experience. John Mackay, the school magazine's editor in 1962/3, pleaded in his final editorial for the 'present library' to be turned into 'a Senior Collegian Common Room' as a means of 'unifying the sixth' and recognising the importance of treating sixth formers 'as students instead of just boys'. I certainly agreed with that, especially since I never became a prefect. More often than not this exalted status was granted to lads like Roger Kitching who had enjoyed success on the sports field, presumably because of the leadership qualities they were deemed to have developed there. In my final year I did reach the dizzy heights of sub-prefect, maybe as a reward for winning a state scholarship. Sadly, I didn't have the bottle to refuse but, as far as I remember, I never made much effort to carry out whatever duties came my way. The only A-Level I sat in 1963 was General Studies and, since I did virtually no work for it at all, hardly distinguished myself in the exam. Instead, I passed the time reading a great deal (particularly novels) and writing loads of history essays for Harold Richardson and James Crump: both were immensely encouraging and never once complained about all the unnecessary marking I inflicted on them. I also became friendly with Michael Gillard (now my form master), even meeting up with him outside school from time to time, and certainly benefited from that. Once I'd obtained a university place I ought to have left school and got a job for a few months. I didn't. Maybe, by staying on to the bitter end, I became more intellectually mature and culturally sophisticated—but I strongly suspect not!

In the early 1950s, John Pearson recalls, Huddersfield College:

> ... took learning seriously and most of us in my class took it seriously too. It was understood that the main aim was to get the best possible university place.

Nothing much had changed by my time and, once I got my A-Level results, it never crossed my mind not to apply to university; moreover, although my best grade had been in English, I never seriously considered reading any subject other than history, despite a spirited effort by Michael Gillard to get me to change my mind. Inevitably, too, I came under considerable pressure to apply to either Oxford or Cambridge. Specifically, I was summoned to A. R. Bielby's study, urged to sit the Oxford entrance exam and assured that my chances of obtaining a place, even perhaps a scholarship or exhibition, were high. This I adamantly refused to do. The headmaster, I suspected, was primarily interested in the school's honours board not me and I certainly felt no sense of loyalty or obligation to him. Anyway, I didn't fancy Oxford at all. Whether rightly or wrongly, I was convinced I would be a complete fish out of water there amidst all the ex-public school boys, as well as liable to be embarrassingly short of money most of the time. Nor did I relish Oxford's old-fashioned history syllabus or the daunting prospect of one-to-one tutorials with remote dons. When Michael Gillard suggested Nottingham (his own old university) and Bristol instead, I didn't have the nerve to resist him as well in favour of the much nearer Leeds or Manchester (tempting because I could have continued to live at home). Of course, in those days, university students got full maintenance grants anyway. Both Nottingham and Bristol called me for interview and, no doubt encouraged by John Mackay, I penned a report of my experiences for the spring 1963 school magazine:

> At Nottingham the keynote was informality: my interview there was essentially a discussion (lasting about forty-five minutes) of various controversial historical issues. The idea was, I have no doubt, to trap me into making some wild generalisations which could then be torn to shreds by the interviewers. Throughout, while on the surface the atmosphere was friendly, I was terrifyingly aware of my every

word and movement being scrutinised. Hence why I left the interview room in a state of exhaustion, only to find that I now had to write an 'off-the-cuff' timed essay on a difficult historical topic.

Clearly, Nottingham wasn't impressed by either me or my essay and I soon received a note rejecting my application. I was more relieved than anything else. Bristol (which I'd been warned in advance to put as my first choice of university or risk almost certain rejection) was obviously less stressful even if more formal:

> At Bristol, formality was the fundamental characteristic of an interview lasting twenty minutes at most. There were no cynical remarks about the weather as there had been at Nottingham, nor did the interviewers encourage me to talk myself into a situation from which there was no escape. Instead, a question and answer technique was adopted, focussing first on history, then more general topics. At the end I felt no more than a sense of relief that the ordeal was over and proceeded to pass the rest of the day in comparative peace of mind.

Since I'd very much liked the feel of both Bristol and its university, when I was offered a place I promptly accepted and I've never regretted the decision. Only after I took up residence in Churchill Hall in the autumn of 1963 did I discover, ironically enough, that Bristol University, like Oxford, had a high percentage of public school students, not to mention a history syllabus closely modelled on Oxford's as well.

Cliff Burhouse recalls that, once he 'became at home' in his 'new environment' at Holme Valley Grammar School, he 'enjoyed every minute of it and was sad to leave' in 1945. Of Huddersfield New College in our time, Bernard Jarvis concludes:

> On reflection, I feel that in a formal sense I was quite well educated. I did learn a lot at school, and not just about literature, and acquired a system of learning which seems to have stood me in good stead ever since.

I very much share these sentiments. 'We weren't in the same form in the lower school', Bernard continues, 'but we were both on the arty (not hearty) and mildly rebellious side of the school'; however, he adds flatteringly:

> ... you were more impressively so and how much more perceptive and alert you must have been as a sixth former than I was. The culture gap between your working class background and Huddersfield New College appears to have been

intellectually stimulating for you since, by the end of our school years, you had developed a more critical and independent way of thinking than your more complacent middle class peers. The almost inevitable tension in class and cultural values seems to have sharpened your perception of your situation in the world: not, I imagine, what Huddersfield New College intended! Two further thoughts arise from this. The first is—and this may well be true—that you were just brighter than the rest of us to begin with and this came through whatever the ambience of the school. The second is the Jackson and Marsden point that, maybe, really bright working class children might thrive in such an environment but not the next couple of trenches down.

While I was a sixth former at Huddersfield New College, in fact, Brian Jackson and Dennis Marsden's *Education and the Working Class* (1962) made a profound impact on me. So did Richard Hoggart's *The Uses of Literacy* (1955). Hoggart's pioneering study of northern working class society and its culture in the mid-twentieth century, drawing heavily on his own experience of growing up in Leeds, struck many chords, not least this comment:

> The scholarship boy has been equipped for hurdle jumping, so he merely thinks of getting on, but somehow not in the world's way. He has left his class, at least in spirit, by being in certain ways unusual, and he is still unusual in another class, too tense and overwound.

Brian Jackson and Dennis Marsden were both Huddersfield boys; both attended Huddersfield College; and *Education and the Working Class* drew heavily on both their own experiences of the school and those of a group of fellow sixth formers between 1949 and 1952. In his *Brian Jackson: Educational Innovator and Social Reformer* (2003), Kit Hardwick (a former student of mine at Huddersfield Polytechnic) commented that Jackson was one of those post-Second World War boys who (under the terms of R. A. Butler's 1944 Education Act):

> ...won scholarships from working class homes, went to grammar schools and in many cases on to university. They came into the world slightly fazed, having amassed a new set of middle class ideas and social mores, yet frequently feeling a nostalgia bordering on guilt for the culture they had left behind.

That was precisely how I felt when I read *Education and the Working Class* very soon after its publication in 1962. The book was massively critical of Huddersfield College (only thinly disguised as Marburton College) and, urged on by Michael Gillard, I penned a highly favourable review for the school magazine. A. R. Bielby didn't veto its publication (perhaps he didn't find out about it until it was too late) but, after it appeared, I received a peremptory summons to his study when he made his displeasure about both the book and my review abundantly clear. I couldn't have been more delighted! As for Jackson and Marsden's conclusions, I particularly took on board the reported failure of so many of their sample of Huddersfield College boys to prosper at university. The principal reason for this, they suggested, was that the effort of getting to university took so much out of working class boys that, once they got there, they were exhausted. Yet, paradoxically, I didn't feel at all exhausted in the autumn of 1963 and, after so much effort, I was absolutely determined to make a success of studying history at Bristol University.

3

Escapes From Reality in Huddersfield

The culture shock of becoming a grammar school boy was a great one for me but it did, at least, provide a daytime escape from the dismal reality of life on a mid-1950s northern council house estate. No doubt my growing interest in literature and history during later years at Huddersfield New College, and eventual decision to read history at university, were part of the same process. And, maybe, there was also an element of escapism in my latching onto medieval and Tudor kings, politics and war rather than the lower end of society. Not that Huddersfield in the 1950s and early 1960s was all that bad. In 1845 Friedrich Engels had described it as 'the handsomest by far of all the factory towns in Yorkshire and Lancashire by reason of its charming situation and modern architecture', sentiments echoed over a century later in John Betjeman's 1964 approval of this 'town of great character and Georgian and Victorian beauty'. In his *Working Class Community* (1968), drawing all its evidence from his home town, Brian Jackson commented:

> Huddersfield has a population of 130,000. Its main industries are textiles and engineering, but it has such a wide spread of employment that it has seldom been liable to serious unemployment. A few miles away are Leeds, Bradford, Halifax, Wakefield, Sheffield. Between them lie great stretches of wild moorland. In its valley, Huddersfield now presents a star-shaped cluster of grimy Methodist chapels, warehouses, factories. The place to see it is from the moorland escarpments above, and the best time is dusk, when the chains of yellow lights light up in active succession, like compass lines along the valley roads. At that moment the canal reflections, the intense blackness of the chapels and chimneys, give the town an unforgettable and unexpected Gothic beauty.

When I allow myself to be positive about the place (not easy), this is much as I remember the Huddersfield of my childhood and adolescence. Several buildings, all reflecting the wealth and prosperity of the town in Victorian times, particularly impressed themselves on my mind: the splendid neoclassical railway station, constructed in the later 1840s, and dominating St. George's Square, home also to the George Hotel and its imposing Italianate facade; the neogothic market hall of 1880, with its central clock tower (complete with gabled spire), several entrances, and both a lower and upper deck sporting a rich variety of stalls; and the town hall, opened in 1881, its deliberately eye-catching internal design more than making up for an unimaginative if solid exterior. More negatively, the endless rows of depressing late nineteenth and early twentieth century working class terrace housing, and the nondescript council house estates that sprang up in the post-Second World War years, are not easily forgotten either. Most memorable of all for me are Huddersfield's two major parks, where I spent countless hours as a child and young teenager. Greenhead Park, the larger of the two and within easy walking distance of the town centre, originally opened in 1884 and featured a small lake, a large children's playground, a bandstand and an open air theatre. Ravensknowle Park, much nearer to where I lived, came into existence when Ravensknowle Hall and its grounds were given to the town by their owner Legh Tolson soon after the end of the First World War. He designated that the hall be turned into a museum in memory of his two nephews who had been killed in the war; the Tolson Memorial Museum, specifically demonstrating 'the influence of all conditions existing in the neighbourhood upon the plant, animal and human life of the town and district', opened in 1922; and the surrounding park, a splendid setting, was certainly a godsend to local working class children like me.

As a little lad in Almondbury I spent a great deal of time on my own, exploring the area and often getting lost in the process. Even by the age of four or five I had a tendency to wander as much as two or three miles from home, almost always by myself and to the considerable consternation of my foster parents, occasionally with alarming results. Once I got hopelessly lost in a large local wood for what seemed like an eternity; I thought I was never going to find my way out; and I had nightmares about it for weeks afterwards. I was certainly fascinated by the fenced off site of the former anti-aircraft battery in Almondbury and, although it was strictly off limits, enjoyed searching its derelict and probably far from safe buildings for clues about the war (perhaps a premature manifestation of my later interest in history). Before long, however, they were pulled down and replaced by prefabs: not interesting at all. Other solitary pursuits included playing marbles and, a great favourite of the time, chalking 'tops' and assaulting them vigorously with whips. Unlike many boys in the post-war years, though, I never got much pleasure out of toy guns and couldn't see the point of pretending to be 'cowboys and Indians'. Around November 5 there were always plenty of fireworks around, not least since two major brands (Standard and Lion) were manufactured in Huddersfield; they tended to be prominently displayed in many shops; and, even as a little boy, I experienced no difficulty in laying hands on them (whether or not I had any money). Clearly, pinching fireworks and petty shop lifting of all sorts was par for the course as far as I was concerned, maybe as a feeble fight back against poverty. I was never caught. Regardless of the danger, moreover, I thought nothing of stuffing my pockets with jumping crackers and bangers from an alarmingly young age. Almost every year, too, there was a travelling fair at Easter and a summer circus, always exciting to wander around even if I couldn't afford the cost of rides or performances. As a boy of thirteen or fourteen, indeed, I occasionally managed to earn a few shillings by doing odd jobs for the showmen (but shovelling elephant dung is not to be recommended, even if the elephants themselves are friendly enough!). Most enjoyable of all were my frequent expeditions, occasionally with Miriam Saunders and Edith Wood, more often on my own, to nearby Castle Hill (so called because it had once been topped by a Norman castle). Huddersfield's best known landmark, it stood about nine hundred feet above sea level and provided splendid views of both the town and its surrounding countryside. Once, I was even caught in a severe thunderstorm there, a truly awesome experience. Since 1899, moreover, the hill had been crowned by the hundred foot tall Jubilee Tower, commissioned and built to celebrate the sixtieth anniversary of Queen Victoria's accession to the throne a couple of years earlier. Unfortunately, during my childhood, it was closed to the public because of its poor state of repair (only reopening in 1960). Almost all these pursuits were solitary and, even after I got to know a few children at junior school, I rarely played games with them and never football. A welcome escape from the grim reality of life in 1950s Britain it may have been for many working class boys, but not for me. I always found kicking a football around tedious to say the least. Even later on, when I occasionally watched Roger Kitching and his more sporty mates playing impromptu games in Ravensknowle Park, I never felt any urge to join in—probably to their relief!

During the Second World War Huddersfield Borough Council began organising summer entertainments and sporting events in Greenhead Park: 'Holidays at Home', first mounted in August 1941. Renamed Summer Entertainments by the early 1950s, they were an irresistible draw for me from an early age, particularly amateur performances in the park's open air theatre, the spectacular firework display on the final Saturday evening and, best of all, Punch and Judy. No doubt a psychologist would have a field day analysing the reasons for, and significance of, my fascination with Punch and Judy by the age of about six or seven and maintained well into my teens. Perhaps unconsciously in search of a father substitute and a man I could admire (John Saunders, in all honesty, wasn't much of a role model), I soon became firm friends with the local children's entertainer 'Professor' Jack Land, a middle-aged man who was a superb puppeteer and no mean ventriloquist as well. I particularly remember, from the age of about eleven or twelve, helping him erect his Punch and Judy booth in the park and never tiring of the performances even over a six week season: Monday evening (two), Wednesday/Friday afternoon and evening (up to five or six), and Saturday afternoon and evening (as many as seven or eight). In his last two or three years (before ill health forced him to retire), he even began paying me a modest amount for my efforts. Roger Kitching became a great enthusiast too, as he recalls:

> I saw Professor Land's so often that, whenever I watched another Punch and Judy show that didn't have the same characters and stories as his, I regarded it as highly suspect. I even came across crocodiles which did not squirt water at the audience: abominable! And how hilarious it all was: Punch beating up Judy, feeding the baby to the crocodile and eventually being tricked himself by Joey the Clown.

I felt exactly the same. Most Thursday evenings, Children's Talent Spotting Night in the open air theatre, there was a bonus as well: Jack Land almost always did a solo turn with his ventriloquist's dummy during the judging. Eventually, I became a competent enough puppeteer myself; I took to deputising for him if he became exhausted by the last show or two on a Saturday; and once, at his urging, I even mounted my own Punch and Judy show (borrowing his booth and puppets) as part of a concert in a local church hall. I learned the basics of ventriloquism from him too and, in later years, occasionally employed my residual skills to liven up history lectures. In the 1950s, moreover, a middle-aged man could befriend a lonely boy without suspicion. Today, no doubt, he'd be deterred by fear of being labelled a paedophile (which he most certainly wasn't). Is that progress? I continued to see Jack Land now and again as an adult and, when he died not long after my return to Huddersfield in 1972, I penned a short appreciation of him for the *Huddersfield Examiner*. Yet clearly, or so it seems to me in retrospect, my own delight in the make-believe world of Punch and Judy (with its rich cast of characters ranging from the stick-wielding Mr Punch himself, his long-suffering wife Judy and his uncooperative dog Toby to the baby-eating crocodile, Joey the clown, Mr Bombardier Wells the boxer and the hangman Jack Ketch) was pure escapism.

Soon after I went to grammar school I persuaded Miriam and Edith to buy me a model railway set: not a Hornby-Dublo (metal locomotives and rolling stock, so too expensive) but a Triang (plastic and cheaper). I eventually ended up with quite an impressive layout and lots of locos, if not always by entirely legitimate means. I also enjoyed myself hugely drawing up complex running schedules based on real British Railways timetables of the time. Roger Kitching, indeed, has a particularly evocative memory of our electric train sets:

> I had a Hornby set which was quite classy but expensive and trying to add to it was frustrating. You had a Triang set which had the advantage of being much cheaper and your layout was better. I seem to remember that someone bought me a Triang footbridge, which looked silly on my railway but suited yours, and we did some kind of deal. Do you recall, too, making a plan of Huddersfield with an underground system? Not only did you do that, you then began to produce a timetable and tried to ensure connections for the various trains. Next time I asked you about it, though, you'd moved on to other things.

Perhaps out of this grew a mounting interest in railways more generally, particularly trains and locomotives running through Huddersfield. Manifesting itself most obviously in train-spotting, I soon became interested in the history of railways as well, the various classes of steam locomotives (still hauling the vast majority of trains in the later 1950s) and even stations (of which Huddersfield, with its glorious central facade of Corinthian columns, was more impressive than most). Most frequently, I loitered at the end of Huddersfield station platforms, hoping to see locomotives I hadn't 'copped' before, but occasionally chose to lurk dangerously close to the Huddersfield-Leeds railway line at Fartown in order to watch passing trains instead. This closely matches the behaviour of John Pearson and his mates a few years earlier:

> ... at Paddock, beside the then four-track Huddersfield.-Manchester-Liverpool line, then part of the London Midland region of British Railways. We underlined the engines we saw in well-produced little booklets and, on occasion, we would put pennies (the big old ones) on the rail to be flattened by a passing train. Most of the passenger trains were hauled by unnamed Stanier class locomotives but our main interest was in named engines, mainly Jubilees but sometimes Patriots or even Royal Scots.

Of locomotives regularly passing through Huddersfield, Patriots were definitely my favourites and I was always delighted when one of those put in an appearance. Among the scheduled trains, none sported a better variety of London Midland engines than the 'half-oner', as Roger Kitching fondly recollects:

At the old school many lads often went to the top storey of Highfield (overlooking the railway line) to watch the 1.30pm Newcastle-Liverpool double-headed express go by. Since I didn't stay for school dinners, however, I was one of the few boys who could provide precise details about the locos when I arrived back in college.

'Very occasionally', John Pearson remembers:

... some of us would go to York to see the completely different set of engines operating on the Eastern region. These included the famous and impressive streamlined 'Streaks', with their special whistle note which always made our spines tingle.

A4 Pacifics or 'Streaks' (among them *Mallard*, holder of the speed record for steam locomotives) were also at the top of my preferred list and, before long, I began travelling considerable distances (almost always alone) in pursuit of my hobby: frequently to nearby Leeds, less often to Manchester, Crewe and York, and even, two or three times, to Newcastle-on-Tyne (where Scotland-based locomotives, rarely to be seen further south, regularly put in appearances). When I hadn't the funds to pay for railway journeys, I'd simply purchase a penny platform ticket at Huddersfield, board a train and take refuge in a lavatory if the guard came round checking. There were always ways of getting off stations, too, even if it occasionally involved dicing with death by running across railway tracks. Equally dangerous to life and limb was sneaking into locomotive depots (engines *en masse!*) and, not infrequently, being chased out again by irate railwaymen. Looking back, risk was definitely part of the fun for me and, more by luck than judgement, I never sustained any injury. Just once was I caught red-handed on a train when, fortunately, a tearful story about having lost my ticket did the trick nicely. Only when I reached the age of about fourteen or fifteen did I finally opt for a more-or-less honest lifestyle, mainly because of growing fear of the consequences if I didn't. Neither A. R. Bielby's Christianity-charged homilies nor more subtle middle class conditioning at school played much of a role. My well developed capacity for deception, however, soon found a new outlet: concealing evidence of my emerging homosexuality (another illegal practice and, at that time, a far more heinous offence against society than petty thieving). As for train spotting, like Punch and Judy it was essentially escapism but, as a result of my youthful escapades, I retain to this day a considerable residual knowledge of the last age of steam.

In the later 1940s and early 1950s funds in the Saunders household never ran to full scale holidays away from Huddersfield but I do recollect day trips by coach, and occasionally train, to northern seaside resorts such as Scarborough,

Bridlington and, inevitably, Blackpool. Miriam and Edith always took me together; my mother never came with us; and nor did John. Elsie Dockray regularly took my half-brother Tony on holiday for a week in the summer but, much to my relief, I was never invited along. As for John, not only did he adamantly refuse to go to the seaside, I cannot remember him ever leaving Huddersfield during all the time I knew him. Particularly enjoyable for me were trips to Blackpool Illuminations in late September or early October, and the Pleasure Beach, much better than the travelling fairs that came to Huddersfield each Easter. In later life, indeed, Edith specifically remembered my once persuading her to take me on the Big Dipper, a formidable roller coaster, even though I was only about nine or ten at the time. I found the experience thrilling to say the least but she didn't like it at all and refused ever to go on the ride again. At least once, too, we went to the Lake District for a day: I probably recall this simply because it was such an unusual excursion for us (but not as much fun as Blackpool). During my early teenage years we did have the odd week away (mainly paid for by Edith, I suspect), staying in boarding houses at the same northern seaside resorts more often than not. During one of these jaunts, to Bridlington, Edith later remembered my complaining about how dull it was compared to nearby Scarborough or Blackpool. When I was about fourteen, at my urging, we went to Edinburgh for a few days but, since my mania for train spotting was then at its height, I spent an inordinate number of hours on the platforms of Waverley station. Similarly, during our one and only visit to London together (when we stayed in a very friendly guest house in Balham), I toured the main line stations with enthusiasm. Since this was my first ever trip to the capital, though, I did manage to squeeze in the likes of Buckingham Palace and the Tower of London. Miriam had never been to London before either and, such was her aversion to escalators in underground stations, she refused ever to visit the city again for the rest of her life.

From a very young age Edith often read to me; she obviously enjoyed the challenge; I was a good listener; and I found the make-believe world of the fairy tale a most welcome contrast to everyday working class life during the austerity years of post-war Britain. Once I'd learned to read myself (certainly before the end of my sixth year), I devoured children's books as if there was no tomorrow, especially after I became a member of Huddersfield Children's Library. More reprehensibly, no doubt, I also became addicted to comics of all kinds. Early on, it was the tabloid variety, especially *The Beano* and *The Dandy*, and I revelled in the doings of Biffo the Bear, Lord Snooty, Desperate Dan, Korky the Cat, Minnie the Minx and, of course, Dennis the Menace (slippered by his dad, it seemed, even more relentlessly than Almondbury County School boys). Sadly, like many lads at the time I suspect, I tended to avoid more up-market comics like *The Hotspur* and *The Wizard* but, when I got a bit older, I did become an avid reader of *The Eagle*, perhaps the best of the 1950s comics: the spaceman Dan Dare, ever confronting his arch-enemy the Mekon (evil, green and always to be found perched on his tiny cloud-like space ship), was a particular favourite. Less to my taste were American products such as *Superman* and *Batman* but I read them anyway. Yet the only periodical of any real quality aimed at children—*The Children's Newspaper*—I never read at all and, even as an adult, I've never been a regular newspaper reader. Comics apart, much of my other reading wouldn't win approval in modern educational circles either, particularly. Enid Blyton. In the later 1940s and early 1950s she wrote for a magazine called *Sunny Stories* and, later, her own periodical *Enid Blyton's Magazine*. Not only did I read her latest offerings, hot off the press, I even found a highly dubious second hand magazine shop where, amidst a welter of soft porn (I saw enough bare breasts as a child to weary even the most voyeuristic of heterosexuals!), copies of *Sunny Stories* from several years back could be found and purchased for next to nothing (or simply pinched!). I must have cut a very strange figure indeed, surrounded on all sides by seedy men in search of sexual gratification. The police, I suspect, eventually closed the establishment down, perhaps because of the danger of paedophiles coming into contact with kids like me in a place that peddled both porn and popular American comics. Only once did a chap there show an unwelcome interest in me (perhaps I simply wasn't desirable enough) and, as Miriam and Edith had advised should this ever happen, I promptly ran out of the shop, waited for the man to go, and then resumed my search for tales of Mr Pinkwhistle, Meddle, Noddy, Big Ears and the rest of Enid Blyton's rich cast of characters. When this happened to me again, on an almost empty late evening Halifax to Huddersfield train at the age of about twelve or thirteen, a pathetic middle aged man even pressed a ten shilling note into my hand, presumably by way of compensation for his feeble fumblings. I found his behaviour more puzzling than threatening. Even so, despite the potentially profitable sideline this incident opened up, I felt no urge to become a juvenile rent boy! Far more importantly, by the time I reached the age of eight or nine, I had discovered the Famous Five. Here were real children, or so they seemed to me, enjoying a far more privileged and secure lifestyle than mine yet, at the same time, experiencing adventure after adventure. Compelling stuff indeed. Over a few years I must have read virtually everything Enid Blyton ever wrote and found the world of her imagination entirely to my juvenile taste. Educationalists who, then and now, tend to condemn her books as badly written, snobbish (most of her children had very well heeled middle class parents and often went to boarding schools) and even racist (who can ever forget the evil golliwogs?) completely miss the point. For kids like me, whose lives were so much more mundane and insecure, her stories were wonderful. So were

Richmal Crompton's *Just William* books, a splendid discovery when I was about ten. I found it very easy to identify with William's rebellious streak, still more his capacity for deception and ability to extract himself from tricky situations. What I never enjoyed were stories featuring sportsmen, especially footballers, and nor was I keen on twentieth-century war heroes and their exploits (much beloved of many boys in the 1950s). W. E. Johns' Biggles, for instance, left me completely cold. Julian, Dick, George, Anne and Timmy the dog (the Famous Five) were altogether more to my taste.

Obviously, once I got to grammar school, much better quality literature than Enid Blyton and Richmal Crompton began to become known to me. Early on, I remember, I developed a liking for Joseph Conrad. I can't imagine why! At home, my preferred reading became English crime novels (more escapism), particularly from the vintage years. Agatha Christie was my favourite and I read every Hercule Poirot, Jane Marple, and Tommy and Tuppence story she wrote, and the rest. The fact that Christie's characters were, for the most part, no more than cardboard cutouts, her plotting erratic and her style undistinguished to say the least worried me not a jot. It was the ingenuity of her puzzles that gripped me: a pointer to my later fascination with Richard III and the fate of the Princes in the Tower, perhaps. I also read most, if not all, of the output of Dorothy L. Sayers, Ngaio Marsh (a New Zealander but with a quintessentially English detective Roderick Alleyn, whose stories, an additional bonus for me, often had theatrical settings) and Patricia Wentworth. Not until I entered the sixth form, and encouraged by Michael Gillard in particular, did I develop a real taste for serious literature. All sixth formers at Huddersfield New College were required to study for an O-Level General Paper, in addition to our A-Levels; Mike Gillard was in charge of this and delivered a series of stimulating lectures to the sixth form *en masse* on topics ranging from twentieth-century cinema to the European Common Market; and, most importantly, he issued a substantial list of books we ought to read. Novels figured particularly prominently and I resolved to read as many as I could, making maximum use of Huddersfield's excellent public library as well as scouring second-hand bookshops for paperbacks. The discovery of Jane Austen was a high point here, while Emily Bronte's superbly atmospheric *Wuthering Heights* remains my favourite novel to this day. Other novelists I read avidly between 1960 and 1963 included Kingsley Amis, Charles Dickens, André Gide, Aldous Huxley, Christopher Isherwood, Thomas Mann, Alberto Moravia, Iris Murdoch, George Orwell, Jean-Paul Sartre, William Thackeray, Anthony Trollope and Evelyn Waugh. The pick of the bunch for me, perhaps, were Kingsley Amis, *Lucky Jim*; Charles Dickens, *Great Expectations* and *David Copperfield*; Aldous Huxley, *Brave New World*; Christopher Isherwood, *Mr Norris Changes Trains* and *Goodbye to Berlin*;

George Orwell, *Animal Farm* and *Nineteen Eighty-Four*; Jean-Paul Sartre's trilogy *The Age of Reason*, *The Reprieve* and *Iron in the Soul*; William Thackeray, *Vanity Fair*; and Anthony Trollope, *The Warden* and *Barchester Towers*. Maybe, by the time I departed for university in September 1963, I'd read enough novels to last a lifetime. Hence why I've never enjoyed the genre all that much since.

At home, for most of the 1950s, we had a radio but no television and I soon became an avid listener, mainly to the Light Programme but also, less frequently, the Home Service as well. Since classical music was virtually a closed book to me until the early 1960s, however, I never listened to the Third Programme at all. These were vintage radio years, particularly for comedy. My favourite programmes, as I recall, included *Life With The Lyons* (featuring a dysfunctional family, with Ben Lyon, Bebe Daniels Lyon and their two children, apparently, playing themselves); *Take It From Here* (written by Frank Muir and Denis Norden, and particularly memorable for the comic performances of Dick Bentley, June Whitfield and 'Professor' Jimmy Edwards as the anxiety-ridden Glum trio); *The Clitheroe Kid* (starring a diminutive, and none too young, Jimmy Clitheroe as a mischievous brat); *Educating Archie* (with Peter Brough, an undistinguished ventriloquist who, fortunately, couldn't be seen on the wireless, his dummy Archie Andrews, and a succession of despairing tutors, among them Tony Hancock, Max Bygraves and Beryl Reid); *Hancock's Half Hour* (with Tony Hancock, Sid James, Bill Kerr, Hattie Jacques and Kenneth Williams); and, funniest of all for me, *The Al Read Show* (in which Al Read, a brilliant Lancashire comedian, played a range of unforgettably down-to-earth working class characters, all of his own creation). It was while listening to the Light Programme, too, that I first heard both Gracie Fields and Vera Lynn, who have remained lifelong favourites. Oddly enough, I hardly ever listened to *The Goons* (brilliant as Peter Sellers, Harry Secombe and Spike Milligan were), at any rate until we were warned off the programme by Huddersfield College's headmaster during a Speech Day oration. Another popular programme of the time was *Top of the Form*, a quiz programme for school teams which, John Pearson speculates, Huddersfield College was 'probably too snooty to enter'. As for *The Archers*, by the time Grace Archer lost her life in a fire while trying to rescue her horse Midnight (an episode put out on the same evening commercial television first came on air) I had become an addict, and I've remained so ever since. Towards the end of the 1950s my foster parents at last acquired a rented television set, partly, I suspect, to discourage a now ailing John from going to the pub so often. If so, it worked. Even though the TV tended to be switched on most of the evening, I didn't watch many programmes myself: in particular, I avoided popular ITV game shows such as Hughie Green's *Double Your Money* and Michael Miles' *Take Your Pick* like the plague. Sunday night was the exception (I always did my weekend homework on Saturdays and Sunday mornings), when Val Parnell's *Sunday Night at the London Palladium* (hosted by Bruce Forsyth) featured famous variety acts week after week and Granada Television's *Armchair Theatre* regularly put out plays of a very high quality indeed.

For 1950s boys and girls in Huddersfield the cinema was a great draw; there were plenty to choose from; and targeting children from an early age was clearly a priority. Not only did several town centre picture houses screen minors' matinees on Saturdays, so did many local cinemas (most of which did not survive the relentless advance of television in the 1960s). For two or three years between the ages of eight and eleven I went along fairly regularly, more often than not to the nearby Regal or Lyceum. The Lyceum, a real fleapit if ever there was one, was my favourite, especially once I found a way of getting in at the back without paying (via the almost invariably open window of the gentleman's lavatory). Flash Gordon serials were a particular draw but there were also Laurel and Hardy, Abbott and Costello and the Three Stooges, not to mention all the cartoons (Mickey Mouse, Donald Duck, Goofy, Pluto, Bugs Bunny, Popeye, Tom and Jerry, and Mr Magoo, to name but a few). Rather dreary and predictable short Westerns, featuring such American 'B' movie icons as Roy Rodgers and Hopalong Cassidy, were often part of the fare as well. Occasionally, too, there were mildly romantic pictures but these did not go down well with the Lyceum's juvenile clientele: indeed, love scenes tended to be greeted with howls of derision and already well torn seats might well sustain further rips as well. Now and again Miriam and Edith took me to the cinema of an evening, but not very often, and once I discovered live theatre I went to the pictures less and less. Films increasingly seemed a poor substitute for the excitement of stage performances and, by the time I reached adulthood, it took a truly exceptional movie to get me to the cinema at all. My earliest experience of live performances was probably watching, and listening to, local concert parties in church halls and, during the annual Summer Entertainments, at Greenhead Park's open air theatre. As a sixth former I even began to attend the occasional classical music concert at Huddersfield Town Hall and, belatedly, first sampled the joys of Bach, Haydn, Mozart, Beethoven, Mendelssohn, Tchaikovsky, Dvorak, Rachmaninov and Elgar. I particularly enjoyed piano concertos and the town hall's fine organ was always awesome to hear as well. Undoubtedly, the most memorable evening of all was when I heard Yehudi Menuhin perform a violin concerto. I even got his almost indecipherable autograph afterwards. Far more important, however, was my discovery (years earlier) of Huddersfield's Theatre Royal and its repertory company.

In the 1950s Huddersfield boasted two professional theatres: the Palace and the Theatre Royal. Edith Wood recalled, in old age, going to the Palace regularly as a young woman in the 1920s, when it seems to have been very much a latter day music hall. She also went to the Theatre Royal occasionally to see plays. The Palace burnt down in 1936 but was soon rebuilt as a variety theatre, and such it still was in my childhood. As a young lad Miriam and Edith took me to a few pantomimes there (always in the cheapest seats), most memorably a staging of *Jack and the Beanstalk* when a diminutive giant was equipped, by way of compensation, with a body microphone and his much amplified voice was scary to say the least. Very occasionally, we also went along to a variety show (again, sitting in the 'Gods', only a very few feet below the roof): for instance, I once saw 'Two Ton' Tessie O'Shea, a large artiste with a small ukelele and a powerful singing voice. Roger Kitching, too, remembers his mother taking him to see 'wonderful second rate variety acts' at the Palace, 'about twenty on a bill, ten each side of the interval'. He has early memories of the Theatre Royal too:

> I always felt this was *my* theatre. I saw pantomimes there as a very young child and, once I was five, I could go and see the Huddersfield Light Operatic Society perform, my father usually taking one of the principal parts. As I got older, I used to go along to dress rehearsals. By keeping my head down and not worrying anybody, I had the whole theatre to myself (apart from stage, dressing rooms and orchestra pit), so I could explore. The gallery was unlit and creepy, and the two boxes at the upper circle level were also dark, scary, dusty and full of theatre rubbish. The dress circle boxes were my favourite and, there, I could watch dress rehearsals feeling like Lord Muck.

Roger's father also directed musicals performed by local amateur operatic companies and, indeed, one of the oldest surviving theatre programmes I have (priced 4d) is of a staging of *Me and My Girl* by the Scissett Amateur Operatic Society in February 1961, 'entire production' by Leonard Kitching. As I got older I also sometimes went to plays put on by the Huddersfield Thespians, a first-rate amateur dramatic company.

Even before I went to grammar school I had become a regular theatre-goer. Although long past its prime (if it ever had one), Huddersfield Theatre Royal was home to a local repertory company in the 1950s putting on a different play every week. Every Friday night from about the age of ten I bought a ticket for the Upper Circle, bagged a front seat (not difficult since audiences tended to be sparse for much of the time), and sat through whatever play was on offer that week. Now and again Edith came with me but, more often than not, I went on my own. No doubt this explains why I attracted attention. I even got to know some of the actors (among them Nita Valerie, whose husband Peter Bernard ran the place), frequently went backstage and, very occasionally, watched a performance from the wings. Indeed, one of the earliest photographs I have of myself is a black and white snapshot taken outside the theatre, alongside actors Fred Ferris and Trevor Maskell: it's dated, on the back, Tuesday June 21 1955. The dramatic fare on offer was far from highbrow, however, and over the years I must have sat through more undistinguished north country comedies than anyone else alive! Among performances that particularly stick in my mind are *Sailor Beware* (a very funny Philip King farce which the company obviously enjoyed as much as the audience), *Trilby* (a compelling melodrama, featuring the evil and manipulative Svengali) and *Smiling Thru'*. Of all the plays I saw at the Theatre Royal, in fact, none made a greater impact on me than this unashamedly sentimental romance: a nightmare to perform, not least because the leading actors had to lose fifty years for Act 2 and put them back on again for Act 3, yet even Nita Valerie (no great actress) put in a powerful performance for once. It also contained a haunting song which I've never forgotten:

> There's a little brown road winding over the hill
> To a little white cot by the sea,
> There's a little green gate
> At whose trellis I wait
> While two eyes of blue
> Come smiling thru'
> At me.
>
> There's a grey lock or two in the brown of the hair
> There's some silver in mine too I see,
> But in all the long years
> When the clouds brought their tears
> These two eyes of blue
> Kept smiling thru'
> At me.
>
> And if ever I'm left in this world all alone
> I shall wait for my call patiently,
> For if Heaven be kind
> I shall wake there to find
> Those two eyes of blue
> Still smiling thru'
> At me.

I'm not sure any song has ever affected me so profoundly as this sentimental ballad did when I was about ten or eleven. More grist for a psychologist's mill, perhaps. Now and again there were performances of high quality dramas at the Theatre Royal, even the occasional new play only recently seen in the West End, but never works by the great Elizabethan dramatists Christopher Marlowe and William Shakespeare, Restoration comedies or modern classics by playwrights such as Henrik Ibsen and Anton Chekhov. At Christmas, inevitably, there were pantomimes (in which Nita Valerie's recurrently portrayed Annie Awful consistently lived up to her name!). No doubt these were vitally important for keeping the theatre open, and I dutifully went along to them, but I was always glad when the panto season ended and weekly rep resumed.

'When you told me that you went to the theatre every week and had been doing so for some time', recalls Roger Kitching, 'I was desperate to join you'. I was absolutely delighted and, henceforth, we went to the Theatre Royal together. I can't imagine what Roger's sporty friends made of this but he obviously didn't care and his parents, too, seemed happy enough for him to be out as late as 10.00pm (or even, sometimes, later) on Friday nights, providing he was with me. I also realised, perhaps for the first time, just how much freedom I was allowed compared to many other boys of my age. Roger's memories of our theatre-going are even more vivid than my own:

> I remember I used to meet you at the theatre, we'd pay our shilling at the box office, go outside to the separate upper circle entrance, and climb the stairs. Always the same seats: front row, right of centre. The usherette was there for years. As we got older she was prepared to let us have a bottle of beer each, pouring it beforehand, and in the interval we'd walk into the bar and pay for the 'lemonade', just in case anybody else was there. Usually there was no one but us. We always knew when the play was five minutes from the end because she'd have her coat on and be next to the exit. It then took about thirty seconds to clear the whole of the upper circle. Finally, having smoked ourselves to death in the theatre, it was fish and chips on the way home.

'When the curtain went up', Roger further reminiscences:

> ... we had a lovely bird's eye view of the stage. Where would the carpet be? It was always the same carpet, whether the play was set in an eighteenth century drawing room, a flat in New York or a northern pub. It was always the same cast too, with Nita Valerie bagging all the best older parts, Arthur Leslie (later in *Coronation Street* as landlord of the Rover's Return) as senior male lead, Gerald Cowan as juvenile, and ex-Huddersfield Thespian Kenneth Waller (later Grandad in the TV sitcom *Bread*) often playing comedy roles. By exposing ourselves to this week-in week-out, I think we got a good idea of what made a play tick, as well

as experienced at what worked and what didn't, and why. Also, because the company was so enthusiastic and hopeful, they sometimes took on plays that taxed their abilities fully. Really, it was all about hopefulness—that they would move on from here to the starry heights—as some of them did. It is sad that the company did not get more support. People wanted a live theatre, or always said they did, yet didn't go when it was there.

On the plays we saw together, I find myself in almost total agreement with Roger's own random jottings:

In a typical four weeks we might see a comedy, a thriller, a drama and a comedy thriller. I loved it when it was comedy thriller week:
Specifically, I can remember:

An Inspector Calls
Rivetting. The first time I had seen it and a favourite ever since.

The Ringer
A cracker of a thriller set in foggy London.

The Trial of Mary Duggan
A *real* story from America in which counsel for the defence turns out to be the murderer.

Towards Zero
One of several Agatha Christie plays we saw.

Sweeney Todd
Not the musical but the play. Gloriously bloody and very exciting because the cast came among the audience in the interval and sold meat pies.

The Diary of Anne Frank
I didn't know the story and found it heart breaking. Also, I was mesmerised by the set: an attic cut in half like a doll's house, so that people could be acting in one part while, in the other, actors pottered about quietly in the dark until it was their turn for the spotlight.

The Long, the Short and the Tall
This had an anti-war theme (just about) and I found it quite moving.

The Hasty Heart
Another war weepy, not long out of the West End.

The Corn is Green
Nita Valerie bagged the best part, as the school teacher, and Gerald Cowan played the Welsh boy. She was about 5'8"; he was 6'2"; and so, although the scene when she puts him over her knee and spanks him is not supposed to be funny, it was! Good play, though.

Jane Eyre
Ever so long—getting on for three hours—and the costumes must have cost a bit.

Wuthering Heights
The cast were able to don the same costumes again for another three hour session, with branches banging at the window and women shouting out 'Heathcliff, Heathcliff!'.

The Brontes of Haworth Parsonage
An everyday story of countryfolk, employing the same costumes.

Saturday Night at the Crown
Crap comedy! I only discovered recently that this play was specifically written as a vehicle for Thora Hird. I'm sure she made more of it than the Theatre Royal cast did.

The Happiest Days of Your Life
A splendid romp, helped by the fact that the film had recently been released, starring Alastair Sim, Margaret Rutherford and Joyce Grenfell.

Quiet Wedding
What a glorious set and what a hoot! If farce is done well, it's bewitching.

Sadly, despite all the efforts of Peter Bernard, Nita Valerie and a succession of talented actors, provincial weekly rep in Huddersfield was in its death throes; the Theatre Royal closed its doors for good in the early 1960s; and, before long, it had been demolished as part of an ill thought-out programme of urban redevelopment. Nevertheless, those years of theatre-going in my home town during the 1950s established a habit that, for me, was to last half a century.

No later than 1958, when I was fourteen, my enthusiasm for theatre began to take me beyond Huddersfield, particularly to the Grand Theatre in Leeds and, now and again, the Bradford Alhambra and the Manchester Opera House. Occasionally, Miriam and Edith came with me, more often I went on my own. As a result I gradually came to appreciate that not all plays need be so humdrum and predictable as those so often on offer at Huddersfield Theatre Royal. More importantly, I discovered musicals such as Sigmund Romberg's *The Student Prince*, Rudolf Friml's *The Vagabond King* and Ivor Novello's *The Dancing Years*. Pure escapism writ large! A chance visit with Roger Kitching to a performance of *Trial by Jury* in a local church hall also awakened a lifelong interest in, and enthusiasm for, the Savoy operas of W. S. Gilbert and Arthur Sullivan. Once I discovered the D'Oyly Carte Opera Company, which came regularly to both Leeds and Bradford, I was completely hooked and, by 1963, I had seen all the main operas at least once, more often than not featuring the incomparable John Reed in the leading comic roles. Even more memorable are my visits to Leeds, Bradford, Manchester, even Hull on one occasion, to see a touring production of *Salad Days* by Julian Slade and Dorothy Reynolds. A splendidly whimsical story built around a magic piano and punctuated by a plethora of haunting songs, it remains my favourite musical to this day. The oldest surviving theatre programme I have, appropriately enough, is for a performance of *Salad Days* at Bradford Alhambra in June 1960 (by which time ex-Huddersfield Theatre Royal actor Kenneth Waller had joined the cast). And Roger Kitching remembers that once, when he, I and his mother went to *Salad Days* together, I even illicitly recorded great chunks of it on a portable tape recorder! In 1959, 1960 and 1961 I also made several theatre-going trips to London, travelling on my own by the overnight mail train from Huddersfield (requiring a change at Crewe in the early hours) and returning the next night. Again, I mainly went to musicals, among them West End productions of *My Fair Lady*, *The Sound of Music*, *Irma La Douce*, *Make Me An Offer*, *Fings Ain't Wot They Used T'Be* and *The Most Happy Fella*. Most enjoyably, Roger Kitching and I paid a couple of theatregoing visits to the capital together (probably in 1962 and 1963), staying in a near-brothel on one occasion and following an extraordinarily ambitious timetable of consecutive performances. As Roger recalls, 'we put together crisp itineraries in advance in your smoke-filled bedroom at home, mapping out every part of the 3-4 day trips, carefully accounting for our expenses, and even planning as many as three shows in one day (possible if we caught early matinees)'. His summary of what we saw and his reactions is precise and squares well with my own memories:

> The most magical show we saw was *Lock Up Your Daughters* (twice!): an open revolving stage, with lattice work, which allowed us to see all Sean Kenny's sets at the same time. No wonder I was so disappointed at his set for *Stop the World I Want to Get Off*: just a circus ring and a tent. I remember us seeing Lionel Bart's

Blitz at the Adelphi, and the siren going off right next to us. Incredible set this time, matched by that of *Oliver* (which we also saw): both by Sean Kenny again. You even wangled us a trip on stage at the Adelphi when we were shown just how the set for *Blitz* worked.

Oh What a Lovely War was a wonderful Joan Littlewood creation, wrenching our emotions from laughter to tears, and back again.

The funniest experience I've ever had in a theatre was when we went to see *Beyond the Fringe*. I was hurting by the interval, and it went on, remorselessly. I'd never before heard the Second World War or religion satirised so bitingly. Alan Bennett's sermon was the ultimate!

We also went to see Agatha Christie's *The Mousetrap* and C.P. Snow's *The Masters*, as well as attending a live lunchtime radio broadcast featuring Cyril Stapleton and his Orchestra.

By the autumn of 1963, too, I had sampled many of London's biggest and most prestigious theatres, among them Drury Lane, Her Majesty's, the Haymarket, the New, the Palace, the Palladium and Wyndham's. I even went to the enormous Coliseum one afternoon to see Bob Monkhouse in Cole Porter's *Aladdin*. As a sixth former in 1961 I also made my first ever trip to Stratford-upon-Avon, this time with John Mackay, when we explored the place thoroughly and saw three Shakespeare plays: *As You Like It* (despite memorable performances by Max Adrian and Michael Redgrave, I didn't much), *Hamlet* (with Ian Bannen in the title role) and, for the first of many times, *Richard III* (the king well portrayed by Christopher Plummer, yet to hit the big screen in *The Sound of Music*).

One of the reasons why I could afford so much theatre-going, even trips to London and Stratford-upon-Avon, in the early 1960s was that, from the age of sixteen, I worked regularly during school vacations. It also meant I could start building up a collection of books and records. Even as a child I was well aware of the world of work and what it seemed to entail for ordinary folk: long hours of poorly paid and mindless drudgery in factories. No wonder, once I became a sixth former, I was so determined to make a success of my A-Levels and go on to university. For much of my childhood I regularly visited Edith Wood at the factory where she worked: W. T. Johnson, Woollen Cloth Manufacturers, situated only a stone's throw from the Moldgreen underdwelling where she lived after leaving Almondbury. I got to know some of Edith's workmates and, since no one worried much about health and safety in the 1950s, even the bosses tolerated my presence. Indeed, there was a real sense of camaraderie about the place;

many employees had worked there for years (Edith among them); and I often heard expressions of obviously genuine loyalty to the firm. Perhaps this was well deserved. Edith never contributed to a pension scheme yet, when she retired, she was provided with a modest pension by her former employers nonetheless. From the age of about twelve or thirteen I even managed to earn extra pocket money by doing odd jobs around the factory such as sweeping up or machine-minding, courtesy of Frank Johnson himself ('Mr Frank' to the workforce) who seemed only too pleased to give a helping hand to a working class lad like me who'd managed to get to grammar school. When I reached sixteen he offered me a full-time vacation job but, almost certainly rightly, I felt I was far too puny to spend eight hours a day lugging heavy rolls of cloth around. Instead, I managed to secure temporary employment at Rushworths, a rather classy department store in the centre of Huddersfield, and continued to work there during vacations throughout my sixth form and undergraduate years. A great variety of tasks came my way, from cleaning the store and manning the lift to waiting at table in the store's cafe (the Westgate Lounge) and deputising for the post room manager. The job I least liked was that of kitchen porter, mainly because the café's cook could be extremely sarcastic and unpleasant, especially to so lowly an underling as me. An overweight middle-aged woman, with bandaged ulcerated legs and a tendency to smoke in the kitchen (even, occasionally, dropping cigarette ash into the deep-fat frier), she rarely encountered any customers. Just as well. On one occasion, when she did waddle through the Westgate Lounge, a would-be eater asked me who she was and, when I told him, he promptly fled, declaring there was no way he would consume food prepared by her: Manning the lift was more interesting since I could chat to its users. Mostly they were pleasant enough, although once, when confronted by a snooty and obnoxious middle-aged woman, I deliberately pretended to get the old-fashioned lift stuck between floors and, in order to lower herself to the floor below by way of escape, she ended up exposing her voluminous knickers to public view. Definitely a moment to relish! The best task that came my way, one Christmas vacation, was spending a couple of glorious weeks operating an enormous and complex model railway layout (complete with Thomas the Tank Engine and the facility to engineer head-on train crashes) set up in Rushworths' toy department. As a student, inevitably, I came in for a great deal of good humoured badinage (eventually learning to give as good as I got) and I certainly soon discovered the severe limitations of my practical skills: working overtime on Sundays, when the store was shut, it became only too evident that I was not cut out to be either a carpenter or painter and decorator.

    Despite their reluctance to accept, every week I gave part of my earnings from Rushworths to my foster parents to help cover the cost of my keep for a month or two at least. The rest I spent mainly on theatre-going, books and records. For books I tended to rummage in second-hand bookshops wherever I came across them and gradually built up a nice collection of Penguin paperbacks (especially green back crime novels). I also acquired a rather battered record player, not because I wanted to listen to pop music (early rock and roll had little appeal for me) but so I could play vinyl LPs of musicals. Among the earliest I bought, inevitably, was an original cast recording of *Salad Days*, as well as several of the shows I saw in the West End: *Blitz, Fings Ain't Wot They Used T'Be, Irma La Douce, Lock Up Your Daughters, Make Me An Offer, My Fair Lady, Oh What a Lovely War, Stop the World I Want to Get Off* and *The Most Happy Fella*. My wider musical interests at this time are reflected in other LPs and EPs I purchased, such as *The World of Gilbert and Sullivan, A Souvenir of Marie Lloyd, Al Jolson Hits, The Debonair Jack Buchanan, The Flanagan and Allen Story, Eartha Kitt Show Stoppers, Noel Coward at Las Vegas* and *An Evening With Tom Lehrer*. John Mackay, moreover, recalls visiting me frequently in Moldgreen and spending:

> ... many evenings in a fug of fags in your garret listening to Tom Lehrer and musicals, most memorably *Salad Days*. You were certainly a very good friend. Our tastes were similar and our excitement about literature a shared passion. I don't remember much about our conversations, except that we were on the same wavelength.

Roger Kitching was an even more frequent visitor, emphasising that at the time I had:

> ... two things which I didn't and I envied you for them. You were on a much longer lead than me and could lay your hands on more cash. From early evening, you had the run of Edith's home, so could play LPs at a decent volume. You introduced me to Tom Lehrer and I used to tape lots of your records.

Indeed, he adds flatteringly, 'the natters in your smoke-filled room were seminal for the course of my life'.

Throughout my years as a student at Bristol University (1963—1969), and while teaching at Plymouth College (1969—1972), I spent vacations in Huddersfield. Indeed, on returning north for the first time in December 1963, I had the biggest row ever with Miriam Saunders when I discovered she had thoroughly cleared out the contents of my tiny bedroom. What angered me above all was that she had thrown away not only all my school reports but also a substantial collection of theatre programmes (including dozens of productions at Huddersfield Theatre Royal). After the luxuries of hot water on tap, bathrooms and internal lavatories in a university hall of residence, I also found it difficult to readjust to the inconveniences of sub-standard housing. My lifestyle in Huddersfield remained much the same as it had been as a sixth former, however, including beavering away at academic tasks in my bedroom and, as an undergraduate, continuing to work for a few weeks each year at Rushworths. During the Easter vacation of 1964 it became clear that John Saunders was declining fast but, one lunchtime, I did take him to a nearby pub. This was virtually the only time he and I ever had a couple of pints together and he was so chuffed that I even managed to get him to talk about his experience of the First World War almost half a century earlier (perhaps because he knew his days were now numbered). In May he was admitted to hospital—the same hospital, ironically enough, where I had been born in 1944. When news reached me in Bristol, right in the middle of my first year exams, I promptly returned to Huddersfield. Both Miriam and I were with John when he died of kidney failure in the middle of June and, inevitably, I ended up largely organising his cremation. Neither Miriam nor I felt any very deep grief, I suspect, but he was given a respectable working class funeral. Following his death Miriam and Edith Wood grew even closer than before and, eventually, they opted to live together in my old home in Moldgreen. Edith took to sleeping in my former bedroom most of the time but always happily shared a bed with Miriam whenever I was in Huddersfield. Now both in receipt of pensions, they were probably better off than at any time in their lives; they began going on regular summer holidays together; and after a few years even ventured to the south west, staying with me in Bristol (in 1967 and 1968) and Plymouth (in 1971).

Although increasingly less so as the years went by, I continued to meet up with former school friends like Roger Kitching and John Mackay when I was in Huddersfield. Indeed, once I stopped working for Rushworths in the mid-1960s, Roger himself got a vacation job there for a year or two. By then, however, the store was no longer independent; it gradually lost its distinctive character and discerning clientele; and, eventually, it closed down altogether. What Roger and I could not do was resume our local theatre-going and he paints a sad picture of the end of professional weekly rep in Huddersfield:

> After you'd departed for Bristol, I remember a grand reopening of the Theatre Royal with a six week stint by a Halifax company. The first play was *The Moon is Blue* which, it was suggested, was an adult play not suitable for people of my age. I was cross. I was one of the few people who came to the theatre every week and, just because the revamp meant a much fuller theatre than usual, that should not have involved discouraging lads like me. (Didn't you have a similar experience with *The Little Hut* years earlier when you only managed to sneak in with the help of the usherette?). I had to go in the dress circle, anyway, because the upper circle

was shut and, by the end of the season, audiences were back to their usual size. This, I must confess, gave me a certain amount of grim satisfaction.

After the Theatre Royal closed for good, Nita Valerie did make a desperate final attempt to revive professional repertory in Huddersfield by setting up a new company to perform in a converted dance hall. Sadly, that didn't last long either. Older people, on whom local theatres so much depended, presumably preferred to stay at home and watch TV. I only ever went to the so-called New Theatre once, in April 1966, when I saw the 'world premiere' of *The Lively Oracles* by John Allegro and Roy Plomley. I have no memory whatever of the play but its cast did include Roy Barraclough. Otherwise, during visits to the north, I regularly saw my natural mother, if more out of a sense of duty than desire, and almost always in a Halifax pub rather than her home. I even met up with my half-brother Tony very occasionally but we never had much to talk about, apart from comparing notes about Elsie Dockray's seemingly endless complaints about her life and future prospects. Now and again, in the later 1960s, newer friends even put up with the discomfort of staying with me for a day or two in Huddersfield, among them fellow Bristol University graduate Peter Allender:

> When you were in Huddersfield during vacations, I stayed with you once or twice and remember Miriam and Edith's unquestioning and consistent kindness. In particular, I recall seeing the film *Kes* with you in Huddersfield, the very week it was released, an authentic West Riding experience.

What was never on my agenda was returning to Huddersfield permanently, Yet, in 1972, I did just that.

4

Bristol University Student

University College, Bristol, first opened its doors to students in 1876 and, when granted a charter in 1909, became a fully-fledged university entitled to award its own degrees. In the 1920s, largely thanks to the generosity of the local Wills family (whose wealth mainly derived from tobacco, not least the iconic Woodbine brand of cigarettes), new buildings began to be bought (such as the Victoria Rooms, home to the student union in 1963/4) or built (most notably, Wills Hall, to accommodate male students, and the University Tower or Wills Memorial Building, a massive neogothic structure very much in the grand manner). To say that Bristol University was built on fags is no exaggeration! Bernard Jarvis and I became students at Bristol together at the end of September 1963, he to read English, me history. By then we already knew each other well and, certainly, Bernard's friendship helped make the transition from school to university far less traumatic than had been my move from Almondbury County School to Huddersfield College in 1955. Even so, I found it all very strange, not least living away from home for the first time and in a university hall of residence. Most history teaching in the 1960s took place in the Wills Memorial Building but, for my first couple of years, I lived in Churchill Hall, near the Clifton Downs and a fifteen minute bus ride away. Opened only a few years earlier, it consisted of a series of blocks arranged around a central grassed area, each containing a generous quota of individual study bedrooms; the establishment was strictly single sex (no change from school there); and its buildings had about as much character as a post-war Huddersfield council estate. Not only was Churchill an all male hall of residence, moreover, it was aggressively so, clearly reflecting the substantial percentage of ex-public school boys who lived there. They, in fact, gave the place an extraordinary all-chaps-together-ethos, never more apparent than at formal meals where, smartly dressed in ties and undergraduate gowns, we congregated most evenings and on Sunday lunchtimes. The ex-public school lads were at their worst in the communal bathrooms in the mornings when, wearing only their pyjama trousers (or even less), they could be found scrubbing their bare torsos with untimely vigour. I soon learned to avoid such mass ablutions and, since this ritualised cleansing tended to occur before breakfast, it wasn't difficult: I rarely got up that early! Indeed, although many of these cleanliness obsessives were by no means unpleasing to the eye (a by-product of. all that sport at school, presumably), I avoided contact with them as much as possible. Fortunately, there were plenty of ex-grammar school boys in Churchill Hall as well, among them Peter Allender (a north-easterner from Darlington), whose memories of our early weeks square very well with mine

> During my first term in hall, I found it horribly male, disconcertingly middle class and overwhelmingly southern. I recoiled, in particular, from the muscular Christians who, each morning, would buff their faces to a pink and painful-looking shine. No wonder breakfasts soon became a rarity for me. I liked the food but couldn't stand the communal heartiness so early in the morning or not being able to choose where you sat. Also, if you arrived late, even as the strident terminating bell was ringing plates of food were removed from before your eyes by a tight-lipped termigent. Formal meals were different and a group of northerners soon formed who, along with Ian Faulkner and Mike Stammers, took to sitting at the same table most evenings and Sunday lunchtimes. This became, for me, an island of comfort in what I was finding a bleak and alienating experience. Indeed, but for Keith, Ian, Mike and Bernard Jarvis, Churchill would have continued to be very daunting. The atmosphere was that of a slightly up-market scout camp where many students seemed to be in the process of becoming their fathers. Yet there was also a sense, if not of actual imposture, of lads pretending rather too heartily to be what they were not. Many, it being Bristol, must have carried the burden of Oxbridge rejection, while the real toffs went to Wills Hall or Burwalls anyway. How did we fit in? I imagine we went unnoticed among the would-be accountants, doctors, engineers and solicitors.

At Bristol, recalls Bernard Jarvis:

> ... a group of us started out together in Churchill Hall where, it seemed, there were more students with double-barrelled names than lads from the north of England. Here friendships were formed and earnest discussions took place fuelled by the usual undergraduate cocktail of coffee (or, in Keith's case, tea), cigarettes and booze.

Michael Stammers, who hailed from Norfolk, muses that he and I must have first met because we were both studying history and living in Churchill Hall; my room there, he recollects, was 'spartan, no decoration or ornament'; and, as for me, I 'smoked incessantly, getting through up to sixty cigarettes a day'. Even so, I was obviously preferable to his neighbours in the block where he lived: 'hearties from Portsmouth Grammar School'. Ian Faulkner, an Oxford lad also reading history who lived in the same block as I did, has exceptionally vivid memories of both me and life in Churchill Hall:

> I soon realised that Keith was not a big eater, existing in the daytime on a diet of toast, tea and tobacco. From early on, however, Peter Allender, Bernard Jarvis, Mike Stammers, Keith and I shared the same table at formal evening dinners and I particularly remember the mirth occasioned by the seemingly ancient head waiter. Keith and I also shared a degree of cynicism about the Oxbridge nature of these dinners, manifesting itself in the compulsory wearing of gowns, the high table and the Latin grace ('Benedictus benedicat'). Most evenings in Churchill seem to have been pretty uneventful. After dinner we usually went back to our rooms to do some work or, alternatively, went to someone else's room for coffee. Keith often spent most of the evening working. Indeed, it quickly became clear that he took his work extremely seriously and spent much more time studying than the rest of us. On more than one occasion he was polite but firm with me when he felt I was overstaying my welcome in his room! At about 9.15pm or so, however, Bernard, Mike, Peter, Keith and I soon got into the routine of setting off across the Downs for a brisk walk to the *King's Arms* for a couple of pints. On returning from the pub we invariably went to someone's room. As I remember it, Keith, Peter and I were inveterate late nighters, Bernard and Mike much more responsible and retiring considerably earlier than we did. It was not unusual for the three of us to stay up talking until the early hours when our cigarette consumption was quite prodigious. Keith outsmoked us all, though, and I even heard that, when he left Churchill, his room had to be redecorated and a blowtorch employed to remove all the nicotine from the window frames. What we talked about during these late night sessions I can't recall but I don't think politics and current affairs featured much; nor did coursework; and, as for women and sport, they rated more or less no mention at all. Unfortunately, late nights and being a history student didn't go too well together since, on at least two mornings a week (possibly more) our first lecture started at 9.0am. Keith and I did manage to get to the university for most of these but without the benefit of breakfast. In fact, I can't remember going to many breakfasts at all after my first month in hall and I'm pretty certain Keith didn't either.

My memories of evenings in Churchill Hall are very similar to Ian's, not least our regular visits to the *King's Arms* for pints of beer, more often than not 'brown splits' (a mixture of Georges' draught bitter, an undistinguished local brew, and bottles of brown ale). Amazingly, we obeyed the no-alcohol-in-study-bedrooms rule and, after returning to hall at closing time, stuck to drinking coffee or tea, playing records and engaging in boisterous conversation. If our antics kept the early morning scrubbers awake, that was clearly a bonus, but it's no wonder breakfast was off the agenda most of the time.

Peter Allender, Ian Faulkner, Bernard Jarvis, Mike Stammers and I remained in Churchill Hall for our first two years at university but there was no option for a third. This was a crazy policy. Living out of hall in the second year, with an opportunity to return for our third, would have been far more sensible. Instead, just as the pressure of impending finals was beginning to loom, we were forced to fend for ourselves, as Ian remembers:

> Our group spent our first two years at Bristol reasonably happily in Churchill Hall but, because of university regulations, we had to find other accommodation for the third year. Keith, Bernard, Mike and Peter decided to move into a well-appointed student house, while I shared a basement flat with another third year student.

Even by undergraduate standards Ian's flat was squalid but our accommodation in a university-owned self-catering student house was decent enough and, most importantly, within easy walking distance of the Wills Memorial Building. Mike Stammers and I elected to share a huge room together and, remarkably, we managed to remain friends in spite of all the inconveniences. Fortunately, as he recalls, there was a central curtain that could be drawn to secure a degree of privacy:

> I shared a room with Keith in a university house in the third year. There was a curtain between us. I was flattered that he wanted to share with me but, I suppose, he chose me because I was less obtrusive and, anyway, it was practical that two history and two English guys (Bernard and Peter) shared rooms. Like Keith, I enjoyed working hard and, indeed, I think I modelled my working practices on his. Intensive and highly organised, especially when it came to revision, he had an iron will and an absolute determination to get high marks. I'm sure I owe him a lot in that respect.

By the time I arrived at Bristol University the eminent early medievalist David Douglas, head of the history department there for many years, had retired. This was a great disappointment. I'd read some of his work as a sixth former and was looking forward to hearing him in the flesh. Malcolm Lambert, who inherited Douglas's first year lecturing, certainly has vivid memories of him:

> David Douglas could be quite formidable. In those less bureaucratic days much depended on the will of the professor. He was quite military about the allocation of teaching: he gave you the job and you just got on with it.

Anne Crawford, who was taught by Douglas in his last year at the university, also got the impression that he was 'a despot but a benevolent one who treated undergraduates with an old-fashioned courtesy'. Fortunately, I did get to hear him deliver guest lectures two or three times: a very charismatic performer and, indeed, it was from him that I picked up the trick of lecturing from filing cards, thereby maximising the freedom to wander about and create an impression of spontaneity even when using a fairly full script. David Douglas's successor K. G.(Gordon) Davies was very different: an eccentric chain-smoking ex-Oxford don and seventeenth-century specialist. Yet, as Malcolm Lambert emphasises:

> K.G. Davies had style and, above all, a critical brain. He talked about the immense pleasure of pulling a finger out of the dyke holding up some well-established historical proposition and inundating an entire landscape. Nor was it entirely a joke when he told us how, asked by a visiting parent 'Where is the department?', he was tempted to say 'Le département, c'est moi!'.

My Ph.D supervisor Charles Ross, too, had a high opinion of Davies intellectually. Student reaction to him, however, was decidedly mixed. Anne Crawford, for instance, 'loathed him' and found him 'sneery, far more concerned with showing off his own cleverness than encouraging students'. Janet Nield, an undergraduate in my own year, specifically recalls that:

> K. G. Davies was responsible for just about the worst experience I had at Bristol when I endured a one-to-one tutorial with him. I can still remember my horror, on seeing the tutorial list, that I'd got to see him on my own. When I went to his room he lolled back in his chair, showing his socks and legs, and proceeded to wipe the floor with me.

Perversely, I rather warmed to a fellow nonconformist and heavy smoker who obviously rated my work. I also saw a very different side of him. When, in the middle of my first year exams, my foster father became seriously ill and I had to return home suddenly, he couldn't have been more supportive. He even waived my having to sit the two qualifying papers I'd missed. My most enduring memory, however, is of an immensely witty speech Davies once gave at an Acton (History) Society dinner outlining the 'all-purpose examination answer'. The other professor of history, an economic historian William Ashworth, I never encountered personally at all. As for the rest of the history staff, most of them, like K. G. Davies, were Oxford men and there were no women at all until Maureen Barry arrived at the beginning of my second year.

David Douglas's legacy was an old-fashioned history syllabus very much modelled on that of Oxford, an antiquated examination system and a perverse tradition of hardly ever awarding first class honours degrees (still going strong in 1966, as I was to discover to my cost). Malcolm Lambert muses that, in fact, Douglas:

> ... belonged to an older world. He had a great belief in the unity of history and avoiding snippeting. Yet he hadn't kept up with the sheer volume of quality work and fine articles. This really knocked the kind of syllabus we then had, particularly our huge outlines courses. Douglas never saw this, yet staff and students alike were restive with it.

Certainly, in 1963/4, first year undergraduates were still provided with a notably traditional fare: *Outlines of Medieval English History*, *Outlines of Modern English History* and, for good measure, *Outlines of European History* from the fall of Rome to the end of the Second World War. We were also required to take a subsidiary subject. Inexplicably, there was nothing literary on offer: if there had been, I would have opted for it like a shot. Instead, we had to choose between Latin and Economics. Since I'd only just scraped through O-Level Latin and never touched the subject in the sixth form, I chose Economics: not, in retrospect, the most sensible decision for a future medieval historian (and I never have mastered the language) but, when I first began studying at Bristol, I had no intention whatever of becoming one. The so-called *Principles of Economics* course was deadly and not slanted towards history students at all: it was probably just as well that my foster father's final illness and death enabled me to avoid the end-of-year examination. As for history itself, Charles Ross (Reader in Medieval History and, at the age of thirty-nine, now the senior medievalist in the department), had the unenviable task in our first term of convincing we raw freshers that medieval Europe 476—1500 was worthy of our serious attention and he did so brilliantly. Prowling restlessly back and forth in his aged gown, he presented the major themes of medieval European history (such as the emergence of feudalism, the evolution of the Papacy, the role of religious orders, the crusades, the Empire/Papacy struggles, the rise of monarchies and the nature of medieval culture) clearly and vividly. Very much inspired by these lectures (and presumably benefiting from having studied medieval Europe at A-Level as well), I scored a higher grade than anyone else in the end of term examination. Seemingly, then, even at Bristol University I was no intellectual lightweight. Regrettably, Patrick McGrath (whose main published work, I discovered much later, concerned medieval and early modern Bristol) entirely failed to maintain Ross's high standard in his pedestrian lectures on sixteenth and early seventeenth-century Europe. Only when John Cannon took over did the excitement return with a vengeance; his lectures, particularly those on personalities such as Louis XlV, Peter the Great and Napoleon, were both stimulating and entertaining; and, as Janet Nield emphasises, he was both 'very clear in delivery and interesting to listen to'. Not to opt for Cannon's second year European course covering 1648—1848 proved a difficult decision when the time came. The *Outlines of Modern English History* course, beginning in 1485 (traditionally regarded as the end of the Middle Ages in England when the last Plantagenet king Richard III bit the dust at Bosworth and the first Tudor Henry VII secured the throne), enabled Peter Ramsey to explore the highways and byways of Tudor history in about a dozen lectures. Well delivered, and not uninteresting to me (especially a couple on Tudor historical writing), they weren't much help to students who hadn't already studied sixteenth-century English history to A-Level. K. G. Davies, on Stuart England, was similarly idiosyncratic but also exceptionally thought-provoking, ending with a splendid lecture on James II's squandering of his brother Charles II's political legacy and provoking the Glorious Revolution of 1688. Inexplicably ignoring 1688—1714, David Large nevertheless faced an awesome task covering the entire period 1714—1945 in less than fifteen weeks. His lectures were certainly thorough and, fortunately for me, he did not assume prior knowledge; however, his high speed of delivery and delight in detail did not always make for easy listening, let alone effective note-taking. Just as well I was an experienced and proficient scribbler! Indeed, all that Janet Nield can remember of Large is:

> ... the speed of his delivery and our amusement that he would begin his lecture as soon as he walked through the door (and he was still speaking when he went out again!). I thought he was good value for money though: lots of information imparted rapidly.

I also recollect Large's annoyance when someone once brought a dog into the lecture theatre! Malcolm Lambert, who provided the bulk of the lectures for the *Outlines of Medieval English History* course (and there were a lot of them), was both a superb lecturer and a very caring man. Unlike some of his colleagues, indeed, he was not only friendly and approachable but even invited groups of us to his home for nibbles and mulled wine. Although primarily a historian of medieval European religion (especially heresy), he certainly fired my interest in Anglo-Saxon England, particularly the so-called 'Lost Centuries' 410—597 (where surviving evidence is both sparse and notoriously difficult to interpret). Post-1066 he tended to highlight kings and high politics; again, very much to my taste. As Janet Nield rightly emphasises:

> Malcolm Lambert came across as a thoroughly nice chap. He made the effort to be friendly, seemed less remote than many of the others, and his enthusiasm for his subject was infectious.

Eventually, Lambert handed over to Charles Ross who, in no more than a dozen lectures on 1399—1485 (Richard II, sadly, got lost in the transition), brought fifteenth-century kings, politics and aristocratic society alive. I became thoroughly hooked on the period and have remained so ever since.

Many universities had largely abandoned traditional outline history courses by 1963 and, after my time, so did Bristol. No doubt this partly reflected mounting undergraduate discontent, already evident in an editorial of 1965 in the *Acton Magazine* (produced by Bristol history students):

> The present syllabus is burdened with first year outline courses which wander incoherently from theme to theme and leave the undergraduate completely dazed, without the satisfaction of knowing one period of history really well or of being able to follow developments in any particular field.

As for 'additional subjects' like Economics, 'they seem to have been tagged on to the syllabus as an afterthought'. I certainly agreed about subsidiary subjects but not, oddly enough, the outline history courses. On the contrary, they suited me very nicely; most of the lectures were well delivered and their content interesting; and, as a result, I retain to this day a substantial residual knowledge of the whole span of English and European history from Roman times to 1945, a knowledge now sadly lacking in so many younger historians. What was wrong in my time was not so much the outline courses themselves as the fact that we were still being examined on their English history content over two years later in 1966.

By the end of my first year at Bristol enrolment on Charles Ross's second year option covering medieval Europe from about the mid-eleventh century to 1378 had become a foregone conclusion. I was not disappointed. Although Charles was wont to stress in later years his ignorance of the central middle ages, this was certainly not apparent in the lectures of 1964/5: on the contrary, they were not only magnificently structured and confidently delivered but also peppered with evidence of his determination to keep abreast of recent scholarship. For a few weeks, in the middle, he handed over to Malcolm Lambert and so we then had an opportunity to hear him lecture on his own field, most memorably St.Francis of Assisi and the Franciscans. Sadly, neither of the two compulsory second year courses had a great deal to recommend them. Until the early 1960s there had been a very old-fashioned course specifically devoted to English constitutional history but, by my time, this had given way to an extraordinary concoction of ill-assorted lectures by a variety of staff under the catch-all title *Special Aspects of English History*. I suspect it was the product of lack of agreement among the staff about whether or not to ditch constitutional history completely. I wish they had! James Sherborne, a fourteenth-century specialist, and Charles Ross probably took the easy way out. Ross managed to make fifteenth century government and administration at least comprehensible but Sherborne's lectures on 1066-1399, mainly devoted to the royal council, Magna Carta and parliament, were both desperately disorganised and dull. Patrick McGrath clearly couldn't make up his mind where he stood. A virtually week-by-week canter through the meetings of the Reformation Parliament 1529-1536 didn't make for exciting listening but he then suddenly came alive (the only time he ever did in the lecture theatre) when recounting the convoluted history of Elizabethan Catholicism: perhaps, as a Roman Catholic himself, he felt a vested interest in the subject. David Large and John Cannon also settled for a mix. Cannon clearly revelled in the workings of parliament and the electoral system in the century prior to the Great Reform Act of 1832 and so managed to engage our interest; as for Large, he certainly nailed his socialist colours to the mast in sardonic lectures on the nineteenth-century monarchy and public schools all too evidently dedicated to preserving the elitist status quo, not only in England but throughout the expanding British Empire. *English Economic and Social History*, another outline course commencing in 1066 (I never did discover the precise significance of the Norman Conquest here), engendered in me a distaste for economic history that has remained undiluted ever since. Social history, as I understood it, hardly figured in the course at all. Patrick McGrath covered the entire period from 1066 to the end of the seventeenth century but I wasn't a great deal wiser at the end of a term's lectures than I had been at the beginning. Why Peter Ramsey, who published an excellent short survey of *Tudor Economic Problems* in 1965 (and even signed the copy I bought for myself), didn't figure on the course at all is extraordinary. W. A. Cole, lecturing on the eighteenth century, was even worse than McGrath and confused us all utterly. William Ashworth, the cold, unsympathetic and remote professor of economic history, was certainly an expert on nineteenth and early twentieth-century economic history; his lectures were clear and coherent; and he presented a firmly conservative interpretation amidst awe-inspiring detail. Unfortunately, for me, the story he told was dreary beyond measure. No wonder I ended up as a historian of medieval and early modern kings, politics and war!

Political Theory, the only compulsory third year course we had to follow, was the responsibility of the philosophy department. The lecturer was an extraordinarily nervous fellow who, partly because of a tendency to chew his handkerchief and talk at the same time, became virtually inaudible beyond the first few rows of the lecture theatre. Not surprisingly, attendance at lectures was not high! Anyway, most history students I knew regarded political philosophy as incomprehensible, irrelevant or both. Perversely, I rather enjoyed it, particularly Plato (whose critique of democracy disturbed me then and still does), Thomas Hobbes (how could I resist a thinker who considered the life of natural man 'solitary, poor, nasty, brutish and short'?) and John Stuart Mill (whose essay *On Liberty* made an immediate and profound impact on me). In the later 1970s I even taught political philosophy myself for a few years at Huddersfield Polytechnic. We were also required to study another chunk of European history and I chose *Renaissance and Reformation*, covering the later fourteenth, fifteenth and sixteenth centuries. Had the course been taught by Patrick McGrath I probably wouldn't have touched it with a barge pole. I might even have sampled American or far eastern history, also on offer, but I doubt it. As I went out of my way to find out, however, Peter Ramsey was the lecturer. For all their quirkiness I'd enjoyed his first year lectures on Tudor England and he didn't disappoint here either. Unfortunately, Ramsey left at the end of the autumn term 1965. K. G. Davies, even more idiosyncratic, then took charge of the teaching and, so it seemed to us, proceeded to lecture on any vaguely relevant topic he happened to know about, ranging from Rabelais to French government finance. Again, I found most of his lectures intellectually stimulating but, as soon as Ramsey's successor arrived, we were handed over to him. No wonder Tony Antonovics encountered a distinctly frosty reception when he tried to interest us in the Council of Trent and, even thirty years later, he still remembered this most disconcerting start to his long career at Bristol. And so ended what had turned out to be a complete dog's breakfast of a course. Yet, when I first came to teach fourteenth, fifteenth and sixteenth-century European history myself, I found my 1965/6 lecture notes quite unexpectedly thought-provoking. The high point of my final year as a history undergraduate, by a very large margin, was Charles Ross's Special Subject on *Yorkist England*, covering the reigns of Edward IV (1461—1483) and Richard III (1483—1485). Although it was a seminar course, with a firm stress on the reading and evaluation of papers delivered by students, there was never much doubt that Ross himself was in charge of the proceedings. Early sessions were devoted to discussing the sources for Yorkist politics, particularly the major chronicles, and everyone was expected to get hold of and read them, even though, in those pre-photocopying days, there was only one copy of most available. Fortunately, we were a small group of just eight. Vernacular chronicles we read in the original English and, in theory at least, we tackled Philippe de Commines (a major continental source) in French. I managed to pick up a nineteenth century translation in a second hand bookshop. Ross was enough of a realist, however, to sanction the study of Latin sources such as the *Crowland Chronicle* and Dominic Mancini's *Usurpation of Richard III* in English (unlike James Sherborne who required his, understandably tiny, Special Subject group studying Richard II to read several narratives in the original Latin). Once all the sources had been covered—and Ross was adept at ensuring we had all the interpretative material necessary, even resorting to lecturing himself when he deemed it expedient—papers were assigned (on Yorkist politics and government mainly, but supplemented, later in the course, by presentations on economic/ social, religious and cultural history). Oddly enough, I opted to tackle Yorkist government finance and, jointly with Mike Stammers, religion and culture 1461—1485. Charles Ross always took copious notes from student papers himself (partly to ensure they were delivered at a reasonable speed) and, whenever there were omissions, misunderstandings or errors, contrived to plug the gaps while, at the same time, preserving the invariably relaxed and friendly atmosphere of the proceedings. All in all, it was an immensely enjoyable, as well as intellectually stimulating, experience, and at the end the whole class felt enriched by it. What was not available to history students in 1965/6 (unlike, for instance, English undergraduates) was the opportunity to research and write a dissertation. Soon after my time, Malcolm Lambert recalls:

> David Large developed the undergraduate thesis and, under his model, it was a choice and could be dropped if it didn't work out in the preparation period of the long vacation between years two and three. Some final products were excellent and, even if they weren't very good, students frequently learnt a lot.

Certainly, I would have seized the opportunity to tackle such a dissertation myself and maybe, if I had, I would have been altogether better prepared to choose a topic, research and write a Ph.D later.

Not only did the mid-1960s Bristol University history syllabus owe much to the Oxford model, so did its tutorial system. The jewel of Oxford's crown, so that university would have us believe, has long been its weekly one-to-one essay tutorials where student assignments receive rigorous oral examination by expert tutors. Bristol, presumably, didn't have the staff resources to match this but we did submit essays to tutors once a fortnight or so and then found ourselves summoned, usually in groups of two or three (although, occasionally, on our own) for hour-long discussions of our efforts. How valuable such sessions were depended entirely on the individual tutor and how he chose to conduct them. Charles Ross, with whom I did enjoy a number of one-to-one tutorials, was friendly, constructive in his criticisms and, so it seemed to me, generous in his grading. So was Malcolm Lambert. Patrick McGrath, for all his shortcomings in the lecture theatre, could be notably stimulating in tutorials held in his smoke-filled room (he was an inveterate pipe smoker) as he gazed at us from behind a desk piled high with books and all manner of clutter. K. G. Davies, who not infrequently conducted tutorials lying languidly on a sofa and had an awesome reputation for bitingly critical comment, not only seemed to like my work but was also notably generous in offering cigarettes to a fellow nicotine addict. David Large, for whom I wrote more essays than anyone else in my first year, I found rather intimidating (he didn't suffer fools gladly and, once I became hooked on medieval history, I tended to keep reading for modern essays to a minimum) but he, too, rarely awarded me less than solid upper second grades. James Sherborne, although another heavy smoker liberal with his cigarettes, simply terrified me as an undergraduate, as he almost invariably criticised my essays (and everyone else's) in painstaking detail. Yet he also awarded me very decent grades more often than not. Only as a postgraduate, when I got to know him much better, did I come to appreciate his sterling qualities. I last saw him in 1987 (not long before he died) when, lying on the Clifton Downs one hot summer afternoon, he clinically (but constructively) dissected the manuscript of my first book. As a student I enjoyed well-structured, informative and stimulating lectures far more than tutorials. Too often we were switched from tutor to tutor for no very good reason and, occasionally, we were even required to read out our essays. This was a complete waste of time. Tutors must have read, and thought about, assignments in advance if sessions were to be of any real value and, anyway, written comments on them were far more use. Now and again, too, there could be a counter-productive personality clash between student and tutor. Malcolm Lambert, rightly, stresses the particular potential value of one-to-one contacts:

> With two or three, tutorials could fall flat. Yet a really good discussion around an essay could be most helpful. It's also true that the shy and reticent, who could hide in a seminar, had to speak and be questioned direct, especially one-to-one. One could make criticisms in private not possible when others were present, bring on essay writing and get to the guts of an argument. It also meant that—if the personalities gelled—you could help on personal and syllabus problems.

I vividly recall just such a session with him when, towards the end of my first term, I submitted a heavily plagiarised assignment. Since neither Harold Richardson nor James Crump had ever warned us against this in the sixth form I wasn't consciously trying to cheat but, obviously, Lambert couldn't ignore such a heinous transgression of academic protocol. Fortunately, and no doubt deliberately, he went out of his way to see me on his own (rare before the second year), handled the situation with enormous sensitivity, and I certainly learned the lesson. Nevertheless, despite such very positive experiences occasionally, I believe the Oxford-style tutorial can all too easily be over-rated as a teaching mechanism and, overall, I have distinctly mixed memories of many of those I sat through at Bristol.

Bristol University history department modelled its examination as well as its tutorial practices on Oxford. Although, over three years, we all wrote dozens of essays, none of them counted towards our final degree classification. There was no continuous assessment at all. Nor did the many exam papers we sat in the first and second years in any way enter the equation. There wasn't even a Part 1, along Cambridge lines. English had this at Bristol but not history. Instead, over a period of about a fortnight in the summer term of our final year, we sat ten three hour written examinations, covering everything we'd done in the second and third years (and even the English history we'd been taught in the first). Revision was a complete nightmare (all the papers were completely unseen, of course); we received little or nothing in the way of advice about how to tackle it; and at least one student in my year simply couldn't cope and had a nervous breakdown. Ian Faulkner vividly recalls the horror of it all, not least my behaviour and its impact on Mike Stammers:

> As Final Examinations loomed, we all began to respond to pressure in varying ways but perhaps no one felt it more than Mike, living as he did with Keith (whose appetite for work had now become legendary). I clearly remember Mike commenting that he just couldn't keep up with Keith's work rate and being in awe of the fact that he had not only produced 'reduced notes' as an *aide-mémoire* but had now moved on to preparing 'reduced reduced notes'!

'I can't remember much about Keith during the Finals period itself', he adds:

> ... except that, although he was expected to do very well, he made it clear he wasn't enjoying the experience any more than the rest of us. He was also strongly critical of Bristol history department's system of examining students on their complete three years' work in one go at the end of the final year.

To make matters worse for us, the exam papers themselves didn't always bear much relation to what we'd actually been taught and studied. K. G. Davies obviously hadn't helped much here. Although, as Malcolm Lambert recalls, he eventually 'greatly revised and improved the syllabus, broke out of the old conservatism and raised standards', he was also:

> ... keen on ensuring that examining was objective. No one, apart from Special Subject tutors, could have 'proprietary' papers. Questions should in part be set by others. He carried this a bit far and, given the vast possibilities, it could be awkward for students.

It certainly could and, in 1966, it most emphatically was. Perhaps a few senior and long-serving staff like Charles Ross and David Large managed to resist the worst excesses of such a directive: the four papers I sat covering Ross's second and third year options were scrupulously fair and so, much to my relief, was the exam devoted to English history 1688-1945. The English history 410—1307 paper was another matter altogether. Malcolm Lambert must have had very little input at all since many of the questions were on topics entirely unfamiliar to us. The English economic and social history exam contained only a couple of reasonable questions on the pre-Industrial Revolution era (on which I'd concentrated in revision); we had to tackle four; and, out of sheer desperation, for my last answer I ended up drawing mainly on what I'd learned about railways and their impact on Victorian society as a schoolboy! The Renaissance and Reformation paper, largely ignoring the first term of the course altogether, was as idiosyncratic as K. G. Davies himself (so, presumably, he set most of the questions on that). As for political theory, the exam was clearly set with philosophy not history students in mind and there were hardly any questions directly on the set texts at all. Talking to my Huddersfield Polytechnic colleague Pauline Stafford years later, I got the impression that even her hit-and-miss Oxford Finals papers had been fairer than ours. It's remarkable that I emerged from my own ordeal, and such it certainly was, as well as I did.

Prior to the examinations, Charles Ross hinted that I was fully expected to get a first class honours degree but, in the end, the legacy of David Douglas (aided and abetted by K. G. Davies, seemingly) prevailed and I didn't. Amazingly, indeed, although there must have been at least fifty single-subject history students in my year (all with very good A-Levels, presumably), there were not only no firsts but just eight upper seconds. James Opie (ex-Eton:) and I got the 'best' upper seconds and so, jointly, won the university's George Hare Leonard Prize in history. Malcolm Lambert believes that:

... the prime reason for no firsts was the history syllabus: it was too amorphous and students couldn't concentrate enough. Good results were achieved in the Special Subjects, which I thought well taught, but people sank in the outlines.

Indeed, he recollects ruefully:

As soon as I arrived at Bristol I was pursued about the syllabus and the lack of firsts, even invited to a hall of residence on an, ostensibly, social occasion and then interrogated. This was hard, as there was nothing a new arrival and very junior lecturer could do. You were certainly not alone in thinking firsts were unreasonably withheld.

Ian Faulkner, Mike Stammers and I were the guilty parties here, I fear, when we invited Lambert to dinner at high table in Churchill Hall during our second year. Ian himself comments:

In common with everyone else I was delighted when I learnt that Keith had achieved the joint highest degree in our year. That this was an upper second rather than a first was, many of us felt, more a reflection of Bristol history department's peculiar way of doing things than anything else.

In 1967, so Charles Ross told me at the time, the number of top grade papers required for a first in history was reduced and, if Opie and I had taken our final exams a year later, we might well have got firsts. Maybe, though, he was simply trying to brighten me up during a bout of academic self-doubt!

Fellow history undergraduate Janet Nield recalls:

Although our paths never really crossed, I remember that you were regarded as the cleverest student in our year and we all hoped that you would get a first. I think you enjoyed respect from the rest of us for your intellect.

Mike Stammers, of course, knew me well:

Keith dressed conventionally, long tweed overcoat, slightly slouched shoulders and large leather briefcase. He was tall, thin and spoke his mind confidently; he had no interest in sport and despised those who had; and he soon demonstrated his maturity, as well as a degree of scepticism and cynicism (not least about the university establishment).

Moreover, he adds perceptively, 'Keith worked like hell, much harder than the rest of us, as if perhaps he was scared of failing or, maybe, simply determined to succeed'. Peter Allender, in not dissimilar vein, comments:

> Keith worked hard and, what is more, knew how to work effectively. I remember him neatly transcribing what seemed to me already legible and highly detailed lecture notes. He knew how to use books. And he seemed to know where he was going and how to get there.

'The only way you seemed different from the rest of us', echoes Bernard Jarvis, was that 'you worked harder and longer'; however, building on his earlier impressions of me as a sixth former, he also emphasises that I:

> ... seemed more completely formed, more hard-edged and consequently more grown up. You'd seen more than the rest of us and, with hindsight, it showed.

Perhaps a specific memory of Malcolm Lambert says it all:

> I remember when I did some extra little talks on the early English period. I had a multitude for King Arthur and a fair number for one or two other topics. Then came medieval Wales. I thought it interesting but no one else did. You were the only person to turn up! I gave the talk in full just the same and thought you were a keen man. So you were.

Despite my failure to obtain a first class honours degree in the summer of 1966, I nevertheless managed to secure funding for up to three years postgraduate research leading, hopefully, to a doctorate. Hence why, at the last minute, I turned down Bristol University Education Department's offer of a place on its one year teacher training course for graduates. By all accounts I didn't miss much. Bernard Jarvis certainly wasn't overly impressed by it and Peter Allender's experience of a similar course in London was even worse. Yet I did want to remain in Bristol, felt comfortable in the university and didn't fancy Warwick, the alternative possibility, at all. I had an interview there with E .P. Thompson, an eminent social historian, and he suggested I might like to work, under his supervision, on the eighteenth-century aristocracy. I liked Thompson very much (another enthusiastic smoker!) and felt sure that, even if I didn't share his left-wing political views, I could get on with him. The eighteenth-century aristocracy, about whom I'd already learned a little from David Large and John Cannon, appealed to me as well. What I couldn't stomach was Warwick University. Its new campus seemed more like a building site than anything else and, worse still, it was situated in the middle of nowhere, several miles from the nearest towns Coventry, Leamington Spa and even Warwick itself. Without a car I would have felt trapped, I couldn't possibly afford even an old banger and, more to the point, I didn't drive. Nor had I any intention of ever doing so and I never have. So I politely turned down Thompson's offer to become one of his research students. I'm sure I was right. Almost a decade later, as an Open University Summer School tutor, I was obliged to live on Warwick's campus for a week or two and that proved quite long enough. Anyway, although Charles Ross had encouraged me to try my luck at Warwick in the first place, he nevertheless seemed happy enough to take me on himself at Bristol. Unfortunately, I had no specific fifteenth-century research topic in mind and, instead of following my own literary and historiographical instincts, I looked to Charles Ross for inspiration. A Yorkshireman himself, Charles's Oxford D.Phil had been on 'The Yorkshire Baronage 1399—1435'; he retained a considerable interest in northern, especially Yorkshire, history; and, since I was also a Yorkshireman, it seemed appropriate that I work on that county as well. During the later 1950s and early 1960s there had been a great deal of research into the political, economic and social importance of English provincial gentry, particularly in early modern times. Specifically, J. T. Cliffe had completed a London University Ph.D. in 1960 entitled 'The Yorkshire Gentry on the Eve of the Civil War' (eventually expanded and published as *The Yorkshire Gentry from the Reformation to the Civil War* in 1969). There had been very little work done on fifteenth-century Yorkshire gentry. So, when Charles suggested I embark on a study of the greater gentry of Yorkshire circa 1450—1509, I readily agreed. Indeed, I felt flattered since it was obviously a subject close to his own heart and, eventually, my postgraduate research was to provide valuable material for both teaching and publication.

Although I was determined never to work as hard again as I had as an undergraduate, I set about my research in a conscientious enough manner and, over the next two or three years, accumulated a considerable archive of material covering some forty prominent Yorkshire gentry families. Much was to be found in volumes of printed record sources and Bristol University library had most of them on its shelves or, more often, in its stack rooms. There I was to be found most mornings but only rarely in the afternoons, and certainly not if Charles Ross and I embarked on one of our regular lunchtime drinking sessions. I soon discovered, however, that fifteenth-century record evidence was much less to my taste than chronicles or letters and that I didn't enjoy reading original manuscripts at all, particularly Latin records preserved in local and national archives. This was unfortunate since records threw up most of what I needed to get to grips with my gentry families. I visited the Borthwick Institute of Historical Research in York a couple of times, easily reached during my occasional visits to

Huddersfield, and read a fair number of unpublished fifteenth-century gentry wills. Two or three times, too, I forced myself to visit the Public Record Office in London's Chancery Lane for a few days, ploughed through a range of mainly legal records and, perhaps most fruitfully, looked up references for my supervisor Charles Ross (who was working on a biography of the first Yorkist king Edward IV, far more interesting than my Yorkshire gentry). Sadly, as far as my research was concerned, I found the pubs in nearby Fleet Street (still the home of most national newspapers in the later 1960s) altogether more to my taste. Nor did my tendency to stay with Ian Faulkner, my former Bristol drinking crony and now working for a London publisher, help a great deal. Reading fifteenth-century manuscripts is difficult enough at the best of times and virtually impossible when nursing a mega-hangover! Also, in retrospect, I spent far too long digging out more and more material on my families, far too little organising it into potential chapter form for my thesis. The playwright Alan Bennett was a research student of K. B. McFarlane (Charles Ross's D.Phil supervisor at Oxford) in the later 1950s and recalled those years vividly in 1997:

> With a First, a research grant was a formality, so I stayed on at Oxford and for a time even convinced myself I was a scholar, coming up to read manuscripts at the Public Record Office, still in Chancery Lane. But I was more a copyist than a scholar, since that was all I did, copying out medieval records with no notion of what to do with them, and the longer I did it the more dissatisfied with myself and the bigger fraud I felt.

The parallels with my own experience of postgraduate research are uncomfortably close but, unfortunately, I didn't have Bennett's flair and ability to change tracks completely and become one of the later twentieth century's most accomplished and successful dramatists.

By 1969 I had written about twenty detailed family histories of my Yorkshire gentry but virtually nothing that could go directly into a Ph.D thesis. Much the best of them concerned the Plumptons because, not only were the records of this West Riding clan unusually rich, there also survived a substantial collection of revealing family letters. The rest were thorough enough but hardly a thrilling read. Towards the end of my time I also delivered a paper to a research seminar at Bristol University on 'Yorkshire Knights and Squires in the service of Richard III'. Responses to this were largely positive (even from James Sherborne!) and Charles Ross's reactions to my family histories, too, were almost invariably encouraging. The eminent fifteenth-century historian Michael Hicks, who did his first degree at Bristol but then moved to Southampton (for his MA) and Oxford (for his D.Phil) muses:

There are two types of Ph.D supervisors, those who regiment their students and those who let them run. Each suits some research students better than others. Maybe you would have benefited from the former, whereas Charles Ross—an instance of the latter—was not right for you, however congenial.

Perhaps Charles could have pushed me harder than he did but it might well have proved counter-productive. As it was, my three years as a research student proved seminally important in another way altogether by providing a much needed opportunity to come to terms with my homosexuality. Charles Ross understood that and gave me the space I needed. Hopefully, I was equally helpful as he, too, grappled with personal problems. As a result we became great friends and the student/supervisor relationship largely faded into the background. Michael Jones, Charles's research student a decade or so after my time, comments shrewdly:

> The most obvious thing Keith and I have in common was being taught medieval history by Charles Ross. Taught, however, does not do justice to Charles's understanding of his subject and the insight with which he communicated it. So, rather, we were both inspired by Charles the historian. Yet we also got to know Charles the man and here the equation was less simple. In different ways we both suffered from the personal issues Charles was struggling with and, as a result, Ph.D supervision sometimes went drastically by the wayside. Nevertheless, in the long term, both Keith and I gained more than we lost by knowing him so well.

It certainly wasn't Charles Ross's fault that I abandoned my Ph.D in the summer of 1969. By then I had become thoroughly turned off by historical research in general and fifteenth-century Yorkshire gentry in particular. At this stage it was far too late to change topic (which might have revived my enthusiasm) and, anyway, even then I hadn't fully realised that what really appealed to me were literary sources for fifteenth-century England (especially its kings, politics and wars) and historiography. All I now knew for certain was that records-based historical research was not my forté at all. Years later Charles Ross expressed the wish that I'd discussed my growing disillusion with him as soon as it began to set in but I never did. Had I done so early enough, he then assured me, he would probably have let me switch (albeit with trepidation) to a historiographically-orientated thesis: focussing on the historian John Richard Greene perhaps, whose pioneering *Short History of the English People* was first published in 1874 (and reprinted fifteen times over the next decade), or his fellow Victorian James Gairdner, prolific editor of chronicles, letters and records, as well as author of the first scholarly biography of Richard III. Sadly, I simply lacked the self-confidence in the later 1960s ever to raise such possibilities with him.

Not only was I fed up with fifteenth-century historical records by the spring of 1969, I'd had enough of universities as well and certainly didn't want a post in one. All I wished to do was recapture my now seriously tarnished enjoyment of history and, hopefully, pass it on to others. Hence why I began to find myself ever more powerfully drawn to secondary school teaching, particularly at sixth form level. So I started applying for jobs in schools. Since I had no teaching qualification and virtually no teaching experience either (beyond conducting a handful of Special Subject seminars for Charles Ross and tutoring a mature student grappling, ironically enough, with fifteenth-century economic history for a London University External degree), there was no point bothering about state schools. Anyway, I didn't fancy teaching in one of the new-fangled comprehensives that now seemed to be replacing grammar schools and secondary moderns all over the place. This left the independent sector and, despite my working class origins, I had no political or ideological hang-ups holding me back. On the contrary, after my years at Huddersfield (New) College, I was curious to find out what a real public school was like from the inside. I secured an interview at Eltham College and nearly got the job. What told against me, apparently, was my complete lack of knowledge of American history, central to the school's sixth form teaching. Charles Ross drove me to Bideford in north Devon for an interview at an independent school there. Again, the headmaster was complimentary, but turned me down this time because I was too much of an academic! Bideford would have been a nightmare anyway: its railway line had been a victim of Dr Beeching's axe and I would have been a virtual prisoner in the place. Then, much to my surprise, I was offered a job as a junior history master at Plymouth College and promptly accepted the post.

5

Plymouth College Schoolmaster

Dennis Collinson, head of history at Plymouth College during my years there, recalls that 'the headmaster and I had no hesitation in offering Keith his first teaching post'; nor did I have any qualms about accepting the job or, indeed, taking on the potentially problematic role of house tutor in one of the school's two boarding houses. It marked a complete break with my recent past and this was just what I was looking for. Martin Meade-King, a historian himself who had been at Clifton College, Bristol, as a boy and head of history at a prominent London public school before taking the helm at Plymouth, confirmed my appointment in writing (the only contract I ever had) a few days later:

> The post is as Assistant Master to teach History (possibly one form of junior English). The salary will be £40 above the Burnham Basic. The first year will be probationary but, if all goes well, you will then receive an additional allowance. You will also join Mr Collinson in Colson House as House Tutor and will receive free board and lodging in return for your duties.

Clearly, since I had no teaching qualification, the headmaster was taking a calculated risk in employing me but I had few doubts about my capacity to rise to the challenge. Perhaps he believed, rightly, that good teachers are born not made and, certainly, much that was pedalled by so-called educationalists during my many years at the chalkface turned out to be highly dubious. More ominous was a rider to his letter:

> I am not expecting you to acquire skills which are not within your scope and interest but I hope you will follow the example of all our younger masters in seeking to contribute to the out-of-school activities of the school.

The prospect of having to participate in sporting activities (even in a supervisory capacity) had no appeal whatever but I decided that was a hurdle to be surmounted later and, in the event, drama provided an entirely congenial escape route when the crunch came. So, shortly before the beginning of term in September 1969, I duly moved to Plymouth and took up residence in Colson House.

Plymouth College, in my time, certainly comprised a ramshackle collection of buildings. Most importantly, there was what Chris Robinson (author of *Plymouth College: The First Hundred Years*) picturesquely describes as the original 'great grey gothic pile' built in the 1870s and particularly 'well suited to the teaching of medieval history'. Within its walls were 'Big School' (where morning assembly took place), the gymnasium, two staffrooms and many classrooms. Most of my own teaching was located here, appropriately enough, boys seated uncomfortably at battered desks which, like the building itself, looked as if they had been there since Victorian times. There was also a more modern complex, arranged around a sort of courtyard, containing not only more (and much better furnished) classrooms but also the school's refectory. The college owned many of the houses in a couple of adjoining terraces, too, where both the school's library and its two boarding houses were to be found. Inevitably, as well, there were playing fields, mainly given over to rugby in the autumn and spring terms, cricket in the summer, and, on CCF afternoons, the scene of uniformed staff barking orders at boys marching around in the guise of soldiers, sailors and airmen. Needless to say, throughout my years at the school, I was rarely to be found there!

Although an establishment that all too evidently aspired to the ethos of an Eton or a Winchester, Plymouth College at the end of the 1960s enjoyed Direct Grant status. As a result, while the majority of boys were fee-paying, there was also a substantial minority of lads who had passed the 11+, won free places and had their fees paid by the local authority. Any qualms I might have had about teaching in such a school were at least partially allayed by this, especially as some of the free placers (like me at Huddersfield New College a decade earlier) came from working class families. Perhaps inevitably, moreover, scholarship boys tended to dominate the 'A' stream while, in the 'B' and 'C' streams, less able lads whose parents could afford to pay for their children's education very much predominated. Among the boarders there were also significant numbers whose fathers were in the military and whose fees were paid by the Ministry of Defence. Clearly, for me, the contrast between sharing a Bristol flat with an older homosexual partner (as I had between 1967 and 1969) and occupying a single room in a school boarding house in Plymouth surrounded by over fifty boys aged eleven to eighteen could hardly have been greater. Huddersfield (New) College, no doubt very much reflecting the values and priorities of its headmaster A. R. Bielby, had sought to model itself on post-war public schools but now, twenty-four hours a day, seven days a week and, as it turned out, for over two-and-a-half years, I was destined to experience the real thing. Everywhere there seemed to be lads wearing striped blazers, sports gear or, most bizarrely, military uniforms on Combined Cadet Force afternoons. Sixth formers were easily identifiable by their grey suits. And most of the staff wore academic gowns. Yet, once I'd settled in and acquired a rather battered gown of my own, I found it all not only fascinating and immensely challenging but also, in many ways, hugely enjoyable as well.

Dennis Collinson, who joined the staff of Plymouth College in 1953 as a junior history master straight from Cambridge, certainly has very positive memories of Martin Meade-King's determination, as headmaster, to raise standards in the school; moreover, during his own years there, he recollects teaching many academic high flyers, and not just from the ranks of free placers. Bernard Samuels, who taught at the school from 1956 to 1970 (when he left to become full-time director of Plymouth Arts Centre), was, on his own admission, 'a Mancunian besotted with art' whose 'background was hardly akin to the world of Plymouth College'; a lover of music, he frequently escaped to his flat on the school site at lunchtime simply to unwind by playing his cello; and, as for teaching French to boys who were 'mainly the sons of local business people', it was 'not a career I had planned'. Yet, although 'the general values of the school and its clientèle were beyond my ken' and despite 'all my reluctance to be a schoolmaster', Bernard found it for many years:

> ... a very tolerant place and the headmaster more forbearing than perhaps he ought to have been. There was one aspect of the school that I did enjoy greatly, namely the company of a fascinating group of characters, for the most part men who had joined the school in the 1930s, gone through the war and simply returned, seemingly happy to enjoy the easy pace of life in Plymouth and work out the rest of their careers teaching at the place they had joined many years before.

The headmaster himself, for instance, had served in military intelligence during the Second World War; Edgar Russell (mathematics), a highly civilised and much respected member of staff, had fought as a naval pilot, undertaken top secret missions and been decorated for bravery; and Bill Barnes (classics) had retired with the rank of colonel. Several had also achieved distinction in the sporting world, most notably the deputy headmaster Bill Battrick (chemistry). And at least two or three senior masters, had they graduated in the 1960s rather than the 1930s or 1940s, might well have pursued successful careers in higher education.

By the time I arrived in September 1969, Bernard Samuels recalls, even within such a conventional middle class school as Plymouth College (populated, as it was, mainly by lads whose parents could afford the fees and for whom 'a career in estate agency seemed to be the principal way ahead'), attitudes were beginning to change, if not very comfortably. During the later 1950s and early 1960s:

> ... the atmosphere of the staff common room was what would be described nowadays as fairly laid back. Bureaucracy was kept to the minimum. Staff meetings occurred at the beginning and end of term. In between people just got on with the job. By the time Keith arrived, however, traditions were being challenged and the common room, which until then had been more or less at ease with itself, became obsessed with what seemed to me trivial matters such as the length of boys' hair. The management was unable to cope. Special staff meetings were called to discuss a crisis in discipline and the threat to the whole ethos and moral fibre of the school.

Michael Allen, a young English master who joined the staff at the same time as I did, had only recently completed his teacher training practice 'in a rough, inner city secondary modern' and so, for him, 'Plymouth College was a dream, or at least the pupils were'. Nevertheless, he recollects:

> Several of the older staff had taught at the school both before and after the war. There were two common rooms—upper (where older staff tended to congregate) and lower (occupied by the likes of us); the school had a strong military psyche; and there was an oppressive ethos of discipline and punishment. Ted Mercer (a middle-aged Yorkshireman and mathematics master) once described the school's common room as 'the most exclusive club in the southwest' but it certainly wasn't for me and such a remark betrayed the insular arrogance of the place.

Dennis Collinson particularly highlights Martin Meade-King's liberalising tendencies as a source of disagreement between headmaster, school governors and some senior staff from time to time. Yet the head also had his supporters amongst more progressive spirits such as Edgar Russell, Dennis himself and most of the younger masters.

Sadly, I have maintained contact with hardly any of the boys I taught in Plymouth over thirty-five years ago but, among those who are still in touch, Roger Middleton is much the most critical of the school. Now professor of economic history at the University of Bristol, his memories are certainly bleak, not least of:

... the hall where morning assembly took place: high-ceilinged, wooden-panelled, all ordered and hierarchical. There stands the headmaster, presiding over his empire, alongside the masters, generally middle-aged but including a few younger ones as well. Casting our eyes around, while trying to block out the dreadful sound of obligatory hymns celebrating British Christianity, our visual senses are dominated by various trophy boards celebrating sporting and Oxbridge achievements. Next I recollect the rigid hierarchies which were so oppressive: the ordered ranks by year and minor gradations of dress, particularly the dreadful striped blazer making its wearers instantly identifiable as public school boys in need of a good kicking. Then, of course, we have the particular focus of 1960s stress, hair, the absence of it on the teachers and the attempted excess of it on the boys who, relishing small victories, sought both to trumpet the length of their tresses to peers and minimise it to the repressive forces constantly on the look out for any indication of individuality and nonconformity.

For Roger, in fact, Plymouth College represented (and continues to represent):

... the public school ethos red in tooth and claw: a combination of feudal legacy and nineteenth-century educational reform designed to generate obsession with duty, denial of the inner self, fortitude and, above all, courage. In this world character mattered more than intellect and playing the game was a necessary preparation for life's travails.

Yet author, artist and television presenter Chris Robinson, who was also at Plymouth College during the later 1960s and early 1970s and certainly has his own reservations about the 'small southwestern public school' where he was educated, nevertheless admits to having loved the place dearly. Indeed, he has remained a loyal Old Plymothian ever since culminating, in 1995, in his becoming a governor of the school.

'My first remembered meeting with Keith', so Mike Allen recalls, was:

... as one of six new recruits in Meade-King's study: a motley crew, among them Ivor Cleeves (mathematics) and Gordon Hook (PE). I felt distinctly overwhelmed and insecure but braved it out. Keith was older, having spent several years working on an incompleted Ph.D., yet, despite our obvious differences, he and I became good friends very quickly.

I certainly felt older than the others, registering, in particular, how fresh-faced and handsome Mike appeared, how fit and healthy Gordon Hook, and I couldn't help feeling a certain alarm about just what I had let myself in for.

Fortunately (if unexpectedly) Mike and I hit it off right from the start, mainly for the reasons he himself suggests: our shared working class backgrounds, real passion for teaching and, perhaps most importantly, taste for beer. He's probably right too when he asserts, admittedly with the benefit of hindsight, that we were both destined to make 'a significant impact' on the school, as 'a breath of fresh air blowing in from the sixties'. Bernard Samuels, in similar vein, remarks that my arrival was 'timely, the proverbial breath of fresh air, and someone who immediately empathised with my exasperation at the state of the place'. As for the boys, they seem to have been mainly struck by my physical appearance and eccentricities. Roger Middleton, for instance, remembers me 'wearing a suit but in so shabby a fashion as to bring the whole process of morning assembly into disrepute'; moreover, he adds, 'we admired him for this'. I even risked wearing a leather jacket now and again until the headmaster, very gently, asked me to desist! Chris Robinson supplies a nice pen-portrait of how I seemed to the older lads:

> Keith certainly had a very distinctive gait, sort of angular and jerky, not quite from the ministry of funny walks but definitely unusual. Nor was it confined to outside the classroom. I can see him now pacing around Room 4: florid complexion, strong whiff of nicotine, occasionally of booze, young, fair-haired, with a strong northern accent, invariably dressing up a drollery or spewing out a sarcasm. Long fingers, long hands, wringing an interesting mixture of historical fact and emotion from his lean frame as he moved restlessly from one part of the room to another. I seldom recall Keith sitting still—too hyper.

Perhaps, even at the very start of my teaching career, I had grasped the value of projecting an image of myself, if only subconsciously as yet. Later on, it became a deliberate and carefully calculated weapon in my armoury at Huddersfield Polytechnic.

Although Martin Meade-King was almost as remote a figure, for a junior master, as A. R. Bielby had been for a grammar school boy and, rather quaintly I thought, almost invariably addressed staff (as well as boys) by their surnames, he knew all our forenames perfectly well and even used them at social gatherings for staff he occasionally hosted in his house on the school site. Before long, moreover, I came to respect him very much and certainly appreciated his quiet but firm backing for my efforts to bring history alive in the classroom. In particular, he approved of my determination to introduce boys, especially sixth formers, to primary source material. So did my head of department Dennis Collinson, who recalls:

Keith was extraordinarily conscientious in preparing masses of his own material for the sixth form, despite the nose-peaked frowning of the school secretary as her coveted paper supplies disappeared: 'That Mr Dockray! What does he do with it all?'. I had to concoct some elaborate story of his having special dispensation for a teaching scheme to be submitted to the Ministry. When other members of staff brought up the issue at a heads of department meeting, the headmaster would have none of it, declaring forthrightly that he wished other junior staff were as adventurous.

Putting on plays in a school is always fraught with difficulty too, particularly if boys are cast who also happen to be accomplished sportsmen since, inevitably, there are occasional clashes between rehearsals and house/school matches. Hence why, on one occasion, I had a blazing row with the senior PE master. The school gymnasium doubled up as a 'theatre' (there was a stage at one end) and he wasn't at all happy about its regular use for rehearsals in the evenings. Again, the headmaster backed me up all the way. When I obtained a post at Huddersfield Polytechnic, requiring that I left the school at the end of the spring term 1972, it obviously posed a real problem for him and, since there was very little teaching for me there until the autumn, Huddersfield could, and should, have postponed my start date. Meade-King, indeed, vigorously tried to persuade me not to accept the appointment and it was certainly one of the most difficult decisions I have ever had to make. Once it was made, however, he warmly shook my hand, thanked me for my service to the school, and wished me every success in the future. In return for his civilised acceptance of the inconvenience of my sudden departure, supplemented by the offer of an extra month's salary (resulting in my being paid by both Huddersfield and Plymouth in April 1972), I happily agreed to mark well over a hundred sixth form assignments during the Easter vacation.

Bernard Samuels, so he remembers, very much enjoyed 'observing the collection of personalities that made up the common room' at Plymouth College and so did I; moreover, I got on well enough with most of them, even the dinosaurs. Among the latter was Bill Battrick the deputy head: he had a doctorate in chemistry but was well past his sell-by date as a teacher; he was an unreconstructed disciplinarian; and, among the boys, he inspired a curious combination of fear and contempt. Yet, as Mike Allen has reminded me, he 'performed adeptly the role of go-between' when it came to relations between staff and headmaster. Among other middle-aged dinosaurs was Ted Mercer (a bluff northerner whose enthusiasm for rugby was matched only by his resistance to new trends in mathematics teaching), Meyricke Jones (whose unwillingness to enthuse boys about literature was at least compensated for by his success in forcing most of them to master the rules of English grammar) and, most memorably, Nigel Radford. Radford was certainly an old-fashioned schoolmaster in every sense whose teaching of lower school Latin and history was not calculated to inspire any great love of the subjects. Yet he had an excellent track record when it came to getting less able boys through O-Level and I couldn't help liking him, not least for his sardonic sense of humour (most evidently displayed in his school reports and entries in the corporal punishment book). Rather younger, but no less formidable, was Doug Martin (whose nickname 'Muscles', so a Colson House boarder once told me, reflected his almost legendary skill in employing the cane on the buttocks of recalcitrant boys). Roger Middleton vividly recollects French lessons with 'this man who called everyone toad', as does Chris Robinson, although he also emphasises that he was 'well liked for his singing and sporting skills'. My own most remarkable achievement while at the school, perhaps, was to persuade Doug Martin to drag up and play the part of the headmistress in a production of *The Happiest Days of Your Life*. Towards the younger end of the age range, too, there were several masters who were both accomplished teachers and popular with the boys, among them Tim 'Mac' Forsyth (English), Rowland Jones (geography), John Arthur (physics), Ivor Cleeves (who left the school a couple of terms before I did to take a post in a comprehensive) and, perhaps the most charismatic young teacher on the staff, Mike Allen (who chose to spend his entire career at the school). Of Mike towards the end of his long years of service, indeed, Chris Robinson reports that he not only 'taught both my sons' but was 'a real inspiration to the eldest'.

'During Keith's first year at Plymouth College', Dennis Collinson recalls:

> ... I was supposed to write a report on the probationer at work during two lessons. I watched ten minutes or so at two ends of the age range and submitted the following to the head:
>
>> Keith Dockray is a natural. I hope that he stays for a few years. The junior pupils take little notice of his Rabelaisian shoulders, frequently in action during lessons that seem to me happy, disciplined and creative.
>
> There was always joy and humour in Keith's teaching rooms and I could trust him to work easily with pupils of all ages.

In fact, Dennis himself was an inspiration, always ready with practical advice, and both popular with the boys and very much respected by them. Chris Robinson, for instance, remembers him as 'a great teaching phenomenon who seemed to do nothing by the book, inspirational, motivational, independent, liberal and so very different to the vast majority of the masters'. I'm sure I learned far more about the art of teaching from Dennis than I ever would have on a postgraduate education course. Yet he never attempted to turn me into a clone of himself and just as well since, whereas he was at his best teaching informally and encouraging a great deal of class participation, I soon realised my own strength lay in much more formal, front-of-the-class semi-performances, even when teaching lower school forms.

When I was presented with my timetable at the beginning of the autumn term 1969, I found Dennis had given me a range of lower school teaching, as well as a generous number of sixth form hours. Although I was apprehensive about my capacity to interest younger lads in history (particularly the less able), I had few qualms about being able to control classes. After all, since I'd come through the 'B' stream at Huddersfield College and witnessed at first hand the sufferings of ineffectual teachers like 'Bessie' Baldick, I knew all the tricks boys were liable to employ and how to nip any attempted excesses in the bud. I certainly intended to maintain order in my classes (it's impossible to teach effectively without it) and soon realised I could achieve this by the sheer force of my personality and an element of carefully calculated unpredictability. An early indication that my stratagem was working came when, as I was approaching a third form classroom on one occasion, the cry of 'KRUD's coming' reached my ears and, by the time I arrived, almost total silence greeted me. 'KRUD', I declared dramatically as I entered the room, 'has arrived!'. Even more significantly, at the beginning of my second year at the school, I overheard two thirteen year olds (in different streams) discussing their new timetables. 'Oh', said one gleefully, 'we've got Mr So-and-So for Latin' (a master whose class control was notably lax). 'Lucky you', responded the other ruefully, 'we've got Mr Radford and we've got that bastard Dockray for history as well'. 'What were you saying about that bastard Dockray?', I remarked as I came up behind them, 'I must make sure I live up to my reputation!'. In the event, teaching that class proved one of the most enjoyable experiences I had at Plymouth College. As for the nickname KRUD, that (and its alternative Dockers) even followed me to Huddersfield Polytechnic.

Plymouth College, like many secondary schools at the end of the 1960s, retained corporal punishment as part of its armoury of discipline. A few older masters felt entirely comfortable with a sanction they had employed throughout their teaching careers; some, but by no means all, younger staff were prepared to resort the cane now and again; and most boys philosophically accepted its occasional use as well (even, sometimes, urging its vigorous employment on the rumps of their unruly mates or volunteering take a thrashing themselves in preference to alternative punishments). The corporal punishment book, where all beatings and the number of strokes administered had to be recorded, occupied a prominent place in the lower common room and there, too, the school's canes were kept. Entries could provide entertaining reading, moreover, since the 'offences committed' column was very much a vehicle for humour: some transgressions were remarkably trivial (for instance, failure to wear a cap in the street during school hours); others had a certain logic (most obviously, bullying); and, occasionally, they were simply bizarre (such as 'heavy breathing', 'playing marbles with sheep's eyes' and 'interfering with a dead rat'!). Soon after joining the staff, Mike Allen recalls, a middle-aged master offered him practical advice on the art of caning:

> Always bend them over the front desk, young man, and take a run at them, stamping your foot at the same time. It frightens the hell out of them.

Another senior member of staff once told him of:

> ... a distressing occasion when, instead of the crisp sound of cane on bottom, I heard a dull thud. I inserted my hand in his trousers—in front of everyone, you understand—and removed a large biology textbook.

These remarks were delivered in all earnestness, Mike emphasises, lacking any trace of irony or awareness of the incident's absurdity. And I certainly remember a free period when a few of us young masters became so engrossed by a demonstration of the technique of caning (a leather armchair deputising for a pair of buttocks) that we totally failed to register the headmaster's quizzical observation of the proceedings.

Personally, I had no strong opinions either way about corporal punishment, at any rate as far as persistently disruptive lads were concerned; however, since it seemed to me an admission of failure to maintain order by other means, I never caned anyone in the school myself. The nearest I got to it was when thoroughly riled by the thirteen year old son of a member of staff. He thought he could get away with anything, aware as he no doubt was of the convention that staff kids were off the agenda for thrashing. Towards the end of the final history lesson of term, when he had been exceptionally irritating, I despatched him to the staff room to obtain not one but a selection of canes for my perusal. Keeping a close but surreptitious eye on the clock, I examined the rods closely, tested them by a few preliminary swishes through the air, and eventually (to the boy's mounting apprehension) selected the most formidable of them. Then followed the ritual of preparing him to receive punishment, enthusiastically advised on best procedure by the rest of the class. Precisely as planned, just when his backside (complete with chalked line across grey flannels as an aid to accuracy) was in optimum position, the bell sounded for the end of the period. Sadly, I informed him, the beating would now have to be postponed until the following term (although, once the rest of the class had departed, I made it clear that, in fact, the matter was now closed). When I told his father of the incident later, he roared with laughter and remarked that it was about time someone on the staff gave his son a good hiding. By the time the new term arrived, I had completely forgotten the whole affair, at any rate until volubly reminded by the class; however, despite their loquacious urging to the contrary, I now firmly declined to carry out the punishment. As for the lad himself, he proved a model pupil for the rest of the year.

The greatest challenge I faced during my first year as a schoolmaster was a bottom stream first form and it took me a while to get on 1C's wavelength. A syllabus covering prehistory and ancient history about which I knew virtually nothing didn't help and, before I taught the first form 'C' stream again the following year, I persuaded Dennis to let me introduce them to twentieth-century history instead. I didn't know a great deal about that either but, at least, the lads did enjoy the First and Second World Wars, encountering the likes of Churchill and Hitler, and my experiment with a new-fangled multi-choice examination paper at the end proved a success as well. My timetable in 1969/70 didn't include any second form classes (Dennis felt I might experience difficulty in getting down to their level on medieval history) but, when I did teach 2A in 1970/1, it was an entirely pleasurable experience: bright lads, easily enthused, and, anyway, how could I fail with the likes of Richard the Lionheart and King John, medieval instruments of torture, or the Black Death? Most interesting, during my first year, was teaching Tudor and Stuart history to both 3A and 3C: plenty of lively lessons and an opportunity to introduce them to contemporary and near-contemporary verdicts on such fascinating personalities as Henry VIII, Elizabeth I, James I, Charles I and Oliver Cromwell. A lecturer from the education department at Exeter University, who regularly supervised PGCE students on teaching practice, once observed one of these lessons and was entirely complimentary; so, seemingly, my own lack of a teaching qualification didn't matter a damn, not even to him. Teaching an O-Level syllabus covering English history 1763-1846 to fourth and fifth formers was less to my taste but, since most of them were both well motivated and hard working, it wasn't too difficult to rise to the challenge. Notes I'd taken as an undergraduate from David Large's modern history lectures proved invaluable and, as a counter to a stodgy syllabus, John Wilkes, Charles James Fox, the Luddites, even the Hell Fire Club, could always be relied upon to revive any signs of flagging interest brought on by William Pitt the Younger's financial reforms, Castlereagh's foreign policy or the Great Reform Act of 1832.

Everything changed during my final two terms at Plymouth College in 1971/2 when I lost all my lower school teaching (apart from a top stream O-Level class), partly because of the sheer number of boys opting for A-Level history, partly because I now found myself teaching economics as well. My new timetable, in fact, consisted of twenty-five periods of sixth form work a week, four with 5A, and nothing else. I regretted losing 2A and 3A in particular (I'd really enjoyed teaching both in 1970/1) and found the sheer amount of sixth form preparation and marking that now came my way almost overwhelming: hardly surprising, since I had thirty-two students in first year sixth sets, twenty-three in second, and four Oxbridge entrance candidates. Apart from a few periods with the Oxbridge lads (covering, rather improbably for me, controversial topics in medieval and early modern English economic and social history and, more comfortably, personalities and politics during the era of the Wars of the Roses), all the rest of my sixth form history teaching was A-Level: medieval Europe, Tudor and Stuart England and a depth-study of the Norman Conquest. The latter, since it involved introducing students to primary sources such as the *Anglo-Saxon Chronicle, Bayeux Tapestry* and *Domesday Book*, was particularly challenging but, at the same time, immensely stimulating. Many classes took the form of university-style seminars, with students researching and reading papers on subjects ranging from Edward the Confessor, William the Conqueror and the battle of Hastings to English resistance to Norman rule post-1066, the Anglo-Norman aristocracy and church/state relations, and there was certainly a great deal of vigorous discussion. More difficult, as my knowledge of the subject was thin and my interest limited to say the least, was teaching economics. Although, in my first year at Bristol University, I'd reluctantly enrolled on an economics subsidiary subject, very little of it had stuck. The headmaster, in fact, played a major role in persuading Dennis Collinson and I to offer an A-Level in politics and economics, and I ended up teaching the economics element mainly because I knew marginally more about the subject than he did. What resulted was probably the worst teaching I have ever done as I struggled, not always very successfully, to keep at least one step ahead of the class in a far from inspiring textbook.

Dennis Collinson's memories of me as a sixth form master are almost embarrassingly positive:

> Keith made his biggest impact on the sixth form where his use of primary sources dynamited the sixth form mind. His adventurousness extended to introducing the sixth to medieval history and this interest benefited many of them in A-Level

examinations and at university interviews. Students much enjoyed his open approach to them, his liberal mind and his bonhomie.

Bernard Samuels, in similar vein, recalls my demonstrating a 'gusto bordering on the frenetic', being 'colossally enthusiastic' about history and 'not in the least beset by English inhibitions about owning up to intellectual passion'. Yet I certainly had no great passion for economics. Quite the contrary! Mike Allen, indeed, remembers me declaring at the time: 'They want me to teach economics: I know sod all about it'. Chris Robinson, on the receiving end, found me 'a pretty lousy economics teacher', although he does add in mitigation:

> Not that this was Keith's fault, probably. Short straw stuff, I suspect. There was a demand for the subject but there wasn't exactly a long queue in the staffroom waiting for it to be added to the syllabus.

Certainly, no one else volunteered to take it on. Roger Middleton's verdict is about right:

> When I began my A-Levels (in 1971), Keith took me for history and the economics element of the combined economics and. politics course. I now know that economics was thrust upon him at short notice but to his credit it was some time before we noticed that he was but one chapter ahead in R. G. Lipsey, *An Introduction to Positive Economics* (1963) and not following the American text P.A. Samuelson, *Economics* (1970), on to which the more advanced of us had quickly moved.

Even so, he adds, rather disarmingly for a man who has become so accomplished an economic historian:

> It was Keith who introduced me to economic history via the English Civil War when we discussed the storm created by Lawrence Stone's *The Crisis of the Aristocracy* (1965), a ground-breaking work. By extension this also linked well with what Dennis Collinson was doing for the European history paper and the politics part of the joint economics/politics A-Level. I consider my A-Level education with these two the finest teaching I have ever experienced and it was certainly a superb preparation for when I went up to Manchester to read economics and economic history in the autumn of 1973. Both Dennis and Keith treated sixth formers as undergraduates. Gone was the boring note-taking of O-Level. Instead, we had seminars, genuine debate provoking further reading and thought and, above all, a sense that our views might matter. Of the two, Dennis was more

serious about being scholarly, Keith more determined that the light-hearted, the quirky, should be part of the endeavour to find meaning in the past and present. How Keith must have hated the discipline and structure of economics in contrast to the freedom and flexibility of history! Yet, for me, they worked together very well indeed.

Chris Robinson, again very flatteringly, remembers me as 'someone who not only loved his subject' but also communicated my 'enthusiasm for medieval history' in particular 'with a great passion', a 'charismatic history teacher' who showed there was 'something altogether deeper and more intense' than just the assimilation of information; indeed, he muses, it 'must have been because of Keith that I dragged two friends of mine around France's medieval cathedrals eighteen months out of school'. And, like Roger Middleton, Chris also emphasises how well Dennis Collinson and I operated as a team.

When I arrived at Plymouth College in September 1969, Dennis Collinson was not only my head of department but also housemaster of Colson House where I became his live-in house tutor; moreover, just as the school was slowly, if not very comfortably, responding to external social pressures and demands, so were its two residential boarding houses. Under Dennis's predecessor Bill Battrick Colson House had been run on firmly traditional lines. An old-fashioned disciplinarian, he had presided over a strict regime: for instance, all boys, including sixth formers, had to be in bed by 9.0pm and he frequently resorted to corporal punishment. When Martin Meade-King appointed Dennis as Battrick's successor in the early 1960s, he passed over more senior members of staff precisely because, in all probability, they would have resisted pressure to change. As a boarder at a public school himself in the 1940s, Dennis had enjoyed an unusual degree of freedom for the times; he was determined to promote a more liberal regime in Colson House; and, in so doing, he received the headmaster's full backing, despite criticisms by traditionalists on the staff. Residual fagging and the compulsory wearing of khaki shorts during out-of-school hours were phased out; bullying was vigorously targetted; and corporal punishment increasingly became a weapon of last rather than first resort. Dennis also strongly supported the headmaster's resolve to overcome opposition to the concept of weekly boarding (whereby boys whose parental homes were nearby could live in during the week but return home at weekends); it was duly introduced; and, before long, its benefit to the school became obvious.

Perhaps inevitably, Colson's more liberal regime led to a degree of envy and resentment among Mannamead House boys since their housemaster, Nigel Radford, continued to enforce more rigorous rules and allow less freedom. John Arthur, who became house tutor in Mannamead at the same time as I took up residence in Colson, recalls hearing that his predecessor once complained to Radford about Mannamead boys scraping their chairs while he was saying grace. Radford's response, so the story went, had been to cane the entire boarding house, even sixth formers, on a sliding scale of severity (one stroke for a first former, two for a second., and so on). Anecdotal, perhaps, but certainly in line with Roger Middleton's memories of his own 'misfortune to be a boarder' in Mannamead rather than Colson:

> Mannamead House under Radford was the sort of place George Orwell could have captured to perfection in his tart essays on the English and class. It is impossible to recapture now: the discipline (canings were frequent), the routine (from morning bell through to lights out), the rituals, the marching up and down Mutley Plain on our way to Sunday service, and the khaki shorts we had to wear in rare moments of leisure.

As for Nigel Radford's wife, he adds, 'she appeared to us adolescents to have served her nursing apprenticeship in a Nazi POW camp'. Worst of all, he 'painfully' recollects:

> Immediately upon arrival in the house I was bullied. Two boys in particular made my life, and that of others, a total misery for three or four years, even physically beating me up on a number of occasions. Both clearly delighted in dominating the boarding house and, by utilising to the full the informal fagging system still in operation when I arrived there, they created a real climate of fear among the younger boys. Radford, the housemaster until the end of my third year, appeared to do nothing about their excesses; moreover, although his successor (Mike Veale, a physics teacher, who became housemaster in September 1969) was a more liberal spirit, I doubt whether he was fully aware of the depths to which these two could sink.

In a modern law court Roger might well be regarded as a hostile witness but, even under Mike Veale, Mannamead boys did seem to me to enjoy significantly less freedom than ours in Colson.

From the beginning, as a raw and rather bewildered new recruit to community living, I was made to feel extremely welcome by both Dennis Collinson and his wife Diané and, before long, grew very fond of them both. Fortunately, they took to me as well, as Di vividly recalls:

> Keith came to Plymouth College in 1969 to teach history and to live with us as a house tutor in Colson House. All of us (Dennis, myself and our four children,

not to mention sixty schoolboys) liked him immediately. He was young, friendly and lively, always ready for conversation and conviviality even when depressed, and especially if beer and coffee made their appearance on the kitchen table and he had half a dozen cigarettes waiting to be conjured from his pocket.

Dennis's memories are equally positive:

> My wife and I asked Keith to join us in Colson House as our house tutor. This might have been a tediously dog's bodyish sort of a job. The house was in the middle of a city not noted for its sparkling culture or its open spaces. But we never noticed any riots induced by boredom when Keith was on duty and I felt confident virtually from the start that I could safely leave him in charge and very much approved of his calculated flexibility in enforcing house rules. As a chain smoker and heavy drinker, he coped well with the paradox of denying these 'pleasures' to his temporary charges. He probably advised them to go well away from the premises and from his own drinking haunts if they were under eighteen. At any rate we never had any crisis.

Unfortunately, when Di Collinson (who had recently completed a Ph.D) became staff tutor in philosophy for the south-western region of the newly established Open University, she and her husband decided to relinquish Colson House in 1971. I seriously considered moving out myself, uncertain whether I could adjust to a possibly stricter regime under the new housemaster Tom Waldock, a mathematics teacher, and his wife. Since Tom himself was keen that I stay on, however, I agreed and, although he and I never became so close as I had been to the Collinsons, we nevertheless worked together perfectly amicably for over a year; indeed, he proved far more liberal-minded than I had feared, even taking on board my homosexual orientation calmly and sympathetically.

Colson House consisted of three large Victorian terrace houses suitably modified internally for communal occupation. Dennis Collinson and his family occupied most of one of them and the others were largely split into day rooms and dormitories (sparsely furnished with uncomfortable beds) for boys aged eleven to sixteen; sixth formers shared smaller rooms in twos and threes; and I had a large room of my own, reasonably furnished and containing a sink, but lacking separate toilet/bathing facilities or central heating. Eight terms of rather spartan living conditions, surrounded by boys on all sides, certainly proved a real eye-opener for me. Even with the door shut, and my sort of music playing on the radio or record player (I had no television), I could never enjoy real privacy or feel entirely cut off from frequently boisterous lads. Some of the younger boarders, inevitably, found it hard to settle at first and I sympathised very much with their dilemma, certainly more so than one father I encountered: an army officer, and as thick as a plank, he seemed to despise his unhappy, introspective and slightly effeminate son, even recommending regular beatings in order 'to make a man of him'. A few older lads too, like Roger Middleton in Mannamead., obviously hated communal life but learned how to cope as well as they could; again, I felt every sympathy. Yet most of the boys, as far as I could tell, rather relished the rough and tumble of boarding house life and I even came across two or three who showed no enthusiasm at all at the prospect of returning home at the end of term. As for myself, I got on well enough with the majority of the lads and enjoyed talking to them, particularly about their backgrounds, families and home lives; moreover, despite my occasional explosions of anger (more often than not about noise), most of them seemed to like me too. Whether I was a good role model is a different matter altogether but sixth formers, at least, probably appreciated the presence of a 'worldly-wise' figure in their midst and, during my time as house tutor, several felt confident enough to bring their personal concerns and worries to me. I hope I helped!

For most of the week Colson House boys had plenty to occupy their time: ten morning or afternoon school sessions (including Saturday morning); sport on Wednesday and Saturday afternoons; and, in the evenings, more sport and prep (the boarding school equivalent of homework). Even on Sundays boys were required to attend a morning religious service and, since the school had no chapel of its own, this entailed, more often than not, making their way in school uniform to an Anglican church in the city centre. I avoided this weekly ritual whenever I could, much to the envy of many of the boys no doubt, and when talking to senior lads I never sought to conceal my own atheism. Inevitably, with so many boys living in such close proximity, there had to be house rules and regulations. When on duty myself I strove to maintain a light hand on the tiller and anyway, in the last resort, I could always refer matters to Dennis Collinson or Tom Waldock. Nevertheless, I did have to dole out punishments now and again. Most obviously, boys could be despatched early to bed, deprived of privileges or gated; I became adept at thinking up imaginative essay topics for the wayward to tackle (such as 'The Inside of a Ball Bearing'); and early morning circuits of the school playing fields proved a particularly effective deterrent. Very occasionally, too, I resorted to the slipper or, even, the cane. When presented with a series of options, a few lads preferred corporal punishment to the alternatives: indeed, I suspected, one or two positively relished demonstrating just how tough they could be in adversity in order to boast about it to their friends later. Exasperated prefects, not permitted to beat younger boys themselves (unlike their equivalents in Lindsay Anderson's compelling and much talked about 1968 film *If*), pressed now and again for an exemplary slippering or caning and, if I reluctantly agreed, an appreciative day room audience could virtually be guaranteed. Only once when, early in November 1971, a prefect discovered a fourteen year old in possession of illicit fireworks in his dormitory did I lose my temper completely and resort to the rod in earnest. I regretted it later but, so I was assured by his mates (no doubt after close inspection of the results), for a mere novice I hadn't made a bad job of it at all. When it became known many weeks later that I was leaving, my victim of that autumn evening (who was both bright and interested in history) expressed his obviously sincere regret at my imminent departure. Noticing my surprise and guessing the reason, he grinned from ear to ear, confessed the whole incident and my reaction had been deliberately provoked, and declared it had done his reputation no harm at all to be so thoroughly thrashed by me of all people.

Despite all the hours of prescribed activities, Colson House boys did enjoy a fair amount of leisure time and, as they got older, more and more freedom. Unofficially, senior lads could even slope off to the pub on Saturday evenings. There were three within easy walking distance of the school. I regularly drank in the *Fortescue* and, if any sixth formers were foolish enough to venture in there when I was present, I'd make my displeasure abundantly clear (particularly if I knew they were under eighteen); however, I rarely visited the *Hyde Park* or the *Nottingham* (as the lads well knew) and, if I did, I simply turned a blind eye to any Colson sixth formers enjoying a drink or two there. I always kept a stock of beer in my room as well, mainly for my own consumption when on duty in the boarding house, but occasionally I'd invite two or three sixth formers in for a can (and a cigarette, too, if they fancied one). As for the younger lads, Sunday afternoons and evenings tended to present the greatest challenge, particularly if the weather was wet. If it was dry, boys had the run of the school playing fields but, on wet days (all too frequent in Plymouth), boredom could easily set in. Hence why John Arthur (the Mannamead House tutor) and I sometimes took a crowd of lads to the gymnasium, retreated to the top of the wall bars for safety, and let them loose on the equipment to play chaotic games such as 'Pirates'. Occasionally, too, sixth formers took younger boys on expeditions of one sort or another (for instance, rambling on nearby Dartmoor) and, at least twice, Mike Allen, a couple of prefects and I escorted a party of youngsters on the train to Looe in Cornwall: their capacity not only to build sand castles but also pepper the beach with sizeable sea-filled holes was impressive to say the least. Most memorably of all, I recollect two or three end-of-term parties in the house: lots of boisterous games to enable the younger boys to let their hair down, beer and cider for the older lads, and even a few mild hangovers the next morning. Perhaps it was entirely appropriate that the boys presented me with a pair of inscribed pewter beer tankards when I left. Just for good measure, a gift wrapped school cane mysteriously appeared in my room as well, accompanied by an anonymous card urging me to practise my stroke play before tackling student unrest in my new post as a lecturer!

Inevitably, throughout my time at Plymouth College, I sought to avoid as far as I could any involvement in sport. 'Being physically without any real coordination since he wasn't wired up properly', recalls Mike Allen, 'Keith affected a rabid dislike of sport and sportsmen'; Chris Robinson, similarly, speculates that I probably 'hated physical exercise or sport' and wasn't 'well enough coordinated for it' anyway; and I genuinely did indeed loathe most sports, particularly team games such as rugby. Several of the school staff and many boys, by contrast, were passionate rugby enthusiasts. Yet I had no problem with this (and, indeed, became very friendly with Rowland Jones who ran the First XV), providing I wasn't forced to become involved. I never was and, apart from the occasional sardonic comment, I simply ignored the powerful competitive culture generated in the school by sport in general and rugby in particular. What I did do was openly sympathise with the minority of lads who, like me at Huddersfield (New) College in the later 1950s, found themselves forced to participate in team games, whether they enjoyed them or not. Roger Middleton, for one, clearly found sports afternoons torture, just as I had: indeed, he recallso 'during twice-weekly rugby sessions I tried to excel at being utterly useless'. Athletics I found mildly ridiculous, as Dennis Collinson rightly remembers:

> While Keith's judgement of the length of a shot putt was dramatically given to the nearest half inch, I swear he thought school Athletics Day a somewhat pointless, albeit amusing, exercise.

Cricket, by contrast, I didn't mind watching in a desultory kind of way on a sunny summer afternoon and, despite my deplorably defective grasp of the rules, I even volunteered to umpire the occasional match. 'Keith knew more or less nothing about the game', Dennis also remarks, 'but his dismissals were theatrical'. The main reason why I made a half-hearted attempt to learn the rules (though my lbw decisions always owed more to the loudness of the appeals than my own observation of the ball), however, was to enable me to act as umpire for the staff cricket team in its evening away fixtures against south Devon village elevens. This was great fun, not so much because some of the staff were very competent cricketers (which they were) but, rather, on account of the eccentricity of village cricket fields: one, I remember, had an extraordinarily steep slope while, at another, the rules had to be modified to accommodate the presence of an enormous tree. Even so, the best matches for me were those when we were rained off and forced to adjourn early to the village pub for copious quantities of beer.

The antics of the Combined Cadet Force I found simply incomprehensible yet, at the same time, obscurely disturbing. Presumably, before my time, men like Bill Barnes who had seen active service in the Second World War had brought a degree of professionalism and real inside knowledge to the CCF. By 1969 most of the staff who donned military uniforms on Tuesday afternoons had, at most, experienced compulsory national service in the 1950s and the Plymouth College CCF seemed to be very much permeated by that ethos as well. Of course, there were plenty of boys who enjoyed pretending to be soldiers, sailors or airmen on the school playing fields once a week, not to mention learning such socially desirable skills as shooting, particularly lads whose fathers were in the forces or who aspired to a military career themselves. Yet many didn't, among them Roger Middleton, whose deep resentment at having to wear a sailor suit two or three hours a week was only too palpable even then. Over three decades later the rancour remains:

> CCF one afternoon a week, when some of the teachers dressed up in uniforms and barked orders (which the more compliant of the boys sought to follow), was simply bizarre. Having a colonel as a father, and knowing something of the real army, I found it all faintly ridiculous but it was three years before I could escape and do something useful on Tuesday afternoons: visit a blind woman down in the docks to do her shopping and keep her company.

And Roger has a particular memory of 'the idiocy' of Plymouth College in general, and 'the dreaded CCF in particular', when he was told 'I could no longer go sailing because my hair was too long'.

My escape route from sport and possibly even, horror of horrors, the CCF, was provided by drama. Mike Allen, who had no great commitment to games either (at any rate, apart from bridge), shared my enthusiasm for putting on a school play. In the spring of 1970, he recalls, 'Keith encouraged me to co-direct, with him, a production of Robert Bolt's *The Thwarting of Baron Bolligrew*'; moreover, although he insists that 'in reality mine was a minor role as I observed Keith, enjoyed myself and, most importantly, learnt', in fact it was very much a joint undertaking. The production was a great success, at any rate if a review in the local newspaper is anything to go by:

> High standards were achieved last night when the Junior Players of Plymouth College presented *The Thwarting of Baron Bolligrew* by Robert Bolt in the school

theatre. The audience of parents and friends was kept in almost constant laughter as the antics of the bold knights and the villainous baron and his magician grew more and more hilarious. The play was a most suitable choice for such a young cast who displayed a polish rarely seen in school performances.

In March 1971 Mike Allen and I teamed up again in a production of A. A. Milne's *Toad of Toad Hall* although, this time, most of the labour of directing fell to Mike, with me acting as his assistant. In both these productions all the parts were played by junior boys but more senior lads and other members of staff were very much involved behind the scenes. The art master Derek Holland, for instance, designed and built the sets (assisted by an enthusiastic group of boys), Rowland Jones took charge of sound effects and John Arthur organised the lighting. Other lads acted as stage hands (among them Roger Middleton); another group showed real flair and imagination in the make-up department; and Chris Robinson designed the programmes. Indeed, Roger Middleton reminds me:

> I first really got to know Keith in connection with drama and school plays where I eventually ended up building sets. This provides some of my happiest memories of Plymouth College. There was also an art teacher (Derek Holland) and an English teacher (Mike Allen) who were much involved and, around them, one could drop one's guard and begin to learn things worth learning. We had a sense that for them, as for us, drama was a licensed escape from the repressive environment in which we all found ourselves. None were as explicit about their individuality and disdain for convention, however, as Keith. Enthusiastic, irreverent, noisy, smoking and drinking (even in the lounge of the *Hyde Park*, despite the convention that *we* went to that bar): these are all solid memories.

The highpoint of my dramatic endeavours at Plymouth College came in December 1971 with a joint staff/boys production of John Dighton's *The Happiest Days of Your Life*. This was a farce I had first seen at Huddersfield Theatre Royal as a grammar school boy in the later 1950s and, again, as a student in Bristol early in 1966. It had also been made into a film starring Alastair Sim, Margaret Rutherford and Joyce Grenfell. Set in a boys' boarding school forced to share its premises with an evacuated girls' school during the Second World War, this was a near-perfect choice of play for our Christmas Entertainment and, as Mike Allen puts it, could hardly fail to be 'a great success in its context'. To get the production off the ground at all took some persistent persuasion, and not a little gentle arm-twisting, on my part. Dennis Collinson, while surely exaggerating the extent to which I was 'a star of the school stage', particularly highlights my success in 'persuading quite mature members of staff to take part in slapstick comedy'. He was one! Yet, as even he reluctantly recognised amidst protestations about his inability to learn all the lines, Dennis was tailor-made for the part of the headmaster Godfrey Pond (Alastair Sim in the film). Even if, occasionally, he did dry during performances, it didn't matter anyway since he proved himself a master of the art of ad-libbing. Mike Allen also remembers requiring some persuasion to take to the boards since he had never acted before. My greatest triumph, however, was to wear down Doug Martin's initial resistance to playing the headmistress (Margaret Rutherford). Only when I consented to don a gymslip as the games mistress (Joyce Grenfell, whom I unashamedly parodied) myself did he finally capitulate. Once rehearsals got going we soon blossomed into a veritable double act in drag and, in performance, our joint first entrance brought the house down every night! Several parts were played by boys, among them Chris Robinson who vividly recalls that:

> I was one of a handful of sixth form lads who appeared alongside the staff and one of the ones who took a female part. I was the vicar's wife, 'Muscles' Martin was the fearsome headmistress and Keith was Miss Gossage—jolly hockey sticks and all. Happy days, indeed!

Originally, I had intended to direct this ill-assorted company myself but, after a few early rehearsals, I decided it would make more sense to concentrate on making the most of the caricature figure of Miss Gossage. Fortunately, a talented sixth former proved more than able to rise to the challenge of cajolling even members of staff into doing what they were told. Again, the local press gave us a good write-up:

> Plymouth College presented a side-splitting play *The Happiest Days of Your Life* at the school last night. Snappy lines, embarrassing situations and occasional slapstick kept the action moving slickly throughout this John Dighton farce. Stars of the show include Douglas Martin as Miss Whitchurch, Keith Dockray as Miss 'Sausage' Gossage, Michael Allen as Dick Tassell and Ivor Cleeves as Rupert Billings. Sixth former Julian Maitland plays a very convincing schoolmistress called Miss Joyce Harper. College history master Dennis Collinson ends up losing his trousers. The play develops quickly with the entrance of an unwelcome St. Swithins' contingent of females to an all-male school, Hilary Hall. The play elaborates until a hilarious climax is reached: parents hear the Ministry has decided to send pupils from a backward boys' and a forward girls' school to join their children. The play is the first production of sixth former David Yates.

In November 1971 Dennis Collinson urged me to apply for a post as lecturer in later medieval and early modern history at the recently established Huddersfield Polytechnic. I wasn't all that enthusiastic. Despite my demanding teaching load, I was very much enjoying the intellectual stimulus of so much sixth form work; I felt much more at ease in Colson House now than I had a couple of years earlier (and Tom Waldock had recently reduced the number of my duty hours); and I was certainly relishing rehearsals of *The Happiest Days of Your Life*. In the end I did apply, partly because I didn't think I had a cat in hell's chance of landing the job anyway; also, it held out the prospect of an expenses-paid trip from Plymouth to Huddersfield and the opportunity to see Miriam and Edith. I was duly called for interview and, much to my amazement, offered the post. Even then I was in two minds about whether to accept it, not least because Huddersfield Polytechnic hadn't impressed me at all. Indeed, I nearly turned it down and, for the first few years back in the north, not infrequently wished I had. Why did I accept? Devon seemed very remote from the rest of the country and I felt little affection for Plymouth; my salary at the school (£1660 per annum) was significantly less than what Huddersfield was offering (£2195) and there seemed little chance of promotion; the prospect of seeing Miriam and. Edith, now ageing, much more regularly was very appealing; and, perhaps most important of all, there was the ever-present strain of having to conceal my homosexuality and fear of the possible consequences should it ever become public knowledge.

Looking back on my Plymouth College years I have no regrets at all, not even about my virtual incarceration in the school and the need for celibacy. I learnt how to teach and discovered that I wasn't half bad at it; I came to appreciate the value of primary source-based history teaching (and this became the linchpin of my work at Huddersfield); and, in fact, I've never enjoyed any teaching as much as all those sixth form sessions over thirty-five years ago. I hope Dennis Collinson's final assessment is right:

> During his short time as a schoolteacher Keith had a benevolent and profound impact on many aspects of school life. He moved fairly quickly on to Huddersfield but left many in Plymouth, students and colleagues, who valued his friendship and scholarship.

6

Pleasures and Pastimes in Bristol and Plymouth

'Bristol in the 1960s seemed to me a gentle and liberal place', recalls my student friend Peter Allender nostalgically, 'classy but seedy at the same time'. This was very much my impression as well. The city had a long history and its first great flowering, in medieval times, had resulted in Bristol's becoming one of the most important towns in England by the end of the fifteenth century. Despite massive expansion and redevelopment since, moreover, and destruction caused by German bombing in 1940/1, there remained plenty of visible evidence of the city's medieval past. Early on I remember exploring three buildings in particular: Bristol cathedral, the Lord Mayor's chapel and St. Mary Redcliffe church. It didn't take too long to realise that the cathedral was very much a hybrid: Victorian to the west of the central tower, later medieval to the east, and featuring earlier remnants of its pre-Reformation incarnation as St. Augustine's abbey as well, most notably an impressive Norman chapter house and gatehouse arch. Across the road was the Lord Mayor's chapel, all that survived of the medieval St. Mark's hospital, but none the less atmospheric for that. Best of all was St. Mary Redcliffe, an enormous and largely later medieval English perpendicular construction, memorably described by Elizabeth I when she visited it in 1574 as 'the fairest, goodliest and most famous parish church in England'. The historic Theatre Royal in the city centre first opened its doors to the public in 1766 and, before long, I began sampling productions by the Bristol Old Vic Company there. Then, of course, there was Clifton, with its splendid Georgian terraces (among them the spectacular Royal York Crescent), the Suspension Bridge crossing the Avon Gorge (designed by Isambard Kingdom Brunel and first opened in 1864) and the Downs (where I walked off many a hangover during my student days). All in all, I soon concluded, Bristol was far more interesting historically than Huddersfield and living in the city very much to my taste as well. Hence why, when I secured early retirement from Huddersfield University in 1994, I promptly returned.

As an undergraduate at Bristol University I worked far too hard but that didn't stop me enjoying myself too. Mostly, I socialised with a small group of fellow students, among them Ian Faulkner who even remembers our first conversation, at a bus stop as we optimistically awaited the arrival of public transport to take us from the university to Churchill Hall (Bristol buses, then as now, were notoriously unreliable!). He recalls, too, how he, Bernard Jarvis, Mike Stammers, Peter Allender and I, all of us in Churchill, soon became friends. My first encounter with Peter Allender has stuck in his mind as well:

> Two or three weeks into our first term in Churchill Hall, Keith entered my room for the first time and in every sense dramatically. Flinging himself on my bed and pressing an arm to his forehead, he declaimed: 'I wish Vince was here'. Vince was a bluff northerner whose room was opposite his. Keith's possible sexual orientation (if it occurred to me at all) was less on my mind, however, than the fate of the erected telescopic aerial of my new, and then quite rare, VHF portable radio that he now twirled vigorously, as if to emphasise his need for Vince's company. I may have said hello!

'Apart from this dramatic entrance', Peter adds, 'my first impression of Keith was of a breath of northern air, however much flavoured by tobacco'. Bernard Jarvis, in not dissimilar vein, muses:

> My current mental picture of you always catches you in motion and talking at the same time. If I were putting you as a character in a play the stage instructions would involve lots of restless movement and striding about. This is not at all the psychotic pacing to and fro, though, but a sort of not quite controlled energy searching for an appropriate outlet. And the theatrical analogy is not a bad one at all since there has always been a theatrical dimension to your life and lifestyle.

In Churchill Hall, Peter Allender further recalls:

> There soon began a custom of talking long into the night in one or another's rooms. Smoking also became a serious pursuit and, maybe, it was under Keith's influence that Consulate, 'cool as a mountain stream', were favoured for daytime use and Players Number 6, with more bite and coupons, for night-time conversations.

At the top of our pleasure agenda as students, inevitably, was social drinking, as Ian Faulkner fondly remembers:

During our two years in Churchill Hall we drank most regularly in the nearby *King's Arms*. The landlord (who always bore a bow tie and was short, tubby and balding) was called George and, as in many Bristol pubs, the beer was Georges' bitter. I didn't think it too bad but Keith and Peter were often at pains to point out that northern beers were far superior. Occasionally, mainly at weekends, we ventured further afield to drink. In the course of a couple of years we must have drunk in quite a number of pubs, among them the *Coronation Tap* in Clifton (a cider house) and the *Rummer* in the city centre (a cut above the rest of the establishments we visited, famous for its sherry and serving, in terms of our rather unsophisticated early 1960s palates, excellent meals: on a few Saturdays, I recall, we even skipped the evening meal in hall and went there instead to sample the delights of steak, chips, mushrooms and peas). We also discovered the lethal combination of rough cider and sherry (served in large schooners). I'm sure Keith had a much stronger capacity for drink than I had but I'm equally sure that, like me, he was sometimes sick as a result of the cider/sherry combo.

All true! Even after leaving Churchill, as Ian also recollects, we continued to drink together regularly, our main venue now becoming:

… the *White Bear*, near Keith's student house. It was kept by a pleasant couple who interpreted drinking-up time extremely liberally and, most weekday evenings, we met up there about ten o'clock.

Mike Stammers has very similar memories:

In our first two years we drank most often in the *King's Arms*, a pub near Churchill Hall, and occasionally in Clifton pubs such as the *Coronation Tap* (which sold disgusting scrumpy). Then, at lunchtime, there was the *White Harte* opposite the Wills Memorial Building, particularly in the third year when Charles Ross was sometimes in evidence. The *White Bear*, up the hill from our third year residence, became another regular watering hole and by then we were more seasoned drinkers.

'The most notable drinking occasion', he reminds me, was:

… the great sherry excursion, in the second term of our third year, when several of us went to the city centre and drank sherry all evening. This was not wise, as Keith and I both had papers to deliver next day to our Special Subject group. Charles Ross took great delight in ringing us up next morning, summoning us to the seminar room (very late), and clearly relished both rousing us and forcing us to perform despite our hideous hangovers.

No wonder I have detested sherry ever since! Peter Allender specifically highlights our visits to Clifton, 'where real people lived and the pubs were unpretentious and often quiet, even if all you could find to drink was EIPA or, worse still, brown splits'. Very occasionally, two or three of us even ventured outside Bristol, visiting, for instance, Bath, Glastonbury and Wells. What I tended to avoid for the most part was the Student Union Bar, probably wisely in Peter's judgement:

> I don't think Keith missed much by not going to the Student Union. Clive James once wrote about coming to England in the 1960s and living in London where he found himself mixing with 'girls wearing cashmere twinsets and tartan skirts who didn't want me to touch any of them or even breathe out in the same room'. Not quite the dress for a Saturday night bop in the Vic Rooms but the attitude was there.

Even more off limits, as far as I was concerned, were student parties, partly because I wasn't very enamoured of pop music and pop groups (even the Beatles, although they, along with the Rolling Stones, seemed better than most), mainly to avoid any situation where my homosexuality might become evident. Could I trust myself, no doubt after vast quantities of ale and, maybe, a few whiffs of cannabis as well, not to blow my cover if confronted by some desirable young man? Probably not, I thought. Anyway, for all five of our Churchill Hall group, pubs were preferable. Our friendship. moreover, became both deep and lasting; Peter Allender and I went to the weddings of both Ian Faulkner and Bernard Jarvis in the later 1960s; and, remarkably, we have never lost contact since.

As a sixth former at Huddersfield New College I had developed a real taste for amateur acting and, during my first term at university, I sought to maintain this by becoming involved in a freshers' production of a one act George Bernard Shaw play. It was a most enjoyable experience but also very time consuming and so, I reluctantly decided, not to be repeated. Studying must come first. Anyway, major university productions tended to be very much dominated by drama students. Hence why, apart from taking part in a short film directed by fellow history student Dave Spiers, I put acting on hold until 1971. Instead, I resumed my Huddersfield habit of regular theatre-going and there was certainly plenty to see, particularly in 1964 (the 400th anniversary of William Shakespeare's birth), both in the university and the city's three professional theatres: Bristol Old Vic Company seasons at the Theatre Royal and the Little Theatre and touring productions at the Hippodrome. I rarely went on my own. 'Unlike you', Peter Allender recollects:

> ... I hadn't been a regular theatre-goer as a boy. Darlington Hippodrome did not have very much going for it. Only as a student, probably influenced by both you (and your records of musicals) and Bernard, did I discover how much I enjoyed live theatre.

Mike Stammers has similar memories:

> Keith loved the theatre, especially musical theatre, and introduced us to records such as *Oh What a Lovely War*. Encouraged by him, we went to any drama that was on offer, ranging from student productions to many of the plays in repertory at the Theatre Royal and the Little, particularly during the Shakespeare centenary year 1964. This was a golden era, moreover, when there were plenty of top quality actors in the Bristol Old Vic Company, several later to find national fame, among them Jane Asher, Paul Eddington, Terence Hardiman, Michael Jayston, Barbara Jefford, Jane Lapotaire, Frank Middlemas, Richard Pasco, Patrick Stewart, Dorothy Tutin and Peter Vaughan.

'Although I'd occasionally been to the theatre in Oxford', muses Ian Faulkner:

> ... I hadn't seen too many plays before going to Bristol; however, since Keith (along with Bernard, Mike and Peter) was keen on going to productions at the Bristol Old Vic, I was happy to tag along. I generally preferred the cinema but can't recall Keith going to many films. One he did go to see with Peter and I was *El Cid* starring Charlton Heston—but they both insisted we left half way through because they thought it so bad! Keith also seemed to eschew the pop music revolution which took place during our time in Bristol, as well as the R&B and folk scenes. While I and the others bought LPs by the Beatles, Rolling Stones, Animals, Bob Dylan and the like, he was a passionate devotee of musicals, most of which were unfamiliar to me before I met him. Two of his LPs I particularly remember were Julian Slade's *Salad Days* and Joan Littlewood's *Oh What a Lovely War*. I very much enjoyed listening to the latter.

As early as October 1963 I saw the Bristol Old Vic Company for the first time, at the Little Theatre (compact, desperately uncomfortable and part of the much larger and more impressive Colston Hall, a major music venue), in a staging of Peter Shaffer's *The Private Ear* and *The Public Eye*. The Bristol Shakespeare Festival of 1964 saw productions of *Othello*, *Henry V* and *Love's Labours Lost* at the company's main home the Theatre Royal (badly in need of refurbishment and, again, not noted for its comfortable seats or unimpaired views of the stage). I saw all three and, later in the year, *A Midsummer Night's Dream* as well.

Equally enjoyable was a double bill at the Little of Nicholas Udall's hilariously funny *Ralph Roister Doister* and the anonymous but no less amusing *Gammer Gurton's Needle* (both written in the early 1550s). Christopher Marlowe's *Edward II*, also staged at the Little but this time by the Bristol Old Vic Theatre School, was very different, as that king's manifold personal defects are exposed, leading inexorably to his deposition and death. As part of the Shakespeare celebrations, too, Bristol University's drama department mounted productions of several rarely performed early plays and I certainly recollect seeing three of them: *Everyman* (an anonymous late fifteenth-century morality play), John Bale's *King Johan* (a thinly disguised dramatic justification of the early sixteenth-century English Reformation) and *The Fair Maid of Bristol* (first performed by William Shakespeare's own company at Hampton Court before the Stuart king James I in 1604). 1965 saw plenty of theatre-going as well, most memorably a splendid student production (in the Victoria Rooms) of Arthur Miller's compelling play *The Crucible* focussing on the Salem witch trials of 1692 (and, by implication, Senator Joseph McCarthy's anti-Communist witch hunt in post-Second World War America), in which Peter Allender and Bernard Jarvis both took leading roles. At the Little Theatre in 1965 I saw both John Gay's early eighteenth-century musical drama *The Beggar's Opera* and George Bernard Shaw's controversial 1902 play about prostitution *Mrs Warren's Profession*, for which the playwright earned a lifelong notoriety. The contrast between Brendan Behan's powerful Irish prison drama *The Quare Fellow*, which I saw at the Theatre Royal in December 1965, and the Bristol Old Vic Company's next production there, John Dighton's farce *The Happiest Days of Your Life*, could hardly have been greater. *Portrait of a Queen* was also staged at the Theatre Royal in 1965: based on diaries, letters and writings bequeathed by both Queen Victoria and her contemporaries, with a cast including Dorothy Tutin as the queen, Peter Vaughan as Gladstone and Paul Eddington as Disraeli, it rapidly transferred to London's Vaudeville Theatre (where I then saw it for a second time). Visits to Bristol's huge Hippodrome Theatre were rarer but, during my undergraduate years, I certainly saw *Salad Days* there (for the umpteenth time!), David Mercer's *Ride a Cock Horse* (starring Peter O'Toole) and a National Theatre production of William Shakespeare's *Much Ado About Nothing* (with a remarkable cast including Albert Finney, Derek Jacobi, Ian McKellan and Maggie Smith). I still paid the occasional visit to London, too. Probably in 1965, I saw a revival of George Bernard Shaw's early 1930s 'extravaganza' *Too True to be Good* at the Garrick Theatre (with a cast including James Bolam, George Cole, T. P. McKenna and Alastair Sim) and, even better, Spike Milligan's *Son of Oblomov* at the Comedy, in which the unpredictable Milligan was aided and abetted by, among others, Bill Owen and Valentine Dyall. Sadly, however, the imminence of final examinations and the need for intensive revision more or less put an end to theatre-going in the early months of 1966.

Although pleasure was rarely absent from my agenda as an undergraduate, during my years as a research student (as I became more and more turned off by fifteenth-century Yorkshire gentry) it eventually came to occupy centre stage. In my first year as a postgraduate (1966/7) I shared a basement flat in Redland, then the poor man's Clifton, with Bernard Jarvis. Consisting of just two rooms and a tiny kitchenette, this flat's only recommendation was that it was cheap. My room had wooden shutters and, when they were closed (which they were most of the time), no light penetrated; the walls were damp and the floor riddled with dry rot (it was too dangerous to walk on in places); and, when I once turned over the mattress on my ancient double bed, I discovered a highly suspicious stain (the result, so another tenant in the house told me, of an illegal abortion once performed on it!). Woodlice abode there in large numbers and there was no shortage of mice either (occasionally waking me up, even scampering across the bed, during the night). Bernard's room did have more light and a stone floor (an advantage in that house) but the only access to the kitchenette (far too disgusting ever to be used for cooking) and the outside lavatory was through it. Hence why, before long, I acquired a large bottle for the purpose of relieving myself, should I need to, during disturbed nights following heavy beer-drinking sessions, and slopping out became a regular morning ritual in Bristol as well as Huddersfield. Yet neither Bernard nor I, as I remember, worried too much about our living conditions: an interesting and temporary novelty for him, nothing new to me. In April 2004 he recalled that it was 'a good year' but, he asked rhetorically, 'did we really survive the whole year on beer, cheese, white loaves and cigarettes in what was little better than a Spartan cellar?'. The answer is yes! No wonder we used the place mainly for sleeping, not infrequently after evenings in the pub. There was a downside for him, though:

> Over the years there have been times when I've soundly cursed you. I never touched a cigarette until I was twenty-one (more out of a perverse desire to be different than any more worthy motive) but, forty years on, as a result of a drunken night out with you in Bristol, I'm still struggling with the habit!

Needless to say, Redland has long since been gentrified, and our dismal basement flat turned into a highly desirable garden apartment.

As a break from historical research and beer drinking, I did continue to visit the theatre occasionally. In April 1967, for instance, I saw a production of William Shakespeare's *The Taming of the Shrew* at the Little Theatre and, in May, a musical entitled *The Pursuit of Love* at the Theatre Royal. The latter, based on a Nancy

Mitford novel, was written and composed by Julian Slade and I was bitterly disappointed by it. The new show completely lacked whatever had made *Salad Days* so compelling. Former undergraduate mates prepared to slum it for a night or two also turned up in Bristol now and again. Mike Stammers, for instance, remembers once staying with me 'when there was nothing to eat in the flat: this is typical of Keith, who never put a high priority on eating'. Peter Allender, enduring a teacher training course in London in 1966/7, was a regular visitor, as he recalls:

> Often, and usually after a night's drinking, I would make my way to Paddington rather than back to King's Cross and an unspeakable bedsit, and buy a cheap return to Bristol where your basement flat in Redland became a real haven. When in Bristol I felt happy, independent and especially ecstatic about the Beatles' LP *Sergeant Pepper's Lonely Hearts Club Band*, which I played over and over again.

Peter and I also regularly listened to an LP of songs by a South African humorist, *Paddy Roberts at the Blue Angel*, from one of which a few lines have inexplicably stuck in my mind ever since:

> Consider now the elephant cow whose problem is a vexed one,
> 'Cos first she mates and then she waits ten years before the next one.
> Its such a bore especially for a rather oversexed one.
> Love is a wonderful thing!

Why Peter and I found this so irresistible forty years ago I can't imagine. A couple of times we reversed roles and I stayed with him in his far from palatial London pad. A high point of one such trip, for me, was revisiting the Whitehall Theatre where, several years earlier, I'd seen a couple of Brian Rix farces: John Chapman's *Simple Spymen* and Ray Cooney's *One for the Pot*. This time Peter and I saw a hilarious comedy musical *Come Spy with Me*, directed by Ned Sherrin and starring Danny La Rue and Barbara Windsor. We were impressed, too, by Paul Scofield's performance in a Royal Shakespeare Company production of Charles Dyer's *Staircase* at the Aldwych, enjoyed Oscar Wilde's *Lady Windermere's Fan* at the Phoenix (with Coral Browne, Juliet Mills and Wilfrid Hyde White) and sat through a dreadful musical *Robert and Elizabeth* (based on *The Barretts of Wimpole Street* by Rudolf Besier) at the Lyric: Sir Donald Wolfit, in the twilight of his long and distinguished career, could certainly have done without starring in that. Wisely, when research brought me to London again in 1968, I opted for a Joan Littlewood production at the Criterion: *Mrs Wilson's Diary*, an 'affectionate lampoon' of Harold Wilson's Labour government by Richard Ingrams and John Wells.

Bernard Jarvis and my next flatmate Patrick Scott apart, the man I saw most of as a postgraduate was my Ph.D supervisor Charles Ross. I'd already got to know him quite well in 1965/6 and, indeed, the only party I ever enjoyed as an undergraduate was a small gathering organised by Mike Stammers and myself for our third year Special Subject group, in the huge room we shared in a student house, with Charles as guest of honour. He brought along several bottles of wine, drank a fair bit himself and, before long, relaxed completely. Mike also remembers an Acton (History) Society dinner we both attended at which Charles's drinking capacity was even more fully revealed. By the time I became his research student his marriage had fallen apart and he was living alone (apart from his Alsation dog Nero and an exceptionally friendly moggy) in an ill-maintained university-owned flat a few minutes walk from the Wills Memorial Building (where his office was situated and the bulk of history teaching took place). This wasn't to his taste at all. As Anne Crawford (who became his second wife a few years after I left Bristol) stresses, 'one of Charles's strongest traits was his ability to be truly interested in people, listen to what they said and encourage them'. Michael Jones, his last research student, emphasises no less strongly that 'Charles was a remarkable person to have as a friend and possessed several very special qualities: a contagious warmth and generosity, a gift of setting you wholly at ease and a mischievous sense of humour'. Fortunately for me, although vigorously heterosexual and notoriously susceptible to the charms of female students, he had no problem in becoming close friends with a gay young man, especially a fellow Yorkshireman who shared his enthusiasm not only for fifteenth-century England but real ale as well. So friends we soon became.

When Tony Pollard, a far more conscientious and hard-working fifteenth-century research student at Bristol than I ever was, first came across me, he recalls, it was as 'a drinking companion of Charles Ross' and he got the firm impression that I 'seemed to spend more time in pubs than libraries and record offices'. This isn't too far from the truth. Unless he was lecturing in the afternoon (and most of his teaching was in the morning), Charles and a few cronies could regularly be found in the nearby *White Harte* at lunchtimes: Jim Tester, a classics lecturer at the university, was a stalwart; so was Alan Gibson, a BBC cricket commentator based in Bristol; and, more intermittently, Charles's medieval history colleague and Tester's room mate James Sherborne turned up as well. I soon became an honorary member of this exclusive drinking club (honorary in the sense that I was rarely allowed to buy a round of drinks). Meeting in an intimate wood panelled bar (now completely wrecked), we tended to drift in about 12.30pm and remain there until the pub shut at 2.30pm. Occasionally, I would even return with Charles to his flat, grab an hour or two's sleep, and then resume drinking when the *White Harte* reopened at 6.0pm. Years later, when staying with me in Huddersfield (which he did on several occasions in the 1970s and early 1980s), Charles once remarked that, during my postgraduate years, beer put paid to my Ph.D thesis and set back his biography of Edward IV by three years: an exaggeration, yet also containing more than a grain of truth. In not dissimilar vein, Anne Crawford remembers him telling her that as 'an impoverished postgraduate' I seemed to live 'entirely on milk, tomatoes and beer'. There were certainly a few extraordinary escapades. On one occasion we found ourselves locked in Clifton Hill House, a female hall of residence, long after hours. Why I was there I have no idea but it wasn't wise since, as fellow history undergraduate Janet Nield recalls:

> Clifton Hill was much less relaxed in rules and regulations than even other women's halls. We had to go and see the warden to get a late key if we wanted to come in after 11.0pm and special permission was required to have a male in your room.

Charles and I had to make our escape through a first floor window and God knows what would have happened had we been caught by the formidable dragon who ran the place. On another occasion, after many pints, we took his dog for a late evening run on the Clifton Downs; it seemed an excellent idea to walk on the grass in bare feet; and, as for our shoes, we left them under a tree and never saw them again. Charles, typically, insisted on buying me a new pair. Even more bizarrely, I remember taking him more than once to the *Moulin Rouge* in Clifton, perhaps the first gay club to open outside London following the passage of the 1967 Act decriminalising male homosexuality. Charles's mother, a rather strait-laced retired schoolteacher who clearly didn't approve of her son's penchant for pleasure, still lived in Wakefield (his home town), just a few miles from Huddersfield, and I accompanied him on several trips to Yorkshire. I can only imagine his mother's reaction when her son once arrived at her home fresh from an extended lunchtime drinking session with me in Wakefield's atmospheric *Yates Wine Lodge*. How I found my way back to Huddersfield that day I have no memory whatever. Best of all, there was a splendid camping holiday he, I and his then girlfriend spent in France in the summer of 1969, touring the cathedrals, castles and bars of the Dordogne and Loire valleys. This was my first ever trip abroad and I wasn't to set foot on foreign soil again until 1998. Two memories particularly stand out. A visit to Cognac where, after generous sampling of the wares of not one but two brandy distilleries, we arrived at a local camp site completely unable to erect our tent (a challenge at the best of times) for several hours. Another day (and, so Anne Crawford tells me, this became one of Charles's favourite anecdotes), his girlfriend appeared in an exceptionally revealing bikini; my response was to remark that, although I might be gay, I was also human and by no means totally oblivious to so revealing a display of female sexuality; and there was certainly a great deal of hilarity in our shared tent every night. All three of us enjoyed ourselves enormously and it remains one of the best holidays I have ever had.

Early in 1967 Bernard Jarvis introduced me to an elderly German Jew he'd come across in some cafe or other and this meeting was to have a profound impact on my life. Alfred Josephson was one of the most fascinating men I have ever met. Although he seemed physically older, he was probably in his early sixties and, mentally, he was ageless. Shortly before the outbreak of the Second World War he had escaped from a Nazi concentration camp and fled to England where, he soon discovered, his German law degree was no use whatever. Over the years he did a variety of jobs (including working in an aircraft factory during the war) but, by the time I knew him, his only employment was the occasional bit of tutoring for Bristol University's German department. What other sources of income he had I have no idea. Fortunately, his lifestyle was simple and he rarely seemed to need much in the way of food. Highly intelligent, scholarly omnivorous and a bohemian in every sense of the word, he struck me as a modern-day Socrates and, like Socrates, often to be found in the company of young men, as well as serving as a veritable guru to Bristol's gay community. He lived in what was little more than a shack attached to a rather grand Victorian house in Redland only yards from Bernard and I, surrounded by an amazing clutter of battered furniture, dubious antiques and many, many books. There, in a tiny clearing amidst all this chaos, he held court (mainly during the hours of darkness: he often stayed in bed much of the day) to a motley crew of intellectuals, homosexuals, working class lads (occasionally newly released from incarceration), cats and, more and more often, me. Before long I'd got to know this eccentric but entirely irresistible Jewish homosexual very well indeed. When we were alone together (not for long usually, as various creatures of the night tended to knock on his door and demand entrance at regular intervals), we'd talk about virtually every subject under the sun. Alfred had a fund of fascinating tales about Berlin in the early 1930s (very much confirming Christopher Isherwood's portrait of the city in *Mr Norris Changes Trains* and *Goodbye to Berlin*); he had a considerable interest in, and knowledge of, philosophy and music (especially Beethoven); and he knew a great deal, too, about medieval Germany (certainly more than I did). Mostly, we drank endless cups of coffee (essential for me if I was to keep awake) and smoked cigarette after cigarette (the ashtrays were always overflowing) but, occasionally, there'd also be whisky and cannabis. I doubt whether either were acquired legally. And then, one night, he introduced me to Patrick Hope-Scott: another life-changing moment.

Pat Scott, as he preferred to call himself, had had a very comfortable middle class Clifton upbringing; he'd been to nearby Clifton College, a prestigious public school, where he had specialised in music; and his two older brothers were a doctor and a barrister. By the time I met him, however, he had become very much the black sheep of the family. Merely by turning out homosexual, he'd clearly blotted his copy book; he suffered from epilepsy; and his lack of worldly ambition only served to compound these shortcomings: in 1967 he was the manager of a shoe shop. About ten years older than me, very smartly dressed and almost handsome when we first bumped into each other at Alfred's place, he informed me many months later that he had fallen in love with me then and there. Anxious to move out of his mother's Clifton apartment (roomy, almost palatial, though it was), he eagerly seized the opportunity to join me in my less than luxurious abode when Bernard Jarvis's teacher training course ended and he left Bristol. Before long I was summoned to his mother's presence to be given the once over and, rather to my surprise, received her immediate seal of approval. Our living conditions did not. Descending on us in a taxi one Sunday morning, she took one look around her and promptly offered us a ground floor flat in a recently modernised four-storey house she owned in nearby Cotham at the same low rent we were paying in Redland. Pat wasn't overly keen but I persuaded him to accept (damn right I did!) and, after furnishing the place at his mother's expense, we moved in. There I remained until I departed for Plymouth at the beginning of September 1969.

The newly refurbished Cotham flat was in everyway an improvement on the Redland basement; it was only a twenty minute walk to the university library (even less to the *White Harte*!); and, in the summer of 1968, I was only too happy to invite Miriam Saunders and Edith Wood to stay there for a few days with Pat and I. During my undergraduate years they had never visited me in Bristol and I'd discouraged them from attending my graduation ceremony too, mainly because I thought they'd find it too expensive to stay in Bristol and wouldn't enjoy the ceremony anyway. It didn't even cross my mind to invite my natural mother who never visited me in Bristol at all, or Plymouth for that matter. As for the graduation ceremony itself, my own most powerful memory is of a colossal hangover. Miriam and Edith first came to the south west in 1967; they slept in my decrepit double bed in the Redland house; and I joined the mice and woodlice on the floor. Even they found my living conditions a bit primitive. The Cotham flat, by contrast, they found almost luxurious in 1968 and my bed altogether more comfortable. As for me, this time I simply joined Pat in his. Pat, Miriam and Edith hit it off splendidly, so much so that they even invited him to Huddersfield at the beginning of the 1970s (when he and I shared my bed). Alfred Josephson paid a rare visit to the Cotham flat while they were there and this, too, proved a great success. More surprisingly, at any rate for me, they also more than held their own when summoned to Pat's mother's Clifton apartment for afternoon tea. Most of the time, though, Pat and I had the Cotham flat to ourselves, apart from regular visits by a handsome ginger cat who lived upstairs. Until then I hadn't even realised how much I liked cats.

For over two years Pat Scott and I lived together very amicably: indeed, this is the longest period I have ever shared a flat or a house with anybody since first leaving Huddersfield in 1963. We respected each other's privacy while, at the same time, spending a great deal of time together, occasionally in bed, more often in the pub. Foolishly, he'd never told me about his epilepsy (it bore almost as great a stigma as homosexuality in those days) so, when he suffered a seizure in the flat one evening, I was completely taken by surprise; I recognised what it was, however, and knew what to do (not a lot); and, during occasional subsequent fits, my main reaction became turning up the radio, television or record player to mask his stentorian breathing. Pat wasn't supposed to drink alcohol at all, and certainly not in the quantities we did, and one night the inevitable happened: he had a seizure in our local pub. Although I managed to persuade the landlord not to ring for an ambulance but simply allow the fit to take its course, he was so put out that, as soon as Pat recovered consciousness, we were promptly barred from the place. Fortunately, it wasn't up to much anyway. Pubs, nevertheless, remained very much a feature of our life together, not least since Pat was an accomplished pub pianist á la Charlie Kunz. He played occasionally in several pubs, including the *Hatchet* near the Hippodrome Theatre (where, much to his irritation, he was required to wear evening dress), as well as a local rugby club. His most regular venue was the *Old Duke*, just a few yards from the Theatre Royal, where he performed at least a couple of times a week. I almost always went along as well, mainly to sink reasonably well kept pints of real ale but also to keep an eye on the clientèle and suggest appropriate numbers. Selections from musicals usually went down well; so did First and Second World War songs (especially those recorded by Vera Lynn); and, towards the end of the evening, Al Jolson hits never failed. I became adept at stimulating audience participation and, more importantly, soon found I could prize very useful sums out of inebriated customers by going round with a beer mug at closing time. Even today I can still remember the lyrics of innumerable pre-1970 popular songs!

Although the Bristol Old Vic Company had lost many of its finest actors by 1968, I still went along to their productions occasionally. At the Little Theatre, for instance, I saw Molière's *The School for Wives* and John Osborne's *Luther*, and at the Theatre Royal an intriguing (and successful) double bill combining a classical Greek tragedy and a modern English comedy: Sophocles' *Oedipus*

Rex and Peter Shaffer's *Black Comedy*. More often during my years with Pat Scott I went to touring productions at the Hippodrome. In October 1967, for instance, I saw Joe Orton's hilariously funny *Loot* (with Bill Maynard as Truscott of the Yard), only a few months after Peter Allender and I had seen the same play in London (with Michael Bates in the lead). Rather less to my taste was Henrik Ibsen's *Ghosts* (even a first-rate Royal Shakespeare Company production starring Peggy Ashcroft), but I certainly enjoyed Franz Lehar's *The Merry Widow*, a Sadlers Wells Opera staging of Puccini's *La Bohème* and a couple of Gilbert and Sullivan operas performed by the D'Oyly Carte. Most memorably, Pat Scott and I went together to see Emlyn Williams' gripping play *Night Must Fall*, where we witnessed the extraordinary spectacle of a very elderly Sybil Thorndike playing opposite a young (and very handsome) Adam Faith. Near the Hippodrome, moreover, was the *Green Room* club, a favourite after hours drinking haunt of both ours and Hippodrome actors. There, indeed, we briefly met Sybil Thorndike and, over several pints in his case, Adam Faith (even better looking close up). The catch was that, from time to time, Pat might well be collared by the management to accompany at the piano any visiting singer sufficiently inebriated to volunteer a free performance. At the *Green Room*, too, I met both Bob Short, a Bristol pub organist, and Adrian Varcoe, a young accordian-playing drag artiste. A few years later Pat and Bob Short even recorded an LP together, for which Adrian Varcoe wrote the cover blurb:

> Within thirty miles of Bristol there are 883 pubs and 246 clubs (give or take a few). In many of these we might find two gentlemen of the ivories. Bob Short began his musical career in the Royal Air Force, progressing to cabaret on the liner Queen Elizabeth on the New York run before a three year residency in New Jersey U.S.A. Pat Scott had a more formal training by studying music at Clifton College and, coming from a very strong musical family, researching the style of Charlie Kunz and 'Fats' Waller. Bob and Pat have worked together for four years since an initial gig at a New Year's Eve dance. *Twenty Fingers in 'C'* is a unique opportunity to hear the combined talents of two of the south west's finest exponents of the keyboard.

When the LP was issued, Pat promptly sent me a copy in memory of both our years together and my consequently never completed Ph.D!

During my years with Pat Scott I had virtually no contact at all with fellow Bristol University students, not even postgraduates. As a result, the student unrest of 1968 more or less passed me by. Just once, more out of curiosity than anything else, I did wander into the Senate House (the university's main administrative building) during a short-lived student occupation. After a couple of bottles of beer, however, I drifted out again, never to return. No doubt this reflected my already cynical attitude towards politics and politicians. Nor, more surprisingly perhaps, did I embrace the drug culture of the later 1960s, except in a very peripheral manner. I smoked cannabis a few times but it didn't do much for me. I even tried LSD once but with entirely negative results. When I came to next morning, I found I had removed most of my LPs from their sleeves and scattered them all over the floor of my room. Extraordinary! I didn't try it again and never sampled heroin or cocaine at all. Beer and cigarettes were more than enough for me. By May 1969 when I began applying for jobs in independent schools, however, I was tired of having so little money and increasingly feeling the need for a completely new start away from Bristol.

Everything certainly did change dramatically when I became a history master and house tutor at Plymouth College since, during my years there, my whole life tended to revolve round the school. Never again was I to spend so many hours a week planning and preparing lessons, putting together teaching material, marking and, most importantly, at the chalkface. Sixth form teaching, in particular, required enormous amounts of preparation, especially as my preferred option was front-of-the-class semi-performance. Putting on school plays was also immensely time-consuming, and not infrequently stressful, entailing not only rehearsing and countering excessive juvenile exuberance but also securing the cooperation of not always very helpful or sympathetic colleagues to get the show on the road. If carried out conscientiously, the duties of a house tutor could be onerous too. Indeed, the only way I could get away from the boys completely was to leave the school premises altogether. Even my social life, such as it was, tended to revolve around Plymouth College, its staff and the boys of Colson House. English master Mike Allen recalls that, despite our strong reservations about the ethos of the school, 'we enjoyed the camaraderie'; John Arthur reminds me that a favourite drinking haunt of staff in the city centre was the *Burton Boys* pub (whose landlord had formerly taught boxing at the school); and I remember, too, regular lunchtime sessions playing darts with a few colleagues, oddly enough in a sports equipment store room. Dennis Collinson and I very occasionally ventured forth to a real ale pub in the evenings (leaving his wife to hold the fort in Colson House) but my main drinking companions were John Arthur (when we could manage to escape boarding house duties at the same time) and, at least two or three times a week, Mike Allen. Our favourite watering hole was the *Fortescue* pub: only about five minutes walk from Colson House, run by a sympathetic landlord who had a son at the school and, an additional bonus, containing a basement restaurant where, even after closing time, it was possible to get a steak sandwich and a pint or two. Evening visits further afield were the exception rather than the rule. As for vacations, I almost invariably travelled north to Huddersfield for a while, not infrequently stopping off in Bristol *en route*. While there, in August 1970, I even went to see the controversial musical *Hair* at the Hippodrome. I entertained a few visitors in Colson House as well, easy enough when the boys (or, at half term, most of them) weren't there. In the summer of 1971, for instance, Miriam and Edith came to Plymouth (perhaps the longest journey they ever made) and stayed in the boarding house for a few days: they were tickled pink at sleeping in a boys' dormitory surrounded by empty beds. Patrick Scott visited me once, too, and found it difficult to understand how I could cope with living in such close proximity to nicely put together sixth formers. Sheer will power, I assured him! Peter Allender recollects that:

> ... on my one and only visit to Plymouth I slept alone in a large dormitory. I also remember meeting a boy I had taught the year before in Stockton, walking proudly along the Hoe in his new Royal Navy uniform.

Vacations in Colson House were certainly eerie: so many empty rooms and so much silence. No wonder I tended to get away as soon as I could.

Plymouth, the most remote and isolated city in England, has a long history stretching back to the Middle Ages and is always associated with Sir Francis Drake, the defeat of the Spanish Armada in 1588, the sailing of the *Mayflower* to America in 1620 and, of course, the navy. Yet I never took to the place in the way I had to Bristol. The city centre, virtually destroyed by German bombing in 1940/1, had been rebuilt in a singularly unimaginative fashion: its grid pattern made every street look more or less the same and there was a distinct paucity of decent pubs. Only the nearby Barbican, its narrow lanes and historic buildings largely untouched by the war, had any real character and a few interesting hostelries. Culturally, too, the city was a great disappointment, at any rate in comparison to Bristol (the nearest large cultural centre but, since it was 120 miles away, hardly easy of access). Bernard Samuels tells me that, ever since his arrival at Plymouth College in 1956, he had:

> ... devoted a great deal of time involving myself in the struggle in post-war Plymouth to take the arts forward in the city. Plymouth had been rebuilt but, somehow, had managed to leave out the matter of provision for the arts. I abandoned teaching (in 1970) to take on the task of making something of the Arts Centre. This had started up at the end of the war, rather successfully at first, but by the later 1960s it was showing distinct signs of loss of momentum.

I visited the Arts Centre from time to time, particularly when there was drama on offer. I vividly recall, for instance, a production there of a splendid Victorian melodrama *Ten Nights in a Bar Room*, seeing Joe Orton's *Loot* again (for the third time in less than five years) and, at Saltram House a few miles outside the city, very much enjoying an Arts Centre-sponsored *Evening with Dame Sybil Thorndike*. I encouraged sixth formers to go to the Arts Centre as well, particularly disgruntled lads like Roger Middleton who, so he recalls, found it 'a very welcome refuge from Mannamead House at weekends'. Deplorably, in my time, there was no professional theatre in Plymouth. The newly built Theatre Royal didn't open its doors to the public until 1982. Fortunately, visiting companies did occasionally perform at the Athenaeum (mainly a venue for amateur productions). In June 1970, for instance, I saw the Bristol Old Vic Company there in a production of Richard Brinsley Sheridan's *The School for Scandal* and, in February 1971, the Worcester Repertory Company in John Osborne's *Inadmissible Evidence*. Now and again, too, I accompanied Plymouth College boys to productions, even once to the Oxford Playhouse to see William Shakespeare's *Othello*. Another highpoint, in 1970, was taking a group of sixth formers to hear the great historian A. J. P. Taylor, lured to Plymouth as part of the city's celebrations of the voyage of the *Mayflower* 350 years earlier, lecture to a capacity audience on the Russian Revolution of 1917. Altogether less uplifting were occasional visits by Mike Allen and I to Union Street, very much a haunt of prostitutes of both sexes (especially when there were sailors in town), and a refreshing antidote to the ethos of Plymouth College. Of a highly dubious establishment there called the *Pussycat* club, the less said the better. Just before I left the school, though, I simply couldn't resist taking three persuasive senior lads to this den of iniquity, mainly out of curiosity to see how they would react. The place was full of sailors, inevitably, and an exceptionally well endowed black stripper certainly held everyone's attention. About a month later, after I'd moved to Huddersfield, I met up with the same lads for a boozy night out in the West End of London. We ended up in another raunchy night club where Danny La Rue, the brilliant drag artiste whom I'd seen on stage a few years earlier, was very much in evidence. Quite an eye opener for them (and me, too, come to that) and, surely, a most fitting end to my short career as a schoolmaster.

7

Coming to Terms with Homosexuality

By far the greatest dilemma of my teenage years, and much of the next two decades for that matter, was learning how best to live with my homosexuality. In today's more tolerant climate, moreover, it's almost impossible to recapture just how traumatic it was for a northern working class lad half a century ago to find himself condemned to membership of a widely feared and misunderstood minority. Discovering that, for most of recorded Western European history, homosexuals had been oppressed at best, persecuted at worst, hardly helped either. In England, specifically, the so-called 'abominable vice' had been punishable by death until 1861 and, as Oscar Wilde found to his cost, a sentence of two years hard labour could still be imposed for homosexual offences in 1895. Nor did tolerance grow significantly in the early twentieth century. In 1944 indeed, the very year of my birth, the appointment of a Roman Catholic bigot Sir Theobald Matthew as Director of Public Prosecutions soon resulted in vigorous targeting of homosexuals, an initiative the post-war Labour Home Secretary Herbert Morrison seems to have fully backed. His Conservative successor Sir David Maxwell-Fyfe was even worse, declaring in 1953:

> Homosexuals, in general, are exhibitionists and proselytizers, and a danger to others, especially the young. So long as I hold the office of Home Secretary, I shall give no countenance to the view that they should not be prevented from being such a danger.

Prosecutions often relied on singularly dubious evidence (arising, for instance, out of the employment of young police officers as *agents provocateurs*) and even the distinguished actor John Gielgud was not immune: in 1953 he was convicted of 'persistently importuning for immoral purposes'. In the same year the archbishop of Canterbury Geoffrey Fisher declared, in *The Times*, that 'homosexual indulgence is a shameful vice and a grievous sin from which deliverance is to be sought by every means'. And all this was accompanied by an increasingly vociferous popular campaign in the media against, as the *Sunday Pictorial* put it in 1952, 'pansies' or 'mincing young men who call themselves queers', rightly regarded by 'simple decent folk' as 'freaks and rarities'. No wonder the discovery of my own sexual orientation only a very few years later was so unwelcome since, apparently, I was destined to be a complete social outsider, a member of a widely despised minority and, if I ever chose to express my feelings physically, an illegal outsider as well.

Early on, in 1958 and 1959, I simply tried to ignore my emerging sexuality in the hope that I'd grow out of it. Yet it seemed to get stronger all the time and, during my first term in the sixth form at Huddersfield New College in the autumn of 1960, I became increasingly depressed at the utterly bleak and humiliating prospect of remaining an emotional outcast for the rest of my life. Early in 1961 I decided to read up on the subject. At the time the standard work was D.J.West's *Homosexuality* (published in 1955). This was easily available in paperback, just as well since, as my schoolmate Roger Kitching recalls:

> In the otherwise excellent Huddersfield Public Library books about any kind of sex were wooden blocks that had to be removed from the shelf and taken to a young female library assistant of about our own age. She would then give the block to a senior librarian who would scan the would-be borrower before getting the book itself from the bowels of the library. He'd then hand it over with a sniff!

Looking at West's *Homosexuality* again now, it seems incredibly dated but, in 1961, I largely accepted it as *the* authority and didn't like what it said at all. Most experts these days, seemingly, regard sexuality as largely genetic rather than a product of upbringing or environmentally induced (even suggesting that many men are neither 100% straight nor 100% gay anyway). This was not the case half a century ago. D. J. West confidently concluded that homosexual men suffered from 'an abnormal inhibition, the origin of which can often be traced to psychological causes early in life'; for West, indeed, 'the flight from heterosexual relations is a neurotic syptom, produced in much the same way as other irrational fears and inhibitions'. Not very comforting! Nor was the idea that I was suffering from an 'Oedipal complex'. The only crumb of comfort came from the Freudian notion that boys 'who had a weak father or no father at all' were much more likely to become homosexual than other lads. At least that put the blame for my 'condition', 'illness' even, on someone other than myself. The other book I remember reading at this time was Peter Wildeblood's *Against the Law* (also published in 1955). This provided little consolation either, apart from confirming that there were plenty of other homosexuals around, among them even a peer of the realm. Edward Lord Montagu of Beaulieu, Michael Pitt-Rivers and Peter Wildeblood himself had all ended up in prison in 1954, so it seemed to me, simply because of what they were. Would that, then, be my fate too if I ever gave way to my emotions? No wonder, after reading West and Wildeblood, I seriously contemplated suicide. My future seemed entirely blighted, and there was nothing I could do about it.

What was most intolerable for me in 1960/1 was the feeling of total isolation. I'd never received any sort of sexual guidance from my foster parents. Indeed, I can't remember sex ever being discussed at home at all and, I suspect, John and Miriam Saunders would have drawn little distinction between homosexuals and paedophiles. Nor did I ever tell them I was gay and, although Edith Wood may well have developed at least an inkling about my sexuality years later, I'm sure my foster parents never did. Roger Kitching recalls that his mother, too, never realised I was gay 'until, as she was always asking me if/when you were going to get married, I eventually told her when we were in our forties: it came as a complete surprise'. My student friend Peter Allender captures northern working class attitudes of the time nicely:

> My mother used to refer to a young man who lived near us in Darlington with comments like 'he's never married' and 'he still lives with his mother', probably coded comments about his homosexuality. I noticed he dressed smartly, even flamboyantly. Now, no doubt, he would have moved to London, or even Bristol. Anyway, it was through meeting him that I first became aware of difference, if only at the level of dress: he didn't wear overalls like my father or tweed jackets like my teachers. He had, I suppose, style. When his mother died, so my mother told me shortly afterwards, he sat down with a bottle of whisky, took an overdose of tablets, and killed himself.

Even in the 1970s, after I returned to Huddersfield, Miriam and Edith never asked me about my personal life at all. Perhaps they assumed I was one of life's natural bachelors who simply had no interest in love, marriage or the procreation of children, happy instead to rely for companionship on a wide circle of friends of both sexes. My natural mother was cannier. Out of the blue one night, when I was about seventeen or eighteen, she asked me bluntly if I was a 'bum-boy'. Remarkably, I was stung into replying in the affirmative: her terminology was hardly sympathetic! Yet, much to my surprise, she barely reacted at all. Presumably because my sexual orientation had no implications for her personally (she had no desire to become a grandmother), moreover, for the rest of her life she rarely mentioned the subject again (except, very occasionally, to ask me if I fancied some young man or other who happened to come into a bar where we were drinking). The fact that my mother was neither shocked nor ashamed to discover she had a queer son was, I suppose, obscurely comforting; however, she had no interest whatever in any problems I might be experiencing in coming to terms with my sexuality.

Huddersfield New College wasn't any use to me either. Not only was it an all boys school, it had about it an air that sex wasn't a suitable subject for us to concern ourselves about: in a nutshell, muscular Christianity and sex simply didn't mix! Inevitably, there was a certain amount of smutty talk among the younger lads, much of it wildly inaccurate, and we should have received sensitive, well-informed and wide-ranging guidance on what was happening to our bodies and its significance by the age of fourteen at the latest. Yet it wasn't until many of us were already sixteen, by which time presumably at least some of the lads had begun dating girls, that the Methodist lay preacher headmaster A. R. Bielby (of all people) delivered the sex lesson. It was a truly bizarre occasion. What we got was a clinical, largely biological, account of human sexual development, complete with textbook-style diagrams of the sexual organs of males and females and a brief description of their functions. Although he did use the terminology of sex, apparently without embarrassment, it was all very impersonal and he made little or no attempt to grapple with the emotions of sex and relationships (beyond advice such as a warning that, at certain times of the month, we shouldn't expect girls to participate in brisk long walks). For us, trying not to laugh was the main problem; no one dared look at anyone else; and, for most of the time, we all stared firmly in front of us or at the desk. As far as I can remember, sex was never so explicitly referred to in class again unless it simply couldn't be avoided: in English Literature in the second year sixth, for instance, when discussing D.H.Lawrence's *Sons and Lovers*. Of his not dissimilar experience at a Darlington grammar school, Peter Allender comments:

> There was a lot of talk about sex at school and, once Lawrence's *Lady Chatterley's Lover* became available as a Penguin, more to read about it too. My father told me, after the ban on its publication was lifted in 1960, 'I don't mind what I catch you reading, but never let it be that mucky book'. Needless to say, the day after that advice I went out and bought myself a copy. Reading Lawrence's odd depictions of the act itself was the nearest I got to any formal sex education. Sex did not figure on my grammar school syllabus at all.

Even Huddersfield New College was a bit better than that but, needless to say, the headmaster's sex lesson contained no reference whatever to homosexuality, so even the information he did convey was largely irrelevant to me. So, increasingly, was Christianity (despite all the school's efforts to keep us on message), especially once I became aware of biblical homophobia, ranging from the fanatical strictures of Leviticus in the Old Testament to the sterile anti-sexual moralising of St. Paul in the New. By the time I left school in 1963 I was firmly agnostic, if not already an atheist.

Throughout my time at Huddersfield New College I carefully concealed all evidence of my emerging sexuality, not least because I was terrified of becoming a butt of the teenage homophobia permeating the school. Pejorative terms like 'queer', 'pouf', 'poufter', even 'shirt-lifter', were common currency among older boys; moreover, although mainly used thoughtlessly and without much deliberate malice, such expressions were still humiliating for anyone struggling to come to terms with his own 'unnatural' tendencies. I remember one lad in particular making life in the sixth form absolute hell for a slightly effeminate youth (fortunately I wasn't that), regularly lambasting him as a 'poufter'; I deliberately befriended the victim of this campaign of abuse; and, before long, I realised he wasn't gay at all. His rugby playing tormentor, who inevitably became a prefect, was scathing about an exuberant member of staff as well. This man was homosexual, I discovered later, as were at least a couple of other masters. None of the three were in any way open about their sexuality at school, however, presumably because to be so in the early 1960s would have been more than their jobs were worth. As for my homophobic classmate, I avoided him as much as I could, appalled at the possible consequences for me if he ever sussed out the genuine article. Fortunately, he didn't and, so Roger Kitching tells me, he never heard any speculation about my sexuality at school at all. Nor did I myself ever guess that at least one of my fellow sixth formers was gay. Such was the stereotyping of the time, it never crossed my mind that this masculine, athletic guy could possibly be as sexually wayward as I was. Sadly, so I was told several years later, he just couldn't cope with the stigma surrounding his sexuality at all and committed suicide soon after departing for university.

What made the homophobia at Huddersfield New College all the worse was the growing realisation that it was several of my fellow classmates I found sexually desirable, not the girls I very occasionally came across outside school. Only once did I test myself out with a member of the opposite sex: a sales assistant at the department store where I worked during school holidays from the age of sixteen. She was a pretty girl, obviously fancied me and, as a result, I took her out two or three times. That was fine until, one night, we ended up in Ravensknowle Park and she came on to me with vigour. I didn't enjoy the experience at all and never asked her out again. Indeed, it made me extremely wary of girls for years to come until, almost two decades later and only after consuming a generous quota of beer and whisky, I ended up in bed with one of my female students at Huddersfield Polytechnic. Much more to my taste at Rushworths was a nicely put together ginger-headed lad who worked in the hardware department. Sadly, I hadn't the self-confidence to check him out (even though, I now suspect, his response might well have been positive). Otherwise, my very early sexual experiences, if they can be called that, were bizarre to say the least. At the age of thirteen or fourteen, just as puberty was beginning, I befriended an emaciated and profoundly unattractive boy in my class at school. One day, as a diversion from playing with my train set, we suddenly decided to strip off in order to examine each other's puzzlingly changing bodies. It cannot have been a pretty sight but, fortunately, there was no one to observe the spectacle save ourselves. Neither of us could make much of it at all. About the same time another boy was caught mucking about in the showers and, in response, an irate gym master promptly administered a sound spanking to his bare bottom. When it was over the rest of us could hardly miss the fact that he'd emerged from the ordeal with an erection. Less unexpectedly, and much to our amusement, he also had a spectacularly red behind, not to mention a very clear palm print right across it. A more regular source of wonder, and envy, was the awesomely large penis of another lad, distinguished otherwise only for his skill as a clarinetist. And, for me at least, there was always the opportunity to observe muscular sports players cavorting naked around the place: very enjoyable but requiring the utmost caution and self-control. All this was innocent enough and only once did I witness a more overtly sexual incident when, one hot summer afternoon in a remote corner of the school playing field, I stumbled upon a couple of lads demonstrating to a few rather startled onlookers the pleasure potential of mutual masturbation. For me, at least, it was a revelation. What the games master's reaction would have been, had he happened on the scene, hardly bears thinking about.

None of this amounted to anything. More significant, but not much, was my half-brother Tony's behaviour at my mother's house two or three times. For a while after completing his National Service in the RAF he had returned home but, in about 1958, he moved to Manchester. This left my mother on her own in the Sowerby Bridge terrace house she'd recently bought and, now and again, I took to staying overnight with her. One night, when Tony was also visiting, we ended up sharing the only spare bed in the house. Out of the blue, he then began to make mild sexual advances on me. What happened next, and on at least one further occasion, wasn't particularly welcome but I took it in my stride. It didn't ruin my life. Nor did it turn me into a homosexual. I was that already. It did, however, seem to reinforce current notions that gay sex was 'unnatural' and I could certainly have done without that. Tony never married, so perhaps he was homosexual too; maybe he had had homosexual encounters during his time in the forces; and now, frustrated, he simply couldn't resist such a golden opportunity to get his hands on a teenage lad. I don't know. When we met up now and again in later years, he never mentioned what had happened at the end of the 1950s, and nor did I. It was ancient history by then anyway. Yet, on reflection, I did at least pick up a few tips about the range of sexual possibilities open to gay men and stored them away for future use:

Meanwhile, back in the real world, by the time I reached the age of fifteen or sixteen my close friendship with Roger Kitching had blossomed, on my part, into ever deeper love. In all honesty, I did not really understand what was happening to me but, before long, I realised that he was developing emotionally along very different lines. My passion was not, and never could be, returned by this ruggedly masculine, athletic and handsome lad. Teenage love can be heart-breakingly powerful and all consuming and so, certainly, it was for me. No wonder I became so profoundly depressed in 1960/1, desperately anxious to retain Roger's friendship yet terrified he would recoil in horror if he ever discovered the truth. Any lingering doubts I had about myself, moreover, were resolved by a young school doctor who, during a routine medical examination, picked up on certain physical manifestations of adolescent homosexuality. Fortunately for me, if unusually for the time, he fully appreciated the emotional turmoil I was in and proved both sympathetic and helpful. We met up outside school a few times; he talked to me at length about what, it soon became clear, was our shared orientation; and, in particular, he urged me to confide in Roger Kitching, even test the waters by making tentative advances on him. This was a most fearsome prospect but one evening, as we smoked cigarettes in my tiny bedroom, I summoned up all my courage and confessed I was queer. Since Roger had been nurtured in the same homophobic environment as I had, this was a high risk stratagem. What galvanised me more than anything else was the prospect of sharing a room, perhaps even a bed, with him during a visit to London's theatres we were planning. Unknown to me, however, Roger himself had more than an inkling of the emotional turbulence I was going through but, until I provided the opportunity, he too felt unable to raise the matter:

> I can't be sure exactly when I first became aware you were gay. The chance that you were became a possibility, then a probability, and eventually a certainty. We carefully trod around the area, not sure how much the other knew and when, because we thought we were dealing with a matter that might destroy a very close friendship. It wouldn't have and you did try to tune me up. Once, when I was smoking yet another of your cigarettes in your bedroom, you explained that, well aware of the dangers of a certain type of life, you were seriously considering cutting yourself off from everyday society in order to devote yourself to study. Quite

clearly implicit in this was the likelihood of your being gay. That's why, when you did finally tell me prior to our first trip to London, it was so welcome. I thought that was not only brave but quite magnificent. I might have upped sticks and said I didn't want to go. You were deliberately taking that risk and also providing me with a way out. In actual fact, it made no difference whatsoever. There was never a gay issue with us and I was now able to demonstrate, unequivocally, that there wasn't.

Interestingly, Roger also adds:

I'd read Peter Wildeblood's *Against the Law* some time before and it made me so cross, as did the homophobia which seemed to pervade our school.

Twenty years later, no doubt, I would have taken the school doctor's advice to probe the depths of Roger's heterosexuality. I certainly wanted to. In fact, I did just the opposite. When my worst fears were realised and I found, on our first trip to London, that we did have to share a double bed, I insisted on placing a bolster between us to protect his virtue from possible predatory attack during the night! The landlady of the place, a seedy joint to say the least, probably suspected the worst anyway. Ironically, too, while in London Roger and I even met up with the very doctor who (unknown to him) had prescribed his seduction as a remedy for my emotional ills; indeed, as Roger himself recalls, the three of us had a meal together and he also took us to meet a group of his friends in Surrey. On balance I'm glad I had the will power to behave so honourably towards Roger in the early 1960s, even though, for me personally, it might well have been better if I hadn't. Today, no doubt, a couple of teenage lads in our position then would simply shrug their shoulders and enjoy the pleasure potential of the situation without any anxiety at all. Instead, in 1963, I firmly resolved never to let myself fall so agonisingly in love again. I never have. Far too painful.

By the age of seventeen or eighteen I badly needed to experiment sexually with someone other than my half-brother and, as Roger now seemed irrevocably unavailable, I felt I had no choice but to look elsewhere. Even so, my first real sexual encounter did not come until I was almost nineteen when, in a young schoolmaster's flat one night, I at last took my first tentative steps down the road to perdition. He was a good-looking fellow no more than ten years older than me; he and I had common interests, most notably the theatre and literature; and rumour had it that he had had plenty of experience on my side of the line. All I can now remember of the occasion, however, is that I drank a great deal of gin and felt extremely ill-at-ease throughout. After all, not only had I virtually no sexual experience, we were also breaking the law. Nevertheless, I remain immensely grateful to him for taking an interest in me and demonstrating that even a respectable middle class teacher could not only be homosexual but even welcome a gauche gay teenager into his bed for the night. Yet I continued to feel extremely uncomfortable with, as well as increasingly resentful about, my sexuality. Nor, when I stumbled upon and visited a gay bar in Huddersfield several times, did my equanimity and self-confidence grow. On the contrary, I found the establishment both alien and alarming. Not surprisingly, perhaps, it was about this time that I became a heavy smoker; I found nicotine a most consoling drug; and, by the time I left Huddersfield in the autumn of 1963, I was already getting through a couple of packs of cigarettes a day. What I just couldn't bring myself to do in the early 1960s was accept my sexual orientation philosophically, throw caution to the winds and be more open about my preferences. The weight of social disapproval, and the legal implications of becoming a practising homosexual, were much too daunting. So, instead, I resolved to lead a life of self-enforced celibacy and single-minded devotion to study.

When I took up residence in Bristol University's all male Churchill Hall, in fact, homosexuality was still very much the 'unmentionable vice'; throughout my undergraduate years I never encountered an openly gay student; and I didn't disclose my own sexual orientation even to my closest friends. Rather, I deliberately cultivated the image of an immensely studious young man for whom sex was an entirely unwanted distraction. In practice, I avoided social contact with females as much as I possibly could, hoping to avoid the embarrassment of any girl making a play for me, and the only time it happened I backed off rapidly in genuine alarm. By and large my stratagem worked. Ian Faulkner muses that in Churchill Hall:

> Women—and thus sex—were hardly talked about in our small circle and Keith just didn't seem interested at all. I had absolutely no idea then that he was gay and I'm pretty sure I didn't find out until after I left Bristol. I suppose I simply assumed he was a mysogynist who regarded women as a distraction from his studies.

For years, recalls Bernard Jarvis, 'the possibility of your being homosexual never crossed my mind'. Peter Allender seems to have had at least an inkling:

> I don't think we talked about sex very much, even during those late night/early morning sessions as we drank coffee and smoked innumerable Players Number 6 cigarettes. It occurred to me that you might be gay, not a word we used then of course, but I had no idea where that might lead practically.

Anyway, he adds:

> Churchill Hall was not exactly orientated towards allowing us to express our sexuality (whatever it was), other than as a solitary pursuit. If the energies devoted to self-abuse could somehow have been marshalled, then it might have been self-sufficient long before talk of wind farms and a Severn barrage. As for the medics who populated my corridor, they were more interested in beer and cadavers than girls, and setting off fire-hydrants when their frustration hit a peak.

Living in Churchill Hall was certainly a challenge for me, not least since the place seemed to be awash with handsome and self-confident ex-public school boys. Ian Faulkner remembers them too, if in a different context:

> Churchill was home to some phenomenal washers, often ex-public school muscular Christians, whom one encountered in the mornings stripped to the waist and making strenuous use of the communal facilities. Keith evinced a healthy contempt for such people, which I happily shared.

I certainly did despise the public school lads' excessive devotion to hygiene, and their in-your-face Christianity on Sundays, but I wouldn't have rejected a few of them as bedmates given half a chance; moreover, their propensity to strip off, irritating as it might be early in the day, also indicated that, at night, they might well have been very pleasant to grapple with between the sheets. A female contemporary assures me that, despite strictly limited visiting hours at Churchill designed to prevent such hanky-panky, there was no shortage of heterosexual activity there: 'hence why curtains were drawn on Sunday afternoons'. If lads could manage that, perhaps I might have got away with a bit of illicit gay sex as well. Maybe, too, a few of the ex-public school boys, fresh from similarly unorthodox gymnastics in the dormitory, would have been available; indeed, if I'd had the nerve to chat up the occasional Old Etonian or Harrovian, I might have learnt a lot! Sadly, I was far too cowardly and insecure even to test the waters. At the very least I should have been more honest about my sexuality to friends like Peter Allender, Ian Faulkner and Bernard Jarvis. Now I ardently wish I'd shown more courage but, at the time, it seemed not only very difficult to be honest about myself but also potentially dangerous to my future. At the very least, I thought, I might be forced to leave Churchill Hall as a moral degenerate. When I shared a room with Mike Stammers during my final year as an undergraduate, I became even more anxious to keep my sexual orientation under wraps and, seemingly, I succeeded. 'Despite the fact that you were very much the leader of our group in Churchill', he remembers:

... I don't think any of us had the least idea you were gay. Even when we shared a room in the third year I did not guess your orientation. The only hint of your leanings was when you once told us you had been persuaded to dress up in WAF's uniform and sing Vera Lynn songs in cabaret at a Bristol club. Of course, we wanted to come and see this act but you forbade us to attend. Even then I did not put two and two together.

Nor, as an undergraduate, did I live anything approaching a double life. Now and again on a Saturday night, after pleading pressure of work as the reason why I didn't want to accompany friends to some potentially threatening social event such as a student party, I did venture into the only gay pub I knew about in Bristol, but never with the conscious intention of trying to pick up another lad. Where could I take him, anyway, without the risk of blowing my cover? Not that I liked the place. No doubt there were plenty of young potential bedmates there, and even more older men cruising the joint in the hope that this was going to be their lucky night, but the bar tended to be too crowded, too noisy and too overtly camp for my taste. Effeminate men have never appealed to me and, at the back of my mind, I always feared being caught up in a police raid as well. So I rarely stayed long. Nor was I any more adventurous back in Huddersfield during vacations.

Throughout my undergraduate years I led an almost entirely celibate life but, once I became a research student, I began to find abstention and my ever growing sense of isolation more and more intolerable. Apart from my new flatmate Bernard Jarvis, I now knew hardly anyone in Bristol, and certainly no other homosexuals. Our basement flat in Redland was dark, dingy and demoralising. Nor, at that time, did I find it easy to go to the pub on my own and strike up casual friendships with fellow solitary drinkers. The nearest hostelry to where we lived was an appallingly barn-like place anyway. Postgraduate research, by its very nature, is a solitary pursuit as well and my later fifteenth-century Yorkshire gentry didn't yield much by way of consolation: records-led historical investigation, especially in its early stages, tends to be mechanical at best, unutterably tedious at worst. After a few weeks I became so depressed I even consulted a psychiatrist. He was worse than useless, even suggesting I might be 'cured' of my homosexuality if I subjected myself to psycho-analysis, hormone treatment or, most alarming of all, electro-convulsive therapy. I refused, and rejected anti-depressants as well, convinced I'd only end up addicted to them as well as cigarettes. No wonder I have regarded the medical profession with such suspicion ever since! After a great deal of soul-searching, however, I did pluck up the courage to tell Bernard I was gay, even though his own heterosexuality was beyond question: he had at least a couple of girlfriends during the year we shared a flat together. Much to my relief he took my revelations entirely in his stride and, like Roger Kitching before him, showed no inclination to end our friendship, let alone cut and run. Perhaps my homosexuality wasn't so threatening after all, even to a heterosexual flatmate. Nevertheless, my sense of social isolation grew greater all the time; there seemed no solution to my dilemma; and a few weeks down the line I tested Bernard's tolerance to the limit. One night he had the misfortune to return to our flat just at the moment I'd reached the lowest point of my entire life. Never have I come nearer to committing suicide. For some reason I'd been drinking whisky in my dismal room, alone, for hours; Bernard now joined me; and, reprehensibly, I even began to make unwanted sexual advances on him. He handled the situation extraordinarily well under the circumstances and the crisis passed. Soon afterwards I told Peter Allender, then Charles Ross, about my sexual orientation and both of them proved entirely supportive too. Most importantly, Bernard introduced me to Alfred Josephson, the Sexual Offences Act was passed in July 1967, and my life was transformed.

Homosexual law reform had been a long time in coming. As early as 1957 the Wolfenden Report had recommended that homosexual acts between consenting male adults in private should no longer be a criminal offence but it had received a distinctly mixed reception. The editor of a contemporary medical journal, for instance, declared that he would 'hate to be mixed up in any way' with it and wished 'to keep quite clear of Wolfenden and his unsavoury crowd'; the *Daily Mail* commented sourly on these proposals to legalise 'degradation in our midst'; and, as for John Gordon in the *Sunday Exrepress*, he condemned the report out of hand as a 'Pansies' Charter. Nor did Harold Macmillan's Conservative government show any interest in homosexual law reform; prosecution of even consenting adult male homosexuals continued unabated; and, in November 1958, the Home Secretary R. A. Butler declared in parliament:

> There is at present a very large section of the population who strongly repudiate homosexual conduct and whose moral sense would be offended by an alteration of the law which would seem to imply approval or tolerance for what they regard as a great social evil.

When even a largely toothless Sexual Offences Bill was introduced into parliament in March 1962, moreover, it got nowhere. By the mid-1960s, however, public opinion was at last beginning to change, partly thanks to the recently formed Homosexual Law Reform Society. Even in Christian circles homophobia was becoming less virulent and, once Labour returned to power in 1964, the new government at least adopted a neutral position on the issue.

There was still considerable resistance to reform, though, and as late as June 1966 the Earl of Dudley's fanatical homophobia is only too evident:

> I cannot stand homosexuals. They are the most disgusting people in the world and they are, unfortunately, on the increase.

In July 1966 a new bill was launched in parliament and, although the Labour government's official stance remained neutral, Home Secretary Roy Jenkins provided important backing behind the scenes. A year later, as the bill's tortuous progress neared a conclusion, increasingly panic-stricken opponents could hardly contain their hysterical loathing of its content, not least Peter Mahon (MP for Preston South):

> This was a bad bill to begin with, it is a bad bill now and it will be a bad bill to the end of time. It will be a bad bill through time to eternity because homosexual acts are a perversion of a natural function. I believe it is inimical to the decency, dignity and moral fibre of the nation. I am against this bill lock, stock and barrel, root and branch, hook line and sinker, warts and all.

Nevertheless, on 27 July 1967 the Sexual Offences Act, decriminalising homosexual acts in private between consenting male adults over the age of twenty-one in England and Wales, finally received the royal assent. At last, at the age of twenty-three, I was legal!

Obviously, the passing of the 1967 Sexual Offences Act was an important milestone for all English homosexuals but, for me personally, meeting Alfred Josephson was even more so. Not only did Alfred and I find each other's company intellectually stimulating, I found his openness about his sexuality immensely refreshing and, inevitably, he sussed out almost immediately that I, too, was gay. At last, here was someone I could talk to at length about my personal dilemma (and that's very much how I saw it at the time), confident that he'd fully understand where I was coming from. Also, he was different from any other homosexual I'd met: not all that many but, by and large, they'd seemed superficial, predictable and much too eager to dwell on their sexual conquests (whether real or imaginary). Alfred was none of these things. Indeed, since there was never any sexual dimension to our relationship, he maybe qualifies as the strangest father figure any young man could possibly have. Like me, Alfred was interested in the history of homosexuality and the reasons why homosexuals had been an oppressed, even persecuted, minority for so long. As a young man in Germany he'd become confident that the climate there was at last changing, particularly in Berlin during the early 1930s. The Nazis put paid to that. Not only Jews but homosexuals, too, were vigorously targeted for extermination. Nor, when Alfred came to England just before the outbreak of the Second World War, did he find the situation all that much better. Homosexuals in the 1940s and 1950s, he vividly recalled, might not have been liable for the death penalty any more but they were widely regarded as abnormal, as sexual deviants, and if caught might well suffer imprisonment; the police force was riddled with homophobia; and good-looking young cops were positively encouraged to entrap desperate lonely men, particularly in public lavatories. Nevertheless Alfred himself who, as a Jew and a homosexual, had lived for years in the knowledge that he might be arrested and sent to a concentration camp simply because of what he was, philosophically accepted the less draconian oppression he found in England and habitually broke the law. By the time I knew him, moreover, he'd developed quite a reputation for his openness; the local police (and there was a police station nearby) regarded him as an eccentric figure who, occasionally, could provide useful information about criminals they were seeking to track down; and, as for the young men who visited Alfred on a regular basis, the police chose to turn a blind eye. I found all this very liberating, and consoling, and my eyes were opened in all kinds of ways. It was during late night sessions at Alfred's place, for instance, that I first came across polari, the coded language used in homosexual circles to enable gays to talk frankly to each other without fear of detection (particularly important before the passing of the 1967 Sexual Offences Act). This also meant, incidentally, that I could now fully understand at last the exchanges between Julian and Sandy (Hugh Paddick and Kenneth Williams) in the long-running radio comedy programme *Round the Horne*. As for Alfred's regular night callers, several were intriguing to say the least. Among them was a middle-aged civil servant who, I soon realised, had definite designs on me. He was destined to disappointment. A pretty long-haired youth of about seventeen, who lived on an out-of-town housing estate, was another frequent visitor. He eventually more or less moved in with Alfred, whether for sex, security, both or neither, I could never quite decide. There was also an extremely handsome muscular young man in his early twenties who, between short spells in prison for various petty crimes, was not averse to a spot of male prostitution; one night, on the run from the police I suspect, he turned up at my flat; I condescended to let him share my double bed; and, as a reward, I was able to sample his professional expertise first hand and for free. Most bizarrely, a well-spoken elderly man once turned up at Alfred's with a younger man in tow and an instrument of correction under his arm, promptly dropped his trousers and pants, and proceeded to subject himself to a none-too-gentle thrashing. Alfred, completely unperturbed by this noisy spectacle, simply carried on discussing the Emperor Frederick Barbarossa, Friedrich Nietzche, Thomas Mann, or whatever, as if no one else was present. Not surprisingly, I found rising to the challenge of serious conversation virtually impossible under the circumstances. This was my first ever encounter with the strange sub-culture of gay sado-masochism. It was not to be the last!

Alfred Josephson certainly made an impression on all who spent time in his company. My former schoolmate John Mackay, for instance, recalls how he 'gradually became aware' that I was gay and, more specifically, visiting me in Bristol in about 1967 when we went out with 'a rather motley crew', among them 'a fairly elderly German who was clearly enamoured of a very pretty young man'. This, he admits 'unnerved me a bit'. Mike Stammers, too, remembers:

> ... Keith's taking me to meet Alfred—a remarkable German Jew—who ran a sort of informal gay centre in his flat, stuffed with books and other treasures, and characterised by lively discourse. Only then did I finally realise Keith was homosexual and positively warmed to his gay friends. I did not, however, witness any of the scenes of depravity at Alfred's place which he told me about in later years!

'Reading gave me my first real insight into homosexuality', recollects Peter Allender:

> ... especially novels about the intensity of male friendships. Yet, although Christopher Isherwood's *Goodbye to Berlin* in particular had prepared me, it was Alfred, Pat and the *Moulin Rouge* that really opened my eyes. By then, moreover, far from being shocked by the new world I discovered, my reading helped me to enjoy and even embrace difference.

Peter has particulaly vivid memories of visiting:

> ... the *Moulin Rouge*, a little bit of Monmartre in a disused quarry behind Blackboy Hill. Although a gay club, it was very unthreatening. I remember once walking into the gents with Alfred, right into the middle of a carnival scene, with young men changing into dazzling versions of Carmen Miranda and Shirley Bassey. I think I left Alfred in there!

Certainly, for me, those many hours spent in Alfred's company in the later 1960s provided a rich learning experience; I began to feel more comfortable with myself than I ever had before; and when, at the end of the 1970s, I finally made my own homosexuality more-or-less public knowledge and began regularly entertaining students in my Huddersfield house, I very much modelled myself on him. When Alfred died, at a ripe old age in 1990, I sent a letter to his last disciple (a handsome artist at least forty years younger than he was):

Alfred loved you dearly, I know, and you were marvellous for him. As for me, I feel I've lost a very close friend of my youth and I'm sure I'll never meet anyone like him again. Was there ever a finer greeting late at night than Alfred's habitual: 'Ach so! It is you'? The world, did it but know it, has parted company with a modern-day Socrates.

At Alfred Josephson's pad one night, in the spring of 1967, I met Patrick Scott: indeed, I suspect, it was a deliberate piece of match-making on his part. When Bernard Jarvis left Bristol a few weeks later Patrick became my flatmate and, for the next couple of years, we were sexual partners as well. Pat's previous amorous encounters had not been very happy by and large; he fell deeply in love with me; and, throughout our time together, we rarely had a cross word. Nor have I ever endured so many regular hangovers. How Pat managed to hold down a full time job for as long as he did I have no idea. Eventually, he packed it in and, while he was on the dole, our lifestyle became even more frenetic. No wonder my research didn't progress as it might have done. No wonder, either, that cash became increasingly short. Pat's mother certainly couldn't rely on us regularly paying the rent after we moved into a flat she owned. She didn't seem to mind. On the contrary, this rather grand Clifton lady very much approved of me as a steadying influence on her wayward homosexual son who, she once declared imperiously, had hitherto been prone to 'totally unsuitable' flings with local working class lads! Fortunately, money earned by Pat as a pub pianist meant we never lacked for beer or cigarettes. And, ironically enough, he eventually obtained a full-time post at the unemployment benefit office. I was very fond of Pat but never loved him in the way he did me and, despite the fact that we were entirely compatible sexually, I didn't sleep with him as often as I should have done. Nor was I entirely faithful.

Patrick Scott and Alfred Josephson apart, I spent most time with my Ph.D supervisor Charles Ross. Pat wasn't entirely happy about this although, on the odd occasion the two met, they hit it off well enough. Tony Pollard recalls that when he first got to know me in 1966/7 he:

> ... never thought you might be gay. Maybe your spending all that time with Charles Ross put me off the scent. You couldn't be more hetero than Charles—or did I even miss something there?

Anne Crawford remembers Charles 'making one or two vaguely anti-gay remarks' when they were married in the later 1970s and early 1980s; however, she adds, 'that would never have been translated into not wanting the friendship of a beer-drinking Yorkshire medievalist (who incidentally happened to be gay) and of whom he was very fond'. My own impression was that Charles, like many men in my experience (including me), had at least a touch of the bisexual about him; he once told me he'd had one or two encounters with homosexuals as a young man at Oxford University; and he certainly wasn't averse to the occasional visit to the *Moulin Rouge*. He and I even ended up in bed together a couple of times, if more out of curiosity than desire on his part and only after extended beer drinking sessions. Rather more often I slept with a mainly straight lad of about my own age; both of us enjoyed our short liaison; and we've remained friends ever since. His recall of our brief encounters is both flattering and perceptive:

> During your postgraduate years in Bristol I began to understand that life did not always have to be solitary. I learned, not just from you but also from Pat and Alfred, that there was more than one way of seeing the world and that the pursuit of pleasure took forms hitherto unknown to me. Ours has been a lasting friendship of over forty years. It was, for a time, something else. One thing I have learned about relationships makes me entirely sure that, if it had ever become passionate rather than whatever it actually was, the friendship wouldn't have lasted the way it has.

While with Patrick I also had the occasional one night stand, most memorably with a splendidly muscular Welsh fly-half I met in a local rugby club where Pat occasionally played the piano. This needn't cause any surprise. Homoerotic horseplay, even if not recognised as such by its often scantily clad participants, was only too evident in the club as the beer flowed and, for two or three lads, man-handling each other seemed to take priority over fondling the ever present female rugby groupies. Patrick, I'm sure, knew only too well that I strayed from time to time, yet he never complained. When I departed for Plymouth in September 1969 he was clearly devastated but, again, philosophically accepted the inevitable and made no attempt to stop me. Maybe he, like me, realised that our relationship was going nowhere anyway. Nevertheless, when I left, he gave me his copy of a Vera Lynn LP *Hits of the Blitz* (in memory of all the hours I'd spent listening to him play Second World War songs at the piano), signing it 'To Keith, in sincere gratitude and affection for 2½ wonderful years'. Whether I deserved such a generous tribute is doubtful to say the least but we remained friends, and continued to see each other now and again, for the next fifteen years. He died in 1985.

Why, during my Plymouth College years 1969-1972, did I revert to more-or-less concealing my sexuality and avoid even casual relationships while I was resident in the city? It was partly a reflection of the times since, although homosexuality had been partially decriminalised in 1967, homophobia remained rampant in society at large. More specifically, it was a reaction to the school's muscular Christian ethos and fear of the consequences if my sexual preferences ever became public knowledge. Not that I was a complete coward. Quite early on I told my young English colleague Mike Allen who, much to my relief, simply shrugged it off as a matter of no importance and we soon became firm allies against the forces of reaction. Bernard Samuels recalls that, in his company at least, I was both 'open and exceptionally straightforward' in talking about my sexuality. When Tom Waldock became housemaster of Colson House I told him too and, rather to my surprise, he scarcely batted an eyelid. As for Dennis Collinson, he reminds me that 'when Keith told me he was gay I think I said something like, "So what", and we carried on with life in an unshakeable friendship'. For the most part, though, I kept my sexuality to myself, not least because homophobic sentiments did surface from time to time in the staffroom, and Dennis, for one, 'never heard any member of staff offering the slightest hint that he thought Keith gay'. Yet, he adds:

> ... it may come as news to Keith that, some years before he joined us, we enjoyed the company of a highly intelligent, civilised and creative member of staff. We all knew about his homosexuality. Except for the Second World War he was on the staff for over thirty years yet I never heard an inappropriate word or phrase in his presence. Only two members of staff thought his sexuality 'wrong or odd' and I am certain they never openly told him so. Otherwise, all I remember is the occasional snide remark about actors or what have you, the sort of thing that might have been expected from any group of men over forty years ago.

Perhaps, then, I was unnecessarily cautious. Even so, I remain convinced that several senior members of staff would have found it very hard, if not impossible, to tolerate an openly gay man in their midst. Among the boys Roger Middleton certainly remembers the college as a 'profoundly homophobic institution', remarking, in particular, that his peers 'frequently referred to objects of their derision as queers and poufs as a matter of routine'; however, he adds, 'I have no memory of Keith's being gay so, I presume, he was extremely careful'. Chris Robinson, by contrast, does recall 'hearing suggestions at school that Keith maybe batted for the other side', but never backed up by any 'hard evidence'. The headmaster Martin Meade-King, I suspect, had at least an inkling too, yet chose to employ me anyway. Had pressure ever been brought upon him to dismiss me, though, could he have resisted? Probably not, I thought, and my sexuality, mounting weariness at having to conceal it and fear of the consequences of its becoming general knowledge (whether justified or not) eventually provided the main reasons for my leaving the school.

Taking a post in an independent school at all was risky enough in 1969 but why, as a practising homosexual, did I also subject myself to the torture of living in close proximity to virile and athletic sixth formers in Colson House? Free accommodation mainly: I had acquired a considerable overdraft by the time I left Bristol. Resisting temptation was far from easy and it's no wonder I deliberately avoided the showers when I knew senior lads were likely to be there. Yet resist it I did. Moral or ethical scruples, I fear, hardly entered the equation at all. Rather, and far less admirably, only sheer will power and abject cowardice at the possible consequences of any lapse restrained me; moreover, since the age of consent for homosexual acts was twenty-one, even the oldest sixth formers were under age and that weighed heavily with me too. Perhaps inevitably, juvenile homophobia occasionally surfaced in the house (instilled in some, no doubt, by reactionary military fathers) and, when it came to my attention, I did at least summon up the courage to challenge that. Now and again, too, I felt obliged to confront masturbation. For instance, in response to a sheepish complaint from a member of the domestic staff about sticky sheets, I once instructed a dormitory of lads to curb their urges or, at the very least, make sure their nocturnal emissions did not contaminate the bedding. On another occasion, responding to a decibel level unusual even by third or fourth form standards, I happened upon a veritable wanking contest. Reprehensibly, no doubt, I merely prescribed early morning circuits of the school playing field as a more wholesome means of burning off excess energy. How I kept my face straight I shall never know and what a contrast to a former boarding house master I heard about: he had maintained a strict rule that no boy should ever be found on another lad's bed, apparently, and considered even self-abuse (let alone mutual masturbation) a sufficiently heinous offence to merit a severe caning. As far as I was concerned, the odd spot of masturbation in response to the onset of puberty was a natural enough phenomenon anyway, especially in an all male environment. Only once, when I almost bumped into a couple of sixth formers passionately cuddling and kissing each other, did I encounter more overt sex. Virtually in tears, they begged me not to initiate any action against them. They need not have worried. All I did was warn them not to sleep together in the house (they shared a tiny room but it had no lock) and suggest they restrict any future amorous encounters to nearby Dartmoor on Sunday afternoons. What added an ironic dimension to their teenage affection was that one of the pair was a star of the school rugby field! Clearly, my advice was not quite in line with orthodox public school counselling but certainly right in their case. These two lads, so I learned many years later, already loved each other deeply and, even after a couple of decades, remained a devoted partnership. The only time I came near (but not that near) to being tempted myself was when another sixth former, a non-Colson lad this time, came to see me in the house one evening and, out of the blue, began to make mildly amorous advances. That he was struggling hard to cope with his own emerging sexual orientation (just as I had at his age a few years earlier) was obvious and, shortly before leaving the school, I did at least introduce him to a gay bar in the city centre, if only to reassure him there were plenty of other young homosexuals around. Not that I frequented such establishments in Plymouth or ever risked smuggling anyone into Colson House for the night. Mike Allen reminds me that:

> John Betjeman, before he died, was asked what he would have done differently. 'More sex', he replied. Keith might have benefited from more of the same during the time I knew him.

I might indeed! Instead, during my schoolteaching years, sex was a rare vacation pleasure, reserved for occasional visits to Bristol. Only once I'd settled back in Huddersfield in the 1970s did bedroom entertainment of all sorts become a semi-regular feature of my lifestyle.

8

Huddersfield Polytechnic Lecturer

When I arrived at Huddersfield Polytechnic for interview on the morning of 29 November 1971, I wasn't impressed by the place or its ethos at all. Nor, despite the promise of very positive references from Dennis Collinson, Martin Meade-King and Charles Ross, did I rate my chances of getting the post as lecturer in later medieval and early modern history: indeed, as a mere schoolmaster who had not even finished a Ph.D let alone published anything, I couldn't really understand why I was there at all. Since Tony Pollard, another former research student of Charles Ross but with both a completed doctorate and several years teaching at Teesside Polytechnic under his belt, was also a candidate, I felt his appointment must be a foregone conclusion anyway, I knew Tony slightly and, after an ill-organised and, so it seemed to me, rather pointless morning, he and I adjourned to the nearby *Zetland* pub together. After consuming at least four pints and now caring even less than before about landing the job, I suffered not a trace of nerves during an early afternoon interview. On the contrary, I soon became extremely argumentative, vigorously defending Direct Grant schools on the one hand while, on the other, expressing my strongly-held opinion that polytechnics should be primarily teaching institutions, providing the opportunity for able working class students from deprived backgrounds and poor schools, in particular, to embark on degree courses, even in arts subjects. Misleadingly, I also gave the impression that I couldn't wait to resume work on my incompleted Ph.D. After the interview was over, I felt I had put in a spirited performance but not one likely to bear fruit. Two days later I received a letter from Malcolm Bond, the polytechnic's registrar, offering me the post. Not without serious, and as it turned out justified, reservations I took the plunge and accepted. John O'Connell, in December 2005, vividly recalled my interview and the 'bravura performance' that got me the lectureship:

My memory is that the interviewing panel consisted only of Mary Dennell, Vice-Principal (Personnel) and I, as head of the then Divsion of History and Politics. It became a chatty affair and, perhaps when you calculated you had created the right atmosphere—or, maybe, you had ceased calculating anything by then!—you asked Miss Dennell: 'Do you mind if I smoke?'. It happened that Miss Dennell herself was an inveterate smoker. Even so, she surprised me by readily agreeing. It might have been otherwise and it could not happen now.

'What different memoirs you might now be writing', he added sardonically, 'if Miss Dennell had not been a fellow smoker!'. As for a tongue-in-cheek Tony Pollard, he can't resist a touch of irony either: 'I will maintain to my dying day that you only got the job because you were cheaper!'. One thing is for sure. A chain-smoking young schoolmaster, without either a doctorate or academic publications, wouldn't even make it to the short list for such a post today, let alone get it.

At the end of March 1972 my former school teaching colleague John Arthur drove me and my worldly goods (such as they were) from Plymouth to Huddersfield; I installed myself in a virtually unfurnished 1930s semi-detached house purchased (on the basis of just photographs) mainly because I couldn't see the point of paying rent to anyone else; and, at the beginning of the summer term, my twenty-two years at Huddersfield Polytechnic/University got underway. Formed by the merger of Huddersfield College of Technology and Oastler College of Education, Huddersfield Polytechnic came into existence on 1 June 1970, as one of thirty new teaching-orientated higher education establishments designated by the government. At that time it had just over 2000 full-time equivalent students, ranging in level from craft courses to doctoral research, and numbers actually fell during the first two years of the polytechnic's existence. Nor did the college have a great deal of success early on in winning approval from the Council for National Academic Awards (CNAA), recently created validating body for the non-university sector of higher education, for new degree courses. Only four had been approved by 1972. Fortunately, one of them was a BA (Humanities) degree but, since this wasn't scheduled to commence until the autumn, during my first term I did virtually no teaching at all, and not much else either. Even before I was appointed, in fact, the Division of History and Politics was grossly overstaffed; most of my new colleagues had only been in post a few months themselves; and at that time the division's student/staff ratio stood at just 6:1. As John O'Connell ruefully recalls, 'we were overstaffed throughout the 1970s and generously staffed in the 1980s as well'.

When, towards the end of a heavy and demanding final term at Plymouth College, I received a letter from John O'Connell setting out my commitments for the summer term at Huddersfield, I was amazed at how little seemed to be required of me. The only specified teaching was for an old-fashioned University of London External BA (General) degree: a couple of lectures on European overseas expansion in the sixteenth century for a first year class of twenty-four students and a weekly tutorial group of just four students covering topics in early modern history; a bit of teaching of Tudor economic history to the second year; and a few revision classes for final year students. Apart from the BA (General), the division's only other teaching of note was for a Certificate in Education, validated by the University of Leeds, both in Huddersfield (mainly in rooms situated above a Coop department store) and a polytechnic outpost at Bermerside Hall, near Halifax, catering for mature students wishing to enter the teaching profession. Bizarrely, since I didn't have a teaching qualification myself, I was required to spend a term observing my new colleague David Wright's supervision of a couple of education students on teaching practice: this, so O'Connell's letter informed me, was 'so you will be happier taking teaching practice supervision on your own thereafter'. My only other task was to talk to a Certificate in Education Year 1 class about their forthcoming second year course on *Reformation and Society*. And that was it. Hardly enough to justify a full-time lecturing post, let alone John O'Connell's perhaps tongue-in-cheek concluding comment: 'I hope you do not find this daunting'. Peter Durrans, one of my history colleagues at Huddersfield for almost a decade, also remembers his:

... surprise, on returning from Canada in 1971, to find that the BA (Humanities) degree I had been recruited for was not yet even approved. This meant that my limited teaching initially consisted of trips to Bermerside for the Certificate in Education and the dreadful External London degree.

When it came to the crunch, I only ever supervised one student on teaching practice, ironically enough at Newsome Secondary School (very near my new home) where, over a decade later, I was to serve as a school governor from 1984 to 1986. My emphasis in supervision, drawing on what I'd learned at Plymouth College, was very much on the practical: how to make history interesting while, at the same time, maintaining firm control over unruly elements in the classroom. Seeking to undermine any progressive teaching clap-trap the student might have imbibed from *avant-garde* education lecturers was a bonus. Since I didn't enjoy the experience all that much, however, I wasn't sorry when no more teaching practice supervision came my way, probably because staff in the education department could cover it all quite comfortably themselves. As for *Reformation and Society*, I taught that just once as well, and then only for a term, as I did a first year course at Bermerside on *Western Europe in the Early and Central Middle Ages c.400—1300*, deputising for my early medieval history colleague Pauline Stafford. Clearly, there were too many staff chasing too little teaching during my first two or three years at Huddersfield and this, no doubt, helps explain the determination of my early modern history colleague Andrew Turnbull to protect his patch against all intruders. No wonder, even after teaching commenced on the new BA (Humanities) degree, I felt far from secure. Hence why I mounted a Certificate in Education Year 3 Special Study on *England under the Yorkists 1461—1485* at Bermerside in 1973, and ran it again in 1974 and 1975. By then, at last, I had acquired a respectable timetable teaching on all three years of the BA (Humanities) degree.

Polytechnics were meant to be primarily teaching institutions and, for most of my time at Huddersfield, teaching did indeed take priority over research, and rightly so. Equally important, for me, was enthusing students about medieval and early modern history, particularly working class teenagers from non-academic backgrounds who, for one reason or another, hadn't obtained high grades at A-Level. Since this was where my own main interest lay, and despite growing pressure by the 1970s for history teaching to concentrate on the lives of ordinary folk in the past, I tended to focus on kings, high politics and war, not least because of the richness of contemporary and near-contemporary sources. Even at Plymouth College I'd gone out of my way to introduce boys to the primary source material on which historians depend when trying to recreate and explain the past, and I was even more determined to do so at Huddersfield. Early on, this was no easy task, and it took me some time to master the art of selecting from the range of sources what worked and what didn't and, no less importantly, how best to present such material to students. Nor, until about the mid-1970s, did most of the students seem very good; there weren't all that many of them; and, as fellow history lecturer Bill Roberts rightly recalls, 'for two or three years quite a few of us felt uncertain about the value of what we were doing and anxious about our future prospects'. In 1973 and 1974, indeed, I seriously considered returning to school teaching and, if a job had become available at Huddersfield New College (my old grammar school, now transformed into a sixth form college), I would almost certainly have applied. I even contemplated applying for public school posts outside Huddersfield. The main reason why I didn't was my reluctance to up sticks again while Miriam and Edith were still alive; also, I wasn't overly keen to return to teaching O-Level and A-Level syllabuses not of my own devising. Another option I toyed with at this time was obtaining a qualification in student counselling but, in the end, I decided against that as well. As the years went by, I frequently found myself counselling students at the polytechnic anyway, particularly, once I'd come out as a homosexual myself in 1979, those who seemed to be struggling to come to terms with their own sexuality. Fortunately, by the later 1970s, we were beginning to attract much better students, and in increasing numbers, as polytechnics came to be viewed less unfavourably by even decent schools and, more importantly, history at Huddersfield began to establish a reputation for itself. The BA (Humanities) intake of 1976, superior to any of its predecessors, growing confidence in my ability to teach well at degree level, and an ever warmer and closer relationship with my two medieval history colleagues Pauline Stafford and Tony Saul, proved pivotal for me as well. Until the possibility of securing early retirement at fifty, and returning to Bristol, became an appealing prospect, I never considered getting out of the polytechnic again.

What I found most depressing during my years at Huddersfield Polytechnic, especially early on, was the institution itself, its senior management and the dismal ethos of the place. The director Kenneth Durrands was a self-opinionated, bombastic engineer and, although he chose to call himself 'the rector' (in order, so John O'Connell recalls, to have a title 'in line with that used by heads of similar institutions in EEC countries'), he had few man-management skills, rarely mixed with academic staff (let alone students) and chose to surround himself with a group of cronies who, by and large, simply seemed to do as they were told. Clearly, he had precious little sympathy for, or interest in, the arts but, however reluctantly, was forced to recognise that—in contrast to many science and engineering options—subjects such as English, history and politics did have real potential when it came to student recruitment. It is surely significant that, of only four CNAA validated degrees approved by the time of my arrival at Huddersfield, BA (Humanities) was one. Once the Local Government Act of 1973 brought the polytechnic under the control of Kirklees Metropolitan Council on 1 April 1974, moreover, the stage was set for years of conflict between its management and the local authority, not to mention intermittent student militancy. Specifically, between 1974 and 1979 overstaffing and endemic financial problems poisoned relations between Durrands, the polytechnic's board of governors and Kirklees council, all in the context of a Labour government itself beset by seemingly intractable inflation-driven fiscal difficulties and their consequences. Between 1979 and 1981, accompanied by a torrent of adverse publicity in the *Huddersfield Examiner*, the polytechnic's problems escalated into a full-scale crisis that seemed to threaten not only the rector's position but the very existence of the institution. In March 1981, indeed, the CNAA threatened that, unless the polytechnic put its own house in order, it would withdraw approval for its courses. Only when Kirklees reluctantly agreed to finance a large-scale early retirement/redundancy package, in order to raise the polytechnic's student/staff ratio to 10:1, did the crisis temporarily pass.

The machinations of senior management, despite a firm determination to have as little as possible to do with the politics of the institution or its pseudo-democratic power structure, impinged even on me. Not that I had any personal dealings with Durrands and his henchmen. I was far too insignificant for that and, anyway, preferred to keep a low profile. Indeed, during all my years at Huddersfield, I cannot recollect ever speaking to the rector or even encountering him very often. When I once did, if an incident recalled by my former politics colleague Brendan Evans is anything to go by, the circumstances were hardly conventional:

> I remember you once being in my office describing a porn film from Amsterdam. You'd fallen asleep while watching it and, so you told me just as Kenneth Durrands came into the room, woke up just in time to be confronted by a large penis on the screen.

Of the rest of the directorate in the 1970s, only Stewart Armstrong, who became Durrands' deputy in 1974, seemed worthy of much respect. Eventually, in April 1978, he fell from grace and resigned. Otherwise, the so-called pro-rectors included Tom Gaskill who, for years, fought an up-hill struggle to oversee the polytechnic's ailing finances until eventually losing the rector's confidence as well; Frank Barr, a taciturn and humourless man who joined the polytechnic when Holly Bank Technical Teacher Training College merged with the polytechnic in 1974; and, least impressive of all, John Patterson, a fact brought home to me with a vengeance in the autumn of 1975. Although I had no real need or desire to rise up the greasy pole John O'Connell, now head of the Department of History and Political Studies, put me forward for promotion from lecturer to senior lecturer; I was rejected; and, at John's suggestion, I reluctantly appealed against the decision. It was a bizarre and pointless exercise, especially since, with John Patterson as chairman, a repeat of my bravura performance at interview in 1971 was always likely to prove counter-productive. As before, I took the offensive and for the same reason. I didn't care whether I was promoted or not. My argument that, if teaching and putting together teaching material counted for anything I deserved promotion more than most, was never likely to impress, especially as I couldn't resist hinting that the appeals procedure was probably nothing more than window dressing anyway. No wonder my appeal was rejected but, perhaps fortunately for my self-esteem, I never received any explanation why. I determined never to enter the promotion stakes again, and never did, eventually proceeding automatically to senior lecturer when I reached the top of the lecturer scale in 1978. So a senior lecturer I remained for the next fifteen years. Ironically, when I expressed the desire for early retirement at the age of fifty in January 1994, a member of the then directorate offered me, out of the blue, promotion to principal lecturer, presumably as a bribe to get me to stay. Needless to say, I wasn't interested at all by then.

Certainly, during my first decade at Huddersfield Polytechnic, there was plenty of room for criticism of the behaviour of top management; as for the recurrent in-fighting between the directorate, polytechnic governors, Kirklees Metropolitan Council, even the CNAA, none of the parties emerge with much credit. Even someone like me, who never became engaged in the politics of the place, couldn't ignore what was going on, and a series of letters I exchanged with Charles Ross and Anne Crawford in 1980/1 capture my sense of despondency and foreboding nicely. On 9 December 1980, for instance, I declared:

> Huddersfield is the centre of dreadful gloom at present. Unemployment is running at unheard-of levels, with the collapse of textiles and the malaise of engineering and chemicals. The polytechnic, which must have the rottonest management of any higher education institution in England, seems poised to indulge in massive redundancies and, I suspect, the arts will be particularly hammered.

Anne, in response, assured me that both she and her husband would keep their fingers crossed, helpfully adding that, if the worst came to the worst, 'Charles, of course, will give you the best possible reference'. On 19 January 1981 I reported, in similar vein, that:

> ... as for the ghastly redundancy issue, we now know we must lose three out of eighteen staff in the department this autumn and, probably, more in 1982. I think I should survive the first axe but, as a medievalist/ early modernist, I'll probably be dangerously high on the second list.

'Redundancy is still threatening', I wrote again in April 1981, but 'so far they seem to be concentrating on the over-50s'. Fortunately, when my fellow medievalist Tony Saul obtained a post at the CNAA, that lifted any imminent threat to Pauline Stafford and myself but, of course, there was no possibility of his being replaced. Yet even in the midst of the crisis, so Tony Payne (a politics lecturer at Huddersfield between 1979 and 1985) recalls:

> ... you did have a certain pride in the polytechnic. You told me that you found it awkward at the time of Durrands and the financial scandals—which were all over the *Examiner*—to go to your local pub because the locals would have a go at the poly. I remember that we devised the line that you should say that this was just the bosses not real workers in the institution. I don't know whether you ever used it.

I did indeed adopt just such a stratagem but, always, emphasising my pride in the history/politics department, never the polytechnic itself. Bill Stafford, a historian of ideas and colleague throughout my time at Huddersfield, tells me he is:

> ... reminded of E.M.Forster's remark, 'If I had to choose between my friend and my country, I hope I would have the courage to choose my friend'. I think you would always prefer your friend to any abstract collective whatever. Indeed, I doubt whether you have ever felt any loyalty to any institution.

He's probably right.

'When we first came to Huddersfield', recalls my former history colleague Keith Laybourn, 'it struck me what an immensely talented group of historians—academics and teachers—had been assembled in 1971 and 1972'. The memories of Peter Durrans, too, are:

> ... very positive. It was a very exciting time academically and John O'Connell (my old school mentor) had assembled what was probably the best polytechnic department in the country.

This was very much my impression as well. In particular, there were several young scholars only recently out of university themselves and still in the process of completing their doctorates, among them Keith Laybourn himself, Tony Saul, Pauline Stafford, Bill Stafford, David Taylor, Andrew Turnbull and Philip Woodfine. Inevitably, though, they had little teaching experience and only a limited grasp of what relatively low calibre students needed if they were to prosper in higher education. For a time, in all honesty, I hadn't too much idea what I was at either, such was the contrast between a well-established public school and a struggling new polytechnic. Fortunately, there were also a few staff who, between them, had clocked up many years at the chalkface, and not just in higher education.

John O'Connell had been in education for over two decades by 1972 and, as I soon came to realise, he had the battle scars to prove it. A working class lad from Bury in Lancashire, he had graduated in history from Manchester University in 1949. After fourteen years as a schoolmaster he left Penistone Grammar School, where he'd been head of history, in order to join the staff of Huddersfield College of Technology in 1964; he became a principal lecturer at the newly-established polytechnic in 1970; and there he remained until 1989 when he retired as professor and head of the Department of Humanities. Throughout the 1970s, pressurised from above by the directorate and below by his own staff in history and politics, he somehow managed to manoeuvre us successfully and relatively unscathed through frequently troubled waters, despite all the brickbats that came his way. Endless meetings and administration occupied most of his working hours, often from early morning until well into the evening, but he never ceased teaching completely and, although I didn't appreciate it at the time, having an institutionally orientated former schoolmaster and further education lecturer as leader of a group of largely young and inexperienced academics was probably a plus rather than a minus. What I certainly benefited from personally, as a teacher first and foremost, was the freedom he gave me to play to my strengths. Only recently has he admitted that, at the time of my appointment, he 'thought we had a clear understanding' that I would resume work on my unfinished Ph.D and 'felt let down' when he realised I 'felt no obligation' to do so. Perhaps I should feel a degree of guilt at misleading him but I don't since, once I began writing for publication in the late 1970s and 1980s, I drew heavily not only on my earlier doctoral research but also on all the teaching material I'd been given the opportunity to put together.

Peter Wood, subject leader in history, was another former schoolteacher who had also taught at Sunderland Polytechnic before coming to Huddersfield as a principal lecturer. I felt a considerable empathy with this practical and down-to-earth north-eastern refugee from the start, particularly his extensive use of primary source material in teaching nineteenth and twentieth-century social and economic history and his encouragement of my source-orientated approach to later medieval/early modern England. Bradford-born David Wright, a grammar school master in his native city for much of the 1960s and a specialist in modern British and European history, came to the polytechnic in 1971 after a short spell at a Leeds teacher training college. A perceptive historian, enthusiastic researcher and first-rate traditional teacher, he played a key role in establishing the BA (Humanities) degree and, in the later 1970s, an MA in history, and certainly inspired his younger colleagues. I was particularly impressed by his enthusiasm for introducing students to literary and philosophical texts for Victorian England, not least the works of John Stuart Mill, and his firm support for the Open University and its pioneering inter-disciplinary courses. It gave me great satisfaction, after David's premature death in 1995, to co-edit a volume of historical essays in his honour. Bill Roberts, once a British civil servant in Malaya and a historian of the far east, also had school teaching experience, as well as a real flair for administration. For years he shouldered the burden of BA (Humanities) course leader, proved adept at diffusing potential conflicts between disciplines on a multi-subject degree and calming bruised egos, and a master of the art of putting together the massive amount of largely pointless documentation required for CNAA validation. He even persuaded me try my hand at teaching Chinese and Japanese history: Perhaps my closest colleague in the 1970s was Peter Durrans. A former pupil of John O'Connell at Penistone Grammar School, he'd taught at a Canadian university prior to obtaining his post at Huddersfield in 1971. A historian of nineteenth and twentieth century history, especially British imperialism, he was only a couple of years older than me, very much shared my enthusiasm for teaching and, like me too, enjoyed meeting up with more personable students outside the classroom (more often than not in the pub). When he and his wife Hazel, whom I also got to know very well, departed for Sunderland at the beginning of the 1980s, I missed them very much. All these men were experienced teachers; I learned a lot from them; and they certainly played an important part in helping convince me of my capacity to operate effectively at degree level.

Professionally, it was clearly desirable that I work amiably and constructively with the three young historians whose teaching and research interests were closest to mine: Pauline Stafford, Tony Saul and Andrew Turnbull. With Pauline and Tony there was never a problem and we soon became firm friends but I never managed to hit it off with Andy. Pauline Stafford, who became professor of medieval history at Liverpool University not long after I left Huddersfield, had a not dissimilar northern working class background (in Leeds) to my own. There the resemblance ended, however, for she was a brilliant scholar who, soon after joining the polytechnic's staff in 1971, polished off her Oxford D.Phil and, before long, began publishing articles in historical journals, thus laying the foundations for a distinguished academic career. Tony Saul, a native of East Anglia who had taught for a year in a direct grant school before coming to Huddersfield, had already got to know Pauline and her no less intellectually formidable husband Bill during their years together at Oxford University. A conscientious and systematic researcher into fourteenth-century English urban records, particularly those bequeathed by Great Yarmouth, he, too, soon completed his doctorate. No wonder, early on, I felt distinctly inferior to both of them! Andrew Turnbull, a seventeenth-century specialist whose research interests focussed on the politics of Charles II's reign, was an all too evidently ambitious but, at the same time, insecure young man who soon made it clear he had no intention of letting me get even a foothold in later sixteenth and seventeenth-century history. Only after he left the polytechnic, and wasn't replaced, did Tony Saul and I rapidly take over the teaching of early modern English and European history beyond 1550. Amazingly, there were also a further four recently appointed young historians in post, all of them modernists, as well as an older man Dennis Walters who never fitted in at all and eventually accepted early retirement terms. Bill Stafford, who married Pauline while they were both still at Oxford, was a historian of ideas and former student of Sir Isaiah Berlin; indeed, he once lured the great liberal philosopher to Huddersfield, an invitation Berlin enthusiastically accepted, so he told us, as a means of escaping the hot-house atmosphere surrounding the election that very day of his successor as president of Wolfson College, Oxford. Philip Woodfine, the only Cambridge graduate amongst us, was an eighteenth-century specialist but, out of necessity, much of his timetable for many years was devoted to teaching nineteenth and twentieth-century American history. David Taylor was an economic historian, specialising in the history of agriculture since the Industrial Revolution. Before long he departed for Teesside Polytechnic, only to return to Huddersfield years later, as head of history, when Peter Wood retired. Last, but certainly not least, there was Keith Laybourn. A Barnsley working class lad who progressed to the polytechnic via Bradford and Lancaster universities, he specialised in modern labour history, especially trades unionism, and, for several years in the 1980s and early 1990s, he and I were destined to share an office. All in all, the place seemed to be awash with historians and it's no wonder John O'Connell felt we were so seriously overstaffed in the 1970s. Yet, as Bill Roberts recalls:

> Although the history group was a disparate bunch, in general we got on well. Looking back, we should also feel proud of setting a standard of history teaching in a polytechnic which was a distinct improvement on that served up in most older universities.

I couldn't agree more.

What of my politics colleagues? For two or three years Brendan Evans, a Manchester modern history/ politics graduate of almost exactly my own age whose research interests were now focussing more and more on twentieth-century politics, taught American history. Before long, however, he became subject leader in politics and, fortunately for us all, then played a pivotal role in securing the addition of a politics option to the BA (Humanities) degree. Bill Stafford, who had a particular interest in political philosophy, was also instrumental in pushing our credentials to teach politics; David Wright, Andrew Turnbull and David Taylor also contributed to the new option; and even I taught political and social theory for a few years, albeit mainly to history rather than politics students. From the beginning politics proved a popular subject, reflecting a time when intelligent teenagers were often far more politically aware and committed than they are today, and certainly helped boost student numbers in the department from the mid-1970s. No wonder several history staff, anxious to boost their own puny timetables, were so willing to contribute to its teaching. Even so, the need for politics specialists was obvious and when David Clark, Labour MP for the Colne Valley (a constituency incorporating several outer suburbs of Huddersfield), lost his seat in 1974 he rapidly joined us as a senior lecturer in politics. He proved a tremendous asset who brought with him not only a real flair for teaching and empathy with students but also a rich vein of inside knowledge, and splendid anecdotes, about the inner workings of the British political system. I particularly enjoyed several conversations with him about Victor Grayson, charismatic and probably bisexual MP for the Colne Valley between 1907 and 1910, who vanished without trace in 1920, never to be heard of again, and about whom David eventually published a fascinating book in 1985. Unfortunately for us, David Clark became MP for South Shields in 1979 and returned to Westminster; throughout the years of Labour turmoil during the 1980s and early 1990s he maintained his integrity as a middle-of-the-road socialist; and, following Tony Blair's dramatic victory in the 1997 general election, he became a cabinet minister. In September 1976 Steve Smith, an outstandingly able and ambitious young man who was destined to progress via the Universities of East Anglia and Wales (Aberystwyth) to the Vice Chancellorship of Exeter University, was a specialist in international politics, particularly its theoretical dimension, and managed to engage the interest of even average students in this most intellectually challenging of areas. I hit it off with him right from the start and particularly enjoyed mildly sending up both Steve himself and his research. Seemingly, as he has recently recalled, he enjoyed the experience as well:

> Keith made a profound impact on me. I arrived in Huddersfield, at the age of twenty-four, for my first lecturing job and there I found this amazingly out-going, confident (or so it seemed), knowledgeable, opinionated, lovable colleague. Above all he was loud: you could hear him three rooms away with the doors shut. I learnt a lot from him, not least his first conversation with me: 'Now listen, Steve, never get so far away from the bloody lectern (in lectures) that you can't get back before you have to make your next point which, of course, you've forgotten'.

Sadly, Steve only stayed at Huddersfield for just over a couple of years. Andrew Taylor, son of Jack Taylor (leader of the Yorkshire miners during the 1984/5 strike against pit closures) and, appropriately, himself researching the politics of coal in the twentieth century, obtained a post at the polytechnic in 1978 and remained throughout my time there. He was particularly struck, so he recollects, by my 'foghorn laugh and heaving shoulders' which reminded him of Edward Heath! More flatteringly, he adds:

> I remember listening to your lectures occasionally and thinking them bravura performances. I certainly tried to learn from you, especially your dictum that lecturing was a public performance, which meant one had to know one's lines, feel nervous in order to get the adrenalin flowing and care about the audience. Your

grasp of what seemed to me obscure corners of British history was also an object lesson in subject enthusiasm.

And Tony Payne, a young specialist in third world politics who joined the department the year after Andrew Taylor, suggests, no less gratifyingly, that I was 'the easiest of the historians to get to know and very helpful to someone learning the job'.

Although, for most of the time, history and politics worked together amicably enough and, once the politics option came on stream in 1975, many students opted for a combination of the two subjects, there was inevitably occasional rancour in such an overstaffed department; moreover, once politics began to prove more popular than history at a time when specialist politics teaching staff were very much in a minority, this led to even more serious divisions. Several politics staff remember me as always trying to cross the divide and frequently seeking to pour oil on troubled waters. Brendan Evans considers that, 'while neither of us was extremist on the issue', the 'silly history/ politics split' did become a barrier between us for several years:

> Your great contribution at this time was as a bridge-builder and healer, by using your personality and humour within an otherwise divided department. I particularly remember when, during one rancorous history/politics meeting, you said: 'Let's get the gloves off. No, let's not bother, let's go to the pub instead'.

Tony Payne has similar memories:

> In respect of history/politics tensions and rivalry, I recall you as someone who tried hard to bridge the gap and did so by the force of your personality. I also remember once when your temper briefly snapped. We were having a rare departmental meeting in Z Block, all of us sat in rows at desks with John O'Connell at the front. We were discussing the problem of students changing subject at the end of the first year and I commented—fairly gently as I remember—that this was not a departmental problem but a history one (because politics was doing better). You interjected, 'Well, if we're going to take the gloves off, let's take them off', but then did not follow it up and the moment passed.

Perhaps Andy Taylor has the same incident in mind when he recollects my:

> ... tendency to smoulder, then explode, usually over some inconsequential issue. Your firepower—which could be formidable—could have been much better directed!

Fortunately, as the years went by and student numbers increased, such disputes gradually faded away.

Since I tended to avoid them whenever I possibly could, I have no personal recollection of any departmental meeting during all my years at the polytechnic, nor any records of their deliberations. Maybe I occasionally glanced at the minutes of such meetings before binning them but, more often than not, Bill Roberts or Peter Wood simply told me by word-of-mouth anything resulting from them that I needed to know: not a lot! It's no wonder, however, that both could find me exasperating to say the least. Bill Roberts, indeed, vividly recalls:

> ... those long years when I was course leader of BA (Humanities) and attempting to achieve some degree of uniformity among my colleagues. With some, this was impossible. With you, the situation was simply challenging. You hated meetings, refused to fill in forms, and generally did things your own way. As for routine matters, your usual response was, 'Well, seeing it's you, I suppose I'll do it'.

Peter Wood makes much the same point:

> Charitably, I suppose, the time you spent on teaching preparation accounted for your reluctance to play a full part in the demanding round of committees which provided the administrative framework for a multi-subject degree and which did so much to dampen the spirits of the rest of us. I'm sure there were times when I took a less sympathetic line on this than I do now! Your initial explosions on matters such as new regulations, while understandable, were not always helpful and the history team should probably have been relieved that you so often avoided meetings.

Nevertheless, he adds in mitigation:

> You were not without considerable administrative skills when it suited your purpose. Your careful attention to the organisation of first year tutorials, handouts and final grades, in particular, solved what was in many ways our most difficult problem. There, your touch was as certain as your hand on a pint glass at the start of an evening.

Indeed, he concludes, 'for a non-sportsman you were always a good team member'. Perhaps Andrew Taylor has it about right:

> One of your most puzzling traits was to respond to any change, crisis or threat with, 'I don't bloody care!'. Yet when it really mattered—for instance, concerning students—you did care and care deeply.

Interestingly, Andy also remarks on what he perceived to be my tendency to hold certain history colleagues in quite unnecessary awe and Tony Payne, too, believes I treated at least a couple of them with far too much reverence. Perhaps they have a point. For a few years at least I did feel rather a poor relation, as a mere ex-schoolmaster whose overriding interest was teaching not research, amidst a bunch of young historians who seemed so much more scholarly than I was. Yet John O'Connell's conclusion that, during the 1970s, 'History and Politics was one of the most successful departments in the polytechnic', not least by being 'the first to gain CNAA approval for a Master's degree course' in history, must surely be right as well. For all our gripes at the time, moreover, his own painstaking perseverence in adversity was probably vital to our success. Nor, as Bill Roberts reminds me, should I forget the role of our departmental secretary for several years, Nancy Alexander, 'with her Marjorie Proops glasses and fag, for ever beating the hell out of her typewriter' on our behalf.

Throughout the 1970s the survival of history at Huddersfield was heavily dependent on the maintenance of a flourishing BA (Humanities) degree. This was CNAA-validated and, even before taking up my appointment, I journeyed north, ostensibly to help secure its approval. For all the use I was I might as well have stayed in Plymouth but, clearly, everyone was immensely relieved when the new BA got the go-ahead, even the polytechnic's senior management. What struck me then, and on subsequent visitations, was the sheer amount of documentation the Council for National Academic Awards required and the complexity of regulations governing the operation of its degrees. Much of it seemed little more than window dressing and so it proved. Once teaching got underway practical modifications to theoretical statements of aims, objectives and methods of delivery of courses inevitably proved both necessary and desirable. New regulations came and went over the years but, for the most part, I either never learned of their existence at all, picked my way around their content or simply ignored them altogether. As Peter Wood shrewdly recalls:

> The Humanities degree was rather like the European Union. New regulations could usually be watered down with the passage of time or so modified in practice that little of consequence was changed.

Bill Roberts also emphasises, rightly, that the polytechnic top management's lack of interest in humanities:

> ... gave us extraordinary freedom to invent our own courses and deliver them as we saw fit. True, there was the CNAA to keep happy but, although bureaucratic in its methods, it was at least based in London and even periodic visits (despite

involving a lot of irritating preparatory work) never caused us any major traumas. In fact, we operated largely as a self-directing entity.

And, CNAA or no CNAA, he adds:

> ... many of us were, or became, critical of the teaching methods we had experienced as students and, of course, old-fashioned finals exams. We wanted to get away from all that and most of us were firmly committed to broadening access to higher education as well.

I certainly was. Education had given me opportunities denied to most working class kids in the 1950s and 1960s, especially if they were bastards brought up in relative poverty, so why not give even more of them the same life-transforming chances in the 1970s?

When teaching on the new BA (Humanities) degree commenced in the autumn of 1972 there were just four subjects on offer: History, Geography, English and French. Each student opted for three subjects out of four in their first year (spending about a third of their time on each) and, thereafter, two in a major (two-thirds)/minor (one-third) combination. Although it was possible to follow a pass degree pathway, and the seriously intellectually challenged or bone idle might occasionally have little or no choice in the matter, most students worked for, and obtained, an honours degree at the end of their three years. Before long, moreover, student choice was expanded as further subjects were added to the menu, most notably Politics, Philosophy, Economics, Oriental Studies and Drama. All this created a powerful spirit of competition between subjects both to recruit students in the first place and then hang on to them at the end of the first year, preferably as majors rather than minors. Vivienne Haley, who became a BA (Humanities) student at Huddersfield in the autumn of 1977, certainly has vivid and splendidly irreverent memories of the annual recruitment jamboree, not least my own role in it:

> As a young and impressionable first year student I remember well the process of going to Huddersfield for the first time and having to select subjects from the range of humanities. History was always on the list because I quite liked it and, since I'd found it fairly easy at school, it seemed an obvious option. What other criterion does an eighteen year old girl use to select the subjects she is going to study for the next three years? Anyway, accompanied by five or six like-minded new girlfriends, I mooched from classroom to classroom to hear what each lecturer had to say in order to drum up numbers for his or her option. Among them were Peter Durrans, in a white safari suit and black polo-neck sweater,

who looked like James Bond in *Out of Africa*; Keith Laybourn, dishevelled and likeable, but whose subject matter seemed very dry; Bill Roberts, none of whose intriguing array of initials obviously fitted the name Bill; and John O'Connell, who came across as humorous and kindly but apparently more interested in the Latin and Greek roots of words than history. Then there was Dockray! Prowling like a caged tiger in an over-small cage of a classroom, back and forth, back and forth, his speed of turn at the end of each width of the room increasing as did the passion with which he spoke. Eventually, with a final flourish, he sat forcibly on the end of the desk at the front of the room as if daring us to opt for history. Only it wasn't a desk. It was a table with a large board placed over the top and, as soon as he sat on one end, all the papers and documents on the other (and there were thousands of them) flew into the air and scattered themselves around the room. How Keith didn't fall to the floor I shall never know—but it was close! With his horrified (and/or tittering) colleagues looking on, he dusted himself down, aimed a parting comment in the general direction of the ceiling, pulled an amazing face, and strode out of the room. We were hooked! Sexy to us girls he might not be, but fascinating and funny, idiosyncratic and cynical, alarming and erratic, he would always be.

Over the years, in fact, I often found myself at the forefront when it came to selling history (especially medieval history) to new students and, in sharp contrast to attending meetings, it was both fun and rewarding.

Not only was there a premium on student recruitment, and intermittent tension between history and politics, there were also rivalries and jealousies between us and other departments, as well as within those departments themselves. Staff who had made the transition from further to higher education in 1970 seemed particularly prone to bickering. Most notably, there were occasional run-ins between John O'Connell and Harry Robinson, head of geography, a down-to-earth Yorkshireman, canny political operator and powerful promoter of his own subject and its staff. Harry nevertheless seemed to enjoy having his leg pulled, even by a junior historian such as myself! There was certainly much in-fighting amongst the English staff but also real enthusiasm for teaching: Hugh Robertson, for instance, won over many students to Elizabethan and Jacobean literature; Mike Wade could hardly fail to score a hit when launched into the risqué later seventeenth-century poetry of James Wilmot Earl of Rochester; and Steve Evans, once a journalist, certainly had real empathy with many students. French always had difficulty recruiting but it, too, had its dogged defenders, not least the engaging Glyn Williams. Inevitably, there were eccentric figures as well, most memorably the philosopher Stuart Linney (whose presence at any meeting virtually guaranteed it would not be short) and the mercurial and tempestuous head of drama David Mann. How Bill Roberts managed to maintain his equanimity, or even his sanity, during his many years as course leader of BA (Humanities) I have no idea. I couldn't have stuck it for a month!

Plymouth College had sported a ramshackle collection of buildings; so did Huddersfield Polytechnic; and not all its accommodation was situated on the main Queensgate campus, hemmed in as it was by an arterial road and the Huddersfield Narrow Canal. The oldest building on the Queensgate site, inherited from Huddersfield College of Technology, dated back to 1883. Despite its not unimpressive Victorian facade, however, the Ramsden building (as it was known in my time) had little to recommend it internally and its classrooms, in particular, left a great deal to be desired. Of considerable age, too, was the Student Union Building, formerly St.Joseph's Roman Catholic school, a dingy structure hardly likely ever to inspire its current occupants. The campus was also home to St.Paul's, an architecturally undistinguished ex-nonconformist church, now visibly delapidated and, for a long time, a bit of a white elephant. Eventually it was refurbished as a concert venue, specialising in the performance of execrable contemporary music. Otherwise, there was an ill-assorted collection of more modern buildings, mainly dating from the later 1950s and 1960s, including two tower blocks (the Textile and Engineering Towers), a peculiarly shaped building known as Z Block, and the Great Hall complex. Not long after my arrival the massive Central Services Building, overlooking the canal, was constructed. Formally opened in May 1977, it contained a new student dining room and many study bedrooms, the library, lecture and seminar rooms, a suite for the rector and his cronies (served by a separate lift!) and myriads of offices to house the institution's ever burgeoning army of bureaucrats. Away from the main site, the polytechnic also occupied a small campus at Holly Bank (following the merger with Holly Bank Technical Teacher Training College in 1974); accommodation above a town centre department store and in the local YMCA building (to which, eventually, drama staff and students were exiled); and, several miles away on the outskirts of Halifax, Bermerside Hall. Time consuming as it was to travel there by public transport, Bermerside was much my favourite teaching location, particularly since sessions there almost invariably ended in a nearby pub. As Keith Laybourn recalls:

> For several years early on we both operated at the Bermerside outpost in Halifax one day a week. You taught final year mature students fifteenth-century history in the mornings and I then caught them for their dissertations in the *Murgatroyd Arms*.

Even better, the earliest of many excursions to Richmond and Middleham castles Keith and I were to organise over the years were with these mature students and, again, there was always ample time to sample the local Theakstons beer. We made sure of that!

When I first arrived in Huddersfield I became one of fifteen or sixteen humanities staff pigged down together in a large desk-laden staff room in Z Block. John O'Connell's determination, and our success in securing approval for the BA (Humanities) degree, produced a dramatic improvement within months when the history staff moved *en masse* into the so-called Workshop Block. A large warehouse-like structure, the part we occupied consisted of several hastily constructed classrooms and a series of tiny offices. It was hardly classy accommodation but, as John has reminded me, we did now become 'the only department in the polytechnic with individual staffrooms'. My own claustrophobic windowless room was sandwiched between those of Bill Roberts and Keith Laybourn, as both vividly recall. 'Do you remember', asks Bill rhetorically:

> ... when we had adjacent cubbyholes in the Workshop Block and sometimes had tutorials at the same time? I was trying to give up smoking at the time and the smoke of your mentholated cigarettes used to curl over the partition. What was far more distracting, though, was the sound of your voice getting increasingly excited over some medieval document or other. My students' attention would begin to waver, I'd start talking louder, but I could never win.

Keith Laybourn's memories are strikingly similar:

> In the Workshop days our rooms were small and liable to disintegrate if water leaked down from the high ceilings onto our little cubicles. I even seem to remember that on one unbelievably wet day rain water all but dissolved one of our cardboard rooms. Otherwise, my main remembrance is of how thin the walls were. On numerous occasions our teaching blended. Once, indeed, when asking my students the reasons for the General Strike of 1926, the answer promptly came back from you next door: 'The Black Death'!

Eventually, in 1978, we returned to Z Block and occupied much of the third floor, refurbished from classrooms into substantial single occupant tutorial rooms. Again, I found myself next door to Keith Laybourn (although the walls were now thicker) and when, a few years later, growing student numbers, the need for more classrooms and the increasing amount of floor space required by pestilential computers forced staff to double up, he and I then moved in together and subsequently shared what amounted to a seminar room for over a decade.

Throughout the 1970s Tony Saul, Pauline Stafford and I worked together very closely indeed and I can't remember us ever having a serious disagreement.

Tony Saul, indeed, recalls that:

> The nine years (1972—1981) I spent with Keith at Huddersfield Polytechnic were professionally one of the most exciting and stimulating periods of my working life. The foundations of the department were laid, new courses were devised, publications were commenced and the confidence of the CNAA was secured. Central to this was the camaraderie and professional collaboration of the medievalists, Keith, Pauline and myself. We learned a great deal from each other and developed/shared teaching materials of a very high order. We really were a team.

Yet this was far from inevitable in 1972. Peter Wood believes 'the efforts of Pauline, Tony and yourself enabled medieval history to flourish in what could have been a hostile environment'. As for Pauline Stafford, she flatteringly emphasises the importance of my role in particular (while showing undue modesty about her own):

> What a huge relief it was when you and Tony were appointed! Before that, I doubted the future of medieval history at Huddersfield, after it never. I certainly have no doubt that you were extremely important in ensuring the success of medieval history and making Huddersfield one of the very few polytechnics/ new universities where it has flourished. You had, and have, a passionate enthusiasm for the subject which communicated itself to students and to colleagues. I am quite certain I could not have made it succeed without you (though I am also fairly sure you could have done it without me). Indeed, I wonder whether I'd have persevered as a lone medievalist at Huddersfield, and whether I'd have had a medieval constituency among the students, had it not been for you.

A former politics colleague tells me that he 'could never work out' whether I 'didn't realise how much advantage Pauline took' of my 'support, cover and generosity' or if I 'knew full well and didn't mind'. In fact, I never saw our working relationship in those terms at all. Of course, since Pauline had young children at the time, I helped wherever I could to enable her to balance career and family responsibilities but it was no big deal and, in reality, we complemented each other very well indeed. I may have produced more teaching material for the courses we taught jointly and perhaps spent marginally more hours in the classroom during an average week but Pauline put together plenty of her own as well and, unlike me, she was also very active on the research front; moreover, and this really was a bonus, Pauline was an accomplished Latin scholar whereas I wasn't and, whenever I sought her assistance, she'd always happily translate problematic passages from medieval Latin chronicles for me. Tony Saul, too, produced a considerable amount of material all three of us used. All in all, Pauline, Tony and I formed a splendid team. We each played to our strengths; we liked and respected, as well as learning a great deal from, each other; and, as time went on, we defended our medieval corner with ever mounting confidence and robustness.

As far as teaching was concerned, Peter Wood particularly remembers my use of contemporary source material, 'something which I fully supported'; indeed, he adds, 'I feel your efforts here were an inspiration to us all'. 'You were most influential in your emphasis on documents in teaching', echoes Pauline Stafford, 'particularly your use of chronicles'; moreover, she recollects, 'this was not something I had encountered before in an undergraduate and postgraduate career more dominated by record sources'. Pauline's doctorate had been devoted to an analysis of the government of tenth-century England, in fact, and her early published work dwelt mainly on early English administration, law and coinage. If, as she suggests, I encouraged her to widen her areas of interest, I'm delighted to accept the compliment:

> I've never lost the interest in chronicles you helped stimulate. Indeed, it was largely thanks to you that my work took the direction which it has followed. It was you who asked me to speak to the Huddersfield branch of the Historical Association and it was in response to what I thought you would appreciate that I wrote the paper 'Sons and Mothers: Family Politics in the Early Middle Ages'. It was that paper which, once published, attracted attention to my work. I feel I owe you a lot.

Tony Saul is even more flattering:

> Keith brought home to a wide audience, not just his immediate professional circle, the role of chronicles and letters in putting together the story of late medieval England. For those brought up on the concept of the primacy of record sources, whether of central or local government, this was a revelation and, for me, the realisation that the Peasants' Revolt of 1381 could not be understood without the chronicle sources was certainly so.

The phrase 'putting together the story of late medieval England', he adds, 'could be construed as simply telling a series of good tales in the H.E.Marshal tradition but Keith showed that the real story could not emerge without detailed knowledge, careful scrutiny and substantial scholarship'. Certainly, it seems to me, what gave Huddersfield medieval history teaching its appealing and distinctive edge, not just in the 1970s but throughout my time there, was the determination of Pauline Stafford, Tony Saul and I to introduce students to a variety of source material from their very first term. Nowadays such an approach is virtually taken as read in many university history departments but that was not the case at all thirty years ago.

Since BA (Humanities) students had to choose two out of three subjects at the end of the year, first year courses clearly had to grab, and maintain, their interest. Also, if medieval history was to flourish at the polytechnic, Pauline Stafford, Tony Saul and I all agreed it was essential that students, hardly any of whom were likely to have encountered early history in the sixth form (even in the 1970s), should have no choice but to study it and find out what it was like. Hence *Medieval to Modern*, a course introducing them to four major areas of Western European history *circa* 1300—1550: English and French kings, politics and war; economic and social history; the Italian Renaissance; and the later medieval church and early Reformation. Tony Saul and I shared the political history lectures (although I did the bulk of them); Tony and Pauline Stafford covered a variety of economic and social themes, such as the Black Death and its impact, social protest movements and the fifteenth-century economy; Pauline introduced students to the Italian Renaissance, not least the flowering of art and architecture; and I gave free vent to my cynical humanist-driven conclusions about later medieval popes, early Protestant reformers and the religious life of the times. All three of us conducted seminars/tutorials across the board, teaching the same groups throughout the year and, hopefully, getting to know our students well as a result. We also put a lot of work into preparing interesting and stimulating teaching material. What I most enjoyed was lecturing and the bigger the audience the better. For me, in fact, lectures were essentially theatrical performances, opportunities to provide intellectual entertainment and, if I managed to fire their interest, encourage students to follow up topics in textbooks, monographs and historical journals. I soon learned, too, that peppering lectures with short quotations from literary sources, particularly focussed on the personalities, private lives and even sexual antics of kings such as Edward II (1307—1327), Edward IV (1461—1483) and Henry VIII (1509—1547), always helped stem any signs of flagging interest, as well as providing essential light relief from the wrist-aching business of taking notes. I always lectured at radio broadcast speed, rarely wrote anything on the blackboard apart from names and, even after overhead projectors appeared, scorned their use. For a few years I did experiment with providing summaries of my lectures but, eventually, abandoned the practice as counter-productive. What I did do, more and more, was consciously structure lectures around the content of primary source material-dominated handouts put together to provide basic reading for follow-up seminars/tutorials. This proved a highly successful stratagem and, indeed, provided a model for all future BA courses I mounted at Huddersfield.

No doubt as anxious as the rest of us to boost his timetable, by the mid-1970s Bill Roberts had succeeded in putting together, and securing CNAA approval for, a new BA (Humanities) option in Oriental Studies. I knew nothing of far eastern history but, so Bill recalls, 'my charm—or your inebriation—led you to agree to teach on the Oriental Studies option'; indeed, he adds, 'I still have some of your Chinese and Japanese teaching notes'. For several years thereafter we shared *Historical Background of the Far East*, a first year course covering the history of China and Japan from early times to the late nineteenth century. Bill and I taught seminars/tutorials across the board and split the lecturing between us (although Keith Laybourn also gave a few lectures for a year or two). My contribution consisted of half a dozen lectures on Chinese history from the late Han period (25—221AD) to the end of the fourteenth century and twelve covering the evolution of Japan from prehistoric times to *circa* 1640. What I particularly enjoyed was drawing comparisons between what was going on in China and Japan and developments in Western Europe at the same time, as well as exploring contacts between East and West over the centuries: for instance, points of similarity and difference between the decline of the Roman Empire in the West and the Han Empire in China, the European 'Dark Ages' and the contemporary Chinese 'Age of Confusion', the impact of Buddhism on China and Christianity in the West and, in the thirteenth and fourteenth centuries, Western missions to China and the threat posed to the West by the powerful Mongol dynasty. Comparisons and contrasts between Japan and the West were even more fascinating, particularly the development of feudalism and feudal societies, independently but at roughly the same time chronologically, in both Japan and Western Europe. Equally intriguing was the arrival of Christian missionaries in sixteenth-century Japan, the fate that befel many of them in the early seventeenth, and the growth of Japanese isolationism culminating in the 'closed centuries' c.1650—1850. I also became interested in the literary sources for medieval Japanese history, particularly those for the fifteenth century, and how they compared with English equivalents. More specifically, I was fascinated to discover that, roughly at the same time as England under Henry VI, Edward IV and Richard III was suffering the traumas of the Wars of the Roses (c.1455-1485), Japan also dissolved into civil war during the shogunate of Yoshimasa: the Onin War (c.1467—1477). This culminated in what Bill Roberts flatteringly describes as my 'master stroke': the publication, in 1979, of an article entitled 'Japan and England in the Fifteenth Century: the Onin War and the Wars of the Roses'.

By the mid-1970s I was also teaching the eleventh, twelfth and thirteenth centuries to Huddersfield history students. For a term in 1974 or 1975 I enjoyed myself hugely covering the whole span of Western European history from the fall of Rome to the end of the thirteenth century with a group of first year Certificate in Education students at Bermerside. Similarly, in 1975/6, I put on a two term course entitled *Medieval Monarchs in Action c.500—1500* for the Huddersfield branch of the Workers Education Authority at a local sixth form college. Concentrating on the personalities, priorities and subsequent reputations of a string of medieval rulers over a period of about a thousand years, I started with the semi-mythical King Arthur and progressed, via Charlemagne, the Anglo-Saxon kings Offa of Mercia, Alfred the Great and Edward the Confessor, the Norman and Angevin kings of England, the Capetian kings of France, and the Salian and Hohenstaufen emperors in Germany, to the later Plantagenet rulers of England in the fourteenth and fifteenth centuries. An enthusiastic group of mature students, I soon discovered, particularly relished analysing and evaluating passages from a wide range of literary sources such as Bede's early eighth-century *History of the English Church and People*, Einhard's *Life of Charlemagne*, Asser's *Life of Alfred*, the *Anglo-Saxon Chronicle*, Joinville's *Life of St.Louis* of France and Jean Froissart's *Chronicles* of England, France and the Hundred Years War in the fourteenth century. So did I. When Pauline Stafford began planning *The Making of the Middle Ages*, a new second year course for BA (Humanities) students covering *circa* 800—1300, I enthusiastically volunteered to teach a chunk of it. Since Pauline was the expert on early medieval history, it obviously made sense for me to concentrate on the central middle ages c.1050—1300. For three or four years I taught blocks on the Empire and the Papacy c.1050—1250, Feudal Monarchy in France and England (covering the rule of the Capetians in France 987—1314 and the Normans/Plantagenets in England 1087—1307) and, as a specifically designated 'problem of historical evidence', an entirely document-based unit devoted to Henry II, Thomas Becket and Church/State relations in Twelfth Century England. Later on, as Pauline's interest in and desire to teach medieval marriage, women and society developed, I abandoned the Empire/Papacy theme and substituted a block on the Papacy, Sex and Morality (enthusiastically seizing the opportunity to lecture on both prostitution and homosexuality!). Again, all my seminars/tutorials, not just the Becket unit, concentrated on the analysis of primary source material, particularly the evidence provided by contemporary and near-contemporary chroniclers such as St.Anselm (on William Rufus), William of Malmesbury (Henry I), the *Gesta Stephani* (Stephen), Gerald of Wales (Henry II) and Matthew Paris (John).

At about the same time as I began teaching *The Making of the Middle Ages* with Pauline Stafford, Tony Saul, Philip Woodfine and I inherited from Andrew Turnbull a second year BA (Humanities) course *Britain and Europe c.1550—1760*. Tony ran the course and, in its earliest version, he covered themes in Western European history from the mid-sixteenth to the later seventeenth-century; he and I, together, tackled later Tudor and Stuart England (to 1688); and Philip shouldered the burden of teaching the last sixty or seventy years of the period. Apart from a document-based 'problem of historical evidence' analysing Elizabeth I's last years c.1588—1603, I focussed on the Origins of the English Revolution c.1603—1642 and Revolution, Restoration and the Later Stuarts c.1642—1688. This gave me ample opportunity to examine the era's fascinating historiography (particularly the interpretations of Whig and Marxist historians), explore its dramatic political twists and turns and, most of all, enjoy getting to grips with the enigmatic personalities of both the Stuart kings themselves and such controversial power brokers as Strafford, Laud and Oliver Cromwell. By 1978/9 Philip Woodfine (as he inherited more and more American history teaching from Brendan Evans) had dropped off the course and, revamped as *Crisis and Recovery: Aspects of British and European History*, it now lost its early eighteenth-century block. Neither Tony Saul nor I had any desire to take that on. All I did, in fact, was restructure and slightly extend my coverage of the Stuart century: Origins of the Civil War c.1603—1642; Civil War, Interregnum and Restoration c.1642—1660; and the Later Stuarts, the Glorious Revolution and its Impact c.1660—1701. Only when Tony Saul departed in 1981, and I took over sole responsibility for early modern history at Huddersfield, did I seize the opportunity to put together a new course very much reflecting my personal predispositions and prejudices throughout.

No doubt concern to expand my timetable, widen my range of teaching and secure my future explains why, in 1974/5, I teamed up with Bill Stafford to put on a third year BA (Humanities) course on *Political and Social Theories*. I was very much the junior partner and my credentials to teach political philosophy at all, let alone at third year degree level, were thin to say the least. Brendan Evans, interestingly, comments:

> You rightly stressed teaching over research and were devotedly backed by students. Yet, maybe, you took on too much teaching at times, both to support others and to cover areas you yourself enjoyed such as Oriental Studies and Political Philosophy.

'Although you taught brilliantly', he adds, 'perhaps this diluted your expertise'. Maybe so, but I certainly found teaching political theory both stimulating and rewarding for several years. Once the course became available to politics and philosophy (as well as history) students, however, David Wright joined us and, gradually, my contribution lessened until, early in the 1980s, I dropped off the course altogether. Employing both historical and philosophical techniques, students were required critically to examine a series of classical texts, most notably Thomas Hobbes' *Leviathan*, John Locke's *Second Treatise on Government*, John Stuart Mill's *Utilitarianism* and *On Liberty*, and a selection of philosophical, political, social and historical discourses penned by Karl Marx. Bill did the vast bulk of the lecturing but we both took seminar/ tutorial groups. Since I couldn't make head nor tail of parts of Rousseau's *Social Contract* and, anyway, felt repelled by notions of *forcing* men to be free, for three weeks students were offered a choice between Rousseau and Plato's *Republic*. Here I did the lecturing, concentrating on what Plato had to say about the nature of justice and injustice in the state and society, the role of education, and his theory of ruling (not least his criticisms of democracy and penchant for philosopher-kings exercising power in an ideal state). I'd been fascinated by Plato's political ideas since my undergraduate days; I felt a considerable empathy with Hobbes' bleak conclusions about man and society, and enjoyed exploring the seventeenth-century context of both his *Leviathan* and Locke's *Second Treatise*; and I relished, too, conducting seminars on Marxism (very much in vogue in the 1970s, of course), mischievously exposing ignorance and misunderstanding among left-wing students in particular. J. S. Mill's powerful case for maximising individual liberty in Society had an obvious personal appeal and relevance for me and, when David Wright added the *Subjection of Women* to the menu, I felt very much on Mill's wavelength there as well. Not surprisingly, I was at my best when tutoring less able students who, struggling as they often did with the philosophical dimension of the course, needed a great deal of encouragement and guidance; bright students, especially if they had a real philosophical bent, not infrequently left *me* at sea! As Bill Stafford remembers, he and I also enjoyed arguing with each other, particularly about Thomas Hobbes:

> You were an out-and-out Hobbesian in theory: indeed, you and I used to argue about this, with me maintaining that not all human motivations are selfish, you (with your normal cynicism) defending Hobbes; moreover, in your own conduct you generally did do what you wanted and could be very obstinate about doing what you didn't want to do. Yet, as Coleridge might have put it, the man was better than his theory. You liked your colleagues and students, so what you wanted to do did not involve Hobbesian aggression, competitiveness or ruthless go-getting at all. You were perfectly capable of wanting the good of your colleagues and students and, as I used to insist, this is *not* selfishness.

I hope he's right.

What I most wanted at Huddersfield, almost from the beginning, was the opportunity to teach an in-depth primary source-based course on later fifteenth-century England. The chance soon came when, in 1973/4, I put together *England under the Yorkists 1461—1485* for third year Certificate in Education students at Bermerside. Very much modelled on the Special Subject I'd experienced at Bristol University in 1965/6, it focussed throughout on contemporary and near-contemporary records, letters and, most particularly, chronicles, and how their detailed study could enable historians to reconstruct the political history of the age. Inevitably, too, personalities were very much to the fore, not just the Yorkist kings Edward IV and his brother Richard III but also Edward's politically active queen Elizabeth Woodville and great magnates such as Richard Neville Earl of Warwick (Warwick the Kingmaker). The Yorkist economy, church and government also figured prominently. *England under the Yorkists* ran at least three times and it proved as much a learning experience for me as it did, hopefully, for the students; in particular, I learnt many valuable lessons about how best to organise and teach such a course.

BA (Humanities) students who majored in history were required to take a primary source-based Special Subject in their third year but such courses were not available to minor students. Instead, they were required to tackle *Problems of Historical Evidence*. First coming on stream in 1974/5, its format very much resulted from the enthusiastic collaboration of Keith Laybourn and myself: two consecutive modules very much focussing on sources for regional and local history. Initially, students had no choice of subject matter. In the first half of the year I taught *The Pastons, the Plumptons and their England c.1450—1500* before handing the class over to Keith for *Reform or Revolution?: The Emergence of the Working Class in Yorkshire c.1800—1926*. Peter Wood recalls:

> Your treatment of the *Problems of Historical Evidence* course was, I felt, particularly inspired and, when the opportunity came to produce a module myself, I gladly took it. I hadn't appreciated the amount of preparation I had taken on but enjoyed every minute of the teaching.

My experience of teaching *England under the Yorkists* at Bermerside had highlighted the problem of students having to rely on single photocopies of printed editions of chronicles and published selections from records and letters. *The Pastons, the Plumptons and their England* was largely based on two surviving collections of later fifteenth-century gentry letters and records: the Pastons, a Norfolk family, and the Plumptons, who hailed from the West Riding of Yorkshire. This time, however, instead of expecting students to rely on printed editions, I put together a series of substantial handouts, consisting of passages arranged thematically, and then structured both lectures and seminars around them. Such a task proved very time-consuming, as I typed out all the passages myself, but it was well worth it, especially as it enabled me to introduce supplementary primary source material from central government records relating to the two families and further evidence about the Plumptons I'd gathered as a research student in the later 1960s. Since both families, especially the Pastons, became embroiled in politics and the Wars of the Roses, there was plenty of scope to explore the interaction between centre and provinces in later fifteenth-century England and, more specifically, the impact of politics and war on the ruling elites of two very different counties. The Paston and Plumpton archives also threw a great deal of light on the private lives and social behaviour of the two families, including their marriages, family relationships and connections with fellow gentry and nobility; their involvement in local government and concern with law, litigation and the lawlessness of the times; their estates and the financial problems of fifteenth-century landowners; and their personal interest in, and promotion of, a range of religious and cultural activities. All in all these family letters and papers provided a rich mix for students to get their teeth into and most of them seemed to enjoy the experience. Once I began planning a third year Special Subject (again covering later fifteenth-century English history) for major students, however, it seemed sensible to put together a new *Problems of Historical Evidence* module as well. Hence why, towards the end of the 1970s, *Yorkshire and the Civil War* replaced *The Pastons, the Plumptons and their England*.

Towards the end of the 1970s, too, Tony Saul persuaded me to contribute to an MA course he was mounting on *London and York c.1376—1485*. I felt very uncertain about this, and took some convincing, partly because I had no great interest in or knowledge of urban history, mainly because I didn't have any sort of postgraduate qualification myself. Soon after the MA in History received CNAA approval and teaching commenced in the autumn of 1976, I had contributed a two hour lecture/seminar session on English Medieval Chronicles c.1100—1500. This I did know about and felt confident enough to teach even at master's level. So, I concluded, the best way I could help Tony was to offer a single session on the Nature and Content of the London Chronicles and a further three on London and the Wars of the Roses c.1450—1471, again particularly revolving around the content of contemporary and near-contemporary narratives put together in the capital. Again, too, I put together meaty handouts of selected passages from the chronicles and structured the classes around them. When Tony left in 1981, however, that put an end to the course and I didn't teach MA students again for several years. My own Special Subject *England in the Age of the Wars of the Roses c.1450—1487* was a different kettle of fish altogether. I taught variations on this virtually every year from 1978/9 (when it first came on stream) to 1993/4 (when I took early retirement); moreover, the very substantial booklets I put together for the course eventually provided the main raw material for a trilogy of published source books.

Three BA (Humanities) students I taught between 1976 and 1979 have independently sent me reminiscences of their time at Huddersfield Polytechnic, not least memories of my teaching and its impact on them. I hope they are not being deliberately flattering! 'Like so many in the mid-1970s', recollects Andy Hook:

> ... I was the first in my family who had taken a very nervous step towards studying for a degree. Armed with my low grades at A-Level and my working class aversion to the multi-cultural state, I was confident I could hack it in a town like Huddersfield. But would I be able to win through in a highbrow academic climate? Well, a few hours, weeks, pints later with several similarly inclined students was all that was needed.

Even so, he emphasises, there was another key ingredient to his survival, namely:

> ... the quality of teaching I received. It would have been no good to me if the academics had delivered their expertise and then retreated to the study. I needed to be taught. Keith's great contribution for people like me was his appreciation that we were willing but needed guidance and structure. The lively seminars, the engineered debates, the thorough lecture outlines, the Wars of the Roses source booklets, gave people like me a chance. The enthusiasm, however, was in equal measure to his demand for commitment. I have taken on board that stratagem and made it a cornerstone of my own teaching. It was an important experience which shaped my own professional outlook.

Since leaving Huddersfield, in fact, Andrew Hook has enjoyed a very successful career teaching history in comprehensive schools in the midlands. So has his fellow student and close friend Neil Scott whose own background and memories of the polytechnic are strikingly similar:

> In September 1976 I was a very average student who had been taught by some very below average teachers. I had just endured two years of dictation on Social and Economic History 1700—1950 and was led to believe that history was a collection of facts where success depended on the ability to remember as many of them as possible. After two years of that, I still had little idea of what an interpretation (or a primary source) was. I was then introduced to medieval history by the Yorkshire Bastard! What a revelation! Each lecture started with a brief historiog-

raphy, followed by factionalism, rumour, skulduggery of every kind. I particularly remember the primary source packs which I continued to use in my own teaching for years. The fact that I quickly became totally absorbed by the later middle ages was down to the use of good materials and a teaching style that was both scholarly and entertaining. Most importantly, it was presented by someone who was totally committed to his students rather than some university lecturers who viewed them as a hindrance to their research.

Neil also recollected another student in his year who, in an essay for me on the origins of the English Civil War, recklessly suggested that 'all the historians' interpretations are bollocks, just to keep lecturers in jobs'; my response, apparently, was to fail the assignment with the comment 'intellectual thuggery does not make up for a total lack of knowledge'. Another member of my 1978/9 Special Subject group was Graham Townend, an exceptionally able working class lad from Leeds. Ironically, he had attended the same grammar school as Alan Bennett a quarter of a century earlier and, although it turned into a comprehensive during his time there, his memories of Leeds Modern (or Lawnswood as it became) are remarkably similar to those of the playwright. Unfortunately, his poor choice of A-Levels apart from history meant that, whereas Bennett went to Oxford University, Graham ended up at Huddersfield. He almost made a bad choice of Special Subject as well; indeed, I remember most unprofessionally warning him off the Second World War (an uninspiringly constructed and indifferently taught course) and urging him to tackle the Wars of the Roses instead. It paid off. He obtained a first class honours degree, went on to Edinburgh University and, a few years later, completed a Ph.D there. Certainly, he has exceptionally fond memories of 'the wonderful experience of studying history, particularly medieval history, at Huddersfield Polytechnic', not least my own teaching there in the later 1970s:

> Keith was an outstanding teacher of medieval history who brought the subject to life in a way that none of his colleagues was able to match. His lectures and seminars sparkled with energy and genuine excitement. It was a pleasure and a privilege to have him as a teacher during what, for me, was the most enjoyable experience I have had in higher education.

Several former colleagues at Huddersfield, too, have memories of my teaching and dealings with students during the 1970s. Keith Laybourn, for instance, recalls that:

> In your early years at Huddersfield you often gave the impression of being a

hard taskmaster, very demanding of students and almost uncompromising. You rightly stressed that students should always aspire to high standards in their work. However, as most of them soon realised, you were always willing to help those who had a genuine desire to learn.

'One of the things that students liked about you', echoes Tony Payne, 'was that you were quite disciplined with them in the sense that they always knew what they had to do to do well'; however, he adds, 'it mattered to you a lot to be popular with them, too, and you worked hard at that'. John O'Connell particularly remembers the 'theatricality' of my teaching style, my 'dramatic gestures' that made me 'an electrifying teacher', and concludes that I was 'an outstanding teacher in the histrionic mould'. Similarly, Peter Wood recalls:

> As a teacher you were always lively and enthusiastic. Your success owed something to your liking to be centre stage but I soon realised that behind your flamboyant delivery there was massive preparation, even down to a last minute rehearsal of lectures.

Steve Smith's verdict is interesting, not least since it's based on only a couple of years, 1976—1978:

> Keith was a fiercely intelligent man who loved his teaching. His students adored him. He was always making them laugh and learn. I loved working with him. He inspired generations to study history and, though he was sometimes criticised for teaching it as if all that mattered were kings and queens, he had a passion for his subject that was infectious and profoundly genuine.

Perhaps the final word on my first decade at Huddersfield should go to Tony Saul, who left the polytechnic in 1981:

> For many Keith was the best of all academic colleagues and there are some who learned more from him about the craft of the 'rounded' historian than they ever did in more formal learning contexts. He was generous in sharing material and teaching experience. His enthusiasm was infectious and his advice invaluable. He showed how the bright and hard-working student could be encouraged and enabled to develop. Less hard working students were given fewer places to hide than they might have liked. Many of his pupils owe their success in the academic and wider worlds to his challenge and inspiration.

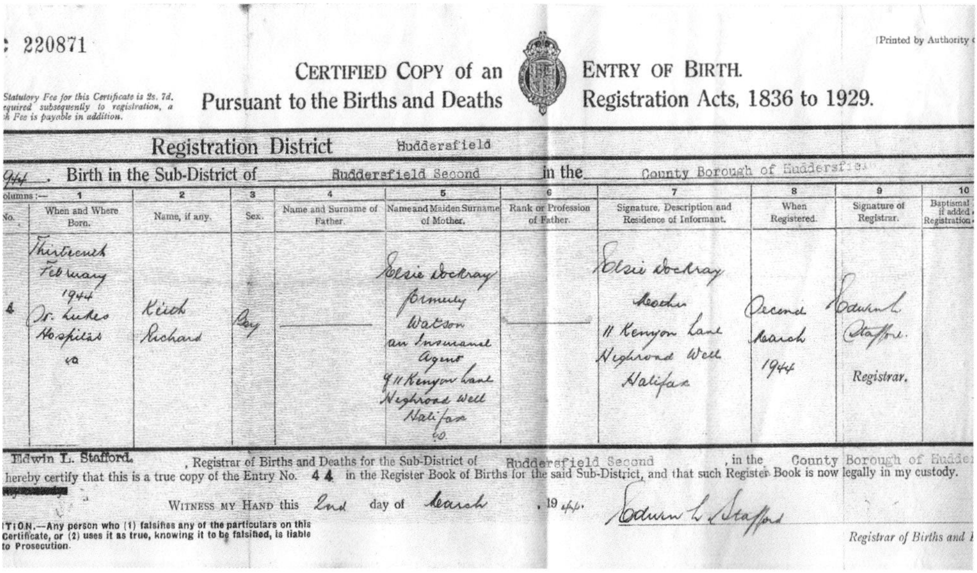

: 220871

[Printed by Authority

Statutory Fee for this Certificate is 2s. 7d. required subsequently to registration, a h Fee is payable in addition.

CERTIFIED COPY of an ENTRY OF BIRTH.
Pursuant to the Births and Deaths Registration Acts, 1836 to 1929.

Registration District Huddersfield

944. Birth in the Sub-District of Huddersfield Second in the County Borough of Huddersfie

olumns:— 1	1	2	3	4	5	6	7	8	9	10
No.	When and Where Born.	Name, if any.	Sex.	Name and Surname of Father.	Name and Maiden Surname of Mother.	Rank or Profession of Father.	Signature, Description and Residence of Informant.	When Registered.	Signature of Registrar.	Baptismal if added Registration
4	Thirteenth February 1944 St. Lukes Hospital	Keith Richard	Boy	————	Elsie Dockray formerly Watson an Insurance Agent 11 Kenyon Lane Highroad Well Halifax	————	Elsie Dockray Mother 11 Kenyon Lane Highroad Well Halifax	Second March 1944	Edwin L. Stafford. Registrar.	

Edwin L. Stafford, Registrar of Births and Deaths for the Sub-District of Huddersfield Second, in the County Borough of Hudde hereby certify that this is a true copy of the Entry No. 44 in the Register Book of Births for the said Sub-District, and that such Register Book is now legally in my custody.

WITNESS MY HAND this 2nd day of March, 1944. Edwin L. Stafford

Registrar of Births and

TION.—Any person who (1) falsifies any of the particulars on this Certificate, or (2) uses it as true, knowing it to be falsified, is liable to Prosecution.

1. KRD's birth certificate, establishing his credentials as a Yorkshire bastard.

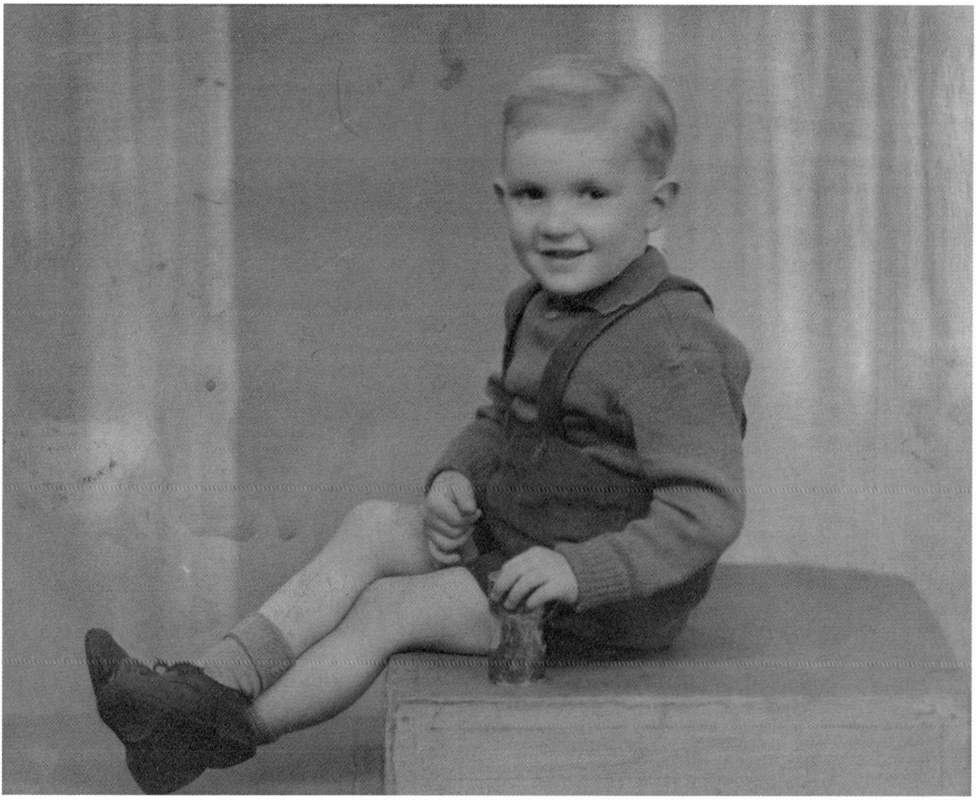

2. Earliest surviving photograph of KRD.

3. John Saunders, outside Huddersfield council house, Huddersfield, mid-1950s.

4. Actors Fred Ferris (left) and Trevor Maskell (right), with KRD (centre), outside Huddersfield Theatre Royal, June 1955.

5. Huddersfield College, October 1955.

6. Form lY, Huddersfield College, October 1955. Front row: 'Garry' Gowans; middle row: Roger Kitching (second from left), John Mack (third from right), KRD (first from right); back row: Michael Duke (sixth from left).

7. Staff, Huddersfield College, October 1955. Front row: Harold Richardson (second from left), 'Joss' Browning (fourth from left) A. R. Bielby (centre), Ted Darke (third from right3, 'Bessie' Baldick (first from right). Middle row: 'Benny' Barker (fourth from left), 'Garry' Gowans (fourth from right), Frank Oromondroyd (third from right). Back row: 'Ivor' Barron (first from left).

8. Yard containing Moldgreen house, Huddersfield, later 1950s.

9. KRD and Edith Wood, later 1950s.

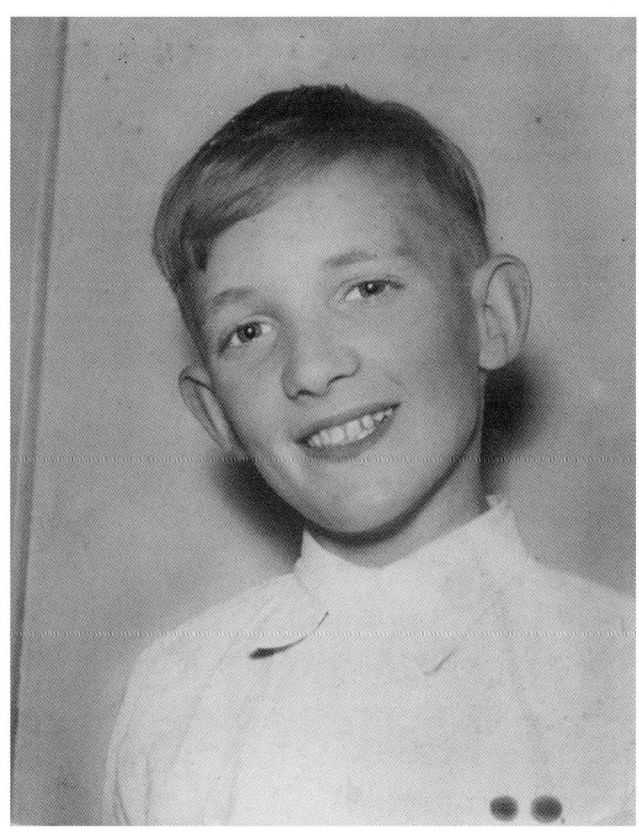

10. KRD, later 1950s.

11. 1.30pm 'Double Header' Newcastle to Liverpool express, arriving at Huddersfield station; later 1950s.

12. A4 Pacific ('Streak') locomotive, arriving at York station, later 1950s.

13. Upper Sixth Arts, Huddersfield New College, September 1961. Front row: KRD (first from left), John Mackay (third from left), Harold Richardson (centre). Back row: Bernard Jarvis (fourth from right).

14. Staff, Huddersfield New College, September 1961. Front row: 'Ivor' Barron (third from left), Michael Gillard (fifth from left), Ted Darke (seventh from left), A.R. Bielby (centre), Frank Oromondroyd (seventh from right), 'Garry' Gowans (fifth from right), Harold Richardson.(third from right). Middle row: Tony Hague (first from left), James Crump (fourth from left). Back row: Alan Thorpe (first from right), 'Benny' Barker (fifth from right).

15. Roger Kitching and KRD, 1962/3.

16. KRD as Charles VI of France in William Shakespeare's *Henry V*, Huddersfield New College, 1963.

17. Huddersfield New College State Scholars, *Huddersfield Examiner*, 1963: Jeremy Anscombe (left), KRD (centre) and W. S. Sheldrick (right).

18. Churchill Hall, Bristol University,1960/5. Front row: Michael Stammers (left), Ian Faulkner (right). Back row: KRD (left), Peter Allender (right).

19. KRD, student house, Bristol University, 1965/6.

20. KRD *en route* to student house, Bristol University, 1965/6.

21. Michael Stammers, student house, Bristol University, 1965/6.

22. Peter, Allender, student house, Bristol University, 1965/6.

23. Bernard Jarvis, student house, Bristol University, 1965/6.

24. Caricatures by Ian Faulkner, mid-1960s: KRD (left) and K. G. Davies (right).

25. KRD's Graduation Photograph, 1966.

26. Miriam Saunders (left), Edith Wood (centre) and KRD (right), later 1960s.

27. Patrick Scott (left) and KRD (right), *Hatchet* pub, Bristol, 1968.

28. Patrick Scott *Hatchet* pub, Bristol, 1968.

29. Alfred Josephson (left) and KRD (right), Cotham flat, Bristol, 1968.

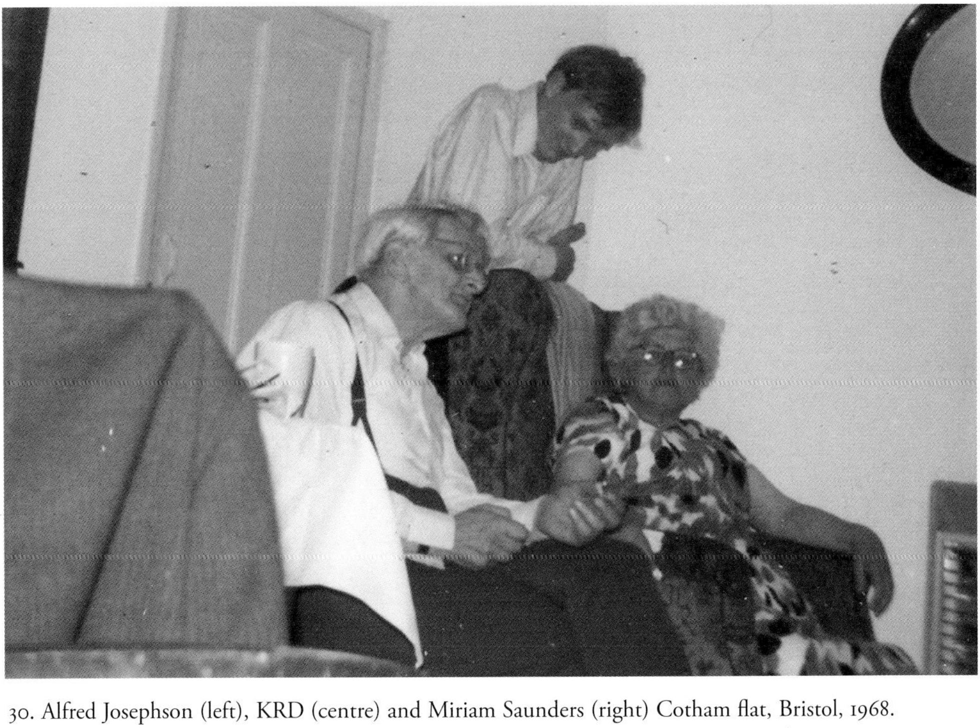

30. Alfred Josephson (left), KRD (centre) and Miriam Saunders (right) Cotham flat, Bristol, 1968.

31. Alfred Josephson (left), Edith Wood (centre) and Miriam Saunders (right), Cotham flat, 1968.

32. Charles Ross (left) and KRD (right), France, 1969.

33. KRD (left) and Charles Ross (right), France, 1969.

34. Charles Ross, France, 1969.

35. Plymouth College, 1970.

36. KRD, Colson House, Plymouth College, 1970.

37. KRD, Colson House, Plymouth College, 1970

8. Curtain call, *The Happiest Days of Your Life*, Plymouth College, 1971: Chris Robinson (first from left), Mike Allen (second from left), Dennis Collinson (fourth from left), Doug Martin (fifth from left), Ivor Cleeves (fourth from right) and KRD (third from right).

39. Post-production party, *The Happiest Days of Your Life*, Plymouth College, 1971. Front row: Chris Robinson (centre), back row: John Arthur (first from left), Ivor Cleeves (fifth from left), KRD, (seventh from left), Mike Allen (third from right).

40. Miriam Saunders (left) Patrick Scott (centre) and Edith Wood (right) outside Moldgreen house, Huddersfield, early 1970s.

41. Miriam Saunders (left), KRD (centre) and Edith Wood (right), outside Moldgreen. house, Huddersfield, early 1970s.

42. Elsie Dockray, Newsome house, Huddersfield, later 1970s.

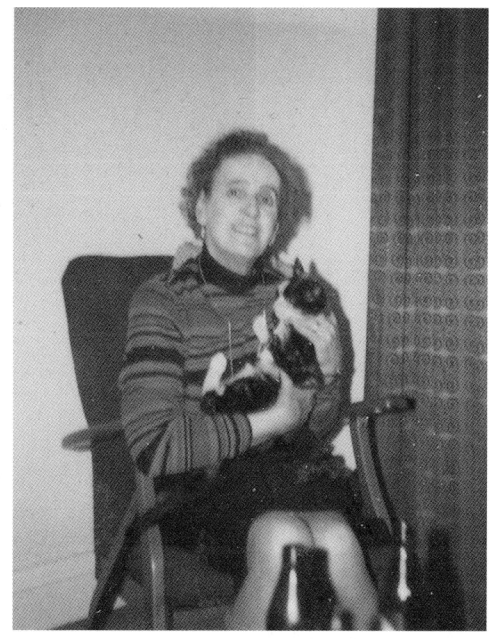

43. Elsie Dockray and Puss Puss, Newsome house, Huddersfield, later 1970s.

44. Edith Wood (left), Tony Dockray (centre) and Miriam Saunders (right), Newsome house, Huddersfield, later 1970s.

45. Tony Saul (left), John O'Connell (centre) and Peter Durrans (right), later 1970s.

46. Peter Wood (first from left), John O'Connell (second from right) and Peter Durrans (first from right), later 1970s.

47. Peter Durrans (second from left), Keith Laybourn (third from left) and Pauline Stafford (second from right), later 1970s.

48. Nancy Alexander (first from left) John O'Connell (second from right) and Pauline Stafford (first from right), later 1970s.

49. Darrolyn Lowe (first from left) and Alison Shaw (centre), later 1970s.

50. Special Subject group, Middleham Castle, 1979: KRD (first from left), Andy Hook (second from right) and Graham Townend (lying on wall, first from right).)

51. Special Subject group, Middleham Castle, 1979: Graham Townend (lying in front), Andy Hook (second from left) and Neil Scott (first from right).

52. KRD wearing a Campaign for Homosexual Equality badge, party at Newsome house, Huddersfield, November 1979.

53. KRD (left), Vivienne Haley (centre) and Peter Durrans (right), *Coach House* club, Huddersfield, December 1979.

54. KRD and Hazel Durrans, Newsome house, Huddersfield, January 1980.

55. Puss Puss, January 1980.

56. Edith Wood (left), KRD (centre) and Miriam Saunders (right), *Fountain* pub, Newsome, Huddersfield, March 1980.

57. History and Political Studies Department, Huddersfield Polytechnic, 1980. Front row: Peter Wood (second from left), Pauline Stafford (third from left), John, O' Connell (centre), Nancy Alexander (third from right), Bill Roberts (second from right), Brendan Evans (first from right). Middle row: Philip Woodfine (first from left), Peter Durrans (second from left), Tony Saul (third from left), David Wright (centre), Bill Stafford (second from right), Keith Laybourn (first from right). Back row: Steve O'Loughlin (first from left), Tony Payne (second from left), Andrew Taylor (third from left), KRD (third from right), Robert Perks (second from right).

58. Peter Allender and KRD, Bristol, early 1980s.

OXFORD UNION 1823-1983

Friday 4th November 8·15pm

That Richard III was more sinned against than sinning

Rosalind Nicholson — Magdalen

Nicholas O'Brien — Merton

Keith Dockray

Julian Lloyd — President Cambridge Union

Jeremy Potter — Queens, author of 'Good King Richard?'

Dr A J Pollard

HRH Richard Duke of Gloucester

Desmond Seward — author of 'England's Black Legend'

Tellers

Ayes
Richard Warren
Christ Church

Noes
Nicholas Botterill
Christ Church

59. Oxford Union Debate on Richard III, Oxford University, November 1983.

60. Stratford-upon-Avon, July 1984: Lloyd Powell (front), Martin Holmes (first from left), David Matthieson (second from left), KRD (second from right), Mark Munday (first from right).

61. Last photograph of Edith Wood (left), KRD (centre) and Miriam Saunders (right), Newsome house, Huddersfield, April 1985.

62. Graduation Day, Huddersfield Polytechnic, 1985: Peter Wood (first from left), Bill Roberts (second from left), Robert Perks (third from left), Keith Laybourn (fourth from left), Philip Woodfine (fourth from right), Tony Payne (third from right), Brendan Evans (second from right), KRD (first from right).

63. Richard Bell (with Laurel and Hardy!), 1990/1.

4. Snubby, Bristol house, August 1991.

65 Snitch, Bristol house, August 1991.

66. Graduation Day, Huddersfield Polytechnic, 1991: Keith Laybourn (left), Brendan Evans (centre) and KRD (right).

67. University of Huddersfield.

68. Steve Garrett and KRD, Bristol house, 1992.

69. Peter Allender and KRD, Bristol house, 1992.

70. Brendan Evans and KRD, joint 50th birthday party, Newsome house, Huddersfield, March 1994.

71. Bill Stafford (left), Tony Saul (centre) and Pauline Stafford (right), 50th birthday party, March 1994.

72. Peter Durrans (first from left), Bill Stafford (second from left) and Andrew Taylor (fifth from left), 50th birthday party, March 1994.

73. Keith Laybourn (left) and Brendan Evans (right), 50th birthday party, March 1994.

74. Kit Hardwick (first from right) and Peter Davies (third from right), 50th birthday party, March 1994.

75. David Taylor, 50th birthday party, March 1994.

76. Hazel Durrans (second from left) and Peter Allender (third from left), 50th birthday party, March 1994.

77. Graduation Day, Huddersfield University, 1994; Steve Garrett (third from left), Barry Goodwin (fourth from left), KRD (fifth from left), Philip Hastie (fourth from right), Dean Southam (third from right).

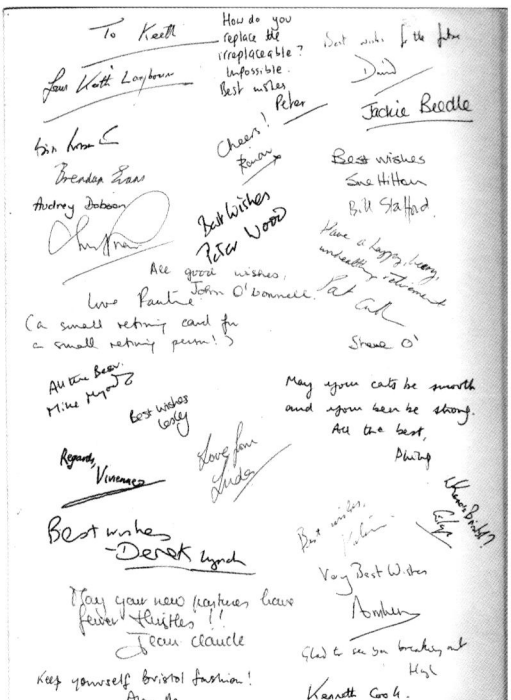

78., 79. and 80. KRD's retirement card, Huddersfield University, 1994.

81. *Representation and Reality of War*, book launch, *Albert* pub, Huddersfield, May 1999: Tony Saul (first from left), Peter Durrans (second from left), Keith Laybourn (third from left), Hazel Durrans (third from right), KRD (second from right), Michael Bartholomew (first from right), Bill Stafford (front).

82. *Representation and Reality of War*, book launch, Huddersfield, May 1999: Bill Roberts (first from left), Jan Roberts (second from left), Tony Saul (centre), Rosemary Saul (second from right), John O'Connell (first from right).

83. *Representation and Reality of War*, book launch, Huddersfield, May 1999: KRD and Hazel Durrans.

84. Peter Allender (left), KRD (centre) and Alan Sutton (right), Chinon, France, July 2000.

85. Alan Sutton (left), KRD (centre) and Peter Allender (right), Tours, France, July 2000.

86. KRD (left) and Peter Fleming (right), contemplating the battlefield of Nibley Green, July 2001.

87. Peter Fleming (left), KRD (centre) and an archer, Nibley Green battlefield, July 2001.

88. Fifteenth-century conference, University of the West of England, September 2001.
Front row: Linda Clark (first from left), Alan Sutton (second from left), Tony Pollard (third from left), Anne Crawford (second from right), Rowena Archer (first from right). Back row: KRD (first from left), Margaret Condon (second from left), Ralph Griffiths (third from left), Diana Dunn (fourth from left), Michael Jones (second from right), Michael Hicks (first from right).

89. Reunion of 1966 Bristol English and History graduates, Bristol, July 2002: Bernard Jarvis (first from left), KRD (second from right), Peter Allender (first from right), Michael Stammers (front).

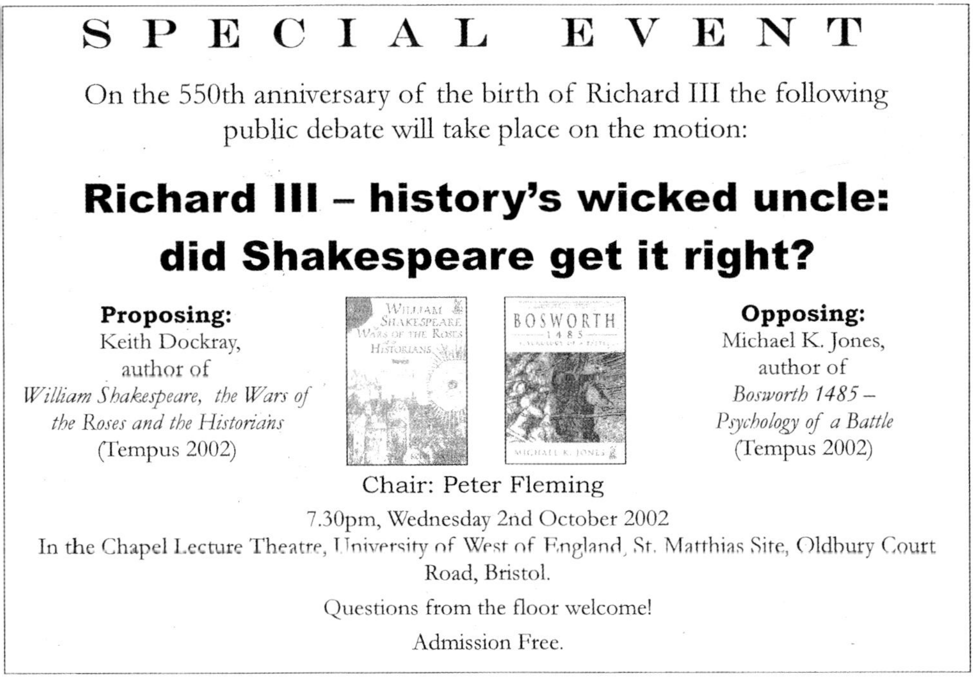

SPECIAL EVENT

On the 550th anniversary of the birth of Richard III the following public debate will take place on the motion:

Richard III – history's wicked uncle: did Shakespeare get it right?

Proposing:
Keith Dockray,
author of
William Shakespeare, the Wars of the Roses and the Historians
(Tempus 2002)

Opposing:
Michael K. Jones,
author of
Bosworth 1485 – Psychology of a Battle
(Tempus 2002)

Chair: Peter Fleming
7.30pm, Wednesday 2nd October 2002
In the Chapel Lecture Theatre, University of West of England, St. Matthias Site, Oldbury Court Road, Bristol.
Questions from the floor welcome!
Admission Free.

90. Richard III Debate, University of the West of England, October 2002.

91. 'Black Stanier' locomotive, Severn Valley Railway, 2003.

92. Smoky, 2004.

93. KRD's final public performance, University of the West of England, December 2004.

94. KRD, towards the end of an extended session in the *Sportsman* and *Annexe* pubs, Bristol, 2005.

95. KRD (left) and Roger Kitching (right), August 2007.

96. KRD (left) and Roger Kitching (right), August 2007.

97. KRD (left) and Peter Allender (right), August 2007.

98. KRD (left) and Steve Gould (right), discussing the typescript of *Memoirs of a Yorkshire Bastard*, *Annexe* garden, 9 August 2007.

99. Debbie Gwilym (left), KRD (centre) and Lyn Sheppard (right), discussing the typescript of *Memoirs of a Yorkshire Bastard*, *Annexe* garden, August 2007.

100. *Annexe* garden, August 2007: Neil Wellman (front), Mark Jones (first from left), Marisa Stevens (second from left), Keith Tucker (third from left), Alan Stevens (fourth from left), (fifth from left), Lyn Sheppard (fourth from right), Steve Gould (third from right), Debbie Gwilym (second from right), Dave Moore (first from right).

9

Huddersfield Polytechnic/ University Lecturer

Throughout the later 1970s endemic financial problems and overstaffing, exacerbated by the behaviour of Huddersfield Polytechnic's director Kenneth Durrands and his henchmen, had bedevilled relations between the institution and its controlling local authority Kirklees Metropolitan Council, eventually culminating in a full-scale crisis. This was only resolved when, in 1981, Kirklees undertook to finance a major early retirement/redundancy package, resulting in the departure of signicant numbers of older staff (among them no fewer than six heads of department). Internal reorganisation also meant that history and politics were now subsumed into a large and unwieldy Department of Humanities, one of twenty new departments spread over five faculties, with John O'Connell as departmental head and, before long, dean of faculty. Closer to home, as far as I was concerned, was Tony Saul's departure for the CNAA, his non-replacement and the resulting need for Pauline Stafford and I to revamp our teaching and courses. Even so, in the early 1980s (and, indeed, for the rest of my career at Huddersfield), I continued to maintain a low profile in an institution still wracked by internal conflicts and on-going battles between its directorate, board of governors and the local authority. During the later 1980s, however, both Kirklees and the Council for National Academic Awards became increasingly irrelevant as Margaret Thatcher's Conservative government enabled polytechnics to obtain more and more autonomy. As a result, in February 1988, Huddersfield Polytechnic began validating its own first degree courses and, in April 1989, the institution was granted corporate status. This was by no means a painless process. Decision-making power became even more concentrated in the hands of the polytechnic's directorate than before, a mixed blessing to say the least. Growing independence, moreover, brought new financial problems and the need, once again, to cut staff numbers. This culminated, at the end of the spring term 1989, in the biggest exodus of senior staff (including, this time, John O'Connell) since 1981. At the same time, under mounting government pressure to extend access to higher education, student numbers rose steadily, reaching about 8000 by the end of the 1980s; moreover, since history and politics experienced few difficulties in recruiting 'bums on seats', we took on more than our fair share, not least me. As early as October 1984 in a letter to Robin Storey (professor of medieval history at Nottingham University), indeed, I reported ruefully on my very heavy teaching timetable, amounting to some seventeen hours a week. Our recruitment potential was increased still further in 1989 when we inaugurated a new BA (Historical and Political Studies) degree. Soon afterwards, as a result of another round of academic reorganisation in the polytechnic transforming twenty departments in five faculties into nine schools, we also became part of a School of Music and Humanities under the deanship of Brendan Evans.

The impact of rising student numbers is nicely reflected in Richard Bell's memories of his first year as a BA (Humanities) student:

> By 1988, at the age of twenty, I had developed a deep interest in history and had heard that the history department at Huddersfield was highly regarded. I became increasingly disappointed during my first year (1988/9), however, as I came to feel that all we were there for was to make up numbers in order to satisfy the Thatcher government's policy of cramming as many students as possible into the system. It had all the flavour of a conveyer belt of learning by rote.

Interesting, too, is Richard Davies's penultimate report, as external examiner in History, in July 1990. 'I am sad', he declared, that the Huddersfield history staff:

> ... seem to become fewer each year and, whilst I am delighted to note the important publications that several have made in the last academic session, I wonder very seriously how long they can maintain this contribution to the country's scholarship as well as what is clearly an impressive and popular teaching contribution to the polytechnic's programme. Huddersfield stands in the first rank of polytechnics and, if it were to claim university status, the History Department has been, and remains, a jewel in its crown. At the moment the department stands in the very unusual position of having eager, energetic scholars who also happen to like students and obviously get an appropriately eager response; they are cheerful and full of enthusiasm about their students, courses and personal research; and they do not make conversation by whingeing about their lot.

Nevertheless, declared this accomplished fifteenth-century historian (himself at Manchester University):

> I feel very strongly that I must not wait for their prompting before I warn the polytechnic that it should not rejoice in such stamina, still less load on yet more pressure. It is one thing to build on such strengths, quite another to overload them. The Huddersfield staff will doubtless see me out next year with their habitual high standards, personal integrity and generous nature. I do not want my successor to have to face a crisis.

This warning, unfortunately, fell on deaf ears.

Although, by the time it became a university in 1992, the polytechnic's finances had at last been placed on a reasonably sound footing, student numbers continued to grow inexorably in the early 1990s. In 1991/2 alone there was a 16% rise, resulting in a total student population of over 10,000. Compared with an average annual increase of about 4% over the previous twenty years, this amounted to a veritable explosion in student enrolment and, inevitably, also resulted in mounting accommodation problems. As early as December 1990 I declared, in a letter to Ralph Griffiths (professor of medieval history at the University of Wales, Swansea), that 'Huddersfield Polytechnic is, as always, awful, and getting worse'. In October 1991 I wrote to him even more gloomily:

> ... we're now in the second week of term: 160 students studying history in Year 1 and I also have 30 in Year 2, 15 in Year 3 and 5 MA students, giving me a personal student/staff ratio of 27:1.

In another letter, this time despatched from Bristol to my dean of school Brendan Evans in August 1992, I specifically remarked on the 'mounting horrors of the University of Huddersfield', expressing the hope that he had now recovered from what even I found 'the most stressful academic year ever'. And, in October 1993, I wrote to Tony Pollard at the University of Teesside:

> ... we come to the end of the second week of term amidst more chaos than I ever remember: far too many students, not enough rooms big enough to hold them, and appalling bureaucratic bungles such as grossly inaccurate student lists. We've even had to hire the theatre in Huddersfield Arts Centre to accommodate some first year lectures. Any lingering doubts I had about applying for early retirement at the end of this academic year have certainly been dispelled over the last few days. Appropriately, the university has just acquired the local lunatic asylum and, no doubt, we'll be high on the list of departments to be sent there. They won't need to declare a change of use!

By then Huddersfield had been a university for over a year, a change of status I had greeted with no enthusiasm whatever, rightly fearing its serious implications for the future balance of priority between teaching and research in the institution. Inevitably, the transition had been accompanied by a vigorous debate about what name we should adopt but, sadly, my mischievous suggestion to Brendan Evans that the new university be called First University College Kirklees (FUCK) never became a contender; instead, more mundanely, we became the University of Huddersfield.

During 1992 and 1993 my irritation about the way higher education was evolving mounted steadily. So did gloom about Huddersfield University and my future prospects/role there. Student numbers continued to rise, as did the relentless tide of managerialism. This manifested itself most intrusively in increasing emphasis on the need for quality assessment of lecturers, not only annual staff appraisals but also moves to promote regular observation and evaluation of classroom teaching. Insofar as I could, I ignored such developments and resisted, in particular, any attempt to interfere with how I chose to deliver lectures and conduct seminars/tutorials. I certainly wasn't prepared to listen to senior staff (particularly educationalists) whose promotion had often owed little or nothing to their teaching skills; indeed, so it seemed to me, many of them lacked both charisma and any real empathy with students. Fortunately, since both my second and third year BA (Historical and Political Studies) options were invariably over-subscribed and student feedback on my teaching often embarrassingly complimentary, I got away with it. David Taylor (now head of history and, as the absurd new jargon of the early 1990s dubbed him, my line manager) and Brendan Evans (dean of school) knew perfectly well that I was one of the most popular and successful history lecturers anyway, so they were happy enough to leave me alone. Nor did I relish the ever greater emphasis on research, an inevitable consequence (now we were a university) of the need to attract additional funding dependent on external assessments of the quantity and quality of staff publications. New appointments also became increasingly linked to this Research Assessment Exercise, so it seemed very unlikely that my equivalent would ever be offered a full-time job again. Since all the historians at Huddersfield were active on the research front, even me to a limited extent, in 1992/3 our seven full-time and 0.6 part-time staff obtained a very creditable rating; indeed, as there were now less of us, and more students to teach, than at any time during my years there, it verged on the miraculous. Positive financial consequences soon followed. When I wrote to Bernard Alford (professor of economic history at Bristol University) in July 1993, I reported:

> We seem to be awash with money at Huddersfield for the first time in years. The history/politics department here has recently been given clearance to make four

new appointments, as well as being granted a generous part-time hours budget for the 1993/4 academic year. No doubt the powers that be have been shamed into it by the fact that we got the best research ranking in history of any of the ex-polytechnics (despite operating, this year, at a student/staff ratio of almost 30:1).

The most obvious benefit to Pauline Stafford and myself was the appointment of Patricia Cullum as an additional medieval/ early modern historian and, during my final year at Huddersfield in 1993/4, the cash to employ two former mature students (Cliff Burhouse and Kit Hardwick) to help bear the burden of first year medieval seminars/tutorials. Yet, for me, our success in the Research Assessment Exercise seemed a distinctly mixed blessing. Not all the extra funding we had generated found its way back to us but, nevertheless, we were expected to perform even better on the research/publication front next time round. This put pressure on history staff to devote even more time to churning out monographs and archive-based articles for learned journals since it was just this sort of dry-as-dust history that carried most weight. It wasn't what I wanted to write at all. Nor had I any desire to obtain a sabbatical term, a rare luxury during our polytechnic days but now, as we became more research-orientated, increasingly available. Even if I did apply for and get one, I suspected, my research time would probably be devoted more to quaffing real ale than deciphering fifteenth-century manuscripts. Several features of our new BA (Historical and Political Studies) degree weren't much to my taste either, most notably a compulsory 'Skills Unit' students had to take in their first year and the requirement that they undertake 'Work Experience' in the final term of their second. All my history/ politics colleagues, however, seemed to welcome university status and Bill Roberts, for one, is notably up-beat about the early 1990s at Huddersfield:

> Obviously, inadequate funding and over-bureaucratisation threatened students' education in the broadest sense but the way we taught larger numbers had real merit. Huddersfield was never going to offer an Oxbridge experience but we organised our teaching well and, in our different ways (some, like you, doing the charismatic stuff, others adopting a more inclusive style), encouraged students both to think and write effectively.

'For all your own ever-growing fury at the direction higher education was taking', he adds, 'you carried on teaching just as you always had'. True enough but, by the end of 1993, I had become determined to get out of full-time lecturing if I possibly could in 1994.

The scope and content of my courses changed considerably in the 1980s and early 1990s, reflecting greater knowledge of and enthusiasm for some themes/topics, lessening interest in others, and factors beyond my control altogether. Most importantly, Tony Saul's departure at the end of the 1980/1 academic year, and his non-replacement, meant that for more than a decade Pauline Stafford and I were the only medievalists at Huddersfield. This had obvious implications for our teaching on the BA (Humanities) degree, not least at first year level, and we now seized the opportunity to shorten the chronological span of *Medieval to Modern*, narrow the scope of its content (most satisfactorily, as far as I was concerned, by jettisoning later medieval French political history) and restructure the course into three sections: English Kings, Politics and War c.1307—1509 (for which I wrote a brand new set of lectures); Society and Economic Change c.1300—1500 (Pauline); and the Italian Renaissance (Pauline) and Pre-Reformation Church (me). Even more overtly than before, lectures were designed to provide a stimulating introduction/ overview and, particularly, cover topics to be followed up in seminars/tutorials focussing on primary source material and the examination of current historical controversies. Pauline and I continued to teach seminars/tutorials across the board and, since this might involve taking as many as five or six classes on the same topic per fortnight, it was a great relief to both of us when, after a year or two, Philip Woodfine volunteered to shoulder some of the burden. When the BA (Historical and Political Studies) degree came on stream in 1989 we made sure a compulsory first year later medieval course (renamed *The Last Centuries of the Middle Ages*) was retained. At the same time we brought in further changes to its content, mainly in order to reflect Pauline's ever deepening interest in and knowledge of women's history. Out went almost all the economic history (much to my relief), the Italian Renaissance (I was rather sad about that) and, in 1992/3, the Pre-Reformation Church as well. As a result, during my last couple of years at Huddersfield, our attention came to focus entirely on Later Medieval English Kings, Politics and War and Continuity and Change in Society during the fourteenth and fifteenth centuries. This further slimming down of scope and content allowed us to explore topics we enjoyed teaching in greater depth than before and students clearly benefited considerably.

Throughout the 1980s and early 1990s, as in the 1970s, I continued to give top priority to countering the negative impact of uninspired teaching new students might have encountered at school. Even more importantly, I remained as determined as ever to get them to enjoy both the intellectual challenge of later medieval history and the fact that it was great fun to study. Hence the amount of time and effort I put into first year teaching. Joanna Cole, who became a BA (Humanities) student at Huddersfield in the autumn of 1986, recalls:

> On my arrival at the polytechnic I attended an introductory lecture to the history course given by Keith. Both I and my fellow students were fascinated by him and

his ability to bring the subject to life as he paced backwards and forwards along the front of the lecture theatre, flapping his arms around enthusiastically. I was hooked and remained so for the whole of my time on the course.

A mature student Cliff Burhouse who, after a career in industry, decided to try his hand at an arts degree, similarly recollects:

> I first met Keith in September 1988 when I enrolled at the then Huddersfield Polytechnic Humanities department. Intending to study English (with History), I attended the fifteen minute presentations by lecturers who explained their particular syllabuses before we started our courses: Philosophy, Politics, Drama, English. Then came History. In stalked this rangy individual in a cloud of cigarette smoke giving a first impression of great energy. The performance which followed was explosive, as he prowled back and forth, waved his arms and laughed loudly with shaking shoulders. He completely won me over. From that moment I reversed my intentions and decided to major in History (with English). I think I would have studied flower arranging if he had offered it!

'Throughout my time at the polytechnic', he adds, 'I looked forward to his lectures and enjoyed them more than any others; moreover, his generous encouragement helped enormously to dispel my fear of failure, natural enough in a fifty-eight year old changing course after a lifetime in industry'. Richard Bell, who also arrived at the polytechnic in September 1988, was particularly struck by the contrast between me and his A-Level history teacher:

> I remember meeting you in my first year and, although the classes were enormous and unwieldy, you nevertheless managed to keep us interested and entertained. After studying in my local sixth form, where my tutor's idea of teaching was to read aloud to the class *verbatim* from E. L. Woodward's Oxford History of England volume *The Age of Reform 1815—1870*, you can imagine the impression your teaching style made on me! You were never still behind the desk, stalking to and fro with that awkward jerkiness which would become so familiar, and your rich voice had an intense, almost theatrical, quality. It came as no surprise to me when I learned, later, of your deep love for the works of Gilbert and Sullivan.

For Peter Broome, whom I taught between 1991 and 1994:

> One lecturer at Huddersfield stood out: the eccentric Keith Dockray. He always told us how it was and was honest about his teaching, even warning us once that the lecture he was about to give was crap because he hadn't updated it in ten

years. Yet, in fact, his lectures and tutorials—straightforward, to the point and funny—were outstanding.

And Steve Garrett, another student at Huddersfield during my last few years there, remembers:

> I first saw Keith in the autumn of 1990. He was seated in a corner of the *College Arms*. As a first year undergraduate studying transport and distribution I didn't know him but certainly knew of him. He was widely admired by students at Huddersfield mainly because he broke down the barriers between staff and students.

In the autumn of 1991 Steve switched to history and, so he tells me, it was my 'infectious enthusiasm for fifteenth-century politics' that:

> ... reignited a thirst for historical knowledge in me. I had lost this in the quagmire of nineteenth-century British social and economic studies at A-Level—the main reason why I had ended up studying transport and distribution! Keith gave me back the desire to read good history for pleasure. The essays and exams then became an exciting challenge rather than a task, and it was Keith who inspired me to obtain a first class honours degree and teach the subject myself—an achievement mirrored by so many of his students.

First year lectures were clearly crucial here, as several former students have reminded me, including Richard Bell:

> In your lectures you would be in a world of your own, spewing out all the history at a rate of knots almost too fast to record. I'd take my eyes off you for a second at the point when your head was bobbing down at your notes and, quick as a flash, you'd have spun round and be half way through a name on the blackboard when I next looked up. Then you'd crack a joke and your shoulders would heave up and down as you snorted out a laugh.

Not that my lectures always went to plan, at any rate early on, as Vivienne Haley recalls from her first year in 1977/8:

> Keith's prowling backwards and forwards was seen to best effect when he warmed to his subject teaching in one of the big lecture halls at Huddersfield. Wide enough, with flights of steps at each side, he could expend great amounts of energy marching around, even venturing up the stairs, checking his lecture

notes at the end of each pass. Higher and higher he climbed as the story he told unfolded, and further and further from his notes, until inevitably, one day, he forgot his lines and had to gallop down nearly the entire flight in order to find out what came next.

Occasionally, too, even I failed to hold the attention of all the students, particularly as numbers of first years relentlessly rose in the later 1980s and early 1990s. Indeed, on one occasion, I became aware that a couple of them were enjoying an animated whispered conversation. I deliberately broke off in mid-sentence, caught the attention of the entire room, and invited them to take over since, presumably, they knew more about the subject than I did. Acutely embarrassed, they hastily declined my offer, amidst considerable hilarity from the rest of the audience. I was never distracted again!

Now and again, we allowed mature students at Huddersfield to commence their degree studies at second level. Just such an entrant was Kit Hardwick, a semi-retired businessman, who became a BA (Historical and Political Studies) student in September 1990 and enrolled on my early modern course. He vividly recalls why:

> After taking a course in local history at York I had come to two conclusions. The first, that I wanted to do a degree, and the second, that I wanted to know more about the fifteenth century. While browsing through the history shelves in a bookshop, I was amazed to find a collection of late medieval letters, *The Plumpton Correspondence*, with an introduction by some guy at my local polytechnic. That settled it. A few months later I found myself sitting in a classroom with the same guy about to start lecturing me on Tudor history. My first impression of this tall, larger-than-life academic prowling to and fro behind a long desk as he surveyed us, a mixed group of some twenty or so students, was that he was a sort of Floyd on history; moreover, the comparison with the extrovert west country TV chef, raconteur and all-round boozer turned out to be remarkably prescient in view of what I was to discover about Keith over the years that followed.

Kit was probably lucky to get a place on my second year course at all. In the early 1980s, when I didn't set limits on numbers, I frequently ended up with uncomfortably large groups for a course I now taught entirely on my own. By the later 1980s, aware of the fact that one or two of my modern history colleagues were recruiting fewer 'bums on seats' than me, I put a maximum of twenty-four on it. After all, there were several nineteenth/ twentieth century specialists, whereas I was the only early modern lecturer. Even so, if individuals pleaded with me, I almost always let them on. Jo Cole didn't realise this in 1987.

'It was only because I was desperate to get on Keith's Year 2 course', she recollects, 'that I made history my major at all'; however, she continues ruefully:

> ... due to his popularity as a lecturer his second year course was over-subscribed almost immediately and I missed out on the chance to study under him that year. I was in awe of many of the lecturers and followed the rules and instructions we were given to the letter. Consequently, when I was told his course was full and I hadn't been successful, I took that to be it.

'I had no idea then that I could have grovelled to you', she adds, but 'if I had known I would have been on my hands and knees immediately'. Richard Bell, who was more fortunate in 1989, has a splendidly evocative memory of the experience:

> The lectures and seminars you gave in the second year were always stimulating if, sometimes, frightening. I remember one bleary-eyed morning seminar—why did they have to start at such an unspeakable hour as 9.15am? —when everyone was unusually unresponsive. You'd tried, several times, to draw out of us the month when the Long Parliament first sat in 1640; your eyes then fixed on me and I blurted out 'November'; and, although I wasn't sure if it was right, it seemed to satisfy you.

Like Richard, I also disliked early morning seminars and, particularly if I had a hangover, it didn't take too much to try my patience. In extremis, when confronted by ignorance and silence rather than well-informed discussion, I occasionally resorted to the FOFO stratagem: 'Fuck Off and Find Out'. Even better, in the early 1990s, I managed to get both my second and third year courses scheduled to run in the evenings.

Tony Saul's departure in 1981 had presented Pauline Stafford and I with a real dilemma as far as second year teaching was concerned. Should we abandon early modern history, or not? Pauline had no desire to teach post-1500 and I was loath to relinquish the central middle ages. Yet it would have been foolish indeed to cease offering a course on the sixteenth and seventeenth centuries, a popular period with students, and it would also have left my third year option for history minors, *Yorkshire and the Civil War*, very much out on a limb. So, reluctantly, I dropped off *The Making of the Middle Ages* in order to take sole responsibility for a revamped course *Politics, Reformation and Revolution in Britain and Western Europe*. Even though I had a set of lectures covering Stuart political history and historiography, and Tony Saul bequeathed me photocopies of all his on later Tudor England and Western Europe c.1550—1714, the amount of new work required proved considerable. Although I certainly drew on Tony's lectures, his interests weren't always mine and, so, I eventually settled for examining just three central and inter-related themes in British and Western European history, pushed back the course's start date to c.1520, and chose to end it in c.1660. My three themes were carefully chosen, as much to conceal my ignorance of early modern Europe as anything else: Personality, Politics and the Pursuit of Power (covering the differing reputations, aptitudes and achievements of rulers such as the Emperor Charles V, Francis I of France and Philip II of Spain and, more comfortably, Henry VIII, Elizabeth I, James I, Charles I and Oliver Cromwell in England); the Reformation (highlighting Protestant and Catholic reform in Germany, Switzerland, France and England during the sixteenth century, especially the roles of men like Martin Luther, Ulrich Zwingli, John Calvin and Ignatius Loyola, and the impact of religious reform on Western European society); and War, Rebellion and Revolution (concentrating on the causes, nature and significance of war and rebellion in the sixteenth and early seventeenth centuries, with particular attention to Tudor rebellions, the French Wars of Religion and the Thirty Years War). This new course culminated in a study in some depth of the historiography, causes and nature of the English Revolution c.1640—1660 and, even more than before, I structured lectures and seminars around primary source material. Truth to tell, I always felt a bit of a fraud teaching sixteenth and early seventeenth-century European history, not least since I made little effort to keep abreast of recent research, and it was certainly a relief when, one year, the eminent early modern historian Anthony Fletcher (who stepped in as external ecaminer at the last minute) was very complimentary about the course, how it had been taught and the quality of both student assignments and examination performance. Gradually, as the years went by, the English history content of the course increased and, when the BA (Historical and Political Studies) degree came on stream at the end of the 1980s, I took the opportunity to ditch Western Europe entirely. For a couple of years I then taught two separate modules (*Politics, Reformation and Society in Tudor England 1485—1603* and *The English Revolution 1603—1660*), eventually combining them, in 1992/3, as *Politics, Reformation and Revolution in Tudor and Early Stuart England*: Henry VII, Henry VIII and the Origins of the English Reformation c.1485—1536; Politics, Religion and Society c.1536—1603; James I, Charles I and the Origins of the English Revolution c.1603—1640; and the English Revolution c.1640—1660. During her first and my final year at Huddersfield (1993/4), moreover, Patricia Cullum had the misfortune of having to share the course with me; she took over the lectures on religious themes (handling them far more sympathetically than I ever had); and we split the seminar burden between us.

What I most enjoyed at Huddersfield in the 1980s and early 1990s was teaching third year courses and, even better, getting to know my students well both in the classroom and, not infrequently, socially as well. In the early 1980s I continued to offer *Yorkshire and the Civil War*, a course for minor history students that first came on stream in 1977/8 and ran for the last time in 1984/5. This twelve week module very much reflected my growing enthusiasm for evaluating, and teaching, literary sources, as well as my shared belief with C. V. Wedgwood (an eminent twentieth century historian of seventeenth-century England) that 'the behaviour of men as individuals is more interesting than their behaviour as groups or classes'. It came about when I discovered there was a series of particularly rich narrative sources available for seventeenth-century Yorkshire history in general, and the early 1640s in particular, and I devoted several months in 1976/7 to putting together a substantial collection of passages from contemporary and near-contemporary histories, memoirs, diaries, letters and records. The Royalist Edward Hyde Earl of Clarendon, for instance, included much interesting (if not always reliable) coverage of Yorkshire society and events in the county during the 1630s and 1640s in his mammoth *History of the Rebellion and Civil Wars in England*. The motives, behaviour and achievements of William Cavendish Duke of Newcastle, Royalist commander in the north for much of the early part of the civil war, are presented for our admiration by his wife Margaret in her *Life* of her husband. The bravery, integrity and considerable eye for detail of Sir Henry Slingsby, a distinguished Yorkshire gentleman and dedicated Royalist, make his diary an invaluable source for c.1638—1648. Sir Hugh Cholmley of Whitby, a prominent opponent of Charles I's government in 1640/1 who ended up as Royalist governor of Scarborough, composed valuable memoirs of his experiences in order to justify his conduct to his family. The Parliamentarian general Thomas Lord Fairfax, second-in-command to his father Ferdinando during the northern campaigns of 1642—1644, penned a notably vivid and personal short memorial of these military actions after his retirement. And I soon became aware, as well, of three no less interesting accounts bequeathed by Yorkshire Puritans: John Hodgson, a minor Halifax gentleman who served as a captain in Fairfax's army, set down his prejudices, grumbles and experiences during the war in a small pocket book; Joseph Lister, a West Riding clothier, is a splendidly partisan chronicler of Bradford's sufferings during the war; and John Shaw, vicar of Rotherham, left fascinating reminiscences of both his own experiences in the war and those of the city of Hull. Clearly, such literary sources provided much scope for comparative study and the problems posed for historians by accounts displaying clear personal, political and religious bias; they certainly appealed to me; and students, too, seemed to enjoy reading and writing about them. In the book I put together for the course, however, I also included material from printed collections of records, official and semi-official letters, and private letters as well, in particular *Calendars of State Papers, Domestic*, and the *Fairfax Correspondence*; I felt this was essential if students were to be in a position to evaluate narrative sources effectively; and so it proved. Apart from discussing the sources themselves, lectures and seminars examined a series of themes and recent scholarship relevant to them: Yorkshire society in the early seventeenth century; the causes and nature of discontent in Yorkshire 1640-1642; the lead-up to civil war January—August 1642 (with particular attention to Hull and York); how and why Yorkshire society divided; military events in Yorkshire August 1642—July 1644 (especially in Bradford, Hull and York); the battle of Marston Moor on 2 July 1644 and its aftermath; and the impact of war on Yorkshire society. Apart from my Special Subject, moreover, no course I taught at Huddersfield engendered so much enthusiasm among students. Even so, after running it for eight years and exhausting its potential, I eventually laid it to rest in the mid-1980s.

In 1978/9, for the first time, I offered a Special Subject to final year major history students on the BA (Humanities) degree: *England in the age of the Wars of the Roses*, covering the period c.1450-1487. It was a natural development from *England under the Yorkists*, the third year Certificate in Education course I'd taught at Bermerside between 1973 and 1976, but far better prepared and organised. I was determined not only that it would be popular and successful but also, hopefully, enjoy a much longer shelf life. So it proved. Over a period of several months in 1977/8 I put together a series of booklets (running to several hundred single-spaced typed pages), containing passages from records, letters and, most importantly, contemporary and near-contemporary chronicles, annals and histories, one for each block of a carefully structured course. These very much reflected my determination that students should concentrate on the study and evaluation of primary sources in order to unravel the complicated political and military history of a notably turbulent age. No less central to my planning of the booklets was a desire to maximise the opportunity to get to grips with contemporary and near-contemporary estimates of such controversial figures as the pious if ineffectual Lancastrian king Henry VI (1422—1461), his formidable wife Margaret of Anjou and his leading aristocratic critic Richard Duke of York who, between them, precipitated the country into civil war; the pleasure-loving yet politically astute Yorkist king Edward IV (1461—1483), his scheming spouse Elizabeth Woodville and his powerful ally Richard Neville Earl of Warwick (the Kingmaker) who, eventually, turned against Edward and briefly restored Henry VI to the throne (1470/1); and Edward IV's brother Richard III (1483—1485), perhaps the most enigmatic ruler England has ever had, who ruthlessly deposed, and perhaps killed, his nephew Edward V in 1483, only to suffer a similar fate himself two years later at the hands of the first Tudor king Henry VII (1485—1509). Rather ambitiously, I also put together booklets covering government and administration, religious life and the cultural history of the times in order to facilitate the study of non-political themes as well. Tony Saul, who had volunteered to teach the course for three weeks in the spring term, similarly assembled a collection of documents focussing on the later fifteenth-century economy and society. My own experience of studying a fifteenth-century Special Subject at Bristol in 1965/6 had been that, once Charles Ross had delivered a few introductory lectures on the sources, most of the ensuing seminars had taken the form of students delivering papers, followed by class discussion. In 1978/9 I rejected this model. Student papers, I felt, were fine providing they were conscientiously prepared and vigorously delivered but, if not, they could all too easily dampen rather than arouse enthusiasm in the class as a whole, even provide a positive barrier to others getting to grips themselves with the topics they covered. Instead, I opted for a combination of lectures delivered by me and tutor-led seminars revolving around the document booklets. Like Charles Ross, though, I did devote about a month's early teaching to introducing students to the sources before embarking on the history proper. This did involve throwing them in at the deep end, however, and source lectures and seminars, by their very nature, could certainly prove both hard-going and intellectually challenging. Nevertheless, I concluded, such an opening block was essential and, when writing to my fellow fifteenth-century historians Ralph Griffiths and Tony Pollard in October 1993, I ended both letters with precisely the same *postscript*:

> Now I must blow the dust off my third year Special Subject lectures and prepare for this evening's exercise in evangelism. Yet, I fear, an opening performance on 'Central and Local Government Records' is unlikely to have them rolling in the aisles crying out for more:

Jo Cole, indeed, recalls that in 1988:

> … I almost quit your third year course in the first term. It was only due to your persuasiveness and support that I carried on. I even came to see you expressing a desire to switch courses but you refused to let me, arguing that I hadn't given it enough time to make such a decision.

Fortunately, she now recognises that it was the right decision to persevere:

> I am so grateful that you stood your ground as you were absolutely right. I ended up thoroughly enjoying *The Wars of the Roses* and it provided me with a real love for history.

What did become evident, within a year or two of the course coming on stream, was that it was seriously overloaded. Hence why, when Tony Saul left in 1981, I decided to jettison the economic, social, religious and cultural blocks and, at the same time, renamed the course *The Wars of the Roses* in order to reflect its narrower scope. As the years went by, and my own knowledge of the sources for later fifteenth-century political history grew, further modifications followed. When the BA (Historical and Political Studies) degree came on stream, and I began to offer the course to MA students as well as third year undergraduates, I abandoned the 1450s and it now became *Edward IV, Richard III and Yorkist Politics 1461—1485*. And in my very last year at Huddersfield, in 1993/4, I even cut out Richard III and taught *Edward IV, Politics and the Wars of the Roses 1461—1483*. In all its incarnations, though, the course worked extremely well. Hence why I ran it for year after year. Nor was it the only medieval Special Subject on offer at Huddersfield in the 1980s and early 1990s. Throughout these years Pauline Stafford taught *The Unification of England*, another document-based course, analysing the nature of tenth-century English unification and its legacy and focussing, in particular, on Cnut's early eleventh-century Danish conquest and the Norman Conquest of 1066. Students, not infrequently, complained that they had to choose between the two and, during his years as External Examiner, Richard Davies clearly liked both, reporting in July 1990:

> The medieval Special Subject papers were, as usual, well answered by just about every student in terms of knowledge, evidence and clarity of purpose. Primary evidence was always to the fore and students spread their answers across the range of questions.

During my last four or five years at Huddersfield I taught later fifteenth-century English history to a mixed group of final year BA and MA students. This started off as an experiment but, once it became clear that it worked very well, I carried on with the practice. The fact that all lectures and seminars now had to be timetabled on Thursday evenings suited me very well, too, and no undergraduate ever complained about the hours either. Most of them, on the contrary, seemed to enjoy being taught alongside MA students and, even more, the fact that once teaching ended we invariably adjourned to the pub. It did mean, though, that pressure to get on the course increased relentlessly and, in my final year, I took on twenty-four students, far more than the conventional Special Subject at older universities. Theoretically, for undergraduates, it was a case of 'first come, first served', as Jo Cole recalls:

> By the time I reached the end of my second year (in 1988), I had become wiser about how the course application system worked. I made sure my form for your

third year course was handed in almost as soon as I received it to ensure I was successful this time.

'Imagine how I would have felt', she adds, 'if I'd failed to get on to either your second or third year courses'. In 1993 students even queued up with their completed forms waiting for the departmental office to open; indeed, so I was told, several had drunk most of the previous night at a local club to ensure that, even if in a deplorable condition, they were at the university with plenty of time to spare: As always, and unknown to them, I made sure any student I wanted got a place on the course anyway. Since they had to endure me at least three consecutive hours a week (two lectures and a seminar), sometimes more if I overran (as I not infrequently did once I had an open-ended evening slot to play with), students certainly needed stamina. Caretakers, too, occasionally had to draw on their reserves of patience and tolerance if seminars drifted on towards 21.30 or even later, as they were only too prone to do if discussion became lively and I lost track of the time. Since I always went out of my to be friendly and approachable, there was never any friction between us; I often joined caretakers in their cubbyhole for a cigarette; and, if they came over to the pub when their shift finished, I went out of my way to buy them a pint or two as well. No wonder, after such extended evening sessions, students themselves were often only too pleased to adjourn to the *Zetland* or *College Arms*. Jo Cole, for instance, recalls that *The Wars of the Roses*:

> ... proved to be very challenging and very hard work but Keith's enthusiasm for his subject and the entertaining way in which he delivered his lectures made the amount of effort worthwhile. Although his seminars were well organised, moreover, he always encouraged us to share our ideas, theories and points of view. One highlight of the Thursday evening sessions was that they often continued after the official time in one of Keith's favourite drinking haunts, the *Zetland*, where his students would continue their lively debates and discussions in his company.

Kit Hardwick, similarly, recollects that 'in my final year I joined Keith's class on the Wars of the Roses which involved an almost week-by-week analysis of some twenty years in the 1460s and 1470s using primary documentary sources'; unfortunately, he adds, although he 'greatly enjoyed this', because 'Keith's sessions were held in the evenings, in order to catch my train home, I had to miss the post-class sessions in the pub'. Now and again my room mate Keith Laybourn did come along and, he remembers, 'by detaching himself from the lecture or seminar situation, Keith then further inspired students with his jovial, if sometimes intense, discussions in the pub'.

After Tony Saul left in 1981, for the next thirteen years I taught the Special Subject entirely on my own. Most years in the later 1980s and early 1990s, however, I did manage to entice at least one fellow fifteenth-century historian to Huddersfield to give a guest lecture. In November 1990, for instance, I wrote to Colin Richmond at Keele University:

> I have a group of fifteen doing my Special Subject this year, a mix of eleven third year undergraduates and four MA students. They seem a nice bunch and, as they get into the sources, they're now beginning to talk well and, by mid-February, they should be confident enough to take even you on.

'A sizeable part of the group also tend to come to the pub afterwards', I added, 'one of the bonuses of evening teaching'. When Colin agreed to come along for a session, I replied:

> I'm glad you fancy a trip to Huddersfield, even in the middle of winter. I always think its very good for students to hear someone else occasionally. They must get fed up with listening to me. I certainly do.

And, when Colin delivered a splendidly provocative lecture, the students did indeed come up trumps, both in the seminar room and, afterwards, in the *College Arms*. A visit by Tony Pollard in 1993 followed a similar pattern. As for Michael Jones, whom I'd known since he was a research student of Charles Ross in the later 1970s, he came to Huddersfield several times and always stimulated his audiences with sparkling performances. Since I tended to lecture from fully written out scripts or piles of filing cards, moreover, students were particularly impressed that Michael could talk authoritatively, and with awesome recall of detail, entirely without notes. Inevitably too, whenever he came to Huddersfield, he and I ended up drinking whisky back at my house well into the early hours. After one such visit in the autumn of 1987, indeed, I wrote to James Sherborne (who had taught both Michael and I at Bristol):

> Towards the end of last term I had Michael Jones to stay and persuaded him to talk to my Special Subject group. He gave a splendidly original lecture on 'Somerset, York and the Wars of the Roses'. Many pints of good Yorkshire beer were drunk during the course of Mike's visit as well, of course, and there was much Bristol nostalgia in the air.

Towards the end of my time at Huddersfield, despite my aversion to so-called progressive teaching, even I experimented a little. Most memorably, in 1993/4,

I organised a couple of role-playing sessions for my Special Subject group, inspired by observing Keith Laybourn's success in bringing the 1920s and 1930s to life in the classroom by this means. Each student adopted the persona of a major participant in Yorkist politics and was required to address the group in the role he or she was playing, bearing in mind questions such as:

> What sort of a person am I?
> What are my personal and political motives, objectives and expectations?
> How justified is my behaviour in trying to secure my aims?
> Do I make any obvious errors of political judgement?
> How successful am I in securing my ends?
> How far are my character, motivations and objectives fairly reported in contemporary and near-contemporary sources?

In the ensuing debates I simply played the role of non-partisan chairman. These sessions proved great fun, not least since they were enlivened by the swigging of cans of beer and bottles of wine, as most participants took to their roles with enthusiasm, vigorously defending their own political behaviour on the Yorkist stage while energetically criticising that of their fellow actors. Even the caretakers seemed amused by the noisy spectacle as, inevitably, we overran on both occasions. Perhaps the students even learned something from such role-playing. At any rate several of the undergraduates went on to put in first class honours finals papers; most of the rest got to upper second standard; and, as for the postgraduate MA students, they all passed very comfortably as well. I couldn't have ended my teaching career at Huddersfield on a higher note and Steve Garrett, whom I taught in this final year, certainly has very fond memories of the experience:

> Keith was in essence a teacher, not just a lecturer. Always willing to help his students do better, he may have been perceived by some as favouring the elite minds but, in reality, he gained a great deal of pleasure from seeing students of all abilities better themselves. His talents, moreover, went beyond engaging the imaginations of his audiences during lectures. Seminars/tutorials always proved entertaining and academically rigorous, often prompting lengthy discussions that spilled over into student pubs, even on to Keith's house.

For most of my time at Huddersfield BA students had the option of tackling an undergraduate dissertation. I was entirely in favour of this, not least because, had I had the opportunity to write one at Bristol University in 1965/6, it would surely have helped prepare me for the discipline of postgraduate research (or, maybe, deterred me from embarking on a Ph.D at all!). Yet, unlike Keith

Laybourn who seemed to revel in supervising long studies, I soon found I didn't enjoy it much at all. Nor was I a very good supervisor, particularly if I didn't have much interest in the subject. Fortunately, most students opted for nineteenth and twentieth-century topics and, if they did choose to test the waters with me, I became adept at emphasising the difficulties they might encounter once embarked on a later medieval or early modern subject. Nevertheless, if undergraduates had the determination to wear down my resistance and ignore my warnings about the minimum supervision they could expect, I usually did take them on. Joint supervision, too, could sometimes yield interesting results. In the mid-1970s, for instance, an enthusiastic and hard-working mature student Darrolyn Lowe (whom I'd already got to know socially) successfully tackled the Elizabethan poet, patron and eminent man of affairs Sir Philip Sidney under the supervision of myself and English literature lecturer Hugh Robertson; similarly when, in 1978/9, Neil Scott became fascinated by Victorian perceptions of medieval history, Pauline Stafford and I encouraged him to research and write a first-rate study of Edward Freeman, William Stubbs and William Rufus. Once I began teaching a fifteenth-century Special Subject, I'd occasionally let one of my Wars of the Roses students embark on a dissertation on a linked topic: in 1983/4, for instance, an extrovert and engaging Sheffield lad Lloyd Powell talked me into letting him loose on Edward IV's 1475 expedition to France while, a decade later, Steve Garrett tackled the minority and personal rule of Henry VI. As I emphasised in my report to the External Examiner, Steve subsequently submitted 'the most accomplished research-based dissertation' by an undergraduate I'd read for years; moreover, I added, this was all the more commendable since I had volunteered 'remarkably little supervision beyond providing a willing ear when he felt the need to talk about his on-going research (in the pub more often than not) and encouraging him to persevere when the sources were proving intractable'.

What I never had any interest in at all during my years at Huddersfield was encouraging students to embark on postgraduate research, at any rate if it involved taking them on myself. Since I'd never successfully completed an MA let alone a Ph.D, I was hardly qualified to supervise postgraduate theses anyway. Occasionally, students did approach me about postgraduate studies and, of course, if I thought they were up to it I'd always supply references for other institutions. Yet, as I wrote to an outstandingly able former BA (Historical and Political Studies) student when, in October 1992, he sought my opinion about the wisdom of embarking on postgraduate research:

> I'm rather iconoclastic on the whole subject of research for higher degrees (hence why I never take on research students). I'm inclined to think you'd be better

advised to obtain a professional qualification somewhere, with an eye to a career. If you decide on research, you'd certainly find the fifteenth century tough going. Research is not thrilling—on the contrary, it's a hard and often lonely slog—and working on fifteenth-century England is a particularly daunting prospect: boring record sources (some of them in Latin), appallingly illegible handwriting and a distinct lack of the sort of 'personal' material that helps keep the researcher going when things get tough. If you do decide to embark on it, you'll need to be very careful in selecting a topic and I'd certainly contemplate crossing the 1485 divide into Tudor history—a natural extension of your studies at Huddersfield anyway.

Not wishing to dampen his enthusiasm too much, however, I did add a post-script:

> All this is not meant to be negatively discouraging, simply realistic. If you're absolutely sure then, of course, embark on a programme of historical research. I'm sure you've got the capacity—and the determination—to study for, and obtain, a higher degree in history and, needless to say, I'll pen a very positive reference for you.

Seemingly, too, I did play an indirect role in, in encouraging Kit Hardwick to embark on research, albeit under Keith Laybourn's supervision (not mine) and into the life of former Huddersfield College boy Brian Jackson whose seminal book *Education and the Working Class* (co-authored with Dennis Marsden) I myself had reviewed for the school magazine thirty years earlier:

> I'd spent a fruitless year after graduating trying to find a suitable research topic that did not involve working away from home. During a social call on Keith in the department his room mate Keith Laybourn overheard my tale of woe. 'If you want to do a Ph.D', he said, 'go and talk to this woman. They're looking for someone to write a biography of their founder'. And with that he handed me a folder from Hazel Wigmore, director of the National Children's Centre in Huddersfield, and it led to my doctoral thesis on the life and works of Brian Jackson, local boy more-or-less made good.

Indeed, he added in January 2004, 'going to the polytechnic at the age of fifty transformed my life and I've enjoyed the last few years teaching there enormously'. Even after I left Huddersfield, I kept track of Kit's research and, when he'd obtained his Ph.D, happily accepted an invitation to attend his degree conferment. This was not a new experience. Although I found them immensely tedious to say the least, I'd regularly attended degree ceremonies in Huddersfield

Town Hall during the 1980s and early 1990s, mainly to show solidarity with former students of mine, meet their parents and, most importantly, enjoy a final drinking bout with some of them. This time, however, I was upgraded to the 'Royal Box' (courtesy of Brendan Evans, by then Pro-Vice Chancellor of the university), despite my unconventional apparel. 'I'd never seen Keith dressed in anything other than casual wear prior to this', Kit recalls, 'and remember being hugely impressed by his bottle green corduroy suit, an outfit entirely in keeping with his flamboyant character'. Soon after Kit's biography of Brian Jackson was published in 2003, he came to Bristol, presented me with a signed copy in my local pub and, so he tells me, after an extended afternoon drinking session was 'quite glad to be able to recover slowly on the train back'.

Throughout my time at Huddersfield course assessment was based on a combination of assignments submitted during the course and unseen three hour examinations at the end. I always found this a very satisfactory combination, nicely tailored to students' varied skills, and for my last decade or so settled for a 50% course work/50% examination ratio. Even when, near the end of my time at Huddersfield, it became possible to have 100% course work for third year options, I rejected the opportunity to go down that route; however, since I'd suffered myself from such a system at Bristol University, I had no desire to move to 100% examinations either. I did vary the format of assignments a good deal over the years, though, eventually settling for a combination of short, sharp essays (1000—1500 words) and exercises in documentary analysis. Nor did I subscribe to the idea that exam questions should be completely shrouded in mystery until students turned the papers over. Early on, at Bermerside, I experimented with telling mature students the precise questions in advance but soon found it didn't work. They simply tended to 'learn up' answers and it showed. What I did do in the 1980s and early 1990s was tell examinees which topics would appear. I couldn't see the point of them revising material that wasn't going to figure on the papers anyway. John O'Connell, indeed, remembers that:

> ... late in my time—?1987/1988—you told me on the eve of that year's final examinations that, though you wouldn't dream of telling your Special Subject students what the examination questions were, you did tell them what topics would be asked about. I was shocked, though I knew staff in other subjects (English comes to mind) were considerably more explicit in what they said in their final tutorials.

Had John known I occasionally became personally involved with students, no doubt he would have been even more shocked! Those few close colleagues who did have an inkling about my nefarious antics never criticised my unprofessional behaviour (if that's what it was), at any rate not to my face, and I never found it difficult to separate what went on in the classroom from what I got up to outside it. If, as happened three or four times over the years, I had to mark the work of such students, I sought to be scrupulously fair. Not only did I never give them extra help, I always made sure their assignments were double marked internally and sent to the external examiner as well. The danger lay not in any temptation to be too generous, oddly enough, but to overcompensate by being too mean. I remember one undergraduate dissertation in particular. Initially, I gave it a bidding mark of 69%, right on the IIi/I borderline; Pauline Stafford raised it to a clear first; and the external examiner accused us both of being stingy and awarded an even higher mark. Neither of us queried his decision. We only argued with externals if we felt students were being harshly treated. For the most part, anyway, history staff hit it off very well with external examiners. Early on, Paul Coles of Bradford University was immensely and importantly supportive of us as we found our feet; later, towards the end of the 1980s, Richard Davies was no less helpful, not least in examination boards where students' final results were determined. Despite my aversion to meetings, and tendency to avoid most of them, I never missed these. They were important. Nevertheless, they could prove immensely irksome. On one occasion, for instance, the philosopher Stuart Linney insisted on a long and pointless discussion of just what 'a mark' was; the idle and seriously dim too often had their bleeding heart supporters; and, now and again, pleas for mitigation could be bizarre to say the least. Most memorably, a student once submitted pseudo-medical evidence seeming to suggest she'd under-performed in her examinations primarily because of personal trauma occasioned by the size of her boyfriend's penis! It didn't work. Inevitably, I had occasional run-ins with externals, not least Richard Davies, but they never amounted to much and were invariably settled amicably enough. The trouble with Richard was that he was a fellow fifteenth-century historian, knew altogether too much for comfort about the Wars of the Roses, and couldn't resist exercising his sardonic humour at my expense. In response to comments in his report of duly 1989, I was even stung to reply:

> As always your wit sparkles and I enjoy your digs at me. The trouble is I'll probably now be black balled by any high-ups who happen to read it. The likes of me are not well thought of in the polytechnic and, even though I've long since abandoned any hopes of promotion (or even desire for it), I do still enjoy teaching students who, by and large, I find interesting and stimulating. If I didn't I'd get out of higher education tomorrow.

Suitably chastened no doubt, Richard promptly sent me a soothing note declaring, 'I thought I smothered my remarks in sufficient hyperbole to prevent anyone being able to question the quality of history teaching at Huddersfield'. Anyway, he added, 'I'll buy you a consolatory drink next year' and, certainly, his report of July 1990 couldn't have been more supportive:

> I find examining with colleagues in the History Department at Huddersfield a most satisfactory exercise, by reason of the high standards set in the courses and the splendid responses the students make. Accordingly, I have made little mark on the content and structure of courses or on procedures of assessment and marking because I have found nothing in my time to criticise and plenty to learn from. Any suggestions I have made have been considered very open-mindedly by the department and responded to as much as possible. With the staff so consistently in touch with current work in their respective fields, it has been particularly impressive to see the speed with which current historical themes and 'latest work' get into exam papers and answers; so has the fact that the 'latest' is rightly not always hailed as the 'greatest' by either students or staff.

Several former colleagues and students at Huddersfield remember my lack of sympathy with administrative procedures in general and the workings of bureaucracy in particular. I often ignored rules and regulations altogether, not least cut-off dates for student assignments. Occasionally, I accepted them (in brown envelopes!) as much as three weeks after final submission deadlines, even as late as the commencement of examinations. Cliff Burhouse, at the end of the 1980s, gained the distinct impression that:

> Keith took little or no notice of rules, regulations or, indeed, anyone in authority. He got away with it thanks to a unique personality, eccentricity and very good results.

Even outsiders got wind of my refusal to conform. Mike Stammers, my friend of student days who himself rose to the very top echelon of management at the Merseyside Maritime Museum, sounds almost envious when he writes of my 'hatred of bureaucracy, red tape and, when at Huddersfield, anything that got in the way of his subject and teaching'. Tony Pollard, who certainly didn't escape onerous administrative roles at Teesside Polytechnic/ University, seems particularly struck by the fact that I 'never sold out' to 'the managerialism, the bureaucracy and the instrumentalism' of the place, choosing rather to 'honour the students, the teachers and open access' to higher education, even suggesting that my 'outspoken and, I am sure for your more malleable colleagues, infuriating stubbornness in giving two fingers to bureaucracy, modish jargon and the whole tribe of managers' maybe 'helped others to keep a level head'. Brendan Evans, who probably suffered more than most from my cavalier behaviour, seems to have been one of them. 'When I became dean of faculty at Huddersfield in 1989' he recalls:

> ... your role was keeping me sane. You would come into my office of an evening, take the piss out of business documents, minutes of meetings and the like, and point out that much of it was very silly anyway.

More often than not, moreover, such untimely interventions would put an end to Brendan's efforts for the day as we rapidly adjourned to the pub. Yet I was by no means a complete anarchist. 'Despite your lack of sympathy for administrative procedures', emphasises Bill Roberts, 'you never deliberately screwed anything up'. 'You presented yourself to the world as a dissipated devil-may-care hedonist, constantly hung over, with no time for bureaucratic routines', Bill Stafford recollects; yet, he adds:

> ... in practice you were extremely tidy and well-organised, your notes in good order, your handouts meticulously prepared and always ready on time. I don't remember that you ever missed a class or other duty.

Pauline Stafford even goes so far as to declare:

> Although you would have scorned any sort of administrative role in the department, you would actually have been very good at it, and that's not meant to be an insult. You ran your own courses, and those we taught jointly, extraordinarily efficiently. While my own notes and files often seemed to me to lack all system, I was always impressed by and envious of yours: lectures and seminars typed up, filed away. It seemed a bit of a paradox to me then and still does now looking back: your exhuberant personality, your impatience with external controls and interference, sitting alongside your own precise organisation. There was a part of you, and of your life, which was very controlled.

This is probably a very fair assessment. I am an efficient enough organiser but detest the procedures of administration. If it has to be done and I can see the point of it, I'm better at administration than many but it has always been a chore for me. No doubt if I'd needed the money and been forced to go for promotion at Huddersfield, or if I'd cared a damn about status, I would have taken on far more administration than I did. As it was, it seemed perfectly reasonable to leave most of it to principal lecturers or those aspiring to enter the ranks of senior staff. Precisely because I tended to be well organised and methodical but with anarchic tendencies ever lurking beneath the surface, moreover, I'm sure I would have found an institutional administrative role utterly intolerable.

Looking back on my years at Huddersfield Polytechnic/University, what I remember most fondly is all the teaching I did, the colleagues with whom I worked closely and, of course, those many students I got to know well both in the classroom and outside it. As for their memories of me in a professional context, they show a remarkable degree of consistency. Keith Laybourn, for instance, recollects that my lectures and seminars were:

> ... greatly admired by both staff and students. They were driven by a genuine desire to encourage interest and understanding in the topic, and characterised by insight, clarity, directness, structure and, above all, enthusiasm. Passion, passion, passion: that is what you offered to staff and students alike in your considered and tightly prepared performances.

'Although in theory your vigorous lecturing style could have been a turn-off', remarks Brendan Evans, 'as practised by you it was electrifying and inspiring'. 'I remember you as being the most humorously cynical member of the department', recalls Vivienne Hemingway (a part-time lecturer and research assistant at Huddersfield towards the end of my time there), 'yet also the one whose seminars and lectures were always popular and who probably had more time for students than most of your colleagues'; even so, she adds, 'you could be pretty scathing about both at times!'. Bill Roberts, in similar vein, declares:

> I have vivid memories of you as a charismatic teacher and heard many anecdotes about your teaching methods, in particular your response if a student had the effrontery to turn up to a tutorial unprepared—told to bugger off! Some of the anecdotes, I'm sure, came from you, and were often accompanied by comments on the shapely posteriors of some of the male students.

Pauline Stafford, closest of all my Huddersfield colleagues academically, recollects that:

> ... as a historian, I always felt that you were particularly interested in the people in the past. You were a constant reminder that people mattered but not people in the sense of the masses, the great unwashed, who never really interested you. That has always been your greatest strength as a historian.

Even so, she adds perceptively:

I have often wondered whether your lack of sympathy with the religious dimension of human experience was a bit of a drawback when it came to the study of the Middle Ages. It certainly meant you had more enthusiasm for Edward IV than Henry VI!

'You were a great colleague', she concludes flatteringly, 'if occasionally a slightly difficult one; I certainly learned from you the importance of teaching and engaging students' enthusiasm; and that the only way to do that was to have the enthusiasm yourself'. As for Brendan Evans, whose role in helping me secure early retirement proved pivotal, my departure from Huddersfield in 1994 was 'much deplored by me, the school and, particularly, the students and staff in history'.

Reminiscences of former students at Huddersfield suggest I didn't change all that much over the years. In the later 1970s Graham Townend gained the powerful impression that:

> ... here was someone who shared my intense passion for the past, someone who taught history because it was interesting and important. You loved your subject, your teaching and, in the sense you wanted to bring out the best in them, your students as well. Unlike so many in higher education, you had grasped the real truth. It was the students who mattered. Whether you were a brilliant administrator, or had a publication list as long as your arm, was irrelevant. The students were the beginning and the end as far as you were concerned.

Vanessa Cook experienced my teaching between 1982 and 1985:

> You fired my imagination and opened up a whole world of later medieval history to me. It was everything I expected and wanted history to be: full of intrigue, unanswered questions, conundrums and passion. It wasn't just political history either but economic, social and cultural as well, and your skill was to help us visualise the past and then tie it all together. I still get a real buzz from reading about or going to places associated with Richard III in particular. For the world you opened up to me, you have my profound thanks.

Julie Bungay, who studied history at the polytechnic between 1984 and 1987 before entering the teaching profession herself soon afterwards, paints an exceptionally graphic, and very personal, portrait of how I seemed to her twenty years ago:

> In lectures your preferred teaching style was to pace along the front of the room, never making eye contact with anyone, but they were always well planned, self-

contained, vigorously delivered and finished on time. Your tutorials were well focussed and interesting. You had an excellent subject knowledge and were prepared to share it at any opportunity. I soon found, too, that you could be charming and considerate. You were obviously interested in your students as people but could also be mischievous and take delight in winding us up. I liked your sense of humour and you were always keen to quip and play to your audience: for instance, I remember you calling me a 'softy southerner' and a 'long-haired loony lefty', and once referring to another student as 'a thick Geordie pillock'. Despite your generally warm-hearted and supportive teaching, moreover, we always knew there could be a hard edge to you. You definitely did not suffer fools gladly, especially if they had not prepared adequately for your tutorials, and you would watch your students intently, looking for any signs of wandering or drifting off. Personally, as both a teacher and a historian I found you inspiring.

Among students I taught between 1988 and 1991, Margaret Swann 'thoroughly enjoyed' history at Huddersfield and found me 'an excellent lecturer, an inspiration to me and, I am sure, many other students'. 'Somebody, somewhere, once said that you never forget a good teacher', echoes Richard Bell, 'and I think you were a damned good teacher and I have great memories of my time in Huddersfield'. 'Keith's performances became well known and much loved', emphasises Cliff Burhouse in similar vein; moreover, his lectures had great substance and his scholarship was widely admired'. In 1993/4, when Cliff was doing some part-time tutoring himself, he even stood in for me as a lecturer on one occasion:

> Keith rang me at home at some early hour to tell me in a soft croak that he had lost his voice and would be unable to deliver a lecture to first year students later that morning. Before cancelling, he wondered if I could do it for him, notes provided. I was flattered, excited and, curiously, not nervous. I did wonder, though, how I would pace it to avoid finishing in minutes or running out of time. He promptly offered to sit in and signal if required. All went well and I enjoyed the experience immensely.

I particularly appreciate the comments of another student I taught in the 1980s:

> You weren't an intellectual snob who turned his back on those of us who were not naturally academic. Instead, you encouraged us to have faith in our abilities and believe we were more than capable of achieving what we wanted, even if we had to work that bit harder to get it. Many of my teachers at school thought a degree

was beyond my capabilities. I had almost begun to think so myself by the time I got to Huddersfield and, without your help and encouragement, I might not have done. I consider it a real privilege to have been taught by you.

Perhaps Steve Garrett, one of the last students I taught at Huddersfield, should have the final word:

> Many of Keith's close colleagues at Huddersfield admired the way that he continued almost to live the life of a student throughout his professional career. At the time I didn't think this to be such a difficult achievement. Later in life I see that Keith's incredible attention to detail—talented and meticulous in planning and organising his teaching—allowed him the leisure time he so much enjoyed. For many of his ex-students it is of great comfort to think that Keith continues to sit in pubs, discussing history and politics in his uniquely entertaining way. For many of us, work and family lives have long since taken over, something that Keith constantly predicted but, in our inexperienced youth, we all denied.

10

Early Historical Research and Writing

'Knowing how in later years you became extraordinarily dedicated to completing tasks you set yourself', mused my former Huddersfield colleague Bill Roberts early in 2005:

> ...it seems odd that you gave up so immediately and so completely on your Ph.D. Did you ever think of going back to it later?

Certainly, during my years as a schoolmaster in Plymouth between 1969 and 1972, my thesis remained firmly on hold, partly because I found teaching history to public school boys far more enjoyable and challenging, partly because living in a school boarding house surrounded by boisterous lads was hardly conducive to serious uninterrupted study and writing, and partly because I was thoroughly fed up with later fifteenth-century Yorkshire gentry anyway. Nevertheless, I was disappointed at the outcome of my three years postgraduate research and, when interviewed for the Huddersfield post in November 1971, strongly implied that my Bristol Ph.D was still very much alive; I probably could have put together a second or third rate thesis in the early 1970s without too much difficulty; and even as late as 1975, when challenged by academic management at the polytechnic, I asserted that 'my Ph.D could be revived at any time and I may resume work on it eventually'. In fact, by then, I had no intention of doing anything of the kind. Instead, early in 1976, I took the bull by the horns and terminated my candidature. About the same time Tony Pollard, pursuing his own interest in north-eastern England during the fifteenth-century (which was to culminate, in 1990, in a major book on the subject), contacted me about my postgraduate research and, in response, I happily gave him *carte blanche* to read and make use of the series of histories of prominent gentry families I'd knocked together in the later 1960s. Thirty years later Tony recalled:

> I will always be indebted to your generosity and unselfishness over your unpublished research. Yet I did not realise, at the time, that you were in effect giving it to me.

I certainly have no regrets about this since, even if I'd stuck doggedly with fifteenth-century northern history and published far more extensively on it than I have, I could never have advanced our knowledge of northern politics and society as fundamentally as Tony has.

The most substantial of my manuscript fifteenth-century gentry family histories concerned the Plumptons of Plumpton near Knaresborough in the West Riding of Yorkshire: indeed this, and the research on which it was based, helped inspire my third year BA (Humanities) course *The Pastons, the Plumptons and their England c.1450—1500*, first taught in the autumn of 1974. This rekindled my interest in fifteenth-century Yorkshire gentry in general, and the Plumptons in particular, sufficiently to contact John Taylor at Leeds University who, in 1975, published an important article on 'The Plumpton Letters 1416—1552' in the journal *Northern History*. No doubt as a result, in May 1976, I received a letter from his former student Shirley Walker (who had written an interesting MA thesis on the family correspondence in 1962) expressing interest in 'the information on Yorkshire families which, I believe, you have collected'; we met later in the year and I lent her several files of material; and, in June 1977, she declared:

> I enjoyed browsing through your valuable notes on Yorkshire gentry and found them immensely useful for obtaining a clearer picture of West Riding society in the fifteenth century. There certainly isn't anything in print to compare with all this accumulated information.

Meanwhile, since even my younger history colleagues at Huddersfield were now beginning to publish and I felt under increasing pressure to do so myself, I decided to have a go at writing an article on the Plumptons for the popular historical magazine *History Today*, focussing on the links between politics, marriage and inheritance during the period covered by the family's letters and papers. I hadn't much expectation of success but, when my colleague Tony Saul read an early draft, his comments were unexpectedly positive. I also sent a copy to John Taylor in July 1976 and, again, received an encouraging response. Even so, I was pleasantly surprised when 'The Troubles of the Yorkshire Plumptons' was accepted and, in due course, published in July 1977.

For most of the 1970s, 1980s and 1990s, even when not very research active myself, I regularly attended fifteenth-century conferences and met up with those who were. Peter Hammond, for many years research officer of the Richard

III Society and eventually its president, and his wife Carolyn, the society's long-time librarian, recall my motives nicely:

> We have seen you at many 15th century conferences and remember you once explaining your philosophy in going to them: attending conferences was fun, a painless way to learn things, and a good opportunity to catch up on the gossip.

Even while still a schoolmaster in Plymouth, I journeyed to University College, Cardiff, for a pioneering gathering of fifteenth-century historians in September 1970. Attended by some fifty specialists in fifteenth-century British history, drawn from twenty-nine universities and other institutions in the United Kingdom and North America, it proved a fascinating occasion. Hearing high quality papers by prominent scholars (including my own mentor Charles Ross), and listening to the stimulating discussions they provoked, was rewarding enough but I remember, even more vividly, individuals and their behaviour: the autocratic organiser Stanley Chrimes, for instance, whose imperious exercise of professorial authority was more than enough to secure the opening of a closed bar; Bertie Wilkinson, to whom I certainly endeared myself one evening by slipping him a whole series of illicit gin and tonics; and Jack Lander, who soon convinced me that I wasn't the only gay historian of fifteenth-century England. Present, too, was Fred Brooks, an elderly shambling Yorkshireman with large hairy ears and a tendency to pick his nose absent-mindedly during the reading of papers. Four years later, at a weekend conference on Anglian and Viking Yorkshire held in Scarborough in October 1974, I encountered him again and discovered, rather to my surprise, that he was a learned and compelling lecturer. Indeed, it was mainly in order to hear Brooks again that I signed up for another conference in Scarborough in October 1975, this time on Yorkshire Monasticism. Once more, I wasn't disappointed but most memorable was the extraordinary spectacle of Brooks, who must have been well into his seventies, contriving to fall asleep while delivering one of his own lectures. Nodding off while listening to tedious papers is an occupational hazard at academic conferences but this was a one-off variation. Admittedly, it occurred in an overheated conference room furnished with very comfortable armchairs after a substantial Sunday lunch but, nevertheless, the embarrassment potential was considerable. Fortunately, in response to a bout of judicious coughing by the audience, Brooks awoke after a few minutes and continued to talk about the suppression of Yorkshire's monasteries in the 1530s, apparently oblivious of his short lapse into unconsciousness. During this conference, too, he led an afternoon trip to Rievaulx and Byland abbeys where he demonstrated both his deep knowledge of medieval religious architecture in Yorkshire and a total disregard for the unpredictability of autumn weather in north-eastern England. Particularly fascinating were his memories of Rievaulx during his first visit (in the 1920s) compared with the cleaned-up excavated ruin of 1975, and his determination, at Byland, to condemn two or three recent studies of the abbey as seriously flawed. September 1976 found me back on more familiar territory, however, when Charles Ross, Tony Saul and I all attended a high-powered three day residential Anglo-French colloquium on later medieval history at the University of Sheffield.

In 1977 Charles Ross set about organising a symposium to meet at Bristol University in July 1978; his avowed, and successful, aim was to promote 'an informal and friendly gathering' where younger scholars of fifteenth-century England, not least former Bristol University students such as Ralph Griffiths, Tony Pollard and Michael Hicks, 'would have the opportunity to read and discuss papers of their own'; and, much to my surprise, Charles asked me to contribute. My first reaction was to refuse, citing heavy teaching commitments by way of excuse for avoiding what, I felt, might well prove an intellectually humiliating experience. Charles wasn't prepared to allow me such an easy cop out. My second response, that I might do something on fifteenth-century Yorkshire gentry, was no good either. Tony Pollard had already collared that subject! Still Charles wouldn't take no for an answer; I visited him in Bristol towards the end of 1977; and, during a heavy beer-drinking session reminiscent of my years as his research student, he persuaded me to put together an hour of academic entertainment for the conference on the final morning. The result, very much a product of teaching rather than serious research, was 'Japan and England in the Fifteenth Century: the Onin War and the Wars of the Roses', an intellectual divertissement amidst much worthy scholarship. When it came to delivering the paper, moreover, I rapidly became fixated upon the not inconsiderable challenge of preventing James Sherborne, who had taught me as an undergraduate, nodding off before it was over: not easy, but I succeeded. Despite its obvious methodological flaws the paper elicited an unexpectedly positive response, not least from Charles Ross's wife Anne Crawford who recently recalled:

> My first clear memory of you is at the Bristol conference in 1978 when you delivered a paper on fifteenth-century Japan that can only be described as a *tour de force*. I still think it's one of the most stimulating and thought-provoking pieces I've ever heard.

When Charles persuaded his friend Alan Sutton to publish the conference proceedings, he insisted that my paper appear alongside the rest, commenting in his introduction to the ensuing volume *Patronage, Pedigree and Power in Later Medieval England*:

In discussing the comparisons and contrasts between England and Japan in the later middle ages, Mr Dockray modestly makes no great methodological claims, merely (he suggests) an identification of some remarkable similarities in the evolution of two societies a whole world apart geographically but not dissimilar economically and socially. The contrasts are no less interesting. If England lacked the splendid succession of concubines and catamites so prominent in Japan (rather mutedly presented in Mr Dockray's *written* text), at least she was spared the bloodshed, starvation and mass popular suffering which occurred during the Onin War.

Although I had no confidence in my ability to secure publication in serious historical journals, and wasn't even sure if I wanted to, I did test the waters in the later 1970s and 1980. It was an entirely depressing and demoralising experience. Almost immediately an appallingly written and unbelievably tedious article (arising out of my postgraduate research) on the Constables, a prominent gentry family from Flamborough near Scarborough in North Yorkshire, was rejected more or less out of hand by the *Yorkshire Archeological Journal*. Perhaps, nevertheless, I should have persevered with Yorkshire material collected for my never completed thesis or at least stuck to the fifteenth century. I didn't. Instead, I gave free vent to my burgeoning enthusiasm for literary sources and historiography (already evident in the Japan/England paper), particularly medieval chronicles and Victorian historians of the Middle Ages. Even more perversely, I chose to focus my attention on the probably homosexual second Norman king of England William Rufus (1087—1100). The result, in 1979, was an article on 'William Rufus, the Victorians and the Present' and it is surely no coincidence that this was the same year I myself tentatively came out as a homosexual. Unfortunately, I wasn't at all clear what audience I was writing for and, as Tony Saul pointed out after reading a first draft, I contrived to fall between two stools:

> It seems a little too heavy for *History Today* but it might be worth trying. My own inclination would be to footnote it and try one of the historical journals, or perhaps even one of the journals combining literature and history.

Pauline Stafford's reaction to a footnoted version was to register a series of not unreasonable criticisms but also record her 'overall impression' that 'this is good' and suggest I 'bat it off somewhere'. I had no luck with *History Today*. The magazine rejected not only a reader-friendly unfootnoted version of the Rufus article but also a light-hearted analysis of 'Courtly Politics and Society in Ancient and Medieval Japan'. I was particularly disappointed at the lack of interest in the latter, not least since it grew out of first year Oriental Studies lectures that had gone down extremely well at Huddersfield. I have never submitted an article to *History Today* since. In January 1980, when I sent the footnoted version of William Rufus to Charles Ross, I captured my prevailing state of mind nicely in an accompanying letter:

> William Rufus, as one of our abler gay kings, has always had a certain appeal for me (perhaps analagous to the vigorously straight Edward IV for you) and I'm also increasingly fascinated by Victorian historians. I'm not entirely happy with this article but very disinclined to translate it into the arid prose so beloved of most historical journals these days (which explains, presumably, why so much of their content has ceased to have any appeal to students!).

Charles did not pull his punches in response but there was clear encouragement as well:

> If the quotations from chronicles and historians are heavily sliced, and coverage of recent reappraisals of William Rufus expanded, this might make an article for *History*. Yet it would fit even better into a book on Victorian approaches to medieval history. Why not have a go at that? You obviously enjoy the subject and it is a good field of study.

Maybe I should have embarked on a programme of reading for a book on *The Victorians and the Middle Ages* (I wish I had) but, instead, I persevered with the article. When a lecture on 'William Rufus, the Victorians and the Historians' went down well with the Huddersfield branch of the Historical Association, I decided to take Charles Ross's alternative advice, revised the paper along the lines he had suggested, and submitted it to the HA's journal *History* in July 1980. Within ten days Keith Robbins, editor of *History*, rejected it; so, soon afterwards, did Antonia Gransden, editor of *Nottingham Medieval Studies*; and the article fared no better at the hands of the editor of *Clio*, an American interdisciplinary journal of literature and history. None of the three was utterly damning. Robbins declared he had 'studied it with interest', Gransden that she had 'read it with considerable enjoyment', and *Clio's* editor, too, judged it 'cogent and interesting'. Nevertheless, all three of them rejected it outright. Hence why, at this point, I gave up and determined never again to submit an uncommissioned article to a learned journal. I never have and probably just as well for my selfesteem and future as a historian. The sort of history I wanted to write, and have had published since the mid-1980s, simply isn't formulaic enough or sufficiently archive-based to meet the requirements of such periodicals.

By the time he got to know me in the early 1980s, recalls my former Huddersfield colleague Tony Payne:

> You always took a strong line about not wanting to do research. I was never sure about that. I think maybe part of you did want to have a go on that front but you'd marched yourself so far up the hill, rhetorically, that it was difficult to go back on yourself and get stuck into research when the ethos of the polytechnic changed.

There's certainly more than an element of truth in this and, indeed, Tony himself played an important role in encouraging me not to abandon research and writing altogether after the setbacks of 1979 and 1980. Even more pivotal was Pauline Stafford, whose own musings of early 2004 are probably spot on:

> I found—and find—it amusing how determinedly you cast yourself as someone who did not write and was not a researcher. Yet in the long run you have produced so much. I often wonder what would have happened had you begun your postgraduate career with a congenial topic utilizing narrative sources. In reaction to it you cast yourself as a non-researcher—and then did the work.

At the end of 1980 Pauline herself asked me to contribute several short biographies to a *Dictionary of British Women*. She was editing the early medieval section to 1100; Anne Crawford was handling the period 1100—1500; and so, fearing possible redundancy at the time, I asked her for a few more. Anne's response, in mid-January 1981 was both prompt and practical:

> Of course you may have some medieval women. I would not be doing the job but for you anyway! I want to do most of the royal ladies myself but what I do have unallocated are six religious women. You are not the first name that springs to mind for them, as being deeply sympatico, but then neither am I.

In fact, I wrote eight mini-biographies of religious women for Anne, including the early fifteenth-century English mystic Margery Kempe, commenting in an accompanying letter of April 1981:

> I'm afraid I've rather let myself go on Margery Kempe, not least her 'tendency to indulge in frequent bouts of noisy, uncontrolled weeping' which 'were no doubt instrumental in finally persuading her husband to forgo his conjugal rights'. I couldn't resist it—but the criticisms seem well documented.

I also penned a whole batch of biographies of political women and tended to be critical of them as well: for instance, I described the early twelfth-century Empress Mathilda, daughter of Henry I of England, as 'haughty, domineering and German-speaking' and Alice Perrers, mistress of Edward III (1327—1377), as a 'rapacious woman' who, on the king's death, 'is said to have stolen the very rings from his fingers'. The *Dictionary* was published in 1983. Later in the same year, at the suggestion of my politics colleagues Brendan Evans, Tony Payne and Andrew Taylor, I delivered a public lecture on 'Politics, Society and Homosexuality in Post-War Britain' which, in 1984, was published by the polytechnic. Similarly, as Bill Roberts recalls, in 1990:

> I persuaded you to contribute to the Huddersfield Pamphlets in History series. Your pamphlet on *Elizabeth I: Myth and Reality*, the first half guilefully presenting the positive view, the second tearing her reputation to bits, was a gem.

During the early 1980s I began to deliver more and more guest lectures, particularly to branches of the Historical Association, and also became more adventurous in my choice of topics. Perhaps the best of them was 'Religion, Sex and Morality in Western Europe during the Middle Ages' which, as I remarked in my letter to Anne Crawford of April 1981, I had just agreed to give to both the Huddersfield and Bradford branches of the HA, adding that 'if the Bristol branch is interested, I'd be happy to perform there too'. The president of the branch, so Anne informed me a few days later, 'jumped at your proposed subject'; in February 1982 I duly travelled to Bristol and delivered the lecture to a substantial audience; and, as at Charles Ross's symposium in 1978, once more managed to keep James Sherborne awake throughout. 1983, the five hundredth anniversary of Richard III's seizure of the throne, also found me trying my hand at historical debate: in the Guildhall, Gloucester, at the end of August and, in November, at the Oxford Union. On both occasions, admittedly with tongue in cheek, I spoke vigorously in favour of the motion 'Richard III Was More Sinned Against Than Sinning'. Even more interesting, in 1983/4, I became involved in the making of a four hour television programme for Channel 4, *The Trial of Richard III*, eventually transmitted on Sunday 4 November 1984. All this did wonders for my self-confidence and, no less importantly, helped open up new publication possibilities.

Charles Ross's fifteenth-century conference at Bristol University in July 1978 had been a most enjoyable and rewarding experience and so were its successors; I got to know more and more later medieval historians; and, no less importantly, I began to develop all sorts of valuable connections. In particular, I formed enduring friendships with three of Ross's former students, Ralph

Griffiths, Michael Hicks and Tony Pollard, all of them fellow performers at the Bristol symposium. Indeed, it was Ralph Griffiths, who had taught there since the early 1960s, who organised a follow-up symposium at University College, Swansea, in July 1979 where, once again, the principal aim was to encourage younger scholars to present the results of their research (although Charles Ross himself was also prevailed upon to deliver a paper). Four years later, in July 1983, a similar conference met at Reading University (the last Charles Ross was to attend); both my former colleague Tony Saul and future collaborator at the University of the West of England Peter Fleming presented papers; and, I noted at the time, this gathering amply demonstrated 'the continuing vigour of research into fifteenth-century history and the growing number of scholars involved in it'. Colin Richmond organised another in this sequence of colloquia at Keele University in July 1985 (where the highlight, for me, was meeting up with a couple of former students Neil Scott and Lloyd Powell in the nearby *Sneyd Arms*) and, as I reported to my Huddersfield colleagues soon afterwards, so did Michael Hicks at Winchester in July 1987:

> Dr Michael Hicks, a young but already distinguished later medieval historian who teaches at King Alfred's College, Winchester, organised this conference with commendable efficiency and ensured that the twenty or more research students present had ample opportunity to contribute to notably interesting and fruitful discussions.

Always acutely conscious of my own minimal efforts on the research front, I rarely contributed much, if anything, to such discussions; I tended to judge papers as much by coherence and vigour of delivery as originality of content; and, for me, the social mixing at conferences (whether in bars or during late night drinking sessions back at halls of residence) was often more enjoyable and rewarding than the hours spent in lecture or seminar rooms. I certainly had no desire to organise a fifteenth-century symposium at Huddersfield and never did.

As well as colloquia designed to encourage younger scholars of fifteenth-century England, the 1980s also spawned larger scale conferences along the lines of the Anglo-French gathering at Sheffield in 1976. At the first of these, held in York University's Derwent College in September 1982, I met Robin Storey, professor of medieval history at the University of Nottingham who, during a final plenary session, volunteered to mount a follow-up conference at Nottingham in September 1984, focussing on gentry and lesser nobility in later medieval Europe. Just three days later, before my nerve failed me, I despatched a cautiously probing letter to him:

Charles Ross has urged me to offer a paper for your 1984 colloquium on fifteenth-century gentry, so I'm doing so at once while his comments (in a telephone conversation yesterday) are still fresh in my mind. In the later 1960s I did a fair bit of work, under Charles' expert guidance, on Yorkshire knights and squires in the later fifteenth century. For various reasons I never turned this stuff into a thesis (much to his annoyance, I fear) and, although I've published odd bits and pieces since, most of it still remains locked in the depths of a filing cabinet. Maybe I can knock together a reasonable paper from it. You'll no doubt get much better offers than this, though, so I'll quite understand if you prefer them to the relatively unsophisticated effort I'd probably turn in.

Storey's response was most encouraging but, when I suggested a paper with the title 'Marriage, Inheritance and Political Affiliation among the Yorkshire Gentry during the Wars of the Roses', he commented:

> The title is fine as a description, though more solemn than to my taste. You won't find Charles Ross taking exception to it but 'Plumpton Pie' would be more in my line.

'Have no fear', I replied with some relief, 'behind a suitably erudite title may well lurk not a little light-hearted stuff, especially if you allot the paper to an hour of delivery clearly calling for such treatment'. For over a year I didn't give the matter much further thought; by then any serious new research was out of the question; and so, in January 1984, I wrote to Robin Storey again:

> I'm inclined to agree with your earlier comment that my original title is too solemn. More entertaining (and easier to write) would be 'Why did Fifteenth-Century Gentry Marry?: the Pastons, Plumptons and Stonors Reconsidered', so let's settle for that. No doubt my lecture will still contain plenty of northern stuff, especially about the Plumptons and their connections, but at least I can also draw on useful (and sometimes amusing) examples in the other two major collections of surviving gentry letters. Hopefully, too, I'll be able to attempt a reinterpretation of the letters in the light of recent work on the family, love and society in medieval and early modern times.

When Storey sent me the final conference programme in May 1984, he emphasised that I had been deliberately allocated 'a post-prandial after-dinner slot'. I was certainly pleased about that. Even so, when I wrote to my former school and university friend Bernard Jarvis in July (arranging to meet up with him in Nottingham where he now lived), I commented ruefully that this was possible because 'I've been daft enough to agree to talk to what seems to be an alarmingly high-powered symposium at the university'. I duly delivered my lecture, in a deliberately theatrical manner and with beer rather than water to help keep me going, extravagantly taking issue (as I reported to my Huddersfield colleagues afterwards) with 'conventional views on later medieval marriage as essentially a matter of business and status-enhancement' and suggesting that 'love and affection were frequently more important than is usually allowed in leading fifteenth-century gentlemen and women to take the plunge'. It seemed to go down well; Colin Richmond, as I also noted at the time, then 'diverted us greatly in the bar with a graphic account of his sufferings as a research student'; and, an additional bonus, my paper duly found its way into a volume of conference proceedings, *Gentry and Lesser Nobility in Late Medieval Europe*, published in 1986.

Perhaps the most important factor encouraging me to write and publish in the early 1980s was membership of the Richard III Society. Although no great admirer of England's last Plantagenet king, I hadn't much sympathy either for Tudor portrayals of Richard III as a ruthless master of intrigue, a callous murderer of rivals ranging from the saintly Henry VI to his own innocent nephews the Princes in the Tower, and a tyrannical, even wicked, ruler. Hence why, towards the end of the 1970s, I became a member of the society and have remained so ever since. Its proudly declared aim is:

> .. to promote in every possible way research into the life and times of Richard III, and to secure a reassessment of the material relating to this period, and of the role in English history of this monarch.

Fortuitously, one of the few positive outcomes of my postgraduate research had been to unearth a great deal of material concerning Richard III's interest in, and connections with, the north of England in general and Yorkshire's lesser nobility and gentry in particular; indeed, in 1969, I had even delivered a paper on 'Yorkshire Knights and Squires in the service of Richard III' to a research seminar at Bristol University. A by-product of that had been the dreary article on the Constables of Flamborough rejected by the *Yorkshire Archeological Journal*. The most interesting member of this wealthy northern family, Sir Marmaduke Constable, had served Richard III in both Kent and the midlands. So, early in 1980, I put together a short biography of him and sent it to *The Ricardian* (quarterly journal of the Richard III Society). Not only was it promptly accepted, and published in December 1980, the editor Anne Sutton even expressed the hope that I would 'bear *The Ricardian* in mind for future work'. My own reaction, when sending a copy of the article to Charles Ross, was 'Dockray in print again, suitably insignificantly'. Another product of my Ph.D research had been a substantial file on the Conyers of Hornby, a prominent family from Richmondshire in north Yorkshire who became embroiled in rebellion against Edward IV in 1469; more interesting, as far as I was concerned by the early 1980s, was the contradictory treatment of the rebellions of 'Robin of Holderness' and 'Robin of Redesdale' in contemporary and near-contemporary chronicles; and the outcome of renewed investigation, in December 1983, was a second *Ricardian* article on 'The Yorkshire Rebellions of 1469'. A light-hearted exchange of letters with Tony Pollard about the precise identity of 'Robin of Redesdale' was a most enjoyable bonus.

When the Richard III Society's research officer Peter Hammond asked me to give a paper to a society conference at Jesus College, Cambridge, in April 1984 (marking the quincentenary of the king's reign), I once more rummaged through my postgraduate research notes. The result was 'Richard III and the Yorkshire Gentry c.1471—1485'. It seemed to go down well, not least with Peter himself (who later described it as 'an excellent paper'!); moreover, Peter also recalls, it was probably at this conference that he and his wife Carolyn 'experienced for the first time Keith's peripatetic style of lecturing, pacing to and fro across the stage, with a large stack of note cards which he didn't actually seem to need'. Michael Jones, who also gave a paper, has even more vivid memories. 'I first got to know Keith about twenty years ago', he recollected in March 2004:

> ... at a conference organised by the Richard III Society. To be honest, I was more than a little frightened of this larger-than-life Yorkshireman with his booming voice. I had rarely encountered anyone who was so honest, who said exactly what he thought, and who so deeply detested any form of pretension. Keith never 'bought into the system' and, over a number of drinks, it was his good humoured irreverence that was so enjoyable. Underneath the banter, Keith had an extraordinary gift of accepting people exactly as they were, for better or worse, and his wonderful sense of humour was a breath of fresh air (much needed sometimes in the fog of cigarette smoke!).

My own memory, no less vivid, is that Michael and I got completely plastered in the college bar one night and had enormous difficulty finding our rooms when we finally staggered out into the night in the early hours. This was to have a sequel at a later conference when Michael, having failed to collect the key to his own room in a hall of residence, ended up crashing out on the floor of mine.

The Cambridge paper of 1984 was eventually published in a 1986 volume of conference proceedings, *Richard III: Loyalty, Lordship and Law*, edited by Peter

Hammond himself. By then I'd written another, and rather better, article on 'The Political Legacy of Richard III in Northern England', again deriving in part from my postgraduate research. The opportunity had come when Ralph Griffiths asked me to contribute to a *festschrift* he and James Sherborne were putting together for Charles Ross (who retired as professor of medieval history at Bristol University in 1982). Correspondence between Ralph and I at this time is revealing. In June 1985, just after I'd sent him the completed paper, he wrote to me:

> I've just finished reading your piece. You've done a good and thorough job and it will be a valuable extension of our pitiful knowledge of the change of regime in 1485. The problem of balance in the volume might arise, though, since you run to 11,500 words. There are a lot of details and a wealth of examples, relevant ones admittedly, but I might have to come back to you later for some pruning or rearrangement or excision. But don't panic and become suicidal:

My relief, when responding early in July, is palpable:

> I'm glad you think the paper is basically OK. Quite a lot of work did go into it. On the length, is it really 11,500 words? I didn't think I was capable of writing so much! Of course, if necessary, I can prune/rearrange/ excise the piece, but I'm equally content that you hack at it yourself.

The paper did turn out to be too long; Ralph himself performed a splendid job of editing it down; and his reaction to a prompt return of the proofs was: 'What an obedient lad you are!'. The *festschrift* was eventually published towards the end of 1986 under the title *Kings and Nobles in the Later Middle Ages: A Tribute to Charles Ross*. Sadly, by then, Charles himself was dead.

Charles Ross's murder on 3 April 1986 at the age of sixty-two came as a profound shock to me. It was he who had first fired my interest in fifteenth-century England in the 1960s and, although disappointed at my failure to complete a doctorate, he remained a close friend throughout the 1970s and early 1980s. More than anyone else, too, it was Charles who encouraged me to return to my postgraduate research files with an eye to publication. I regularly visited him in Bristol and, after he married Anne Crawford (another former student of his) in the mid-1970s, stayed with them several times. Indeed, Anne recalls:

> We were always delighted to see you when you came to stay with us in Redland, but I do remember Charles being a trifle put out when you once rolled back very drunk in the early hours of the morning—probably jealous because he hadn't been out with you!

Charles and I had certainly drunk vast quantities of beer together in the later 1960s and, occasionally, hit the whisky or gin as well. By the end of the 1970s, however, his fondness for vodka had turned him into a virtual alcoholic, a fact brought home to me with a vengeance when we were both scheduled to address a fifteenth-century conference in Wakefield, his home town, in April 1983. Although he still managed to convey his old enthusiasm for, and knowledge of, fifteenth-century northern history, it was a well below par performance; by the time we set off for Huddersfield (where he was staying with me overnight) he must already have been well over the legal limit for driving; and, *en route*, I even insisted we stop off at a pub for a couple of pints of beer (which seemed preferable to his swigging yet more vodka in the car). Back at my house a great deal more alcohol was consumed; I had a severe hangover next morning; and how Charles managed to get back to Bristol in one piece that day I have no idea. Soon afterwards drink put paid to his marriage and, although he and Anne remained close and he continued to see his young son James regularly, Charles moved into a cramped Bristol flat with another woman he had known for years. By September 1985, however, he had embarked on a new book and was seriously trying to curb his drinking, sufficiently so to attend a talk I gave to the Yorkshire branch of the Richard III Society in York. Although he didn't know it, what he heard was a lecture version of my *festschrift* paper and, much to my relief, he was very complimentary about it. The last time I saw him, only a few weeks before his death, was when he and his new companion, a fellow alcoholic, stayed with me in Huddersfield: it was a splendid evening but, I fear, did nothing to aid his efforts to cut down on alcohol. I did let slip, however, that a *festschrift* in his honour was in the final stage of preparation and he was clearly delighted. At the beginning of April 1986, in a letter from Ralph Griffiths mainly concerned with the *festschrift*, I learned that 'Charles seems to be trying to keep to a strict *regimen*' and 'is beavering away at his new book'. The very next day, so Peter Allender remembers, 'when watching the local television news in Bristol I was startled to see a picture of Charles and shocked to hear of his murder'. The first I knew of it, in fact, was when Peter rang me in Huddersfield the same evening.

'Professor Charles Ross, a medieval history expert', was 'stabbed to death by his lover when she cracked under the strains imposed by alcoholism', reported the *Independent* at the conclusion of her trial in November 1986. In the meantime many historians, including myself, had journeyed to the Lord Mayor's Chapel, Bristol, for a memorial service on 4 July. Ralph Griffiths spoke for most of us when he declared in an address that Charles was 'a social and economic historian, a student of politics and institutions, and he knew his church'; he was 'immensely learned and dedicated in a modest sort of way'; and he was:

... never happier than when listening (for he was a good listener) and discussing problems of medieval society informally, with pipe and pint, and with a seriousness that was never allowed to fall into pretension or pomposity on the part of either student or mentor. To Charles the study of history was serious fun and his own enjoyment of it was infectious.

A few years later, in December 1990, I myself wrote to Ralph:

I've just agreed to write a 7000 word appreciation of Charles Ross for a new medieval history journal (publication April 1992). Perhaps it was you who suggested me to the editor? I'm certainly very glad to do it.

Ralph, in response, sent me a copy of the address he had delivered at Charles's memorial service, and very helpful it proved to be. Several months later, in September 1991, I sent first drafts of my appreciation to both Ralph and Anne Crawford, commenting in an accompanying letter:

I'm not entirely satisfied with this but it will have to do. If you detect any significant errors, I'll alter it accordingly, and also take out anything you think unseemly. I've thought carefully about the personal stuff and put most of it in footnotes. Charles's friends will obviously read between the lines in places but I think the stories and anecdotes do aid understanding of his success as a teacher and writer. I'm sure Charles, in his modest way, would accuse me of exaggerating his contribution to fifteenth-century history and squirm at some of the hyperbole but I think his friends will agree with the vast majority of it.

The responses of both were positive. 'It is splendid', declared Ralph, 'so congratulations: you've done just the job I knew you would'. Anne replied, in similar vein, 'I thought it excellent, a combination of the personal and scholarly which is appropriately Ross-like'. As for Judith Loades, the editor of *Medieval History*, she too was complimentary when I sent her the final version:

Thank you so much for the splendid appreciation of Charles Ross—exactly what I was looking for. It was obviously a piece that was very important to you and it shows. Terrific!

Steve Garrett, a student of mine at Huddersfield in the early 1990s, specifically remembers that 'in the era I knew Keith he clearly missed his much loved mentor Charles Ross', while Mike Stammers (who himself took Charles's Special Subject at Bristol in 1965/6) comments:

I think the contact with Charles Ross inspired Keith and, after graduating, Ross became a friend and more. Ross's loss, I believe, has made Keith carry his flame.

Tony Pollard is more speculative:

I have always thought you put yourself too much in Charles Ross's shadow, as if what he achieved was a substitute for what you, following in his footsteps, might achieve. Was he the father-figure you never knew? And, since he was not your natural father, was it impossible to do like other sons do and depose him?

Maybe Tony has a point but, re-reading the 1992 appreciation fifteen years later, my conclusions still seem right:

Charles Ross has left an irrevocable stamp on the recent historiography of fifteenth-century England. No one knew more than he about the Yorkist age, particularly its kings and aristocracy, and he revelled in the unfolding of its detailed history. His talent for teaching and his gift for writing, his pragmatism and firm rejection of narrow ideology-led history, and his rare capacity to inspire as well as instruct, are fondly remembered by all who knew him. Above all, he had a tremendous capacity for friendship, and his dry sense of humour, his fondness for good stories (and ability to recount them) and his ready generosity ensured he had friends in plenty.

Perhaps Charles Ross's disappearance from the scene, and the emergence of a new breed of young scholars ruthless in their determination to create waves and make their mark, helps explain the changing atmosphere at fifteenth-century conferences from the later 1980s. This first became palpable at a colloquium hosted by Manchester University in July 1989. The day after it ended, in a letter to Colin Richmond at Keele, I commented:

The Manchester conference was an enjoyable gathering on the whole. I found most of the lectures, papers and discussions stimulating, and devoured my usual high quota of alcohol. What I did *not* like was what seemed to be a novel and nasty tone emanating mainly from the Cambridge contingent. Their evident lack of tolerance, I fear, can only reflect the advance of Thatcherite notions ('is he one of us?') into academia. Charles Ross would not have approved at all. After all he inaugurated this sequence of conferences with a stress on friendliness and informality. Perhaps the spirit of F. R. Leavis [a waspish English don at Cambridge University in the 1940s and 1950] has transferred its malign and destructive influence from the English to the History school.

On the very same day, and in similar terms, I also wrote to Richard Davies, one of the organisers of the conference. In reply Richard admitted that he, too, had sensed 'a Cambridge versus the Rest air'; as for Colin, who had been the victim of several barbed remarks himself, he responded with characteristic vigour:

> I suppose I would have expected you to write so promptly. If any fifteenth-century historian is human, it is you (that's a compliment!). Like you I was disturbed by the whole scene at Manchester. Thank Christ you and I are out of the McFarlane/ Ross stable. These Cambridge folk seem puny. Small minds have to be stopped. Ross and most of his pupils (*all* I know) have the large variety. We get up the noses of those who think of themselves as 'professional historians'! It must be Cambridge that does it. Huddersfield, like Stoke, broadens the mind.

Even the mild-mannered Ralph Griffiths, a couple of years later, felt moved to remark on 'the unfeeling and hypercritical section of the fifteenth-century community'.

The next academic conference I attended, on 'English Provincial Society and its Institutions c.1250—1650' at Bristol Polytechnic in September 1990, was much pleasanter. Its success owed a great deal to the organisational skills of Peter Fleming and, indeed, it was here that I really got to know him. The other bonus was the presence of Jack Lander. I hadn't encountered him in person since 1970 at Cardiff but had always enjoyed his work. Now retired and back in England after many years at the University of Western Ontario, he proved splendid company, not only in the bar in the evenings but also early in the morning as both he and I pulled ourselves together over tea and cigarettes in the hall of residence. Even so, after Manchester, I was rather wary of going to another fifteenth-century conference. What made the difference was that, in September 1992, the venue was Oxford University's Manchester College and the organiser Rowena Archer, another former pupil of Charles Ross. As I wrote to the American historian Joel Rosenthal, who was booked to give a paper, early in June 1992:

> I do intend to go to Oxford in mid-September for Rowena's conference: indeed, I've more or less been given a 3-line whip! I don't know how many of the papers I'll be able to face but I'll certainly be at yours. Let's hope some of the other drinkers will be there as well (Mike Jones immediately springs to mind). No doubt you and I will manage a modest pint or two come what may. Presumably that's why you're coming to England anyway, for the beer:

As it turned out this was the most relaxed fifteenth-century gathering I'd been to for several years, most memorably a visit to Broughton castle where Lord Saye and Sele (whose forbear of the same name, as we didn't fail to remind him, had been murdered by Jack Cade's rebels in London in 1450!) took us on an entertaining and revealing tour of his ancestral pile. Since the next conference, at Durham University's Trevelyan College in September 1993, was partly organised by Tony Pollard and focussed on later medieval English political history, I felt duty bound to attend that as well. Most of the papers were interesting enough but, as I noted at the time, 'sessions in the bar—and in my room post-midnight for the inner circle of the Ross connection—were even more rewarding and enjoyable'. Unfortunately, the Cambridge mafia also turned out in force. 'Although I was sorry not to see you at Durham', I wrote to Ralph Griffiths soon after returning to Huddersfield, 'at least you were spared the spectacle of observing the Cambridge contingent in action once more'. Indeed, Durham left such a sour taste in my mouth that I didn't attend another fifteenth-century conference until 1996.

In the later 1980s and early 1990s, rather to my astonishment, I found myself more and more in demand as a guest lecturer. Just a fortnight after Charles Ross's murder in April 1986, I returned to the chantry chapel on the bridge in Wakefield where he and I had performed together almost exactly three years earlier. Preluding my lecture with a brief appreciation of Charles himself, I then went on to talk about 'Marriage, Love and Sex in Fifteenth Century England', ending with a selection of lurid evidence from church court records on topics ranging from abortion to adultery, bastards to brothels. During the course of the day, too, I was interviewed live on Radio Leeds and, apparently, caused not a little consternation back in the studio by telling a series of risqué stories hardly suitable for day time listeners in the mid-1980s. The best of them, derived from the register of an archbishop of York, concerned a certain John whose wife had applied to the ecclesiastical authorities, in 1433, for annulment of her marriage on the grounds of her husband's impotency. This required that he be 'inspected' by seven women in turn, the first of whom we're told:

> ... exposed her naked breasts and, after warming her hands at the fire, held and rubbed his penis, and stirred him up insofar as she could to show his virility and potency, admonishing him for shame that he should there and then prove and render himself a man. Yet, she then declared, throughout his penis remained scarcely three inches long, registering neither increase nor decrease.

When the other six had no more success, they cursed John for his failure, walked out, and his wife was promptly granted a divorce! A splendid story but not, perhaps, Radio Leeds' normal Saturday fare. A few days later Richard Knowles, organiser of the conference, sent me a note expressing his:

> ... sincere thanks for a splendid talk. I know for sure that all the people present enjoyed it immensely. And I hope Radio Leeds did not bother you too much.

I subsequently gave the lecture on several more occasions, most memorably to the Manchester Medieval Society in March 1988, when I added by way of preamble:

> When I was asked to talk to this society, I offered either a serious academic lecture or this relatively light-hearted survey originally put together for a non-specialist audience. Your chairman felt sex should take precedence over scholarship, a verdict with which I'm strongly inclined to agree, so here goes.

Another lecture of the later 1980s, eventually published in 1995, was 'Edward IV: Playboy or Politician?' and, again, sex figured prominently. This received its first hearing at Leeds Art Gallery in April 1989 when, so a member of the organising Yorkshire branch of the Richard III Society told me, it was 'much appreciated by all there', among them my own Huddersfield colleague Pauline Stafford. A few months later I gave it again, this time to the Nottingham branch of the Historical Association at the invitation of fifteenth-century historian Ian Arthurson, and, a real bonus, also met up with Bernard Jarvis once more. As I wrote to Ian at the time:

> I rang my friend Bernard Jarvis in Nottingham and he can put me up overnight. Indeed, he asked me if he could come along to the lecture himself and bring his teenage son (who, apparently, is in the first year sixth and studying the Tudors to A-Level). Is that OK?

Bernard and his son duly turned up and seemed to enjoy the talk. 'Edward IV: Playboy or Politician?' was to surface several more times in the 1990s. 'The Yorkshire Plumptons and their Letters in the Fifteenth Century' had a number of outings as well. Originally put together for a Historical Association Day School on *The Wars of the Roses in the North* at York University in November 1989 (where Tony Pollard was a fellow speaker), it faced its most potentially critical audience at the Knaresborough Historical Society in April 1990 since the Plumptons were very much a local gentry family. In fact, it went down well and resulted in an unusually well-informed discussion. Tony Pollard had obviously enjoyed it as well; I gave a revised version to his MA group at Teesside University in June 1994; and, so he assured me, 'the presentation was just right' (remarkable, if true, since I'd stayed with him and his wife the night before and was nursing a not inconsiderable hangover!). What I could never face was the long flight to America. Joel Rosenthal, professor of history at New York State University, first invited me to perform at an international medieval conference at West Michigan University, Kalamazoo, in 1990, assuring me that, although he couldn't extol the local beer, the regional wine was 'probably at least as good as the Romans got from the vineyards along the Old Kent Road'. Sadly, I replied, 'I must decline since my aversion to long distance travelling these days verges on paranoia'. He tried again in 1993 but, once more, I turned down the invitation because 'I'm just not able to cope with long distance travel'. A pity perhaps, especially as I was promised full expenses on both occasions, but I've never had any desire to visit the United States anyway.

At the end of June 1986, I penned a cautiously probing letter to Anne Sutton, editor of *The Ricardian*:

> Next year is the anniversary of the accession to the throne of William Rufus in 1087. Over the last year or two I've been considering points of comparison between Rufus, as one supposedly archetypal medieval villain, and Richard III, as another. In particular, I've been looking at contemporary and near-contemporary assessments of the two, how Victorian historians (in particular) built on them, and how/why traditional views of the pair have been modified in the twentieth century. I know you normally only publish stuff that's strictly on the fifteenth century but I think Rufus, too, might be of considerable interest to *Ricardian* readers in view of the similarities between his traditional treatment and that of Richard III. I wonder, therefore, if you'd consider a piece for publication next year on 'William Rufus, Richard III and Historical Tradition'.

What I'd done, in fact, was dig out my unpublished 1979 paper on 'William Rufus, the Victorians and the Present' and this seemed an excellent way of recycling the material. Anne's response that 'an article along the lines you suggest would be of interest to *The Ricardian*' provided all the incentive I needed; Pauline Stafford's expertise and advice helped save me from error in interpreting the sources for William Rufus; and, in April 1987, I duly despatched the final result, commenting:

> I've tried to write it very much with *Ricardian* readers in mind and it has proved more difficult than I'd anticipated. I haven't had so much trouble since my last venture into comparative history (comparing England and Japan in the fifteenth century) in the late 1970s.

Anne's reaction, 'I've enjoyed reading the article and I'm sure Ricardians will too', couldn't have been more gratifying and it was duly published in September

1987. Since about the end of 1984 I had also been toying with the idea of writing a book on *England and the English in the Fifteenth Century* for the publisher Alan Sutton. Although the subject was interesting enough, progress was so minimal that in August 1989 I decided to offer a spin-off article, 'Patriotism, Pride and Paranoia: England and the English in the Fifteenth Century', to *The Ricardian* instead; again, Anne Sutton accepted what was, as I put it at the time, 'originally intended as the opening chapter of a now defunct book'; and the paper appeared in print in September 1990. At the invitation of Pam Judkins, keeper of archeology, I delivered a lecture at Wakefield Museum early in October 1991 on 'The Battle of Wakefield and the Wars of the Roses' as part of a Day School on *The Battle of Wakefield 1460*. Tony Pollard was a fellow performer and, as I remarked in a letter to Ralph Griffiths a few days later, once the conference was over he and I 'retired to a nearby pub and mulled over the horrors of higher education'. Pam Judkins herself seemed very pleased at the day's success:

> Thank you for your talk on Saturday. It was very good of you to give up your time and quite beyond the call of duty to produce such a good handout of extracts from contemporary and near-contemporary sources. I found that really useful as the material is not easily available anywhere in print and I'm sure I'll be needing it again. I felt the day was successful and members of the audience I spoke to certainly enjoyed it.

By the time I gave the lecture again, to the Huddersfield Military History Society in March 1993, an expanded version of that, too, had found its way into print in *The Ricardian* (incorporating substantial chunks from the major primary sources). Tony Pollard immediately sent me a note declaring he had 'just read your battle of Wakefield'; moreover, he added, 'it has the same panache as the Lancastrian leadership at Hull' in 1460, albeit 'historical not military in your case'. This was praise indeed from the most accomplished scholar of fifteenth-century northern history of my generation and I was delighted. Soon after publication in June 1992, alongside a complementary article on the battle field's topography by local historian Richard Knowles, the Richard III Society issued a pamphlet containing both; in October 1992 Pam Judkins reported that 'we are selling it at Wakefield Museum and local sales have been quite good'; and it was even reprinted in 1999.

By the later 1980s I was also regularly penning book reviews, mainly of new work covering later medieval politics and society, for *The Ricardian*. This was both enjoyable in itself and intellectually rewarding, as well as yielding free copies of often expensive books. From the start I set myself three main tasks: to put books into their historiographical context, provide a brief summary of their content and, wherever possible, be positive about them and avoid embarking on a critical ego-trip of my own. Anne Sutton seemed to like my approach. In August 1988, for instance, she acknowledged receipt of a 'prompt and excellent review' of Denys Hay's *Renaissance Essays*, adding 'I must use your reviewing talents more often'; similarly, in March 1989, not only did she thank me for 'an excellent review' of *The New Monarchy; England 1471—1534* by Anthony Goodman but also remarked that 'it is marvellous to have a reviewer who does not need reminding they've had a book 6-12 months'. Declaring in response that 'flattery will get you everywhere', I even agreed to review a substantial *History of Parliament: The Middle Ages* since, 'although I tend to avoid reading books about institutions, it would be both good for my soul and a useful way of bringing me up to date on the subject'. By then I also felt confident enough to add:

> I gather Tony Pollard's book on *North-Eastern England during the Wars of the Roses* should appear early in 1990. May I put in a request to review it for *The Ricardian*? I'm really looking forward to reading it.

Anne complied and I wasn't disappointed by a 'splendid book' where, 'while displaying formidable scholarship throughout', Pollard 'never ceases to be both readable and thought-provoking'. In 1991 she also sent me a new textbook by the well-established Oxford historian Maurice Keen, *English Society in the Later Middle Ages*, commenting that my subsequent review was, 'as always, one members of the Society will enjoy'.

For a couple of years in the later 1980s I also found myself reviewing books on later medieval England for the *Times Higher Education Supplement*, an opportunity almost certainly resulting from the fact that Pauline Stafford knew its literary editor Brian Morton. Unlike *The Ricardian*, or learned journals for that matter, *THES* reviewers were even paid! Since the first book I received (in September 1987) happened to be a first-rate study of the later medieval English nobility by Chris Given-Wilson, moreover, my review was almost entirely positive, so much so that Andrew Wheatcroft of Routledge and Kegan Paul (the publisher) even sent me a note declaring:

> I was delighted with your review of Chris Given-Wilson's book, as I know he was. In fact, I have been on the point of writing to you for some time because there are one or two projects that I would very much like to discuss with you.

James Sherborne of Bristol University, who had so often put my undergraduate essays under the microscope in 1964/5, also responded enthusiastically:

I thought your review of Given-Wilson's book read extremely well. It certainly has the desired effect of encouraging others to read it.

Both these responses certainly encouraged me to carry on reviewing. Perhaps the book I most enjoyed reading for the *THES* (in September 1989) was *Richard III: A Study of Service*, a 'fine work of traditional scholarship' by a young Cambridge historian Rosemary Horrox. Indeed, as I wrote to her at the time:

> Hearing on the grapevine that publication was imminent and anticipating (rightly!) that the book would be both scholarly and readable, I urged the literary editor of the *Times Higher Education Supplement* to ensure it was reviewed there. Rather to my surprise, not only did he take my advice but sent it to me rather than Tony Pollard or another luminary of the 'respectable' end of the medieval fraternity. Don't worry! Although I'm sure I wouldn't be your choice of reviewer—after all, you and I must represent the two extremes of professional historians (the formidable and dedicated scholar firmly in the Oxbridge mould as opposed to a committed populariser-cum-simplifier of fifteenth-century history lacking any great interest in, enthusiasm for or even deep expectations of, archives on major topics)—I can still just about recognise a quality book when I see it. No doubt the reason why I get monographs to review from time to time (very good for me, I'm sure) is that I do always try to provide a context and never indulge in the futile scoring of minor academic points. My contempt for elitist Oxbridge-type history grows ever more powerful and medieval history must certainly demonstrate its relevance to modern society or go under.

Rosemary's reply, thanking me for saying 'such nice things' about her book, was equally forthright:

> I do know what you mean about the Oxbridge mafia. I suppose I'm a fringe member—although I tend to think that if I'd been a fully paid up mafioso (so to speak) I might have found a job by now. As it is, I'm still free-lancing here—which at least is possible, although when I look at my teaching load/annual income and compare it with that of salaried colleagues, I can't help feeling exploited.

Rosemary courageously stuck in there and, eventually, she did obtain a full-time salaried post at Cambridge, and rightly so. By the end of 1989 however, I was beginning to find regular reviewing for the *THES* a bit of a chore and so, when I was sent an almost impenetrable study of lordship in later medieval England, I penned the only seriously hostile review I've ever written. 'I did not like this book at all', I wrote to the literary editor, 'but I hope you decide to publish the review as I've taken the opportunity to mount a blast against dry-as-dust history'. Even now, I stand by my conclusion absolutely:

> A. J. P. Taylor remarks, at the end of a revealing autobiography which should be compulsory reading for all historians of the dry-as-dust tendency, that, for him, 'writing history has been Fun on a high academic level'. This is certainly history 'on a high academic level', conscientiously researched and coherent within its own narrow terms of reference; sadly, it is also history at its most dreary and incestuous, and no fun at all.

For whatever reason, this turned out to be the last book I ever reviewed for the *Times Higher Education Supplement.* By the time I left Huddersfield in 1994, however, I was beginning to be asked to review for learned journals, even the prestigious *History*.

'The very first time I met you', recollects the publisher Alan Sutton:

> ...was at Swansea in 1979. I recall being attracted by your outspoken and anarchic manner and, as a fellow smoker and drinker, it was easy to latch on to your company when other wimpish and good-behaving academics were scurrying quietly away to their quarters. Other early conferences followed a similar pattern and we seemed to get on rather well, despite your ridiculing me as a budding tycoon while, meanwhile, poor academics such as yourself starved.

In fact, apart from Anne Sutton and *The Ricardian*, it was meeting and eventually becoming a close friend of Alan that most encouraged me to get down to some serious writing in the 1980s. Critically important was a weekend Alan spent with me in Huddersfield in April 1986 when, after an hour or two browsing through documents put together for my Special Subject at the polytechnic, the notion of *Richard III: A Reader in History* was born. A few weeks later I received a letter from him confirming that Alan Sutton Publishing had now firmly decided:

> ... in favour of doing the *Richard III Reader*. It will be very much an experiment taking us into a new market. I envisage secondary school, undergraduate and also general trade interest. If we can ensure the success of this volume, moreover, we might even publish a series, so please try and devise a structure that could be used for subsequent readers.

By the spring of 1987 the book, dedicated to the memory of Miriam Saunders and Edith Wood 'who enabled me to survive an unpromising beginning', was complete; I came up with a format that did help spawn a series; and two of my Huddersfield colleagues Keith Laybourn and Bill Roberts soon penned volumes for it. Indeed, Bill recollects that it was through me he 'first met Alan Sutton and, as a consequence, gained a foothold in publishing'; moreover, he adds reflectively, 'many years later we met up again at the *Fountain*, one of the scrattiest pubs in Huddersfield, a curious spot to entertain a publisher'. The arrival of the proofs of *Richard III: A Reader in History* coincided with a visit to Bristol in the late summer of 1987 when, so James Sherborne recalled a few weeks later, he and I spent a sultry afternoon reading them on Clifton Downs; James and I also visited Charles Ross's very elderly mother (ensconsed in a retirement home where we found her reading Jane Austen!); and, when the book was published early in 1988, he expressed the belief that it would be 'valuable, useful and well received'. Sadly, within a couple of years, he was dead. A positive review in *The Ricardian* was obviously to be hoped for and eventually, in June 1990, even Richard III Society luminary John Saunders concluded that it was:

> ... a solid introduction to a difficult and complicated subject and will be particularly beneficial to those seeking to use and study primary source material for the first time. To have such a range of extracts from contemporary material in one compact, reasonably priced book is a good idea, and it certainly fulfils its aim of being an informative and valuable addition to the literature on Richard III.

More unexpected, and more immediate, was a slightly tongue-in-cheek interview I gave to a *Huddersfield Examiner* reporter at the end of March 1988:

> Tomorrow sees the publication of Keith Dockray's first book, *Richard III*, an investigation of the truth about the king via the many documents of the time. The 44-year-old author, a senior lecturer in history at Huddersfield Polytechnic who lives at Newsome, argues that Richard gained his reputation largely as a result of hostile southern establishment opinion and Tudor propaganda, culminating in Shakespeare's play of the early 1590s:
>
>> In the north Richard was popular but, once he became king because of his northern connections, those in the south resented the fact that he introduced many northerners into positions of authority. Then after his removal from the throne, the Tudor propaganda machine was put on full throttle against him.
>
> Mr Dockray, who has spoken in favour of the much maligned king in an Oxford Union debate and on television, insists that Richard III is not guilty of many of

the murders he is supposed to have committed. There's even a question mark over whether he had any involvement in the murder of the Princes in the Tower although, since they were a danger to him because of their own claim to the throne, Mr Dockray concedes that in this violent and brutal age he could well have been responsible for their untimely end:

> Even so, he was not the wicked monster Shakespeare portrayed. I would sum him up as an ambitious, ruthless man who was nevertheless capable of good government and of attracting loyalty, particularly in the north, and who was unlucky to lose his throne at the battle of Bosworth in 1485.

I also aired my views about Richard III on national radio but, since the interview was recorded at 7.30 in the morning for transmission later in the day, I never heard it because I was lecturing at the time! More satisfying than either interview, anyway, was Tony Pollard's decision to recommend my book as a text for his Richard III Special Subject at Teesside Polytechnic. There was also a spin-off when Judith Loades of Headstart History asked me to write a pamphlet for her on Richard III which, as I told her shortly before publication in 1992, was:

> ...very much based on the documents and commentary in my *Richard III: A Reader* in History. Alan Sutton (whom I saw the other week) seems happy about this, no doubt anticipating a few further sales of the book on the strength of it. What I have done is reorganise the material substantially and tried to take on board new stuff that has appeared since 1987. I hope the result is, at least, clear and coherent enough to whet the appetites of the uninitiated.

Again, I particularly appreciated Tony Pollard's response to the pamphlet:

> *Richard III* is a very neat job. In fact I might well read it out aloud in a couple of weeks time when I conduct a seminar on recent writings about the king at a Historical Association conference in Durham! An excellent short introduction for all students.

Alan Sutton, as well as commissioning new books on fifteenth-century England and publishing several volumes of conference proceedings in the 1980s, was also keen to reprint classic works that had long been unavailable outside well-established libraries. This included Victorian editions of primary sources and, towards the end of 1987, he and I came up with the idea of reissuing in a single volume three short chronicles covering the years 1469—1471 (when

Edward IV both lost his throne and won it back again); early in 1989 I wrote a short introduction discussing their possible authors, dates of composition, content and value to historians; and, towards the end of the year, *Three Chronicles of the Reign of Edward IV* was published. At my suggestion, Alan also decided to reprint the only existing edition of *The Plumpton Correspondence* (originally published in 1839); again, I penned a new introduction; and the book appeared in 1990. More bizarrely, this time at Alan's suggestion, I also ended up editing a book on Victorian peasants. 'I have a book called *The English Peasant* by Richard Heath', he wrote in June 1987:

> Published in 1892, it is a rather strange book in many ways. It is made up of articles printed in periodicals over the twenty years before 1892, including some rather amateurish medieval stuff. Heath was not a professional but the nineteenth-century pieces are rather nice: he wandered around England interviewing peasants! If you are interested in taking it on, I'll send you a photocopy of the whole book to delete chunks and edit the rest. I would like to end up with a book of 192 or possibly 224 pages, incorporating contemporary photographs, and amounting to about 70,000 words. It should be a nice easy job. The only real work would be a 4000 word introduction putting the articles into context.

I knew nothing about nineteenth-century peasants, and cared less, but Alan offered a not ungenerous fee and it sounded an interesting challenge. So I accepted the commission and, in the end, enjoyed the experience more than I had expected, particularly penning the introduction and concocting passages such as:

> Immorality haunts the pages of Heath's essays, but only rarely is he explicit: more often than not his readers are left to make what they can of hints and innuendos. Clearly Richard Heath, in common with so many other later nineteenth-century commentators, was inclined to exaggerate the prevalence of immoral behaviour; they were far too ready to to equate 'immodesty' with 'immorality', men, women and children living together in unavoidably cramped conditions were not, as a result, inevitably victims of overwhelming lascivious desire; and clergymen in particular were altogether too ready to detect cohabitation and consequent illegitimacy lurking everywhere. Even the everyday sight of animals copulating in the fields was naively identified as a perverted stimulus to immorality!

The Victorian Peasant, a splendidly produced and superbly illustrated volume, was published in 1989, including a heart-felt expression of gratitude to:

... my colleagues Keith Laybourn and Peter Wood for answering my no doubt often naive questions and commenting on the introduction. Hopefully, they have prevented me, as a mere medievalist entering the stormy waters of Victorian rural history, making too many crass errors!

Perhaps inevitably, *The Victorian Peasant* was more extensively reviewed than most books on fifteenth-century England, even in the *Independent* newspaper (where, much to my relief, I was judged to have 'made judicious use of Richard Heath's work').

Not only did Alan Sutton publish *Richard III: A Reader in History* and put other historical projects my way in the later 1980s, he and I also became close friends; he visited me in Huddersfield several times; and, for a while, I even became a shareholder in his publishing company. Alan himself recalls how, when staying with me in Huddersfield in April 1986:

> I mentioned the plight of Alan Sutton Publishing Limited. This was the point at which your true spirit came out for, despite ridiculing businessmen, you joined in the spirit of assistance and helped keep the ship afloat as a worthwhile cause to support and, hopefully, gain from.

Unfortunately, in 1987, in order to raise much needed further cash, Alan was forced into a deal with the Guernsey Press Company under which existing shareholders like me lost out badly. I accepted the loss of almost £4000 philosophically enough but, as a letter he wrote in October 1990 makes clear, Alan himself had felt very uncomfortable at the time:

> May I thank you once again for all the assistance you gave at a difficult time in the company's history. Although events did not turn out as we would have wished, without your assistance the company would not have survived.

And, years later again, he even confessed that I had been more understanding than he deserved! Alan's continuing problems with the company he himself had founded some fifteen years earlier came to a head in 1993 when, he recalls, 'I visited you in Huddersfield on Sunday 19 September *en route* to the Durham conference predicting, quite rightly as it turned out, an explosion the following week'. The outcome, in fact, was Alan's resignation as managing director. Almost immediately I despatched a robust letter to his successor:

> As a historian who has much admired Alan's publishing enterprise over many years, and know how much the company owed to his flair and judgement (partic-

ularly in its early days), I am naturally astounded at the manner of his departure. At the time when Guernsey Press was in process of negotiation, and at Alan's urging *in the interests of the company*, I sold my share holding in Alan Sutton Publishing at a very substantial loss. Naturally, in the circumstances now prevailing, I can feel little loyalty to, or sympathy for, the parent company.

At about the same time I also wrote to Ralph Griffiths:

No doubt you've heard of the upheavals at Alan Sutton Publishing, culminating in Alan's departure from the company. I was so appalled at the behaviour of Guernsey Press that, after consulting Alan, I sent a critical letter to the new managing director. As a man who, like me, has always appreciated Alan's pivotal role in the renaissance of fifteenth-century studies over the years, you might find it of interest.

Ralph's response was equally forceful:

Like you I was very distressed at the news of Alan's departure and have written to him, and the company, very largely along the lines of your letter. It is a tragedy for Alan to have to sever his links with the firm which he launched and inspired and, as you say, it is difficult to calculate the debt which lots of 15th-century historians, especially young ones, owe to his interest (and indulgence!) over many years.

Alan's own reaction was:

Is it not wonderful? The only letters and expressions of support I have received are from the fifteenth-century coterie. Thank you for sending your letter to the company. I am sure it rattled the cage a little and, while it may make little difference in the final analysis, it certainly made me feel better.

For me, the upshot of all this was that, for several years, I had virtually no contact with Sutton Publishing (as it became soon after Alan's departure) and I was certainly delighted when, years later in 2007, he bought back the company.

By the time I left Huddersfield in 1994, despite such a shaky start on the research front, I felt I had begun to earn a modest reputation for myself as a published historian. This was brought home to me most dramatically when I received a letter from a Japanese historian Hisao Ono telling me that my appreciation of Charles Ross (1992) had recently been translated into Japanese for publication in a Japanese journal. A regular correspondence and exchange of articles ensued culminating, in September 1998, in our meeting up and spending a pleasant afternoon exploring medieval Bristol together. Even more remarkable, or so I felt at the time, was my election to a fellowship of the Royal Historical Society. In May 1992 I wrote to Tony Pollard:

> Two of my colleagues have recently persuaded me to apply for the fellowship of the Royal Historical Society. Keith Laybourn got the form and more or less forced me to fill it in. I can't really believe I'm eminent enough and, only the other day, I discovered that you are an influential voice in that august institution. Please don't feel embarrassed if it falls to you to block it!

A few days later Tony replied:

> Your application for election as a Fellow of the RHS came up at a meeting of Council yesterday. You should be hearing good news shortly. I certainly did not attempt to block it! You have no need to feel that you are not eminent enough. It all depends on how you choose to judge eminence. Surely it isn't just a publication list as long as your arm but also how you are valued by your peers. Well, the RHS certainly takes that view.

After I'd been duly elected, I again dropped him a note:

> I am now a Fellow of the Royal Historical Society! If I ever indulged in letters after my name (which I don't) it amounts to a trebling of length. Seriously, though, I'm flattered to join the ranks of respectable historians after all these years.

What I value even more, despite all the hyperbole, are the judgements of former Huddersfield colleagues. Brendan Evans, for instance, recalls that over the years we worked together 'you quietly and increasingly produced high quality publications, credible as pure historical research yet, at the same time, never losing focus on the needs of students and generating enthusiasm for history'. Keith Laybourn is even more flattering:

> Your enthusiasm for teaching extended into your writing. Although you always denied an interest in writing anything, and still do, you have been a prolific writer, whether it be on Richard III, Edward IV, Shakespeare, or various combinations of all three. You have even compared the Onin War with the Wars of the Roses. I have read most of what you have written and, whilst not an expert in your areas of publication, admire the clarity, composition and perception of your writing. It is accomplished, humorous, generous to other writers, and a blessing for students who need a guide through all the mass of detail and interpretation that is history.

And, Keith adds anecdotally:

> Your writing is compelling and has left its mark on a generation or more of students. Indeed, I once met a student in the library of Nottingham Trent University (I was there as an external examiner) who was most impressed that I not only knew Keith Dockray but actually shared a room with him. What kudos and status I gained in his eyes!

As for my former medieval colleague Tony Saul, his conclusions are wider in scope but not dissimilar in essence:

> Keith made light of his scholarship. Fortunately, the wider academic community, his colleagues, his students and his publishers did not. Among Keith's many qualities is his ability to enthuse his listeners, whether in formal university or conference settings or in wider contexts. Reaching the wider audience and making medieval history (or the English Civil War, or Gilbert and Sullivan) fun is one of Keith's fortés. Friends or local history societies, especially if they asked for something on Richard III and/or the Princes in the Tower, were seldom refused. To Keith the prospect of travel was sometimes more daunting than the preparation or delivery of the talk. Members of the Ricardian fan club were handled gently and left with thoughtful challenges to their preconceptions. Keith's 'outreach activities' were recognised by television companies and he was much sought after as an adviser in preparing documentaries and debates. Publishers formed a steady queue on his doorstep, only to be sent away disappointed.

While I was at Huddersfield, in fact, teaching and verbal 'outreach activities' always took priority over research, writing and publication. Only during the last decade or so has this changed significantly.

11

Pleasures and Pastimes in Huddersfield

Until I unexpectedly secured the lecturing job at Huddersfield Polytechnic in 1972, I had no intention of ever again living in my home town. On my return I found the place had changed considerably, and not for the better. True, Huddersfield's splendid railway station was still there, and so was St.George's Square, the first sight greeting passengers as they emerged through its portico of Corinthian columns. Its rather less distinguished late nineteenth-century Town Hall also remained untouched. Unfortunately, recent redevelopment of the town centre had been less kind to other fondly remembered buildings. The superb Victorian Market Hall had been demolished by municipal vandals in 1970. So had the Theatre Royal, where I had spent so many happy Friday nights as a lad. The Palace Theatre was still there but, sadly, now downgraded to a bingo hall. Virtually all the town's cinemas had been closed. Rushworths, the department store where I had worked as a sixth former and undergraduate, had bit the dust. Even Huddersfield's fleet of trolley buses, despite hill-climbing capacities entirely suitable for its steep gradients, had vanished. The last of them ran in 1968. Yet, perversely, I bought a house very near the top of just such a hill!

Although I had no strong desire to become a house owner, I wanted even less to pay rent to someone else. Hence why, before returning north at the beginning of April 1972, I purchased (entirely on the basis of photographs and for the princely sum of £3650) a standard 1930s three bedroom semi-detached. The house's lack of any real character worried me not a jot; it took only about twenty minutes to walk down to the polytechnic; and, since there was a reasonably frequent bus service up the hill, I could easily avoid an unwelcome climb at the end of the day. Newsome, where my new home was located, had a pleasantly village-like atmosphere, several shops and, most importantly, two or three decent pubs. I even served as a governor of the local comprehensive school for a couple of years in the mid-1980s. As for the house itself, I treated it in a notably cavalier fashion for over twenty years. A severe winter early on did galvanise me into installing central heating; I had the place rewired while I was at it; and, so great was the resulting mess, I even had the house redecorated (for the one and only time). Otherwise, since I had no practical skills, whenever anything went wrong (however minor) I always had to summon the assistance of others. Usually, they were local tradesmen I'd got to know in the pub; also, as my former student Vivienne Haley reminds me, for several years she too was conveniently placed 'to help out with technical matters like hiring vans, moving furniture and fitting washing machines'. The large rear garden I simply ignored for most of the time, only occasionally getting the resulting jungle hacked down in the interest of maintaining reasonable neighbourly relations.

A great bonus of my returning to Huddersfield was that I saw Miriam Saunders and Edith Wood at least a couple of times a week; indeed, they became frequent visitors to my Newsome house. Virtually every Friday morning they got the bus from Moldgreen and, by the time I returned home from the polytechnic at teatime, they'd usually have done my washing and ironing, as well as cleaning the house. Even my former colleague Bill Roberts recalls that, whenever he happened upon them there, 'they always seemed to be busy doing things around your house' and, perhaps as a result, were 'never easy to engage in conversation'. Miriam and Edith certainly pampered my neurotic cat quite outrageously in the later 1970s. As a child I never had pets and, although I didn't dislike either cats or dogs, I had no desire to acquire an animal until a stray black cat chose to adopt me in 1974. Sadly, he was killed within weeks by a passing car but, rather to my surprise, I found I missed having him around. Hence why, before long, I acquired a young tortoiseshell moggy Letitia (or Puss Puss as I usually called her since this was the only name she'd respond to). She became very fond of me (and I of her), tolerated Miriam and Edith, and detested any other visitors to the house; indeed, she even took to lurking at the top of the stairs, snarling and spitting at anyone daring to approach her! When I was away (for instance, at Open University Summer Schools) Miriam and Edith tended to move into the house completely, partly to look after Puss Puss, partly to throw themselves into cleaning the place even more thoroughly than usual. I also got into the habit of taking them to a local pub most Friday evenings. Since neither had ever visited pubs much before, this was very much a new departure for them but, clearly, not an unpleasant one. Miriam tended to opt for soft drinks (although, occasionally, might risk a port and lemon). Edith obviously enjoyed a weekly gin and tonic and even inexpertly smoked the odd cigarette now and again if the fancy took her. Nor did I shirk from introducing them to middle class friends and they got on particularly well with Peter and Hazel Durrans, as Hazel recollects;

I can't really remember when we first met Miriam and Edith but they soon became what we affectionately called 'the two old dears'. After our daughter Katie was born in 1975, they often baby sat for us and came to Katie's parties. They were appreciative of everything done for them and always thrilled when we took them out for tea in Holmfirth.

During the 1970s I often joined Miriam and Edith for a few days during their annual jaunt to the seaside, no longer staying in cheap boarding houses but very decent hotels (for which they developed a real taste in old age). In about 1973, for instance, after teaching for a fortnight at an Open University Summer School in Norwich, I took the train to Great Yarmouth where I found them happily settled in a seafront hotel: one evening, I remember, we saw a summer show starring Norman Wisdom (whom they didn't like at all) and the splendid pub-style pianist Mrs Mills (whom they loved). A couple of years later, in 1975, we stayed at the Norbreck Hotel, perched on the cliff top overlooking Scarborough's north bay: all three of us very much enjoyed a *Jolson Summer Review* at the Floral Hall Theatre and, even more, the brilliant impressionist Mike Yarwood's *Summer Spectacular* at the Futurist. Miriam and Edith really liked the Norbreck and so did I: it had a friendly bar with both real ale and attractive barmen! We even spent Christmas there one year. 1977 saw us just down the road from Scarborough, at Bridlington, where we once more saw Mike Yarwood, this time at the Spa Theatre. And, inevitably, we revisited Blackpool at least once, in 1979, sampling the Bachelors and Nolan Sisters at the ABC Theatre (very much to their taste), Russ Abbott at the North Pier (much more up my street) and Freddie Starr at the Opera House (thoroughly disliked by all three of us). In the 1970s, too, Miriam and Edith occasionally accompanied me to Leeds Grand Theatre, particularly to see performances of Gilbert and Sullivan operas by the D'Oyly Carte Opera Company. They even came along to the odd guest lecture by me in Huddersfield, a mystifying experience for both of them no doubt, as well as a production of William Shakespeare's *A Midsummer Night's Dream* in 1977 (when I played Oberon).

Although they never complained, it had become increasingly evident by the end of 1977 that Miriam and Edith, now both in their seventies, were finding their living conditions (particularly not having an inside lavatory and bathroom) more and more intolerable. Hence why, since they were very reluctant to leave Moldgreen (where they'd lived for so long), I bought them a modernised terrace house not far from their old home in February 1978. Peter Durrans and I even hired a small furniture van, and shifted their battered furniture ourselves, in order to minimise the stress of the move. They insisted on paying me rent but, since they got it all back in rebate (I made sure of that), the arrangement suited all three of us and, for about three or four years, they seemed very happy there.

Seeing Miriam and Edith so often in their later years was a real bonus: indeed, the opportunity to do so had been a prime motive for accepting the post at Huddersfield Polytechnic in the first place. Less to my taste was the fact that my natural mother lived only a few miles away in Sowerby Bridge. I hadn't liked her much as a child and now found her company wearing to say the least. Nevertheless, I met up with her regularly in a Halifax pub in the 1970s. At least there, as she insisted on telling the same not very interesting stories over and over again, I could swill real ale and observe the good-looking young men who seemed to frequent the place. I rarely introduced her to any of my friends and most of them probably didn't even know she existed. An exception, clearly, was Bill Roberts, who specifically remembers that she:

> ... once came to the house we had in Greetland (near Halifax) when she talked nineteen to the dozen. I think we had at least one baby present at the time which, I imagine, flummoxed her.

During these years, too, I met up with my half-brother Tony now and again, either at my mother's house or in the pub. Such meetings mainly served to confirm that all we had in common was a taste for beer and, maybe, a shared sexual orientation (though we never discussed this). Once or twice I even brought my mother, Tony, Miriam and Edith together at my Newsome house. Everyone was very polite! Like me, my mother was a chain smoker and no mean drinker (especially of bottled Guinness) but, when she stayed with me for a few days over Christmas 1978, it soon became evident that her memory was deteriorating and confusion beginning to set in. A few weeks later she was dead at the age of seventy-three and, when I reluctantly viewed her lifeless body in its coffin, I felt remarkably little emotion beyond a certain relief at her passing. Over the next two or three months I probably saw more of my half-brother than I ever had before, even though the ritual of organising her funeral, sorting out her affairs and selling her Sowerby Bridge house largely devolved on me. Hardly anyone turned up for the funeral at a local crematorium (delayed for three weeks, as it was, by the 1979 Winter of Discontent), apart from Miriam and Edith, Tony and myself. Bill Roberts recalls coming along as well and, afterwards, 'going to your mother's place in Sowerby Bridge to help you clean it out'. Since I had no affection whatsoever for the town, I visited Halifax just once more after 1979 and that was to see Billy Connolly in performance at the civic theatre there. I only ever met my half-brother again once as well, by accident in a Manchester bar in the early 1980s. Over twenty years later, in May 2005, a uniformed policeman turned up at my Bristol house one morning to inform me his corpse had been discovered the day before in a Manchester bedsit. I experienced no emotion at all about the passing of a man I scarcely knew. The closest we had ever been, in fact, was when he seduced me as a teenager! Nor did I feel any sense of obligation towards him. Manchester Social Services arranged his cremation, assuring me he had left sufficient cash to cover the cost, and I didn't travel north myself. A few weeks later, but reluctantly, I claimed what cash remained in his savings account (not a lot) simply to prevent it passing to HM Treasury.

Living on my own, and not knowing all that many people in Huddersfield after almost a decade away, my recreational as well as professional life largely revolved around the polytechnic, my departmental colleagues there and, increasingly as the years went by, students I got to know. Most obviously, I tended to go along to any drama productions they became involved in, ranging from Aristophanes' risqué Greek farce *Lysistrata* and Thomas Middleton's early seventeenth-century *Women Beware Women*, via Restoration comedies such as Sir George Etherege's *She Would If She Could* and *The Man of Mode*, to John Gay's evocative early eighteenth-century compilation *The Beggar's Opera* and the splendidly atmospheric musical *Cabaret* (loosely based on Christopher Isherwood's stories set in early 1930s Berlin). I even took part in a couple of productions myself, partly because of fond memories of directing and acting at Plymouth College, partly because I believed drama at the polytechnic should be accessible to all, staff and students alike. What provided the opportunity was getting to know Darrolyn Lowe, a mature student of mine in the early 1970s whose husband Ken played the outrageous Sir Foppling Flutter in *The Man of Mode*. Through them, I got to know the play's director, drama lecturer Sally Robertshaw; she was instrumental in setting up a Polytechnic Students Drama Society; and, when she decided to stage Ben Jonson's 1606 play *Volpone*, she not only persuaded the talented Ken Lowe to play the title role but also cast me as Corvino, a far from admirable merchant. Several other members of staff took part as well and the production was staged in the Student Union Hall. It proved an entirely enjoyable experience, despite a few hair-raising moments: most memorably, during one performance, the breasts of the very well endowed girl playing my wife suddenly popped out of their tight fitting into full view; she completely froze in sheer embarrassment; and her equanimity was only restored when I firmly forced them back into place! Another drama lecturer Sheila Connor was also involved in the production of *Volpone* and it was she who, in 1977, persuaded me to play Oberon in an open-air staging of *A Midsummer Night's Dream*. This was a production sponsored by Huddersfield Arts Council and mounted in the town's Greenhead Park as part of local celebrations of Queen Elizabeth II's silver jubilee. Its cast comprised an eclectic mix of professional and amateur actors, not to mention local school children masquerading as fairies. Rehearsals were chaotic throughout and, in the end, it was a minor miracle that our efforts turned out as well as they did. Ken Lowe played William Shakespeare's Puck to my Oberon (whom I portrayed as a supernatural sadist) and we certainly had a great deal of fun, not least during a performance when, by the final scene, my boy fairies had become distinctly the worse for wear as a result of illicitly drinking cans of beer in my cave! Several history/politics colleagues came along out of curiosity, including Pauline Stafford (who flatteringly recalls my 'magnificent Oberon in Greenhead Park') and Brendan Evans (who asserts it was 'an unforgettable experience'). Yet when, over twenty years later, I let it slip to the landlord of my local pub in Bristol that I'd once played Oberon, his reaction was: 'That's about right, King of the Fucking Fairies'. Since I'd found learning all the lines a complete nightmare, however, I decided this would be my last acting role, and so it was.

Throughout the 1970s and 1980s, my social life very much revolved around beer drinking, whether in Newsome and town centre pubs, clubs, or during extended after-hours sessions back at my house. Early on, I particularly frequented the *Wellington*, not least since it was only a couple of hundred yards from where I lived. It was very much a local working class pub, with a regular clientèle and run on firmly traditional lines by its splendid middle-aged landlady, and I became very much part of the furniture there for a while. Illegal after hours drinking was very much the norm. Once casual customers had been ushered out at closing time, the doors were locked and serious beer consumption began, sometimes well into the night. At least once, indeed, a group of us were still there at dawn, when the landlady was even cajoled into cooking a full English breakfast to help sober us up. No wonder I so disliked nine-fifteen lectures and seminars during my first few years at the polytechnic! No wonder, either, that my colleague Pauline Stafford specifically remembers 'some heroic recoveries from the night before' (although, she adds, 'the show always went on, however bad you felt'). After the landlady of the *Wellington* retired and the pub began targetting a younger passing trade, many of us regulars transferred our custom to the nearby *Fountain*. This was a very basic no frills drinking joint, but the ale was excellent and the conversation frequently animated. Occasionally, I even took colleagues and students in there and this, no doubt, helps explain Tony Payne's memory of my 'capacity to go down to the pub and get on well with ordinary people', something 'most university folk can't and probably don't want to do'. I was also an occasional patron of other local pubs: the *Clarence*, for instance, a slightly more up market establishment but not renowned for the quality of its beer; the *Golden Fleece*, in nearby Berry Brow, sporting a comfortable lounge preferred by most of my polytechnic colleagues; the *Victoria* (or *t'Bum Royd* as Newsome folk called it), sometimes enlivened by the playing of a pub pianist and where my former Bristol flatmate Pat Scott once entertained an appreciative Saturday evening crowd; and, when I could face the awesomely steep hill leading up to it, the *Castle Hill Hotel*, a ramshackle Victorian pile. When visiting Miriam and Edith in Moldgreen, I occasionally sampled the not very distinguished local pubs there as well. And whenever we met up during one of his regular trips from Cornwall to Huddersfield to see his mother, my former school mate and theatre-going buddy Roger Kitching and I generally rendezvoused at the *Jolly Sailor*, if only to sample its excellent Tetley bitter.

Inevitably, the two town centre pubs I most frequently patronised were those just across the road from the polytechnic: the *Zetland* and the *College Arms*. Ex-student Vivienne Haley has a particular memory of the former:

> Funny things always seemed to happen around us when Keith was there. Sitting in the bar of the *Zetland* pub one day around a table, we were having a pint or five when a big piece of the ceiling fell down on top of us. Shrouded in clouds of plaster dust and crumbled lathes and paint, Keith calmly picked a piece of plasterwork out of his glass and stood up. 'My round, I think', he declared matter of factly.

No wonder, by about the mid-1980s, I'd come to prefer the *College Arms*: less barn-like, better beer and a most engaging Asian landlord. Sometimes, too, I visited the *Albert* (across the road from Huddersfield Town Hall and run by a middle-aged landlord who not only sported a bow tie but also regularly played opera tapes in the pub) and the *Commercial*: this was the favoured haunt of my colleague Keith Laybourn, not least because (almost uniquely in Huddersfield) it sold Samuel Smiths' bitter. Now and again I drank in the polytechnic student union (despite its tendency to serve badly kept beer in plastic glasses) and even the staff bar (main plotting venue for an inner clique of members of the college branch of the further and higher education trade union NATFHE); more infrequently, I visited the *Greyhound*, Huddersfield's most overtly gay bar; and then, of course, there were town centre clubs such as the *Coach House* and *Johnnys* for after hours drinking. An incident in the *Coach House* at the end of the 1970s particularly sticks in my mind. A group of final year BA (Humanities) students and I must have been drinking for hours; I went to the loo to get rid of the last pint or two; and there I found one of them passed out on the floor, penis still in hand, and liberally sprinkled with urine (presumably both his and that of others). Having summoned assistance, we somehow got him out of the lavatory (not easy since he was a big lad and a complete dead weight when plastered), manoeuvred him down a long flight of stairs (not a simple operation since he struggled and must have come very near to rolling from top to bottom) and, finally, deposited him in a taxi, paid its justifiably apprehensive driver in advance, and despatched him home. And Julie Bungey, a student at Huddersfield in the mid-1980s, certainly remembers 'spending much time in your company, sometimes in pubs (the *Zetland* and *College Arms*), sometimes in *Johnnys* night club'.

Peter Wood, head of history at the polytechnic for most of the 1970s and 1980s, recalls that my 'social skills made any communal activity something to look forward to' and believes my unrestrained laughter on such occasions 'will be remembered by everyone'. Certainly, I very much enjoyed socialising with history/politics colleagues and regularly did so. Partners sometimes came along as well: Bill Roberts' wife Jan, for instance, recollects that 'you gathered people around you easily, even if it was almost always at the pub'. During the 1970s my closest friend on the staff was Peter Durrans and, before long, I got to know his wife Hazel equally well. 'You were very much at the centre of the historians' social life at Huddersfield', Peter recollects:

> ... insisting on the need to 'wind down'. As I recall, we went out for a drink every week, often more than once. We usually had lunch together at work as well.

Hazel's memories are even more vivid:

> I always associate Peter, you and I with drinking sessions, right from first meeting you in 1972. We would meet at 5.30, drink all evening and play the fruit machine in the *Wellington* in Newsome. One Christmas you came to us, we drank gin late into the night, and I even ended up putting you to bed. And what were you and I doing, another night, snogging in the back seat of the car when Peter was driving?

For a couple of years in the later 1970s Steve Smith regularly joined us and he obviously relished these occasions:

> I enjoyed many drinks with Keith over the years. He was also a popular attendee at student parties where he would show a quite unexpected knowledge of which women I, and other colleagues, might find attractive. I have profoundly happy memories of my time with him in various pubs, mimicking our colleagues, and laughing out loud. I don't do that much now but, when I next meet Keith, I just know I will.

Steve's successor as a lecturer in politics, Tony Payne, also remembers that:

... you, Peter Durrans and I were a regular drinking group for quite a while, occasionally with my wife Jill, more often with Hazel Durrans, sometimes with Robert Perks and Jane or Andrew Taylor and Dawn. I enjoyed these evenings and have never quite replicated since the group sense we had then.

Rather more unexpectedly, for much of the 1980s I became a regular drinking companion of the polytechnic's Anglican chaplain Kenneth Cook who, as Julie Bungey recalls, 'liked to minister to the faithful in local pubs and clubs'. I certainly have very fond, if occasionally rather hazy, memories of Ken, not least his sympathetic counselling of students, regardless of whether or not they were Anglicans. I also admired the fact that, once he'd hung up his dog collar for the day, he could be so splendidly unclerical (especially when boozing in the *College Arms* or *Johnnys*). Indeed, he and I visited *Johnnys* so often that we were eventually given gold cards by the management enabling us to get in free whenever the whim took us. Not surprisingly, religion was off limits as a topic of conversation (much to his relief, I suspect), although I did attend the occasional carol service he organised in the polytechnic's St.Paul's venue, as well as spending several Christmas Day afternoons and evenings with him and his mother. When he departed from Huddersfield to become vicar of a splendid historic church in Lincoln, Brendan Evans and I went along to his inauguration and we attended, as well, the twenty-fifth anniversary celebration in May 1994 of his ordination to the priesthood. After I moved to Bristol he visited me at least once and I was immensely sad to learn of his sudden death in January 2006. Late night drinking in Huddersfield town centre certainly had its problems, though, not least getting home long after the last bus to Newsome had departed. Occasionally, I cadged a lift from a fellow drinker, one of whom recalls:

> ... the dreadful time when I was driving you home and definitely hit a policeman's foot as he stood by his car. As I looked through the rear mirror he was pointing me out to his partner. God knows why he didn't pursue me and end my driving career. We drunkenly thought it a great joke at the time!

More often, I simply got a taxi: indeed, I used the same firm so often that a remarkably rapid service at a reduced rate eventually became virtually guaranteed.

More and more as the years went by, I threw professionalism to the winds and started drinking regularly (and not infrequently to excess!) with my own students. This tendency began with Darrolyn Lowe and her friends in the mid-1970s, both in the pub and in the splendid seventeenth-century New House Hall she and her husband part-occupied in the otherwise unsavoury

Huddersfield suburb of Sheepbridge, and where I also attended several far from conventional parties. From the autumn of 1978 the die was cast irrevocably, as Neil Scott remembers:

> Socially, you certainly got on well with our year in Year 3, 1978/9. Very early on Andy Hook and I were walking past the *Commercial* and you were standing at the bus stop. Andy suggested we ask you over the road for a quick pint. Three hours later we were absolutely plastered and, soon after that, boozing at the *Commercial* on Thursday night became a regular routine for quite a big group of us.

This is confirmed by Andy Hook himself who also believes that:

> The excessive drinking sessions in the *Commercial* cemented a real sense that we were all in it together. I really enjoyed the cut and thrust of debate and discussion with lecturers like Peter Durrans and yourself. I usually got so plastered on the Sam Smiths' bitter that I often couldn't remember a single point of interest next morning, never mind twenty-five years later. Somehow it doesn't really matter.

Other members of the group included Graham Townend and Robert Perks, both of whom managed to obtain first class honours degrees as well as enjoying Thursday evenings to the full. Since the vivacious Vivienne Haley and extrovert Lesley Burkey both entered their third year as humanities students in September 1979, sobriety remained firmly off the agenda in 1980 too. Indeed, Viv reminds me that, even after leaving the polytechnic, she found herself 'periodically lured back to Huddersfield for dubious weekends' to recharge her batteries, more often than not 'getting very drunk with a perpetual student called Dockray'. And so it went on. 1983/4 was an exceptionally alcoholic year, courtesy not least of Martin Holmes (a pleasure-loving and most engaging lad from Liverpool), David Mathieson (excellent company and a street-wise southerner right down to his finger tips) and Lloyd Powell (whose Sheffield origins, and capacity to charm almost everyone he met, were no less evident). Vanessa Cook remembers how, in 1984/5, she:

> ... had a marvellous time with Keith in Huddersfield, not least great evenings spent in the *College Arms* getting drunk, talking about Richard III, and contemplating life, love and human kind.

Paul O'Grady, a mature student of 1985/6, was no less agreeable both in the classroom and the pub. As for Julie Bungey in 1986/7, not only does she remember our frequent evenings of alcoholic excess but also has vivid memories of several of her fellow students: 'a manic depressive Norfolk farmer's son with a prominent chin', for instance, 'a three-piece polyester suit wearing and briefcase carrying obsessive from Orpington who got on everyone's nerves with his humourless intensity', and 'a blond good-looking Durham lad who went on to be a television presenter'.

Now and again colleagues and friends took pity on this superficially sad bachelor who, seemingly, preferred beer to food and lived alone with only a neurotic cat for company. Peter and Hazel Durrans, for instance, invited me to lunch or dinner at their home many times in the 1970s; Bill and Jan Roberts were very hospitable as well; and even a man as indifferent to what I ate as I was couldn't fail to appreciate the quality of food available at dinner parties hosted by Bill and Pauline Stafford. Very occasionally too, at any rate during my early years back in Huddersfield, I reciprocated and subjected myself to the torture of cooking half-decent meals for others in my own house (while, at the same time, making sure there was plenty of booze to wash them down). Jan Roberts recalls, indeed, that on such evenings I could be quite conventionally hospitable; her husband Bill's most vivid memory, by contrast, is of a night when, 'after a good few drinks in the pub', he and I:

> ... went back to your place and began drinking whisky. When I left in the small hours you had just about passed out and I was in a deplorable condition. I bumbled into work next morning but, and this did not surprise me, there was no sign of you. When the next day you were still not to be seen, I began to worry a little, knowing the state I had left you in. And when, on the third day, you did not appear again, I became convinced that you were dead—at which point you did show up!

Yet, amazingly, I can't remember ever missing a class because of over-indulgence during my entire time at the polytechnic. The nearest I came to it, probably, was in 1984 when, after drinking throughout the preceding night with two or three of them, I staggered into college for a Special Subject session; somehow I got through it but it was a far from vintage performance; and, once the ordeal (for both me and the students) was over, we all adjourned to the *College Arms* to recover.

By the end of the 1970s I had begun to invite students back to my house more and more often, usually after extended drinking sessions in town centre pubs. Invariably, plenty of canned beer was then consumed, often topped up with whisky or gin, and, now and again, a joint or two of cannabis. A former sixth former at Plymouth College, who visited me not long after I moved to Huddersfield, recalls my house as 'a dark place, with no television, plenty of books, and what seemed to be a complete collection of Agatha Christie paperbacks'. Alison Shaw, whom I first met when I was her Open University tutor in the mid-1970s, specifically recalls:

> ... the first time I came to your house for a meal and offered to wash up afterwards only to find a kitchen stacked to the rafters with dirty dishes because you never washed up unless you had to. I also remember being impressed by your loyalty to the Quentin Crisp school of housework!

Nevertheless, she adds, 'we had loads of good nights together', not to mention 'writing off many a Christmas Day after spending Xmas Eve with you'. Julie Bungey recollects that in 1986/7:

> ... you occasionally invited me and other students back to your house in Newsome. My main memories of your home are the red velvet curtains, the massive book collection all over the house, the cats (Snubby and Snitch), the drinks cabinet, a pile of beer cans in a corner, a typewriter, and a garden gnome occupying a niche in the front room. I remember you playing records during late night sessions, mostly musicals. You drank a lot but I don't remember you ever being really drunk. The alcohol seemed to have a heightening effect on you initially but, as the night wore on, your mood would become more reflective.

Inevitably, during all the years I lived there, my Huddersfield house witnessed many bizarre happenings. Two stand out from the rest. One night a group of students turned up, three or four lads accompanied by an attractive and very well endowed young lady whom, it rapidly became clear, they all fancied like hell. No doubt wishing to inspect the goods more closely, they suggested a game of strip pontoon; she readily agreed (although with a distinctly sardonic look in her eye); and I settled back (fully dressed and with every intention of remaining so) to enjoy the spectacle. Since the girl was far more sober than any of the lads, before long they were down to their underpants (less in one case) while she remained largely clothed. At this point she declared she was shattered and I suggested she crash out in my spare room. Once she'd departed upstairs the lads' minds rapidly turned to the possibilities of seduction until, eventually, the drunkest of all decided (against my advice) to chance his arm. Ten minutes later he was back, pitifully declaring that she had responded to his unwelcome advances by biting his eager penis. The truth of this statement, moreover, was evident for all to see! No less outlandish is this sequence of events related by another former female student:

Two of us had had a boozy night out with Keith somewhere. It was about 4.0am and well past time for bed. Suddenly there was a knock at the door. Keith answered it to find a youth of about nineteen or twenty, dishevilled and drunk, standing there, swaying slightly. Slurringly, he said he was lost and needed to call a cab to get home but had no money. Keith invited him in while he called a taxi for him. The lad sat on a chair in the front room with us waiting for his cab. We introduced ourselves and asked the young man how he'd got into such a state. He couldn't remember where he'd been but, somewhere in his ramblings, came the statement that his girlfriend had thrown him out. 'I'm not surprised', says one of us, 'you wouldn't be much use to her in that state anyway'. Of course, with the bravado of youth and alcohol, he claimed that he would be and proceeded to drop his trousers and pants to demonstrate his capabilities. Keith walked in with a glass of beer in his hand, only to find this young lad semi-naked in his front room. The look of astonishment on his face was classic Keith. How had we got this poor unsuspecting boy to remove most of his clothing in only the time it took for him to pour a beer? We took it further, pretending to kiss and caress each other to show the lad that, even if he'd been sober, he wouldn't have been much good to us since we didn't like young men. You could see the look of alarm on his face when he suddenly thought he had wandered into some sort of brothel or S&M parlour in Newsome of all places. It was when Keith told him that we didn't mind foursomes that the lad lurched to his feet and made a bid for the door. Luckily for him, the doorbell rang about the same time. 'I think my taxi is here', he gasped, desperately clutching at his jeans, underpants, belt and shoes—by now hopelessly entangled—as he fell out of the house and into the taxi driver's arms. 'Take him home', said Keith imperiously, 'and here's a fiver for the fare'. Taxi driver and lad disappeared into the night and we have visions of them still driving around Huddersfield to this day trying to find where he lived!

These two young women were amazing. Even if we never managed a foursome, we three certainly ended up in bed together at least once after a drunken trek home from the pub one night through desolate fields of dead brussels sprouts. Needless to say, hilarity was the predominant emotion throughout. As to what these two buxom wenches got up to another night on Table 13 in a local Huddersfield Italian restaurant after closing time (aided and abetted by a couple of hairy young Neopolitan waiters), the less said the better. Suffice to say, I never sat at Table 13 again!

In November 1979 I organised a party at my Newsome house, partly as a convenient way of returning hospitality, partly to mark my tentative coming out as a homosexual. Almost all my history/politics colleagues from the polytechnic turned up; so did several Newsome drinking cronies; and I also invited along a selection of past and present students. The food on offer was Marks and Spencers' best and, needless to say, a vast amount of alcohol was consumed. Needless to say, too, the party lasted well into the night; two or three of my colleagues didn't miss out on such a golden opportunity to over-indulge; and, as for the students, they certainly let their hair down with vigour. Indeed, so one of a male contingent who had only recently graduated from the polytechnic recalls:

> Several of us met up in Huddersfield earlier in the day and, by the time we arrived at your house, we were already very well oiled. Nor did we slow down then and, eventually, a couple of us ended up passing out and sleeping it off in the double bed in your spare room.

Five years later, in 1984, Brendan Evans and I laid on another party at my house (less potential for damage than at his!), this time to celebrate our joint fortieth birthday. Our friendship had been growing for some time and, as Brendan puts it, 'approaching our joint fortieth year trauma made us identify with each other even more; you visited me and my wife Astrid at home a few times; and the culmination was our great party'. Indeed, so successful was this alcoholic jamboree, we mounted a repeat performance for our fiftieth a decade later.

Although, not least as a result of my experience of communal living in Plymouth College's Colson House, I much preferred to live on my own once back in Huddersfield, I did give refuge to polytechnic colleagues from time to time. Early on a young twentieth-century European history/politics specialist Alex Pravda stayed with me for a few months. Obviously a highly intelligent fellow who seemed destined to go far in the academic world (as he did), he was phenominally hard-working, Even so, that didn't prevent us spending many enjoyable evenings in the pub together. His former wife Imogen Martin recollected over thirty years later:

> My acquaintance with Keith in 1972/3, though brief, left an indelible impression. Here was a man who could expatiate about Gilbert and Sullivan with blissful disregard for the ignorance and/or indifference of the audience, yet who showed unstinting kindness and hospitality to a new colleague and, on occasion, his wife.

A few years later Alan Martin, another polytechnic colleague (who specialised in the teaching of English as a foreign language), also shared my house for a while; he and I, moreover, regularly met up in various pubs throughout my years in Huddersfield. As for Steve O'Loughlin, a politics lecturer who rented a room from me for a while as well, he even managed to restore a degree of order to my perpetually overgrown garden. Over the years, too, I occasionally took in students for a few weeks, more often than not so they could enjoy a reasonably quiet environment in the lead-up to final examinations. I have vivid recollections of one lad in particular. He hadn't exactly overworked himself for most of his three years at the polytechnic but he was bright and certainly wanted to leave with a decent degree. Not that, even in his last term, he gave up sex! Over no more than three or four months he enjoyed several one night stands. Yet even his stamina flagged at least once. One Sunday morning he suddenly materialised in my study stark naked, pointed despairingly at his drooping penis, and declared desperately that it had completely ceased to function. In response I pointed out that this might just reflect the amount of alcohol he had consumed the night before, supplied him with a mug of strong black coffee, and despatched him back to bed to try again. An hour or two later he and a rather sheepish-looking young lady appeared (fully dressed this time) and, in celebration of his clearly successful return to virility, we all three adjourned to a local pub for lunch. Otherwise, during the exam season, he seemed to survive mainly on amphetamine tablets; the drug obviously did the trick; and he obtained a very creditable upper second class honours degree.

Former students, anxious to recapture their carefree early years away from home, occasionally turned up at the polytechnic and I was only too happy to welcome them, embark on tours of fondly remembered drinking haunts, even provide overnight accommodation now and again. From time to time, too, I supplied bed and a modicom of board for friends from elsewhere in the country, particularly the south west. Charles Ross, for instance, stayed with me several times. So did Patrick Scott who, during his visits, invariably met up with Miriam and Edith as well. On his final trip to the north in August 1980, accompanied by Peter and Hazel Durrans, we even took them to Scarborough for the day. Since both remind me of their visit, Dennis and Di Collinson obviously had an unforgettable experience when they once came to Huddersfield. 'One summer when we were planning to drive to Scotland for a family holiday', Di recollects:

> ...Keith generously offered an overnight stay for six of us in his Huddersfield house. We knew he lived alone, but would we find his two 'mothers' Miriam and Edith turning up with freshly ironed shirts for him, or a steaming hotpot? No, because by then Keith was looking after them rather than they he. What we did find, in his plain and tidy house on a steep Huddersfield road, were beds and blankets for all of us, the most delicious bacon ever, and a beloved cat, eccentric to the tips of her whiskers: a familiar, perhaps, who began life in the thirteenth

century, but spurned all our efforts to ingratiate ourselves with her and, whether from contempt, disgust or merely habit, retired to live and eat in a closed wardrobe for the duration of our visit.

Dennis vividly remembers, moreover, that when he and Di offered to buy some takeaways for the evening:

> We all piled into our motor caravan and drove to Keith's favourite 'Chinese'. Two of us disembarked to look at the menu and give orders. As we approached the door it was thrown open violently and a young man rushed out closely followed by another wielding some sort of large knife and screaming in clear if incompehensible Cantonese or Mandarin. A notice quickly appeared at the window: 'Sorry: Closed for Food'. Hastily beating a retreat to our vehicle, visibly shaking with Keith's shoulder vibrations, we were informed by him that they were always having family differences. 'A pity', he added, 'since they serve such good food.'

Apparently, after I'd assured them there was another equally good Chinese restaurant on the other side of town:

> In we piled again and drove off. We arrived at a quiet part of the town. The restaurant looked charming with chintzy curtains. Inside a pleasant young couple greeted us. The wife gave us some menus and we got on with the exciting business of salivating over the thought of our first Huddersfield 'Chinese' meal. The place was very quiet as we studied the bills of fare, so quiet that perhaps only two or three of us noticed the exquisitely pyjamaed small boy of perhaps three or four coming down the stairs from what we assumed were the family's private rooms. It was a delightful scene, the mother gazing fondly at the small boy. Suddenly, what seemed to be all Chinese hell was let loose. The father had seen the child. He screamed at the mother. She responded rapidly and volubly, all, as before, in a Chinese language. Our eyes switched from one parent to the other and to the little boy still quietly descending. The parents obviously blamed each other for the son's getting out of bed. They came to the front of the counter, the sweet young woman smiling but livid and ushering us out in very rapid Chinese. The handsome young man, also highly perturbed, shared the ushering, saying: 'Sorry. Closed for the evening', and constantly reiterating 'No more food'. We beat an ordered if hasty retreat to our vehicle with Keith, ever the analytical historian, vainly pointing out that we had had no food at all. History was obviously not the young man's strong suit. He turned on his heel and shut the restaurant door with a crash. We drove off. Keith did suggest a third 'Chinese' out of town but the children had espied a fish and chip shop. We bought some and ate them back at Keith's. They were excellent.

Peter Allender and his wife Jean also visited me in Huddersfield at least twice during these years. Indeed, Peter recalls, 'on one occasion when our son Tom was quite small (probably August 1979) Miriam and Edith baby-sat while we went to the pub'; both he and Jean remember visiting nearby Holmfirth and Emley Moor with me; and, maybe in the mid-1980s, Peter reminds me 'how much Tom and Rob liked the chips in the *Castle Hill* pub, especially when you introduced them to the tasty "crozzly" bits'.

Although as a teenager I had relished short railway journeys on steam-hauled trains (for instance, Huddersfield to York or Crewe for train-spotting, even the occasional theatre-going jaunt to London), by the later 1960s I was beginning to develop the aversion to long-distance travel that has remained with me ever since. Hence why I have only very rarely ventured abroad and never further than France and the Low Countries. Nor have I ever had much of a taste for holidays, at any rate beyond three or four days. What I did enjoy, throughout my years at the polytechnic, were staff/student history trips. I remember, for instance, an excursion to Fountains abbey and Ripon cathedral (worth visiting for its splendid misericords alone). Keith Laybourn, similarly, recalls an occasion when the 'Cartwright Hall trio' (Bill Roberts, Keith and myself), accompanied by a group of Oriental Studies students, visited a Samurai Exhibition in Bradford where he soon found himself dressed up in samurai armour (although not, he adds sadly, allowed to handle the sword!). In about 1974, ominously, Keith and I organised the first of many expeditions over the years to Richmond and Middleham castles. This first trip, he reminds me, was 'by mini-bus and involved about eight Bermerside students, David Wright, myself and you (sporting long flowing cavalier hair at the time)'. After touring Richmond castle and consuming a great deal of Theakstons' beer, 'we then proceeded to Middleham where David led a race up and down the moat', resulting in 'an exasperated attendant confronting you, the soberest of us, and asking, "How are we expected to keep kids in order if we can't control you lot?"'. On another occasion, he reminiscences:

> We ended up in the *Black Swan* in Middleham. It had an old range and a dartboard. We played darts, and you took photos of me against the bar with about twenty empty beer glasses. Eventually, the two elderly ladies who ran the pub let us out of the back door about 4.0pm (well after afternoon closing time) so we could, at last, rapidly peruse the castle.

And after yet another visit to the Wensleydale castles, he adds, 'Bill Roberts and I, desperate to release distilled Theakstons, had to find a tree to hide behind in a Leeds suburb on our way home'. Students, too, remember these outings fondly. Andy Hook, for instance, particularly stresses how Middleham trips in the late 1970s helped 'blur the edges between student and lecturer'; as for Vanessa Cook, her 'most wonderful memories' of student life in the early 1980s are of such excursions:

> The first was to Middleham and Richmond castles, with a stop off in Masham and the Theakstons brewery. That was the only time I've ever got so drunk that I couldn't remember where I lived! The other great history trip took in Scarborough castle and Rievaulx abbey. Again, much alcohol was consumed, many cigarettes smoked (and not just the tobacco variety!), and lots of information shared with students. Your love of Richard III certainly went hand in hand with a taste for pleasure:

For me, the most enjoyable trip of all was a few days I spent in Stratford-upon-Avon with a group of ex-students in July 1984. During their second and third years in 1983 and 1984 I'd got to know Martin Holmes, David Mathieson, Mark Munday and Lloyd Powell very well, boozing regularly with them both in Huddersfield bars and back at my house; they seemed keen to celebrate both the end of their studies and my fortieth year with an excursion somewhere; and I suggested William Shakespeare's birthplace as an apt venue, combining as it did plenty of culture and a plethora of pleasant pubs. They enthusiastically agreed, booked us into a small licensed hotel, and off we went. It proved a most exhilarating, if exhausting, break, as I wrote to Bernard Jarvis soon afterwards:

> I've just returned from a few days in Stratford-on-Avon with a group of ex-students, a splendidly sociable and alcoholic lot. I'm still recovering. We saw *Henry V* and *Richard III*. Kenneth Branagh was competent enough as Henry V but the production was a bit pedestrian at times and over long. *Richard III* was brilliant, especially Antony Sher's portrayal of the king (on crutches!). I doubt whether I shall ever see a better performance.

Throughout the 1970s and early 1980s I regularly visited theatres in the north of England, particularly in Leeds but also, now and again, in Bradford, Oldham and Manchester. Huddersfield itself, sadly, no longer had a professional theatre but I did occasionally go along to amateur productions in the town: in 1976, for instance, I saw the Huddersfield Thespians' staging of Noel Coward's mid-1930s trilogy *Tonight at 8.30* and the Amateur Operatic Society in Franz Lehar's light-hearted 1905 operetta *The Merry Widow*. Now and again, too, minor professional companies came to Huddersfield Arts Centre: in 1983, indeed, I saw the Keswick-based Century Theatre in productions of both Oscar Wilde's *The Importance of Being Earnest* and Willy Russell's award-winning comedy *Educating Rita*. Leeds sported two professional theatres: the Grand, where touring companies performed, and the Playhouse, home to its own repertory company. At Leeds Grand, in 1981, I saw Lehar's *The Merry Widow* again, this time performed by Opera North, not to mention musicals such as Rodgers and Hammerstein's *Oklahoma* and Stephen Sondheim's *Company* (both in 1980). About the same time I sat through only the first half of Peter O'Toole's notorious mangling of the title role in Shakespeare's *Macbeth* and saw Opera North, for a second time, in a production of La *Bohème*. Alison Shaw accompanied me to both these, later recalling both O'Toole's 'dire performance' and my laughing at her sobbing through the Puccini. I'm certainly struck by the variety of what I saw at Leeds Grand in the 1970s and early 1980s, ranging from John Vanbrugh's Restoration comedy *The Provok'd Wife* and Oscar Wilde's *Lord Arthur Savile's Crime* (1980) to the D'Oyly Carte Opera Company (in its last years) performing Gilbert and Sullivan (1976, 1979 and 1980). Leeds Playhouse tended to be more adventurous in its offerings: in 1973, for instance, a staging of Georges Feydeau's farce *A Flea in Her Ear* and, in 1982, Richard O'Brien's cult musical *The Rocky Horror Show*. I even once went to Leeds City Varieties, decked out in period costume, to experience a recording of BBC Television's long-running *The Good Old Days*. Bradford's Alhambra Theatre was more difficult to get to and took longer (there were no direct trains from Huddersfield to Bradford by the 1970s) but I did see a few touring productions there, most memorably a terrific rendering by the Royal Shakespeare Company of Cole Porter's *Kiss Me Kate* (surely one of the best musicals ever written) in 1987. Oldham Coliseum, a splendid theatre lucky to survive the 1960s, was even more difficult to get to without a car but I did manage it a few times: in 1976, for example, I saw Alan Bennett's *Habeas Corpus* there and, in 1984, Joe Orton's last play *What the Butler Saw*. The most moving production I experienced at the Oldham Coliseum, accompanied by Bill and Jan Roberts, was Martin Sherman's *Bent* in 1980. Its bleak portrayal of the persecution of homosexuals in Nazi Germany certainly stunned even a largely middle class, middle-aged audience the night we saw it. Otherwise, I particularly recall seeing Walter Greenwood's atmospheric portrayal of northern working class life in the 1930s in *Love on the Dole* (with Keith Laybourn and his Special Subject group in 1980) and Christopher Marlowe's *Doctor Faustus* (1981) at Manchester's Royal Exchange Theatre. In Manchester, too, I saw a production of Claude Debussy's opera *Pélleas et Mélisande* at the Royal Northern College of Music in 1985, not to mention enjoying concerts by the city's Halle Orchestra in Huddersfield Town Hall from time to time. Another vivid memory is of once accompanying Bill and Pauline Stafford to York to see the *York Cycle of Mystery Plays*, performed against a backdrop of the ruins of St. Mary's abbey one rainy evening. As for other excursions during these years, Peter Durrans has unearthed:

> ... cryptic diary references from the 1970s to a visit to Bradford to see Gilbert and Sullivan's *The Gondoliers* at the Alhambra (when you insisted on visiting a pub in the city centre where the toilets were padlocked!), a trip to Soho with Alex and Imogen Pravda and an expedition to Bailey's Casino in Sheffield.

During the visit to Soho I seem to remember venturing into a London strip club for the one and only time in my life while, at the Sheffield casino, Pauline Stafford and I teased more cash out of a one-arm bandit than the rest won at the roulette table. What Peter particularly recalls, however, are several weekends in Blackpool (when the town's annual 'Illuminations' were switched on), featuring 'late night drinking and, on one occasion, playing boule in the Savoy Hotel foyer until the early hours'. Peter's wife Hazel's memories also include 'the trips to Blackpool, drinking till all hours in the cocktail bar of the Savoy and then trying to play boule on the beach next morning', not to mention she and I once taking a tram to nearby Fleetwood in a deplorably hung over condition. Bill Roberts, too, remembers:

> ... a notable trip to Blackpool to see the lights. You came with Jan and me and five kids. Somebody must have gone on the train and I was supposed to be returning that way as the car, a Renault 4, was not big enough to take us all. Unfortunately, I missed the train so we all had to come back in the car—how, I don't know.

My own main memory of this day out is taking Bill's two young sons on the Big Dipper (a formidable roller coaster) and having to hang on to them like grim death during the first hair-raising descent (there were no safety belts in the 1970s). How the three of us survived the experience remains a minor mystery to this day.

By the 1970s I no longer enjoyed visiting London as much as I once had but, on occasional trips there, I almost invariably took in a show or two. In 1973, for instance, I saw a production of J. B. Priestley's compelling 1940s play *An Inspector Calls* at the Mermaid Theatre, directed by the Mermaid's original founder Bernard Miles; in 1977 I very much enjoyed *Side by Side by Sondheim*, a compilation of songs from musicals by Stephen Sondheim, at the Garrick Theatre and, rather less to my taste, *A Chorus Line* at the imposing Drury Lane Theatre Royal; and 1978 found me at the Mermaid again, this time to see *Every Boy Deserves a Favour*, 'a piece for actors and orchestra' by Tom Stoppard and André Previn. As Alison Shaw remembered years later, she and I visited London together in both 1980 and 1982:

> Our trips to London were certainly great fun. The first time we stayed in Paddington and kept the night porter busy until the early hours supplying us with

alcohol. We didn't get much sleep anyway because of the platform announcements continually coming from Paddington station. The second time we stayed near King's Cross station in an establishment where everyone else rented rooms by the hour and all the plumbing ran through our bedroom—so little sleep there either! We saw *Cats* with the original cast, *The King and I* with Yul Brynner, and *Dr Faustus*. We ate and drank a great deal; you bought loads of books; and we had to walk everywhere because you loathed the tube!

In 1980, in fact, Alison and I not only saw Christopher Marlowe's *Doctor Faustus* at the Fortune Theatre and Rodgers and Hammerstein's *The King and I* at the London Palladium but also a production of my favourite Noel Coward comedy *Private Lives* at the Duchess. In 1982, as well as Andrew Lloyd Webber's superbly staged *Cats* at the New London Theatre (with Brian Blessed, Bonnie Langford, Paul Nicholas, Elaine Page and Wayne Sleep all in the cast), we also saw another Noel Coward comedy, *Design for Living*, at the Globe. Like Alison, I recall the semi-brothel with noisy plumbing in King's Cross (where our sleeping dilemma was compounded by sharing a double bed). My most vivid memory, however, is the performance of *The King and I* we saw together, not least because I found myself sitting next to an old lady who was virtually in tears from the start and whose participation in the action rose to an alarming crescendo during the king's death bed scene.

During the mid-1980s, if surviving hotel bills and theatre programmes are anything to go by, I must have visited London four or five times. In August 1984, when I stayed at the distinctly run down County Hotel in Upper Woburn Place and even witnessed a fist fight between a couple of members of staff during breakfast one morning, I saw *The Clandestine Marriage* (an eighteenth-century 'comedy of high manners and low intentions' by David Garrick and George Colman) at the Albery Theatre and a spirited revival of Leonard Bernstein's American musical *West Side Story* at Her Majesty's. Before the end of the year I also saw Alan Bennett's *Forty Years On* (with a cast including both Paul Eddington and Stephen Fry) at the Queen's Theatre and the vintage Rodgers and Hart musical *On Your Toes* at the Palace. In the autumn of 1985 I saw two hilarious comedies, Richard Harris's *Stepping Out* at the Duke of York's Theatre and Michael Frayn's *Noises Off* at the Savoy, as well as Robert Lindsay in an exuberant new rendering of Noel Gay's 1937 musical *Me and My Girl* at the Adelphi. 1986 offered an even greater plethora of riches. Not only did I revisit the County Hotel (or Fawlty Towers as it might not unreasonably have been renamed), I saw Antony Sher once more (this time in Harvey Fierstein's *Torch Song Trilogy* at the Albery Theatre), Noel Coward's *Blithe Spirit* at the Vaudeville and even an English National Opera production of Mozart's *The Marriage of*

Figaro at the London Coliseum. Throw in T. S. Eliot's *The Cocktail Party* at the Phoenix Theatre and Christopher Hampton's *Les Liaisons Dangereuses* at the Ambassadors for good measure, and 1986 was clearly a vintage London theatre-going year for me. On at least a couple of these mid-1980s trips to London, moreover, I stayed with David Mathieson in his flat not far from King's Cross station. After graduating from Huddersfield in 1984 he had embarked on a Ph.D under the supervision of Brendan Evans; he soon became a research assistant to the Labour MP (and future cabinet minister) Robin Cook; and he certainly knew central London inside out. Most memorably, I recall boozing right through the night with him on one occasion, starting at the appropriately named *Brahms and Liszt* pub in the West End, drinking for several more hours after closing time in an Oxford Street jazz club, and ending up in another pub near Smithfield meat market (licensed to open for a couple of hours very early in the morning). No wonder we then treated ourselves to a full English breakfast in a nearby cafe to sober up!

In February 1984 I found myself in London for a very different reason: the filming by London Weekend Television of *The Trial of Richard III* (on the charge of murdering his nephews the Princes in the Tower), a 4-hour epic for transmission by Channel 4 later in the year. A few months earlier the programme's associate producer Mark Redhead had met me, ironically enough, in the Tudor bar of Huddersfield's George Hotel. Over a few very pleasant pints we discussed the project at some length and, as he recollected in a book about the programme penned by producer Richard Drewitt and himself, 'although on balance Keith Dockray felt the weight of historical evidence pointed towards Richard's guilt in the matter of the princes, nevertheless he was broadly sympathetic to Richard and volunteered to speak in his defence'. Over the next few weeks I supplied a fair amount of material pointing to the possible unreliability of contemporary and near-contemporary chronicles, as well as positive evidence of Richard III's popularity in the north of England, all of which I felt might be useful to the defence. In the end, however, I didn't appear in the programme. Tony Pollard, who proved a formidable witness for the prosecution, mischievously accused me twenty years later of 'ducking out' of the ordeal, commenting that, 'as your subsequent career has shown, this was due either to a quite unjustified fear of the camera or, alternatively, exceptional wisdom about the lure of television'. In fact, as the day of filming drew ever nearer, I became increasingly convinced that I myself would make a far better prosecution than defence witness, and virtually admitted as much in a letter to the defending barrister Richard du Cann. 'Given the defence line proposed and the decision that the jury will be asked to make a judgement on the *balance of the of the evidence* rather than *beyond reasonable doubt*', I wrote, 'I'm not at all sure I'm going to be much use to you';

nevertheless, I added without much conviction, 'having committed myself to the defence, I'll certainly do the best I can'. Richard du Cann, probably rightly, decided not to risk it, again as recorded by Richard Drewitt and Mark Redhead in their book:

> On a visit to the set on the evening before the trial, the defence counsel revealed he had decided not to call Mr Dockray. He explained that, though Mr Dockray would have much of importance to contribute as far as an assessment of the chronicles was concerned, if the prosecution asked him the fundamental question, 'Do you believe that Richard III probably killed the Princes?', he could not be expected to lie.

However, they add gratifyingly:

> Keith Dockray took this news with his usual equanimity and cheerfulness. His considerable work for the defence was not wasted, moreover, since many of his observations on the chronicles and the northern aspects of the case were included in the defence counsel's cross-examination.

As Peter Hammond (at the time research officer of the Richard III Society) recalled twenty years later:

> The filming of *The Trial of Richard III* was a great occasion, where they had decided you were not sound enough on Richard to be a witness for the defence (ie. might say he could have murdered his nephews!) and I had firmly refused to do more than provide evidence. So we both sat and watched instead.

Among the audience, too, was the present Richard Duke of Gloucester. On reflection, I would probably have been worse than useless anyway, as a result of a mega-hangover brought on by several hours drinking with a former student the night before! It was certainly a fascinating experience, not least because the studio reconstruction of Court Number 4 of the Old Bailey (and, no doubt, its atmosphere) was so unnervingly realistic, and the presiding judge Lord Elwyn Jones (a former Labour Lord Chancellor) so wryly sardonic throughout. An additional bonus for me, moreover, was meeting up again with Kenneth Waller, who played the court usher, and reminiscing about his Huddersfield Theatre Royal repertory years at the end of the 1950s. As for Richard III himself, despite not deigning to put in a personal appearance, he was found not guilty by the jury.

Apart from visits to nearby northern cities and towns (theatrically inspired more often than not), student trips, and occasional jaunts to London, Bristol and elsewhere, I tended to avoid travel in the 1970s and early 1980s as much as I could. Several journeys I did make, moreover, were sparked mainly by professional considerations, most obviously attending conferences. And I never even considered venturing abroad during these years. I did visit Nottingham two or three times and stayed with Bernard Jarvis, his wife Val (whom I'd known as an undergraduate in Bristol) and their two sons: at the end of 1976, for instance, when we all went to see *Sleeping Beauty* at the Nottingham Playhouse and., again, in September 1984 (after delivering a paper at a conference), when, I seem to remember, Bernard and I strove hard to recreate our student days by visiting a string of pubs. More adventurously, in July 1979, I visited Bernard's parents in North Wales and stayed with them in Tan-y-Bwlch near Blaenau Ffestiniog (where they now ran an antiques and craft shop). As a sixth former I'd found Bernard's mother fantastic, totally unfazed by her son's befriending a working class lad from what was little better than a Huddersfield slum, and always welcoming. His father, by contrast, had always seemed a rather remote and forbidding figure. Only when he once gave Bernard and I a lift to Bristol in his Land. Rover during our student days did I realise he could be both friendly and possessed a wry sense of humour. By 1979, no doubt relieved to have escaped from his high-powered job at the ICI in Huddersfield, he had chilled out completely (even smoking the occasional cigarette); he and I spent a very pleasant day visiting Welsh castles (the only time I've ever been to Harlech, the last Welsh fortress to hold out for the Lancastrians against Edward IV in the 1460s); and all three of us very much enjoyed a steam-hauled trip on the Ffestiniog railway from Blaenau to Porthmadog. A visit to Cambridge University to talk to the Richard III Society in April 1984 provided the opportunity to stay for a couple of days with Ian Faulkner and his wife Carole who lived nearby. As I wrote to Bernard Jarvis soon afterwards, 'Ian's local pub, I'm glad to say, seemed to have no conception of closing time, so it was a pretty alcoholic occasion (for which I'd already primed myself during the conference in Jesus College bar!)'; moreover, Mike Stammers recalls 'Ian telling me about the time Keith stayed with him and Carole in Lode when he talked about a night of group sex between male and female students at Huddersfield in the hearing of almost the whole pub'. Surely not! On another occasion, at the end of the 1970s not long after he left the polytechnic, I remember spending a few days with Steve Smith in Norfolk, sampling the delights of rural medieval churches and local pubs. And Vivienne Haley has a vivid memory of my staying with her in Northamptonshire in the early 1980s soon after she bought 'a terrace cottage with no heating', when I insisted she buy a heater and refused to let her out of the shop until she did; however, she adds:

I'm sure Keith will remember this weekend for another reason. Opposite my house lived an old lady, larger than life, with her ageing husband and a live-in friend. I invited her over to a party and, just before festivities commenced, she arrived and sat opposite Keith in a comfy chair (she was over eighty). 'I don't get invited to many parties', she declared, 'so I've put these on specially'. Then, cackling, she lifted her skirts high and exposed an enormous pair of union jack bloomers. Keith nearly had apoplexy as he got a full view and certainly choked on his beer! 'What a splendid woman', he declared afterwards.

1983, the five hundredth anniversary of Richard III's seizure of the throne, resulted in invitations to both Gloucester and Oxford to participate in public debates on the motion 'Richard III was more sinned against than sinning'. On both occasions I found myself supporting the contention and, fortunately, there were no professional barristers present to subject my ramblings to clinical cross-examination. In Gloucester's splendid Guildhall I was teamed up with Jeremy Potter, chairman of the Richard III Society, against Tony Pollard and Michael Hicks; the debate was lively and entertaining; and we won the vote at the end. I had real reservations about taking part in the Oxford Union debate at all and adamantly refused to don evening dress; however, my doubts were overcome and even my wearing of a green corduroy suit sanctioned without demur. Again, the proposers included Jeremy Potter (and our opponents Tony Pollard) but, this time, we were led by Richard Duke of Gloucester. Chatting to him beforehand, I was unexpectedly impressed by his knowledge of even so distant an ancestor and he certainly put in a convincing performance. Since, by the time we entered the debating chamber, I was already well oiled on mulled wine, I found I had no inhibitions at all, highlighted the king's northern credentials and popularity in Yorkshire with gusto, and reacted to vigorous but good-natured heckling at one point by declaring in stentorian tones: 'Richard III couldn't get a hearing in southern England in 1483, Mr President, and nor can I in Oxford in 1983'. The place exploded with laughter. Tony Pollard, as at Gloucester, found himself on the losing side, and firmly believes that, in 'a bravura performance', I 'stole the show by outrageously putting on the Yorkshire'. It was all great fun and, by the time I rolled into bed in a classy hotel several hours later, I was probably as plastered as I have ever been. Fortunately, along the way, I had also acquired a pleasantly muscular ex-public school Oxford postgraduate student for company!

When, in July 1978, I travelled to Bristol for a fifteenth century conference organised by Charles Ross, I stayed at the St Vincent Rocks hotel in Clifton, a mere five minutes' walk from Brunel's magnificent suspension bridge spanning the Avon Gorge. This reminded me of just why I so much preferred the city to

Huddersfield and, over the next decade, I visited Bristol virtually every year, staying with Anne and Charles Ross more often than not. Two or three times, too, I journeyed on to Devon at the invitation of Di and Dennis Collinson, now enjoying the rural life near Ivybridge. This was always a pleasure, not least the occasion when I also visited Plymouth Arts Centre (where Bernard Samuels and I traded anecdotes about our years at Plymouth College) and toured the city's recently built Theatre Royal (where the charming and intelligent actor Bernard Bresslaw, a friend of the Collinsons, was appearing in pantomime at the time). At least once, too, I visited the college itself and met up with former colleagues such as Mike Allen and John Arthur. Peter Allender, whom I invariably saw whenever I visited Bristol, had shared the same flat as I had with Patrick Scott in the early 1970s. Indeed, probably in 1979, he recalls our visiting:

> ... the new *Green Room Club* at the end of King Street where there was a confrontation between Pat and someone he knew. In an unlikely way he started to square up to Pat. There were a group of Bristol Old Vic actors standing by the bar (Pete Postlethwaite among them) who diffused the situation by taking up mock boxing stances and having a pretend fight.

A few years later he also remembers his wife Jean driving us and their two young sons to:

> ... the *Anchor* at Oldbury-on-Severn when it had a garden, an orchard with a donkey, and wasn't too crowded. The boys Tom and Rob enjoyed playing there, and one of them kicked a football which landed in your pint, spilling most of its contents on your trousers. There was a split second while they waited for your response, which was to light a cigarette, laugh loudly, and suggest they buy you another beer. Since then they have found you an intriguing and entertaining friend:

Later that same day, he adds, we visited Berkeley castle and, on another occasion, went even further afield, driving up the Wye valley to Monmouth and Goodrich castle. Probably in 1983 Peter and I met up with Pat Scott for the last time. By then, sadly, he had contracted emphysema but that didn't prevent us embarking on a bit of a pub crawl, ending up in the *Dugout*, an underground mixed straight/gay club not far from the university. In the spring of 1985 Patrick died; I couldn't make it to his funeral but did pen a letter of condolence to his brother Jimmy (a medical doctor and general practitioner); and, in reply, he emphasised that Pat had been:

... following a steadily downhill path over the past few years and the eventual outcome was no surprise. His breathing became increasingly difficult and the oxygen cylinder was never far away. Despite the sadness, I am glad his sufferings are over.

Jimmy and I met up in a Clifton pub when I did visit Bristol a few weeks later; I met Alfred Josephson for the last time during this trip as well; and, maybe., it was also then that I first conceived the idea of coming back to live in the city someday.

What kept me in Huddersfield more than anything else in the early 1980s was the deteriorating health of Miriam Saunders and Edith Wood. In June 1981 I had to postpone a trip to Bristol because, as I wrote to Anne Crawford, 'my foster mother has become ill and, I fear, may be showing early signs of senile dementia' and Brendan Evans recalls that, probably about the same time, 'you abandoned plans to visit Norwich with us because Miriam was ill and you wanted to support her'. My diagnosis proved correct and, over the next few months, the symptoms of Alzheimer's became more and more pronounced: Miriam became very forgetful and increasingly confused; Edith, who was several years older anyway, found it ever more difficult to cope with her behaviour (such as wandering out into the street at night wearing only her nightgown); and so, reluctantly, in May 1982 I secured her admission into Oakes Villa, a residential home for the elderly run by the local authority. Towards the end of 1983 Edith, too, was clearly deteriorating; her eyesight, in particular, became very poor; and, since she was now on her own in my Moldgreen house, the problems of even day-to-day living were obviously becoming too much for her. I did what I could and even suggested she come and live with me in Newsome but she wouldn't hear of it. Then one evening when I was visiting her she suddenly declared, out of the blue, that she was lonely, couldn't cope any more, and wanted to join Miriam in the residential home. Fortunately, a former student of mine was now working for Kirklees Social Services; I contacted her; and together, despite a long waiting list, we managed to get her admitted to Oakes Villa in December 1983. This left me with a furnished but untenanted terrace house in Moldgreen; for a few months I let it to a gay friend of mine but, when he lost his job, he could no longer pay the rent regularly; and, eventually, he insisted on moving back home to live with his elderly parents. I toyed with the idea of letting the place to students (it was within walking distance of the polytechnic); however, when the electricity failed and I was told it badly needed rewiring, I sold the house instead in January 1985 (for almost double what I'd paid for it seven years earlier). Meanwhile, I visited Miriam and Edith regularly in Oakes Villa and, as far as I could tell, they were both reasonably contented there. I got on well with most of the staff (especially a jolly middle-aged woman whose party piece was playing the banjo), befriended several other residents and, now and again, even escorted a few of them to a nearby pub for a drink. I also became involved in fund-raising for the home, most memorably by hosting a version of television's *The Price is Right* one evening in a local church hail. Central Television provided us with a recording of the show's signature tune; the staff at Oakes Villa showed much ingenuity in constructing games; and a number of Huddersfield shops were prevailed upon to supply the prizes. Rather to my surprise, I enjoyed myself hugely and the audience were notably generous in their donations. Very occasionally, I even brought Miriam and Edith to Newsome by taxi for the day but, eventually, had to stop since such visits so disorientated Miriam. At this time, too, I came to the firm conclusion that I had no desire whatever to survive into old age myself. Hence why, over the last twenty years, I have studiously avoided increasing the risk of doing so by, for instance, eating healthily or stopping smoking.

During the early months of 1985 Miriam's physical and mental heath gradually worsened; by June she hardly recognised Edith or myself; and, early in July, she lapsed into a coma and died a couple of days later. I felt very sad at the passing of a woman who had always done her best for me but also relieved that her now virtually meaningless life was over. I organised the funeral; Edith, although deeply upset and not all that well herself, insisted on coming along to the last rites at Huddersfield crematorium; and even Miriam's rather prim and proper niece, whom I hadn't seen for years, gave the proceedings her seal of approval. About the same time my eccentric and anti-social cat Puss Puss became very ill. Brendan Evans, indeed, recalls 'bringing the car round to your house one Saturday night and taking you to the vet's' and my 'understandable grief' when she had to be put out of her misery. I vowed never to get another but my resolution was undermined almost immediately when a colleague told me a friend of his was looking for a home for a couple of kittens; he drove me to see them; and, inevitably, I promptly acquired Snubby and Snitch, a pair of utterly delightful tabbies. Soon after Edith insisted on coming to the house for one last time simply in order to meet them. Otherwise, I continued to visit her regularly in Oakes Villa. She remained *compos mentis* to the end and her rich fund of entertaining stories about her early life always made such visits a pleasure. Even so, as she became almost blind and increasingly immobile, she told me more than once that she now had no desire to hang on to life. My second foster mother, for such Edith had surely been, passed away in January 1987, just short of her eighty-seventh birthday, only minutes after cracking jokes with the staff. Again, I felt a powerful mixture of sorrow and relief. Throughout her life Edith had been devoted to Roman Catholicism and I was determined she be afforded a full Requiem Mass. Fortunately, I knew the polytechnic's Roman Catholic chaplain Peter Dauber (he and I occasionally drank in the same pub together) and he did her proud. I was amazed by how many people turned up to the service (including not only several members of staff from Oakes Villa but also my dean of faculty John O'Connell, the joint owners of the textile mill where Edith had worked for almost fifty years and her greatest school friend). Back at my house the seriously elderly had recourse to whisky (purely for medicinal purposes, of course!) and I sent them home reasonably contented after playing an audio-tape of Edith (on top form) I'd recorded a few years earlier. Bill Roberts, who came along to the funerals of both Miriam and Edith, comments:

> I was always impressed by the kindness you showed to Miriam and Edith, from the time when they used to come round to your house in Newsome to do some cleaning for you, then later in the house you bought for them in Moldgreen, and finally in the residential home where they lived.

Yet, now both were dead, there was very little to keep me in Huddersfield.

12

From Huddersfield to Bristol

During the 1970s and early 1980s my social life in Huddersfield largely revolved around drinking, particularly sinking pints of real ale in pubs. In later years at the polytechnic nothing much changed. I still regularly visited local hostelries in Newsome, especially the *Fountain* once my colleague David Taylor and his wife Thelma bought a house nearby at the beginning of the 1990s. As my quota of evening teaching increased, however, I tended more and more to frequent pubs in the town centre. Favourite among them remained the *College Arms*, just five minutes walk from my office, and this continued to be a prime watering hole for students I taught as well. Richard Bell, for instance, fondly remembers 'extra curricular activities' at Huddersfield when:

> ... Keith's interest in booze was roundly reciprocated. The *College Arms* was often the resort of a small clique of us in 1990/1 after receiving yet more wisdom at his hands and, sometimes, two or three of us would go back to your place. You made us cheese sandwiches on one occasion and, so big were they, Kirklees Council could easily have missed some of its kerbstones that day—but how good they tasted to the inebriated! There I discovered your strange obsession with frog ornaments and even stranger enthusiasm for Gilbert and Sullivan. I clearly remember, too, once leaving your house in the early hours one morning, making my way down the very steep Newsome Road to my digs, and distinctly hearing the sound of a fox barking somewhere across the valley as I fought to put my key in the door. A striking memory!

My room mate Keith Laybourn and I continued to drink together regularly, more often than not after evening teaching sessions, and, as he recalls, we became even greater friends than before:

Whilst at Huddersfield we were two of the closest friends that could be imagined. In a sense we were both isolated and lonely in our backgrounds, striving to be liked, and perhaps this similarity of origins, and temperament, brought us together in genuine understanding and friendship. We were dubbed the 'Two Keiths', partly because we shared a common sense of humour. Indeed, we played up to the 'Two Ronnies' model to such perfection that we could put on a show of an hour or two, setting each other up and adopting the straight man role in turn.

And, he adds, 'we can still do that: I remember the two of us being quite outrageous at a pub quiz night in Bristol years after you left Huddersfield'. Brendan Evans and David Taylor not infrequently joined Keith and I in the *College Arms*; so did a younger colleague Peter Davies; and a couple of departmental research assistants Sue Cox and Vivienne Hemingway were not averse to a few drinks either. Sue Cox, indeed, specifically remembers our 'enjoying massive meals together at the *Victoria* pub in Holmfirth', as well as 'drinking in the *Greyhound*, the gay bar on Manchester Road, where we always found it amusing that people simply couldn't make us out'. As for Vivienne Hemingway, with whom for some mysterious reason I seemed almost invariably to end up discussing hairy rugby players, she recollects that:

> Outside work you were gregarious and sociable. I was on the outskirts of your group, not one of the 'inner circle', but I certainly remember being introduced to Gilbert and Sullivan, Flanders and Swann, and Tom Lehrer, back at your house after the pubs shut.

My taste for social drinking with students became, if anything, even more pronounced than before during my last years in Huddersfield. The fact that such behaviour wouldn't have won many plaudits from the polytechnic's senior management, and my sexual antics even less, worried me not a jot. On the contrary, as time went by I revelled more and more in defying convention. I certainly got to know a splendid bunch of students, ranging from Richard Wright (a most engaging local lad who never quite knew what to make of my playfully provocative comments about his muscular physique) and Robin Harris (a serious-minded but sociable mature student from Nottingham) to Kerry Grieves (who later admitted to missing Huddersfield mainly because she'd been 'able to go into any pub in the town and know at least half a dozen mates would be there') and Jean Mountain (a retired police inspector who embraced the liberation of student life with enthusiasm). Occasionally, such friendships had unexpected spin-offs. In about 1987, for instance, Paul Darlison and Mark Swain, both accomplished beer drinkers, rebuilt a collapsed wall in my back garden. Memorably, too, in 1991 Aidan Jones and Anthony Kavanagh, a couple of splendidly out-going and sociable lads, persuaded me not only to attend a history/politics Christmas function they organised in an out-of-town hotel but also set the tone for later proceedings in an after dinner speech. Perhaps my opening remarks did just that:

> I really don't know why I've been invited to fill the gap between your over-indulgence in food and, no doubt, over-indulgence in whatever else is on offer in this superior establishment. Certainly, I'd hate to keep you from the serious business of chatting up the opposite sex—or even, for the more adventurous among you, the same sex. Either way, I doubt whether Marsden runs to gin-flavoured condoms or battery-operated dildos, so you might as well listen to me as a safer alternative.

And never, during all my years at Huddersfield, did I get to know a better crowd of students than my last ever Special Subject group in 1993/4, ranging from Philip Hastie (an immensely good-humoured and laid back north-easterner whose pronounced Geordie accent I ribbed mercilessly) and Dean Southam (an engaging, intelligent yet self-deprecating lad who seemed to find my homosexuality both fascinating and obscurely threatening) to Barry Goodwin (a sardonic mature student from south-eastern England who philosophically anticipated disaster lurking around every corner) and Steve Garrett (whose bewitching charm and obviously sincere concern for the welfare of others even ran to persuading his father to move me and my worldly goods to Bristol in September 1994).

Since the mid-1970s Keith Laybourn and I had regularly organised student history trips, particularly to the Wensleydale castles of Richmond and Middleham, and we continued to do so in the later 1980s and early 1990s. According to Richard Bell, history was clearly not at the top of the agenda during one such excursion:

> I remember a visit to Middleham castle which you organised, probably in my second year (1990). After setting off in some delapidated coach you handed round leaflets on Richard of Gloucester's lordship of Middleham. I think I was the only swot who gave the leaflet more than a cursory glance. On arrival, there was an unholy sprint through the ruins and then the real business of the day began: a consideration of the finer things of life from the best side of the bar. Thus, most of the trip was spent in one of the pubs nestled in the shadow of the castle.

In 1991 I visited Middleham again, this time specifically for the launch of Tony Pollard's splendid book *Richard III and the Princes in the Tower*; I met up with the Oxford historian Rowena Archer there; and we were both reduced to near hysteria by the local guide's eccentric commentary during a tour of the castle. Appropriately, in my very last term at Huddersfield, Keith and I decided to mount one final expedition to Wensleydale. Its beginnings were not auspicious. The night before three or four students had drunk very late at my house. Eventually, about 4.0am, the last of them departed; I promptly passed out; and, not surprisingly, I failed to make it to the university for the coach just five hours later. Keith Laybourn guessed what had happened (not too difficult!), persuaded the driver to make a diversion up Newsome Road, forced me to get on the coach, and off we went. Knowing this was my swansong several other colleagues (including Bill Roberts and Pauline Stafford) also came along; there was much gleeful repartee at my expense; and, perhaps inevitably, that time I never made it from pub to castle at all. When one of the students revisited Middleham in 1995, so he informed me on a National Portrait Gallery card featuring Richard III in person, 'it brought back memories of that great day at the castle last year'; however, he added, 'the castle is far more interesting when you're plastered!'. This reminded me of another occasion when this lad got so drunk at my house that even a cold shower and a vigorous spanking failed to revive him significantly. In the end his girlfriend and I simply dumped his stark naked body in a nearby bed. His hangover next day was truly spectacular, a condition no doubt compounded by his inability to remember just how he'd acquired a mildly sore backside as well.

During my later years in Huddersfield, as before, I occasionally provided overnight accommodation for visitors from elsewhere in the country. Alan Sutton certainly stayed with me several times: in 1987, for instance, and again in 1993. Colin Richmond reminds me of 'a happy seminar' at the polytechnic in February 1991:

> ... followed by whisky at your house until the early hours, and then having to get up at 6.30 or so in order to get back to teach at Keele at 9.0 or 10.0. I also recall the wonderful bacon butties in the station buffet!

Towards the end of my time in the north Bernard Jarvis and his mother, both of whom I'd known for at least thirty years, decided to revisit his home town and stayed with me for a few days. Barbara Jarvis, now an elderly widowed lady, particularly enjoyed herself, not least when joining me in gently ridiculing her eldest son one morning for smoking a cigarette in order to recover from an exhausting run. Peter Allender certainly remembers a visit he once made with his wife and two sons, probably at the end of 1988, particularly the antics of Lesley Burkey and Viv Haley:

The clearest memory I have is of New Year's Day. I've never seen anyone look as green as Vivienne did. Entering the room just as you took the lid off a large dish of stew, she promptly retired to bed, not to be seen again until the next morning. We stayed up until the early hours as Lesley regaled us with all manner of lurid tales. Jean and the boys, who'd also gone to bed by then, were kept awake by our unrestrained laughter!

A year or two later, Viv certainly got her own back:

My parents and I had eaten at a favourite restaurant in Huddersfield and then gone on to *Johnnys* night club. We met Keith and a couple of guys there, quite by accident, and one of them asked my mother to dance. Being fleet of foot she said yes and the two of them then waltzed around the bar much to the delight of the crowd there: an elegant lady of 60+ dancing with a flamboyant queen! My father and Keith looked on amazed. Keith came back to my place that night and my last memory, as I went to bed, is of Keith and my mother settling down with a bottle of gin under two quilts on the lounge sofa, talking animatedly. What they talked about all night I don't know but my mother went to bed at 6.0am (according to my father who had been there for hours!). The next day—New Year's Day—I remember we had roast lamb for lunch but Keith and my mother just sat there pushing peas around their plates in an ineffectual manner, unable to eat anything. The gin bottle was empty, of course.

As I became more and more tired of living in Huddersfield, and increasingly unhappy at the way higher education was evolving, my consumption of beer reached awesome proportions. Drinking whisky or gin late at night also showed signs of becoming regular rather than occasional. Vivienne Hemingway, indeed, recalls that my colleague David Wright (himself a heavy smoker!):

... at one time counselled you (if that's the right word) about your drinking and smoking because of the effect on your health. I think you moderated both for a short time but I don't think it lasted.

Perceptively, she also remarks that 'I always got the feeling that your sociability and gregariousness masked something else, a desperate need to be accepted and liked perhaps'. Only after I retired to Bristol in 1994, and began to enjoy writing almost as much as teaching, did I reach some sort of equilibrium for a few years.

Drinking apart, theatre-going continued to provide a great deal of pleasure during my last years in the north, not to mention an always welcome escape from the realities of everyday life. As in the 1970s and early 1980s, I visited Leeds most regularly, mainly because it was the easiest venue to get to without a car. In 1988 and 1991, for instance, I saw performances by the New D'Oyly Carte Opera Company at the Grand Theatre. The old company, originally founded by the Victorian impresario Richard D'Oyly Carte specifically to perform the comic operas of W. S. Gilbert and Arthur Sullivan, had come to an ignominious end a few years earlier: its very last performance had been at London's Adelphi Theatre on 27 February 1982. I'd enjoyed Gilbert and Sullivan ever since my teenage years, so I was delighted when a new company was formed, and *The Yeomen of the Guard* (1988) and *Iolanthe* (1991) were both splendid productions. No less escapist and enjoyable was *King's Rhapsody* (1988), the first Ivor Novello musical I'd seen for over a quarter of a century, while the Royal Shakespeare Company and Opera North combined in 1991 to stage Jerome Kern and Oscar Hammerstein's *Showboat*, surely the best American musical of the 1920s, not least for its almost unique blend of superb melodies and critical comment on contemporary society. Very different was *Back With A Vengeance*, when the 'almost legendary' Barry Humphries took the theatre by storm in November 1988 as both the irresistible Dame Edna Everage and the boorish Australian cultural attaché Sir Les Patterson, and *The Rocky Horror Show*. Sue Cox certainly remembers 'our visit to *The Rocky Horror Show* at Leeds Grand, trying on hats in some department store before the show and then, during the performance, the theatre balcony swaying with people dancing'. I recall, even more vividly, the astonishment in a nearby pub when a group of lads dressed in fishnet tights and girls in very short skirts masquerading as usherettes put in an exuberant appearance. More seriously, Jo Cole reminds me of a trip to Leeds with my 1988/9 Special Subject group to see 'three of Shakespeare's Wars of the Roses plays in one day' performed by the English Shakespeare Company. This is the only time I've ever spent ten almost continuous hours sitting, in ever mounting discomfort, in a packed theatre. *Richard III* was one of the plays we saw and, in 1990, I went to a National Theatre production of the same play in the same theatre, imaginatively set in the 1930s with Ian McKellan in the title role (a performance he was later to recreate on film). Occasionally, too, I went to Leeds Playhouse: in 1988, for instance, for the regional premiere of Alan Bennett's *Kafka's Dick* and, after it was reincarnated in the much superior Quarry Theatre as the West Yorkshire Playhouse, a stage version of Cole Porter's tuneful 1950s Hollywood musical *High Society* in 1991.

Apart from Leeds Grand and the West Yorkshire Playhouse, the only other professional theatre reasonably accessible from Huddersfield was Bradford's Alhambra and there in 1988 (courtesy of Brendan Evans and his car) I saw, for the one and only time, Noel Coward's rarely staged 1929 operetta *Bitter Sweet* by the New Sadler's Wells Opera Company. The contrast with Rodgers and Hammerstein's *South Pacific*, which I saw at the same theatre a few months later, was striking to say the least. Trevor Nunn's production of Tim Rice's *Chess* in 1990 was different again. At the Alhambra in the same year I also saw the English Shakespeare Company again, this time in *Coriolanus*; in 1991 I couldn't resist yet another production of Noel Coward's *Private Lives*; and, in 1992, I was bowled over by Nigel Hawthorne's powerful portrayal of the Hanoverian king in Alan Bennett's *The Madness of George III*. Occasionally, I went further afield than Leeds and Bradford. In 1988, for instance, I visited Sheffield's Crucible Theatre for a dramatised version of Emily Bronte's *Wuthering Heights* (not very impressive) and, in 1992, a rather more successful rendering of Charlotte Bronte's *Jane Eyre*, as well as accompanying Jean Mountain to *Elvis: The Musical* at the city's recently reopened Lyceum Theatre (almost as atmospheric as *The Buddy Holly Story* which I'd seen a year or two earlier). As for an open air staging of the *Wakefield Cycle of Mystery Plays* in July 1988 against a backdrop of the ruins of Pontefract castle, it was rendered all the more interesting by the reactions of my companion, the polytechnic's Anglican chaplain Kenneth Cook. I also crossed the Pennines at least three times during these years to see major productions in Manchester: *Tosca*, *The Phantom of the Opera* and *Les Miserables*. Although, by the late 1980s, I was finding London more and more stressful, I still visited the city now and again, more often than not for professional reasons. By then, since Anne Crawford had now left Bristol and obtained a post at the Public Record Office, I tended to stay overnight with her and her young son James in Acton. Usually, too, I took in a West End show: it seemed almost sacrilegious if I didn't. 'I've always been slightly surprised and impressed by your keenness for the theatre', Anne muses, and 'enjoyed sharing several visits with you'; however, she adds, 'I'm damned if I can remember which productions we've seen together'. Nor can I but, perhaps, they included Noel Coward's *The Vortex* at the Garrick Theatre in 1989 (the only time I've ever seen Coward's most harrowing play) and William Shakespeare's *Much Ado About Nothing* at the Queen's in 1993. As for Huddersfield, it hadn't had a professional theatre since the 1960s but I still went to amateur productions in the town from time to time: early in 1994, for instance, I saw the Huddersfield Thespians in a production of Tennessee Williams' *The Glass Menagerie*. And, for reasons that now entirely escape me, I even went to Huddersfield Town Hall for An *Evening with Ken Dodd*, a test of both his stamina as a traditional comic and that of his far from young audience since the show didn't end until after midnight.

A few months after reaching my fiftieth birthday in February 1994, I not only early retired but sold my house in Huddersfield and moved to Bristol. This dramatic transformation in my life had been a long time in the making.

Indeed, what had kept me at the polytechnic in the 1970s and early 1980s more than anything else had been my reluctance to leave Huddersfield while Miriam Saunders and Edith Wood were still alive. Following Miriam's death in July 1985 and Edith's in January 1987, this was no longer a consideration; the fact that I had never married or fathered children meant there were no family pressures on me; and, over the next few years, my desire to make a clean break from the place where I felt I'd spent far too many years of my life already became almost overwhelming. Providing I secured even a relatively low pension income and a bit of part-time teaching, moreover, money wasn't likely to prove a problem. Ever since returning north in 1972, my annual expenditure had been consistently below my income and, by accident rather than design, I'd accumulated a considerable nest egg; the sale of my Moldgreen house in January 1985 had produced a tidy sum as well; and the outstanding mortgage on my own home in Newsome no longer amounted to a great deal. Throughout the 1970s and early 1980s the semi-detached adjoining mine had been occupied by an elderly lady. Despite my overgrown garden continually encroaching on hers, she and I got on well but, by the mid-1980s, she was finding it increasingly difficult to cope on her own. For a year or two I did what I could to help until, in the summer of 1987, she decided to enter sheltered accommodation. Her house was promptly put up for sale. Since I had now paid off the mortgage on my own Newsome property, I decided to put in an offer, if only to guard against the possibility of getting noisy neighbours. As a result it became mine, for £23,000, in March 1988. For a while it remained empty; Robin Harris, a recently graduated student friend, occupied the place virtually rent free for a few weeks in the summer and, in return, did some repairs and decorating; and, in September 1988, I let the house to three final year BA (Humanities) students, two of whom had already opted for my Wars of the Roses Special Subject. This set the pattern for the next few years. I always opted for female students, at least one of whom I was teaching at the time, and charged a rent below the going rate for student tenancies in Huddersfield. The logic behind this was that girls were more likely to look after the place than lads and, since their landlord was also a polytechnic lecturer, think twice about not paying the rent on time. So it proved. Most of the time, too, they were reasonably quiet, apart from the occasional party (fine by me, as long as I was invited along). Boyfriends were a bonus, especially if they had DIY skills, and there never seemed to be any shortage of them. One year, indeed, there were so many lads coming and going in the mornings that an old lady living across the road even expressed concern that the place had become a brothel! Occasionally, too, I put up visitors there during vacations, including Peter Allender and his family over a New Year break when, he remembers, the house was extremely cold since it had no central heating. I took out a new mortgage to buy the property but rent more than covered monthly repayments and my bank balance was further boosted as a result. After four years, however, I'd had enough of the place; in July 1992 I sold it to the daughter of a local shopkeeper I knew for £32,500 (a tidy profit on my investment); and this turned out to be a very wise move since, so I learned a few years later, part of an external wall eventually collapsed as a result of subsidence.

When Alfred Josephson (the German Jew who had played such a crucial role in helping me come to terms with my homosexuality in the later 1960s) died in the spring of 1990, I travelled to the south west for his funeral. Held at a crematorium near Bath, it was a moving if rather bizarre occasion. The service was Jewish (even though Alfred had no religious beliefs) and, as for the substantial congregation, it comprised an unlikely mix of members of Bath's Jewish community and Bristol homosexuals (several of whom made no attempt whatever to disguise their orientation). Afterwards, many of us adjourned to Alfred's family home in Bath. There, for the first time ever, I met his surviving brother (who, despite being over ninety years old, nevertheless cadged two or three illicit cigarettes from me) and talked to Alfred's last boyfriend (a young artist in his early thirties who was clearly devastated at his mentor's death). During this trip I stayed with Peter Allender in Bristol and, whilst there and virtually without premeditation, I decided to buy a house in the city myself. Since even a decent flat in historic Clifton was beyond my financial means, I settled instead on searching out a suitable property in the Bishopston/Horfield district where Peter lived. As he himself recalls, although this was an area 'we hardly knew as students when Bristol was the Downs, Clifton, Redland and Cotham', I'd rather taken to it when visiting him in the later 1980s; in the weeks that followed Alfred's funeral he became 'a kind of estate agent', sending me information about local houses coming on to the market; and, as for 'the house-buying day' itself, it was certainly memorable:

> Like me, Keith was amazed at some of the properties the owners had the nerve to put on the market. One seemed all right when we entered but became more like an abandoned building site the further we went around it. Then there was the 'gnome house' whose dotty owner, surrounded by garden gnomes on all sides, obviously had no intention of selling: 'I loves my 'ouze', she kept declaring. Next, we went to the 'brown house', numbingly redolent of its last owner, deceased some months or even years past. To lighten our spirits—and especially Keith's—we spent lunchtime in the nearby *Forester's Arms* and, over a couple of pints, wondered whether it was worth seeing the last remaining property, about which the young estate agent seemed less than enthusiastic himself. Actually, I think we both took to this house as soon as we entered it, despite the proximity of

Bristol prison. It had a properly lived-in feel, lots of rooms, even some comfortable furniture the previous owners had left.

No doubt the proximity of the prison, coupled with well-publicised riots within its walls a few months earlier, explained the modest asking price: £57,000. The notion of living near a prison rather tickled my fancy and I would probably have paid the asking price if I'd had to. Mainly to test the waters, I put in an initial offer of £53,000; it was promptly accepted; and, in November 1990, the house became mine. Although there was a certain amount of rather battered furniture there already, more was clearly needed. Vivienne Haley, not for the first time, proved immensely helpful as she herself vividly recalled in 2004:

> Soon after Keith bought his house in Bristol, we hired a furniture van, visited a second hand furniture store in Huddersfield, loaded it up and set off for Bristol. Erroneously as it turned out, I had thought the journey from Yorkshire to Bristol was about three hours. Not so. Keith was unable to sit in a van cab for longer than about forty-five minutes at a stretch, so we had to stop several times to get a drink and replenish his ciggy supply. Eventually, when we arrived in Bristol, we had to unload the van and get everything into the house. 'Can we go and get a washing machine while we've got the van?', asked Keith, trying to look innocent, as though it hadn't been on his list of things to do from the beginning. Despite the fact we had been on the go since before 7.0am and it was now starting to get dark, it seemed like a fairly good idea so, accompanied by Keith's friend Peter Allender and Peter's two young sons, off we went. The item was chosen within fifteen minutes. Keith paid for it from a great wad of bank notes he'd previously stashed in his back pocket. Clearly, his hatred of electronic progress didn't stretch to washing machines but did prevent his paying for them by any form of plastic. With the item safely in the back of the van and lashed vaguely to the sides, Keith and the boys volunteered to travel in the back. Everything seemed fine to me as we drove along, stopping at traffic lights, swaying round corners, squeezing this enormous vehicle between parked cars, until we pulled up outside the house. When they emerged, however, Keith looked very wobbly and seasick, while the boys followed whitely. Nevertheless, we all went out to dinner that night and, inevitably, had far too much to drink.

Nor was this the end of our escapades, as Viv also reminds me:

> Next day Keith and I set off back to Huddersfield with the van, and a very cold and icy day it was. When we got near Oldham, setting off across the Pennines without a fortifying drink seemed madness, so we made a detour to the pub.

This put us onto a very minor road across the 'tops'. It started snowing. We battled on. The wind began to howl, battering at our now empty feather-light van and pushing us all over the place. Knowing we were near the highest point, and that it was now downhill all the way into the outskirts of Huddersfield, we kept going. Neither of us really knew what happened next but, with a combination of wind and ice, we found ourselves sliding off the road and facing a steep drop of hundreds of feet to certain death. How we didn't go over the edge I have no idea but, badly shaken as we were, a recuperative drink or two proved essential when we finally reached our destination.

Now I'd acquired a house in Bristol, what was I going to do with it? Soon after completion I wrote to Ralph Griffiths:

> I've just bought a rambling terrace house in Bristol, very near Horfield prison. I'm going to let the place to students in term time and probably live in it myself during summer vacations.

Instead, early in 1991, I let the house to a Bristol schoolteacher I knew at a significantly lower rent than three or four students might have paid. On balance, this seemed a much better arrangement since I could depend on him to look after the place; the rent was more than enough to cover mortgage payments; and, most importantly, he was perfectly happy to share the house with me whenever, and for however long at a time, I visited. Between 1991 and 1994, in fact, I spent as much time in Bristol as I could, more often than not taking my cats Snubby and Snitch with me. Fortunately, northern friends seemed only too happy to provide a long-distance taxi service in return for a few days free accommodation in the south west. Indeed, as a letter to Brendan Evans sent in August 1992 indicates, the place occasionally turned into a veritable cross between a cattery and a hotel:

> Snubby and Snitch—who, like me, seem to prefer this house to that in Huddersfield—have so far concentrated their destructive tendencies on just one chair and, so far at least, shown no interest in wallpaper stripping. Sue Cox is turning up here later today. I'm meeting Tony and Rosemary Saul for a pub lunch in Bristol tomorrow. Vivienne Haley and Lesley Burkey are descending on me this coming weekend and David Mathieson next week.

During my sojourns in Bristol in the early 1990s, inevitably, Peter Allender soon became a regular drinking and theatre-going buddy. He recalls, for instance, our visits to the nearby *Kellaway Arms*, even though it was 'run by a landlord of quite determined charmlessness' and the regulars in its tiny lounge bar seemed 'a thoroughly miserable lot'. The *Golden Lion*, nearest hostelry to my house, retained at least the vestiges of a traditional local pub in the early 1990s and we also occasionally visited the *Annexe* (destined to become my main drinking haunt a few years later). Now and again, too, we visited pubs in Clifton, Bristol city centre and, whenever we went to the theatre there, Bath as well. In 1991, 1992 and 1993 I saw over twenty productions either in Bristol or Bath, more often than not with Peter. In the early 1990s, he recollects, 'the Bristol Old Vic was going through a good phase, with Bristolian Timothy West in charge and his wife, Prunella Scales, making many appearances'. At its historic if none too comfortable Theatre Royal we saw, for instance, Rodgers and Hart's 1940 musical *Pal Joey* (nicely recapturing Chicago's sleazy night life at the end of the 1930s) and Eugene O'Neill's *Long Day's Journey into Night* ('a play with the aptest of titles', Peter remembers, 'and a part for Prunella Scales as far away from Sybil Fawity in the BBC TV sitcom *Fawlty Towers* as can be imagined'). The Hippodrome, nearest Bristol equivalent to Leeds Grand and Bradford Alhambra, was the favoured venue for major touring productions, particularly musicals: Peter and I saw *My Fair Lady* there in 1992 and *Me and My Girl* in 1993. Occasionally, straight plays also came to the Hippodrome, among them Peter Shaffer's *Lettice and Lovage* ('lost in the enormous Hippodrome auditorium', Peter recalls, 'but probably not worth finding anyway'). Increasingly, however, the theatre we most enjoyed visiting was Bath's Theatre Royal, only recently (and very comfortably) restored to its former glory. In 1991, for instance, I saw Derek Jacobi and Robert Lindsay in Jean Anouih's *Becket*; in 1992 Jacobi appeared there again, this time in Hugh Whitmore's compelling *Breaking the Code*; in 1993 Timothy West put in a memorably powerful performance in Brian Phelan's *Himself*; and, as for a star-studded production of Oliver Goldsmith's *She Stoops to Conquer* directed by Peter Hall, Peter Allender particularly remembers 'a wonderful over-the-top performance' by Donald Sinden and a no less 'scene stealing' one by Miriam Margolyes as Mr and Mrs Hardcastle. I often dragged visitors along to the theatre as well: Vivienne Haley and Lesley Burkey accompanied me to a spectacular staging of Gilbert and Sullivan's *The Mikado* at Bristol Hippodrome; Steve Garrett came along with Peter Allender and I to Oscar Wilde's *The Importance of Being Earnest* at the Bristol Old Vic (when, Peter reminds me, we occupied a box adjoining the stage and were even invited to toss roses at the feet of Zena Walker's Lady Bracknell during curtain calls); and, with both Peter and Jean Mountain in tow, I went to *The Rocky Horror Show* again (this time at Bath's Theatre Royal when, for Peter at least, 'the audience were often more interesting than what was happening on the stage'). Of all the productions I saw between 1991 and 1994, however, none is more memorable than Joe Orton's *Entertaining Mr Sloane* in July 1993. Kenneth Waller, whom I'd known since his years in repertory at Huddersfield Theatre Royal at the end of the 1950s and last met at London Weekend Television studios in 1984, was in the cast. By 1993 he had won national recognition as the eccentric and irascible Grandad in Carla Lane's BBC TV sitcom *Bread*, so it was without much expectation of a response that I rang Bath Theatre Royal's box office and left a message for him. Almost immediately he rang me back and suggested we meet for a pub lunch, prior to the matinee for which I'd already obtained a ticket. Not only did we then spend a pleasant and nostalgic hour or two together, after the performance I went backstage, met his fellow actors (including Barbara Windsor) and very much enjoyed a guided tour of set and stage, enlivened by Ken's sardonic comments on the theatre's shortcomings and inconveniences for actors. Sadly, he and I never had the opportunity to meet again.

'Because you popped into my office one evening hot foot from Bristol', recalls Brendan Evans, 'I think I was the first to learn of, and be surprised by, your early retirement plans, sensible as they proved to be'. This was probably at the end of 1990 when, as I wrote to Ralph Griffiths, 'I've now fully decided to pack in full-time teaching, if I possibly can, when I get to fifty in 1994 and return to Bristol, the only place where I've ever really enjoyed living'. Over the next few years my determination to get out as soon as I could in no way diminished. The fact that I spent several weeks in Bristol during the summers of 1991, 1992 and 1993, making me unavailable for any vacation duties in Huddersfield, also helped provide a handy element in my later case for 'premature retirement in the interest of the efficient discharge of the employer's functions'. Each year, too, I became more and more reluctant to return to the north of England. Early in September 1991, indeed, I wrote from Bristol to Anne Crawford at the Public Record Office:

> I do see buying a house in Bristol as the first step on the road to early retirement. Unfortunately, I shall have to return to Huddersfield soon and prepare for the rigours of a new academic year.

In August 1992, in a letter to Brendan Evans, I asked rhetorically whether 'there is room these days for a chain-smoking, semi-alcoholic in what passes for academia in the so-called University of Huddersfield'; moreover, in the same letter, I also mooted the possibility of immediate resignation or resigning at the end of the 1992/3 academic year rather than 'hanging on until 1994 and, hopefully, getting early retirement'. When I arrived back in Huddersfield I talked to Brendan at some length in his capacity as dean of school, I remember, and was persuaded to carry on. Even so, when writing to Mike Stammers in November 1992, I commented:

I spent over eight weeks at my Bristol house this summer, including about four on my own while my schoolteacher tenant was away. Ian Faulkner, whom I hadn't seen since 1984, came down for a weekend of nostalgia. Even on my own, I found Bristol in every way preferable to Huddersfield, certainly far better than the glorified technical college I work in, now masquerading as a university. I'm going there again this coming weekend and, since I've persuaded a second year student with a car that he'd enjoy a visit, I shall be saved the horrors of British Rail. Next week I'm due to be cascaded with marking—another pleasure I can do without! Next summer I expect I'll be in Bristol for most of July and August, even if I have to pretend to be ill for several weeks!! I've certainly got my eye firmly set on early retirement as soon as possible.

Developments at work over the next year only served to reinforce my determination to apply for early retirement at fifty, not least another bout of widely publicised turmoil and conflict within the university's upper management, eventually culminating in the resignation of its long-time director Kenneth Durrands (or vice chancellor as he'd become in 1992) at about the same time as my own departure. I also began to sense that Pauline Stafford, like me, was beginning to get itchy feet and, before long, would start applying for posts elsewhere. This made the prospect of remaining at Huddersfield even less appealing and I was certainly not surprised to hear, three or four years after I left, of Pauline's appointment to the prestigious chair of medieval history at the University of Liverpool. Inevitably, since I made no attempt to disguise it, colleagues, even students, were now becoming increasingly aware of my despondency as well. Andrew Taylor, for instance, recalls how he 'did worry towards the end of your time at Huddersfield that you were so obviously unhappy'; whether this was 'the job, your personal life or a combination I don't know' but 'I should have done more to help'. Similarly, Steve Garrett remembers that:

> In the era I knew Keith he was in personal turmoil. He missed his much-loved mentor Charles Ross and was sickened by the way higher education was supposedly modernising. All he wanted to do was get out.

And, clearly, by the time I wrote to Peter Fleming at the University of the West of England early in July 1993, any lingering doubts I may have had had been completely dispelled:

> I have taken the momentous decision to apply for early retirement at the end of the 1993/4 academic year. I've not lost interest in teaching and writing but I have definitely had enough of Huddersfield and profoundly dislike the particular

CAT scheme the university is to introduce in 1994/5 [Credit Accumulation and Transfer, the latest fad in higher education, involving setting up an ill thought out modular degree programme throughout the university]. Also, I now find the pressure of coping with ever increasing student numbers—and associated marking!—leaves little time for much else. I shall be at my Bristol house from 9 July to 1 September and would be delighted to hear from you there. If nothing else, it would be nice to meet for a drink and, no doubt, an exchange of horror stories about recent trends in higher education.

Part of the reason for writing to Peter (whom I'd first met at a fifteenth-century history conference in the early 1980s) was to enquire about the possibility of getting part-time teaching at the University of the West of England. His reply was most encouraging:

> While it's not good news that you're fed up with Huddersfield (ah! those heady days when CATS was just a musical), it is that you're finally effecting your move to Bristol. Of course, it's unsafe to predict these days what's going to happen in higher education a month hence, let alone a year, but I should imagine that your prospects would be pretty good. In a year or two a new module on *Elites, Polities and Society in England c.1370—1540* will appear on our BA (History) degree. At the moment I'm down to run it on my own but, finances permitting, your assisance would be greatly appreciated.

Once I returned to Huddersfield in September 1993, I soon set about trying to persuade Brendan Evans, my dean of school, to back my quest for early retirement. At first he didn't want to and, indeed, tried to dissuade me. Once he became convinced that I was in earnest and might well resign anyway if my application was unsuccessful, however, he reluctantly promised his support. As a result, during the 1993 Christmas vacation we spent an evening in my local pub concocting both a letter making my case for early retirement and his response to it. Towards the end of January 1994 I submitted my request to the university's senior management and certainly didn't pull my punches:

> I find myself ever more out of sympathy with current trends in higher education. I disapprove strongly of so-called progressive teaching methods (which we seem under increasing pressure to adopt) and remain firmly committed to a traditional lecture/tutor-led seminar structure, examined by conventional written assignments and unseen three hour examinations. I abhor the present stress on 'skills', 'teaching objectives', 'relevance to the world of work' (and the rest!), rather than the advancement of learning and knowledge for its own sake. Furthermore, I am

adamantly opposed to the CAT scheme the university is in the process of implementing. There is no way my kind of detailed, source-based later medieval/early modern history can be taught in 10 (or even 20) credit modules: if I tried it would result in 'Mickey Mouse' options of little academic value and teaching such six or twelve week modules would represent, for me, the betrayal of everything I've tried to do, or found worthwhile, in teaching since I first embarked on my career in 1969. I am entirely out of sympathy, too, with the national policy of increasing student numbers at all costs, regardless of whether staff can cope with the burgeoning work load or provide undergraduates with the quality of education they have a right to expect. The result can only be a production line mentality in higher education.

Having lambasted higher education in general, and the university's priorities in particular, I then turned to my own teaching where, clearly, I simply couldn't resist over-the-top rhetorical flourishes:

Increasingly, I find myself out of step with what is regarded as 'important' in later medieval/early modern English history (let alone Europe, or the wider world, which I now have no interest in teaching at all), particularly the lives of the masses and women's history. My interests remain what they have always been: kings, nobility, gentry, high politics and war. I neither know nor care about peasants (whether male or female!) in my period: their dreary lives have never turned me on and I can't convey to students (even with my histrionic talents!) an enthusiasm that simply isn't there. Indeed, I'm amazed I still recruit as many students as I do on my courses. It's certainly not because I set out to make them trendy: quite the contrary! Perhaps it's a combination of outright masochism on their part and the challenge of surviving classes taught by the dinosaur of the department. I suspect students do well on my courses (as they frequently do) because they're too bloody terrified of me to slack (although, to be fair to myself, I can still manage a charismatic lecture performance on a good day). Yet I fear that, should I continue at the university beyond the current academic year, I might become more and more unreliable, letting down both colleagues and students, and that would be a sad end to a largely enjoyable and productive career.

Finally, I summed up my 'case for early retirement at fifty' in terms that allowed for no misunderstanding:

I find myself suffering from ever increasing stress and growing lack of sympathy with current trends in higher education. I have no family and no responsibilities to anyone but myself. I am no longer happy in Huddersfield and fear that, in the not too distant future, I might find it increasingly difficult to make a full and committed contribution to the university. Better to retire now, by mutual agreement, lest I become a complete liability in the future and face the possibility of an ignominious dismissal.

Eventually, both my letter and Brendan's supportive response found their way to the desk of one of the university's pro-vice chancellors. When I was summoned to see him, he immediately confessed to being taken aback by such devastating honesty! Fortunately, I knew him reasonably well since he'd been promoted through the ranks and, perhaps as a result, our ensuing conversation was both friendly and informal. Out of the blue, he promptly offered me promotion to principal lecturer. I politely declined. When he then made it clear there was no possibility of pension enhancement (not least, he hinted, because of the cost of financing the vice chancellor's imminent resignation package), I emphasised that I wanted to leave anyway. At that point he grinned broadly, declared he knew when he was beaten, warmly shook hands, and promised to do everything he could to facilitate my smooth departure. It worked and, a few weeks later, I was granted premature retirement on 31 August 1994, with a tax free sum of £23926 and a pension entitlement of £7975 per annum. So, the deed was done and, knowing my escape was now guaranteed, I enjoyed my last few weeks teaching full-time at Huddersfield enormously. Rather to my surprise, I also realised that I genuinely cared about the future of history at the university in general and the well being of my own patch in particular. Fortunately, this did seem assured. Later medievalist Pat Cullum had been appointed the previous year; the powers-that-be soon sanctioned my replacement; and early modernist Tim Thornton, my successor, struck me as an immensely personable, able and committed young man.

Securing early retirement made the party Brendan Evans and I organised to celebrate our fiftieth birthdays in February 1994 all the more enjoyable for me. Held at my house, it was very much a repeat of our fortieth year jamboree in 1984. Virtually all our current history/politics colleagues turned up. Former polytechnic lecturers Peter Durrans and Tony Saul made the journey to Huddersfield as well, accompanied by their wives Hazel and Rosemary. Inevitably, too, I invited along a selection of past and present students, among them Peter Broome, Steve Garrett, Vivienne Haley, Cliff Burhouse and Kit Hardwick (who recalls the party as 'one of many splendidly alcoholic occasions I just about remember sharing with Keith'). Peter Allender, musing that 'for a future recluse Keith certainly had a wide circle of acquaintances', also travelled north for the junketings (despite not feeling too well), only to discover 'the impossibility of finding a quiet corner to sleep' even after midnight. Next morning, nonetheless, he had completely recovered and, by the time Brendan Evans turned up to help in the late afternoon, we'd managed to clear away the debris and restore the place to at least a semblance of normality. So, before long, we simply adjourned to the pub and embarked on another drinking session. Then, shortly before the end of the summer term, Brendan invited me, along with close colleagues and their wives, to his house for an informal gathering and presentation to mark my imminent departure from the university. About thirty also signed a huge card. 'Now that you're retiring it's time to take control of your life and decide which direction you're going in', declared a caption on the front while, inside, a signpost simply pointed to three pubs. Very appropriate! Equally apt were comments such as, 'may your new pastures have fewer thistles', 'glad to see you're breaking out', 'may your cats be smooth and your beer be strong', 'have a happy, beery, unhealthy retirement' and, ironically from Pauline Stafford, 'a small retiring card for a small retiring person'. A very pleasant evening ensued, if a little overwhelming at times.

Once the summer term was over clearing out my office at the university proved a nightmare and took days; the house was no better and, in the end, I took a great deal of stuff to Bristol that ought to have been junked; and I finally left Huddersfield on 10 September 1994. Appropriately, two former students played key roles in getting me to the south west. Vivienne Haley vividly recalls that:

> Keith's final move to Bristol involved taking both him and his two neurotic cats in the back seat of my car. Why I was doing this I have no idea. Highly allergic to cats as I am., we drove the whole way there with the windows open, and arrived frozen and asthmatic.

Steve Garrett, whose father (most fortuitously) possessed a removal van, similarly remembers how he had 'the pleasure of moving Keith's books and chattels to Bristol, a place where he needed to return in order to feel closer to the people and times that had once made him so happy'. All that remained was to sell my Newsome house. It went on the market the day after my departure and, despite its run down condition, by the end of October had been sold for £38,500: not a bad return on the £3650 I'd paid for it in 1972.

Although I have never suffered a pang of regret at my decision to get out of my home town and full-time teaching, during my first year in Bristol I did continue working at a distance for the University of Huddersfield. The circumstances that led to this were extraordinary. In 1993/4 Pat Cullum and I had had a splendid bunch of second year BA (Historical and Political Studies) students taking *Politics, Reformation and Revolution in Tudor and Early Stuart*

England and I'd enjoyed teaching a couple of very lively and committed seminar groups. Several of them had set their sights on taking my Special Subject the following year and, when news leaked out of my impending departure, there was considerable disappointment. Brendan Evans and David Taylor then came up with an unexpected suggestion. How did I feel about taking on a group of students studying fifteenth-century English history at a distance à la the Open University? I wasn't all that enthusiastic but, since the remuneration on offer was not ungenerous and included four expenses-paid trips from Bristol to Huddersfield during the 1994/5 academic year, I came up with the notion of an Independent Study Unit entitled *Politics, War and Government in Late Lancastrian and Yorkist England c.1450—1485*. Anyone opting for this, it was made clear, would be required to attend an extended briefing session during the final week of the summer term 1994. This mainly took the form of four 1¼ hour lectures introducing them to the principal primary sources for later fifteenth-century England, recorded at the time and then available on tape in the department for the rest of the year. Additionally, on the same day, I arranged to see each student individually for about twenty minutes to discuss the four inter-related assignments they would write, and have assessed, during the autumn and spring terms. These, restructured into a coherent whole, would then be submitted as a veritable undergraduate dissertation early in the summer term 1995. Students had to provide me with their home addresses; I supplied them with mine in Bristol; and I also undertook to ensure my availability for consultation by telephone during a two hour slot every week. On each of my visits to Huddersfield, moreover, I promised to lay on one-to-one tutorials. It was a bold experiment and I wasn't entirely sure it would work but, by and large, it did. Of the dozen or so students who took the risk, four or five put in upper second class work and a couple got firsts. Since 1995, however, my academic connections with Huddersfield have virtually ceased, apart from commenting on two or three Ph.D research proposals. I made several social visits to my home town in the later 1990s (more often than not staying with David and Thelma Taylor in Newsome) but, by 2000, I could no longer face the train journey. In all probability, I shall never visit the north of England again.

13

Open University Tutor in Yorkshire and the South West

By the time I left Huddersfield for Bristol in September 1994 I had already been an Open University part-time tutor for well over two decades. This had happened more by accident than design but it did mean that, right from the start, I found myself involved in the most original and important new initiative in higher education in the later twentieth century. Indeed, the establishment of the University of the Air (as it was originally to be called) by Harold Wilson's Labour government at the end of the 1960s is among its most enduring achievements and, certainly, far more commendable than its enthusiasm for destroying grammar schools and misguided social engineering in promoting nation-wide comprehensives. Di Collinson, who had recently completed a Ph.D in philosophy, became the first staff tutor in Arts for the new university's south-western region in 1970 and she must bear prime responsibilty for recruiting not only me but also her own husband Dennis into its part-time ranks: patronage, perhaps, but maybe essential if she was to obtain a team of tutors enthusiastic and committed enough to get the show on the road. Indeed, as I remember, living in Plymouth College's Colson House with her and Dennis as I was at the time, neither I nor he had much choice in the matter. And Dennis himself recollects how, during the university's first five or six years, Di 'worked tirelessly in setting up a vast teaching structure for the Arts in the south west', as well as 'managing to write a great deal of OU teaching material invariably praised by students'. In retrospect, I'm immensely grateful to her since becoming an Open University tutor in 1971 proved to be vitally important for the future direction of my career. Little did I suspect, though, that I'd still be working for the organisation thirty years later!

The Open University, particularly in its early years, broke new ground all over the place. Centred at Walton Hall, on the outskirts of Milton Keynes, it had a central core of academics but their main function was not teaching or even research. Rather, it was their responsibility to put together first, second and third level courses, and course material, designed to be studied at a distance by mature students under the guidance of part-time staff in the new university's nine regions. Most of the full-time staff's labours, in fact, were devoted to researching and writing course units, carefully structured to enable students to work on their own, and in their spare time, building up academic credits over the years until, eventually, they'd accumulated enough to be awarded degrees. Otherwise, there were prescribed set books for most courses; television and radio programmes; records and, later, cassettes; and a strictly limited number of hours of face-to-face tutorials held in nearby host institutions such as universities, polytechnics and further education colleges. All first and many third level courses also had annual residential Summer Schools while, for the rest, there tended to be two or three Day Schools instead. Needless to say, too, students and tutors had to contend with a veritable army of largely Milton Keynes-based bureaucrats employed to ensure the whole elaborate organisation functioned smoothly and efficiently. They didn't always succeed!

During the Open University's first year in 1971 I tutored *A100 Arts: A Foundation Course*, a multi-disciplinary course designed to introduce students new to humanities to history, art history, philosophy, music and literature. Early units examined, with varying degrees of success, the methodologies underpinning the study of these disciplines, followed by a series of case studies focussing, for instance, on William Shakespeare's *Hamlet*, the sixteenth-century art historian Giorgio Vasari, the seventeenth-century philosopher Réné Descartes and the early nineteenth-century composer Felix Mendelssohn. For the last eight weeks or so the course homed in on the theme Industrialisation and Culture *circa* 1830—1914, presenting students with the opportunity to get to grips with the historical debate about industrialisation, art and industry, and D.H.Lawrence's *The Rainbow*. This worked extremely well, in sharp contrast to a strand running throughout the course seeking to introduce them to logic: this proved so complete a disaster that it came near to blighting the course as a whole. Fortunately, since many tutors (including me) couldn't make much sense of the logic units either, they were able to reassure panicking students. And, despite distinctly rough patches, A100 did manage to achieve its main objectives and ensure healthy recruitment to second level humanities courses.

Since I taught it only once as a correspondence tutor, my memories of A100 tuition are hazy to say the least. I was certainly enthusiastic about the new enterprise, even encouraging my Plymouth College colleague Mike Allen to embark on an Open University degree and, so he assures me, offering him 'critical and typical' support early on. Unfortunately, foundation level tutors in

1971 didn't have a great deal of face-to-face contact with students, nor did they even mark all their assignments. Yet, from the beginning, what I most enjoyed about Open University teaching was the opportunity to deliver occasional lectures and conduct seminars/tutorials. Early on, inevitably, the majority of students were probably older than I was but I never felt intimidated by this. On the contrary I made it clear that I was in charge and always maintained firm control of sessions, never allowing them to degenerate into vapid nit-picking about the course material or assignments. Most students seemed only too happy with my approach, even when I chose to ignore tuition guidelines emanating from Walton Hall (as I all too frequently did) and follow my own instincts instead. Dennis Collinson certainly has positive memories of my Open University teaching, based not only on our early experiences of 1971/2 but also the mid-1990s when, after I returned to the south-west region, we once more found ourselves tutoring the same courses:

> At the Open University Keith magnetized many students in hour, two hour and three hour sessions. He was always keen and willing to help out in teaching areas where he had little prior knowledge by reading massively around subjects unfamiliar to him [such as a lecture on the Origins and Nature of the French Revolution delivered to A202 students in Exeter in March 1972] . His dictum seemed to be: 'Keep one step ahead and don't be afraid to admit ignorance to students'. I have some hope that that may have come from me! Mature students loved his novel and refreshing approach to academic study, especially in the early days of the university.

My most vivid memories of A100 are of Summer Schools held at host universities such as East Anglia, Warwick, Keele and York. Again, it was Di and Dennis Collinson who first encouraged me to apply to be a Summer School tutor in history; I was duly accepted; and, as a result, I spent a fortnight at the University of East Anglia in the summer of 1971. Di and Dennis, too, did a couple of weeks in Norwich that year (Di as A100 Course Director, Dennis as a history tutor like me) although, much to my disappointment, not at the same time as I was there. Nevertheless, I enjoyed the experience so much that I went on to teach at Summer Schools for the next five or six years until A100 was replaced by a new foundation course A101. Inevitably, in 1971, there were teething troubles but, despite the tendency of John Purkis (A100 Course Director during my fortnight at UWE) to panic when problems arose, there were no major hiccups. Most of the organisational difficulties encountered in 1971 had been ironed out by 1972 when a specifically produced Summer School booklet also explained just what students could expect to gain from their week of intense residential study: firstly, further exploration of each individual discipline and its methodology; secondly, a focus on 'the Renaissance period covered by units students will be studying around the time of the Summer School (Vasari, *Hamlet* and Descartes), when it is hoped that history will provide the cross-disciplinary link'. This suited me extremely well. For a seminar on the philosophy of history (repeated three or four times each week with different groups), I put together a short handout of my own, setting the tone with Catherine Morland's comment in Jane Austen's *Northanger Abbey*: 'I often think it odd that history should be so dull, for a great deal of it must be invention'. Thereafter, I included passages from Karl Marx and Friedrich Engels' 1848 *Communist Manifesto* (for the Marxist interpretation of history); Lord Acton's up-beat Whig assessment of history's future (in the *Cambridge Modern History*, 1896); E. H. Carr's critical discussion (in *What is History?*, 1961) of R. G. Collingwood's compelling dictum that the philosophy of history is concerned neither with 'the past by itself' nor 'the historian's thought about it by itself' but, rather, 'the two things in their mutual relations' (most fully explored in Collingwood's *The Idea of History*, 1946); and G. R. Elton's no nonsense practical exposition of what historians actually do (in *The Practice of History*, 1967). Students had already been introduced to many of these ideas by Arthur Marwick, the Open University's first professor of history, in his units for the course and set book *The Nature of History* and, as a result, splendidly lively seminars resulted, raising both historical and interdisciplinary issues. For a seminar on the Renaissance era (again repeated several times) I relied on a stimulating essay '*Hamlet* and History', penned by the Open University's professor of literature Arnold Kettle, and a number of contemporary and near-contemporary historical documents. This, too, seemed to work very well. From 1974 history teaching at A100 Summer Schools focussed much more firmly on the later stages of the course, including introducing students to its final block Industrialisation and Culture 1830-1914. I could still hold a round of seminars on sixteenth/seventeenth century themes, fortunately, such as the Later Italian Renaissance; *Hamlet*, Shakespeare and his England; and English Society c.1560—1660. Conducting so-called 'Workshop' sessions on Industrialisation and Culture, by contrast, presented me with a real dilemma, as my ignorance of the subject went hand-in-hand with a lack of any real interest in it. Since the Open University did supply a series of interesting passages from the likes of William Cobbett, George Eliot and Charles Dickens, and well-chosen documents illustrating conditions in London and Manchester, however, even however I rose to the challenge reasonably well. By 1976, indeed, I felt confident enough to offer a lecture on John Stuart Mill and the Role of Women in Victorian Society!

Open University A100 Summer Schools were certainly hard work for staff and students alike. Not only did tutors conduct seminars, moreover, they were also required to mark and discuss with students a short piece of written work each week. Worst of all, if I chose to teach two consecutive weeks at the same host university (as I did every year but one), there were only a few free hours between the departure of one set of students on Saturday morning and the arrival of a fresh and enthusiastic bunch on Saturday evening (when the first round of seminars was also scheduled). Nor was there only teaching and marking to be done. Most weeks I became involved in at least one afternoon excursion with students, most memorably, one year, to the recently opened National Railway Museum in York. And, in my last year as a Summer School tutor, I even laid on a two hour entertainment entitled *The Topsy-Turvy World of Gilbert and Sullivan*, illustrated by a tape of songs from the Savoy Operas and enlivened by a great deal of enthusiastic audience participation. Inevitably, too, there was a great deal of drinking at Summer Schools. Many students were married, often with families, and not surprisingly determined to enjoy to the full their unaccustomed freedom from normal routine. They were certainly great fun to drink with in the bar of an evening, as were both fellow tutors (such as, one year, Arnold Kettle's son Martin) and full-time Open University staff doing their required annual stint at Summer School (most memorably, literature specialist Brian Stone and historian Clive Emsley). Rumour had it there was a fair bit of sex as well! Indeed, at the commencement of my second stint at the University of East Anglia, there was even an exposé in that Sunday's *News of the World* of alleged sexual antics on campus the previous week. Perhaps, had I been heterosexual, I might have been able to engineer the occasional study bedroom frolic for myself. The opportunities were certainly there, particularly for tutors. Sadly, on reflection, I chose to conceal my homosexuality at Summer Schools and so, presumably, did most gay students as well. At any rate I never encountered an openly gay young man, let alone slept with one (although I do recollect, on one occasion, playing a leading role in getting three nuns slightly tipsy!). In my final year as a history tutor I managed to coincide with Di Collinson for a week and, as she recalls, I certainly didn't seek to hide my sexual tastes from her:

> Keith and I once found ourselves working at the same OU Summer School at the University of York. Wednesday afternoon and evening were free so, when the day came, we went into York together to do the sights. We spent most of the afternoon rooting around in dark, second hand book shops, gradually filling a capacious hold-all that Keith, with foresight born of complete self-knowledge, had brought with him. As evening drew on we embarked on the day's peak experience: doing the

rounds of the gay pubs in York. Keith knew them from a previous visit. It pleased me greatly that he took it for granted, and rightly so, that I was entirely happy to accompany him on the tour. For me it was a unique and unforgettable experience.

Yet, perhaps, it was just as well I wasn't openly gay at Summer Schools: a heavy teaching load, combined with a generous quota of beer every evening and remarkably little sleep, was quite exhausting enough. Indeed, I eventually gave up teaching at them not only because A100 came to an end but also because, now in my early thirties, I already lacked the stamina to carry on!

From 1972 to 1980 I tutored *A201: Renaissance and Reformation*, a multi-disciplinary second level course covering the period circa 1300-1600. Rather more successfully than A100, moreover, it managed to reconcile the differing aims and interests of its team of writers (for instance, art historians wishing to concentrate on Renaissance Italy and literature specialists anxious to home in on Elizabethan England) and, perhaps, reflected the growing self-confidence of full-time Open University staff in putting together distance learning material. Most memorably, the perceptive young art historian Catherine King enjoyed considerable success in stimulating student interest in the changing status of the artist in Renaissance Italy, iconography and, in particular, the fascinating Leonardo da Vinci. No less compellingly, ex-Jesuit Francis Clark put together a series of first-rate units covering the origins and nature of both Protestant and Catholic Reformations in sixteenth-century Europe, as well as assessing the roles of religious reformers such as the German Martin Luther, the French John Calvin and the Spaniard Ignatius Loyola (founder of the Society of Jesus). Students were given the opportunity, too, to sample Renaissance music, political philosophy (Machiavelli's *The Prince*), science (the Copernican Revolution), Tudor poetry, and Elizabethan/Jacobean drama (Marlowe's *Doctor Faustus*, Middleton's *The Changeling*, Jonson's *The Alchemist* and Shakespeare's *King Lear*). Employing outside experts to pen particular units, such as Maurice Dobb to present a Marxist perspective on the controversial theme of Europe's transition from feudalism to capitalism during the fourteenth, fifteenth and sixteenth centuries, and John Larner to share his deep knowledge of the evolution of Florentine society between 1382 and 1494, also proved successful. Inevitably, the quality of course material did vary but, by and large, A201 went down well with the majority of students. As for me, I enjoyed teaching the course hugely, probably learned as much as the students, and felt genuinely sad when it ran for the last time in 1980.

When I first began teaching A201 I was still in Plymouth and, even after I moved to Huddersfield, I continued to mark the same group's assignments at a distance for the rest of the year. Thereafter, for over twenty years, I worked for the Open University's Yorkshire region, based in Leeds. Both the university itself, and its huge team of part-time tutors, were very much feeling their way in the 1970s. This was particularly so, in my case, when it came to A201 tutorials and Day Schools. Open university tutorials, like Summer Schools and, indeed, Day Schools, were held in host institutions and, most years, I managed to teach groups at Huddersfield Polytechnic (although, occasionally, they were based in Leeds and, at least once, Bradford). The location of tutorials depended on recruitment and where students lived, and I usually managed to get Huddersfield-based groups because I didn't drive and so found it difficult to get to other study centres (particularly if, as was frequently the case, sessions were scheduled to take place in the evenings). It soon became clear, moreover, that what most students preferred was the combination of a formal mini-lecture on a central theme of the course, followed by a discussion of the same topic. What they didn't like were loosely organised talking sessions, particularly if they slavishly followed the content of course units. Nor did there seem much point in chatting to the group as a whole about assignments so, instead, I usually made sure I was *in situ* at least half an hour before tutorials were scheduled to begin in order to tackle any problems individuals were experiencing (even though there was no payment for this). I never consulted students about the academic content of sessions either but, rather, chose topics (such as the historiography of the Renaissance and the origins of the Reformation) that happened to interest me, seemed likely to generate enthusiasm and, most importantly, ought to promote vigorous class discussion. By and large, the stratagem worked very well and, over the years, I rarely had any complaints. Tutorials apart, A201 also offered (in lieu of a Summer School) three Saturday Day Schools (in March, July and September), held at Leeds University for students in the Yorkshire region. These comprised a series of lectures and seminars by part-time staff and, occasionally, full-time Open University academics or visiting lecturers such as the eminent late medievalist Barrie Dobson of York University. Here students could encounter the teaching of men and women whose specialist discipline was different from that of their own tutor. I particularly liked lecturing to large groups (for instance, on Politics and Culture in Renaissance Florence and Protestant Reformation and Society) and, as students frequently made clear, such Day Schools were both popular and immensely valuable. I even tutored (and visited) over the years three or four A201 students incarcerated in Wakefield jail and recall, in particular, a highly intelligent prisoner who became fascinated by the splendour of fifteenth-century Florentine buildings, no doubt as a welcome distraction from the grim Victorian architecture surrounding him. As for Alison Shaw, an A201 student in 1977 who became a close friend, she certainly seems to have appreciated my approach:

I always regard our friendship as a product of the *Educating Rita* syndrome. Dizzy OU student entertained and inspired by a tutor whose passion for his subject motivated her to do some of her best work and pass with flying colours.

Although both A100 and A201 professed to be interdisciplinary courses, neither fully succeeded in integrating history, art history, philosophy, music and literature into a coherent whole. Perhaps this was virtually impossible in practice anyway but *A203: Seventeenth-Century England: A Changing Culture*, which I taught between 1981 and 1989, almost pulled it off. Again, this was a second level course. Indeed, I taught at second level throughout my time in Huddersfield, mainly because third level specialist history courses never covered the fifteenth, sixteenth and seventeenth centuries. There simply weren't enough later medieval/early modern historians, either at Walton Hall or among regional full-time staff, to mount such a course. I always thought this was a missed opportunity for, there is no doubt, many students I taught over the years would have jumped at the chance of taking such a course and, indeed, the opportunity to study the early and central middle ages as well. A201 had tried to cover too many topics, spread over too long a time span, no doubt reflecting the fact that it had been put together by a team of individuals all determined to leave their mark. This was to prove a problem, too, for *A205: Culture and Belief in Europe 1450—1600* (which I taught in the Yorkshire region between 1990 and 1994) and *A305: The Renaissance in Europe: A Cultural Enquiry* (tutored in Bristol in 2000 and 2001). A203 had a much shorter chronological timespan, as well as largely confining itself to Stuart England and its culture so, perhaps, this helps explain why it came nearest to success in the interdisciplinary stakes. No doubt, too, it benefited hugely from the joint-chairmanship of Christopher Hill (recently retired Master of Balliol College, Oxford, and a prolific and highly respected historian of seventeenth-century England) and Anne Laurence (an enthusiastic young historian of the period just beginning to make her mark at Walton Hall). Indeed, the course team as a whole was impressive, including not only other full-time staff at the centre such as Tim Benton (art/architecture), Anne Hughes (history) and Arnold Kettle (literature) but also, and importantly, regional staff tutors like Joan Bellamy (literature) and Di Collinson (philosophy). No less crucial in holding A203 together so effectively was its essentially Marxist baseline, again no doubt reflecting Christopher Hill's leadership. Throughout, in fact, A203 focussed firmly on what seventeenth-century society and its culture were like in an age of great change, its content clearly strengthened by the fact that units were 'hammered out in discussion' between the course team's membership while, at the same time, their 'many disagreements' were preserved in the 'varying points of view' expressed in the end result. Students were certainly introduced to an impressive galaxy of seventeenth-century writers and writings, including the metaphysical poetry of John Donne, Thomas Middleton's *Women Beware Women*, Thomas Hobbes' *Leviathan*, John Milton's *Areopagitica* and *Paradise Lost*, John Bunyan's *Pilgrim's Progress*, George Etherege's Restoration comedy *The Man of Mode*, John Dryden's satirical political poem *Absalom and Achitophel* and John Locke's *Second Treatise on Government*. They sampled seventeenth-century art, architecture, music and science. And with Christopher Hill's own *Century of Revolution* (1961) as an immensely stimulating and controversial set book, students were given ample opportunity to get to grips not only with the origins and nature of the English Revolution in the 1640s and 1650s but also the restoration of Charles II in 1660 and its consequences. Yet, throughout, A203 sought to make explicit links and interconnections between disciplines, even spelling out clearly in the course guide that it was:

> ... an interdisciplinary course. It is not a history course. We have used history as a hook on which to hang the study of society in an age other than our own, but we are looking at culture in a broader sense in that society.

The result was certainly a stimulating course but I did have distinct reservations about it even so, not least the content of history units. What I most regretted was the lost opportunity to engage with the fascinating political personalities of the age, a regret shared by many of the students I taught, and by Dennis Collinson, too, who specifically recalls the 'personality angst' seemingly shared by several members of the course team. I certainly sought to remedy A203's shortcomings, particularly regarding the personalities of James I, Charles I, Oliver Cromwell, Charles II and James II, in the lectures, seminars and tutorials I put together for it. Years later, in a letter to Anne Laurence, I remarked:

> You'll no doubt be distressed to learn that I remain as firmly attached to the importance of personalities in later medieval/early modern history as ever. Why have Walton Hall historians always been so scared of them?

Anne declared, in reply, that she was '*not* unsympathetic to personalities', just 'reluctant to give them sole responsibility' for events. Yet, she added, 'I think we all agreed on reflection that we hadn't given Oliver Cromwell enough space in A203'.

Joan Bellamy, a member of the A203 course team and author of some of its teaching material, was a full-time staff tutor in the Yorkshire region in 1981 and played an active role in planning, promoting and teaching the course there in its early years. In February 1981 I wrote to her offering to contribute a lecture on the Historiography of the English Revolution to an A203 Day School at Leeds University the following month, adding:

> I would, as is my normal practice, put together a summary of the lecture and/or illustrative documents for the students and, if time allowed, take questions at the end.

I also remarked that, at Day Schools, 'my pet hate is trying to hold discussion sessions with large ill-prepared groups, and I certainly think we should avoid that'; nevertheless, providing a short handout of passages from primary sources could be sent out to students in advance, I undertook to conduct a seminar on King, Parliament and the Constitution in Early Seventeenth Century England—A Struggle for Sovereignty?. Joan promptly accepted my offer. My contribution to a September Day School later in the year followed a similar pattern: a lecture on the Glorious Revolution of 1688 and, rather rashly, a seminar on John Locke's Political Philosophy. In July, meanwhile, I had put my money firmly where my mouth was by lecturing (with illustrative documents) on the Enigma of Oliver Cromwell. Not wishing to do any further preparation, I continued to contribute the same lectures and seminars to A203 Day Schools at Leeds University (1982—1985) and Leeds Polytechnic (1986-1989) until the course came to an end.

At the beginning of 1981, in an introductory letter to the first group of A203 students I tutored, I described myself as 'a veteran Open University course tutor' and emphasised that 'my current teaching at Huddersfield Polytechnic covers both seventeenth-century history and political philosophy'; however, I added, 'the interdisciplinary approach of A203 is refreshingly new to me and so, like you, I anticipate learning a great deal as the year progresses'. I also listed the topics to be covered in tutorials, 'not negotiable but all central to the course, controversial and interesting', enclosed a handout of short passages from primary sources for the first of them (Crown, Court and Country in Early Seventeenth-Century England), and explained my aim of trying to:

> ... cater for all tastes by combining 'holding forth' myself with group discussion. If we can achieve a 'half and half' lecture/discussion situation, that would be ideal.

A few days after meeting these students for the first time, I wrote to Joan Bellamy:

> Sixteen people attended my first tutorial in Huddersfield last Saturday morning. As far as I can judge the tutorial went OK and, certainly, my impression was that the students are very much looking forward to the course and like what they've read so far.

Enclosing handouts with my letter for later tutorials (to be copied at the regional centre in Leeds and despatched to my group), I also remarked that, 'if you think this material may be of interest to other tutors, do let them have copies too'; however, I added, 'the only one that may be of real interest is the May effort (The Road to Civil War c.1640—1642) since it includes some not easily accessible Yorkshire material for the lead-up to the Civil War'. In keeping with the spirit of the course, moreover, I didn't limit myself to historical themes: sessions were devoted to Thomas Hobbes' political philosophy, for instance, and John Milton's *Paradise Lost* (an in-depth analysis of the first two hundred lines of Book 1). I also gave over the whole of the final tutorial to Examination Questions and Techniques. A203, like all the Open University courses I tutored over the years, had an unseen three hour examination at the end (equally weighted, at 50%, with course work); mature students all too often found such exams intimidating; and, therefore, I sought to calm nerves and boost confidence as much as I could. Specifically, I tried to advise them on how best to revise; stressed the need always to answer questions firmly, directly and concisely; and, rather unwisely since it amounted to little more than inspired guesswork on my part, even contrived to come up with a few suggestions of topics that might reasonably be expected to appear on the paper. Usually, as I remember, most students departed from such tutorials a bit happier than when they arrived:

A205: Culture and Belief 1450—1600, which I tutored during my last five years in the Yorkshire region, was the Open University second level course I least enjoyed teaching. This was partly because personalities seemed even thinner on the ground than in A201 and A203 but mainly because there was altogether too much religion and culture for my taste. The course sought to focus not on events but, rather, address 'general historical questions' about a period when 'key aspects of European culture underwent major changes' via the medium of 'four broad themes' and 'seven narrower topics'. None of the broad themes appealed to me all that much: Religion and Secularization; Authority; Cultural and Social Change; and Regionalism and Wider Perspectives. Of the narrower topics, at least I knew a fair bit about humanism, religious reform and printing, while magic and witchcraft were fun, but women, minorities and popular culture carried with them too many undertones of later twentieth-century political correctness for my taste. A205 wasn't a bad course academically; set books such as Marlowe's *Doctor Faustus*, Shakespeare's *Richard II*. and Montaigne's *Essays* went down well (even if Spenser's *Faerie Queen* left many students cold); and even I felt at home with some of it, most notably sections covering politics, religion and society in France, and the exercise of royal and religious authority in the British Isles. Yet I wasn't sorry to switch to tutoring two new single-discipline courses, on seventeenth-century history and fourteenth-century art history, when I moved to Bristol in 1994.

My main consideration when choosing tutorial and Day School topics for A205 was, obviously, relevance to the course but I also sought, wherever possible, to recycle what I'd taught on A201 a decade earlier and draw on lectures/seminars/handouts put together for BA (Humanities) students at Huddersfield Polytechnic. Whenever and wherever I could, I contrived to drag in personalities as well and, unlike A203, all my tutorials were on historical themes: for instance, I devoted sessions to Christian Humanism in Western Europe c.1450—1530 (structured, in part, around a series of extracts from letters written by Erasmus of Rotterdam), the sixteenth-century Catholic Reformation (particularly highlighting the role of Ignatius Loyola and the Jesuits), and the Early Printing Press, its products and importance. Unashamedly, too, I drew on my knowledge of later fifteenth-century and Tudor England for tutorials on Religion, Society and Culture in Pre-Reformation England and Courtly Politics, Patronage and Culture in Elizabethan England. As for Day Schools at Leeds Polytechnic/Metropolitan University, I revived an A201 lecture on Protestant Reformation and Society and a seminar on Martin Luther's Religious, Political and Social Ideas (based on extracts from Luther's own writings); recycling material from Year 2 teaching at Huddersfield, I delivered lectures on the Origins and Nature of the French Wars of Religion and Elizabeth I: Myth and Reality, and a seminar on Philip II of Spain; and, as for a seminar on Historical Truth and Dramatic Licence in Shakespeare s History Plays (with particular reference to *Richard II*), it very much reflected my mounting interest in the historical content of William Shakespeare's Plantagenet cycle.

By the time A205 came on stream in 1990, Joan Bellamy had retired and Michael Bartholomew was the Yorkshire region staff tutor in charge of the new course. He and I hit it off very well even if, as he ruefully recalls:

> ... your style made life a bit difficult now and then. Picture the scene. It's lunchtime at Leeds Polytechnic and you are scheduled to give the 2pm lecture. At 1.30 you stride in (you are never late: that would offend your professional standards). From fifty yards away you see me and boom out:
>
> > I feel like death. I haven't read the course units. This course is moribund. I haven't a clue what I'm going to lecture about.
>
> Students look a bit startled. At 2pm, however, there you are in the lecture theatre, shoulders back, and you launch into a *tour de force*, as usual. The pre-lecture drama was a necessary part of the run-up—but the lecture itself was always immaculate.

The Open University tutor's most important function was reading, commenting upon and grading student assignments. Yet for me this was always a chore; I frequently ignored rules and regulations governing the submission, marking and return of assignments; and I rarely succeeded in getting work back to students as quickly as I should have done. Sometimes, indeed, I was disgracefully casual about it, as Dennis Collinson recalls:

> If I had one serious disagreement with Keith over academically-related matters, it was with what I felt to be a too casual attitude over deadlines in returning mature students' essays. I sympathised since I was also guilty but I'm sure he underestimated student dependence and longing to read tutor comments as a boost to flagging self-confidence.

Not that I sought to cover up my deficiencies. In February 1981, for instance, in a letter to Joan Bellamy, I remarked on my 'customary snail-like progress' in returning assignments, vowing that 'I must improve this year' (but I'm sure I didn't!); similarly, when writing to Lucille Kekewich (staff tutor in Arts for the London region) years later, I gloomily referred to 'the pile of unmarked bloody essays lurking on a far corner of my desk'. My Huddersfield colleague Bill Roberts, an Open University tutor for almost as long as I was, vividly recalls 'the many dark hours OU tutors spent avoiding marking assignments' and how:

> ... over many years we shared our views on the machinations of the university. Being a conformist I used to try to mark my assignments on time but I was always impressed by what appeared to be your cavalier attitude to such matters. You would say you had had a pile of unmarked assignments on your desk for weeks, that you had at last got round to looking at them, and had been so shocked that you'd gone straight to the pub; or, alternatively, that you had knocked off a whole batch in a morning (it took me two days!).

'As for monitoring forms and the behaviour of some full-time OU staff', he adds, 'we shared our frustrations and enjoyed abusing the system'. What irritated me more than anything else, in fact, was occasionally holier-than-thou monitoring of assignment marking, particularly when it resulted in unhelpful quibbling about tutor comments on essays or unjustified criticism of grades awarded. Usually, I rapidly consigned such monitoring reports to the wastebin but, now and again, I did foolishly allow myself to be stung into reacting. Mike Bartholomew, indeed, specifically remembers a monitoring report penned by 'a rather humourless' Walton Hall historian:

> It was a bit nit-picking. I sent it on to you and you bounced it straight back, with 'Bollocks' written across it from corner to corner.

Irritating, too, was the very small minority of students inclined to telephone tutors, even very late in the evening, about amazingly trivial matters. Fortunately, most Open University students were splendid and often expressed warm appreciation of the teaching they received; Bill Roberts remarks, 'I am sure many OU students will remember you with affection'; and even Mike Bartholomew, despite all the problems posed for him by my deplorably wilful and headstrong behaviour on occasion, seems to have enjoyed the experience of working with me:

> Once I got to know you, it became clear that you were a special case. What made you special was a brilliant teaching style and rapport with the students, coupled with an airy indifference to the bureaucracy and rules of the OU. Tutor-marked assignment cut off dates?—forget about them. No smoking rules?—ignore them. Monitoring reports?—treat them with disdain. Yet the students liked you and were aware they were being taught by someone a bit special.

'I think that's what we're all looking for when we're students', Mike adds, 'someone who occupies an intellectual world that we aspire to and who, without condescension, makes us believe that we might be able to inhabit it too'.

When I returned to the south-west region in 1994, I wasn't at all sorry to find that A205 already had its full quota of tutors but delighted at the prospect of working with Di and Dennis Collinson again. Even so, I did continue to contribute to A205 Day Schools between 1995 and 1999 (when the course came to an end), mainly in Bristol but occasionally in Exeter, offering much the same lectures and seminars as I'd delivered in Yorkshire. After a couple of years Di retired and I awaited the appointment of her successor with some trepidation. Not all regional staff tutors were as supportive of part-timers as Di Collinson, Joan Bellamy and Mike Bartholomew. I needn't have worried. Peter Elmer, the historian of science who took over from Di, was very much in the same league and, as early as December 1997, I received a most welcome note from him:

> I would like to thank you for your contribution to the success of A205 in 1997. Your efforts are greatly appreciated, both by the faculty, students and myself.

Indeed, it was largely down to Peter (and London staff tutor Lucille Kekewich) that I joined the course team, as student assessor, of a new third level interdisciplinary course *AA305: The Renaissance in Europe: A Cultural Enquiry* towards the end of 1998 and carried on working for the Open University until 2002.

During the later 1990s my tight finances required more part-time earnings than a few hours per annum teaching at A205 Day Schools generated. Hence why I eagerly accepted Di Collinson's offer to tutor two new half credit courses in 1995: A220 and A354. *A220: Princes and Peoples: France and the British Isles 1620—1714* was the first specialist history course I'd taught for the Open University. Indeed, it was the first purely history module not focussed on the nineteenth and twentieth centuries. Instead of the seven or eight assignments required for full credit courses such as A201, A203 and A205, however, since A220 was weighted at half credit it prescribed only four (although 50% of the assessment was still based on an unseen three hour examination). Teaching both A220 and A354 together was roughly the equivalent of tutoring a single full credit course: just as well, since I found eight assignments per year more than enough to cope with! A220 was very much the brainchild of Anne Laurence and Lucille Kekewich, who were responsible between them for almost half the course material (although there were other contributors as well, even the Open University's long-serving professor of history Arthur Marwick). The course's central aims were to examine what kinds of states evolved in France and the British Isles between 1620 and 1714; how they developed; and whether traditional portrayals of France as an absolutist state, Britain as a limited monarchy, by 1714 stand up to critical examination. The first block of units concentrated on why, how and with what consequences events on both sides of the English Channel in the 1620s, 1630s and 1640s resulted in bloody internal conflicts (the Civil Wars in Britain and the Frondes in France); a second block considered society and culture in seventeenth-century Britain and France; particularly focussing on local communities; and a third, aptly entitled Parliaments and Kings, looked at how, why and to what extent the French and British states evolved along different lines between the 1660s and 1714. Throughout, moreover, there was an emphasis on the sources, both written and visual, available to historians of the era; the course held together well, despite a few dull and uninspiring patches; and Lucille Kekewich certainly reported on it very positively in a newsletter to students in 1998:

> The course has proved very popular with students since it started in 1995. In that year we were amazed and delighted to find that, instead of the anticipated six hundred, we had nearly a a thousand students and those kinds of numbers have remained steady in subsequent years. The course results have been equally gratifying, despite the fact it is notoriously difficult to do well in history. Perhaps this reflects the way we have tried to combine a fairly traditional approach, a substantial element of architecture and court culture, and the newer opportunities offered by multi-media teaching.

For A220 tutorials in Bristol, held on Saturday mornings at the University of the West of England, I drew on lectures and seminars originally put together for my Huddersfield students or recycled material from A203 and, as always, sought to highlight personalities. Resulting sessions, all based on newly prepared handouts containing passages from both primary and secondary sources, included Kings, Courts and Politics in Early Seventeenth-century England and France; Origins of the English Civil War; The Frondes; Oliver Cromwell and the English Revolution; Charles II, James II and the Glorious Revolution; and Louis XIV:. Myth and Reality. What made teaching A220 particularly enjoyable was that Dennis Collinson was a fellow tutor and, as in 1971/2, we were able to exchange ideas and compare experiences. Over a period of more than a quarter of a century Dennis had performed many roles for the Open University, as acting/assistant staff tutor, counsellor/senior counsellor, examination scriptmarker and tutor (both in the south-west region and at Summer Schools), so his positive verdict on my own efforts is all the more satisfying for that:

> Keith's apparently heretical judgements on established historical figures, often couched in the broadest and most colourful of language, drew many OU students on board their new academic venture, and one saw them blossoming under his tutelage. He was especially sympathetic and helpful to those who had few or no formal academic qualifications. They learned to make judgements and to research material to support them because they knew that Keith, despite his throwaways, had always done meticulous research to support his own.

I tutored A220 for the last time in 1999.

Alongside A220 in 1995, Di Collinson also persuaded me to tutor a new half credit third level art history course *A354: Art, Society and Religion in Siena, Florence and Padua 1280—1400*. My credentials to teach such a course were thin to say the least; indeed, Bill Roberts remembers me once declaring, in Huddersfield, that 'Renaissance painting is a bit of a blind spot'! Nevertheless, I accepted Di's offer not only for obvious financial reasons but also because I relished the challenge of tutoring at third level for the first time; moreover, I'd almost always been impressed by the contributions of art historians like Tim Benton and Catherine King to multi-disciplinary courses and, additionally, I very much liked the look of A354. The course material took the form of four study guides, two splendidly illustrated volumes of perceptive essays penned mainly by members of the course team, and a series of television programmes and videos. The art of Siena, Florence and Padua during the early Italian Renaissance provided the central core of the course and there was plenty of analysis of major works such as Duccio's high altarpiece (the Maestà) for the cathedral of his native city Siena and the Florentine Giotto's Arena Chapel frescoes in Padua. Yet the architecture, painting and sculpture of these three cities was set firmly within a wider historical and cultural context. Underpinning all, in fact, was the conviction that fourteenth-century art should be studied 'not only as an autonomous tradition of artistic styles, techniques and interpretative skills but also as a practice in which such artistic concerns were affected by wider social, political, religious, intellectual and cultural contexts'. Hence why I felt just about self-confident enough to become a tutor on what turned out to be, perhaps, the best Open University course I ever taught.

Putting together a series of tutorial topics, and accompanying handouts, for A354 that wouldn't betray my ignorance of 'artistic styles, techniques and interpretative skills' too much certainly proved a challenge. Fortunately, the course material did contain plenty of promising historical and historiographical content that was to my taste and, in my introductory letter to students, I decided honesty was the best policy:

> So excellent is the treatment of painting, sculpture and architecture in the splendid course material (and the guidance given on individual works of art) that I shall concentrate attention in tutorials on historical context and historiography.

Thus, although I certainly discussed specific buildings, sculptures and paintings with students (for instance, the Palazzo Vecchio in Florence, the Arena Chapel in Padua, the reliquary of the head of St. Zenobius in Florence Cathedral, Duccio's Maestà for Siena Cathedral, Orcagna's Strozzi altarpiece and Giotto's Ognissanti Madonna), they weren't the main focus of my classes. Rather, I offered sessions on Italy c.1280—1400 and the Origins of the Renaissance in Art; Politics, Religion and Art in Siena c.1280-1348; Florentine Politics, Society and Art c.1280—1348; Giotto: Myth and Reality; and The Black Death, Art and Society in Florence and Siena c.1348—1400. In these tutorials, too, I went out of my way to introduce students to contemporary literary sources (such as Giovanni Villani's *Chronicle of Florence* and Giovanni Boccaccio's *Decameron*) and the conclusions of art historians ranging from Giorgio Vasari in the sixteenth century to Millard Meiss in the twentieth. In the very first year I taught A354, however, it came as a considerable shock to find I had a student whose knowledge of art history was far greater than mine! Fortunately, Peter Clarkson, who attended all the sessions, proved an ally not a threat, vigorously contributing to discussion and helping enthuse both me and the rest of the class. It came as no surprise when, soon after graduating, he became an Open University tutor himself. I taught A354 for just four years. Recruitment figures for 1999 were disappointing and, as a result, it was necessary to lose a tutor in the south west region. Although I don't think I was at the top of Peter Elmer's hit list, I promptly volunteered to put my head on the block since, by then, I was beginning to find tutoring two very different courses at the same time a bit of a nightmare.

Throughout my Open University career I tended to treat rules and regulations with contempt, enjoyed either ignoring or breaking them, and revelled in the resulting bewilderment of their enthusiastic enforcers. Di Collinson recalls my antics vividly:

> Anyone who has taught or studied with the OU will know how tightly structured are its courses, tutorials and study programmes. Keith managed to break every rule in the book without being dismissed or disciplined in some appalling way. He would accept very late essays from students and return marked assignments very late too, thereby reducing the monstrous OU central computer to a frazzled burnt-out heap. He never hesitated to condemn a whole study book as utter rubbish if that was his opinion of it. Sometimes, because of other commitments or personal plans, he would lay down his own instructions to his tutorial group for the submission, structure, content and length of essays, ruthlessly promising failure or hellfire for any student who did not conform to his requirements. In short, Keith was a superb and much loved tutor.

Clearly, my unorthodox behaviour can hardly have endeared me to the Open University's central administration at Walton Hall. Nor did I ever relish visiting Milton Keynes myself. Travelling there could often prove a nightmare, particularly early on when the nearest mainline railway station was miles away at Bletchley. As for the campus itself, it had plenty of buildings, including a library, and masses of offices to house both academic staff and a huge army of bureaucrats. Only rarely, though, could more than a handful of students be found there. Most Open University tutors probably hardly ever visited the place either, not least since meetings to launch new courses tended to be held in London. My own occasional trips to Walton Hall were mainly for examination scriptmarker briefings and, since these invariably occurred on Saturdays, the campus tended to be virtually deserted: very eerie! Between 1973 and 1977 I was a scriptmarker for A201; in the early 1980s I marked A203 exams; and, in the 1990s, I was employed in a similar capacity for A205 and A220. From the beginning I tended to be critical of Open University unseen examinations, not because they existed at all (on balance, I regarded them as a necessary plank in establishing and maintaining the credibility of OU degrees) but, rather, because of the questions set and the guidance notes provided for scriptmarkers so as to ensure uniformity of standards. Nor was I alone in my criticisms. Bill Roberts, for instance, recalls that one of his:

... few contributions to the way that venerable institution, the Open University, worked came one summer when I was summoned to London to a big post-mortem on an *A202: The Enlightenment* exam. I must have felt very annoyed (probably because we'd been discussing its unfairness) and came out with a criticism that actually led to a major change. I suggested it was a nonsense that some topics were tested twice (both by course work assignment and in the exam) while others didn't figure at all. To my amazement the system was altered accordingly. What a claim to fame!

Too often, it seemed to me, questions for A201, A203 and A205 tended to be very difficult, sometimes verging on the impossible, probably reflecting the fact that such multi-disciplinary exams were put together by teams of specialists. I recall, in particular, a music question that seemed to make no sense at all; nor did the scriptmarker notes; and, on the day of the briefing, there was no music specialist around to enlighten us. Fortunately, hardly any students were daft enough to attempt it! Scriptmarker notes, again often provided by subject specialists, varied enormously in value. Sometimes they could be immensely helpful but, too frequently, they tended to be too prescriptive or set impossibly ambitious targets for higher grades, or both. Hence why, at briefing meetings, they were often modified or even, occasionally, set on one side altogether. If in doubt, when actually marking, I always tended to follow my instincts anyway. A great bonus of Open University exam scriptmarking, and there weren't many, was that, for many years, Dennis Collinson and I found ourselves working together; we almost always agreed about the questions and their level of difficulty; and, during the fortnight or so of intensive marking itself, we tended to ring each other up, compare notes and help boost our sometimes flagging self-confidence. As for the Walton Hall briefings, Dennis's memories are certainly sharp:

> We formed an examining team together in the early OU days under the chairing of a staff tutor whose meetings consisted of asking if we understood the ramifications of the questions, if we had any difficulty in interpretation, and if we agreed with him that some of the questions concocted by the Examination Board were pretty stupid. Declaiming that he knew far less about the fifteenth and sixteenth centuries than the pair of us, he generally declared the meeting closed and hauled us off to the bar after half an hour. Keith regarded this as highly civilised behaviour, in contrast to later meetings when student numbers and intrusive scrutineering increased. It would be both blasphemous and libellous to repeat some of his comments after five hour examiners' meetings. Outside adjudicators, fortunately, always graded our work as excellent!

At least, by the time I was marking A220 scripts in the later 1990s, questions tended to be clearer and more precise, while both Anne Laurence and Lucille Kekewich (who tended to handle scriptmarker briefings for the course) put a great deal of emphasis on the importance of sheer common sense when it came to assessing and grading answers.

During my time the Open University never fully appreciated just how much it depended on its part-time tutors for the successful delivery of courses or the wealth of teaching experience and academic expertise they often brought to the job. Indeed, so it seemed to me, a major function of regional staff tutors (admirably performed by Di Collinson, Joan Bellamy, Mike Bartholomew and Peter Elmer) was to keep us calm and committed, particularly in the face of mountains of paper emanating from the centre. Towards the end of the 1990s we were redesignated Associate Lecturers but, in practice, this made little difference and certainly didn't bring remunerative benefits (the opposite, if anything). Once I retired from full-time teaching in 1994, I began to become involved with the Open University in other ways as well. Initially, this was down to Lucille Kekewich, staff tutor in the London region and a fellow fifteenth-century historian. In 1996, for instance, I did a short stint as a part-time assistant staff tutor, employed to help Lucille 'in short-listing and interviewing staff for history courses' and, as a result, spent a very pleasant day or two at the London regional office. Then, in 1997, Lucille (who was course leader at the time) persuaded me to edit the annual newsletter for students proposing to embark on A220 in 1998. The practice of sending out newsletters designed to enthuse students, breathe new life into ageing courses and draw attention to recently published books, was well established. As early as 1982, indeed, I'd contributed 'The Historiography of the English Revolution' (based on a Day School lecture and handout) to an A203 newsletter. Almost as soon as she heard I was to edit the A220 newsletter, Anne Laurence wrote to me:

> I gather you are to do the newsletter for A220 for 1998. That's very kind of you. I'll send you anything I come across during the next few months, but without any supposition that you'll include it, just in case it's something you don't happen to have seen.

'I was more than happy to accede to Lucille's request to oversee a new A220 newsletter', I replied, 'and will, of course, be more than grateful for anything you send me'; moreover, I added:

> I'm finding early retirement entirely satisfactory. Part-time teaching for Bristol University, the University of the West of England and the Open University is

enjoyable; not having to attend long boring meetings or worry about research assessment exercises, financial crises and the rest even more so.

In the end, although I did include material Anne sent me in a survey of recent publications on the seventeenth century and a book review by Richard Salter (a fellow tutor for A220 in the south-west region), most of the newsletter was my own work. I enjoyed penning an obituary of C. V. Wedgwood, a prolific historian of seventeenth-century England who had recently died, particularly emphasising that 'few twentieth-century historians have matched either Wedgwood's flair for writing readable yet often learned history or her capacity to convey a real sense of enjoyment of the past for its own sake'. Even more satisfying was writing a short article (based on teaching material I'd put together for the course) on 'Kings, Courts and Politics in Early Seventeenth-Century England and France', not least because (as I wrote to Lucille) it gave me the opportunity 'deliberately to take a very different line from the course material and try to highlight how much fun early seventeenth-century political history can be'. When the newsletter was complete and I sent it to her, Lucille declared she had 'very much enjoyed it, especially your article', even adding that it was 'a great improvement on last year's'.

Perhaps the most interesting challenge that came my way at the end of the 1990s was an invitation from Lucille Kekewich and Peter Elmer to join the course team, as consultant/tutor assessor, of *AA305: The Renaissance in Europe: A Cultural Enquiry*, a new third level interdisciplinary course the Open University Arts Faculty was putting together. Although I didn't at all relish the prospect of regular meetings at Walton Hall, I accepted out of genuine curiosity to see from the inside just how OU courses were put together and why they turned out as they did. By the time Peter Elmer took over the chairmanship of the course team in March 1999, there seemed a real possibility that AA305 would not be ready in time for a start date of 2000; several first draft chapters for the three books around which the course was to be structured needed a great deal of further work if they were to be any good; and the vitally important study guides to accompany the course books had yet to be written. Indeed, Peter freely admitted to me in private that the main reason why I'd been coopted was because I was a very experienced Open University tutor who would be prepared not only to inject a dose of robust common sense into discussions but also back him, if necessary, in knocking obstinate heads together . Thus, for instance, I firmly supported the proposition that, as in most Open University courses, there should be a three hour examination weighted at 50%, providing students were given more indication than usual of just which topics would appear. Vague, idealistic notions of substituting a project or dissertation, supervised by tutors, would have proved a nightmare in practice for a course expected to recruit hundreds of students. After a great deal of argument the majority decision was that, despite all the problems unseen exams could pose for mature students, it was the better option. Peter Elmer certainly proved a perceptive, hardworking and firm course leader. He needed to be! Most dramatically, he scrapped an almost impenetrable opening section of *Book 1: The Impact of Humanism*, substituting a clear and coherent historiographical chapter 'Inventing the Renaissance: Jacob Burckhardt as Historian' penned by himself; he drastically revised and rendered student-friendly a vitally important first chapter 'Court Culture and the Renaissance' for *Book 2: Courts, Patrons and Poets*; and, as well as personally editing *Book 3: Challenges to Authority*, he also provided two of its most fascinating sections 'Did Science have a Renaissance?' and 'The Dark Side: Occult Philosophy, Magic and Witchcraft'. Peter's deputy chairman Richard Danson Brown (a young literature specialist) was equally practical and student-orientated, not least when penning splendid chapters of his own on 'The London Stage' and '*The Witch of Edmonton*'. And, no less importantly, the course manager Roberta Wood, who had the unenviable task of ensuring everything was published in time for AA305's commencement, was both immensely well organised and extremely efficient.

AA305 certainly turned out better than A205, the last Open University interdisciplinary course I'd tutored, and made real progress towards achieving its stated aims:

> To engage with the debate as to the precise meaning of the term 'Renaissance'.
> To appreciate distinctive features of the cultural developments associated with the Renaissance.
> To assess the extent to which the adoption of Renaissance values either challenged or sustained traditional notions of religious, political and cultural authority.
> To examine the factors which determined how the Renaissance was received and adapted by early modern Europeans, and to make comparisons between people and places.

Inevitably, even after all the rewriting of 1999, the course still had its weaknesses: the art history sections., by and large, were disappointing (at any rate in comparison with A354); *The Merchant of Venice*, rather than the tailor-made *Hamlet*, seemed an odd choice of Shakespearean play to focus upon (although Richard Danson Brown did his best); and, as for the case study of an obscure sixteenth-century Spaniard Lazarillo de Tormes, it left both me (and the students) more perplexed than anything else. As usual, too, the course enjoyed only mixed success in the interdisciplinary stakes; it tried to cover far too much ground; and there weren't enough personalities for my taste (although Lucille Kekewich was stimulating on Machiavelli and so was Anthony Lentin on Montaigne).

I tutored AA305 just twice, in 2000 and 2001. As always, what I most enjoyed were the face-to-face teaching sessions, all scheduled to take place on Saturdays and switched, in my final year, from the University of the West of England to the more convenient city centre site of Bristol College, a further education establishment. Since many students had to travel quite a distance, wherever possible I offered morning and afternoon sessions on the same day—exhausting though it was for all of us! As far as the organisation of classes was concerned, I stuck to the format that had worked well for so many years: an hour's lecture followed by an hour's discussion based on both the lecture and a pre-circulated handout of passages from primary and secondary sources. As always, too, I made sessions central to the themes of the course while, at the same time, reflecting my own interests and recycling relevant material originally put together for A201 and A205: Contemporary Perspectives on the Renaissance; Jacob Burckhardt, the Renaissance and Twentieth-Century Scholarship; Renaissance History and Historians; Machiavelli; Fifteenth-Century Burgundy and the Burgundian Court; Politics, Patronage and Culture in Fifteenth-Century Florence; Courtly Politics, Patronage and Culture in Elizabethan England; Erasmus, Christian Humanism and Religious Reform; Luther, Zwingli and Religious Reform; and Montaigne, Education and Classical Learning. I ended, again as usual, with a two hour session on Examination Questions and Techniques. In December 2001, after completing AA305, a member of my last ever tutorial group wrote to me:

> I would like to thank you very much for your tutoring of the Renaissance course this year. The notes from your tutorials and comments on my assignments were extremely helpful when revising for the exam. Even though I found the amount of reading rather overwhelming at times, I really enjoyed the course.

Two Open University students I taught in Bristol, and got to know socially as well, certainly have strikingly similar memories of the experience. Prior to the commencement of a teaching session, Jane Smith remembers:

> Keith would be outside the building smoking like it was going out of fashion. Once he entered the room, however, he became focussed and organised; he gave formal lectures and wouldn't tolerate chat or questions until the end; and his depth of knowledge about a variety of topics helped me and fellow students enormously, even if we got writers cramp trying to take notes. Everyone I knew admired and respected him as a tutor. As for his advice on exams, it stood me in good stead for the rest of my OU career.

'Keith was my tutor for both A354 and AA305', recalls Angela Cooper, 'and proved something of a culture shock; his lectures were formal but brilliant, delivered on the move and with only occasional glances at his notes; and, afterwards, he was both patient and very helpful with our questions, as well as giving invaluable advice on exam techniques'. Moreover, she adds:

> Keith's out of class comments could be hilarious and disarming. I remember once, after emerging from a session, discussing how I might raise money for an OU art history trip to New York. In the crowded foyer he responded:
>
> > Well, you could always become a rent boy, couldn't you? Or maybe not, since you're the wrong sex!
>
> The expressions on the faces of several elderly matrons were a picture. I'll also never forget Keith sitting in my garden, surrounded by admirers listening to him holding forth on history while, at the same time, being continually pestered by my lunatic collie bringing his ball to be thrown. He obliged without batting an eyelid, or allowing himself to be interrupted in full flow, even when the dog tried to hump his leg!

My thirty-one years teaching for the Open University ended, sadly, with a whimper not a bang. Although I still enjoyed classroom sessions, by the summer of 2001 I'd come to the conclusion that I simply couldn't face another year marking assignments. It was also becoming clear that, before long, tutors like me who were computer illiterate and didn't have an e-mail address would cease to be employable by the OU anyway. When he learnt of my decision to retire from tutoring, Peter Elmer sent me a most appreciative letter, thanking me for all my years of service to the university and help to him in particular. This certainly contrasted sharply with the deafening silence of the establishment at Walton Hall. In both 2000 and 2001, as well as teaching AA305, I'd also served as monitor of the marking of a group of tutors in south-eastern England: an interesting experience when, remembering my own years of irritation at sometimes negative and insensitive monitoring of my own work, I bent over backwards to be as positive as I could about marking and grading. Even after I'd given up teaching the course myself, I monitored another group of AA305 tutors in 2002. In 2000 and 2001, too, I was an AA305 examination scriptmarker and, for financial reasons, I decided to apply for one final time in 2002. Not only was I rejected for the first time ever, to add insult to injury I was offered, instead, appointment as a reserve scriptmarker. This would have meant holding myself in readiness as a last minute substitute in case another scriptmarker dropped out. Naturally, I refused. Perhaps such cavalier treatment simply reflected the fact I was no longer an AA305 tutor; or, maybe, it represented payback time by a member of the course team whose toes I'd trodden on when tutor assessor in 1999. I never found out. At all events my rejection as a scriptmarker in 2002 was virtually the last I heard from Milton Keynes until, at the end of the 2002/3 financial year, I received a P45. This typified the lack of loyalty to teaching staff or appreciation of their efforts by management in higher education institutions throughout my years working in the sector. No wonder I never felt any sort of loyalty or obligation towards them!

14

Part-time Lecturer in Bristol

Over a year before I moved back to Bristol I contacted my former Huddersfield colleague Tony Saul, who had risen to the upper echelons of management there, about the possibility of obtaining part-time lecturing at Gwent College of Higher Education; he seemed enthusiastic to get me on board; and, as a result, I began teaching at Gwent in the autumn of 1994. Transformed into University of Wales College, Newport, in 1996, Gwent CHE was situated on a pleasant site at Caerleon, a short bus ride from Newport. In September 2005 Tony recalled his prime objectives at the college:

> Opening up access to higher education was always close to the top of my agenda. This often meant encouraging and admitting students with fairly modest academic backgrounds. It didn't do much for A-Level point score profiles and all the rest but it did mean students, especially mature ones, had the chance to study at their local college or university. Huddersfield and Gwent were not Oxford or Cambridge but they had equally valid missions.

I entirely sympathised with such sentiments and, for a couple of years, I found teaching at Gwent CHE a most rewarding experience and enjoyed meeting up regularly with Tony as well (more often than not in the same Caerleon pub to which I occasionally adjourned with students). Many of the students were both committed and hard-working, and not a few warmly appreciative of the teaching they received. As for the head of history Ray Howell, he was a first-rate lecturer who had real rapport with students and was always determined to do his best for them. This wasn't easy, not least since his excessive dependence on the services of part-time staff made mounting coherent courses very difficult. Also, there was a significant minority of students who struggled academically and needed all the help and guidance they could get. I certainly admired Ray very much; he and I hit it off well; and, throughout my time at Gwent, we were very much on the same wavelength. What I didn't relish at all, however, was travelling from Bristol to Caerleon by public transport. This meant getting a bus to Bristol Parkway station, a train from Bristol to Newport, and another bus from Newport to Caerleon: a stressful and time-consuming journey, rarely taking less than a couple of hours each way. I certainly couldn't manage it now!

In both 1994/5 and 1995/6 I found myself teaching on two second year modules at Gwent: *Introduction to Medieval Studies* and *Kings, Parliament and People*. Since the college operated an American-style semester system (under which the academic year was split into two virtually independent halves), both ran from October to February. Unfortunately, the modules were timetabled on different days so this involved making twice-weekly trips when I was teaching on both; buses were unreliable (particularly at the Bristol end) and trains frequently late (indeed, on one occasion, I never made it from Bristol Parkway to Newport at all when a passenger selfishly elected to commit suicide by throwing himself out of a train in the Severn Tunnel); and, since I wasn't paid expenses, the cost of travelling made quite a dent in my earnings. As for the topics covered in the modules, they reflected the rather ill-matched expertise of available teaching staff as much as anything else, and there was no thematic continuity. For my own classes, more often than not, I revamped lectures, seminars and handouts originally put together for Huddersfield or Open University students. On the medieval course, for instance, I lectured on English Kings, Magnates and Politics c.1307—1485; Edward III, Henry V and the Hundred Years War; and Later Medieval Economic, Social, Religious and Cultural History. Splitting the fifty odd students into four seminar groups, and teaching each for three consecutive weeks, I also sought to introduce them to the history of, and major sources for, Lancaster, York and the Wars of the Roses c.1450—1485. For the early modern module I focussed, predictably, on James I, Court and Politics 1603—1625; Charles I and the Road to Civil War 1625—1642; and Oliver Cromwell and the English Revolution 1642—1660. Again, I tried to draw attention to a range of primary sources for the period, as well as its fascinating historiography. In the end of semester exams for both courses, two things stood out: more students opted for my questions than anyone else's and, although there was a fair sprinkling of upper second class answers, the standard overall was rather lower than what I'd grown accustomed to in Huddersfield.

What I most enjoyed at Gwent CHE, between March and December 1995, was supervising a Research Study group of ten Year 2/3 students working on Richard III. Although this was never clearly explained to me, I took this to be a combination of a Huddersfield-style Special Subject and Independent Study

Unit. My aim was to get the group to study in depth a range of conflicting, often partisan, primary sources for Richard III, both before and after he seized the throne in 1483, supplemented by extensive reading in secondary sources. Allocated a three hour slot on Friday afternoons, I devoted the first three weeks to delivering half a dozen lectures introducing the sources for, and historiography of, Richard III. Students were required to attend these (and they did!) while, at the same time, reading my *Richard III: A Reader in History* (1988) and at least one recent biography of the king. Thereafter, I saw each individually to discuss a definite programme of study for the summer term and the first semester of their final year. Once everyone was embarked on their research, I then held weekly seminars with the group, provided individual supervision and advice as their work progressed, and, since I was now visiting the college only once a week, supplied them with my Bristol address and telephone number. In the autumn term I was given a 16.30—18.00 slot on Mondays to see their studies through to a conclusion. Students submitted two linked long essays, eventually combining them (with an introduction, conclusion and bibliography) into what amounted to an undergraduate dissertation. The results were splendid: two or three students produced very high quality work and even the weaker ones managed to reach their maximum potential.

My two years teaching at Gwent ended ignominiously when, in the summer of 1996, I was peremptorily sacked as a part-time lecturer. Presumably this linked to Gwent becoming University of Wales College, Newport, and the financial implications of the college's new status. It was certainly a messy business and did no credit to the college at all but, sadly, it was only too typical of the behaviour of institutions of higher education by the later 1990s. In the second semester of 1996 I began supervising another Research Study group on Richard III, foolishly assuming that, as in 1995, I'd see the students through to the conclusion of their studies. Had I had even an inkling of what was to happen a few months down the line, I would never have taken the group on in the first place. Also, Ray Howell and I agreed informally that I would continue to contribute, along the lines of 1995/6, to the Year 2 teaching programme for 1996/7. When the college subsequently reneged on these arrangements, I felt both the students and myself had been very shabbily treated but, sadly, accepted the inevitable. There the matter would have ended if one of the Richard III group hadn't written to me, early in the autumn term of 1996, outlining the collective grievances of the group and complaining of the lack of expert supervision they were now getting for their work. Even then I was loath to react, fearing I might put my long-standing friendship with Tony Saul at risk, but for once principle prevailed. In deliberately formal terms I wrote to Tony, referring to 'the appalling treatment your students have received (not to mention part-time staff)' and suggesting that, at the very least, he should take over supervising the Richard III group himself. When Tony replied, in his capacity as Vice Principal (Academic), his letter consisted mainly of extracts from a report about the matter cobbled together by the Faculty of Education, Humanities and Science. It was a classic of its kind, very defensive, and resorting to the familiar device of hiding behind the precise wording of regulations governing the college's joint-honours degree. For me, one short passage said it all:

> The impression given by K.Dockray's letter is that he has been encouraged to see the long essay as being more significant than it really is within the validated scheme. All information regarding the nature of the history course has been conveyed to him from the history staff.

In other words, no blame could be placed on the shoulders of management and, by implication, it was all Ray Howell's fault. I wasn't impressed, commenting tersely in response that, 'regulations or no regulations, these students have received a very raw deal'. So they had but, hopefully, they'd learned enough before the college dispensed with my services to do justice to themselves anyway. I never found out. Not that I blamed Tony Saul personally for what had happened; he had always striven to present the human and humane face of management, encourage his staff and protect students from the consequences of financial constraints and cutbacks (even if he'd failed this time); and, despite our academically-related spat of 1996, he and I have remained friends and continued to see each other occasionally.

From a purely personal point of view I wasn't sorry to be no longer teaching at Gwent: the older I got, the more stressful travelling became (especially so complex and unpredictable a journey by public transport as that between Bristol and Caerleon). Fortunately, too, it didn't affect my finances all that much since, for the 1996/7 academic years I'd secured new teaching in the history department of Bristol University. As long ago as June 1993 I'd written to Bernard Alford, head of the Department of Historical Studies, enquiring about the possibility of part-time teaching. His reply had been disappointing, as I acknowledged at the time:

> Many thanks for your letter and its sympathetic, if for the present negative, response to my enquiry about part-time teaching. It's sad to hear that one of our senior history departments is subject to such severe financial restraints.

Yet, I'd added, 'please do bear me in mind should your financial constraints become less tight in the future'. Despite this set-back, once I returned to Bristol

I soon got to know the three medievalists in the department anyway, mainly as a result of attending lectures and seminars mounted by the university's multi-disciplinary Centre for Medieval Studies. I was impressed. Ian Wei, the most senior of them (although still only a young man), was a first-rate lecturer who even managed to breathe life into twelfth and thirteenth-century intellectual history; Marcus Bull brought a strong strand of down-to-earth common sense to his teaching of medieval political and religious history in general and the Crusades in particular; and Brendan Smith, a most engaging young Irishman, not only managed to convey his own enthusiasm for medieval Ireland to students but also the frontier societies of Wales, Scotland and Spain. All were very friendly and so, despite his baptism of fire at the hands of myself and fellow history undergraduates in 1966, was Tony Antonovics, as well as always willing to share his deep knowledge of Renaissance Italy in general and Florence in particular. It was always a pleasure, too, to talk to the economic historian Roger Middleton (whom I'd taught as a sixth former at Plymouth College) and Ronald Hutton, an outstanding scholar (especially of seventeenth-century England) and a charismatic lecturer who was truly inspiring not only in the classroom but on radio and television as well. Yet, sadly, by the later 1990s the history department no longer had a specialist on fifteenth-century England and, as a result, the legacy of Charles Ross had been largely squandered. This did have a real bonus for both me and Peter Fleming at the University of the West of England, however, since there was virtually no competition for access to the university library's rich stock of printed primary and secondary sources for later medieval England.

Out of the blue, early in June 1996, I received a telephone call from Ian Wei offering me a couple of seminar groups during the 1996/7 academic year on a second/third year course *Identity and Community in Europe 1000—1400*. Since I hadn't taught pre-1300 history for over fifteen years, and had made little attempt to keep abreast of recent scholarship, I had understandable reservations about my capacity to take it on and, as I wrote to Ian at the time, 'I wouldn't want to commit myself to teaching for you unless I was sure I could do it reasonably competently and, most importantly, interestingly'. Once I'd read through the course handbook, however, I couldn't resist, not least because, as I emphasised to Ian, 'I think it's great that you, Brendan and Marcus manage to work together so closely and amicably'. Ian, in turn, responded:

> I'm delighted to hear you are willing to join us. Your proposed list of seminar topics is splendid and fits perfectly with the sort of stuff the rest of us do.

Indeed, he added, 'I have the impression that you work in the same spirit as we do and I'm sure that you will strengthen the team'. What tempted me most of all, however, was the novelty of teaching students who, in theory at least, must be intellectually superior to most of those I'd encountered elsewhere.

Identity and Community was a cleverly structured and intellectually challenging course covering a range of inter-related political, religious and social topics in Western European history c.1000—1400, seeking to address such questions as:

> How did medieval people define their sense of identity?
> How did they organise themselves into groups and were some groups more important than others? Did medieval people's perceptions of how societies were organised match with what was happening in practice?
> What sort of evidence survives for the study of such matters and what problems do historians face in interpreting it?
> How far do the political, religious and social categories favoured by modern historians correspond with how medieval people viewed themselves and their world?

Over thirty lectures provided the course's solid backbone; their quality ensured both high attendance and positive student response; and I seized the opportunity to sample a fair number of them myself, most memorably Ian Wei's interactive sessions devoted to minorities in medieval society such as Jews, lepers, heretics, prostitutes and homosexuals. I even contributed a lecture of my own on medieval women. Seminars were held fortnightly over twenty weeks; attendance was compulsory (I certainly approved of that); and penalties ensured there were few absentees. Four sessions had to be devoted to the course's set texts: the early medieval monastic rule of St.Benedict; Gerald of Wales' twelfth-century *History and Topography of Ireland*; Christine de Pisan's later fourteenth-century proto-feminist *Treasure of the City of Ladies*; and a selection of passages from contemporary chronicles and records on the English Peasants' Revolt of 1381. Otherwise, I chose topics that, while clearly linked to major themes of the course, also happened to fire my own interest and, more importantly, seemed likely to stimulate vigorous discussion:

> English Kings, National Identity and the Community of the Realm c.1050—1300
> Anglo-Scottish Relations, the Hundred Years War and the English National Community c.1300—1422
> Politics, Society and the Urban Community: Fourteenth-century Florence
> Aristocratic Society and Chivalry: An Elite Community?
> Women: Identity Denied?
> Homosexuals and Prostitutes: Oppressed Minorities and Community Rejects?

For each seminar, too, I put together a series of questions for students (and me!) to think about and, inevitably, short passages from primary sources around which discussion could be focussed. This proved surprisingly enjoyable since it took me back to chronicles I'd hardly looked at for years such as the *Anglo-Saxon Chronicle* and Matthew Paris, as well as a range of other fascinating literary sources and records: Peter Damian's hysterical exposition of ecclesiastical homophobia in his mid-eleventh century *Book of Gomorrah*, for instance, and St.Aelred of Rievaulx's contrasting early twelfth-century tract *On Spiritual Friendship*; Pope Urban II's speech launching the First Crusade, delivered at Clermont in 1095; Andreas Capellanus' mid-twelfth century *Art of Courtly Love*; and even Henry II of England's 1162 Ordinances for regulating the Southwark Brothels.

A few weeks after I commenced teaching *Identity and Community*, I wrote to Tony Saul:

> I'm very much enjoying teaching at Bristol University, not least because all three medievalists are such splendid young chaps. I'm not used to students who are both very bright and voracious readers (it's the public school education many of them have received, I expect) but it's a most stimulating (if occasionally alarming) experience. Thank goodness my residual knowledge of European history 1000—1400 is rather greater than I'd feared.

I certainly did enjoy teaching *Identity and Community*. By and large, the students were intelligent, enthusiastic and hard-working; their lively contributions to discussion were almost invariably well-informed and, not infrequently, peppered with humour; and they tended to be gratifyingly appreciative of any help or advice I could give them. Since classes took place in the late afternoon, moreover, several of them soon got into the habit of regularly adjourning to a nearby pub with me afterwards. This had a particularly pleasant spin-off. As a Bristol student myself in the 1960s, I'd regularly attended lectures mounted by the Acton Society, run by and on behalf of undergraduates. The society was still going strong in the mid-1990s and, early in 1997, I felt genuinely flattered by an invitation to address it; the turn-out was impressive, not only students but several full-time staff as well (including the three medievalists); and my historiographically orientated lecture on 'William Rufus: A Much Maligned King?' seemed to meet with general approval.

Identity and Community was very different from the traditional medieval courses I'd studied at Bristol thirty years earlier. The department's assessment and examination arrangements, too, had moved on, although written assignments carried far less weight than an unseen three hour examination at the end. A real bonus for me was that Bristol University's payment scales for part-time lecturers were more generous than Gwent's (or the University of the West of England for that matter): the hourly rate for lectures/ seminars was higher; there was specific remuneration to cover time preparing classes; I was given a few paid office hours so I could see students individually about their work (and Brendan Smith happily let me use his room); and, best of all, every assignment marked generated a fee. Even so, I probably put in considerably more hours than I was paid for and, when the appointment of a fourth full-time medievalist rendered my services superfluous to departmental needs, I wasn't altogether sorry. Among the most engaging students I taught at Bristol in 1996/7 was an articulate and amusing ex-public school lad who, soon after graduation, obtained an internship at the J. Paul Getty Museum in Los Angeles 'researching historical projects for which a knowledge of the classical and medieval periods is very useful'. Sending me a splendid illustrated art history catalogue 'as a token of my appreciation for last year', he also wrote in November 1997:

> I never got the chance to thank you for seeing me through the *Identity and Community* medieval course. At the beginning of the year I was really dreading it but, now, I have been converted. It really is a fascinating period and seminars were a great way to get to know and discuss it.

In response, I declared:

> I'm so glad you've become hooked on the medieval era. Like you, I really enjoyed our seminars last year and, for a middle-aged gay historian who still retains the vestige of a sense of humour, you were certainly the ideal student: a splendid combination of beauty, brains and banter!

Altogether less demanding than *Identity and Community* but no less enjoyable was the teaching I did for Bristol University's Department of Continuing Education in the later 1990s on a part-time course for mature students leading to a Certificate in Arts: The History of Renaissance Art. Just how Cathy Oakes, staff tutor in Visual Arts, latched on to me I'm not sure but it was probably down to the Open University and my tutoring of *A354: Art, Society and Religion in Siena, Florence and Padua 1280—1400*. My function was to deliver occasional lectures/seminars on Saturdays designed to provide historical background/ historiography for the course's specialist art history content. Apart from a session on the Rise of the Mendicants in November 1998, it required little new preparation: Early Renaissance Italy (February 1996 and November 1998), Later Renaissance Italy (January 1997 and October 1999), Later Renaissance Florence

(February 1997 and October 1999) and Fifteenth-century Burgundy and the Burgundian Court (July 1997 and February 2000). As far as I could tell the students enjoyed some solid history and, certainly, participated enthusiastically in the discussions following my lectures. Again, too, I was impressed by the remuneration on offer and the university's speed in paying what it owed.

During the decade following my return to Bristol in 1994 the institution for which I worked most, and got to know best, was the University of the West of England. Like Huddersfield, it began life as a polytechnic in 1970 and, before long, embarked on the construction of a new purpose-built campus on the outskirts of Bristol. By the time I taught Open University students there in the later 1990s, the Frenchay campus had become UWE's prime site. Sadly, though, its complex and confusing array of ultra-modern buildings was singularly nondescript and uninviting. Between 1976 and 1978 two local teacher training colleges were merged with the polytechnic: Redland (where I taught in 1994/5 and 2000/1) and St.Matthias (where the history department was based). Again like Huddersfield, Bristol Polytechnic was granted corporate status in 1989 and, in 1992, became a university. Peter Fleming, who joined the polytechnic's staff in 1985, recalls ironically that, among the names considered for the new university, were:

> ... the University of Avon (just in time for the abolition of Avon County Council), Merchant Adventurers University (obviously suggested by people who hadn't realised that the Bristol Merchant Adventurers Company's history of slave trading might send out the wrong message to potential students from ethnic minorities) and the University of the M4/M5 Interchange (not seriously, but it would have helped people find their way there: who knows where the West of England is, precisely?). In the early days UWE was affectionately known as the University of Woe, but my favourite was coined by a BBC Radio Bristol hack who once introduced me on air as coming from the University of the Rest of England.

Student numbers at Huddersfield had expanded dramatically in the later 1980s and early 1990s but at nothing like the same rate as Bristol. Even by the mid-1980s it had more than 10,000 students; this had risen to almost 15,000 by 1992; and, by 1994, the university had more than 18,000. Hence, no doubt, why I was an eagerly welcomed new recruit to the history department's part-time staff.

Peter Fleming, my fifteenth-century colleague and colloaborator at UWE for a decade, recalls that:

> ... during my first few years at Bristol I did all my teaching, and spent nearly all my time, at the Redland (Education) campus; in 1993 I mounted a third year

medieval course *The Pastons and Fifteenth-Century England* on the B.Ed; and, when I had a sabbatical in 1994/5, you took it over.

I hadn't taught on the equivalent of a B.Ed degree since the mid-l970s but, despite far from inspiring accommodation, the students turned out to be both interested and committed; moreover, although I couldn't resist the temptation to portray myself as a diehard opponent of progressive teaching (even advocating, tongue-in-cheek, a return to corporal punishment in schools), they soon saw through me. As for the course itself, it was very similar to the *Problems of Historical Evidence* module I'd put together for Huddersfield BA (Humanities) students two decades earlier. So, I dug out my aged lectures and handouts for *The Pastons, the Plumptons and their England c.1450—1500* and found, much to my relief, that they still retained a certain freshness even after twenty years. All I needed to do in addition was put together a new course guide, containing questions for students to think about and updated bibliographical information, and explaining my aims and objectives:

> This course is designed to introduce students to the political, economic and social history of fifteenth-century England through the study in depth of a particular kind of source material: family letters and papers, written in the vernacular, and first appearing in the fifteenth century.

Mostly, as at Huddersfield, I concentrated on the East Anglian Paston family and their letters but, not least since I'd written a new introduction to a 1990 reprint of the nineteenth-century edition of the Plumpton letters and papers, I still devoted about a third of the time to this Yorkshire gentry family, emphasising throughout that 'together, these two collections of letters form an unrivalled archive for fifteenth-century history'. Peter Fleming who, in line with UWE history department's care in such matters, double-marked all course work, comments flatteringly:

> You transformed the course, very much for the better. I had been putting too much focus on a close reading of the letters (which was inappropriate for B.Ed students) but you gave it a broader perspective.

From the beginning I made it clear to Peter Fleming that I had no desire to teach first year UWE students. Yet, in 2000/1, I ended up doing just that on the B.Ed at Redland (now renamed BA QTS) when I took on a module entitled *The Tudors*. I wasn't overly enthusiastic but agreed mainly to help relieve pressure on full-time staff in the face of rising student numbers and, even more, the need to provide study leave so as to boost the department's research and publication rating (and, in the process, generate extra income). Drawing heavily on lectures and handouts originally put together for second year students at Huddersfield, I produced a substantial new course booklet, including (since I was now teaching the material to a first year group) a long introduction which was, in essence, a summary of my lectures. As with *The Pastons and Fifteenth-Century England*, I had a weekly two hour slot spread over a couple of terms and, in line with my normal practice, I split the time equally between lectures and seminars. I also deliberately concentrated on just five major topics, all reflecting my own knowledge and interests: Henry VII and the Establishment of the Tudor Dynasty 1485—1509; Henry VIII and the Consolidation of the Tudor Dynasty 1509—1547; Politics, Reformation and Counter Reformation 1529—1558; Elizabeth I and the Triumph of the Tudor Dynasty 1558—1603; and Politics, Protestantism and Roman Catholicism 1558—1603. As always, too, I sought to introduce students to primary source material, particularly documents that might prove useful to them in their own teaching (for instance, on the personalities of Henry VIII and Elizabeth I). It proved a far more enjoyable and satisfying experience than I'd anticipated.

Much the most stimulating teaching I did at UWE was on BA and MA courses mounted jointly with Peter Fleming at the St. Matthias campus (the pleasantest of the university's sites, not least on account of its core of Victorian buildings). Peter remembers our first meeting, probably at a fifteenth-century conference hosted by the University of Reading in 1983:

> I was a rather timid postgrad feeling intimidated by all these grand figures, most of whom I'd previously known only as authors' names on book covers and articles. It's a fair bet we bumped into each other in the bar! Strangely, you didn't want to talk about the workings of the 1405 parliament or the procedures of the Exchequer of Pleas and that was a great relief. I can't remember what the topics of conversation were—though I could hazard a guess—but that's probably the sign of a good evening. Our paths crossed occasionally thereafter at other conferences where you were always good company and a refreshing change from some of the more earnest.

Certainly, from the start at UWE, we hit it off splendidly and soon found our approaches to, and interests in, fifteenth-century history complemented each other extraordinarily well. During his own early years at Bristol Polytechnic, Peter recalls, there was virtually no pre-18th century history taught, apart from the B.Ed at Redland, but gradually later medieval/early modern history did creep into the BA history syllabus at St.Matthias:

We developed *Elites, Politics and Society in Pre-Reformation England* for the BA and *England during the Wars of the Roses* for the MA. My original idea with both courses was to do something rather more social than they actually turned out. What made the difference was your input since, as I remember, you gave me an enormous amount of help and advice in planning them, and I hoped you would play a major role in teaching them too (which, of course, you did).

The result of your intervention, he adds, was 'wholly positive'; the 'political spine' it provided was 'absolutely necessary, particularly for those students (90% of them) who had no previous experience of fifteenth-century history'; and, 'in terms of teaching, the results were excellent'.

Together, Peter Fleming and I taught *Elites, Politics and Society c.1370—1509* to second and third year history students four times in all: 1995/6, 1997/8, 1999/2000 and 2001/2. As Peter himself wrote in the course guide:

> This module studies the political, social and economic history of the final years of medieval England from the viewpoints of its elites: the king and royal family, the landed elite of aristocracy and gentry, and the mercantile urban elite. The first half of the module consists of a study of high politics over the period. This provides the chronological framework essential to any understanding of the period and also introduces the central issues which will be taken up in the second half, organised thematically. Throughout emphasis is placed on the use of primary sources, as well as consideration of the historiography of this era.

On the organisation of the course, he emphasised that it:

> ... consists of lectures introducing the major themes and approaches for each session, seminars based on secondary reading and primary sources, the latter provided in two volumes of extracts, in translation where necessary. The first ten seminars use materials from the volume extracts; thereafter seminars are based on a combination of extract material and secondary sources, since it is our contention that the best introduction to the political narrative of the period is provided by primary sources, particularly chronicles.

Although it was Peter who penned these paragraphs, they very much reflected our joint philosophy in mounting and teaching *Elites, Politics and Society*. My chronologically-structured lectures on later medieval English kings, politics and war in the first half of the course were not dissimilar in content to those I'd delivered for so many years on the first year medieval course at Huddersfield, but rewritten and restructured for second and third year students. Most of the primary material in the two volumes of extracts was also originally put together for Huddersfield students. Inevitably, I particularly focussed on the kings, the literary sources available for their study, and their historiography: an ageing leopard does not easily change his spots! Peter provided the thematic lectures which followed, all of which I attended and much enjoyed, covering topics such as the Black Death and its impact, popular rebellions (such as the Great Revolt of 1381), warfare and society, chivalry and, reflecting his own ever mounting interest in later medieval urban history (especially Bristol's), towns and politics. Both Peter and I took seminar groups, occasionally together, a very stimulating experience for us and, hopefully, for the students as well. During the very first year the course ran, in 1995/6, James Lee was among its students, as he recalls:

> I was in my second year when the now (in)famous double act of 'Dockray and Fleming' taught me *Elites, Politics and Society in Late Medieval England*, a very demanding undergraduate course by anyone's standards, with an intense focus on primary source material (a characteristic Dockray trait). We were all particularly amazed at how Keith managed to gyrate whilst delivering his lectures. Legs, arms, wrists would all extravagantly gesture towards students and/or thin air as the comic/tragic events of fifteenth-century politics emerged from his intriguing inch-high mound of card-index lecture notes. We were equally amazed at how Keith managed to incorporate sex into every lecture. To this day I can't shake off the image of Edward IV as a highly sexed (possibly, according to Keith, bisexual) rampaging brute of a man from my mind. Edward was one of Keith's most memorable creations. Piers Gaveston (Edward II's playboy manipulator), Margaret of Anjou (the 'matriarch') and Henry VII (Keith deplored how 'boring' and 'sensible' he was) also spring to mind. He would paint a cast of fifteenth-century figures, each apparently nonchalently, but nevertheless meticulously crafted. There's real aesthetic and pedagogic artistry in that. History is so much more engaging when its personalities are evoked.

James was probably the ablest and certainly the most engaging undergraduate I taught at UWE; he soon embarked on a Ph.D supervised by Peter Fleming; and, much to my delight, he obtained a full-time post at the university himself in 2007.

In 2002/3 Peter Fleming mounted a new BA history course *Culture, Authority and Crisis in England and her Neighbours*, focussing on England, its dependent territories and its neighbours (Wales, Ireland, Scotland, France and Burgundy), and aiming to 'explore how political and social authority was asserted and contested in the period between the Black Death of 1348 and the end of the Middle Ages', an era 'characterised by demographic crisis, political conflict and social fluidity'. Designed particularly to appeal to third year undergraduates, and very much reflecting recent trends in fifteenth-century historiography, it deliberately adopted a multi-disciplinary approach, 'using literature and literary scholarship and, to a lesser extent, evidence from the visual arts, to complement a core of social and political history'. When Peter asked me to contribute, and since I was working on a historiographically-orientated biography of the victor of Agincourt at the time, I came up with the notion of a case study of Henry V, War and Nationalism. As I subsequently declared in the course handout, the life and reputation of England's second Lancastrian king 'bring together most of the themes dealt with in this module': hence why it was entirely appropriate to devote its final five weeks to putting Henry V's heroic image, warlike character and military achievements under the spotlight. For this case study, moreover, I put together my last ever teaching material: almost thirty pages of extracts from contemporary and near-contemporary lives of Henry V, English and French chronicles, poems, letters and government records. As always, too, I laid on a series of interlinked lectures and seminars, covering three major themes:

Henry V: Images of Heroic Kingship
Henry V, War and Chivalry
Henry V, Nationalism and the Dual Monarchy of England and France

Peter Fleming sat in on most of the seminars; we managed, between us, to stimulate a good deal of vigorous discussion; and the students not only seemed to enjoy the experience but also, as their examination answers showed, achieved real depth of understanding,.

Perhaps the most enjoyable and rewarding teaching I did at UWE over the years was a twelve week MA module on *England during the Wars of the Roses c.1450—1471*. Again, this was very much a joint enterprise with Peter Fleming and, soon after we began teaching the course for the first time in the autumn of 1996, I reported enthusiastically to Tony Saul that 'the MA at UWE seems to be going very well: an able group of committed students making for very lively seminars'. In the three hour evening slot available each week, Peter and I adopted the tried and tested formula of a lecture followed by a linked seminar; we split the lecturing between us; and we presided over the seminars together. In the very necessary mid-session interval, most of us adjourned to the student union bar (the only social venue available on the St.Matthias campus in the evenings) where, not infrequently, written assignments were discussed. In a newly written set of half a dozen lectures, I concentrated on introducing students to Henry VI, Edward IV and the political twists-and-turns of the 1450s and 1460s, particularly as reported in contemporary and near-contemporary literary sources. Seminars were based on document booklets originally put together for my Special Subject/MA students at Huddersfield, reinforced by carefully chosen 'focus documents': very short extracts from chronicles, letters and records specifically intended to stimulate discussion. Peter Fleming's lectures (all of which I attended, as he did mine) and seminars tended to be more thematic and designed, in part, to introduce students to current historical controversies about the fifteenth century. This mix proved highly successful and, when the module ran again in 1998/9 and 2000/1, we stuck to it. In 2003/4, however, I found myself teaching *England during the Wars of the Roses* on my own. I took some persuading, mainly because I didn't at all relish evening journeys to and from St.Matthias (especially having to change buses in Bristol city centre). Fortunately, although Peter was on sabbatical, he needed to visit the university at least once a week; the MA evening was as good a time as any; and, so, he happily undertook to drive me there and back. For what was obviously going to be a one off, however, I was loath to put in hours of new preparation. Instead, I simply expanded my existing six lectures into twelve and structured seminars around the content of my own recently published source books: *Henry VI, Margaret of Anjou and the Wars of the Roses* (2000) and *Edward IV* (1999). Unofficially, Peter Fleming often came along to the seminars and this certainly helped ensure my views could never entirely dominate discussion! I enjoyed teaching the half dozen students who completed the course, and they all passed comfortably enough, but over the weeks I became increasingly convinced that I was now past my prime as a teacher. Also I was finding the proliferation of pointless bureaucratic rules and regulations in the university more and more intolerable. So, when the module ended, just three weeks prior to my sixtieth birthday, so did my years as a part-time lecturer.

During over thirty years teaching at degree level, Peter Fleming was the only historian of fifteenth-century England with whom I worked closely and, for me, this was an entirely enjoyable and satisfying experience. Gratifyingly, he obviously felt the same. 'We had courses that worked extremely well', he recalls, and 'we also complemented each other in terms of teaching styles and interests'. Even so, he adds, 'the two of us together in seminars could sometimes be a little overpowering for students, not on account of the sheer weight of our combined knowledge and intelligence, but simply because they couldn't get a word in edgeways!'. There's certainly more than an element of truth in this but our repartee had positive as well as negative consequences: if we disagreed about a source, or a historian's interpretation of events, I'm sure this served to boost students' self-confidence to put their own oar in (as well as encouraging originality in written assignments). No one has been more perceptive than Peter in his verdict on me as a teacher, particularly in the lecture theatre:

You're pretty well a textbook case of how not to teach, but only insofar as how the textbooks tell us we *should* do it. Lectures are suspect. We should certainly not stand in front of a group of students and read from our notes. Lectures, if they have to happen, must be inter-active; they should not be about simply imparting information but about facilitating learning; and we should forever be using visual aids (the overhead projector hardly counts: these days it's got to be whistles and bells laptop computers and data projectors with websites). So—you were a dismal failure and would have scored *nil points* in one of those 'how to teach' courses inflicted on new staff. Which is why you were so popular with students. You didn't give a lecture, after all, you put on a performance. Personally, I agree with the educationalists that lectures are a bad medium: it's much more effective for students to read a book or an article. Yet you've got to get them to do it in the first place and lectures are a superb way of enthusing them to do so—or yours were, anyway. One of the reasons why I turned up at your lectures when I didn't have to was that they were always informative *and* entertaining.

'And when it came to assignments and dealing with students', he adds, 'you were a fund of common sense: indeed, common sense was one of the most important qualities you brought to your teaching'. Perhaps the last word here should go to James Lee, whom I first taught in 1995/6 (as well as regularly socialising with him and his fellow students in the union bar) and have met up with now and again ever since:

> I have never seen anyone simultaneously so thoroughly enthused by their work and by the act of conveying that enthusiasm to students while, at the same time, so willing to be openly disapproving and condemnatory about anything that takes their fancy. Keith's honesty was a true delight to us impressionable nineteen year olds!

'Without needlessly pummelling the proverbial bush', he concludes, 'the teaching of Keith Dockray and Peter Fleming made me want to be a historian'.

There were many reasons why, in February 2004, I came to the firm decision to stop teaching at the University of the West of England. Now aged sixty, I was finding it increasingly difficult to rise to the sheer physical challenge of delivering lively and entertaining lectures; maintaining focus, and sustaining vigorous discussion, in seminars was no longer as painless as it had been in my prime; and, as for marking assignments and examinations, it had become a tedious chore. Also, I'd had enough of evening teaching and travelling to and from the university and, since my bank balance had continued to rise every year since 1994, I no longer needed part-time earnings. Most of all, mounting managerialism and irritating bureaucracy (despite Peter Fleming's gallant efforts to protect me from it) had begun seriously to impair the pleasure of teaching at UWE. This had become ever more apparent while teaching the MA in 2003/4. For a start I was given a huge and entirely unsuitable room, lacking even the small tables necessary to create a seminar-like atmosphere. Most weeks, indeed, there wasn't even a table for me and I had to purloin one from another classroom. Early on, too, an enthusiastic and obviously able mature student was forced to withdraw from the module because an absurd regulation meant he couldn't continue to be an examination invigilator if he was taking a course at the university himself. Another rule was that student assignments had to be nameless. This seemed to me an insult to the professionalism of academic staff; blind marking, I strongly believed, was not in the best interests of students; and, so, I deliberately subverted it. Yet another irritating regulation required that all written work had to be transmitted to me initially, and then returned to students, via the departmental office (even though the office was usually shut by the time we arrived for evening classes). Peter Fleming, fortunately, volunteered to relieve me of this potential hassle. Then, to cap it all, there were increasingly vexatious hurdles to be jumped in order to secure payment for work done. Presumably designed to prevent overpayment, in practice they simply tended to delay money reaching my bank account swiftly. Nor were UWE's remuneration rates particularly generous. In theory, at least, payment was made only for student-contact hours; there was no formal provision for either preparation or marking; and the university didn't pay travel expenses. Fortunately, part-time contracts could, at the department's discretion, specify a few more hours than were actually taught and, not least because I did a lot of formal lecturing (unlike many part-timers), mine almost invariably did. My final dealings with UWE's financial bureaucrats were also my worst. In June 2000 and April 2003 Peter Fleming and I played major roles at sixth form conferences on Tudor history mounted in the university. After thirty odd years in higher education I found it most rewarding to encounter sixth formers again and, so, I happily agreed to do another, on Henry VIII and the English Reformation, in April 2004. Both Peter and I gave short introductory lectures (when I contrived to suggest, mischievously, that the main cause of the Henrician Reformation was Anne Boleyn's breasts!); we helped supervise groups of sixth formers working on documents supplied by us; and then we listened to, and commented upon, their presentations to the conference as a whole. Again, it proved a very enjoyable and successful day. Unfortunately, the first payment claim I submitted to the finance office turned out to have been written on the wrong form and was rejected; when I resubmitted, on the right form this time, my claim was lost in the bureaucratic machine; and, despite Peter Fleming's urging me to stick at it,

I decided it simply wasn't worth the hassle of battering my head against a seemingly brick wall and gave up the battle. So I was never paid at all for my last ever teaching at UWE. And, apart from reviving my *Topsy-Turvy World of Gilbert and Sullivan* for a final public performance at St.Matthias in December 2004, I've hardly been near the university since.

Throughout my three decades in higher education, I very much enjoyed teaching medieval and early modern history at degree level, as well as penning a series of articles and books on fifteenth-century England very much drawing on my experiences in the lecture theatre and seminar room. Yet, clearly, I was always an obstinate and wilful square peg squirming to avoid fitting into a series of round holes. Now, if I was still in the university business, I'd probably be an even more determined member of the awkward squad. The low priority afforded to teaching in many universities these days is deplorable and concentrating on it is almost certainly the kiss of death to any hopes of promotion; full-time academic historians spend far too much time on study leave, not nearly enough in the classroom; and, instead of enlightening undergraduates and a wider public about the past, they too often seem to hide away in archives and studies, churning out frequently tedious articles and monographs primarily aimed at attracting research funding (so they can then write yet more turgid fact-laden stuff of interest only to themselves and fellow specialists). Too much teaching is now in the hands of part-timers or people on short-term contracts and, although I obviously benefited from this trend myself between 1994 and 2004, it doesn't augur well for history's future. Nor does the continuing failure to attract enough able working class students into university history departments, or the relentless growth of managerialism in higher education. Pointless meetings have proliferated out of control and, by comparison with the flood of internal e-mails to which academics are now subjected, even the endless memoranda of yesteryear seem modest. The paucity of history provision in many schools these days, apart from an almost obsessive attention to the First and Second World Wars, is also ominous. Yet, however bleak history's future sometimes looks, the continuing popular appeal of the past is only too evident in the programme schedules of television channels.

15

Later Historical Research and Writing

'In the last few years', I wrote to the Cambridge medieval historian Rosemary Horrox in September 1989:

> ... I've been persuaded to write more than I did in the 1970s and early 1980s (when teaching was always my top priority), mainly because too many academic historians these days seem only to address each other rather than sixth formers and undergraduates. Yet, surely, the latter must be attracted to medieval history and its sources in the next decade if it is to survive outside public schools and Oxbridge. That's why I always aim at them and a wider audience (even though my simplifications no doubt infuriate purists). What has happened to classical studies in recent years (hardly taught at all in state schools anymore) should be a lesson to us all. Medieval history could very easily go the same way, and will, if medievalists remain too stuffily locked in the ivory tower of traditional scholarship. Hence why I'm glad the Richard III Society continues to flourish. Medieval history is worth reading and studying and it is down to us to ensure it retains, and expands, its place in sixth forms, colleges and universities.

During the early 1990s the situation did not improve; indeed, if anything, it got worse, not least as far as fifteenth-century history was concerned. The emergence of a revisionist school of neo-constitutional historians didn't help and, as I remarked in a letter to the Canadian scholar DeLloyd Guth in April 1997:

> The revisionists have a lot to answer for and I'm not really all that sympathetic to the avalanche of fifteenth-century research now in progress (the 'getting to know more and more about less and less' syndrome). It's about time teaching rather than research went to the top of the higher education agenda—but, sadly, all the pressures these days are the other way.

'I share virtually all your sadness about a lot of what currently passes for revisionism', he replied, 'very much the pit-bull approach, even when it is readable'. I returned to the subject when writing to DeLloyd again later in the year:

> Have I any further thoughts on the Oxbridge revisionists? Mainly negative, I'm afraid. What depresses me most about much very recent stuff is that it's widening the divide between academic and popular treatment of the period, a potentially disastrous development as far as the future health and appeal of fifteenth-century studies are concerned. Why is so much recent record-based history so narrow in focus and so tedious?

No wonder, once early retirement from Huddersfield reduced my teaching load and I had more time to devote to writing, I deliberately set myself the tricky task of straddling the divide between academic and popular history. Not that I was in any way dedicated, as my Bristol neighbour Mark Jones mused early in 2004:

> We eventually discovered that Keith was a medieval historian of some repute, with a string of academically sound publications to his name. So that was where the near inaudible sound of typing at four o'clock in the morning was coming from: another book on the way. 'This is definitely the last book I write', says Keith, yet a few months later we hear the faint sound of a smoking typewriter again. There's a sort of inevitability about it.

'Every book you have written you've declared to be your last', echoed publisher Alan Sutton in December 2005, 'but you can never resist the temptation to embark on another—and that is as it should be'. Dennis Collinson, my former Plymouth College and Open University colleague, commented in March 2004 that 'those who know Keith's writing will appreciate how beautifully clear it is and how persuasive his analyses'. At about the same time Peter Hammond, now president of the Richard III Society, declared:

> You certainly have a talent for teaching, both directly to an audience and indirectly through your writing. Too many historians think of themselves (consciously or unconsciously) as writing down to a 'popular' audience, unless they are being deliberately 'scholarly', when they can be incomprehensible! You are never either. You are just trying to communicate your own enthusiasm and knowledge, and you do it well.

The judgement of Keith Stenner, another luminary of the Richard III Society, is remarkably similar:

As an ardent late medieval enthusiast, my first introduction to Keith Dockray came via the enjoyment of his impressive canon of books and essays which are erudite, succinct, accessible and honest. They are also consistently generous in acknowledgement of the influence of others, reflecting Keith's self-deprecating nature and liberality of spirit.

And Mark Jones supplies a particularly splendid anecdote:

> A couple of years ago I was travelling to Dalaman airport at the end of a holiday in Turkey. The rep on the coach was a Turkish university student specialising in some aspect of medieval history for his dissertation. His supervisor had recommended, he said, a specific text by K. Dockray. 'Oh yes', I remarked, 'I live next door to him'. The student looked at me as though I was mad. Thinking back, it probably did seem a bit unlikely!

Once I got out of full-time university teaching in 1994, I no longer felt under any pressure to attend fifteenth-century conferences, and didn't feel much inclination to do so either. I did give a short, and very derivative, paper on 'The North of England and the Wars of the Roses' to a gathering at Liverpool Institute of Higher Education in April 1995 but mainly because an expenses-paid trip to the city enabled me to meet up with former undergraduate friend Mike Stammers and ex-Huddersfield student Steve Garrett. A decade later Mike recalled:

> ... Keith's coming to Liverpool for a conference. I attended an afternoon session where he performed wearing a sky-blue tracksuit: a less suitable garment for the biggest non-sportsman I know is difficult to imagine! This was followed by six or seven pints of beer (without any food) with Keith and a bright ex-student of his. The session ended with me going home, incoherent, in a taxi: a most dramatic reintroduction to Dockray-style drinking!

Peter Fleming, my former colleague at the University of the West of England, reminisces:

> On the professional level you've helped me develop as a historian. First of all, it's wonderful to have someone close by with shared interests in the fifteenth century. Secondly, because you know everyone in the field who's worth knowing (in Britain anyway), I've got to know lots of people—and lots of people better than I would otherwise have done—through you.

Meeting up with friends and catching up on fifteenth-century gossip, in fact, was the main reason why I still journeyed to the occasional conference in the later 1990s. This was certainly my prime motive for accompanying Peter on a nightmare car drive to Aberystwyth in July 1996. I have only the faintest recall of the papers I sat through but remember vividly an extended beer-drinking session with Steve Smith, my Huddersfield Polytechnic colleague of the later 1970s, professor of politics at the University of Wales college at the time. Steve himself also recollected, in April 2004, that 'the last of many drinks I enjoyed with Keith over the years was in a Welsh Nationalist pub in Aberystwyth when he proceeded to explain (loudly) why he so much disliked Welsh nationalism'.

At Aberystwyth I also met up with Tim Thornton, my successor at Huddersfield University, and a few days later wrote to him offering to give a paper at the symposium he was organising there in September 1997; however, I couldn't resist adding:

> I think you're very brave (or do I mean foolhardy?) to risk putting on a conference at Huddersfield—but, perhaps, these days the faceless bureaucrats are less obstructive than they used to be. The talk I have in mind ('James Gairdner: A Colossus of Victorian Historians of the Wars of the Roses, Richard III and Henry VII') won't be too intellectually demanding, so might I have the after dinner slot on Saturday evening? It's not a good time for complex research papers and, if my previous visits to Huddersfield since 1994 are anything to go by, I'll probably be severely hung over during the day—a condition not conducive to a good performance! Anyway, a few ex-colleagues might enjoy coming along to what will probably be the last ever Dockray lecture at the university.

Tim readily agreed; the lecture was duly delivered; and several former history and politics colleagues did indeed turn up. I couldn't resist an opening preamble:

> Since I taught medieval and early modern history at this impossible institution for almost a quarter of a century, I felt morally obliged to offer a contribution to this colloquium. Unfortunately, since I'd already contrived to land myself with part-time teaching for three different universities in 1997, any serious research was out of the question. Anyway, perhaps alone among Charles Ross's research students over the years, I inherited his considerable distaste for spending long nicotene-deprived periods in musty archives. So, since one of my great pleasures ever since I was a student has been reading Victorian histories of the Middle Ages, James Gairdner seemed a promising subject, especially for a post-prandial discourse.

Soon after returning to Bristol, I wrote to Tony Pollard at Teesside University:

> I had an amazingly hectic weekend in Huddersfield. What with drinking with David Taylor [an ex-colleague of both Tony and myself] well into the night on both Friday and Saturday, meeting up with other former colleagues and friends, and ending up at Tetley's brewery in Leeds with Bill and Pauline Stafford on Sunday lunchtime, I was lucky not to sleep through Bristol and end up in Penzance on the train journey home.

About the same time I reported to Ralph Griffiths in Swansea:

> A sobering thought, isn't it, that Tim Thornton got the fifteenth-century crowd to Huddersfield within three years of succeeding me: it never crossed my mind to organise such junketings in over twenty years there. My lecture on James Gairdner seems to have been enjoyed by the older generation at least (dunno about the youngsters: they seem far more serious-minded than I ever was at their age). Whether it will appear in any published proceedings I don't know and don't mind either way. No wonder I've never acquired any sort of reputation—apart, of course, from heavy drinking, chain-smoking and, perhaps, giving the occasional entertaining lecture!

Ralph responded by declaring he had enjoyed the Gairdner lecture and also suggesting that I 'follow up some of the other giants of the earlier age, never forgotten when I was a student but pushed into the background since by pygmies'. A few years later I very much had this comment in mind when I contributed a paper on the historian C. L. Kingsford (1862-1926) to a *festschrift* in his honour. As for the Gairdner lecture itself, I decided it would fit very uneasily into a volume of largely archive-based conference proceedings, offered it to *The Ricardian* instead, and there it was duly published in March 1999: very appropriately, perhaps, since James Gairdner was Richard III's first truly academic biographer.

Huddersfield, and my former colleagues there, were occupying my mind for another reason in the later 1990s. David Wright, who had taught at the polytechnic throughout the 1970s and 1980s, died suddenly at his home in Gloucestershire in December 1995. A generous, supportive and self-effacing man, he also had the rare capacity as a historian of combining deep scholarship, immense readability and a capacity to render complex subjects (even the French Revolution!) intelligible to the most average of students, both in the classroom and in print. He was a long-serving Open University tutor as well and, on a personal level, I much appreciated his sympathy and support as I struggled to come to terms with my sexuality once and for all in the 1970s.

Mike Bartholomew, Arts staff tutor for the Open University in Yorkshire, came to Bristol and drove me to Stroud for David's funeral where, so he assures me, I 'gave a warm and eloquent little speech'. A few days later I travelled north for a memorial service in Shipley, near Bradford, and it was then that Keith Laybourn and I first conceived the idea of editing a volume of historical essays in his honour. Nine months after, in September 1996, I wrote to Keith:

> Over the last two or three weeks, as much to keep me out of the pub at lunchtime as anything else, I've knocked together a paper on 'Bradford, Leeds and the Civil War in the West Riding of Yorkshire: Literary Sources and their Interpretation'. Hopefully, it can be my contribution to the David Wright volume if we ever get it off the ground. I doubt whether any historical journal would accept the piece: it isn't 'Ph.D history' and that's all journals seem to publish these days (hence why I rarely read them anymore). There's not much new research in it but, as far as I know, no one has ever written about literary sources for the West Riding campaigns 1642—1644 in quite this way before. Anyway, you might enjoy it, especially the Bradford bits.

In fact, as I admitted in a footnote, the essay had its genesis:

> ... in a final year BA course on *Yorkshire and the Civil War* which I taught at Huddersfield Polytechnic for several years in the late 1970s and early 1980s, a course that owed much to David Wright's encouragement. I have drawn heavily on my lectures (first written in 1977) and on a collection of primary sources I put together to provide material for seminar discussion.

Early in December 1996 Sutton Publishing expressed a strong interest in publishing the *festschrift*, providing we came up with a themed collection of papers; Keith thought war might provide an appropriate and appealing unifying theme; and I suggested *The Representation and Reality of War* as a promising title. We now approached potential contributors and soon assembled a list of authors, almost all of them former colleagues and students of David himself, and topics on relevant themes. As a result the book became as much a celebration of a group of people who had worked closely together for years as a tribute to David, among them Brendan Evans, Bill Roberts, Bill Stafford, Andrew Taylor and Philip Woodfine. Suttons now firmly committed themselves to publication; Keith Laybourn and I jointly penned an introduction highlighting David's personal qualities, his teaching and his writing; and *The Representation and Reality of War: the British Experience* duly appeared in the spring of 1999. Keith also organised a 'celebration of the life of David Wright' and book launch in an upper room of the *Albert* pub in the centre of Huddersfield; many of David's former colleagues, students and friends turned out; and it proved a most enjoyable occasion, not least for me since I met up with several people I hadn't seen since 1994.

Ever since my postgraduate years in the later 1960s, I had frequently consulted the *Dictionary of National Biography*, a multi-volume work conceived in the late nineteenth century and very much a product of Victorian pride in ancestry and past achievement. By the early 1990s, however, it was badly in need of up-dating and the Oxford University Press now set itself the awesome task of doing just that. I very much approved and, over a period of some six or seven years, penned a series of short articles on later medieval/early Tudor nobility and gentry for it myself, amounting to about 15,000 words altogether. Of course, I wasn't nearly eminent enough to be offered any of the big historical names but I did get the opportunity to write about several prominent northerners and their families (including, yet again, the Yorkshire Plumptons). By and large it was an instructive and rewarding experience; moreover, when a Cambridge-based associate editor made a series of piffling criticisms of one of my articles, my robust response was, 'Take it or leave it': the research editor Henry Summerson took it and, indeed, even commissioned me to write several more biographies. *The New Oxford Dictionary of National Biography*, all sixty volumes of it, was finally published in September 2004.

In 1987 Alan Sutton, of Alan Sutton Publishing, had published my first book *Richard III: A Reader in History*; over the next few years he also put several other historical projects my way; and, when he was virtually forced to resign as managing director of the company in September 1993, I expressed my disgust at the manner of his departure in no uncertain terms. His successor's response was conciliatory:

> Because of your long and close association with Alan, I respect the reasons for the tone of your letter. I hope that in time you will accept and understand what has happened and that we at ASP might look forward to a renewed relationship.

Several years elapsed, in fact, before I had any further dealings with Sutton Publishing, as it was soon renamed. When I did it was down to Roger Thorp, a young history editor Alan himself had appointed, who wrote to me in October 1996:

> You might be pleased to hear that we are considering a reprint of *Richard III: A Reader in History* for next year. If this goes ahead, I wondered how you would like it to be done. In one way or another I would imagine it ought to take into account

material and information that has come to light since it was first published and tackle issues raised by reviewers. Do you think this would be best done through a fully revised, reset and possibly expanded edition, or would you prefer simply to add a new preface and update the bibliography? Let me know your thoughts.

Soon afterwards Roger and I met up in a Bristol pub and the result was *Richard III: A Source Book*. In the end, moreover, I did make substantial changes to my original book, both seeking to incorporate the fruits of recent scholarship and adding a number of extra documents. In 1987 I had expressed my gratitude to students and colleagues at Huddersfield Polytechnic (especially Pauline Stafford) 'who have long sustained my enthusiasm and indulged my eccentricities'; now I declared that:

> My gratitude to former colleagues and students at the University of Huddersfield remains as strong as ever, and I must now additionally thank Peter Fleming, Peter Allender and students at both the University of the West of England and University of Wales College, Newport, for helping to keep my interest in fifteenth-century politics in general, and Richard III in particular, alive and kicking. Moreover, despite the very best of feline endeavours, my two delightful cats Snitch (now sadly deceased) and Snubby have not managed to prevent either the original book or this new edition being completed.

The book was published in September 1997 and, as I reported to Tony Pollard a few weeks later, it 'sold far more than I expected'. About the same time Dennis Collinson persuaded me to visit south Devon and talk to a local history society about the fate of Edward IV's sons ('Did Richard III murder the Princes in the Tower?'); I photocopied, and distributed, the relevant chapter of my book; and, perhaps, that helped generate a few more sales. So, no doubt, did a hardback edition produced for the Ancient and Medieval Book Club. *Richard III: A Source Book* was remaindered early in 1999, a puzzling decision by Suttons since, only a year later, it was reprinted. So too, in 2002, was the pamphlet on the king I'd written in 1992 where, in a new foreword, I commented:

> No doubt the next decade, like the last, will see further advances in our knowledge and understanding of the last Yorkist king, as yet another generation of historians falls prey to the fascination of Ricardian lore. Good luck to them!

In March 1989 the American historian Joel Rosenthal asked me to write short biographical entries on Edward IV, Edward V and Richard III for an ambitious *Medieval England: An Encyclopedia* project; I duly obliged; and, after an amazingly long delay, the huge volume was eventually published in 1998. At the end of the 1980s, too, at the request of the Yorkshire branch of the Richard III Society, I put together a lecture entitled 'Edward IV: Playboy or Politician?'. Early in 1990 I even sounded out Alan Sutton about a follow-up, on Edward IV, to *Richard III: A Reader in History* and he expressed considerable interest. Nothing came of this, partly because of pressure of teaching, and Alan's peremptory departure from his own publishing company in 1993 seemed to kill off the idea once and for all. What I did do, a couple of years later, was turn my Edward IV lecture into an article for *The Ricardian* (published in December 1995). I also continued to give the lecture itself occasionally: for instance, to the Bristol branch of the Historical Association and in Oxford (where I spent a most enjoyable evening with Rowena Archer). In November 1997, shortly before he left Suttons for Routledge, I once more met up with Roger Thorp in a Bristol pub, this time seriously to discuss *Edward IV: A Source Book*. He was enthusiastic and, soon afterwards, his successor Christopher Feeney gave me the final go-ahead:

> I am delighted to tell you that your book on Edward IV was accepted for publication at our December publishing meeting this morning. We have done very well with *Richard III: Source Book* and I look forward to working with you on the next in what might become a nice mini-series. Who knows?

By the end of May 1998 the book was finished, as I reported to Ralph Griffiths (who had been most encouraging, and helpful, about the project throughout):

> I've now finished *Edward IV: A Source Book*, amazingly quickly for me. I hope it will serve its prime purpose of highlighting Edward's fascinating personality and the action-packed high politics of his reign, as well as providing a useful introduction for sixth formers and undergraduates to the main primary sources and the problems they raise.

The book was published at the end of March 1999, and, almost immediately, I received an unexpected but entirely welcome letter from Jack Lander (by then the most eminent living historian of the king):

> I have just finished reading your book *Edward IV*. May I congratulate you on a really splendid volume which I am quite certain will be indispensable to anyone teaching or studying Edward's reign—not only for the selection of documents from original sources but also for the judicious and very fair way in which you present and adjudicate between the differing views of modern writers. Admirably done!

'This is a book for those historians who see history as scenes in a play which focuses on individuals, their actions and motives', declared Penny Tucker in a review published in *The Ricardian* in December 1999; moreover, 'anyone new to the debate on Edward IV has here a clear, compact, vigorous and frank introduction to the position today and the sources which have mainly informed it'. A few years later, in his own refreshing exploration of the king's reputation (*Edward IV*, 2004), Michael Hicks concluded that I had brought to the subject:

> ... a first-hand familiarity with the period over many years, an exhaustive reading of the secondary literature, and a capacity for trenchant criticism, perceptive insights and, on occasion, shrewd discrimination between opposing views. Often he offers the most rapid and sure-footed access to current issues for and against.

Edward IV: A Source Book also had a light-hearted spin off: 'Edward IV and Henry VIII: A Yorkist Grandfather and Tudor Grandson Compared', a lecture eventually published by Judith Loades in *Medieval History* in 2002.

Perhaps the first clear indication that I had established a modest reputation for myself had been in May 1992 when Tony Pollard asked me to contribute an essay on the origins of the Wars of the Roses to *The Wars of the Roses*, a volume he was editing for Macmillans' well-established 'Problems in Focus' series, specifically requesting 'a summarizing overview, pithy and to the point, the sort of thing students will be using for years to come and which I know you would do well'. I was a bit cautious in response, commenting:

> The origins of the Wars of the Roses is not a subject on which I can claim any particular expertise (although I've taught it for years to both first and third year students). As long as you don't anticipate any substantial new research or startlingly original revelations, however, I think it might be fun to have a go at.

Tony's reaction to receiving a synopsis of the chapter's probable content was:

> What promptness! An acceptance and a synopsis in the same mail. I'm delighted on both counts. The synopsis is just the sort of thing I hoped you would come up with, based, as you say, on years of teaching the subject. That will give it the directness and approachability to students the topic demands.

Before sending the completed paper to Tony in March 1994, I received positive responses to its content from several third year Special Subject students; even so, I urged him to:

... reject it if it's too far from your requirements. I have no particular attachment to it! Yet, I suspect, students seeking a quick fix for an essay on the origins of the Wars of the Roses will latch on to it like a shot—no doubt to the annoyance of their tutors.

'It's certainly a bit late to start worrying about my academic reputation', I added, 'especially since I never have before'. Gratifyingly, Tony assured me that 'the article seems just right for the volume' and *The Wars of the Roses* was duly published in 1995. I even got paid £175 for it!

In January 1998, while working on *Edward IV*, I floated the idea of penning a third source book on the Wars of the Roses era, building in part on my 1995 'Problems in Focus' paper. Christopher Feeney showed immediate interest, as I remarked to Michael Hicks at the time:

> Suttons now seem keen that I complete a trilogy of source books, going straight on to *Henry VI, the Wars of the Roses and the End of the Lancastrian Dynasty* as soon as I've finished *Edward IV*. Perhaps I will but, if I do, my now largely moribund Latin will perforce ensure the predominance of vernacular and already translated sources. Since I spent so many years at Huddersfield teaching English political history 1450—1485 from contemporary and near-contemporary sources (especially narratives)—and am still doing so at UWE—maybe I should do it. A trilogy of student-friendly source books (*Richard III*, I gather, is used from GCSE to MA level) is certainly the most appropriate legacy I can leave. How bloody pompous that sounds!

In July 1998 I wrote in very similar terms to Tony Pollard, adding that 'I find source books quite fun to do and, I like to think, they do serve a useful function, not least in bridging the gulf (sadly growing at present) between academic and popular history'; Tony's immediate response was that I 'should definitely go on and complete the trilogy' since such books are 'not only useful to students but also lazy academics'; and, by the time I signed a contract with Suttons in December, work on the book was well underway. Throughout I was much encouraged by Ralph Griffiths, himself author of *The Reign of Henry VI* (published in 1981 and as near a definitive history of 1422—1461 as we can ever hope to have), despite his rueful comment that 'we don't see eye to eye on poor Henry and his capacious shoulders bearing the weight of practically all undesirable things in the fifteenth century'. As early as September 1998 I wrote to him:

> *Henry VI, the Wars of the Roses and the End of the Lancastrian Dynasty* is progressing nicely and I'll try not to be *too* hard on Henry VI. It won't be easy! Instinctively,

my sympathies lie with 'sinners' (like Edward IV) rather than 'saints' and, in that sense if no other, I'm a true chip off the Charles Ross block. No doubt this book (like its two predecessors) will appal old-fashioned, traditionally-minded and academically-elitist scholars (if it should ever come to their attention!). Sadly, some of the younger generation seem to have similar views and even the ex-polytechnics these days appear to value research more than teaching. Yet, it seems to me, if fifteenth-century English political history is left entirely in the hands of the 'purists', it's liable to become unteachable and, ultimately, untaught beyond the privileged portals of the old universities.

Ralph's response was no less outspoken:

I'm glad to hear the Wars of the Roses is progressing so well. Why so gloomy at its possible reception? The only possible criticism of the approach you are adopting might come from those teaching courses that require students to get to grips with a particular source (or sources) in the round rather than those for whom selections of texts are more appropriate. So crusade away and keep up the good work.

As for Henry VI, he added, 'he's too often treated out of context, and that increasingly irritates me, but I expect the worst from your pen, not least because I'm sure he wouldn't have been a smoker even if tobacco had been discovered!'. A few months later, in May 1999, I wrote to Christopher Feeney:

Surveying the work I've done so far on the source book, I'm strongly inclined to change the title to *Henry VI, Margaret of Anjou and the Wars of the Roses*. Henry's queen is figuring much more in the documents/commentaries than I'd anticipated; having her name on the cover might help sales; and the suggested change would slightly shorten a long title.

Christopher responded positively:

Why not let the mighty Margaret have her moment in the sun? I think it could very well help sales and I like the idea of a slightly shorter title. You'll be pleased to hear that *Edward IV: A Source Book* went very well at the American medieval conference in Kalamazoo. I could have sold a boxful if I'd had them.

Even so, as I wrote to Tony Pollard a few weeks later, I wasn't finding the going easy:

I'm beavering away at *Henry VI, Margaret of Anjou and the Wars of the Roses* but finding it much trickier than its two predecessors. I've certainly had my bloody fill of source books. Three is definitely enough:

The book was completed in the autumn of 1999 but, shortly before publication, came an irritating hiccup, as I complained to Christopher Feeney:

> I must object in the strongest possible terms to altering the title of my book to *Henry VI and the Wars of the Roses* at the very last minute and without any consultation with me. The original title accurately reflects the book's content. The new one does not. Moreover, I find it incredible that your Sales Department (which, I gather, is responsible for the change) really believe removing Margaret of Anjou from the cover will *increase* sales:

My original title was restored and the book duly published, in both hardback (primarily for the History Guild) and paperback, in March 2000. And, without any prompting from me, Tony Pollard penned a splendid review for *The Ricardian*, published in June 2001:

> Keith Dockray has completed his excellent trilogy of the Wars of the Roses with a volume which deals with events, battles and personalities from 1450—1471. It offers a clear delineation of the chronology and an excellently balanced summary of scholarly debates backed up by a judicious selection of sources. The introductions both to the whole volume and to the individual sections form as good a short summary of the state of learning at the end of the twentieth century as one could hope to have. The trilogy now stands as an essential port of call for all who come to the second half of the fifteenth century for the first time.

'I'm not attending Michael Hicks' fifteenth-century conference at Southampton in September', I wrote to Tony Pollard in June 1999:

> Reprehensibly, no doubt, I just can't take a weekend of Ph.D history anymore. Presumably, if Peter Fleming hosts the 2001 conference at the University of the West of England, I'll get drawn into that (if my lifestyle hasn't finally caught up with me by then!).

This is precisely what happened. Peter organised the symposium; I attended most sessions, even chairing at least a couple; and I certainly enjoyed the social side (not least a late evening beer-drinking bout in a spectacularly undistinguished local pub). Peter and I subsequently wrote a report on the proceedings for *The Fifteenth Century: Authority and Subversion*, published in 2003. A quarter of a century earlier, we noted, Charles Ross had organised a pioneering colloquium on fifteenth-century history at Bristol University:

> In September 2001 Bristol, once again, provided the home for a symposium: not Bristol University (where Charles Ross's legacy has become just that, a legacy) but the University of the West of England. Organised by Peter Fleming (a former student of Ralph Griffiths), with Keith Dockray's enthusiastic encouragement, the conference was attended by some sixty delegates. Despite the reluctance of modern plumbing to produce a regular supply of hot water at the twist of a tap, the university's Gothic revival campus of St.Matthias in the quiet suburb of Fishponds provided a most pleasant setting for a series of almost uniformly high-quality papers. The symposium also saw the biggest reunion of the Bristol connection for years. Charles Ross, sadly, had died in 1986, but his spirit was well represented by the likes of Rowena Archer, Margaret Condon, Keith Dockray, Diana Dunn, Ralph Griffiths, Michael Hicks, Michael K.Jones, Tony Pollard and Alan Sutton, and crowned by the presence not only of Ross's widow Anne Crawford but also their son James.

An unexpected souvenir of the conference was a photograph of the Bristol connection taken by my friend Peter Allender. A few weeks later I sent copies to the rest of the group and received enthusiastic responses: Michael Hicks, for instance, remarked that 'UWE 2001 went very well, I thought, the Bristol connection was out in force, and what a nice photo'; similarly, Ralph Griffiths expressed himself 'glad to have the splendid photo (even if I am the soberest one there) and, fortunately, no one looks at all decrepit'. The high point of the conference for me was chairing a session at which both James Ross and James Lee delivered splendidly coherent and well-researched papers. I had known James Ross since he was a small boy, meeting up with him regularly when I stayed with his parents in Bristol and, after his father's death, with his mother in London. As for James himself, he recalled in May 2005 that 'my memories of you from an early age are the smell of cigarettes, lots of drink and, more recently, a stinking hangover last time I stayed with you in Bristol'. I was delighted when he obtained a place to read history at Oxford University in the mid-1990s, secured funding to embark on postgraduate study there three years later, and settled for research into fifteenth-century history. 'I believe he intends to investigate the fifteenth-century earls of Oxford', I wrote to Ralph Griffiths in July 1998, adding, 'is there a Ross dynasty in the making here?'. It seemed most appropriate that Rowena Archer, one of his father's former students, should be his supervisor. And I was certainly pleased and flattered when he asked me to comment on a section of his thesis, as well as in no way surprised when he was duly awarded his doctorate and, following in his mother's footsteps, obtained a post at the National Archives. Seemingly, or so he tells me, I may also have been of assistance to Peter Fleming's research student James Lee (whom I'd taught myself as an undergraduate at UWE):

> Whenever I've plucked up courage to ask Keith a serious historical question (not easy for a young pretender when confronted by his many years of history teaching and writing), he has not hesitated to reply courteously, positively and helpfully.

I appreciate even more James's comment that:

> At academic conferences I've tended to make a beeline for the 'Dockray zone', a unique blend of hearty and earnest laughter, plumes of smoke, pint glasses stacked high on a wobbling table, and flowing conversation interjected with some token asides on late medieval history. I'm sure for many this is the side of academic history conferences to be avoided but, for undergrads, postgrads, dejected late medievalists and any bystanders feeling out of sorts for the evening, this is the place to talk freely and humanly about things academics aren't supposed to discuss.

The UWE conference of 2001 was certainly one of the most enjoyable fifteenth-century gatherings I ever attended; I haven't journeyed to such a symposium since; and, now I'm fully retired from academia, it's very unlikely I will again.

In December 2000 I received a letter from Livia Visser-Fuchs, close friend and collaborator of *The Ricardian*'s long-time editor Anne Sutton, asking me if I would like to contribute to a *festschrift* in her honour. I was delighted to do so. Anne had played a major role in enabling me to get into print in the 1980s, even accepting idiosyncratic articles for *The Ricardian* which would probably never have seen the light of day otherwise. In the 1990s, although probably sufficiently well established by then to have had at least a sporting chance of winning over pedantic editors of learned journals, I preferred to submit my historiographical essays on Edward IV and James Gairdner to Anne. Interesting members of the Richard III Society was a far more worthwhile objective, I felt, than trying to impress dry-as dust academics! I also continued to write reviews for *The Ricardian* and not only of books that seemed tailor-made for me (such as Michael Hicks' biography of Warwick the Kingmaker in 1999 and a study of late medieval Northallerton, in Yorkshire, by Christine Newman in 2000): for instance, in 1995, I reviewed a short study of medieval chivalry and, in 1995, a fascinating collection of essays by Phillip Lindley on the development of

English sculpture in the thirteenth, fourteenth and fifteenth centuries. When Cambridge University Press published a new edition of the Plumpton letters and papers by Joan Kirby, I specifically requested Anne to let me review it (and, in the end, did so for both *The Ricardian* and the journal *History* in 1998). I even toyed with a northern topic for her *festschrift*, returning to my Ph.D files for the first time in years, as I wrote to Livia at the end of 2000:

> My days of doing cutting-edge research—insofar as they ever existed!—are now thankfully over. However, for a number of years I've been toying with the idea of writing an article on 'The Lancashire Harringtons and the Wars of the Roses'. Successive heads of the family were firm supporters of the Yorkists, particularly Richard III, and their story is quite a lively and interesting one.

Within a few weeks, however, I'd thought better of it and settled for Joan of Arc instead. Several years earlier in October 1995, at the request of my former colleague Peter Davies (a specialist in twentieth-century French history), I'd journeyed to Huddersfield for a *Joan of Arc Evening* and lectured on 'Joan of Arc: Myth and Reality'. At the time, when told of my professed resolve 'to control myself on the subject of angelic voices and transvestite tendencies', Tony Pollard responded in similar spirit:

> I assume your appearance in full armour at Huddersfield has not yet occurred. What I want to know is: will you allow the ladies of the court to inspect you?

In fact, I put on a typical Dockray performance, delivering a talk punctuated by quotations from contemporary, near-contemporary and more recent verdicts on France's fifteenth-century heroine. It went down well; I thought it might appeal to Anne Sutton; and, when sending an expanded and footnoted version to Livia Visser-Fuchs in May 2001, I commented:

> As you'll see, I'm very much in a 'history for people rather than academics' mode (I usually am these days) but, although hardly breaking new ground, it reads quite well (so a couple of friends assure me) and both Anne and *Ricardian* subscribers might enjoy it.

Her response, gratifyingly, was 'it's fine, very readable and not too difficult for those Ricardians who are maybe going to be bombarded with esoteric stuff'; *Tant D'Emprises—So Many Undertakings: Essays in Honour of Anne F. Sutton* was published in 2003; and my short appreciation of Anne, one of many included in the volume, was profoundly genuine:

During the long period of Anne's editorship *The Ricardian* has become firmly established as a respected academic periodical. Presenting the results of original research by both amateur and professional historians (unlike most historical journals), it has also gained a well-deserved reputation for excellent reviews and invaluable notices of recent publications on fifteenth-century England. Perhaps Anne's greatest achievement has been her strenuous, and no doubt immensely time-consuming, efforts to ensure contents that are not only scholarly but interesting and readable as well.

Ever since the 1970s, as my interest in contemporary and near-contemporary chronicles for fifteenth-century England grew, so did my fascination with William Shakespeare's Plantagenet history plays of the 1590s and the sixteenth-century narrative sources (such as the chroniclers Edward Hall and Raphael Holinshed) on which the playwright drew for their plots. This developed alongside a burgeoning enthusiasm for historiography more generally. Hence why, when I was asked to write an article for the *History Teaching Review Year Book* (journal of the Scottish Association of Teachers of History) in August 1996, I promptly offered to knock together:

> ... a piece on 'William Shakespeare, the Wars of the Roses and Richard III', suggesting—a little mischievously but not without justification—that Shakespeare might not have been all that far off the mark in emphasising the *dynastic* dimension of the Wars of the Roses in general and the self-seeking ruthlessness of Richard III in particular.

The editor Andrew Hunt, commenting that 'it sounds a nice provocative mixture and will be eagerly read by the members of SATH', gave me the go-ahead; on receipt of the completed piece he remarked 'I like the look of your article and how it reads'; and it was duly published in June 1997. Later in the year I sent a copy to Ralph Griffiths, judiciously emphasising that:

> ... it is in no way original but it has provoked several letters (all positive I'm glad to say). Whether I actually *believe* what I've written is an open question but it was fun to do—and, perhaps, it has stimulated a few hairy Scots to invest in *Richard III: A Source Book*. In December I'm giving a lecture version to the Bristol branch of the Historical Association, so that could be a sobering experience (especially if any English Literature people are there!).

I was pleased to learn soon afterwards that Ralph had 'read it twice, with profit as always', and also that he himself believed 'William Shakespeare is a much better historian—if an inferential and oblique one—than many give him credit for'.

By the end of 1997, in fact, I was already contemplating a book on the historical content and historiographical significance of Shakespeare's fifteenth-century history plays, maybe for the publisher Alan Sutton who had so encouraged me in the later 1980s.

After his peremptory departure in 1993 from the publishing company he had founded and which bore his name, Alan Sutton, in true entrepreneurial fashion, had dusted himself down and set up a new company Tempus Publishing. By 1999 it was flourishing and, in August, both Peter Fleming and I were invited to attend 'a special birthday party' at Tempus 'to celebrate with Alan Sutton twenty-five years of publishing local and national history'. A couple of months earlier Alan had expressed interest in publishing *William Shakespeare, the Wars of the Roses and the Historians*, 'a book aimed at the more popular end of the history market and very much focussing on Shakespeare's Plantagenet history plays, their derivation and their influence on/treatment by historians since the 1590s'. Again, too, Ralph Griffiths was very encouraging. 'Wasn't it at the Huddersfield conference in September 1997', he asked rhetorically:

> ... that you first mooted the Shakespeare book? I'm with you in appreciating Shakespeare as a historian—and it's interesting to speculate on some of the scenes that are hardly in Hall and Holinshed.

Early in September 1999 Jonathan Reeve, history editor at Tempus, sent me a draft contract; I wasn't at all impressed by its terms; and, very much on the spur of the moment, promptly despatched it back to him:

> I've brought this into line with my last contract from Suttons. If my alterations are unacceptable, then it will save me the bother of writing the book. After all, it was only Alan Sutton's persuasiveness that led me into offering to write the bloody thing in the first place!

On the same day I also wrote to Alan himself:

> I received a draft contract for the Shakespeare book today that was distincly author-unfriendly and nearly rejected it out of hand. If the contract is not substantially altered, I'm afraid I shall offer the book to another publisher or, more likely, forget about it altogether. Do I really want to write any more books anyway? A vast amount of work for very little financial return!

'Of course', I added, 'this has nothing to do with our personal friendship and I hope to see you again in the near future'. My alterations were all accepted and I was even paid an advance on royalties. A few weeks later I wrote to Christopher Feeney at Suttons:

> As you know, Alan Sutton is an old friend of mine and, after several pints earlier this year, I agreed to do a book for Tempus entitled *William Shakespeare, the Wars of the Roses and the Historians*. The fact that he offered a better royalty rate than Suttons may also have been a factor! It's due to be completed not later than September 2001.

I even met the deadline, commenting in a letter to Tony Pollard at the end of November 2001:

> You won't agree *at all* with my sympathetic treatment of Shakespeare's perspective on fifteenth-century kings, politics and war but I have, at last, committed to print my views on the aridity of so much recent 'pseudo-scientific' history.

The book closed, in fact, with a firm statement of my belief that:

> ... the relentless quest by professional historians for pseudo-scientific answers to the questions posed by fifteenth-century England and its sources has made them apt to forget that history is, and should be, a literary art as well as a painstaking search for truth (and here, surely, they have much to learn from amateurs!). Certainly, no mere historian will ever paint a more compelling and dramatic picture of England's Lancastrian and Yorkist kings, and the Wars of the Roses, than William Shakespeare.

William Shakespeare, the Wars of the Roses and the Historians was published in June 2002. Obviously, a favourable review in *The Ricardian* was particularly to be hoped for and, in December 2002, the Richard III Society's new research officer Wendy Moorhen supplied just that:

> This book should appeal to a wide readership, as there is something for those interested generally in Shakespeare, for those approaching the plays from the literary viewpoint but without much knowledge of the period, and for students of history... The book is written in a lively and readable style and, although a rather curious mixture of Shakespeare, original sources and historiography, it is nonetheless enjoyable and the kind of work to be expected from a historian who has already provided so many useful source books... In his opening paragraph the author suggests that without Shakespeare nobody outside 'a few elite schools, universities and the Richard III Society' would have known of the wars. Perhaps

this could be taken a stage further—would there be a Richard III Society without Shakespeare's history cycle?

Even more pleasingly, at the end of 2003, Ralph Griffiths sent me a copy of a review he had penned, commenting 'I agreed to do it partly so I could say a word about your work: have I got it right?'. Again, his conclusions were largely positive:

> Keith Dockray sets out to re-assess Shakespeare as an interpreter of the Wars of the Roses in the light of the welter of historical research over the past thirty years into kings, kingship and nobles in late fifteenth-century England, especially the work of Charles Ross and those inspired by his writings (including Dockray himself)... Captivated by Shakespeare as he is, Dockray stresses the compelling drama of the history plays and the playwright's sophisticated understanding both of human nature and the human condition; he does not expect modern interpreters of the fifteenth century to approach Shakespeare's success in portraying the age of Lancaster and York for London audiences; and yet he applauds, and rightly, those who have sought to make its history accessible. Indeed, in his own volumes of contemporary sources placed in an interpretative framework, he himself has already done more than many. This new book, attractively written and, at times, racy, is laced with humour, as well as appreciative of, rather than carping at, the researches of others.

William Shakespeare, the Wars of the Roses and the Historians had two very pleasant spin offs. Early in June 1999, when he attended a lecture I gave on Edward IV to the Gloucestershire branch of the Richard III Society, Peter Hammond had asked me to perform at a big bash the society was organising at York University in April 2002 to celebrate the 550th anniversary of the king's birth. I agreed and, a few days later, Peter wrote to me:

> It was good to see you again. It was so long since we had met that Carolyn and I almost wondered if we would recognise you but, when we did meet, it was as if there had been no intervening gap. We greatly enjoyed your talk, as did other people we spoke to. About your lecture at York, I think a full fifty minute Friday evening talk would be a very good way to open the proceedings. We can offer you the full weekend at the university and travel expenses with the compliments of the society.

Since, by the time I confirmed my willingness to speak at the conference in July 2001, *William Shakespeare, the Wars of the Roses and the Historians* was nearing completion, it seemed a shrewd move to lecture on 'William Shakespeare, Richard III and the Historians' and take along a stack of leaflets advertising the book! As the event drew nearer, the prospect of a long train journey became ever more daunting, however, so I was massively relieved when Peter Fleming decided to attend the conference and offered to drive me to York. Even then, it proved stressful, especially when we hit severe traffic congestion outside the city. Hence why I resolved never to travel north again. Once there however, and faced by a large but appreciative audience, I pulled out all the stops, setting the tone with a few preliminary remarks:

> I'm delighted to be giving what may well be my last public lecture to the Richard III Society. It's nice to see so many friends and acquaintances here but, even so, I feel like a singularly insecure Daniel in a potentially lethal lions' den talking on this subject. Hopefully, I'll emerge with life and limb more or less intact at the end.

An unexpected bonus was Tony Pollard's turning up to the lecture; another was an extended afternoon boozing session in a York pub next day; and the society laid on a splendid Saturday evening conference dinner in the citys fifteenth-century Merchant Adventurers Hall. A few days later Wendy Moorhen sent me a most welcome letter:

> Thank you for joining the society at the recent conference in York and delivering a very entertaining paper in such an energetic way. It proved to be an excellent start to the conference and all the feedback I have had has been very positive.

And, she added, 'I am glad you were able to make it to the conference dinner and provided me with an excuse for a cigarette break'! Before long, moreover, I was holding forth on Richard III's reputation again, this time in Bristol, as I wrote to Michael Hicks early in September 2002:

> Michael Jones and I are going to lead a public debate at the University of the West of England on 2 October on the motion 'Richard III—history's wicked uncle: did Shakespeare get it right?'. Since it's fallen to me to present the case for the Tudor villain (not my usual stance), I'll probably be expelled from the Richard III Society as a result!

The debate was very much the brainchild of Michael Jones who had recently published *Bosworth 1485: Psychology of a Battle*, a compelling, if deliberately mischievous, reinterpretation of the last Plantagenet's character, motives and behaviour. I hadn't taken part in a public debate since performing at the Oxford Union in the autumn of 1983; moreover, whereas then I had spoken in defence of Richard III, this time I took the opposite line: such is the versatility of historians! Peter Fleming bravely volunteered to chair the debate. Inevitably, I found myself on the losing side, not least since members of the local branch of the Richard III Society turned out in force. Nevertheless, prominent Gloucestershire Ricardian Keith Stenner, for one, certainly seems to have enjoyed my performances over the years:

> Keith's trade mark of prowling the lecture podium like a caged tiger can prove intimidating to the uninitiated. However, this trait only serves to give additional emphasis to the imparted word which Keith always delivers with passion and total commitment.

When writing *William Shakespeare, the Wars of the Roses and the Historians* in 2000 and 2001, I found myself increasingly ill-at-ease with Shakespeare's heroic portrayal of Henry V (1413—1422) and ever more sceptical about the admiration for the king displayed by so many historians. Alan Sutton and Jonathan Reeve liked the idea of a short, historiographically-orientated but critically conceived biography of the victor of Agincourt and, in October 2001, I signed a contract with Tempus to write just that, commenting in a letter to Tony Pollard soon afterwards:

> I've just signed a contract to write a 'popular' book on Henry V. It will, no doubt, be a characteristically Dockray product: not much original research, very historiographically orientated, and containing lots of passages from contemporary and near-contemporary chronicles and lives. Like you, though, I anticipate ending up highly sceptical about the 'medieval hero-king' tradition.

Tony was typically encouraging, as was Ralph Griffiths who commented, indeed, that '*Henry V* is a good thing to do in a sceptical frame of mind'. Michael Hicks, too, responded favourably:

> We professional historians have a lot to answer for. The reading on Henry V has become excessive and altogether beyond the capacity of the modern student or even ourselves of forty years ago for our weekly/their fortnightly essay. If you can guide them through that, you will be performing a really useful service.

Much of the literary source material for Henry V was available in English, fortunately, but even I had to resort to translating occasional passages from Latin and French: most decidedly *not* a labour of love! The amount of secondary reading certainly was enormous. And, of course, I had never taught Henry V as a Special Subject. As a result, the book proved more difficult, and took longer, to write than I had expected. When I finally despatched the completed manuscript to Jonathan Reeve at the end of July 2003, I commented:

> With a great sense of relief that the bloody thing is finished (at last!), I enclose the typescript of *Henry V*. Reading it through, it seems rather more academic than I'd expected it to turn out—but not excessively so, I hope. Apart from the odd article or book review in the future, I think I've just about written myself out on the fifteenth century. Anyway, five books in eight years seems more than enough.

Soon afterwards I wrote to Ralph Griffiths:

> *Henry V* is now complete (publication next summer). A typical Dockray product: no original research beyond printed sources but I think I tell the story (especially as presented by chronicles and lives) quite vigorously. I certainly enjoyed writing the historiography sections and putting the boot in a bit. I ended up reluctantly admiring the king as a ruler and a general (though with strong reservations) but disliking him as a man. Not my type at all. Give me Edward IV any day!

When the book was published in June 2004, I promptly sent a copy to Keith Laybourn and his response was all I could have hoped for:

> I have read your book on Henry V and thought it splendid. On receiving it I immediately ordered two copies for the university library which should now be on the shelves!

Not long after my *Henry V* appeared, so did Malcolm Mercer's *Henry V: The Rebirth of Chivalry*. Since he chose to highlight the evidence of records in the National Archives rather than literary sources, the two complemented each other nicely, and I was certainly pleased by his judgement on mine as 'a fascinating biography offering new insights into Henry V's life and career'. When Michael Jones embarked on a short study of *Agincourt 1415* (published in 2005), we talked about the project at some length, and his comment that I had provided 'an excellent introduction to the full range of chronicle sources for the king's reign' was no less welcome. More unexpectedly, even a review in the academic journal *History* judged the book 'well-crafted and thought-provoking'. Equally pleasing were the verdicts of former student Graham Townend and historian Michael Hicks. 'I thoroughly enjoyed *Henry V* from beginning to end', declared Graham, and 'found your portrayal of the king interesting, persuasive and a timely warning about military adventurers through the ages'. An 'appropriately skeptical modern life', concluded Michael in the American medieval history journal *Speculum*, as well as 'an accessible, informative and often perceptive introduction to the narrative sources'. As for the *Oxford Times*, it simply judged that I had unravelled 'the man behind both image and conquest in a superlative book': an amazingly positive assessment, to say the least. And the hardback of *Henry V* did sell sufficiently well, apparently, for Tempus to publish a paperback version, under the title *Warrior King: The Life of Henry V*, in May 2007.

Towards the end of 2001, while Peter Fleming and I were enjoying a drink together in a Bristol pub, our conversation turned to Ralph Griffiths (who was nearing retirement as professor of medieval history at Swansea) and we came up with the idea of jointly editing a *festschrift* in his honour. Alan Sutton promptly committed himself to publishing the volume; several of Ralph's friends and admirers among the ranks of later medieval historians, including Michael Hicks, Tony Pollard and Colin Richmond, enthusiastically agreed to contribute; and *People, Places and Perspectives: Essays on Later Medieval and Early Tudor England in Honour of Ralph A. Griffiths* was duly published in September 2005. Charles Ross had first introduced me to Ralph in about 1967 or 1968 when I was a research student and, over the next thirty years, he and I met regularly at fifteenth-century conferences. During these years, too, I benefited greatly from Ralph's infectious enthusiasm for later medieval history, marvelled at his industriousness in writing it and, most of all, enjoyed his company. It was he who persuaded me to contribute to a *festschrift* for Charles Ross in the mid-1980s and, in the early 1990s, encouraged me to write an appreciation of him; he sent me occasional books to review for the *Welsh History Review*; and his advice and suggestions when penning my trilogy of later fifteenth-century source books, *William Shakespeare, the Wars of the Roses and the Historians*, and *Henry V* were invariably helpful and positive. He was warmly appreciative, too, of a talk I gave on Shakespeare's *Henry V* at a one day conference held in his honour at the University of Wales, Swansea, in May 2003. So it was a real pleasure to help edit *People, Places and Perspectives*. Peter Fleming and I penned an introduction to the collection covering Ralph's long teaching career at Swansea, his prolific output as a historian, and his wider role in promoting history (for which he had recently been awarded an OBE). Peter also contributed a paper of his own, appropriately on Bristol during the Wars of the Roses, and so did I, on the historical legacy of C. L. Kingsford (1862-1926). This, too, was an apt choice of subject. A few years earlier I had written a short article on Kingsford for the *Oxford Dictionary of National Biography* and, again encouraged by Ralph (whose own interest in historiography was considerable), even toyed with the idea of a book on later Victorian and early twentieth-century historians of fifteenth-century England. *People, Places and Perspectives* was presented to Ralph at a conference in Swansea in September 2005; I couldn't face the prospect of even a two hour train journey to south Wales but Peter Fleming did the honours on behalf of both myself and Alan Sutton; and, a few days later, I received a typically warm appreciation of our efforts:

> I am just about recovering from the shock of being presented with this splendid book: how did all of you manage to keep its existence a secret? I am, most sincerely and affectionately, deeply grateful for your central part in its production and for all those nice things that have crept into your and Peter's introduction. Shock and gratitude have now turned into a turbulent combination in my mind of humility, inadequacy, embarrassment, pride and utter pleasure at the writers willing to write, editors to edit, and the number of you willing to perjure yourselves in the gentlest of introductions. It is overwhelming!

Both Peter and I were delighted, in turn, by fifteenth-century historian Hannes Kleineke's review in *The Ricardian*. 'An interesting and varied collection', he declared; 'the quality of the contributions is a mark of the respect and affection of the contributors for Ralph Griffiths'; and the result is a volume with which 'the editors and Professor Griffiths can afford to be pleased in equal measure'. Its publication would never have happened, moreover, without the encouragement and backing of Alan Sutton. Nor, for that matter, would I myself have written even as much as I have. Hence why I shared his own satisfaction when, early in 2007, he bought back Sutton Publishing (the company he himself had originally founded in 1978) and, as chief executive of the NPI Media Group, became head of the leading history and heritage conglomerate in the country.

Apart from *People, Places and Perspectives*, and two or three book reviews, since completing *Henry V* in 2003 and stopping teaching in 2004, I've virtually abandoned the fifteenth century. The only exception has been to respond to requests from Peter Hammond, Wendy Moorhen and Anne Sutton of the Richard III Society. In the summer of 2004, as I remarked to my former school and university friend Bernard Jarvis at the time, Peter Hammond asked me to pen:

> ... an appreciation of Paul Murray Kendall's *Richard III* for publication next year (the fiftieth anniversary of the book's first appearance in 1955). My copy, so the inscription reminds me, was a twenty-first birthday present from Roger Kitching and John Mackay and it was probably the book that first fired my interest in fifteenth-century England in general and the last Plantagenet in particular. I'm

now inclined to regard it as the best 'popular' biography of the king ever written, even if its author was a bit too inclined to over-imaginative reconstruction of ill-reported events. More importantly, it's an object lesson in how to communicate well-researched history to a wide readership, a capacity many young historians urgently need to develop if academic history isn't to degenerate into an incestuous and irrelevant intellectual game.

Peter Hammond's response, when I sent him the completed piece, was entirely positive:

It is splendid, a marvellous description of the book and one which will make anyone who has not read it go straight to it. It is a great book, I think, and attracted a lot of us in the way you describe, determining if not an academic career certainly a path which we have followed ever since.

In January 2005 Wendy Moorhen made a further request:

We need a concise introduction to the Wars of the Roses from the political perspective for a new Richard III Society website. I thought it would be rather good to have this from a 'name' within the academic community and wonder if you might consider writing it for us.

'I'm not sure I qualify as a name', I responded:

... but, I suppose, lots of members do possess my *Richard III* source book so, perhaps, I'm not a bad choice to write such an introduction. It's ironic, though, that I myself am completely computer illiterate and happy to remain so. In the early nineteenth century I'm sure I would have been a Luddite; indeed, I might well have protested against the wheel! So all you'll get from me is a typescript.

I duly penned a breathless scamper through the Wars of the Roses, remarking on delivery that 'it's hardly original but doesn't seem to read too badly' and, so I was told, it made its way to an electronic light of day early in 2006. Perhaps even more improbably, I also commented at some length on a Key Stage 3 Education pack aimed at 13/14 year olds, again sponsored by the Richard III Society, on 'Richard III: Hero or Villain', remarking enthusiastically that 'this is a splendid project and its aims entirely commendable'. Once more, my efforts were well received. Reading this material also helped inspire an article of my own on 'The Hero and the Villain?: Henry V and Richard III', a light-hearted exercise in comparative history, which appeared in the society's *Ricardian Bulletin* in 2006/7.

At Anne Sutton's request this time, I also penned yet another book review for *The Ricardian* (2007). I was suitably impressed by the academic quality of *The Fifteenth Century: Image, Belief and Regulation in Late Medieval England*, a collection of 'nine papers by both well-established scholars and relative newcomers to the fifteenth-century scene', but couldn't resist remarking as well that, 'surely, fifteenth-century history can be both scholarly and stimulating, intellectually challenging yet also enjoyable to read, even humorous and entertaining now and again'. When the Richard III Society held its annual general meeting in Bristol in October 2004, I put in an appearance at that too; however, regretfully, I declined an invitation to address a further gathering in York in September 2006, part of the celebration of the fiftieth anniversary of the society's refounding in 1956. My lecturing and travelling days (especially in the now fast emerging era of non-smoking public buildings and trains) were, I felt, well and truly over!

Most of what I have written over the last two or three decades has grown out of teaching at least as much as research, as well as reflecting my conviction that, while obviously reflecting their own economic, social, religious and cultural environments, medieval and early modern men and women were fundamentally no different from their twenty-first century successors. I have barely set foot in an archive since I was a research student in the later 1960s (although Anne Crawford did once give me a guided tour of her then place of work the Public Record Office, now the National Archives, at Kew!). I find much records-based history ever more tedious and unappealing. Nor do I have a great deal of time for those professional historians who doggedly insist on writing mainly for each other. What I've always tried to do, particularly since I retired from full-time university teaching in 1994, is to pen intellectually sound but hopefully readable history. Whether I have succeeded is for others to judge and several have recently done just that, among them two of my fellow students at Bristol University in the mid-1960s. Bernard Jarvis, indeed, assures me that:

> ... in your books a pretty unusual cocktail of authoritative understanding and an accessible friendly style, with a bit of fun thrown in, make for an excellent read. We used to joke at one time how every history book, however obscure, always made a play for wider readership by claiming, in its blurb, that it would be of considerable interest to the general reader when, patently, it wouldn't be. You've killed the joke, though, because that's just what you do.

Mike Stammers, who has written a great deal of history himself, comments:

> Keith has become one of the authorities on late medieval England. He does not hold with fancy theories, especially literary/philosophical stuff of the French and

Post Modernist type. He also has little time for economic and social history. He has set out his stall for narrative history and time will probably prove that he was right to stick to his guns. In spite of making life difficult for his publishers by refusing to embrace computer technology, he has produced an admirable collection of books and articles, especially since his return to Bristol. They amount to a substantial history of fifteenth-century politics, based on evidence he has sifted and assessed over years of teaching, and remarkably accessible. What a legacy!

Tony Pollard, in not dissimilar vein, comments:

> I always think of you as the modern expert on narrative sources for the second half of the fifteenth century, summed up in your three source books and demonstrated in such pieces as your reconstruction of the battle of Wakefield. Indeed, I remember you telling me once that you still consider narratives to be the core, the foundation, of all work on the period and that we must, of necessity, come back to them time after time,

Michael Jones suggests an interesting variation on this:

> Keith was never going to plough the archives transcribing obscure and dusty documents. His gifts as a historian come, rather, from his flair as an actor. He understands that teaching is in part performance, and a bravura performance at that. Yet he also has the instinctive skill to let authors of narrative sources speak for themselves and, in both his teaching and published work, he has given them the opportunity to do just that. In the academic climate of our time this gift may seem demeaned by the epithet 'traditional', but I think traditional is a rich compliment.

As for Peter Fleming, not only does he generously refer to 'the esteem in which you are held by sensible people' in the field of fifteenth-century studies, he also emphasises that:

> ...you like to go on about your hatred of archives, and you don't follow the latest fads in historiography, but this hasn't meant any diminution in the respect and, more importantly, genuine affection in which you are held. This is for several reasons. Firstly, you have an unrivalled knowledge of chronicle sources for the political history of fifteenth-century England and of much else besides.Secondly, you write extremely well on this subject. Thirdly, and perhaps most importantly, there's no humbug or pretence about you, and people respect that. You're also very generous intellectually, as Tony Pollard recognised in *The Worlds of Richard III* (2001):

> ...I would like to acknowledge my debt to Keith Dockray who began working on the late fifteenth-century gentry of Yorkshire long before I stumbled upon them. He has never published as much as he should of his early studies but, from the beginning, he generously made the results available to me. If I have been able over these years to make a small contribution to an understanding of the worlds of Richard III, as much is owed to Keith's unselfishness as my own endeavours.

> I could supply plenty of examples from my own experience but I won't—for the sake of saving us both the embarrassment!

Michael Hicks, interestingly, finds it 'very sad that Keith values himself so little and, apparently, under-rates what he has done'. Colin Richmond suggests that I have 'enriched fifteenth-century English history' by my writing and, just as much, my 'lively and unorthodox presence—waking us dry old sticks up!'. And Ralph Griffiths, when he learned I was embarking on a chronicle of my life and times, specifically urged me to:

> ... think of the people, young and old, you have informed, influenced and entertained, and the enjoyment you and they have experienced along the way. To have moved historical understanding along a mite is an enduring thing and, now, future historiographers will have your *Memoirs* to work with and ensure your immortality. A horrifying thought!

16

Pleasures and Pastimes in Bristol

As soon as I received my early retirement lump sum and the proceeds of selling my Huddersfield semi-detached, I paid off the mortgage on my Bristol house. Yet, even on a low pension and especially when supplemented by part-time earnings, I soon found I had more than enough to live on; indeed, far from having to draw on savings, over the decade 1994-2004 they continued to grow. As for the Bristol house itself, it suited me very well: plenty of rooms (essential to accommodate guests, not to mention all the books I brought with me from the north); a rather delapidated garage (which I rented out for a while before, eventually, selling it to a neighbour in 2007); and a tiny garden (its smallness one of the most appealing features of the property!), now a favoured meeting place for local cats with a taste for jungle conditions. A freehold double-fronted end terrace built about 1900, the house had once incorporated a corner shop, as local barman Steve Gould recalls:

> I knew Keith's house long before I met him, when part of it was still a shop. Indeed, as a schoolboy, I often bought sweets there on the way home.

A few years down the line I turned the ex-shop into a very comfortable study. Kit Hardwick comments how, in the mid-1990s, he found:

> ... Keith and two enormous cats settled in what looked like a former corner shop near Bristol jail and convenient for his local pub. He very kindly put me up there a couple of times in a bedroom full of bookshelves, positively heaving with just about everything ever published on medieval England and doubtless much else besides.

Unfortunately, he adds 'by the time I got to bed I was usually too far gone to examine them in detail!'. For all my mounting eccentricities over the years, moreover, I got on reasonably well with neighbours. Frank Chlebko, for instance, recalled in April 2004:

> I have known Keith for ten years and more, initially as a neighbour and subsequently in the *Annexe* pub. I greatly respect him, value his friendship and hope, for many years to come, to enjoy beer-swigging conversations with him in the pub and back at his house listening to his wonderful 78 gramophone records.

'In October 1998', recollects Mark Jones:

> ... I moved next door to Keith with my partner Jan. The previous owners had warned us, with waggling eyebrows, that there was a weird chap next door, and we began to wonder whether moving there had been the right decision. Then we met Keith. After a brief introduction over the garden wall, where all we could tell was that he was somewhat sozzled, we made his better acquaintance in more typical surroundings: the local pub! It didn't take too long to discover that Jan and I had several things in common with him: the ability to live side by side with dust, a love of cats, and an abhorrence of children in pubs. As for Keith himself, he seemed quite happy that his new neighbours did not plan to have children and even more pleased when we told him we intended to have cats instead.

For a non-driver the house could hardly have been better situated: in particular, nearby Gloucester Road abounded in shops and there was also a frequent bus service to the city centre. Even so, living near a prison did prove a rather mixed blessing, particularly when, towards the end of 1996, news broke that its status was to be raised from local nick to top security. There was considerable opposition from nearby residents and with every justification; a public meeting was held; and, as a result, a committee to liaise with the prison authorities was set up (of which I became a member for a while). In August 1997 I wrote to David Clark, a former colleague at Huddersfield Polytechnic and now a member of Tony Blair's new Labour government, in no uncertain terms:

> Somehow, I've found myself on a local residents' committee trying to resist the arrogant and insensitive decision to upgrade Bristol Prison to Category A. Since then our lives have been appallingly disrupted by happenings both within and without its walls, ranging from the enormous noise of construction work and the appearance of new security cameras infringing our privacy to the serious exacerbation of parking problems in the area. To put it bluntly, making a prison like

Bristol Category A is crazy and we're determined to fight the consequences for us.

I never received a direct reply but lip service, at least, was paid to local concerns and a few of our suggestions acted upon; nevertheless, the prison did become a top security establishment and at outrageous cost to the taxpayer. For the next few years, as a result, armed convoys became a familiar sight until, very quietly, the prison was eventually downgraded to Category B status again. All this, in theory, hardly added value to my house. Yet, in practice, house prices in the area have rocketed over the last decade and, only recently, a property developer keen to convert the place into two flats offered me an extraordinarily large sum for mine. Tempting, perhaps, but not sufficiently so to compensate for the horrors of having to move elsewhere.

Even after I took up permanent residence in Bristol in September 1994, I would happily have shared the house with the schoolteacher friend who had lived there since 1991: it was certainly big enough. When it came to the crunch, however, he decided to move out, leaving me and my two cats Snubby and Snitch as sole occupants. Bill Roberts, indeed, recalls knowing the pair of them 'both in their magnificent prime and in old age'. Snitch, sadly, died in 1996 but Snubby soldiered on until 2002. Although not the brightest of cats, he was immensely affectionate and I certainly missed having him around. Hence why, a few weeks after his death, I acquired Smoky, a seven year old black male with whom his owners were reluctantly forced to part when their baby developed an allergy to cats. He, too, soon became very attached to me and, despite his unpredictable nature and chronic inability to grasp that I wasn't covered in thick protective fur, I rapidly took to him as well. It certainly seemed appropriate, when my biography of Henry V was published in 2004, to record in the preface that during its writing 'my fabulous felines Snitch (1985—1996) and Snubby (1985—2002) could no longer disturb my labours but Smoky, my latest familiar, has striven hard to prove himself a worthy successor'. In January 2007 Smoky, too, died. Nicky Bramhall, the local vet who had operated on him and saved his life in 2004, immediately sent me a most welcome letter:

> How very sorry I was to hear of the death of Smoky. I know how much he meant to you and how much he will be missed. He was a lovely cat and I hope it is of comfort to you to know he had a happy caring home. I hope that in time your sadness at his loss will be eased by happy memories of a very special friend.

I did miss Smoky terribly, and it felt very strange not to have a cat around the house after more than thirty years; nevertheless, I've firmly resisted the temptation to get another since, if I died during his lifetime (a near certainty!), his future well-being could not be guaranteed. Fortunately, one or two local moggies have taken to visiting me now and again and, as my neighbour Mark Jones reminds me, I often meet up with his two cats as well:

> Keith, very luckily for us, is a cat lover and happily looks after ours a couple of times a year when we go away on holiday. We repay his kindness by buying him cigarettes!

What I certainly haven't lacked since 1994 is a regular stream of visitors from all over the country. Roger Kitching, whom I've known ever since we became grammar school boys together at Huddersfield College in 1955, has frequently stayed overnight. Our shared taste for real ale and the theatre, especially musicals, always make such visits immensely enjoyable, not least the opportunity to reminisce about our youth and wallow in nostalgia about a gentler but now irrevocably lost world. Highlights must certainly include his driving me to Swansea in May 2003 for a conference in honour of Ralph Griffiths (his former history tutor in the mid-1960s) and, in December 2004, his coming along to my last ever public lecture (appropriately, on Gilbert and Sullivan's portrayal of late Victorian England) at the University of the West of England. Roger himself comments:

> What I value about our friendship is that it is based on such firm foundations that it would be almost impossible for it to be wrecked. It seems we can always pick up where we left off even if there are a couple of years intervening.

My dedication of *Henry V* to him in 2004 was profoundly genuine:

> To Roger Kitching for his encouragement, understanding and friendship over almost fifty years.

It was Roger, too, who enabled me to re-establish contact with John Mackay, another grammar school friend, at the end of 2003. When John visited me in November 2004 (our first meeting in almost forty years), Roger came along as well, and the place soon became even more soggy with nostalgia. Another school and university friend Bernard Jarvis has also stayed with me two or three times and Mike Stammers, whom I first met in the autumn of 1963, has become a regular visitor. Mike recalls two trips in particular:

> In 1996 I was a member of the crew of the *Brocklebank* when we brought the tug to Bristol's Maritime Festival. Keith, Peter Allender and Peter's son Robin came

on board in Bristol; we explored the *SS Great Britain* together; and then, inevitably, we visited a string of dockside pubs: a splendid afternoon and evening in the fairground atmosphere of the Festival.

A few years later, he adds:

I recall Keith attending an exhibition of pictures about the Falkland Islands on the *Great Britain*. He was wearing a black leather jacket with a red polo-neck sweater; he had more hair then and it was swept back; and he observed the proceedings with an eagle-like stare. I'm not sure what he was thinking at the time but, as the platitudes rolled out, it was probably something like: 'This is all balls!'. In fact, that could be his motto in more ways than one!!

Both Bernard Jarvis and Mike Stammers came to Bristol at the same time in July 2002, joining Peter Allender and I at an informal reunion of a small group of 1966 Bristol University history and English graduates. Ian Faulkner, another friend of student days, couldn't make it to that but he, too, has certainly made the journey to Bristol several times over the last decade. From my Plymouth College years, Mike Allen has enjoyed the occasional afternoon boozing session with me in Bristol and I've met up with former physics master John Arthur two or three times as well. Ex-colleagues and students at Huddersfield Polytechnic, as well as other northern friends from the 1970s, 1980s and early 1990s, have also put in an appearance from time to time. Bill and Pauline Stafford, Peter Davies and former college chaplain Kenneth Cook have all visited me at least once. Bill Roberts and his wife Jan, regular visitors to the south west, usually seek me out during their jaunts: indeed, Bill tells me, he has a 'splendid photograph' of me standing on the architecturally breathtaking Royal York Crescent in Clifton. Imogen Martin, whom I first met when her husband lodged with me in Huddersfield for a while in 1972/3, vividly recalls her occasional visits to Bristol:

Here was a man who, despite his professed revulsion from young children, could enthral and engage my nine-year-old daughter with scurrilous tales of sexual misdemeanours observed, unawares, in the Clifton Camera Obscura and, in this way, earn her unflagging devotion. Indeed, here was a man who put himself out to entertain a woman and her assorted children whenever they, on a whim, deigned to call!

And it has certainly always been a pleasure to welcome Keith Laybourn who has stayed with me several times, even enduring a tour of medieval Bristol on one occasion. The list of former students who have met up with me in Bristol over these years is longer still, among them Richard Bell, Peter Broome, Julie Bungey, Cliff Burhouse, Jo Cole, Vanessa Cook and Graham Townend. Fellow fifteenth-century historians Anne Crawford, James Ross and Michael Jones have all stayed overnight with me, and I've met up with others, too, when they've visited the city, among them Rowena Archer, Ralph Griffiths, Michael Hicks and Tony Pollard. Perhaps the most regular visitor in recent years has been publisher Alan Sutton, particularly between 1999 and 2002 when his Portuguese personal assistant Pedro Cordeiro stayed with me several times too. Alan himself muses that, after my move to Bristol, 'we became closer and I always enjoyed your mocking of me, fully aware that most of it was intended in a friendly manner'. As for Pedro, he was certainly a splendid young man and very easy to have around the house; his English improved by leaps and bounds during the years I knew him; I encouraged him to embark on an Open University degree; and I was touched when he gave me a signed copy of the photograph book he put together illustrating the history of his home town Ponta Delgada in the Azores. Fortunately, even if guests have sometimes become a bit boisterous late at night (as heavy beer drinking sessions in the pub have been followed by whisky-imbibing back at the house), my next door neighbour Mark Jones doesn't seem to have minded:

> Very occasionally, and this is how we know Keith has someone visiting, we get to hear sporadic strains of Doris Day from the wind-up gramophone (he has a nice collection of 78s) or Tom Lehrer from the record player. I wish he'd turn them up a bit: we really have to strain to hear the words!

During the decade 1994—2004, either in Bristol or Bath, Peter Allender and I accompanied each other to the theatre on about sixty occasions. Indeed, as Peter emphasises:

> These ten years marked the high point of our theatre-going. It's remarkable just how regular it was. The main difficulty we had was deciding what *not* to go and see.

And I saw over twenty further productions, either on my own or with other people, as well. At Bristol Old Vic's Theatre Royal Peter and I saw at least four Shakespeare plays: a sparkling rendering of *Twelfth Night* (1994), enjoyed both by us and Peter's teenage son Robin; *Much Ado About Nothing* (1996), perhaps my favourite Shakespearean comedy; an irritatingly trendy treatment of *Macbeth* (1997); and a more satifyingly traditional staging of *Henry IV Part 1* (2002). We also saw several other period dramas: *Brief Lives* (1997), based on the seventeenth-century writings of the idiosyncratic John Aubrey and much enhanced by a splendidly imaginative set; Georges Farquhar's cheerful early eighteenth-century romp *The Beaux Stratagem* (1996) and John Gay's *The Beggar's Opera* (2002), of about the same vintage; Fanny Burney's puzzlingly neglected early nineteenth-century comedy *A Busy Day* (2000) and *Frankenstein: A Truly Monstrous Experiment* (2001), a surrealistic modern entertainment inspired by Mary Shelley's gothic masterpiece written shortly after the end of the Napoleonic Wars; and, in 1995, Peter even managed to overcome my reluctance to enter the gloomy world of Anton Chekhov's *Three Sisters*. In complete contrast, in 1998, we saw *The Ghost Train*, when Ian Lavender took the lead in an atmospheric production of fellow BBC sitcom *Dad's Army* actor Arnold Ridley's 1925 play. Reginald Rose's compelling *Twelve Angry Men* (1996) had a superb cast (including Timothy West, Tim Healy and Kevin Whately) and we even went along to Tony Robinson's extraordinary *Maid Marian and her Merry Men: The Musical* in the same year. At the Bristol Old Vic, too, I saw Terence Rattigan's gripping wartime play *Flare Path* (1995); Cliff Burhouse and I went to see *Neville's Island*, 'a comedy in thick fog by Tim Firth', when he visited me (also in 1995); and Peter Weiss's *Marat/Sade* (1996) certainly provided a chilling and unforgettable theatrical experience. As for the adjoining New Vic studio theatre, Peter Allender particularly recollects Bristol Old Vic Theatre School productions we saw there sporting 'enormous casts of extraordinarily talented students': John Marston's 1605 play *The Dutch Courtesan* in 1996, for instance, a nineteenth-century stage adaptation of Oliver Goldsmith's 1766 novel *The Vicar of Wakefield* in 2002 and, the following year, a brave attempt to breathe life into William Shakespeare's rarely performed *King John*. Inevitably, too, almost all our visits to the Bristol Old Vic involved post-matinee recuperation in nearby King Street pubs such as the *Old Duke* and *Naval Volunteer*. At the Bristol Hippodrome over these years I also saw a string of musicals, among them Rodgers and Hammerstein's *Oklahoma* (1994), Willy Russell's *Blood Brothers* (1995), Leslie Bricusse's *Scrooge* (1996), Tim Rice and Andrew Lloyd Webber's *Evita* (1996) and George Gershwin's *Crazy for You* (1997), as well as the occasional opera such as Verdi's *Il Trovatore* (with Peter Allender, Pedro Cordeiro and Alan Sutton in 2003). The pubs nearest the Hippodrome, however, tended to be crowded, noisy and only too resistible!

Over thirty of the productions Peter and I saw together between 1994 and 2004 were at the splendid Theatre Royal in Bath. 'I loved the routine we established when visiting Bath', Peter himself recalls, commencing with:

> ... the ten minute train journey from Bristol, walking to the theatre past the abbey, and time for a pint before the performance (hopefully only one) in the

Garrick's Head. Until about 2001 this was a genuine pub, as well as a theatrical one—photos of famous actors and actresses who had played next door, posters all over the place. The odd living famous face was also sometimes to be seen at the bar. Keith Waterhouse was a regular, brooding over a mineral water. The only time I ever saw him smile was when you once greeted me from the door and he obviously recognised a fellow emigré from the West Riding of Yorkshire. Then the *Garrick's Head* was vandalised and turned into a soulless wine bar, robbing it of its atmosphere, most of its customers and, sadly, a great barmaid of the old school: well-preserved, as long as you didn't get too close, probably the wrong side of sixty, yet smiling, friendly, efficient and full of character.

Particularly after the *Garrick's Head* was wrecked, Peter also remembers that:

> ... we would round off the play with more pints in one of the little pubs with which Bath seems to abound (the *Volunteer Rifleman's Arms* and the *Coeur de Lion* were our favourites), before the train back to Bristol and a taxi from Temple Meads to the *Annexe* (for yet more pints!). One night, indeed, when there were no trains to be had from Bath, we had to get a taxi all the way back to Bristol.

Again, we saw a most eclectic range of productions, not all of them to our taste: an adaptation of Evelyn Waugh's *A Handful of Dust* (1994) which, Peter recalls, he 'slept through, apart from a few loud moments', as he was 'suffering badly from jet lag' at the time; an appalling rendering of Shakespeare's *Antony and Cleopatra* (1995), with Vanessa Redgrave as a virtually sexless Cleopatra and a set that most nearly resembled an ancient Egyptian rubbish dump; and *The Shakespeare Revue* (1997), a most peculiar and irritating concoction, not to be excused by Peter's comment that, since he was marking A-Level at the time, nothing could have distracted him anyway. Most of the plays we saw in. Bath during these years, however, were well worth the journey and several had first-rate actors in leading roles: in 1994, for instance, David Suchet's portrayal of the great English comic Sid Field in *What a Performance* was entirely convincing; Miriam Margolyes was perfectly cast in the title role of Frank Marcus's *The Killing of Sister George* and so was Leo McKern in Harold Brighouse's *Hobson's Choice* (both in 1995); Alan Bates' performance in Simon Grey's *Life Support* (directed by Harold Pinter in 1997) was superb, as was Tom Conti's in Keith Waterhouse's hilarious *Jeffrey Bernard is Unwell* (directed by Ned Sherrin in 2000); and Richard Briers obviously relished playing Prospero in Shakespeare's *The Tempest* (2002). Touring companies, moreover, brought plays by some of England's finest dramatists to Bath over the decade: Christopher Marlowe's *The Jew of Malta* (1999); William Shakespeare's *Henry V* (1997); John

Vanbrugh's *The Provoked Wife* (1994) and *The Relapse* (1998); Oscar Wilde's *Lady Windermere's Fan* (2000), *The Importance of Being Earnest* (2001) and *A Woman of No Importance* (2002); Noel Coward's *Hay Fever* (1999), *Star Quality* (2001) and *Present Laughter* (2003); J. B. Priestley's *Dangerous Corner* (1995) and *I Have Been Here Before* (1996); Terence Rattigan's *The Browning Version* (2000); Joe Orton's *What the Butler Saw* (1995); Tom Stoppard's *Rosencrantz and Guildernstern are Dead* (1996) and *The Real Inspector Hound* (1999); and Alan Bennett's *Forty Years On* (1997), *Talking Heads* (2000) and *Single Spies* (2002). Other plays ranged from Molière's *School for Wives* (1996) and *Tartuffe* (1998), William Wycherley's Restoration comedy *The Country Wife* (1997) and Edward Ravenscroft's *The London Cuckolds* (1998) and Henrik Ibsen's *Hedda Gabler* (1997), to Michael Frayn's *Noises Off*, John Mortimer's *A Voyage Round My Father* and Arthur Miller's *Broken Glass* (all in 1995). And, although the Theatre Royal's stage was far from ideal for big American musicals I also saw Rodgers and Hammerstein's *Carousel* in Bath in 2000 and, in 2001, Leonard Bernstein's *West Side Story*.

Ever since the late 1950s I had gone out of my way to see Julian Slade and Dorothy Reynolds' whimsical musical *Salad Days* whenever opportunity arose. Roger Kitching, regular theatre-going buddy of my teenage years, was also very fond of this hauntingly tuneful show and, in 1994, he deliberately journeyed from Cornwall to Bristol so we could enjoy seeing it together once more and, for a fleeting moment, recapture our long lost youth. We were not disappointed! When a sympathetic revival directed by Ned Sherrin came to Bath Theatre Royal in 1997, I naturally went to that as well. A few years later I was to see *Salad Days* yet again, almost certainly for the last time. Originally written as an end-of-season entertainment for the Bristol Old Vic Company in 1954, June 2004 marked the fiftieth anniversary of its first staging and the BOV Theatre School, most aptly, now decided to put it on once more in its old home. Peter Allender and I simply couldn't resist going along to a matinee. In a letter to Roger Kitching the week before, indeed, I remarked that 'I'm really looking forward to seeing it'; however, I added, 'I hope they don't bugger about with it: I shall feel strongly inclined to heckle if they do'. After the performance I wrote to him again:

> *Salad Days* was a bit jazzed up (but not appallingly so) and the cast used body mikes (which I don't like). Nevertheless, it was a very enjoyable afternoon. The theatre was packed. About two thirds of the audience seemed to be aged 55-90+ (wheelchairs and zimmer frames everywhere) and the rest BOV students: virtually nothing in between: The lads and lasses in the stalls were very lively too, reacting vigorously to the antics of their mates on stage. Reprises lasted for ages and many of the audience joined in. All great fun.

This seemed a most fitting end to half a century of theatre-going and I haven't been to a live production since.

At the beginning of November 2004, I despatched yet another letter to Roger Kitching:

> I'm booked to give my last ever public performance at the University of the West of England on Wednesday 15 December (for the Historical Association and UWE history students): a two hour entertainment entitled *The Topsy Turvy World of Gilbert and Sullivan: Late Nineteenth-Century England as Portrayed in Musical Theatre*, illustrated by D'Oyly Carte recordings of some of the comic songs. I've done it before (the last time in Huddersfield just before I retired to Bristol) and deliberately encourage audience participation by distributing handouts of the relevant lyrics. Perhaps you'd like to come along?

This two hour extravaganza was almost thirty years old by 2004, in fact, and my enthusiasm for Gilbert and Sullivan had an even longer pedigree. Indeed, the very first time I saw a Savoy Opera was as a young teenager when Roger Kitching and I went along to an amateur staging of *Trial By Jury* in a Huddersfield church hall. I was hooked. Soon afterwards I enjoyed the first of many performances of the operas by the D'Oyly Carte Opera Company and over the next few decades saw virtually all of them (popular ones such as *HMS Pinafore, The Mikado, Iolanthe* and *The Gondoliers* on numerous occasions). In 1998 I even persuaded Peter Allender, no great lover of Gilbert and Sullivan, to accompany me to an unorthodox West Yorkshire Playhouse touring production of *The Pirates of Penzance* at Bath's Theatre Royal and, at the same theatre in 2001, I also saw a splendidly performed *Yeomen of the Guard* by Carl Rosa Opera: this, and the rarely performed *Patience* (lampooning Oscar Wilde and the aesthetic movement he virtually personified) are perhaps my favourite Gilbert and Sullivan operas. As for my own two hour entertainment (explaining and illustrating the rich satirical content of the operas, on topics ranging from the law, the army and the navy to the idiosyncracies of later Victorian political life), I first put it together in about 1976 for an Open University Summer School at York. I gave it another airing at Huddersfield Polytechnic soon afterwards, as Keith Laybourn reminds me:

> I particularly remember you giving a superb double lecture on Gilbert and Sullivan, during which you and the audience were regularly replenished with beer. This certainly helped encourage the community singing!

A few months before moving to Bristol, I dug it out again, this time for a largely student audience assembled in a conference room above a Huddersfield pub.

For the final performance at UWE, my neighbour Mark Jones put together a new CD for me; Peter Fleming operated the technology; and several friends, among them Peter Allenders, Roger Kitching, Mike Stammers and a regular drinking mate Keith Tucker came along. An apt swansong, perhaps, to so many years revelling in musical theatre *and* trying to show that not all history is boring and impenetrable.

Although I've never had any interest in making a name for myself in the media, I have dabbled a bit in radio and television, particularly since moving to Bristol in 1994. Radio interviews on historical topics are pleasant enough to undertake occasionally and, as recently as June 2005, I recorded a few snippets about Richard III's father Richard Duke of York at the BBC in Bristol for a Radio 4 programme *Making History*. Television, by contrast, isn't to my taste at all and I don't come across particularly well on the box. Even so, in 2000, I only narrowly escaped serious exposure on Channel 4. Early in the year I travelled north to Granada Television in Manchester to discuss three possible programmes on the Wars of the Roses. I came up with a range of suggestions about approach and content, especially focussing on the roles of Henry VI, Edward IV and Richard III, and even expressed a cautious willingness to act as historical adviser. Further meetings followed in Ludlow and Bristol. Then, and much to my surprise, it was suggested I might present the series. I wasn't very enthusiastic, not least because of the amount of travelling around the country it would inevitably entail. I did agree, however, to submit myself to the ordeal of making a so-called screen test. Filming took place at Micklegate Bar, in York, and Sandal Castle, near Wakefield, in September 2000. I didn't enjoy the experience much and soon became convinced., too, that I wasn't very good. The only consolation was visiting Huddersfield for a final time and meeting up with Michael Jones in Wakefield: indeed, I even conducted an interview with him amidst the ruins of Sandal Castle, acutely aware that he was much better in front of the camera than I was. In another sequence, I also insisted on smoking a cigarette, perhaps unconsciously hoping to emphasise my political incorrectness as a would-be presenter. If so, it worked. The commissioning editor at Channel 4 didn't take to me at all and the series was never made. I was massively relieved!

In the spring of 2001 I received a telephone call from a Clifton-based company Available Light Productions concerning *The History Trail*, a series of television programmes planned for ITV (West) in the autumn. Specifically, I was quizzed about the potential of the battle of Nibley Green. An almost forgotten skirmish fought on 20 March 1470, it was the most dramatic product of a long-running feud in Gloucestershire between the Berkeley and Lisle families; more than that, it has also traditionally been regarded as the last private battle ever fought on English soil. Since I knew little about either feud or battle, I suggested the company contact my UWE colleague Peter Fleming who did. Soon afterwards a meeting was arranged with the production team; well primed in advance by Peter, he and I went along together: and, for reasons that escaped me then and still do, I ended up as the programme's joint presenter; indeed, we now found ourselves dubbed 'two Bristol historians who have spent their professional lives trying to uncover many of the darker secrets of the Middle Ages'. Shortly before filming commenced in July 2001, the director put together an outline of the programme's content, emphasising that:

> As this is a history trail, we need to bring out the sense of following the story and discovering things (almost all of which we will already know, of course!). I would like us to discover where the battlefield is as part of the trail rather than show the audience straight away. Hence why we really need to begin at Berkeley castle.

So we did, with Peter and I talking on camera to both the castle's current owner (still a Berkeley) and the family archivist. At the probable site of the battle itself we interviewed a local expert on the skirmish, quizzically observed an archer in period costume shooting arrows at a water melon, and even feigned enthusiasm for an ancient tree where, according to legend, local children had watched the action from the safety of its branches. The final sequence of all was filmed in the study of my Bristol house! All very surrealistic but not uninteresting; the director Richard Van Enden certainly knew what he wanted; and, by and large, he got it. The main problem was that England was experiencing a heat wave that summer and we must have sweated buckets. Indeed Lyn Sheppard, a barmaid in my local pub at the time, specifically remembers:

> ... the time you were filming a television programme on probably the hottest day of the year. You walked into the pub with a face like a boiled lobster and blisters on your nose, a sight I will never forget. You certainly needed a pint or two that day!

The programme itself turned out rather better than I'd expected, not least because Peter Fleming proved himself a very competent TV presenter and even I came across reasonably well. A couple of years later he and Michael Wood, a former MA student of ours, published *Gloucestershire's Forgotten Battle: Nibley Green 1470*. In its foreword they kindly remarked that 'Keith Dockray has provided inspiration, encouragement and good humour, as usual', while Peter inscribed the copy he gave me: 'With fond memories of tree-hugging!'.

Early in 2002 Richard Sanders of Spire Films came to Bristol to discuss a programme on Richard III he was making for Channel 4. He and I got well oiled together in a local pub and he departed back to Oxford with several pages of no doubt increasingly illegible notes of our meeting. I had little desire to appear on the box again and certainly didn't fancy a trip to London to film an interview; however, when I was offered a lift from door to door I could hardly refuse. A few days before the ordeal early in November 2002, Richard Sanders wrote to me:

> We are all set for our Richard III interviews. Yours will be fairly general. I know you have done TV before, and I'm sure you are aware of this, but the key is to keep it simple. Bear in mind most viewers will only be dimly aware of who Richard III was. Don't feel the need to be too formal. Blunt is good! Modern analogies always go down well too.

I dutifully followed his advice and, rather to my surprise, enjoyed the experience, not least visiting the Society of Antiquaries' splendid London headquarters for the first time ever and meeting up there with fellow interviewee Tony Pollard. By the time the programme was transmitted on 3 January 2004, however, I'd almost forgotten about it. Tony Robinson presented and, as Tony Pollard wrote to me soon afterwards, the result was:

> ... surprisingly better than I expected. Tony Robinson is quite clever. It seemed to me and Michael Jones that he had got all his information from us, from our recorded interviews, and then worked it up into a neat script. For a while he looked as though he was going to do the Ricardian whitewash, then nicely switched. In his script I recognised all sorts of phrases and ideas that could only have come from you, me, Michael and Anne Sutton.

I was amazed at how many people I knew saw the programme, among them several regulars in my local pub, Keith Laybourn and, even though he was in Spain at the time of transmission, Cliff Burhouse.

'I've never quite understood how Keith can be such a good historian', mused Vivienne Haley in March 2004, 'yet at the same time find travelling any distance so abhorrent'. She certainly has a point and, no doubt, my distaste for visiting archives over the years partly reflected this; so did my determination never to learn to drive or own a car; and my lack of enthusiasm for holidays in general, and venturing abroad in particular, has been an obvious manifestation of the same phenomenon. In recent years, moreover, my aversion to travel has been compounded by smoking bans on public transport, especially trains, since smoking even more cigarettes than usual had always helped counter the stress of getting from place to place. Since 2002, in fact, I've rarely ventured further than Bath and, now, I avoid even the shortest of bus rides if I possibly can. Hence, too, why I've never bothered to get the reduced fare travel pass for the elderly to which I'm presumably entitled.

Professional needs, theatre-going and, occasionaly, responding to invitations from friends explain most of the travelling I have undertaken since returning to Bristol in 1994. For a number of years I steeled myself to endure the four hour train journey to Huddersfield although, as I remarked in a letter to Tony Pollard in September 1995, 'the nicest thing about going back to Huddersfield is the sense of relief, on leaving again, that I no longer have to live there anymore'. My last visit to Huddersfield was in September 2000; Peter Fleming drove me to York for a conference in April 2002; and I haven't set foot in Yorkshire since. Indeed, as I wrote to former Huddersfield student Neil Scott in January 2004:

> I doubt whether I'll ever visit the north again. I've now developed a profoundly deep aversion to travel. I don't drive, as you know, and I hate modern trains: cramped, non-smoking, full of mental defectives on mobile phones and, of course, almost invariably late.

Nor have I visited London since 2002 and I have no desire ever to do so again. The last West End production I saw, perhaps appropriately, was *Gross Indecency: The Three Trials of Oscar Wilde* at the Gielgud Theatre on Shaftesbury Avenue in 1999. Otherwise, since the mid-1990s, I've occasionally joined Peter Fleming and UWE students on coach trips, more often than not to castles in south Wales; I recall visiting none-too-distant cathedrals and abbeys such as Hereford and Tewkesbury; and, courtesy of fellow steam locomotive enthusiast Keith Tucker and his car, Peter Allender and I have made several visits to the Severn Valley Railway and, once, sampled the West Somerset Railway as well. Dennis and Di Collinson persuaded me to visit them in south Devon two or three times and, in 1998, I journeyed to Plymouth (almost certainly for the last time) for alcohol-laden celebrations to mark Mike Allen's fiftieth birthday. Several times, too, I've met up with Tony Saul and his wife Rosemary in Newport, mutually convenient for driving to castles such as Chepstow. By 2005, however, I could no longer face even a short train journey, so Tony and Rosemary came to Bristol that year instead.

Since visiting France with Charles Ross in the summer of 1969, I hadn't been abroad at all. In October 1998, however, curiosity got the better of me and I spent a few days in Amsterdam. I certainly wouldn't have travelled there on my own but, when I asked Peter Allender if he fancied joining me, his enthusiasm soon turned my rather vague notion of visiting the city into reality. Peter organised the trip and, as he recalls:

We flew to Amsterdam from Bristol Airport in a Fokker jet-prop, quite a small plane, and I remember there being quite a lot of turbulence. Yet, although this was your first flight, you took it in your stride: more than I did! On arrival, for some reason, there was a chauffeur-driven Mercedes waiting for us, and its friendly driver even apologised for the rainy weather. 'Holland would be a beautiful country', he declared, 'if only they put a roof over it'.

We stayed in a very pleasant hotel, a converted diamond factory apparently, and centrally situated. Throughout our stay the weather remained wet and windy; indeed, the streets seemed to be littered with abandoned blown-inside-out umbrellas. It hardly bothered us at all. On the first night, after several hours drinking, we got hopelessly lost until finally, at 1.30 in the morning, we were pointed in the right direction by a young girl cyclist. Once Peter realised the canals were circular not straight, however, his sense of direction proved remarkable. Just as well since, left to myself, I would never have found my way anywhere. Naturally, we did most of what was expected of visitors to Amsterdam, including spending a few very pleasant hours in the Rijksmuseum, visiting Anne Frank's house, and enjoying a canal cruise. We even sampled the city's splendid, if rather alarming, trams. One night, too, we rapidly toured its extraordinary red light district, even though sex was not on our agenda. Left to myself, no doubt, I would have been even more adventurous (especially as the area's streets and bars seemed so remarkably unthreatening). I'd probably have sampled the cannabis cafes as well and, maybe, both the Hash Marihuana and Erotic museums. Sadly, Peter managed to keep me on the straight and narrow! What we certainly did do, as he fondly remembers, was visit a range of bars:

> The first bar we went into was called *Nellies* and it was also the only one we sampled where no one spoke English. This did not stop you getting on very well with the bar staff (both male and female), though, and before long the owner (Nellie herself) was taking us through her photo albums. Sadly, we never found that bar again. The bar nearest the hotel was a rather ramshackle place and seemed to be run by students for their friends. Nevertheless, we seemed to fit in there too. And we drank in quite a few other bars as well, among them the very pleasant *Hansel and Gretel*, right opposite the Rijksmuseum.

All in all, despite the travelling, a most enjoyable experience.

In July 2000 Peter Allender and I ventured abroad together again, this time at the invitation of Alan Sutton whose publishing company Tempus had a flat in Tours. Peter captures the essence of our few days in France nicely:

We went by Eurostar, changing at Lille onto the French TGV to Tours. We travelled around the southern outskirts of Paris, stopping at Charles de Gaulle airport station only a couple of hours before Concorde crashed nearby. Alan and Pedro treated us very well, showed us Tours, its impressive cathedral, and a wonderful steak restaurant which was obviously home from home for Alan. Pedro had also discovered the only Portuguese restaurant in Tours, so I was able to enjoy the country's famous salted cod. You firmly resisted the temptation.

Sadly, among my many faults, is a suspicion of fancy foreign food! As Peter also recalls, however, we both enjoyed being driven around the French countryside in Alan's Range Rover (not a common sight in that area) and, even more, visiting 'the medieval house he had recently bought, believed to have been an inn in the time of Joan of Arc'. In November 2001 we visited Alan and Pedro again, this time in Ostend. We flew from Heathrow to Brussels, travelling on to Ostend by train, where we found the pair of them occupying a rather luxurious flat. Apart from visiting a neighbourhood restaurant where Alan was welcomed as a regular, Peter and I inevitably sought out local bars. The first we visited, near the harbour, was pleasant enough, at any rate until a crowd of British lager louts turned up. We fled and, fortunately, then found a quieter bar; we remained there for most of the afternoon; and, in the evening, returned with Alan and Pedro. Peter remembers that:

> ... it wasn't long before you became one of the family and we were even entertained by the owner's pet cockatoo whose party trick was to reduce newspapers to neat strips with his beak. The evening's cabaret was even more to your taste as, for some unknown reason, bar staff and customers (apart from us) celebrated an Ostend Saturday night by enthusiastically cross-dressing and enjoying themselves thoroughly. So did we, watching them.

The high point of the trip, for me, was the few hours we spent in Bruges. As I wrote to Tony Pollard soon after we returned to England:

> I've just spent a very pleasant few days with Alan Sutton in Belgium, most notably discovering the treasures of Bruges for the first time, those splendid brick churches and fifteenth-century paintings in particular. Mind you, I'll probably best remember quite the most repellent Catholic shrine I've ever seen, supposedly constructed to house a phial of Christ's blood and, certainly, completely untouched by the Reformation.

Recollecting our foreign jaunts in 2006, Peter Allender commented ruefully: 'You seemed to take to it all so well, I envisaged a future of our sharing visits to many European cities'. Like him, I certainly enjoyed visiting the Netherlands, Belgium and France, but not the stressful anticipation of travelling or, indeed, the journeys themselves very much: the non-smoking express coach from Bristol to Heathrow, for instance, and the bustling airport itself, I found profoundly unappealing. If I ever venture abroad again, it will probably be to a European country where voluntary euthanasia is legal in order to get myself humanely put down should I have the misfortune to contract a painful terminal illness.

Although abandoning Huddersfield for Bristol in 1994 marked a dramatic change in my life, it was a change of place rather than lifestyle. I continued to spend far more, during an average week, on beer and cigarettes than food, and socialising in pubs remained my principal leisure pursuit. For a few years I enjoyed visiting a variety of Bristol pubs but, gradually, I became less and less adventurous. This was partly the result of advancing years but mainly because so many traditional pubs were wrecked in the 1990s. Big breweries, concerned only to maximise profits, transformed many locals into barn-like establishments with little or no character; televisions proliferated, as did the number of customers mindlessly watching football or similarly tedious sports; irritatingly loud and unpleasant pop music continuously blaring out began to make conversation difficult if not impossible; more and more pubs became primarily eating rather than drinking venues; and, instead of keeping bored and noisy children out, too many managements began positively to welcome them in. The nearby *Golden Lion*, for instance, not only got rid of its quiet lounge but even turned itself into a pseudo-Irish theme pub, glorifying in the name *Finnegan's Wake*. Another became *Bar Oz*, pseudo-Australian this time, catering almost exclusively for a young lager-drinking passing trade.

By the end of the 1990s only the *Sportsman and Annexe Inn* remained bearable, at any rate until about 9-30pm or so. This was a large complex, consisting of two pubs and a separate restaurant, all under the same management. The *Sportsman* was a huge and largely characterless establishment, with an enormous television at one end and much of the floor space occupied by pool tables; however, it did sell well-kept real ale. Its female bar staff tended to be young and friendly, among them Laura Gregory, who recalled in 2004:

> I first met Keith three or four years ago in the *Sportsman*. I found him very funny from the start and knew we'd get on well. We have. Before long he told me he was an academic historian and he didn't fit my picture of what an academic should be like at all: prim and proper, I imagined, not sitting at the bar chain-smoking and swigging pints of beer, occasionally reading, more often talking about sex.

Barmen in the *Sportsman* tended to be young too, as well as pleasantly good-looking lads; they didn't seem to mind my occasionally outrageous banter; and a couple of them even once invited me along to a party where, despite the fug of cannabis smoke, I soon realised I was about thirty years older than almost anyone else there: fortunately, there wasn't a trace of ageism, nor homophobia for that matter. The *Sportsman*, in fact, became my favoured late afternoon drinking haunt for several years, when I often ended up chatting to other middle-aged teatime regulars, amicably sharing the place with local students and muscular pool-playing lads fresh from a day's plumbing, roofing or whatever. For two or three years my neighbour Mark Jones was also a frequent teatime drinker in the *Sportsman* and he certainly paints a vivid picture of how I seemed to him when we met up there:

> Perhaps the first impression one got of Keith, at the hazy, unsteady-legged cusp of afternoon and evening, was of an often theatrically-opinionated, chain-smoking northerner (educated variety) declaiming about something or other—probably the pointlessness of computers and e-mail or the need to legalise voluntary euthanasia—at the bar. The second impression was that, although he had been saying for the previous twenty minutes that the current pint would be his last, he'd then have another, and probably another after that. There was a sort of inevitability about it.

Lunchtimes and early evenings often found me next door in the *Annexe*, very occasionally as part of a single extended session lasting anything up to ten hours. Truly colossal hangovers, not surprisingly, prevented such massive over-indulgence becoming too regular.

For years Peter Allender and I met up at least once or twice a week in the *Annexe*. Indeed, Peter recalls, he had:

> ... drunk intermittently in the *Annexe* since about 1980. During the 1980s, however, both it and the *Sportsman* went through a lean time. Someone even tried to turn the *Sportsman* into a night club until, not surprisingly, the neighbours got it closed. The *Annexe*, meanwhile, became shabby and run down, a speciality being its ripped cushions. One of my friends called it the 'National Front' pub because staff and customers seemed mainly to be crop-headed and prone to express loud, ultra-right wing sentiments whenever the opportunity arose, or even when it did not.

Peter became a regular in the *Annexe* early in the 1990s, by which time it had acquired not only new cushions and carpets but also a customer-friendly management team, Roger Morgan and his wife Carole. Roger, he adds, was:

... one of the best landlords I have ever come across and, in his time, the television was only turned on for special occasions. My abiding memory of Roger and you, though, is of his sitting down with us to watch the Nibley Green TV programme you and Peter Fleming had made.

Neil Wellman, another *Annexe* regular for several years, commented in 2004:

> Originally the skittle alley of the County Ground Hotel, the *Annexe* is now a public bar with a distinct hint of a drinking club and a heady atmosphere of spilt beer, acrid smoke and stale old men. Many believe that Dr W.G.Grace the cricketer once stayed there. Some say he never left!

Neil also regretted the passing of 'the sadly deceased landlord' Roger 'to whom all real ale drinkers were grateful'; as for me, he emphasised that:

> Keith, or rather 'Professor Keith' (his *Annexe* soubriquet) has been a regular for years. He is usually to be seen rubbing shoulders with other bar-side stalwarts or, alternatively, he might be engaged in conversation around one of the tables, sometimes with a group of cronies, at others with an earnest young man.

Lyn Sheppard, also in 2004, reminisced:

> I started work at the *Annexe* as a barmaid early in 1994, under the excellent tuition of Roger and his wife Carole. A backstreet pub, it tended to be rather quiet during a lunchtime session, with mainly regular customers. I probably first noticed Keith soon after I started there. He always struck me as a slightly eccentric character, with his battered briefcase and armfuls of notes. He soon became a regular lunchtime customer. He seemed rather quiet at first, and certainly stood out from our usual lunchtime clientele, but always polite and friendly. I remember him sitting at the bar, pint mug of Boddingtons, packet of cigarettes, and the ever present bag, into which he would delve and pull out armfuls of paper on which he would then make notes. For us southerners he also had the strange habit of asking for a head on his pint and he was quick to complain if I didn't get it right. He also occasionally ran out of fags half way through a session and, in response, Carole got in the habit of bringing in a spare pack: she knew that, even if he'd allegedly only come in for a pint or two, he might well still be there four hours later.

'Keith soon became a favourite with Roger and myself', Lyn added:

> ... because he always had an amusing story to tell and lunchtime sessions were less boring when he was in the pub. He and I soon discovered we were both very fond of cats and used to chat for ages about our respective animals, their strange ways and habits. From there we developed a friendship and he started to talk about his past. I soon learned that he wrote books and lectured occasionally, and that he was an expert on medieval history. Hence why be became known as 'Professor Keith'. He had a way of talking that made people want to hear what he was saying, and we would have long discussions about Richard III. Through him, I found that history could be interesting!

Steve Gould, again in 2004, expressed similar sentiments:

> When I began working at the *Annexe* as a barman in 2000, Keith was already a regular drinker there. Roger Morgan, the typical traditional pub landlord, a dying breed, soon told me he was an academic who taught and wrote history. Hence why he was affectionately known in the pub as 'Professor Keith' or 'the Prof'. I didn't feel intimidated by this and, indeed, if Keith had taught me history at school I might have found it more interesting than I did. Another *Annexe* regular, after seeing Keith on TV one night, remarked that he'd never realised what a clever man he was.

Occasionally, I met colleagues in the *Annexe*, most frequently Peter Fleming, as well as almost invariably introducing the place to visitors from Huddersfield or other parts of the country. Keith Stenner, whom I got to know through the Richard III Society, also recalls that:

> Local lectures often ended with a visit to Keith's spiritual home, the *Annexe*. Here the topic of the evening might either be developed or lost amidst any number of new subjects, all engaged with his ready wit and equally ready cynicism. As a result evenings passed all too quickly, amidst wide ranging conversation, real ale, the fug of rising tobacco smoke and, always, much laughter.

More often than not, if I went to the *Annexe* on my own (as I usually did), I chatted to other regulars at the bar, and an interestingly mixed bunch they were. Among them was a former Huddersfield Polytechnic chemistry student, originally from Barnsley; our paths had never crossed in the north but we often reminisced about both our Yorkshire roots and the college; occasionally our conversations became seriously intellectual; and, more than once, we drank so much together that he ended up crashing out back at my place. Another northerner was on the maintenance staff of Clifton College, so he and I often exchanged anecdotes about public school life and how it had changed (or not) since my years at Plymouth College. Then there were two Dorset men, and an electrician friend of theirs, all of whom did repair work on my house at one time or another. More occasionally, I chatted to an actor and a musician: plenty of common ground there. Several *Annexe* regulars have even committed their impressions of me to paper. Keith Tucker, for instance, recalls that it was he who first nicknamed me 'the Prof, since there were three or four regulars called Keith'; moreover, he adds, 'I enjoyed his company and we had good chats, as well as usually managing to polish off a few pints together'. 'My first impression of Keith', recollects Mike Bush, was:

> ... of an intelligent man but, probably, liable to prove a boring old sod as well. Later, I concluded that, if he had been a history teacher at my school, what a lot I would have learnt. It turned out to be very interesting, in fact, to talk to an *Annexe* regular who was a retired university lecturer and historian, as well as a very likeable gay piss artist.

'A thoroughly nice guy', echoes Dave Moore, 'whom I always enjoyed talking to at the bar, no matter what the subject, and how we laughed at his tales of student drug taking and public schoolmasters thrashing young boarders'. Of course, muses Debbie Gwilym, 'Keith was one of those intellectual bods, but very personable and witty with it: it was always a pleasure to spend time with him and any subject we discussed seemed to produce both laughter and food for thought'. 'Our first impression of Keith', so Alan and Marisa Stevens remember, was that I was:

> ... a quiet man who would sit and observe, making little eye contact at first, tidy in dress and with a briefcase as a constant companion. Later on, under the influence of ale and cigarette fumes and to the accompaniment of taped music in the background, we had many interesting conversations, for Keith was a man who had soaked up and could pass on all manner of information, as well as enjoying a great deal of banter and mickey-taking with us.

Not all conversations in the *Annexe* were confined to the bar. Sometimes a group of us would sit around a table. Two friends of Peter Allender were regular participants: Denis Wright, a sardonic pipe-smoking retired English teacher with a taste for local history, and Simon Forbes, another English teacher, but still condemned to grapple daily with the horrors of modern secondary school life. Neil Wellman, a college lecturer, was another, and his memories are vivid indeed:

My first meeting with Keith is hidden both by the mists of time and many pints but, no doubt, it started with some casual remark or overheard comment. I remember early conversations ranging from Richard III (did he or didn't he murder the Princes in the Tower?), via the never ending battle with new technology (a natural Luddite is Keith) to the difficulty of getting a decent pub sandwich anymore and the evil conspiracy of the medical profession to keep him alive. Later on, while subjects for discussion still included good old standbys such as standards in education (too low), the progress of technology (too far) and the world in general (too fast), they widened to cover a diverse range of more personal and esoteric topics such as Punch and Judy, public school life, the difficulties of proof reading, the sexual proclivities of gay medieval historians (or at least one of them) and what to do when the nanny state finally bans smoking in pubs: he'd emigrate if only his prejudices would let him!

'Throughout these years', Neil concludes, 'one of the pleasures of early evening drinking in the *Annexe* was to see Keith's flannel-clad figure still at the bar after his afternoon stint, stuffing his bar-bought sandwich into his document case ("for later"), and seizing the opportunity for fine talk, intellectual challenge and setting the world to rights once again'.

During the course of 2005 I began to suffer from increasingly deep depression for the first time in many years. I spent more and more time in the pub, chatting to a range of friends and casual acquaintances and drinking vast quantities of beer, yet not feeling much better for it most of the time. When I reached my sixty-second birthday in mid-February 2006, I resolved never to consume alcohol in pubs again and, indeed, only visit them at all in future if friends or visitors insisted. Ironically enough, this was in the very same week the over-powerful health lobby achieved its legislative objective of banning smoking in pubs from July 2007. Traditional English locals have been in decline for years anyway and, no doubt, the smoking ban will eventually finish them off, as they become increasingly hi-jacked by health-crazed middle class folk more interested in food than beer and certainly not the sort of extended beer drinking sessions I enjoyed for so many years. More specifically, ever since Roger Morgan's death in 2003, the *Annexe* had deteriorated. When so many of the pub's regulars turned out for his funeral, me among them, maybe we were already mourning more than just the passing of its long-serving landlord. If so, we were right. In the ensuing months the quality of the *Annexe's* beer became less and less reliable; by February 2006 the pub sported three or four television sets, switched on almost continuously, and it had become virtually impossible to escape their endless diet of sport; and, about then too, the couple of barmen I knew best left as well. As for other nearby pubs, they were even worse, and I certainly had no desire to rub shoulders with lager louts or listen to the irritating ringing of mobile phones. All these considerations helped underpin my decision virtually to give them up after more than forty years. So did the imminent smoking ban. Predominant, however, was the growing conviction that, if I didn't, I might well end up an alcoholic. So far, my dramatic change of lifestyle has proved less traumatic than I had anticipated. Inevitably, I've now become almost a recluse but, remarkably, I hardly miss pubs at all. Anyway, weather permitting, I do still allow myself the occasional couple of hours boozing in the *Annexe* courtyard or garden (more often than not with Peter Allender) where, since the smoking ban came into force, we're rarely on our own for long!

17

Out of the Closet

As a teenager I found it very difficult to come to terms with my homosexuality. I had no desire to be condemned to membership of a widely despised and misunderstood minority but, before long, realised I had no choice in the matter; moreover, I was acutely aware that, if ever caught engaging in sexual activity with another male, I was liable to prosecution, even imprisonment. In response, during my undergraduate years at Bristol University between 1963 and 1966, I deliberately concealed my sexual preferences and led a virtually celibate life. As early as 1957 the Wolfenden Report had recommended that homosexual acts in private between consenting male adults over the age of twenty-one should no longer be a criminal offence but it wasn't until 1967 that the Sexual Offences Act decriminalised adult male homosexual practices, and then only in England and Wales. By then I was already twenty-three years old and, even in the late 1960s and 1970s, I remained cautious about revealing my sexuality to anyone outside a very narrow circle of close friends. Only gradually, as the moral climate became less oppressive in the 1970s, did my self-confidence grow. The 1967 act itself had serious flaws as well. Homosexuality, as such, was not legalised; rather, certain aspects of adult male behaviour in private in England and Wales were decriminalised. The armed forces and merchant navy were explicitly excluded, as a result of powerful lobbying at the time. Field Marshal Lord Montgomery, for instance, had declared in parliament:

> If these unnatural practices are made legal, a blow is struck at the discipline of the British armed forces. Take an infantry battalion. Suppose the men know the officers are indulging in unnatural practices and it is legal and nothing can be done. Take a large aircraft carrier with two thousand men cooped up in a small area. Imagine what would happen in a ship of that sort if these practices crept in.

Legal or not, such practices were certainly not off limits for a few of the sailors I observed in Plymouth's Union Street in the early 1970s! Similarly, a spokesman for the National Union of Seamen had expressed the strong opinion, in 1966, that the presence of homosexuals in the merchant navy 'could give rise to serious conflicts at sea and jealousies which might even lead to violence'. Concern had also been raised about the act's implications for 'authorities at the universities and corresponding institutions': perhaps, remembering my on antics at Huddersfield in the 1980s and early 1990s, this had a certain justification! Scotland, Northern Ireland, the Isle of Man and the Channel Islands were not covered by the act. Homosexuals remained vulnerable to conspiracy charges; any public expression of their sexuality remained firmly taboo; the act encapsulated absurdly restricted definitions of 'consent' and 'in private'; and, since the age of consent was fixed at twenty-one, young homosexuals still remained legally condemned to celebacy. As a result, prosecutions for homosexual offences became more rather than less frequent after 1967, homophobia remained rampant and student friend Peter Allender poignantly remembers that, 'even in the more liberal 1970s,Darlington's first gay pub was trashed within weeks of opening by homophobic soldiers on the rampage from nearby Catterick camp'. Nevertheless, the Sexual Offences Act did help set the scene for further liberalisation of attitudes towards homosexuality in the 1970s (even if not, sadly, the law itself). Unlike the 1950s and 1960s, moreover, homosexuals themselves now felt increasingly able to take the lead in campaigning openly on their own behalf. The Campaign for Homosexual Equality was founded in 1971 and the Gay Liberation Front soon afterwards (although, perhaps, the latter was so radical and outspoken that it actually dissuaded moderate people from becoming more openly tolerant for fear of being branded subversive or anarchist). *Gay News* was founded in 1972 and, before long, I'd become a regular reader. Gay groups emerged within all the main political parties (even the Conservatives), as well as those traditional bastions of working class prejudice, the trades unions. Most importantly, homosexuals in virtually all walks of life very cautiously began to be more open about their sexuality (even come 'out of the closet' altogether).

In the early 1970s, nevertheless, I was probably wise to conceal my own sexuality for the most part, not least from one or two colleagues at Huddersfield Polytechnic. Steve Smith, who became a lecturer in politics at Huddersfield in 1976, certainly recalls a senior historian once remarking that:

> ... he could never work with a homosexual. This struck me as all the more bizarre since you were really beginning to come out sexually at the time. On cue, in you flounced, straight from central casting (as in 'send me as obviously an out/camp/

flamboyant gay man as you can find'). Yet he never seemed to notice, simply saying that was 'just Keith'.

Brendan Evans believes that, for several years, a real obstacle to our becoming more friendly was his feeling that I was probably gay, his 'reluctance to enquire because of the inhibitions of the time', and the blossoming of our friendship once I came out. 'I have no clear recollection of when I first realised you were gay', muses Bill Roberts, but it was 'probably quite early on in our acquaintance'. The first colleague I actually told was Peter Durrans in about 1973, maybe at the urging of his wife Hazel who sussed me out very quickly indeed. Philip Woodfine soon guessed and so did David Wright. David's liberal views on homosexuality rather took me by surprise since, in many ways, he was a social traditionalist: sexual orientation does not matter, he once remarked to me in about the mid-1970s, and people should be judged as people, not in terms of their gender preferences when it came to bedmates. More problematic, or so I thought, were Keith Laybourn and Andrew Taylor, both the sons of Yorkshire miners. Early in 2004 Andy recalled that, when we got to know each other in the later 1970s, I was probably the first openly gay man he'd ever come across; however, he added, 'as far as I was concerned, so what?: it was never an issue for me'. My response to this revelation was typical:

> What a sheltered life you clearly led amidst the coal mines of south Yorkshire. Of course, you must have fondled many a hairy gay buttock in your youth and been the victim of reciprocal embraces. I refer, needless to say, to your pre-polytechnic exploits on the rugby field! Perhaps there's even a connection between our becoming boozing mates and you kissing farewell to oval balls.

For years I misjudged Keith Laybourn, my long-time room mate in the 1980s and early 1990s, completely. I convinced myself that, if he ever found out I was homosexual, it might destroy our friendship. I even warned colleagues who did know never to let on to him! Since I had been here before, as a teenager with Roger Kitching, I should have known better. As Keith himself made clear in a letter of March 2004:

> The fact that you were gay, even if I had known at the time, would have made no difference to our friendship. Since I was from a mining family I'm sure you saw me as coming from an environment which was intensely masculine but, in fact, I always saw myself as someone who cut away from the typical masculine stereotype.

Certainly, when I eventually did tell Keith about my sexual orientation not all that long before I left Huddersfield, he took the news entirely in his stride.

For years I kept quiet about my sexuality when drinking with students too and, no doubt, missed out on many golden opportunities in the 1970s as a result. Yet, perhaps, I needn't have bothered, at any rate if Andy Hook, Neil Scott and Graham Townend are anything to go by. Andy reckons he and his mates sussed me out 'within thirty seconds' of my 'strutting across the lecture theatre with great gusto' during my first lecture to the 1976 intake of BA (Humanities) students; 'if history is detective work', he adds, 'we didn't need any more clues for that one'. Neil recollects that very early on at Huddersfield:

> ... Andy Hook said he thought you might be gay. I said you were just an intellectual and they were all like that. I spent the next three years in a minority of one, saying you were not gay but just an intellectual. I was very naive! I think you 'came out' shortly after we left in 1979. You told me personally in the *Sneyd Arms* at Keele when you were at a conference at the university in 1985.

'Any gossip about you during my student days', comments Graham:

> ... was concerned with your sexuality. It didn't take too long to realise you were a homosexual but that didn't weigh too heavily with any of us. There were the odd silly comments and jokes, so beloved of adolescents who don°t know any better, but the subject never held our attention all that much. Your sexuality was a minor consideration.

My very real fear in the 1970s that, if students found out I was gay, it might seriously compromise or undermine my position as a lecturer probably was largely groundless. In the 1980s and early 1990s, when I was much more open about my sexual preferences, everyone benefited from my more relaxed persona, me most of all.

Soon after I moved to Huddersfield there were a couple of unexpected spin-offs from my Plymouth College years. One Friday teatime in about 1975 a couple of lads I'd taught as sixth formers rolled up at Huddersfield Polytechnic; many pints were consumed; and one of the pair proved entirely unable to cope with large quantities of real Yorkshire ale. After he'd been vigorously sick on the way home and, again, on my doorstep, we manhandled him upstairs, helped him shed his clothes and got him into the double bed in my spare room. He promptly passed out. We both agreed that, rather than risk being vomited over himself, it might be better if his mate slept with me in the other double bed. Although I was probably just as plastered as he was, I remained sufficiently *com-*

pos mentis to realise I was within grasping distance of a very handsome young man. I didn't miss out on the opportunity and he seemed more than happy to sample a new experience as well. When I next met up with him, by which time he was a happily married family man, he told me it was the one and only time he'd ever crossed the sexual divide. Yet, as far as I could tell, he didn't seem to regret what had happened that night at all. What is clear from this, and several similar encounters I've had over the years, is that a straight guy can have the odd gay experience without in any way compromising his own fundamental sexuality. The same goes for me. My powerful homosexual orientation has never been in any way dented by the occasional heterosexual frolic. Another lad I'd taught at Plymouth College also once turned up in Huddersfield and, this time, the outcome was even more unexpected. Again after many pints and back at my house, he reminded me that he'd been a bit of a tearaway at school. As a result several canings had come his way and, ever since, he'd had a real taste for ritualistic punishment! My role in the surrealistic late night entertainment which followed was entirely predictable.

'In the summer of 1972 when we were first at Huddersfield', recalls Philip Woodfine:

> ... you were teaching at a Summer School in York for the Open University. We met up for a drink on the Saturday evening and ended up in York City Rowing Club. After a few drinks I found myself in the urinal, standing beside a stocky-chested leading oarsman and champion drinker. After a minute or two he said to me: 'It's backs against the wall with your mate in there, isn't it?'. I replied, 'Don't worry, you're not his type'. 'Bloody good job', he said, yet adding after a while, 'he can certainly drink though'. The only accolade that mattered. We had a good convivial night and my stock rose in the club, having been regarded as only a moderate pot man up to then.

Philip never mentioned this incident at the time (I didn't even realise then that he'd guessed I was gay) but, clearly, it's just as well I didn't try my luck there! Not much chance of that, even though I was now determined to put an end to my recent spell of near-celibacy. Over the next few years, in fact, I enjoyed a succession of one-night stands, occasionally with men I hardly knew, as well as two or three rather longer sexual liaisons. Sadly, there didn't seem any real alternative. Friends I found sexually attractive seemed invariably to be married and, although I was already convinced that many men are neither 100% straight nor 100% gay, I had no desire to threaten the stable relationships of others. The nearest I came to it was with a fellow actor in *A Midsummer Night's Dream* in 1977 but, in the end, I managed to resist seriously testing the waters. My antics during trips to Blackpool with Peter and Hazel Durrans were more typical and more productive, as Hazel remembers:

> You were more than adept at finding sleeping partners in Blackpool. The time you disappeared from the bar, for instance, only to bounce back a few minutes later having successfully chatted up a waiter.

I certainly remember him too: handsome, muscular and insatiable. I was even more knackered than usual after a night's romp with him! Otherwise, in the 1970s, I occasionally replied to contact ads in *Gay News* (although, perhaps significantly, I never inserted one myself). Several pleasant nights resulted. I recall, for instance, an intense young male nurse from Manchester and a very nicely put together snooker-loving builder from Leeds. Neither these lads nor I were looking for long-term commitment, however, and we had little in common save our sexuality. More firmly etched in my memory are several meetings with a wealthy middle-aged man from north Yorkshire. He was an industrialist who lived in a palatial house near Scarborough, owned a boat and had a well-developed taste for exotic sexual role play. Since he was also a former public school boy, with an interest in both local history and the theatre, we had plenty to talk about between sessions as well. After a few months, however, the novelty of it all wore off; we lost touch; and, no doubt, he soon found himself a new playmate via the pages of *Gay News*. In Huddersfield itself I visited the *Greyhound*, a local gay pub, now and again, but never with any great enthusiasm. Only once did I find an interesting bedmate there when, one night, I noticed an extraordinarily good-looking young man sitting by himself in a corner; he was reading a set text for the Open University course I was tutoring at the time; and this provided a perfect excuse to join him. We hit it off well and, after a few pints, he opened up about himself. Maybe even I was a bit shocked when he told me he was an upmarket rent boy, working out of one of London's classier hotels, who'd obtained a couple of A-Levels at Huddersfield New College a few years earlier and was now anxious to obtain a degree before reaching his sell-by date as a prostitute. He now knew hardly anyone in Huddersfield but still returned to the town occasionally to visit his mother. This lad's fees were well beyond my means and I was amazed, indeed, at just how much he did charge wealthy, mainly foreign, gentlemen for his services. Fortunately, that night, he was on the look out for a younger man who wasn't a punter. I fitted the bill nicely. We met up again several times and even after he went to live in New York, remained in touch. Eventually, encouraged by me, he even completed his Open University degree. More frequently, and in the mainly straight *Commercial* pub this time, I met up with a couple of elderly men who had been a partnership since the early 1950s; among their wide circle of acquaintances was a young bus driver; and he and I had a light-hearted on-and-off fling lasting several years. None of these liaisons amounted to much more than bedroom entertainment, and this suited me very well, but they certainly helped widen my horizons and open my eyes to the sheer variety of sexual pleasure.

In the summer of 1977, for reasons now lost in the depths of time (but surely not in response to medical propaganda!), I stopped smoking. It proved a disastrous error. Before long I came to suspect that my creativity had been seriously compromised by nicotine deprivation; depression set in; and, by the autumn of 1978, suicidal inclinations (absent for over a decade) had also returned with a vengeance. My occasional beer-drinking companions in Huddersfield did include a local psychiatrist but, recalling earlier encounters with an insensitive and unsympathetic (perhaps homophobic) psychotherapist in 1966, I was extremely wary about opening up to him. Eventually, after many pints one night, I did confide in him about my state of mind and, over the next few weeks, allowed him just enough access to my psyche to attempt a diagnosis. To be told I was probably a manic depressive (hence my susceptibility to dramatic mood swings and bouts of hyper-activity) wasn't exactly comforting but he did come up with three pieces of very practical advice: avoid anti-depressants since they merely relieved the symptoms of depression and only temporarily at that; resume smoking cigarettes, if longevity wasn't on my agenda, since nicotine probably was a beneficial stimulant for me; and become much more open about my sexuality. I didn't fancy anti-depressants in 1978 any more than I had a decade earlier and for the same reason: the conviction that I would simply become addicted to them. I started smoking again and have continued to get through two or three packs a day ever since. Most importantly, over the next few months I told more and more people about my sexual orientation. I have rarely received more constructive advice from anyone and, an additional bonus, the psychiatrist and I became regular drinking mates until he moved away from Huddersfield a few years later.

My greatest confidante in the later 1970s was probably Hazel Durrans and, as she recalls, her advice was much the same as the psychiatrist's:

> You were really undecided about whether or not to make your homosexuality public knowledge and we talked at length about it. As I pointed out to you, almost all your friends knew anyway, so why not? You'd really got nothing to lose and everything to gain.

The outcome of all this was what amounted to a coming out party held at my Newsome house in November 1979. Yet, for many of my polytechnic colleagues at least, all it seems to have done was confirm what they already suspected or knew. Steve Smith, for instance, recollects that he 'missed your coming out party but, as far as I was concerned, there was nothing to come out'. Tony Payne, who joined the staff in 1979, comments:

> I don't ever remember being told you were gay. It was just apparent from the outset and not anything that I thought about much at all.

Bill Roberts perhaps says it all:

> I don't think your coming out had a great impact on the regard with which you were held at the polytechnic. Times had changed and attitudes towards homosexuality were different from those we'd grown up with. So, while your coming out was of the utmost importance to you, it was something which those who knew you well took almost for granted.

Maybe, then, all the years of fear and anxiety had been completely unnecessary! In today's more tolerant climate, it certainly seems a strange, almost forgotten, world. Yet, if Christian fundamentalists and Islamic homophobes ever get their way in the future, it could all too easily return. What isn't in doubt is that my decision to come out transformed my personal life. Now I had finally thrown caution to the winds, I could at last enjoy an uninhibited sex life. I never resorted to contact ads again and my visits to gay bars, never frequent, became rarer still. Instead, I could seize every opportunity for bedroom fun and frolics that presented itself, confident that hardly anyone who knew me would be shocked or even taken by surprise anymore. For the rest of my time in Huddersfield I did just that!

In his autobiography *Turning Points*, published in 1976, Lord Wolfenden commented:

> It may well be that it is time to review the whole field of homosexual law reform again, that further changes are due, in one place or another. After nearly twenty years that would not be unreasonable.

Five years later in *Gay Workers: Trade Unions and the Law*, a pamphlet published by the National Council for Civil Liberties in 1981, former Labour cabinet minister Tony Benn pointed out that recent legislation to protect the rights of women and blacks did not cover 'the two million or more homosexuals in Britain' and, in particular, 'serious discrimination against gays' in the work place continued unabated:

> There should be absolute equality in law between heterosexual and homosexual men and women. The present inequality relating amongst other things to the definition of privacy, the differing ages of consent, the exclusion of the Armed Services and Merchant Navy, cannot be justified and must be completely swept away from the statute book. Gay people are also entitled to the same rights in seeking housing or in access to public facilities as any other group.

Unfortunately, by then, Margaret Thatcher's Conservative government was in power and, partly as a result, there was a resurgence of moral conservatism in British society in the early 1980s. Right-wing Tory politicians, advocating a return to traditional moral standards, found ready allies in the religious establishment, spearheaded by the Roman Catholic Church: in 1983, for instance, the Vatican issued a document firmly condemning both masturbation and homosexuality as 'moral disorders' and calling on homosexuals to exercise determined 'self-control'. The arrival of AIDS, widely portrayed in the popular press as a 'gay plague', seemed to add grist to the mill of intolerance. This was certainly not a climate in which further liberalisation of the law in respect of homosexuality could be expected. All that happened in the early 1980s, in fact, was the decriminalisation of male homosexuality in Scotland (1980), Northern Ireland (1982) and the Channel Islands (1983) to bring them into line with England and Wales; there was considerable opposition even to that, most notably the Reverend Ian Paisley's 'Save Ulster from Sodomy' campaign; and all homosexual acts (regardless of whether or not they were in private between consenting adults over twenty-one) remained illegal on the Isle of Man until 1992. In 1988, moreover, there was a step backwards when section 28 of the Local Government Act banning the 'promotion' of homosexuality in schools came into force, enthusiastically backed by Conservative local government minister Michael Howard. Yet, outside Tory ranks at least, there were some promising developments in the 1980s as well: in 1984, for instance, the London Labour MP Chris Smith became the first member of parliament to come out as gay; in 1989 the Stonewall organisation was set up, particularly to fight section 28; and, in 1990, the direct action group Outrage was launched to combat homophobia in both society and its institutions head-on. Lowering the age of consent for homosexual acts was a top priority but there was still widespread opposition to bringing it into line, at sixteen, with that for heterosexuals. John Major, Conservative prime minister in the early 1990s, was at least sufficiently liberal-minded not to block its reduction from twenty-one to eighteen in 1994.

Even after 1979 I didn't broadcast my sexuality from the rafters. All I did was stop trying to conceal it. Most visibly, I began wearing discreet badges featuring a pink triangle (commemorating victims of homophobia in Nazi Germany) or a silver lamda (favoured by contemporary reformers in Britain). Most people didn't recognise the significance of these symbols but, if they asked me (as they not infrequently did), I invariably explained just why I was sporting such labels. When teaching fourteenth-century England to first year polytechnic students, I also began highlighting Edward II's probable homosexual tendencies and their role in moulding his posthumous reputation; similarly, in second year lectures and seminars on William Rufus and James I, I specifically sought to demonstrate how verdicts by contemporary and near-contemporary commentators were coloured by hostility to the rumoured sexual preferences of these kings. Whenever I encountered traces of homophobia in student responses, moreover, I vigorously countered it in terms hinting ever more strongly at my own homosexuality. Inspired by Michael Goodich's *The Unmentionable Vice: Homosexuality in the Later Medieval Period* (1979) and John Boswell's *Christianity, Social Tolerance and Homosexuality: Gay People in Western Europe from the Beginning of the Christian Era to the Fourteenth Century* (1980) in particular, I also began to cover the history of homosexuality in medieval times a bit, most notably in a Historical Association lecture on 'Religion, Sex and Morality in Western Europe during the Middle Ages' (written in 1981): my treatment of the teachings and behaviour of the medieval church was *not* sympathetic! Clearly, by 1983, my homosexuality was common knowledge and, towards the end of that year, I was invited to deliver a public lecture, sponsored by the Huddersfield Polytechnic Politics Society, on 'Politics, Society and Homosexuality in Post-War Britain'. Far more people turned up to hear it than I expected and, although I never explicitly mentioned my own sexual orientation, few can have had much doubt about what it was. Tony Payne obviously came along:

> I remember very strongly you giving a lecture (in an upstairs room of the *Zetland* pub) on the politics of homosexual law reform in the UK. You were unusually nervous and tense because, I guess, it was a more public coming out than perhaps ever before. It is a vivid memory.

Similarly, Brendan Evans comments:

> I well remember a very serious lecture you gave on the case for homosexual law reform. It revealed you in a campaigning role which, while we rarely saw it, was part of your character.

In 1984 the polytechnic published an expanded and footnoted version of this lecture in pamphlet form.

Although always unofficially, as the years went by I became more and more involved in student counselling at Huddersfield. Once my sexual orientation became more widely known after 1979, moreover, gay and lesbian students struggling to come to terms with their own sexuality not infrequently sought me out, whether or not I taught them. Flatteringly, Hazel Durrans even recalls 'having tremendous admiration for you when you started counselling gay folk who needed help'. Even in the later 1980s and early 1990s, homosexually-orientated students did not find it easy to be open about themselves and, until they reached the age of twenty-one, gay lads continued to risk prosecution if they became sexually active, even with each other. My advice to them was simple: ignore the law but be discreet about it. Their fellow students didn't always help much either, as one heterosexual lad I taught rather shamefacedly admits:

> Early on at Huddersfield the lad occupying the room next to mine in our hall of residence opened up to me: the first person he ever told about his sexuality. I boorishly repaid his confidence when, later in the day and pretty drunk, I loudly let the cat out of the bag in the canteen. Disgracefully immature behaviour. Even so, he remained friends with me and, later, he, I and five others shared the same house.

The arrival of AIDS in the early 1980s made for even greater anxiety and, in order to be as helpful as I could, I read widely on the subject. Only in 1987, when the Conservative government finally grasped this wasn't a disease largely confined to homosexual men and intravenous drug users, was an official leaflet 'AIDS: DON'T DIE OF IGNORANCE' issued and a public information campaign launched both in the press and on television. Even during my last year at Huddersfield in 1993/4, two or three students talked to me at length about themselves, most memorably a lad whose parents simply couldn't accept they had a gay son at all.

For a year or two in the 1980s the local police in Huddersfield didn't help much. A former student of mine, now a police officer himself, remembers a cannabis-smoking mate of his having 'a run-in with one of Maggie Thatcher's boot boys' one night 'when he'd been approached and searched on the grounds that his leather jacket, of the sort beloved by bikers, could be regarded as an offensive weapon'. I had the occasional brush with the constabulary myself, most notably a homophobic inspector of the old school. When writing to the German Jew Alfred Josephson in Bristol, I simply couldn't resist resorting to hyperbole:

> The police seem to be conducting a vicious anti-gay crusade in Huddersfield at the moment. As a regular counsellor of gay students these days I've inevitably got involved. I can understand now what it must have been like for homosexuals

in Berlin in the later 1930s. Only the extermination camps are missing and, no doubt, one of our local inspectors would set those up if he could get away with it.

What he did do was target the main gentleman's lavatory in the centre of Huddersfield, employing a pair of good-looking young cops in tight jeans as *agents provocateurs* to trap the unwary into making sexual advances on them. A student I knew fell for the trick, got himself arrested and then came under powerful pressure to plead guilty to such a minor offence. Fortunately, the lad rang me from the police station where, when I arrived, I made it very clear to the inspector what I thought of the behaviour of his underlings and persuaded the student to plead not guilty. The whole story came out in court; I was a character witness; and the lad got off. If looks could have killed, the glare I got from the inspector as we left court would have floored me for ever. I never risked visiting the town centre toilets in Huddersfield again! Not that this was any great deprivation. Even cruising for casual sex in bars, let alone cottaging (trying to make sexual contacts in public lavatories), has never been my forté. Why the playwright Joe Orton so obviously relished such encounters is a mystery to me. I can identify much more closely with the dramatist who subsequently adapted John Lahr's 1978 biography of Orton, *Prick Up Your Ears*, for the screen. 'Living life in Orton's bold, head-on sort of way', declared Alan Bennett in November 2004, was something 'I was never able to do'; more specifically, he added:

> I have never been able to cruise and have never had much inclination to do so. It was partly that, never feeling I would be much of a catch, I saw no point in trawling the streets for someone who might feel differently. And then, too, I was quite hard to please.

Getting to know Kenneth Cook, the polytechnic Anglican chaplain for most of the 1980s, brought home to me with a vengeance the religious and moral quandary facing homosexual clerics. Throughout the time I knew him he was troubled by the dilemma of reconciling his profound Christian beliefs, the harshly homophobic sentiments expressed by several biblical prophets and his sexual orientation. He dealt with it by leading a largely, perhaps entirely, celibate life but it was always very difficult for him. I was never sure whether knowing me, an openly gay athiest who enjoyed a series of casual relationships with young men in the 1980s and made no secret of the fact, helped or hindered him in dealing with his own sexuality. We certainly talked about it often enough and I even had a brief fling with one lad I met through him, if only because the opportunity was clearly there and he wasn't going to grasp it himself. I don't think he was too pleased when he found out, and I'm not proud of my behaviour, but we remained drinking mates nonetheless. The resurgence of homophobic Christian fundamentalism in recent years, even within Anglican ranks, has no doubt only served to compound the misery endured by many gay priests. Very different were my encounters with an astute entrepreneur and businessman in the 1980s and early 1990s, as he himself vividly recalls:

> For someone like myself, too frightened to do anything about my sexuality, exposure to you and your life experiences was rather thrilling. On one visit to Huddersfield you took me to a gay bar to show me what life was like. As it turned out, it was all very innocent, meek and mild—much to my disappointment! The next visit to your den of iniquity was an important milestone in my innocent and naive life. I arrived a little after 8.0pm and we immediately went to the pub. Back at your house it was whisky and chat, followed by my first ever viewing of a gay film—a very sensual French one! I eventually went to bed but it was cold and I had other images floating through my mind. Next day we drove to *Last of the Summer Wine* country [nearby Holmfirth and its surrounding countryside] and that night, after more imbibing, I somehow ended up in your bed. So, during that weekend in Yorkshire, I lost my innocence!

Later on, he adds, 'you were supportive in my attempts to find a boyfriend', even if 'your attempt to seduce him one night after many drinks was not as helpful as it might have been; but, then, I'm aware that an old leopard cannot change his spots!'. Again, despite this deplorable incident, we've remained friends.

By the end of the 1980s I had been openly gay for a decade so, when Robert Perks (a student at Huddersfield in the late 1970s, now curator of oral history for the British Library National Sound Archive) asked me to record a series of tapes for the Hall/Carpenter archive (covering gay and lesbian history), I readily agreed. In March 1990 a splendid young woman turned up at my house in Huddersfield one Friday afternoon; she asked me questions (partly based on written material I had supplied in advance); and, although not nearly as frank as I might have been a few years later, I answered them. We talked for about three hours, drinking gin and tonic for most of the time, so there's a distinct deterioration in quality towards the end. The following day I wrote to Robert:

> I enjoyed talking to Margot Farnham yesterday and was impressed by her degree of preparation for the interview, organisation of the session, and effective line of questioning. Whether I said anything of historical value is another matter!

More cautious than I would be today, I also added:

For my own protection (particularly should I ever return to public school teaching), I must put a restriction on access to the tapes. I don't want to find myself on the front page of *The Sun*: 'Poufter Lecturer Tells All'. Of course, I would always agree to access being given to any historian, researcher or serious writer.

When I began work on these *Memoirs* Robert Perks kindly sent me copies of the tapes. Whether anyone else has ever listened to them I have no idea.

My visits to local gay bars in Huddersfield in the 1980s and early 1990s were rare but, occasionally, I still went along to the *Greyhound*, more often than not at the suggestion of students who fancied a change from the *Zetland* or *College Arms*. I remember, in particular, once spending an hour or two there in the company of a pair of strikingly good-looking straight lads; they seemed to enjoy the admiring glances that came their way; and I was certainly amused by the jealous glares directed at me. Perhaps wisely, neither of them would risk visiting the lavatory on his own! One or two of my younger colleagues also accompanied me there now and again and, as he reminds me, I once took Roger Kitching and a mate of his to the *Greyhound*. Roger realised immediately that we were in a gay pub but his friend remained oblivious to the regular clientèle's all too obvious proclivities throughout. When the *Gemini*, a gay night club, opened in Huddersfield, it had regular student nights and provided an alternative after hours drinking haunt to *Johnnys*. Indeed, for a while, it became a popular student venue; girls found it refreshingly unthreatening; and even straight lads, especially if they had an exhibitionist streak, seemed to enjoy the place as well. I didn't go there very often, except for a few months towards the end of the 1980s when I had a couple of openly gay lads in my third year Special Subject group. The atmosphere in the club tended to be not a little raunchy and a yard at the back even more so. I never ventured outside myself! Live entertainment was laid on in the club now and again, most memorably a speciality act one night featuring a male stripper and an enormous python with distinctly unorthodox tastes. More regularly, I enjoyed the spectacle of watching nicely put together heterosexual male students fending off the amorous advances of flamboyant young queens. The highlight of these visits was a 'wet shorts' evening. Urged on by the rest of us a couple of very drunk straight lads in the group stripped down to the very scantiest of bum-hugging shorts; the requisite wet look was easily achieved with the aid of a soda water syphon; and they even seemed to revel in the intimate man-handling that soon came their way. Unluckily for them, one of the girls with us had brought along a polaroid camera and so, a day or two later when they'd sobered up, we were able to present concrete evidence of their out-of-character behaviour. Needless to say, I couldn't resist providing an over-the-top running commentary on events the lads themselves could scarcely remember!

Once my sexuality became more widely known after 1979 I felt less and less inhibition about letting student drinking mates know if I fancied them, or even telling a few heterosexual friends about my exploits. As early as December 1980 I wrote to Charles Ross:

> At the moment I've got a splendidly handsome and virile new boyfriend, aged 22, who—amazingly—seems to think I'm great, despite an ever-expanding beer gut. Long may this bliss continue!

'Of all the dissolute times in your life', mused Brendan Evans in February 2004, 'the period I recall most vividly is 1984 when, as a head-on challenge to becoming forty, you spent even more time on booze and sex than other years'; Vivienne Hemingway remembers my occasionally telling stories of student bedmates; and, for Bill Roberts :

> ... it was not always easy to judge just how deeply you were involved in the affairs and incidents you'd mention from time to time. You would certainly refer to them with bravado but, maybe, simply to see how shocked a response you could provoke!

Perhaps Bill Stafford gets to the heart of the matter:

> You were one of the most amoral men I have ever come across. You had no time for morality at all, regarding it as utter humbug. Yet, for all your sexual escapades, I don't remember you doing anything that I would regard as fundamentally immoral. Indeed, paradoxically, your amoralism was a kind of virtue. Being incapable of moral disapproval, you never worked yourself up into hostility to anybody else on the grounds of their so-called immorality. Your nature, in fact, was always tolerant and forgiving.

Although, in the 1980s and early 1990s, I slept with a succession of male students, as far as I can remember I never put pressure on anyone. On the contrary, it was almost invariably the lads themselves who made the first overt move, usually by rejecting the offer of a spare bed in favour of joining me in mine for a night of fun and frolics. They were certainly a splendidly mixed bunch! For instance, there was a sinewy young man who never had any difficulty finding willing female partners but, now and again, enjoyed checking out a member of his own sex as well; another, when he caught sight of himself naked in a mirror one night, ironically described his physique as 'small but perfectly formed'; and a third regularly brought along gay videos, presumably because the lads featured in them were far more desirable than I was. All these lads became semi-regular bedmates during their last few months at the polytechnic. There were also plenty of one night stands over the years. I remember, in particular, a bulky lad who had seemed irrevocably heterosexual until, one night, he drank a truly awesome quantity of whisky at my house; he was probably the hairiest young man I have ever examined in any detail; and, for the rest of his time at Huddersfield, I dubbed him 'the animated hearthrug'. Another was an exceptionally able lad who, like many predominantly heterosexual yet also liberal-minded students in the 1980s and early 1990s, lacked any trace of homophobia. One night he made it clear that he was not averse to a discreet homosexual experience. Since his looks were as impressive as his intellect, I was only too happy to play the role of mentor. When, shortly after leaving Huddersfield, he decided to enrol on a teacher training course, I supplied an enthusiastic but entirely honest reference. As always when I agreed to pen references for ex-students, I sent him a copy; however, I couldn't resist adding a sentence I'd judiciously excluded from the original:

> This superbly put together young man will, no doubt, massively send up the masturbation rate among 13—14 year old love sick girls, not to mention proto-gay boys. Even so, providing he is taken in hand by the appropriate seigneurial authority, his male beauty ought not to prove too much of a handicap.

Perhaps, had I included these observations, be wouldn't now be a happily married senior teacher. Altogether less pleasant to recall is a decent-looking but devious extrovert who probably manoeuvred himself into my bed one night in the hope of improving his degree prospects. If so, it didn't work.

A side effect of my coming out was a tendency for gay and lesbian history students to opt for my third year Special Subject, even if they weren't all that interested in the fifteenth century. Only once did I have a roll in the hay with one of them (bisexuals were much more my forté), an outrageously camp young man who made no secret whatever of his sexual preferences: a fellow student, indeed, recalls him being 'mortally offended to be mistaken for a heterosexual' by one of my colleagues! Sadly, so I learned a few years later, he eventually fell victim to AIDS in London. Not many ethnic minority lads studied history at Huddersfield during my time there but among those who did was an Afro-Caribbean who came to the polytechnic, so he recalled in 2005, 'because the town was in a part of Yorkshire I always liked and which reminded me of the area of the West Indies my parents came from'. He was an enthusiastic and hard-working lad, with a well-developed sense of humour, but his cultural background hardly predisposed him to tolerance of homosexuality:

I didn't even realise you were gay until the middle of my second year and that was only when Pauline Stafford told me. As a young man from a very sheltered middle class and fairly religious background, it came as quite a revelation but, by then, it was no longer an issue for me. Two or three years earlier it might have been a completely different matter. My attitude towards quite a lot of things, including homosexuality, changed during the time I was in Huddersfield.

Clearly, I took it upon myself to test the limits of his new tolerance with enthusiasm:

I heard from other students that you'd remarked on my being a very good-looking boy and I certainly remember when you first made your interest in me more explicit. By then, I could accept it as a compliment. In fact, I was really chuffed.

Only once did I sleep with more than one male student at the same time. Both lads had shared my bed singly and, no doubt after comparing notes, suggested we make up a threesome for the night. Rather reluctantly, I went along with this but, it soon became clear, their real objective was to get their hands on each other. After a while, with a suitably sardonic parting comment, I retreated to the spare room and left them to it. Only once, too, did I sleep with a student away from Huddersfield during these years: an ex-public school history postgraduate following the Oxford Union debate on Richard III in 1983. Just how I ended up in bed with him in an Oxford hotel I simply can't recall but, no doubt, massive over-indulgence in alcohol figured prominently in the equation. What I do remember is that, at an Open University examination scriptmarkers' meeting next day, I was well below par.

Obviously, as the years went by in Huddersfield, I began to acquire a bit of a reputation for sexual recklessness, as a former colleague recollects:

Once, when you came to spend the night with us, my second son, a student at the time, was there and we three got drinking. Although I am sure you did not fancy him, I stayed up drinking into the early hours myself just in case!

Actually, I fancied him like hell but even I drew the line at bedding a colleague's son in his own house. At least one polytechnic student, moreover, played his own cards extremely skilfully:

Early on at Huddersfield I found out you were homosexual. This didn't bother me at all and I never felt uncomfortable with it—except once! We'd been drinking in the *College Arms* until closing time and went back to your place. Nothing new in that. Unfortunately, I'd got dead drunk and had to sleep in your spare room. I don't think I could have got home under my own steam and no taxi driver would have risked having to mop out his car next morning. Having stuck me in the room, you hung around optimistically and I resorted to perhaps the commonest and least original ploy in the book. I played dumb and uncomprehending. It did the trick and you flounced out declaring, 'God, you're so naive!'.

Yet, he adds, 'I'm certainly not suggesting you were trying to take advantage of me; I knew your orientation and did not feel in any way threatened; I didn't even feel you were out of order; and, anyway, I'd expected you to proposition me sooner or later'. Over fifteen years later this lean, muscular dark haired young man visited me in Bristol. By then in his late thirties he was, if anything, even better looking than he had been as an undergraduate. Yet, even after several hours drinking real ale in the pub followed by half a bottle of whisky back at my house, he still spurned the opportunity posed by my playful advances, albeit in an entirely good-humoured manner and without a hint of heterosexual repugnance. A splendid fellow who consistently knew his own mind!

During the 1980s and early 1990s I shared a bed, at one time or another, with a string of male students at Huddersfield and my track record certainly wouldn't win any plaudits from present day moralists. Even at the time feminists were beginning to get more and more hot under the collar about male staff sleeping with female students but they had no interest in the more exotic possibility of young men at the polytechnic meeting a similar fate. One of their number whom I taught, towards the end of a long drinking session, even expressed the opinion that, if I bedded the occasional male student, that was fine by her; indeed, it served them right! Maybe my behaviour even had a didactic dimension to it. Some lads, despite more than a touch of the bisexual in their own make-up, still had irrational fears of homosexuality and the threat it posed to their masculinity. Experiencing the occasional gay romp themselves may have helped dispel such sentiments and, if so, I'm glad I helped advance such a worthy cause! Not that such thoughts were ever in my mind at the time, of course. More often than not late night drinking sessions and the enjoyment of each other's company simply acquired a mild sexual dimension, almost by accident. Rarely did such encounters develop much beyond the sheer pleasure of sleeping together and, particularly following the arrival of AIDS, I was always scrupulous in avoiding risky sexual practices (even when partners were prepared to skate on thinner ice than I was). I doubt whether any of these young men felt anything beyond strong friendship and, maybe, fleeting affection for me, coupled with a certain curiosity to explore the potential of an easily available and nonthreatening same-sex experience. Perhaps a few simply took pity on this solitary and ageing gay bachelor.

Discretion was always expected, and assured, and love never entered the equation. Neither the students nor I were interested in long term commitment and most of them went on to lead conventional heterosexual lives. Not long ago I wrote to a former female student, now in the teaching profession herself:

> I feel not the faintest pang of guilt about my blatantly unprofessional conduct over the years. I never sought deliberately to take advantage of students but nor did I see any reason to reject amorous overtures from them. No lad I had a bit of a fling with ever complained or expressed regret afterwards (not to me at any rate) and several have remained friends to this day.

Her reply was equally forthright:

> Why should any student have complained about your unprofessional conduct? After all, you were consenting adults.

Over the last decade or so there has been a remarkable growth of social tolerance of homosexuals and homosexuality in Britain, reflected in further liberalisation of the law. A year after the triumphant return of Labour to office, the age of consent for homosexual acts was at last lowered from eighteen to sixteen in 1998, bringing it into line with that for heterosexuals. This was achieved with a healthy majority of over two hundred MPs (mainly Labour) but not without fierce opposition from mainly Conservative traditionalists such as Nicholas Winterton who, echoing his predecessors of thirty years earlier, still railed against 'unnatural practices' in terms of Christian morality and the need to protect vulnerable young men from their predatory elders. Further reforms followed: the ban on lesbians and gay men serving in the armed forces was lifted in 2000; in 2003 discrimination in the work place on grounds of sexual orientation was made illegal and section 28 of the 1988 Local Government Act banning the 'promotion' of homosexuality in schools repealed; and, in 2005, civil partnerships between gay people were legally recognised. Clearly, young homosexuals today need no longer suffer the agonies I endured in the later 1950s and early 1960s. Yet there's still a long way to go. Changing the law and promoting tolerance is one thing, engendering a society where sexuality is no longer an issue quite another, and there's plenty of homophobia around even now. Homophobic bullying remains a problem in schools and gay teachers continue to find it hard to be open about themselves; the same goes for the police force, the fire service and the military; and the growth of narrow-minded religious fundamentalism in recent years, whether of the Christian or Moslem variety, might well pose a real threat to social liberalism in the future.

Once I moved to Bristol in September 1994 I expected my sex life, so dependent on students for over a decade, more or less to cease. I regarded this prospect with equanimity. After all, I had already proved my capacity to lead a virtually celibate life during my undergraduate years in the mid-1960s and, again, as a schoolmaster in Plymouth between 1969 and 1972. I certainly had no intention of joining the ranks of pathetic middle-aged homosexuals for ever in quest of the unattainable in gay bars and clubs; indeed, during the last few years I've visited such establishments only very rarely and never on my own. As a part-time lecturer I seldom got to know students as well as I had in Huddersfield and hardly ever invited any of them back to my house. Not that I made any secret of my homosexuality. I just didn't advertise it very much. James Lee comments:

> I don't recall much conversation about Keith's sexuality at UWE. Perhaps it's a sign of the times. Over the years, however, as he revealed more and more stories of past taboo scenarios, I realised he was gay without needing, or indeed seeking, confirmation. It's not the most interesting part of him, though, and hasn't really coloured our relationship.

Inevitably, when friends from Huddersfield have turned up in Bristol, the subject has not infrequently surfaced, as Kit Hardwick recalls:

> I remember once sitting listening to my partner Linda and Keith weighing up the male talent in a Bristol pub and, perhaps unsurprisingly, agreeing about most of it. Happily, they didn't get to fighting for possession. Possibly in retaliation, I eventually brought a rather drunken young lady to join our group—only to have her irate girlfriend stalk up and whisk her away again!

Occasionally, too, old flames of yesteryear have visited me and we've briefly become re-acquainted between the sheets; moreover, against my expectations, new opportunities for sexual entertainment have also presented themselves now and again, even a couple of the lads I taught at the University of the West of England.

Among the most interesting of my bedmates since 1994 has been a West Indian schoolteacher in his thirties. Like me three or four decades earlier he had managed to escape from a poverty-stricken working class background but was struggling to come to terms with his homosexuality. Although homophobia was declining in society at large by then, so he assured me, it was still rampant in Afro-Caribbean circles; he came from a closely-knit family but neither his parents nor his siblings knew he was gay; and, very uncomfortable as he was in mainly white working class pubs where racism never seemed far below the surface, we tended to meet up at my house. I was staggered when he told me he'd had no sexual experience at all, apart from a few uncomfortable encounters with women, and I happily helped him remedy that. Yet, as I pointed out to him more than once, he was far too handsome and elegible to be wasting his time with a man over twenty years older than he was. After a while, since he was extremely reluctant to visit gay bars and clubs, I persuaded him to try his luck with a gay dating service. Eventually, as a result, he did find himself a younger partner. Less anxiety-ridden, if more exotic in his tastes, was a fellow beer-drinking enthusiast in his forties whose well-preserved physique always made him a pleasure to grapple with between the sheets and a historian of about my own age who, discovering a bisexual streak in himself late in life, obviously relished the opportunity to explore its potential. There have been a few one night stands as well, inevitably following heavy sessions in the pub. Three particularly stick in my mind. One evening I got chatting to a member of a local band in his early thirties who had had plenty of heterosexual experience but, so he told me, had always been intrigued by gay sex. I hope, now his opportunity had come, he enjoyed it as much as I did. Another casual encounter came when, during a spell of intolerably hot and humid Bristol weather, I took refuge in a pub as soon as it opened for the day. Before long I became aware of a stunningly good-looking young man, splendidly well displayed since he was wearing only the very briefest of cut-down jeans. Taking advantage of the fact that he was drinking with an older guy whom I knew slightly, I joined them, mainly in order to observe his excellent physique close up. I wasn't disappointed! When he went to the bar to buy yet another round of drinks, I remarked on his magnificent frame to his mate. He promptly roared with laughter, adding sardonically that he was sure his son would be delighted to know his years of weight-training in the gym hadn't been wasted. This man knew I was gay. When father and son departed an hour or two later, I decided I might as well make a day of it now. Soon the young man returned to the pub on his own, rapidly engaged me in further conversation and also made it clear his father had told him what I'd said. Far from being alarmed, offended or angry, however, he chose instead to volunteer the information that he wasn't 100% straight himself but had never had the nerve to sample the gay scene. What really inhibited him, he admitted after yet more beer, was that he didn't really know what homosexuals did and was scared of making a fool of himself. Eventually we adjourned to my house and, in due course, the lesson commenced. A chance meeting with a Bristol University student had more bizarre consequences. He'd been a boarder at a public school and, before long, we began comparing my experiences as a master at Plymouth College with his as a schoolboy at Harrow over a quarter of a century later. He seemed especially interested to hear my stories of corporal punishment which he was too young to have experienced at school himself. Not entirely to my surprise, after we'd consumed a generous quota of pints, he confessed to occasional fantasies about himself on the receiving end of a ritualised thrashing. Since I'd been here before, even if over twenty years earlier, I couldn't resist offering to indulge him a bit. He jumped at the chance, obviously enjoyed the experience and, since he was also a very presentable young man, once he'd recovered his equanimity we went on to spend a very pleasant night together. All these encounters, and several others in Bristol since 1994, certainly show that, as social tolerance of homosexuals and homosexuality grew, more and more predominantly heterosexual men began to feel confident enough to test the waters on the other side of the line if opportunity arose. I'm glad I was able to help them explore their bisexual streak!

Although for most of the 1990s I tended to keep my sexuality more or less to myself when drinking in the *Sportsman* and *Annexe*, from about 2000 I threw caution to the winds and became increasingly open about my sexual preferences. Rather to my surprise, I found that even working class regulars seemed comfortable with it and, on the sole occasion I did encounter out-and-out homophobia, I was touched by just how many fellow drinkers went out of their way to sympathise. Even a hunky young man in his mid-twenties, as traditionally macho as they come, remained friendly: one evening, indeed, he told me he had been homophobic in his teens but, now, had no problem at all exchanging quips with an elderly queer. There was certainly plenty of light-hearted and not infrequently sexually-charged banter at the bar! Most memorably, not long before I stopped frequenting the *Sportsman* and *Annexe*, I mischievously asked several male bar staff and regulars one teatime how many of them were circumcised; they all happily supplied the information; and we established that, out of thirteen of us, three had been deprived of our foreskins and ten not. Frank discussion of whether it mattered or not inevitably followed. No less improbably, another night, I was urged by a couple of drinking cronies to chance my arm with an extremely handsome young man who had just come into the *Annexe*. He turned out to be a student at the University of the West of England and, as I soon realised, he was not only very well oiled but completely stoned as well. No wonder it took him quite a while to grasp he was being propositioned and, by then, a whole group of regulars had gathered around us. When my apparent intentions at last dawned on him he panicked, volubly asserting not only his impeccable heterosexual credentials but also his complete devotion to his girlfriend. Eventually he departed with another guy who clearly fancied him like hell. I wonder if his virtue survived the night. One thing is for sure. Such a sequence of events could not have unfolded even a few years earlier.

In 2004/5 I asked several staff and regular customers of the *Sportsman* and *Annexe* to scribble down their impressions of me and how they felt about socialising with an openly gay man. Their responses were illuminating to say the least. Among the bar staff Laura Gregory recalled that:

> ... one of the other staff in the *Sportsman* told me Keith was gay. I didn't guess. It made no difference to me. I enjoy the company of gay men and find them amusing and unthreatening. My partner also used to talk to Keith at the bar. He didn't guess he was gay either but was neither surprised nor alarmed when he found out. Although a prison officer accustomed to a very different male culture, he and Keith still chat together when they meet.

Significantly, perhaps, Laura added that she didn't know of any other regular drinker in the *Sportsman* who was homosexual. Lyn Sheppard, who became a barmaid in the *Annexe* in 1994:

> ... suspected Keith might be gay quite early on, although I might have stereotyped him at first: lives alone with pussy! He also had a certain gentleness which one only seems to find in gay men (but he's certainly not camp or effeminate). So what if he's homosexual? It doesn't matter to those who know and respect him and, if anyone does care, they're not worth bothering about anyway.

Steve Gould, an *Annexe* barman during my later years drinking there, commented in July 2004:

> When Keith is in the pub there's often a great deal of banter, frequently riddled with sexual innuendo. I feel totally at ease with the fact he's gay and he has become more openly so in the time I've known him. Most of the regulars in the *Annexe* now know Keith is gay as well but I've never heard anyone express any real prejudice or malice against him because of his sexuality.

Among such Annexe customers Keith Tucker remembers that:

> ...a little while after I started talking to Keith I heard comments like, 'You know what he is, don't you?'. I hadn't picked up on his sexuality until then, but so what if he is gay? It doesn't matter to me. How people want to live their lives is up to them.

Mark Jones, by contrast, recalls that 'it didn't take me long to work out Keith was gay' and, anyway, 'he told me himself early in our acquaintance: on about pint number four one afternoon'. Mike Bush declared forthrightly in January

2005 that my sexuality was not a problem for him, 'having worked with a lot of gays and enjoyed very entertaining times with them'; moreover, he concluded, 'homophobia is now on the decline except for the odd moron who can't get into the modern world'. 'During the time we've known Keith', recalled Alan and Marisa Stevens at about the same time:

> ... he has openly acknowledged his homosexuality, although it wasn't obvious to us before. Even remarks like 'Alan is a fine figure of a man' cause us no offence. The *Annexe* has an age profile ranging from the early '30s upwards and we hope we don't appear judgemental. Who are we to be so anyway? Why should we judge anyone by their sexual preferences? It is the person whom we know and like that matters.

'I've never felt uneasy or threatened by knowing you're gay', mused Dave Moore; nevertheless, he added, 'although this doesn't apply to the *Annexe*, I don't think homophobia is in decline generally or among older pub customers'. Debbie Gwilym recalled that her first impression of me was of:

> ... a man comfortable with himself: no change there. I've never felt uneasy, threatened or anything else, by his being openly gay. He's fun and interesting.

'I've never thought of the *Annexe* as being homophobic', she further commented, but 'I'm not sure homophobia is in decline generally'. Another *Annexe* regular became almost philosophical:

> I feel homophobia results from the way homosexuality is presented to people in early life, the comments of those around them and the way gay men are often portrayed in films and on TV. I had an uncle who was full of fun. Yet his sexuality was never discussed and, even after his death, never will be. My family's attitude was that homosexuality was something that happened to other families, not ours.

Frank Chlebko, whom I drank with off and for over a decade in the *Annexe*, perhaps deserves the last word:

> The fact that Keith was gay never bothered me in the least and I don't think it bothered him either. His expression of admiration for a good looking young man in the *Annexe* on occasion was no different from similar remarks I might make about an attractive female. The only downside amongst all the amusing tales he told about his homosexuality was, by his own admission, his inability to commit himself to any one partner over the years.

By the time I reached sixty in February 2004 the ravages of time and lifestyle were beginning to show only too clearly. Nevertheless, even during my last couple of years of regular pub drinking, I continued to enjoy chatting to and exchanging quips with young male bar staff, especially if they were also pleasing to the eye. Most memorably, I recollect an exceptionally handsome barman with a superb head, a magnificent torso and an enticingly mobile rear; a sinewy ginger-headed lad whose interests, sadly, seemed entirely focussed on an absentee girlfriend; another youth of classical proportions whose job, irritatingly, largely confined him to the kitchen; and a most engaging sporty tearaway who simply oozed masculinity. Over these years, too, I revelled in conversation with only slightly older bar managers: a serious-minded young man who eventually had the immense good fortune to meet a feisty Yorkshire lass, for instance, and a cynical worldly-wise fellow whose mildly homophobic but entirely good-humoured banter at my expense amused me hugely. All these young men were entirely straight as far as I know and, anyway, even latent bisexual tendencies were hardly likely to be triggered by so increasingly decrepit a voyeur as me. C'est la vie!

For two or three decades I very much enjoyed the challenges and rewards of semi-regular homosexual promiscuity and it's probably true to say that sex is the only sport that has ever come naturally to me. While hardly providing an admirable role model for others, moreover, I have no regrets at all about my lifestyle over so many years. Yet, paradoxically, I only visited gay bars and clubs very intermittently. Nor have I ever felt part of a gay community or, indeed, wanted to become so. By choice, not necessity, my social life has always revolved mainly around heterosexual men and women. Maybe, if I'd felt confident enough to defy society and be more open about my sexuality earlier than I was, I might have found a permanent partner, but I doubt it. I much preferred living on my own, anyway, with just a cat or two for company. Nor do I regret not having had children. Even if I had, I suspect, I would have been a rotten father and, funds permitting, probably despatched my kids to boarding school at the earliest opportunity. I fully support the notion of civil partnerships for gay couples and have no problem, either, with same-sex pairs fostering or even adopting children. Gay marriage, by contrast, I find bizarre, especially if it has a pseudo-religious dimension. Nor am I convinced of the wisdom of homosexuals emphasising their minority status so much. Far better to project themselves as differing from the majority of men and women only in respect of their preferred bedmates. The so-called gay community also seems perversely reluctant to accept the extent of bisexuality among both men and women. Most of my own bedroom encounters over the years have been with men whose predominant orientation was heterosexual. Most of them, too, have been casual and short term, almost in the same category as social drinking, great fun but not to be taken too seriously. Love has never entered the equation. At their worst these liaisons have meant virtually nothing beyond the fleeting pleasure of the moment. At their best they have been an extremely enjoyable extension of friendship, a physical manifestation of male bonding, no more and no less. Yet, maybe, the verdict of a fellow historian and friend of over twenty years, even if a bit on the sombre side, isn't too far from the truth:

> Keith has ploughed a lonely and difficult furrow. This may seem strange, given the deep affection he inspires from his former students and many friends. Yet what strikes me is not the trials and tribulations of the gay historian—although I can see the importance of this to Keith—but the difficulty he has in forming any really intimate relationship. After society began to lessen its homophobia and hypocrisy, Keith's choice of partner spoke for itself, usually younger heterosexual men (like me) who wanted to experiment. In other words we were not really available in the longer term and I think this suited Keith because there was no danger of commitment, Gregarious but restless, Keith now seems to be retreating from a world he doesn't understand or feel comfortable in any more. But then, perhaps, he never did.

Epilogue

All the world's a stage,
And all the men and women merely players;
They have their exits and their entrances;
And one man in his time plays many parts,
His acts being seven ages.
At first the infant,
Mewling and puking in the nurse's arms;
Then the whining schoolboy, with his satchel
And shining morning face, creeping, like snail
Unwillingly to sohool.
And then the lover,
Sighing like furnace, with a woeful ballad
Made to his mistress eyebrow.
Then a soldier,
Full of strange oaths, and bearded like the pard,
Jealous in honour, sudden and quick in quarrel,
Seeking the bubble reputation even in the cannon's mouth.
And then the justice,
In fair round belly with good capon lined,
With eyes severe and beard of formal cut,
Full of wise saws and modern instances;
And so he plays his part.
The sixth age shifts
Into the lean and slipper'd pantaloon,
With spectacles on nose and pouch on side;
His youthful hose, well sav'd, a world too wide

> For his shrunk shank; and his big manly voice,
> Turning again toward childish treble, pipes
> And whistles in his sound.
> Last scene of all,
> That ends this strange eventful history,
> Is second childishness and mere oblivion;
> Sans teeth, sans eyes, sans taste, sans everything.

At first sight there seems no apter opening to this epilogue than the melancholy and sardonic Jacques' 'Seven Ages of Man' oration in *As You Like It*, perhaps my favourite passage in the whole of Shakespeare. Yet, although I have certainly played many parts, I'm not sure I conform to the Tudor playwright's picture all that well. Maybe Peter Fleming, my former colleague at the University of the West of England, is nearer the mark in his Shakespearean analogy:

> Keith reminds me, in some ways, of Sir John Falstaff and his Shakespearean close comedic cousins. No strangers to the chimes at midnight, they have in common an appetite for life, a ready wit, a deep dislike of puritans and puritanism (Toby Belch: 'Dost thou think, because thou art virtuous, there shall be no more cakes and ale?'), a wisdom and profundity about the human condition, and a genius for friendship. Keith has not, to the best of my knowledge, led a pack of highway robbers onto Shooter's Hill, nor rubbed shoulders, or anything else, with the heir to the throne! Nor does he share those traits that lead an audience to laugh at, rather than with, these characters. Nevertheless, like them, he has something else going on underneath the garrulous exterior, whether it should be called a darker, or more profound, or more grounded side, I don't know, but his is most certainly not a straightforward personality.

Oddly enough, I don't seem to have changed all that much since I was a young man. Even as a student in the 1960s, Mike Stammers recalls, 'Keith began to enjoy being notorious and scandalising people'; however, he adds, 'for all his cynicism, he also inspired warm and lasting friendships'. 'A loyal friend and a great companion', echoes Mike Allen, my Plymouth College colleague of the early 1970s, while my then head of department Dennis Collinson's 'memories remain bright of Keith's Rabelaisian shoulders, sharp intellect and our shared, almost schoolboyish sense of humour'. Looking back on our years together at Huddersfield Polytechnic in the 1970s and 1980s, John O'Connell wonders whether I accept that my sexuality is 'the main determinant' of my persona. Perhaps I do and it certainly helps make sense of much of my behaviour since sixth form days. Another Huddersfield colleague Brendan Evans, too, believes homosexuality may provide a major clue to my character; however, he adds, it cannot fully explain my 'enthusiasm for teaching and research, skill as an actor, sense of humour and capacity for friendship'. 'Notwithstanding the sense of theatre which is integral to your persona', declares Peter Durrans, 'the central characteristic I associate with you is your humanity: a rare gift and one I will always treasure'. For Andrew Taylor I was 'a fun colleague and a good mate'; Bill Roberts has 'memories of heavy drinking sessions, a few rather imprudent escapades and some sadder moments'; and, as for Bill's wife Jan, she found me 'a colourful character, compassionate, full of energy, interesting and knowledgeable to talk to' and, above all, 'very forthright' in expressing my opinions. Andy Hook, whom I taught at Huddersfield in the later 1970s, remembers that he and his mates 'warmed to a guy who maintained a professional integrity, shared his love of history and had an openness and honesty we could all relate to'; Cliff Burhouse, who suffered at my hands between 1988 and 1991, concluded in January 2004 that 'in a society no longer catering for individualists, where conformity is the easy way out, Keith is a nonconformist, a one-off in a world of clones, and as such he should be treasured'; and Peter Broome, a member of my very last Huddersfield Special Subject group in 1993/4, recalled in May 2005:

> Keith gave the impression that he didn't give a damn about anything but I always believed that was a cover. In my case, indeed, he helped me through a difficult period in my life and I'll always be grateful for that.

As for others who got to know me over the years, Keith Stenner considers I am 'great fun to be with' and, although my 'cynical stance on modern life and its attendant hypocrisies is rarely absent, it is always rendered in good humour and without malice'. For Michael Jones I am 'highly idiosyncratic' and have 'a unique one-off way of seeing life' yet, at the same time, 'warm and loyal, a friend you can depend on'. And Peter Hammond believes I have 'retained an impressive number of friends', firmly ascribing this to my 'personality and larger-than-life qualities'. All in all, a remarkable consistency in verdicts covering over forty years.

'Perhaps our lives have been intertwined for over four decades', muses Darlington-born Peter Allender, mainly because:

> ... we were both children born into, or in Keith's case brought up by, post-war northern working class families. In some ways we are the victims as well as the survivors of our success. Not many made it to grammar school and university from the sort of areas where we grew up; indeed, a lad might as well have been a giraffe as a scholarship boy and we had to learn, and think in, a different lan-

guage. The price we pay is deracination, in the original Latin sense of uprooted. Will we ever know who we really are?

I can certainly identify with these sentiments but, oddly enough, I have few regrets and, prevailing social attitudes towards lads grappling to cope with homosexuality apart, not much resentment about what happened to me between 1944 and 1963. My early years, spent in relative poverty living with foster parents in a virtual slum, were grim even by the standards of the time. My natural mother was more an irritant than a help. Yet John and Miriam Saunders looked after me as well as they could, and Edith Wood was an entirely positive influence. From an early age I learned to live with disadvantage and developed a degree of self-sufficiency that has remained with me ever since. At primary school I soon became literate, embraced the pleasures of reading, passed the 11+ and won a place at Huddersfield's most prestigious grammar school. By the age of eleven, too, solitary pursuits such as exploring Huddersfield and its surrounding area, watching Jack Land's Punch and Judy shows at every opportunity and weekly theatre-going had become well-established escapes from the day-to-day realities of life on a post-war council house estate. Huddersfield (New) College proved a real challenge but, eventually, I got used to it and settled down reasonably well. Indeed, for all my gripes about the place and its middle class Christian ethos, I received a very decent academic education there; I was encouraged to apply to university; and, courtesy of state-paid tuition fees and a full maintenance grant, I was able to grasp the opportunity. Almost certainly, had I ended up in a secondary modern school or even an urban comprehensive serving the sort of area where I lived, I would have sunk without trace. Had I been required to finance my undergraduate studies by taking out student loans, that avenue would have been closed off to me as well. I simply wouldn't have been prepared to contemplate incurring such debts in 1963. Grammar schools and free university education were a great boon for bright working class kids in post-war Britain providing they were prepared to grasp the chances on offer. When comprehensive schools became all the rage in the 1960s and 1970s (a highly dubious exercise in social engineering favoured by the middle class, I suspect, mainly as a means of saving their thicker offspring from secondary moderns: hence zoning), clever working class boys and girls lost out badly. All Huddersfield New College needed was a more enlightened headmaster than A. R. Bielby and more staff of the calibre of James Crump and Michael Gillard. Nor was the abolition of the 11+ such a universal boon. The main problem, so it seemed to me at the time and still does, was not so much the very existence of a selective exam as its inflexibility, combined with the failure of successive post-war governments properly to finance and staff secondary moderns. As for the more recent near-abolition of university maintenance grants and imposition of tuition fees, that, too, is a sadly retrograde step. During my own teenage years, and here there has been real progress since the 1960s, nothing caused me greater anxiety than discovering I was homosexual and learning to accept the inevitable; indeed, it brought me to the verge of suicide in 1960/1. 'I hadn't realised the financial pressure you were under at Huddersfield New College', commented Bill Roberts in June 2006, 'and that, combined with the class issue and the growing realisation you were gay must have been very difficult: I'm not surprised you became severely depressed'. My childhood and teenage years also helped make me the political, religious and social cynic I have remained ever since. Yet these early experiences toughened me up as well and, eventually, made me even more determined than before to play a poor hand as well as I could.

Michael Barthokomew, whom I first got to know through the Open University in the 1980s, commented in February 2004:

> There is something in the experience of being the first member of a working class family who goes to university that is common to us. There are loads of us about, and we form a sort of free masonry in academe, never fitting in perfectly but no longer fully at ease with the working class world we've left behind either.

I myself emerged from six years at Bristol University in 1969 virtually classless but, fortunately, still able to mix comfortably with working class men and women in pubs while, at last, no longer fazed at all by either middle class folk or their self-interested and self-promoting values. As an undergraduate, although I contracted a few close and enduring friendships, I worked extraordinarily hard and probably earned a first class honours degree even if I didn't get one. My experience of the Bristol history department, its courses, teaching and antiquated examination system, moreover, was to influence profoundly my own approach to undergraduate teaching and assessment at Huddersfield Polytechnic/ University between 1972 and 1994. More immediately, disappointment at obtaining only an upper second after so much effort maybe helps explain the onset of another bout of severe depression in the autumn of 1966 and dented self-confidence in my academic abilities my subsequent failure to complete a Ph.D. (though the ill-suited topic I was working on didn't help much either). What I did at last achieve as a postgraduate student, courtesy of Alfred Josephson and Patrick Scott in particular, was a measure of composure about my homosexuality. By the summer of 1969, however, I badly needed a new challenge; obtaining the post of a junior history master at Plymouth College and house tutor in a boys' boarding house certainly provided just that; and, rather to my surprise, over the next two and a half years I not only learned how to teach successfully but also to cope constructively with the traumas of young teenagers living an almost monk-like existence away from home for weeks at a time. Former pupil Roger Middleton, indeed, speculates that 'for Keith, his Plymouth College years seem to have served as a springboard for a creative life'. As for Chris Robinson, who admits to 'really enjoying Keith's company' when we unexpectedly met up again in Plymouth in 1998, he is inclined to:

> ... lay a fair amount of the blame for my chosen career on Keith and Dennis Collinson. It's great to be able to do something that you're really passionate about and I thank Keith for whatever part he played in the process. I'm sure there are plenty of others around, too, who are similarly grateful.

Ex-colleague Bernard Samuels recalled in May 2004:

> Even after all this time, I still have a strong impression of Keith: the impact of his personality, keenness to talk about his background and upbringing, openness, complete honesty, high intelligence, passion for history and the fact that he obviously possessed the qualities that make for a first class teacher.

Yet, he added, 'I must also put on record my utter admiration for his amazing strength and stamina in being able to maintain his consumption of beer and cigarettes while still sailing through teaching, always producing the goods'. Di Collinson, whose family shared Colson House with me and over fifty boys for more than a year, has even more vivid memories:

> We soon learned that Keith had at least two mothers safely installed in Huddersfield and that he loved cats; that he had iconoclastic and rebellious tendencies; that he wrote beautifully, spoke scurrilously, and drank a lot; and that his only obvious resemblance to Edward Heath was that his shoulders shook uncontrollably up and down when he laughed. He was, and is, never bland. His opinions and arguments pack punch even when they are up the pole, so talking to him is always fun, and also instructive. His historical knowledge and acumen are prodigious. Yet, while he absolutely inhabits whatever he is working on, he also has the gift of being able to walk out and slam the door on it when he wants to.

Di Collinson herself has a lot to answer for in one respect at least since it was she who first encouraged me to become an Open University tutor in 1971. Thirty years later I was still at it. As for her husband Dennis, it was he who persuaded me to apply for, obtain and accept the job of lecturer at Huddersfield Polytechnic in 1972:

Although Keith's schoolteaching seemed entirely congenial to him, I felt strongly that young historians shouldn't become stuck in their first post, however good they were and however enjoyable the work. In Keith's case I convinced myself that he should be teaching at degree level and be given some opportunity for research and writing; moreover, those who have read his articles and books will know how beautifully clear his writing is and how persuasive his analyses.

'If his move back to Yorkshire caused him distress', he adds, 'I apologise profusely but, in the end, I hope he feels the Huddersfield move made good sense for him'. In the longer term it did but, early on at Huddersfield, I felt far from happy. The history/politics department was seriously overstaffed, there weren't all that many students and virtually no high fliers at all. I was loath to take up serious historical research again after my experience of the later 1960s. Only the proximity of a now ageing Miriam Saunders and Edith Wood, making a few close friends like Peter and Hazel Durrans, and my homosexuality, prevented me abandoning higher education and returning to the independent school sector. Perhaps inevitably, I eventually suffered another bout of depression in 1977/8. This was mainly caused by the only serious attempt I have ever made to stop smoking and, once I started again, it rapidly passed. Also, in 1978/9, I began teaching a Special Subject on the Wars of the Roses. Among the members of my very first group were Graham Townend and Neil Scott, both exceptionally enthusiastic and able students. They are certainly very generous in their assessments of me and my influence on them. 'I believe that much of what I am as a teacher today', declared Neil in January 2004, 'is due to my old friend the Yorkshire Bastard!'. Graham's verdict is even more positive:

> As a brilliant teacher Keith didn't have to justify his love of history. It was there for all to see. So was his warmth, kindness, generosity and compassion. It is one of the greatest privileges of my life to have known him both as a teacher and a friend.

'I was immediately struck by you when I first saw you at a polytechnic open day in the summer of 1984', recalled Julie Bungey in February 2004:

> There was something about you that I found attractive. You were certainly good looking, young for your age, tall., short brown hair (slightly thinning), inquisitive brown eyes, and an interesting cadence in your voice. Later on I discovered that it wasn't just history that interested you. You had a wide range of interests, from cats to contemporary politics. You were always interesting to be with, both in and out of the classroom.

'Keith wasn't just my tutor in 1988/9', Jo Cole remembers:

> As my final year progressed he became a very good friend. He was extremely supportive and it is largely the result of Keith's help and encouragement that I walked away with a good degree and went on to pursue a teaching career.

'You should be really proud of yourself', she added flatteringly in September 2005, since 'you so obviously had a very positive influence on many of your students and played a major part in making them what they are today'. One such, seemingly, was Richard Bell whom I taught between 1988 and 1991:

> To listen to someone like you speaking confidently on a subject that interests them and which they have, quite obviously, thoroughly mastered and absorbed is one of life's joys. When about to leave the polytechnic, you implored me to read good history in the future and I have followed that advice to this day.

Among my former colleagues at Huddersfield, Keith Laybourn particularly recalls:

> ...a fearlessness about you which I always admired, a willingness to prick pomposity and defy rules, but also a basic and underlying generosity and sympathy which belied the fearsome and bellicose Keith who sometimes emerged in lectures and tutorials. Much of what I admire in you as a historian comes from your professional attitude and joy in your subject and the kindness of spirit you exude. To me these traits reflect your personality.

Bill Stafford provides a nice illustrative anecdote:

> I remember a couple of occasions when you and I had a row. You, in your usual exuberant manner, went off like a volcano. Yet, very soon after, even though I was almost certainly the one in the wrong, you came and apologised for losing your temper, and we were again the best of friends.

As for Steve Smith, he found me:

> ... one of the most sensitive and caring people you could meet, although it was doubtless he who suggested to Sartre that 'hell is other people'. He could always find time to support you yet, at the same time, always be relied on to laugh at himself as well.

Throughout my years back in Huddersfield social drinking was never far from the top of my pleasure agenda, both as a regular in local Newsome pubs and in the town centre. I spent a great deal of time with colleagues and, more and more as the years went by, students too. Once I came out as a homosexual in 1979, moreover, I rarely succumbed to serious depression any more, as well as having plenty of fun in the bedroom. Obviously, I particularly enjoyed the company of handsome young men but socialising with women could also be immensely pleasurable (and uncomplicated!) now my sexuality was widely known. Alison Shaw, whom I first got to know as an Open University student in the later 1970s, painted a refreshingly honest picture of our long friendship in February 2004:

> Discovering a shared interest in fags and booze, and both having a rather cynical outlook on life, we soon became friends. You had a great ability to make people laugh and not take themselves too seriously. You could be exasperating, provoking, a bit thoughtless occasionally and annoyingly right most of the time, but you were also entertaining and good company. Above all, you were a loyal friend whose support I could always count on.

A few days before her premature death four months later, Alison sent me a final card:

> Goodbye, old friend. Don't be sad. Get out there and enjoy what time you have left—and have a few for me!

Between 1972 and 1981 Peter Durrans, his wife Hazel and I consumed an awesome quantity of beer in each other's company and, as Hazel recollects, my sardonic sense of humour sometimes got the better of me:

> You were certainly forthright on many occasions! At Peter's leaving do, for instance, when I turned up wearing a turquoise outfit complete with gossamer wrap, you quipped, 'it's not a fancy dress party, Hazel' (though I think you meant 'you look really stunning!'). Then there was the time I changed my scent and you accused me of drinking gin. I just couldn't persuade you that it was perfume. Such comments were always made in your usual jocular manner, though, so it was impossible to take offence.

In 1984 and 1985 I remember exchanging many a quip with polytechnic student Vanessa Cook, too, so it came as rather a surprise to learn in December 2005 that I had been:

> ... one of the most important people in my time in Huddersfield. I don't know exactly how, but you gave me confidence in my own ability and confidence, too, to air my own views and opinions. At the same time you helped me realise that it was OK to be me; I didn't have to be like anyone else; and for the first time in my life I even began to like myself. For what it's worth, I know I am a more interesting person for knowing you and I'm sure I can't be the only one.

Former Huddersfield Polytechnic politics colleague Tony Payne raises a matter hardly touched on at all in these reminiscences:

> Politically, I would see you as having deep roots in a kind of working class conservatism and you were certainly hostile to the left. Yet you weren't altogether prepared to play along with the liberal agenda either, despite the gay issue and your own sexuality.

Until I became a sixth former at Huddersfield New College I took virtually no interest in politics at all. At home in the 1950s matters political were hardly ever discussed; I only rarely saw a newspaper (we never had one delivered); and, even as an adult, I've never been a regular reader (not even of the *Guardian*!). John Saunders professed a deep distaste for all politicians, probably first engendered by his experience of the First World War and its gloomy domestic aftermath for working class folk, and never voted in either general or local elections. Miriam Saunders and Edith Wood may have done but, perhaps significantly, I can't remember for sure. As for my natural mother, she certainly disapproved of both the Labour party and the welfare state (hence why she refused to claim child allowance when I was a boy, presumably) but this never translated into serious support for the Conservatives. In the early 1960s I began to listen to radio news bulletins or watch their television equivalent but, as I recollect, tended to find them more irritating than anything else, and I simply couldn't understand at all what prompted a sixth form friend to become an enthusiastic member of the local Labour party. He, in turn, found it most puzzling that an intelligent working class lad like me didn't seem to share his views. As I developed an ever more powerful libertarian streak during my later teenage years, in fact, I found it impossible to feel comfortable with either the Labour or Conservative parties; I felt repelled by the authoritarian tendencies of so many professional politicians when they held power in their hands; and, once I became aware of the apparent intolerance of most of them towards homosexuality and homosexuals like me, I began to despise politicians as a breed. More fundamentally, while recognising that monarchy, despotism or oligarchy might well be much worse, I soon came to the conclusion that even democracy had one major downside for social minorities: its tendency to enshrine in powerful elected institutions the tyranny of the majority. Hence why, by the time I left Huddersfield for Bristol in the autumn of 1963, I had already become the political cynic I have remained ever since. Hence. too, why I've so often voted tactically in general elections (Conservative once, Labour two or three times, Liberal or Liberal Democrat most frequently), mainly in the hope of curtailing the excesses of elected representatives. Sadly, it has rarely worked! No wonder I am such an enthusiastic advocate of proportional representation. Now, after a decade living under an increasingly authoritarian Labour government, I'm probably even more cynical about politics and politicians than I was when casting my first ever parliamentary vote in 1966. Nor is it just politicians I'm inclined to treat with contempt. I feel much the same about any person, people or institutions exercising power over others, whether political, religious, economic or social, a sentiment nicely captured by Vivienne Haley. After leaving Huddersfield Polytechnic in 1980, she recalled in March 2004:

> I worked for several big companies. This seemed to confound Keith entirely and I often got the feeling that he liked to display me as a rare animal in captivity. 'This is Viv: she was a student of mine for a while but now seems to be a capitalist', he'd say, as though the two statements should be mutually exclusive. He'd then mercilessly take the mickey out of anything he saw as immoral or purposeless that I represented. I'm sure he felt I'd crush the working class under my well-heeled shoe if I could. Yet, underneath his critical and denigrating comments about my chosen profession, I have a sneaking feeling he was secretly a bit proud of me.

Perhaps I was but, if so, it certainly went against the grain!

Since I took early retirement and returned to Bristol in 1994, I don't seem to have changed for the worse or, even, very much at all, apart from suffering the inevitable ravages of time. Among my regular drinking companions in the *Annexe*, for instance Dave Moore found me 'a very decent guy'; Mike Bush declared 'you have a great personality, so don't stop smoking, drinking or being gay because, if you did, you'd no longer be you'; and Lyn Sheppard concluded that I was:

> ...a very amusing man who had worked hard to make something of yourself but not forgotten your roots. You're a loner but not lonely. The society around you is materialistic but you are one of the most down to earth people I know. So stick two fingers up at the world, Keith, and carry on as you are.

Peter Fleming, once a colleague in Bristol and now a close friend, speculates:

Underneath that bluff, no-nonsense Yorkshire exterior there is a sensitivity and compassion, for students of course, but also for those who don't quite fit in. Perhaps Keith is a man out of his time. It would be going too far to say that he might have been more at home in an Elizabethan tavern than a twenty-first century pub with big screen TV, smoking ban and fizzy beer, but there's no doubt that the trappings of modernity both puzzle and repel him. Maybe he would feel more comfortable back in the 1950s or 1960s. If all this sounds like criticism, though, it isn't meant to. Rather, it's the recognition of a rare kind of sanity.

James Lee, whom both Peter and I first got to know as a history student at the University of the West of England in the later 1990s, comments:

> Keith is the sort of man who, when you meet him, you feel you've known for years. He's generous, thoughtful, thoroughly entertaining, and an all round nice chap. He knows (whether consciously or not) how to break the ice, how to set people at ease. I remember most vividly our informal chats, sometimes historical, more often than not just about life and what a bugger it can be.

Fellow historian Tony Pollard fondly recollects 'boozy nights we spent together at fifteenth-century conferences', my 'honesty, commitment to teaching and lack of ambition' and, most of all, my 'theatriality and capacity to perform in front of an audience'. Di Collinson obviously had her philosopher's hat on when she wrote in March 2004:

> Keith, or so it seems to me, is a kind of existentialist. Like Hobbes, he knows the life of man can be 'solitary, poor, nasty, brutish and short' but, like Hobbes again, he also knows that laughter is 'a Sudden Glory'. From the dazzling clarity of that rather frightening awareness he chooses to live like Sisyphus—but with added zest!

As for publisher Alan Sutton, he simply concludes:

> Your friendship has been an experience! You are radical, anarchic, luddite in respect of technology, incisive, discursive, dismissive, irreverent and never frightened to speak your mind. If I have to choose one word to sum you up, it has to be outrageous!

Since they are among my oldest friends, perhaps the verdicts of Roger Kitching, Bernard Jarvis, Michael Stammers and Peter Allender carry most weight. Roger, whom I first met over fifty years ago in 1955, particularly highlights my virtually life-long aversion to technology and its significance:

As a young man Keith rejected the opportunity to become involved with the internal combustion engine, not only as a car owner but even as a driver. He could see nothing wrong with a national transport policy based solely on sedan chairs, railways and, at a pinch, trolley buses. So, even then, he thrust himself irrevocably to the very forefront of the ecological and environmentally friendly lobby! Nothing has changed and, as a result, he avoids the problems that beset so many on a daily basis. For him IT is what attractive people have, keyboards are on upright pianos, a virus is a bout of flu and spam is OK in fritters. The *Green Man* is not a pub: he is alive and well and living in Bristol. From one of the most travelled teenagers in our form at Huddersfield New College Keith has now become almost as reclusive as his house cat. He has created a world perfectly adapted to his needs and so rarely has to face the anxieties he feels when he does venture out. When we meet, be it five years, five months or five weeks since the last time, the years roll away. Keith is essentially unchanged. We pick up where we left off and our conversations range easily over the fifty years we have known each other: always the past and the present, never the future.

Bernard Jarvis, a friend since sixth form days at Huddersfield New College, combines perception, irony and generosity in almost equal measure:

> Over the years I've reflected on whether, when you shock people from time to time, you do it because you're amused by their reactions or, maybe, simply don't care about what impression you create. For instance, stubbing out a cigarette on King Arthur's alleged grave at Glastonbury, remarking that, since it wasn't your period, it didn't really matter; or smoking in non-smoking university seminars; or drinking (and more!) with students. I'm still not sure about this. My feeling is that, most of the time, you just do what you believe is right and sod what anyone else thinks. Just occasionally, though, you can't resist the soft target and, as far as I know, that's the nearest you get, as a gay bloke, to being outrageous. I suspect being in an oppressed minority assumes, for people of principle, an exceptionally large role in the way they perceive their relationship with the world though and, perhaps, this is a subtle part of the oppression. I see you as a kind, clever, driven person who writes history very well and is also homosexual. You probably hate the word 'enthusiasm' and stick the word 'infectious' in front of it and you'll probably throw up. Yet you do care about what you are doing; your personal commitment shows; and this pulls people along with you.

Mike Stammers, who had the misfortune to share a room with me during our final year as history undergraduates in 1965/6, remains a bit perplexed even forty years on:

I am not sure whether obstinacy is a Yorkshire gene but you certainly have it, as demonstrated in your lack of enthusiasm for housework, refusal to stop smoking or get a computer; however, obstinacy can also be interpreted as will power: the determination to get the best degree as a student, for instance, and not reveal your sexuality. Like all human beings you are a mass of contradictions. On the one hand you are the most cynical of men. Yet, on the other, you have lavished enthusiasm and scholarship on your chosen career as a historians, as well as real affection on many of those you have taught and befriended.

Peter Allender., whom I first met about the same time as Mike, seems even more puzzled:

I have known Keith for over forty years but still cannot say what he actually is: a gregarious misanthrope; a homosexual who enjoys the company of women and would have liked, perhaps, to be a father; a lecturer who no longer wants to lecture; a writer who seems reluctant to write; and a hard drinker who can stay sober for days or even weeks at a time. Yet, beneath his cynical carapace, lies a generous and sympathetic friend, highly moral in his immorality.

Perhaps, then, I am an enigma, even to myself!

As long ago as January 1994, in a letter to Brendan Evans at Huddersfield University putting my case for early retirement at fifty, I commented:

I an unlikely to make it beyond sixty—indeed, there's a good chance I won't even make that!—and don't particularly want to. For most of the last thirty years I've been hopelessly addicted to nicotine and, during that time, I've rarely smoked less than forty cigarettes a day. It's amazing cigarettes haven't killed me already. No doubt they will in the end. If they don't, alcohol or high blood pressure will. I can contemplate death with equanimity and have no intention of changing the habits of a lifetime. Longevity, for its own sake, has never seemed a desirable objective to me and I find it remarkable that it has become almost an obsession in western society in recent years. I'm not troubled by any intimations of approaching immortality either. I've been an agnostic or athiest ever since my teenage years and I'm now more than ever convinced that religion is mere mythology.

Since 1994 my views have hardened, if anything, and I now find the prospect of progressing to an almost inevitably lonely, probably decrepit and, worst of all, perhaps mentally handicapped old age (my natural mother began to display signs of dementia in her early seventies) in an ever more materialistic and technology-obsessed society profoundly unappealing. I have no desire whatever to end up like the historian A. J. P. Taylor (crippled by Parkinson's) or novelist Iris Murdoch (rendered mindless by Alzheimer's).

My life has turned out to be very much a pursuit of hedonism: the intellectual pleasures of study, teaching and writing sitting alongside the sheer fun of social drinking, smoking and sex. Yet my only serious regret is that, for too long, I hadn't the courage to be more open about my sexuality. Hence why, perhaps, I've never experienced love since I was a teenager nor found, or even seriously sought, a long-term relationship. Happiness, whatever that is, has eluded me too, but my origins and early life in the later 1940s and 1950s, and sexual orientation since, probably made that almost inevitable. Even so, under the circumstances and despite occasional bouts of severe depression, I haven't fared all that badly. Maybe it's an almost inevitable consequence of ageing, though, to take on the persona of a grumpy old man or woman. If so, I'm typical in that respect if no other. I find modern British society, despite its greater tolerance of homosexuality, thoroughly distasteful. In particular, it seems to have become ever more paranoid in the face of real or perceived threats— among them a bewildering catalogue of health risks, drugs-related crime and violence, immigration, terrorism, even climate change—and, in response, government has become increasingly authoritarian. The nanny state, nauseatingly self-righteous, intolerant of dissent and oblivious to the impact of social engineering on individual liberty, has never been more powerful. Everywhere, these days, we are under surveillance from closed circuit television cameras; rules and regulations seek to control more and more areas of our lives and behaviour; and the ever-growing army of faceless bureaucrats has never had it so good. The recent ban on smoking in pubs says it all and here, not surprisingly, I find myself entirely in agreement with columnist Christopher Hitchens and painter David Hockney. The smoking ban, declared Hitchens on the eve of its introduction, is about 'state-enforced behaviour modification' (in effect 'prohibition') and, as a result, 'the little sum of human happiness' has been 'radically reduced'. 'A grotesque piece of social engineering', echoed Hockney, imposed by:

> ...a political and media elite who think they can control everybody. I smoke for my mental health. I think it's good for it and I certainly prefer its calming effects to the pharmaceutical ones. Fortunately, the ban won't affect me much. I'm not very social and, in the world I have created, I will smoke.

For an unreconstructed libertarian and athiest like me, the revival of religious fundamentalism, as well as the emergence of a new secular puritanism, seem no less alarming and, for several years now, I've been a member of the British Humanist Association. Also I find it deeply ironic that, as a homosexual, I may no longer be regarded as a serious threat to the moral fibre of the nation but, as a smoker, I've become a danger to its physical well-being instead. Either way, my life-long status as a social outsider remains intact, while Aldous Huxley's *Brave New World* and George Orwell's *Nineteen Eighty Four* seem to get closer all the time. Hence why, during the last two or three years, I've tended to avoid all unnecessary contact with the world and become more and more of a recluse.

'If Keith is running true to form', mused Michael Bartholomew in February 2004, 'when all we clean-livers are dead, he'll be standing at our gravesides, fag in one hand, pint of beer in the other, saying how terrible he feels'. This seems an unlikely, if fittingly unorthodox, scenario. A former student bedmate, now fast approaching middle age himself, recently suggested that I seek out 'a handsome, intelligent, muscular live-in houseboy with DIY skills', if only to 'help reduce the strain of modern living' for an ageing and ever more eccentric gay historian. Maybe, he added, the 'human equivalent of a domestic tom cat' would suit me best, but with him pandering to my needs rather than the other way round. A splendid notion in theory but would any self-respecting young man relish such a role in practice? Almost certainly not, I suspect. What is actually in store for me I have no idea but a fatal heart attack not too far down the line would provide the most satisfactory exit. If, instead, I contract a terminal disease brought on by years of hedonism, no doubt my last battle will have to be fought against an arrogant, over-powerful and philosophically bankrupt medical profession, single-mindedly dedicated to the preservation of life, of however poor a quality, at all costs. Since I have no family (my half-brother Tony, whom I hadn't seen for years anyway, died in May 2005), no cat since Smoky's death in January 2007 and only a handful of close friends, the timing of my death has few implications for anyone else. All I shall require is pain-killers. Yet the chances of finding a sympathetic general practitioner seem remote. Doctors, sadly, appear to have become government-sponsored high priests of our secular society and, like their medieval religious equivalents, reluctant to tolerate any deviation from the sacred texts and practices of modern medicine. What I do have is an excellent role model. In the early 1990s a highly intelligent drinking mate of mine in Huddersfield developed lung cancer; he refused to submit himself to humiliating medical treatment designed, at most, to prolong his life for a few months; and when his GP refused to accommodate his desire for more powerful pain-killers, he took control of his own destiny. For over a year he bought heroin on the black market (as a criminal lawyer he had easy access to a local drug dealer), gradually increasing his intake until, I suspect, he deliberately took a massive overdose. Hopefully, should I ever get to that stage, voluntary euthanasia will have been legalised in Britain. Hence why I recently joined the Voluntary Euthanasia Society (now Dignity in Dying). The most terrifying prospect, for me at any rate, is lasting long enough to end up involuntarily incarcerated and unwillingly kept alive in an understaffed geriatric ward or a run-for-profit residential care home at my own expense. I'm fast approaching Shakespeare's 'lean and slipper'd pantaloon' stage but, if I stick to an unhealthy lifestyle, I might at least avoid 'second childishness and mere oblivion: sans teeth, sans eyes, sans taste, sans everything'.